Global Business
Information Technology

An integrated systems approach

We work with leading authors to develop the strongest educational materials in business and information technology, bringing cutting-edge thinking and best learning practice to a global market.

Under a range of well-known imprints, including Addison Wesley, we craft high quality print and electronic publications which help readers to understand and apply their content, whether studying or at work.

To find out more about the complete range of our publishing, please visit us on the World Wide Web at: www.pearsoned.co.uk

Visit the *Global Business Information Technology* Companion Website at **www.booksites.net/elliott_gbi** to find:

• Multiple choice questions to help test your learning
• Useful weblinks to relevant sources to take your learning further.

Global Business Information Technology

An integrated systems approach

Geoffrey Elliott
London South Bank University

PEARSON
Addison
Wesley

Harlow, England • London • New York • Boston • San Francisco • Toronto
Sydney • Tokyo • Singapore • Hong Kong • Seoul • Taipei • New Delhi
Cape Town • Madrid • Mexico City • Amsterdam • Munich • Paris • Milan

Pearson Education Limited

Edinburgh Gate
Harlow
Essex CM20 2JE
England

and Associated Companies throughout the world

Visit us on the World Wide Web at:
www.pearsoned.co.uk

———————————————

First published 2004

© Pearson Education Limited 2004

The right of Geoffrey Elliott to be identified as author of this work has
been asserted by him in accordance with the Copyright, Designs and
Patents Act 1988.

ISBN 0321 27012 6

British Library Cataloguing-in-Publication Data
A catalogue record for this book is available from the British Library

10 9 8 7 6 5 4 3 2 1
08 07 06 05 04

Typeset in 9.5/12.5 in Stone Serif by 3
Printed and bound by Ashford Colour Press Ltd, Gosport

The publisher's policy is to use paper manufactured from sustainable forests.

To Valerie, Emrys and Norman
'Forever'

Contents

8   The global business environment — 291

9   Applications for handling data and information modelling — 331

Website resources at **www.booksites.net/elliott_gbi**

For students
- Multiple choice questions to help test your learning
- Useful weblinks to relevant sources to take your learning further

For lecturers
- A secure, password-protected site with teaching material including PowerPoint slides that can be downloaded and used as OHTs

Preface

This book is aimed at providing first year and second year students in colleges and universities with an effective knowledge and understanding of the capabilities of Information Technology (IT) in the global business domain. In many respects information technology is a common international 'language' in the business world. The book is primarily aimed at students studying within the following broad subject areas:

▶ Business information systems
▶ Information technology
▶ Business computing.

This book is particularly useful to students that wish to study modules and courses in information systems and information technology – with emphasis on the international aspects of business IT. The book is also useful to students that are specializing in degrees, diplomas and university foundation studies in business information systems, business information technology and business studies.

It has been my intention in writing this book to try to provide an insight into the manner in which information systems and information technology are embedded into the fabric of business organizations across the globe. In studying information systems and information technology it is important to possess an understanding of the models that underpin information systems development and the methods and techniques used to evaluate information technology effectiveness in the global business domain. In essence the key areas of study within the book are as follows:

▶ The relationship of information systems and information technology in business.
▶ The capabilities of IT, its configuration and global management within business.
▶ The analysis, design and implementation of business information systems.
▶ The use and application of enabling technologies to engineer systems across an organization.

A fundamental motivation in writing the book was to provide a holistic framework of understanding of the applications, techniques and systems used within the global business domain. These form the 'what, how and why' of global business information technology, with emphasis on systems integration. In addition, the book takes into account some of the recent developments in the modern business systems environment that have affected the way business organizations utilize information technology.

Case studies are referred to throughout the book. These are described as 'pause for thought' sections that refer to real world situations and these can be found in each chapter. It is hoped that these sections enable students to link theory with practice within the business domain. This case study material also encourages students to think about the concepts, knowledge sets, technologies and systems being described in each chapter.

In essence, the book strives to broaden a student's knowledge and understanding of global business information technology as they progress through the chapters, hopefully, culminating in a holistic understanding of integrated business information systems. The chapters have been written so that the final section of each chapter leads logically into the next. The emphasis throughout is on providing a large amount of interactive tutorial material in each chapter, supported by numerous short self-assessment questions and longer exercises and group activities at the end of each chapter.

I hope the book is both useful, and more importantly, interesting to students, teachers, lecturers and general readers in the global information systems and IT domain.

Geoffrey Elliott
May 2004

Acknowledgements

I would like to thank Dr David Ellis at the University of Sheffield for giving me the chance, once upon a time, to become what is termed an 'academic' and to Dr Hedley Rees, Professor David Ashton and Professor Don Egginton at the University of Bristol for providing opportunities in academic research. I am also indebted to Paul Lillington for sharing material and ideas, particularly on course content and style. In recent years I would like to acknowledge the help, guidance and advice of Professor Terry Baylis and Professor Christopher Clare in enabling me to grow and develop as an academic and an academic manager. I also particularly acknowledge the kindness and support of Nigel Phillips who co-authored a book with me in wireless information systems and influenced my development as an author. Each person, in many different ways, has contributed a pattern to my life so far.

Publisher's acknowledgements

We are grateful to the following for permission to reproduce copyright material:

Figure 2.1 adapted from A mathematical theory of communication, The Bell Systems Technical Journal, Vol. 27, July/October, Bell Laboratories (Shannon, C. 1948) COPYRIGHT CLEARANCE CENTRE; Figures 4.3, 4.4, 4.6 and 11.1 frame reproduced with permission from AOL; Figure 4.3, 4.4, and 4.5 from DSDM Consortium website (www.dsdm.org); Figure 4.6 from Agile Alliance website (www.agilealliance.org); Figure 5.17 reproduced with kind permission of Dr Shushma Patel, London South Bank University; Figure 5.21 reprinted with the permission of The Free Press, a Division of Simon & Schuster Adult Publishing Group, from COMPETITIVE ADVANTAGE: Creating and Sustaining Superior Performance by Michael E. Porter. Copyright © 1985, 1998 by Michael E. Porter. All rights reserved. Figure 6.9 from *Systems Thinking, Systems Practice*, Checkland, P. Copyright 1981. © John Wiley & Sons Limited. Reproduced with permission. Figure 10.1 from Science Photo Library Ltd; Figure 11.1 from World Wide Web Consortium (W3C) website (www.w3.org); Figure 11.2 frame reprinted by permission of Microsoft Corporation, screenshot courtesy of Eudora (www.eudora.com); Figure 13.2 reproduced with kind permission of the Bank of England (www.bankofengland.com).

Cambridge University Press for an extract adapted from 'Systems Theory' published in *The Cambridge Dictionary of Philosophy* by Robert Audi 1995; Professor Blaise Cronin, Indiana University Bloomington USA for the home page of the School of Library and Information Science at Indiana University; Federal Computer Week for the article 'Dynamic Due' by Brian Robinson published on www.fcw.com 21st July 2003 © FCW Media Group 2003. All rights reserved; Patrick Hiatte and The Burlington Northern and Santa Fe Railway Company for information concerning The Burlington Northern Railroad (BNRR); Robert H'obbes' Zakon for adaptation of Hobbes' Internet Timeline published on www.zakon.org/robert/internet/timeline; The Institute of Internal Auditors Research Foundation, Florida USA for an extract adapted from *Systems Auditability and Control, Module 7: End-User and Departmental Computing*; Bill Jennerich for the article 'Joint Application Design: Business Requirements Analysis for Successful Re-engineering' © 1990 Bill Jennerich www.bee.net/bluebird/jaddoc.htm; JupiterMedia Corporation for an extract adapted from 'Mills: Security Issues Won't Slow Pervasive Computing' by Erin Joyce published on www.internetnews.com 24th September 2003 © 2004 All rights reserved; Brian V Maurice, Independent Outsourcing Consultant for an 'example of a formal Questionnaire'; US State Department for text of the statement issued by President Clinton upon signing the 1996 FOIA amendments into law on 2nd October 1996 as published on www.state.gov 2003; and Peter J Wasilko, Founder, The Institute for End User Computing Inc for an extract on 'End-User Computing'.

We are grateful to the Financial Times Limited for permission to reprint the following material:

Pause for thought 1.2 Long Live e-business: software is finding a new role in helping companies to share information effectively, © *Financial Times*, 6 March 2002.

In some instances we have been unable to trace the owners of copyright material, and we would appreciate any information that would enable us to do so.

PART 1

Information systems theory

Chapter 1

The global information age

Learning outcomes When you have studied this chapter you will be able to:

- ▶ define the information age and understand the importance of information to advanced industrial economies;
- ▶ evaluate the importance of information and knowledge workers in information-based economies;
- ▶ describe the role of information and knowledge management within competitive business environments;
- ▶ outline the nature and characteristics of information and communications technology (ICT) within the global business environment;
- ▶ describe the evolution and integration of business information systems within the global business environment.

1.1 Introduction to the global information age

National economies are engaged in competition with one another on a global scale. This competition is for global markets and a larger share of economic wealth. One of the earliest studies of national economic wealth and competition was by a Scottish economist named Adam Smith in his book entitled *Wealth of Nations* in 1776. Adam Smith stated that the wealth of a nation is dependent on how well a society organizes its production in national businesses and factories. Higher levels of industrial effectiveness, described as productivity, will lead to higher levels of national wealth and consequently higher living standards for the population of a society. This was encapsulated and described as the *industrial age*. In the twenty-first century the wealth of a nation is still dependent upon how well a society can organize its national assets. Chief among these national assets in the twenty-first century are *information* and *knowledge*. The importance of these assets in generating national wealth has led to the twenty-first century being referred to as the *information age*.

We live in an information age, mediated by the tools of *information and communication technology* (ICT), rather than an industrial age mediated by manufacturing and dependent upon the mass production of physical goods. The industrial age primarily relied upon producing tangible goods to sell for a profit. A tangible good is a physical product. In comparison to the industrial age, an information-based economy is one where the majority of businesses are engaged in information work and mainly employ information and knowledge workers. The information age primarily relies upon the handling and communication of intangible products and services. The wealth of information-based economies depends largely on the effectiveness and productivity of information and knowledge workers.

National economies where the majority of wealth is produced by information work are referred to as information-based economies. Within such economies national wealth, which is gauged by gross domestic product (GDP – the total market value of all final goods and services produced in a country in a given year), is created through the storage, processing and transmission of information. This manipulation of information leads to greater understanding and knowledge of the business systems environment. Information has become an important business asset and resource with attached monetary value.

What is an information-based economy?
A national economy where the majority of national wealth is produced by creating, processing and transmitting information.

Information workers can be divided into two sub-categories known as *data workers* and *knowledge workers*. Data workers are those who use, manipulate, process and disseminate information. Knowledge workers are those involved in the creation, distribution and application of new information or knowledge. Knowledge workers are usually formally educated to a higher level than data workers and include the following occupations: architects, authors, engineers, lawyers, lecturers, researchers, teachers and scientists. These workers are distinguished by the fact that they need to have and use creativity, discerning judgement and be able to interpret and apply information. By comparison, data workers normally have a less formal education and are restricted to handling and processing data rather than creating and interpreting information. Information becomes very important in supporting the management and control of organizations and enabling them to action decisions with more certainty. The network of connected information provides greater knowledge of the decision-making environment.

Information-based economies rely on the effective development and use of information systems and information and communications technology – referred to as ICT. The national wealth of an information-based economy will depend upon the efficiency and effectiveness of ICT applications across all business organizations in a national economy.

The information age has come about as a natural consequence of a number of long-term developments within society. To understand the information age we must place it into its historical context. The information age was preceded by the industrial (and mechanical) age, which in turn was preceded by the agricultural (and artisan) age.

▶ **Agricultural and artisan age**: characterized by farming and artisans involved in skilled trades (e.g. tool making, blacksmiths, basket weavers, etc.). The bulk of national wealth was generated through farming and small-scale, skilled trades. Agriculture, and the trades associated with agriculture, predominated economic activity. Any surplus income from farming was used to buy the artefacts of skilled trades people. This was an age prior to the 1820s – before the growth of mechanized transportation and the development of mechanized production.

▶ **Industrial and mechanized age**: dominated by the development of mechanized mass-production techniques and the collection of labour into one place. Large factories, employing large numbers of workers in one place, dominated economic wealth. This was an age of steam engines, steam ships and automated – and repetitive – manufacturing. The industrial age began in England at the start of the 1800s. The practices of the industrial age spread quickly to other countries throughout the nineteenth century. The industrial age produced great economic surpluses that could be re-invested into other areas, such as the building of permanent roads, the construction of drainage and sewage systems and the funding of schools and government institutions (through taxation). The industrial age also brought negative effects, such as the demise of rural communities, the growth of industrial pollution, and a number of social ills that came from crowding people into industrial towns. However, the mechanization of production also brought great economic growth and wealth to industrial nations and set the basis for the living standards that many people in economically developed countries enjoy today.

▶ **Information (and knowledge) age**: began in the 1950s, coinciding with the decline in large-scale manufacturing and production and its role in the generation of economic wealth. Although manufacturing and production are still very important today, the majority of workers in the information age are involved in the creation, distribution and application of information. The tools that they use are information and communications technologies (i.e. computers, telecommunication and networks).

Some of the first computer systems were developed in the 1950s. For example, the Lyons Electronic Office (LEO) computer was the first application of computing specifically for business purposes. It was used by J. Lyons & Company in the UK, a catering company famous for its teashops but with strong interests in new office management techniques. The computer was used to collect centrally, and process, data on the performance of individual shops (e.g. the amount of food and drink sold per day or week, revenue per day and week, and inventory – or stock – levels). In October 1947 the directors of J. Lyons & Company decided to take an active role in promoting the commercial development of computers. In 1951 the LEO I computer was operational and ran the world's first regular routine office computer job. The company LEO Computers Ltd was formed in 1954. LEO II computers were installed in many offices, including Ford Motor Company. LEO III computers were installed internationally in Australia, South Africa and Czechoslovakia. Many other companies followed by installing computers to perform administrative office tasks.

Within information-based economies the majority of workers are 'white-collar' workers (i.e. business managers, professionals, doctors, lawyers, teachers, scientists, etc.) rather than 'blue-collar' workers (i.e. those working in factories or involved in the handling or distribution of tangible goods).

Did you know?

The *Guinness Book of Records* accepted evidence provided by Professor Frank Land, an eminent information systems academic, that the LEO I computer was the first ever business computer. The first of the LEO I's many business applications was the valuation of weekly output of bread and cakes from Lyons' bakeries in the UK, in November 1951.

Source: www.leo-computers.org.uk

The information age is characterized by many things that we take for granted, for instance:

▶ The majority of jobs involve the creation, handling, processing and dissemination of information to enable corporate decision making.

▶ The activities of the information age are facilitated by various tools and techniques referred to collectively as information and communications technology.

▶ The ability to handle information efficiently and effectively is as important to a business organization as the efficient and effective handling of tangible goods.

▶ The value of information is calculated by its usefulness in making informed decisions within the business systems environment.

▶ Information can provide knowledge of the competitive business environment and relies on knowledge workers who have been educated to a high level.

Educational levels are vital to the growth and development of information and knowledge economies. Increasingly, the majority of information and knowledge workers are educated to college or university level. Most graduates from colleges and universities will be using, and often building, information systems using current ICT to support their knowledge-based activities. These knowledge workers need to be ICT literate in order to cope with the business environment of the twenty-first century. To this extent, many universities and colleges are embedding the importance of information skills into college and university syllabuses. The aim is to support the development of information-based economies. There are now many faculties of information science and information systems that not only embed basic information skills into their syllabus but also further address the teaching and learning of a range of information-based studies in their own right. To be ICT literate a knowledge worker should have:

▶ a sophisticated understanding of ICT tools and techniques;

▶ the skills and understanding to use these ICT tools within their correct organizational context;

▶ an understanding of how to exploit ICT for organizational advantage.

Pause for thought 1.1 has been reproduced from the internet home page of Indiana University, School of Information Science, in the USA. It highlights the importance of information skills and understanding in the information age.

PAUSE FOR THOUGHT 1.1

The world of information

For decades, scholars and futurists have predicted an information revolution. Those predictions have come to life dramatically in recent years. We live in an information age, an age in which the ability to generate and access new knowledge has become a key driver of social and economic growth. The conviction is powerfully reflected in the development of the information superhighway and in the feverish rate of take-overs and joint ventures in the telecommunications, cable and computer industries, as the major players position themselves to be in the vanguard of the digital revolution. Such developments are transforming both scholarly and lay perceptions of the value of information.

Historically, information has been treated as a public good, freely available to citizens. That model is coming under pressure, as the full economic and social significance of information becomes apparent. In many developed nations, the information sector is among the fastest growing segments of the economy. The emergence of a dynamic global information industry has created a wealth of opportunities for appropriately educated information professionals, but it has also helped throw into relief a raft of complex public policy issues, such as privatization of government-held information resources, the management of intellectual property rights, and the possible emergence of an information underclass, all of which call for rigorous and informed policy analysis.

The signs of a new age are everywhere: personal computers in the classroom, interactive media in the home, global communication networks, electronic publishing, digital libraries. The statistics are irresistible; the amount of information produced in the last decade alone is greater than all the information created in the past millennia. Public awareness of the importance of information has never been sharper, from national debate on the emerging Infobahn to issues of censorship in cyberspace. The rhetoric of the information age has finally become reality. And that reality translates into unprecedented career opportunities for information professionals who know how to organize, manage, and exploit information assets; who combine analytic and technical skills with a sense of the strategic value of information to organizations of all kinds.

The economic and social well-being of nations depends increasingly on their ability to generate and access new knowledge. Hence, a need exists to create information-literate societies. Being information literate means knowing how information is created, stored, transmitted, and used. The 'informatization' of society is creating demand for specialists who will function as information resource managers and act as guides, interpreters, mediators, brokers, and quality controllers for the ultimate user, who might be a corporate executive, a scientist, or a school child. Today's information professionals do not merely store and locate information, but analyze and synthesize raw information and data to produce customized, value-added services and products for diverse clientele. The field offers a kaleidoscope of career tracks from which to choose, as the mass of position announcements in both the professional and generalist press makes abundantly clear: database design and marketing, information brokering, medical informatics, systems, competitor intelligence analysis. In a sense, the opportunities are limited only by the imagination.

Source: The home page of the School of Library and Information Science at Indiana University website (www.slis.indiana.edu), 1998; reproduced by permission of Professor Blaise Cronin, Indiana University, Bloomington, USA.

The information age

Discuss why in many developed nations the information sector is often among the fastest growing segments of the economy. Write down four reasons why the economic and social well-being of nations depends increasingly on their ability to generate and access new knowledge.

1.2 What is information and communications technology?

The information age is dependent upon information and communications technology (ICT). The constituent parts of ICT are *computers* (both wired and wireless), *telecommunications* (both wired and wireless) and *networks* (both wired and wireless). However, these are merely the tools of the information age. Information and knowledge workers need to know how to use these tools and also what the consequences and effects are of using these tools for business systems activity.

The characteristics of ICT are that it:

▶ transforms business processes, making them more efficient and effective;

▶ can be obvious or embedded in the environment around us;

▶ can be used to create, store and disseminate data;

▶ can be used to translate data into useful information for decision making.

Information is a fundamental resource and is often referred to as the *life-blood* of a business organization. Information is important to all types of organization and the right type of information can sometimes provide a competitive advantage over other organizations in information-based societies. ICT performs a series of fundamental functions within business organizations:

▶ **Data and information capture**: using ICT to capture raw data (i.e. facts, figures, images, etc.). The capture of data (and sometimes information) can take many forms. Data capture is not just about alphanumeric data (i.e. numbers and words). For example, a system may capture a person's image and match it up to a database of images; a system could also be used to collect information from facial images, fingerprints and voice intonation, known as *biometric* identification; a system could also capture data through the use of sensors to scan the number of people entering an area of a building. The methods of data capture are many and varied.

▶ **Data and information storage**: holding data in the most efficient and effective manner so that it can be processed. Data storage techniques and devices can take many forms, for example hard-disk memory in computers (e.g. laptops, wireless personal digital assistants (PDAs), embedded devices in vehicles, etc.), CD-ROM disks and voice storage.

▶ **Data and information processing**: using ICT for quickly and accurately processing large amounts of information. Processing is a functional activity that is largely dependent upon the quality of the technology used (i.e. processing power and memory). The activity of processing involves the conversion and analysis of captured data in order to transform it into information. This information may then be further analyzed to provide greater levels of information content. One of the advantages of computing power is the capability to process different data and information simultaneously and in parallel. This is sometimes referred to as parallel computing.

▶ **Data and information retrieval**: locating stored or processed data and information in the most efficient and effective manner. The good characteristics of retrieved information for decision making are:
  – speed of retrieval
  – information accuracy
  – information relevance to the person or system retrieving the information
  – portability and connectivity of the information (i.e. its ability to be used and integrate into other parts of the system).

▶ **Information dissemination**: communicating information to the end user or transmitting information to another computer-based system, connected by either wired or wireless links. Information dissemination can take two forms: structured information that is dissemination in a fixed and bounded form (e.g. the publication of monthly accounts in a standard format), or unstructured information that is published in varied formats according to the end user's requirements (e.g. the core information is embedded into an e-mail, edited and disseminated in an unstructured form).

It should be clear from this analysis that the activities affecting data and information lead to transformation. From each activity – from data capture to information retrieval and dissemination – some form or transformation takes place.

> **Did you know?**
> The modern English word for information comes from the Latin word *informare* which means to form or take shape.

1.3 Business systems activity in the global information age

The central aim of most business organizations is to generate a profit for the owners or shareholders of the business. Organizations compete with one another nationally and internationally, on a global scale, for a share of business opportunities and markets. Business organizations comprise a range of human resources and technological assets that need to be successfully managed, organized and coordinated for the purposes of generating a profit. Information systems and information technology are part of the resources of an organization that are used to generate income and profit.

The three fundamental resources of any organization are the employees, the structure (or corporate organization) and the technology. These are sometimes known as the three *socio-technical pillars* of a business organization:

▶ people
▶ organization
▶ technology.

The success of a business is determined by how well (i.e. how efficiently and effectively) it manages and controls these three fundamental resources in a *systematic* way. A system is a set of interrelated and integrated components. In the business systems environment the three overarching components are clearly people, organizational structure and technology. Business systems not only interact with each other, they also interact with other systems in the world at large (e.g. education, government agencies, transportation and social systems). The purpose of systematic behaviour is to manage, coordinate and integrate the various components of a system for some particular purpose. The overarching purpose of commercial business systems activity is to make a profit.

What is the difference between efficiency and effectiveness?

Throughout this book the terms efficiency and effectiveness will frequently be used. The two terms are imperative in the measuring of information systems and ICT performance. Evaluating information systems performance requires the use of performance standards. An information systems performance standard is a specific objective or goal of a system.

Efficiency is a relative measure of what is produced divided by what is consumed. For example, the efficiency of a mechanical engine could be measured by the ratio of the work done to the work needed to operate the engine.

Effectiveness is a measure of the extent to which a system achieves its goals or objectives. A system that achieves all its goals is totally effective and a system that only achieves some of its goals is, by degree, less effective.

The components of the three systems pillars of a business organization are described in Table 1.1. These components constitute the elements that need to be considered when dealing with the integration of people, organization and technology. Each of these business pillars will be covered and studied in greater detail in subsequent chapters.

The successful integration of these pillars into holistic business information systems is the driving force behind effective use and application of ICT within the business environment. Consideration of these three pillars is sometimes known as a *socio-technical* view of information systems within a business organization. The socio-technical view of organizations gives paramount importance to people as the major and most significant asset of a business within the infor-

Table 1.1 The three pillars of a business organization

People	Organization	Technology
Career	Bureaucracy	Hardware
Education	Culture	Software
Ergonomics	Competition	Telecommunications
Employee attitudes	Environment	Informatics
Employee participation	Management	
Employee monitoring	Mission	
Statutory regulation	Policy	
Training	Strategy	

mation systems domain. Most business organizations aim to be effective and efficient in maximizing the utilization of all three resources to generate a business profit.

Within the socio-technical perspective, information systems within organizations need to be designed and developed so that people can integrate, use, control and understand the information asset. The study of information systems is an attempt to understand and integrate these three pillars successfully into the fabric of a business organization.

The majority of ICT applications are found within the business systems domain. Business information systems (BIS) are concerned with a range of factors that determine the effective and efficient design, development and integration of ICT to enable a business to meet its full potential in generating an income or profit. Therefore, the study of business information systems activity in the information age relates to that part of the computing domain that intersects with the pure business domain and involves all aspects of the building, maintenance and evaluation of information systems at all levels within a commercial organization.

To understand the use and application of ICT in the business systems domain it is essential to understand how information systems, information technology and business organizational theory integrate for an understanding of the design, use and application of business information technology in the twenty-first century. A business information technology professional in the information age is required to understand the nature of competitive business organizations and also to be able to work with business specialists to achieve ICT-based solutions to an organization's information problems.

The aim of information and knowledge workers within the business domain is to:

▶ successfully integrate the three fundamental resources of people, organization and technology;

▶ develop and maintain well-engineered business information systems;

▶ translate and support business objectives with effective and efficient information systems infrastructures.

Did you know?

The term engineering is deliberately used in business to emphasize the fact that business systems and business information technology are both rigorous academic and skills-based disciplines. It requires technology skills but also, more importantly, the intellectual ability to understand when and how to use ICT to fulfil the objectives of an organization.

Therefore, a BIS professional should act as a conduit at the middle of a spectrum of skills and knowledge found within the disciplines of business and computing. The central aim of the BIS professional is to translate the requirements of business specialists into holistic and tangible ICT-based information systems that can be used for decision making within a competitive business environment. Any BIS professional working within the business systems domain should possess an understanding of the commercial information requirements of business together with a discerning knowledge of how to integrate business practices, procedures and technology into useful information systems for eventual decision making.

> **Did you know?**
>
> The Business Information Systems (BIS) professional is concerned with the analysis, design, implementation and evaluation of ICT-based business systems used for decision making within the competitive business environment.

A central aim of information and knowledge workers is to acquire skills in the engineering and integration of ICT. Information and knowledge workers should fill the vacuum of misunderstanding that often exists between the pure business specialist and the pure technologist within the business environment. This should be coupled with the desire to build systems that have the highest possible levels of information certainty to allow accurate decision making to be undertaken. The need to manage business information systems has, with the evolution of ICT, become subsumed into the whole business function rather than concentrated in a specific department or section of the business organization; ICT pervades the whole workplace.

The prevalence and benefits of ICT in the business domain are often taken for granted by many business organizations. This can be a mistake because business organizations require a strategy for optimizing ICT investment in order to maximize the return on information systems investment. There is no direct correlation between investment in ICT alone and increases in business performance. One organization may spend $10 000 on ICT and increase profits, while another organization spends the same amount on the same technologies but achieves no increase in profits. Therefore, the key indicator is not merely ICT investment but rather how effective the management, control and utilization of information (and knowledge) is to business performance.

There are five key issues within business information systems thinking and practice:

▶ the relationship of ICT to business;
▶ the capabilities of ICT, its configuration and management within the organization;
▶ the analysis, design and implementation and evaluation of information systems;
▶ the management and analysis of information as an organizational asset;
▶ the enabling characteristics of wired and wireless ICT within business.

An understanding of the nature and characteristics of ICT in business goes a long way towards meeting the needs of business and industry in the information age. Trends in business ICT include:

▶ The evolution of computing and ICT over the last 50 years, moving away from large-scale electronic data processing (EDP) departments towards 'end-user' computing.
▶ The growing business need for knowledge workers who possess an understand-

ing of ICT and its application within the business information systems domain.

▶ The growing business need for knowledge workers who possess an understanding of networked systems from a socio-technical perspective.

▶ The development of the concept of intellectual capital and knowledge management (KM) as a human resource vital to all business organizations.

▶ The integration of information systems and ICT to provide a framework for developing knowledge and understanding of business systems activity within dynamic, competitive and global business environments.

1.4 Knowledge management (KM)

Knowledge workers are concerned with the organizational structures, processes and systems for handling information, and its conversion into knowledge, in order to understand effectively the nature of the business environment. This has led to the concept of *knowledge management*. Information systems play an important role in enabling an organization to structure information flows and capture the inherent knowledge base of an organization. The structuring of information and the creation of knowledge bases is so important in the information age that many organizations appoint staff specifically to oversee the task of knowledge management. These people are often referred to as chief knowledge officers (CKO). In effect knowledge workers have become those employees in the business domain that manage the information resources, information architecture and intellectual capital of an organization.

The knowledge base of an organization is normally composed of two components:

▶ formal structured knowledge (e.g. process and procedure manuals, company policy documents, etc.);

▶ informal unstructured knowledge (e.g. ways of doing things, experience of employees' needs, habits and abilities, etc.).

The second category of knowledge resides in the minds of employees; it is informal and not documented or structured. This type of knowledge is termed *tacit knowledge*. Experience and understanding of an organization that resides in the minds of employees is tacit knowledge. This knowledge can be released by encouraging group collaboration among employees and establishing systems that enable knowledge to be shared and integrated into the way that the organization operates.

What is knowledge mananagement?

It caters to the critical issues of organizational adaption, survival, and competence in the face of increasingly discontinuous environmental change. [Knowledge Management] embodies organizational processes that seek synergistic combination of data and information processing capacity of information technologies, and the creative and innovative capacity of human beings.

Source: Dr Yogesh Malhotra, 'Tools@work: deciphering the knowledge management hype', *Journal for Quality and Participation*, July/August 1998.

The concept of knowledge management can also be extended to a macro-economic level by considering its importance and relevance to the national economy. Information-based economies depend upon the efficiency, effectiveness and productivity of knowledge workers. A *knowledge economy* is one that makes effective use of the intellectual capital and knowledge of its population for the economy's collective social and economic development. There are three pillars to the creation of a successful knowledge economy:

▶ nurturing intellectual capital and encouraging the retention of knowledge in organizations to promote economic growth and sustain intellectual competition;

▶ providing and nurturing the development of knowledge banks in organizations to provide a resource of global knowledge that can be adapted and innovated to create new knowledge;

▶ providing support for knowledge workers through education and research that leads to an understanding of knowledge as a national asset.

Business organizations operate by coordinating and managing intelligent interactivity. The twenty-first century is characterized by knowledge as the critical resource for business activity. Organizations have to manage and control the digital convergence of telecommunications, ICT and information content. The pace of change within ICT alone makes knowledge management a challenging activity within the business domain.

What is a knowledge economy?

An economy that makes effective use of intellectual capital and knowledge for its economic and social development. This includes harvesting global and national knowledge, as well as adapting and creating knowledge for an economy's specific requirements.

Information enables business organizations to undertake the activity of decision making. However, information and knowledge are not the same; knowledge resides in human beings not technologies. Knowledge represents the interpretation and contextualization of information by human beings. This activity leads to a human appreciation of the business environment in all its complexity. Humans are in effect *appreciative systems*; they understand the world around them and take decisions based on facts, figures, experience and intuition. Knowledge creation occurs via social interaction and observation of the world around us. Knowledge is embedded in people, from their experiences, and the majority of knowledge occurs from observing historical actions and consequences that formulate into memories and intuition that in turn can be interpreted to provide knowledge for decision making.

To coordinate, control and use knowledge in an organization successfully it has to be managed. The following are a few ways in which knowledge can be managed to encourage its use within the business systems domain:

▶ emphasize the human aspects of business activity in terms of the organization being a community of humans with inherent knowledge of how things work;

▶ manage the creation of knowledge through the encouragement of human imagination and creativity;

▶ encourage human reflection of actions and consequences to deepen the process of conceptualization of decision making as an activity;

▶ encourage communities of practice that are formal and informal human networks inside and outside the organization to deepen knowledge of the wider business environment;

▶ ensure that there are sufficient information channels within an organization to enable the free flow of knowledge between people in an organization.

Good knowledge management occurs in business environments where the intangible assets of human beings (i.e. their experiences and knowledge) are recognized and synthesized through open information systems and the encouragement of human interaction and networking.

What is knowledge management in the real world?

Knowledge management is concerned with the management of human knowledge and understanding of the business environment. It is often referred to as 'knowledge capital' as it constitutes an asset to a business organization. Knowledge is acquired through experience. It is experience of doing things well and of doing things less well that lead to a bank of human understanding, intuition and knowledge.

Knowledge management is about harnessing the knowledge that is valuable and the knowledge that is a fundamental asset to an organization. It is for the individual company to define and determine what information qualifies as intellectual capital and knowledge capital. Knowledge-based assets fall into two categories:

▶ explicit knowledge
▶ tacit knowledge.

Explicit knowledge includes assets such as patents, trademarks, and customer basics. Explicit knowledge consists of anything that can be documented, archived and codified. However, tacit knowledge is more difficult to define and codify. Tacit knowledge includes what is in someone's head; it is their experience and knowledge of what works and what does not work in the relevant business environment. It is what was traditionally called 'professional knowledge'. The challenge with tacit knowledge revolves around working out how to recognize, generate, share and manage knowledge for the greater good.

In the information age the harnessing of knowledge (i.e. the management of knowledge) is aimed at enabling a business organization to encourage innovation and stimulate business ideas. It also aims to encourage participation in the decision making arenas of a business organization. In a well run knowledge based business organization a person's knowledge and experience is valued. Knowledge management tries to encourage employees to share knowledge and understanding of the business environment. This leads to broader and greater understanding. A knowledge based company harnesses both the physical and knowledge capital of a business organization.

PAUSE FOR THOUGHT 1.2

Long live e-business: Software is finding a new role in helping companies to share information effectively FT

Portals are passe. Business-to-business online marketplaces have come and gone and the value of customer relationship management systems is being questioned. What has gone wrong with e-business software? What is next? And why should business managers still take note?

Back in 1999, e-business software was going to change the world. Online marketplaces were heralded as a way to find alternative suppliers and lower prices. There was much talk of 'disintermediation'. Traditional distributors and wholesalers would be out of the picture as businesses switched to buying and selling via the internet, many predicted. Entire industries would be restructured as even small businesses would have worldwide reach. Trade and competition laws would have to be rewritten. Yet most online marketplaces are now history. The opportunities and threats they seemed to pose turned out to be hot air. Customer relationship management (CRM) was de rigueur. This created huge demand for CRM software that drew together all of the information regarding a customer's past and present interactions with a company. Tens of millions of dollars were spent implementing CRM but software industry executives now say fewer than half the systems lived up to customers' expectations. One in five executives surveyed last year by Bain & Co, the consulting group, said CRM initiatives had damaged customer relationships.

It is tempting to write off e-business software as just another over-hyped technology bubble. Yet despite the failures – the software companies that have closed their doors and customer experiences that have gone sour – e-business lives on and some would say its prospects are improving. Several important lessons have been learnt. First, the internet is a business tool but it does not alter business fundamentals. The second is that e-business applications evolved from enterprise software and they too are tools, not magic bullets. E-business automates or streamlines business processes but companies that attempt to map the software to their traditional operating practices make a grave error. It is entirely possible to customise the value out of e-business software by rigidly applying traditional approvals processes, for example, or limiting the ability of employees and business partners to access information. To take full advantage of e-business, companies must be ready to embrace change, even it is disruptive. The old 'command and control' management model is not compatible with e-business. Another tough lesson that many have learnt is that systems integration is complex, time-consuming and expensive – yet integration of legacy systems is essential to maximise value.

However, it is not only e-business users who have learnt the hard way. Software vendors that focused on e-commerce have been humbled as the centre of gravity of e-business has shifted from transactions to information-sharing. Collaboration is the new e-business buzz word and this time it is not just a fad. Rather, the technology is mirroring and accelerating the changing shape of manufacturing and other industries. 'Outsourcing – whether it be of manufacturing or design or any other aspect of a company's operations – is driving demand for improved information-sharing as the fortunes of a company become more closely intertwined with those of its suppliers and business partners,' says Mark O'Connell, chief executive of Matrix One, a supplier of collaboration software. 'Every company is under pressure to squeeze costs out of business processes and to speed new products to market. Our customers are looking for ways to get people to work together more effectively.'

The car industry is a good example. Big US carmakers have set goals to reduce the time it takes to bring a new vehicle to market, from three to four years to only one to two years. This involves radical changes in the structure of the industry. 'About 50 to 70 per cent of design work is now being done outside the big auto manufacturing companies,' says Bob Matulka, director of collaboration at Covisint, an online marketplace created by the car industry. 'There is a great need to tie globally dispersed teams together.' Engineering design changes can play havoc with the product development schedule, he says. 'You can end up with weeks of wasted effort.' An internet-based collaboration environment in which information about design changes is rapidly disseminated can create big cost and time savings. John Warniak, director, e-business speed, at Johnson Controls, is on the front lines. As a leading car industry supplier, his company must now deal with issues such as vendor-managed inventory and advanced quality planning. 'We have to be able to interface with our customers and our suppliers with a common interface. There has to be a single source of truth, of up-to-date information.'

Carmakers and their suppliers are not alone in adopting e-business collaboration. Hewlett-Packard and Compaq Computer are planning their merger in virtual online work spaces, using eRoom software, where documents and messages are shared and saved. Francois Gossieaux, chief executive of eRoom, expects his company's products will increasingly be used for such partnerships between businesses, rather than just internal communications. Even CRM is finding a second wind. Bo Manning, chief executive of Pivotal, which supplies software to the mid-sized company CRM segment, is redefining his products to include 'partnership relationship management'. In other words, relationship management is shifting to include all the constituencies that are important to a business.

Now, B2B stands for 'back to business basics' and e-business is the confluence of best business practices, the internet and software. It is a potent mix, not to be ignored. Those 1999 predictions may yet prove prescient. E-business software is perhaps the most disruptive technology to emerge in the past five years. In the world of technology, that is a very long time.

Source: Louise Kehoe, *Financial Times*, March 6, 2002.

Activity 1.2 Knowledge management

Discuss what is meant by knowledge management (KM). Outline the important aspects of KM. What are the benefits of KM and how should KM be adopted within the business domain? Discuss the main challenges of KM.

1.5 Competitive advantage through business systems

A significant reason why rigorously built business information systems are so important to an organization can be gauged by the following quote that forecasts the business environment of the twenty-first century:

> In the past the economic winners were those who invented new products. But in the 21st Century sustainable competitive advantage will come more out of new process technologies and much less out of new product technologies.
>
> What used to be primary (inventing new products) becomes secondary, and what used to be secondary (inventing and perfecting new processes) becomes primary. (Thurow, 2003)

Business organizations are realizing, especially those operating in dynamic (i.e. continuously changing) business environments, that competitiveness is established not merely by the product or service, but by the quality of the ICT-based information systems that deliver those products (and services) to customers.

Competitiveness plays an important role in the business systems environment. So much so that the term 'competitive advantage' was coined to encapsulate the idea that how the assets of an organization are organized can affect the competitiveness of the organization. Business competition often takes place on a global scale. The globalization of trade means larger markets, more competition and greater environmental uncertainty. For example, globalization has led to greater uncertainty within the information environment, through differing national laws, trading practices, competition policies and cultural attitudes to technology and its use. However, the rewards of global trading can also be greater in terms of increased revenue and profits. Therefore, information systems need to be focused to these global challenges and enable organizations to compete in increasingly competitive global environments.

A significant challenge in business information systems is the need to attain *competitive advantage* both nationally and internationally. The concept of competitive advantage is one that has become synonymous with Professor Michael Porter of Harvard University, USA. Competitive advantage defines the ability of a business organization to compete with other organizations. According to Porter, the competitive advantage of a business is determined, and gauged, by a number of competitive forces. There are five main generic competitive forces:

▶ threat of new entrants to the competitive market

▶ substitute products and services

▶ competition and rivalry between business organizations

▶ bargaining power of suppliers

▶ bargaining power of customers.

These competitive forces affect the relationship and position of competing business organizations within a market. Once these forces are recognized then strategies can be developed to counteract these forces affecting competition.

There are four main strategies that can be used to deal with the competitive forces outlined above. These are:

▶ **Cost leadership**: producing products and services at a lower price than competitors.

▶ **Market niche**: focusing products and services to particular markets or customers so that a business can concentrate on providing better products and services than its competitors.

▶ **Product differentiation**: creating new or different products and services that distinguish (or differentiate) one business organization from another organization.

▶ **Customer and supplier linkage**: locking-in suppliers to the price and delivery structure of the purchasing organization or locking customers into the organization's products or services. Both of these can be achieved by linkages between the business systems of customers, organizations and suppliers inherent in the structure of the competing business organization.

What is competitive advantage?

The advantage that one business has over another business organization due to more effective and efficient use of information systems and ICT to deal with competitive forces.

Information systems and ICT can be used to implement these strategies to achieve competitive advantage. For example, marketing information systems can be developed to enhance the information available from sales and marketing systems. This information can be used to target customers or suppliers to identify market niches for products and services. Such information can also be used to determine the necessary strategies to target products and services to customers.

Business information systems and ICT can also be used to create more attractive products and services. For example, retail banks are one of the main users and providers of ICT for competitive advantage (e.g. internet banking and wireless banking from mobile phones). Banking was one of the first industries to recognize the importance of innovative ICT to make a profit within the business domain. Many of the banking technologies and services that we use are taken for granted, such as credit cards, debit cards, internet banking and the global availability of automated teller machines (ATMs) in every town, city and airport in the world. The globalization of this technology makes redundant the need for travellers' cheques and currency exchange payments since we can get off an airplane and take cash out of globally networked ATM machines. However, all these services would be impossible were it not for ICT and its application to business competitiveness. Banking is a very competitive business domain where banks and financial corporations are constantly looking for ways of providing more efficient and effective customer services. Banks are also constantly reviewing internal and external business systems productivity to gain competitive advantages.

Did you know?

Cash dispensers, known technically as automated teller machines (ATMs), were first developed by Citicorp Bank in the USA in 1977. In the UK, Barclays Bank was the first high street bank to place a cash dispenser outside for customers to use with a cash debit card. The competitive advantage was that customers could have access to banking services 24 hours a day and seven days a week.

ICT can be used to link customers and suppliers to a business organization's systems. In doing so, an organization can develop customer loyalty and make it too costly, or inconvenient, for customers (and suppliers) to switch allegiance to a competitor organization.

Customer linkage can be achieved through the provision of better products and services, with value-added aspects (e.g. after-sales care or automatic product upgrades for customers). Linkage with customers through ICT can be achieved by providing unique services that make it necessary, or desirable, for the customer to maintain a relationship with a particular organization's products and services. In terms of supplier linkage, ICT can be used to incorporate the suppliers' information systems into the purchasing organization's systems. The supplier becomes a virtual part of the purchasing organization's information systems. The supplier becomes technologically linked through its dependence and connectivity with the systems infrastructure of the purchasing organization. This makes it too inconvenient for the supplier to seek costly initial supplier relationships with any other business organizations.

Competitive business organizations recognize that information systems and ICT can be used to *transform* organizational infrastructures. ICT can also be used to define the manner in which an organization conducts business activity in relation to its customers and suppliers. Competitive advantage can be gained by designing and developing business information systems that provide competitive advantage in the global business environment.

Did you know?

It is forecast that there will be 84 million internet banking customers in Europe by 2007. The UK and Germany are Europe's biggest online banking markets, although the Scandinavian markets have the most internet bankers per head of the population. In Sweden and Finland in particular, there are more than 0.4 online banking customers per head of the population. Internet banks constantly try to focus on developing new services and functionality that appeal to the growing population of experienced online banking users.

Source: Based on Datamonitor website (www.datamonitor.com), 28 March 2003.

Activity 1.3   Competitive strategy in internet banking

Discuss and identify three ways in which ICT can be used to deal with the main competitive forces present in internet banking. If in difficulty, search the internet for references to the internet banking industry. Find a case study or article on how internet banks and other online financial institutions compete with one another on a global scale. Discuss how various products, services and systems lock-in (or link) customers to particular internet banks (or financial products). What ICT do banks try to exploit and what competitive advantages are they trying to gain through the use of ICT?

Activity 1.4   Competitive advantage through information systems

Information systems can be used to gain a competitive advantage over other organizations in the business environment. Information systems and technology can be used to develop new markets or products, new ways of dealing with suppliers and customers, and new ways of operating processes and systems practices within the organization. Provide examples of how information systems can be used to transform the processes and practices of a business of your choice. Explain how information systems and ICT can support each of the four competitive strategies of competitive advantage.

1.6 End-user computing

ICT utilization within business has evolved dramatically over the last 50 years. Business has witnessed a number of underlying trends that have changed the way technology is integrated into the business domain. One of the major trends witnessed in the early 1990s was a movement away from large-scale data processing departments towards *end-user computing* (EUC). End-user computing was a popular concept within information systems development in the early 1990s and has recently been revived in the early twenty-first century.

End-user computing is used to describe the fact that in the modern business information systems domain the development of information systems primarily resides with a specific user, or group of users, of an information system. The ownership and development of business information systems is the primary concern of the end users of that system. This concept encourages employees within an organization to take an active role and participate in the analysis, design, implementation and evaluation of information systems. The end users may work with various ICT experts but the end users are primary, not secondary, in dictating the scope and nature of the information systems to be designed and built.

End-user computing is used in the ICT domain to describe the final consumer (or user) of information. End-user computing consists of the *systems* and *tools* given directly to information and knowledge workers that allow them to manipulate and extract their own information; to decide when and how to use ICT applications; and to own and control the information that they use within the organization. The emphasis is on placing responsibility and control of ICT in the hands of the final user, or users, of information.

> **What is end-user computing (EUC)?**
> The ownership and development of information and knowledge systems by the end users of the information.

In the 1950s and 1960s business computing normally took place within defined, large electronic data processing departments where a small number of specially trained computer technicians generated mainly operational data using large-scale mainframe computer technology. However, over time the roles and responsibilities of such staff have become integrated into all aspects of business. Within modern business, computers are not only used in the operational functions of business (e.g. administration, stock control, wage calculation, etc.) but are also used in the management and executive domains of most organizations.

PAUSE FOR THOUGHT 1.3

End-user computing

When we speak of end-user computing, we are referring to the total experience of using information technology to both augment and develop one's own innate skills and abilities. Therefore, we are not simply interested in the user interface per se, but also the underlying capabilities provided by a user's computing environment and how they can be orchestrated and made comprehensible. End-user computing embraces a broad range of technologies and techniques and looks at how they can be integrated and refactored to enhance system stability, security, and flexibility.

End-user computing is about empowering people to derive the greatest benefit from their computer with the least stress. There is no one stereotypical end user, but rather a number of representative user types whose technical skills span a continuum from novice to expert, whose ages, languages, and physical abilities are not uniform, and whose areas of substantive interest vary markedly. But by discovering the commonalities that underlie this rich diversity, end-user computing offers the promise of leveraging work aimed at supporting specific classes of users to the benefit of all. Thus efforts to improve accessibility for the disabled, might for example, lead to novel interaction styles that empower mobile business users and peace officers to do more with ultra-miniature devices.

In short, we focus on the big picture and dwell in the interstices between research domains. We work to knit together communities and create vibrant new ecologies in which technology and technology users can flourish. We do not subscribe to the view that end users are dummies who cannot, should not, and do not want to understand their tools. Nor do we ignore the reality that technologists are themselves end users.

Indeed, we have come to recognize that for decades we have been lowering our expectations as end users at the very same time that we have been pushing the boundaries of the enabling technologies coming out of our labs and R&D centers. Ironically, our very efforts to maximize the impact of our short-term research efforts by reusing old code and providing backward compatibility with ancient systems to minimize the learning curve for those trained on them have, in aggregate, had the perverse effect of holding us back.

We recognize that economic and research policy dynamics have been a factor in these feedback loops, which have stifled deep innovation at the platform level. This has led to an IT training crisis, the spread of maddeningly frustrating buggy software, and the progressive de-personalization of the personal computer. Yet at the very same time we are seeing a renaissance in tools, languages, and libraries for programmers. The trouble is that these facilities are fragmented and do not transition well from the lab into the real world and seldom make an appreciable positive impact at the end user level.

This is why we believe that for the US and indeed the world to realize the full potential of IT and for people to be able to control the role it plays in their lives, we need to break with the past and rethink our computing environments from the ground up.

This is not to say that we should throw out everything we have learned over the last thirty years, but rather that *now* is the time to finally put *all* of our knowledge to use in a principled fashion. This is why we are forming 'The Institute for End-User Computing'.

Source: Institute for End User Computing website (www.ieuc.org), 25 May 2003.

The development of end-user computing

In the 1950s and 1960s task specialization gave rise to three categories of computer professional: the analyst, the programmer and the final user of information. Originally, an enquiry from a user of information within an organization would have been passed to a systems analyst, who analyzed the business problem, then passed it on to a computer programmer to implement a solution. The information would then have been passed to the final user, whose involvement in the analysis, design and implementation of the business information system would have been non-existent. Over time these task-specific *computing intermediaries* have been replaced and often merged into one person: the information end user.

Consequently, career opportunities in business computing have changed dramatically. In the 1970s a computer professional working in a large organization would have started their career as a junior programmer and worked their way up through the ranks to become a systems analyst, then senior analyst through to becoming a project manager. This is not normally the case today, for the following main reasons:

▶ the elimination of task demarcation in terms of computing roles and responsibilities within business organizations;

▶ changes in information systems practices and procedures and changes in how ICT is viewed and adopted in the business domain;

▶ the emergence of service computing for mainly operational systems functions, such as stock control, payroll and even sales and purchase order processing;

▶ the growth of the BIS professional as a facilitator of ICT within business.

What are the desirable characteristics of information?

Information should be:

▶ accurate

▶ relevant

▶ timely

▶ complete

▶ portable.

To be competitive business organizations need to invest resources into end-user computing. We have seen from studying knowledge management that the social and technological innovation that encourages human activity and business development comes from information and, in particular, knowledge. Innovation is what drives business growth and development. The coupling of end-user computing with concepts of knowledge management can be used to try to achieve competitive advantage. In practice, to get the most out of modern ICT-based information systems requires managers who know how and where to apply ICT; staff at every level of the organization being comfortable with using ICT; and somebody to manage the information systems environment and encourage the utilization of knowledge.

Organizational structure

ICT and business information systems theory have been absorbed into the organizational levels (or strata) of business corporations. A general hierarchical organization will have three broad levels of organizational decision making, from top down:

▶ the strategic (or executive) level

▶ the management level

▶ the operational (or functional) level.

Each level exhibits different information requirement characteristics (in terms of the decision timeframe, certainty, risk, responsiveness, information structure and technology). The decision-making levels are highly significant, since the purpose of processing data is to produce information for decision making.

Business information systems fall into three broad categories within the organizational hierarchy: operational systems, management systems and strategic systems. Operational (or functional) systems are responsive and deterministic to the extent that the inputs and outputs are known with certainty. Such systems are usually found in the manufacturing domain, or at the lowest levels of a business organization. Such systems are mechanical, routine and algorithmic in their operation. Examples of such systems in business are inventory (or stock) control, payroll, sales order processing and purchase order processing. By contrast, strategic information systems are often only as accurate as the level of certainty or uncertainty of the predicted probabilities and forecasted events of the business environment. Within strategic information systems the information environment is uncertain and the decision-making functions are unstructured. This level of decision-making is characterized by executive information systems (EIS), decision support systems (DSS), expert systems (ES) and artificial intelligence (AI).

Management information systems (MIS), characterized by medium-term budgeting and forecasting functions, lie somewhere on the spectrum between strategic systems and operational systems. Management information systems are characterized by semi-structured information sets. In operational systems the whole of the decision picture is known; however, in strategic information systems parts of the decision picture are unknown. The aim of all systems is to get as near to decision-making certainty as possible.

In the light of the above, a business information systems professional in modern business systems environments needs not only an understanding of ICT, but also a substantive understanding of the application and characteristics of information systems at each level of the decision-making hierarchy within the modern information and knowledge-conscious business organization.

End-user computing has caused competitive business organizations to move away from the electronic data processing era of historical business computing, when organizations invested in data processing technology to automate their core business systems with no involvement from end users, to an era where information systems empower *knowledge workers* to make informed decisions in highly competitive business environments. This can often mean transforming a business organization's processes and procedures to make it more competitive or to counteract the advantages held by other organizations. Business transformation can be undertaken by the intelligent use of ICT to transform organizational structures and the way in which an organization practises business in relation to its employees, customers and suppliers.

Any business information systems professional should recognize the evolution and application of end-user computing within the business domain, where the final user of an information system is primarily responsible for the construction and development of that business system. Information systems end users are now more likely to be directly involved in the day-to-day decisions of ICT-based information systems and also in their specification and design. Therefore, end-user computing impacts on how information systems are built and used by organizations.

With the evolution of computing the need to manage ICT has become subsumed into the whole business function rather than concentrated in the hands of one person or department of a business organization; ICT now pervades the whole workplace. We have noted earlier that the prevalence and benefits of ICT are often taken for granted. This should be avoided because most organizations require a business strategy for optimizing ICT investment in order to maximize the return on such investment. Business organizations require a clear understanding of how ICT can make business processes more efficient and effective and also deliver new products and services through the strategic application of ICT.

Activity 1.5 Information and end-user computing

Discuss the general qualities that information should possess within information systems and outline considered arguments as to whether there are any trade-offs between these characteristics. For example, is there a trade-off between timeliness and information accuracy? Then provide three examples of information that may provide a business organization with an advantage over other competing business organizations. It is sometimes stated that information is power. In this context discuss whether you believe information should be available to all employees of a business organization or whether only a restricted set of information end users should possess (or own) the information available within a business domain.

1.7 Computing and ICT

Computing and ICT are not interchangable concepts. Computing is part of ICT but not the same as ICT. Traditionally, computing applications were targeted at 'number-crunching', mathematical problems and the routine processing of raw data to provide basic information from raw data. Such computing activities were concerned with structured and algorithmic data processing. ICT differs in definition to computing in that it includes not only computing-based technology but also incorporates the areas of wired and wireless networking and telecommunications. Therefore, the definition of ICT includes all aspects of computing, integrated with technological developments in networking and telecommunications technology.

What is an algorithm?

A defined set of instructions used to solve a problem. Computer code is often divided into algorithms.

ICT involves understanding that computer systems are no longer isolated from other computer systems, but are networked. Many in the business information systems domain talk of the 'networked enterprise' that conceptualizes the connectivity and interrelationship of computer networks with human networking within the business domain. Computer systems can be linked together into various larger ICT-based networks that connect both internally and externally to an organization. Consequently, wired and wireless telecommunication technologies are of significance and importance within the global business systems environment.

What is ICT?

The acquisition, processing, storage and dissemination of vocal, pictorial, textual and numeric information by a micro-electronics-based combination of computing and telecommunications.

Source: Department of Trade and Industry, UK.

ICT includes all aspects of computing technology, including the use and application of computer software and computer hardware. Computer software is the generic term used to describe the programs, algorithms and instructions used by computing technology to carry out commands, functions and activities. The software instructions coordinate the processes and operation of the physical components of computer technology hardware, which includes all the electronics, circuitry, storage media, and data input and output technologies (peripheral devices) included in a computer system. Therefore, computer hardware is the physical computing technology used for inputting, storage and outputting of data and information within an information system's environment. Telecommunications technologies undertake the activity of transferring data and information from one computer system to another computer system, either at a local or remote location. All these aspects of computer hardware, computer software and computer telecommunications will be covered in detail in subsequent chapters and can be considered part of the definition of ICT.

ICT can deliver a number of operational and managerial benefits to a business organization by integrating computing and telecommunications to achieve the following benefits:

▶ increased capacity and speed of data and information processing;
▶ wider dissemination and communication of data between information systems;
▶ effective access to local and remote data storage facilities;
▶ effective and efficient information control, enabling global business competition.

Information technology impacts on business information systems and widens the nature of business practices and competition to the extent that internal and external barriers to trade, such as technological barriers, political barriers and economic barriers, can often be eliminated. Advanced information-based economies, as we saw earlier in this chapter, seek to invest heavily in ICT in order to maintain or increase economic wealth. However, heavy national investment in information technology can only deliver the benefits of increased economic wealth if the population is ICT literate and educated to a level where ICT is developed and applied constructively in business and society in general.

What is ICT literacy?

A thorough knowledge about the use and application of information technology in society.

Therefore, to reap the benefits of ICT in all aspects of society there is a requirement for people to be ICT literate. ICT literacy within the business environment refers to an understanding of how to design, apply and use ICT in order to maximize its benefits. Therefore, ICT literacy extends to a knowledge and understanding of how information is used and managed by individuals and business organizations. This area is often referred to as *informatics*, which includes the study of all aspects of the retrieval, storage and dissemination of information. The importance of informatics in society was alluded to in Pause for thought 1.1. Informatics stresses the importance of information as a valuable and essential part of modern information-based economies.

Activity 1.6 Information and communications technology

Divide up into groups of four people and discuss the importance of telecommunications networks for modern ICT-based information systems. Outline five benefits of using ICT effectively within a business organization and deliver your findings in the form of a report to the other groups undertaking this activity. Compile a list of all the different benefits of ICT found by the various groups.

1.8 Information systems and ICT

An information system within business results from the structured and successful integration of the three main resources of people, organization and technology. Therefore, a business information system is a set of interrelated parts to handle, store and process data that is in turn disseminated to users to provide information and knowledge for decision making and control within the business domain.

There are three underlying components to an information system:

▶ **Inputs:** the collection and capture of raw data, which may be alphanumeric, image-based or voice based.

▶ **Processing**: structuring the raw input into a useful output (i.e. information or knowledge).

▶ **Outputs**: how information is transmitted or disseminated to support the decision-making activity.

What is an information system?

A set of interrelated components that act together to achieve some purpose or goal.

Data and information should not be considered as the same in definition. It is a fundamental fact of ICT that information is data processed for the purpose of decision making. Therefore, information is the result of processing raw data. Figure 1.1 shows the relationship and correlation between inputs and outputs and data and information within the fabric of an information system.

For information to have the appropriate *quality* for decision making it must possess certain desirable characteristics. The ideal characteristics that information should possess to be useful and purposeful can be summarized as:

▶ relevant to the user's needs
▶ accurate and factual
▶ complete and unabridged
▶ timely and delivered to the right person
▶ reliable for decision making
▶ useful to the end user's needs
▶ consistent and comparable over time
▶ understandable to the user
▶ portable and easily transmittable.

Information should be *relevant* for its purpose and to the end user of that information. Information should be *accurate* for the purpose, which means that the information is correct in all ways. Information should also be *complete* with all material available to allow that information to be used by a decision maker.

The data processing activity:

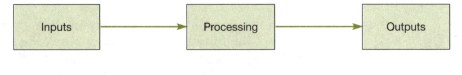

Information represents processed data:

Figure 1.1 ICT activity

Information should be *timely* in order for it to be useful for decision making. For example, information that is produced after an event has expired is worthless. Information should be *reliable*, which will allow decision makers to have confidence in the information. Confidence in information and information sources has to be built up over time. If information was reliable in the past, and communicated effectively, the decision maker will feel confident in depending on the reliability of the information.

Information should be *useful* to user needs – the correct and appropriate person should have access to the right information. The information requirements of different decision makers will vary. It is important that the information is focused to the requirements of the end users of that information. Information should be *consistent* and homogeneous. The method and approach to preparing information should be consistent from year to year (or period to period) and be consistent between different business organizations. For example, the annual financial accounts and statements produced by all business organizations are produced under strict and consistent rules, guidelines and regulations. This allows the financial information of one organization to be compared accurately with another business organization within the same national legal frameworks and time periods. Information should be *understandable* to the end user of the information. The information environment and the language used will influence the degree to which information is understandable to end users. Information should be *portable* to the extent that it can be effectively communicated between information systems and people within an organization.

Information can be internal to an organization or external to the business organization. Table 1.2 lists some of the possible external sources of information and some of the possible internal sources of information affecting a business organization.

Quality information for decision making is an essential asset for any competitive business. However, the measurement of information value is a difficult exercise that is often neglected by many organizations. The purchase cost of the hardware and software aspects of information systems is verifiable and quantifiable. Likewise, any business should attempt to apply a quantifiable measure of cost (or economic return) on the value of information.

Quantifiable value is factual, verifiable by documentation, and measured in monetary terms. On the other hand *non-quantifiable value* cannot be measured with such certainty. It may be the case that the information from an information system adds value to the overall business organization that is not measurable in

Table 1.2 Sources of business information

Internal sources	External sources
Financial accounting information	Business competition
Management accounting information	Customer demand and supply
Marketing information	Economic information
Production costs and expenses	Government information
Human resources information	Cultural and political information
Research and development	Technological information

direct monetary terms. Such value is qualitative rather than quantitative (quantitative value is based on facts, figures and numbers; qualitative value is based mainly on intuition and judgement). For example, a marketing information system may store and analyze demographic, social and economic information on customers for transmission to managers for decision making concerning product development in the future. Such information may also be of significance to other sectors of the business domain, both internally and externally. Therefore, the marketing system has added indirect benefit to other sectors of the organization. The benefits of an information system may have a ripple effect across an organization and its external environment affecting customers, suppliers and other competing business organizations.

Activity 1.7 Information quality and value

The quality of information affects the quality of decision making within a business organization. Put yourself into the role of a manager deciding whether to buy new equipment for a factory manufacturing computer components. Discuss and list all the possible information sources the manager would consult to establish a set of criteria for decision making. Explain the qualities that the information set should possess. Define whether the information set may include quantifiable and non-quantifiable information and highlight some of the problems associated with measuring intangible information value.

1.9 Business and society in the global information age

This chapter has emphasized how important ICT is to business. The majority of modern business organizations are intrinsically information-based. Information is the life-blood of a modern business organization. This section expands on the ideas of business to look at some of the historical developments of business and ICT within society.

We noted earlier in this chapter that the information age evolved from the industrial age of the nineteenth century, which in turn evolved from the agricultural age preceding that century. Up until about 1825 the majority of the population around the world was engaged in agricultural labour. However, that year was a milestone in the industrial revolution. In 1825 the first railway line, built between Stockton and Darlington in England, heralded the start of a revolution in travel and the beginning of an industrial age based on manufacturing. Railroad networks expanded very rapidly throughout the nineteenth century. Railroads in the USA began effectively with the Baltimore and Ohio railroad in 1830. This development, along with the growth of large-scale industrial manufacturing, signalled the coming of the industrial age where the majority of the population would be employed in heavy industries such as steel, coal, shipbuilding and engineering. However, in the twentieth century, and particularly since the 1940s, the industrial age has declined in importance and has been replaced by the information age where the majority of the workforce is involved in some form of information (and knowledge) handling, processing and dissemination.

This age is often referred to as the *post-industrial society* or by the shorthand description of the *information society*.

Information has become a saleable commodity in its own right, with many modern organizations engaged in analyzing and processing information to be sold to other organizations for profit. For example, some financial organizations have large research departments to study the performance of company equities or national economic performance. These organizations are part of the *information industry*. The information society description should not be confused with the information industry. The information industry refers to organizations that earn money from buying, selling and trading information.

Did you know?

The information age began with Samuel Morse's development of the telegraph transmitter and receiver in 1837. It was the first instrument to transform information into electrical form and transmit it over vast distances. The data was transmitted in Morse code (a series of dots and dashes). The first experimental commercial telegraph line was between Washington, DC, and Baltimore, Maryland, in the USA in 1844. Soon bankers and business professionals realized that the speed of information exchange could be used for business advantage; for example, making use of the speedy receipt of stock price changes and other vital business information. This technology shortened the time for decision making and increased the pace of the business day.

Business organizations are often referred to as being information-based to the extent that information retrieval, storage and dissemination are the reason for their existence as a commercial organization. Information is a particularly important commodity in the financial and banking sectors. The information age has led to the study of the science of information, referred to as *informatics*, and covers the study of information mediated by ICT.

The growth of the information society has been fuelled by two factors:

▶ **Supply-side growth**: developments in computing and ICT.

▶ **Demand-side growth**: market forces and competition among business organizations that has added impetus in the acquisition of quality information.

Therefore, the demand for information that possesses all the qualities of accuracy, timeliness, relevance, usefulness, understandability and portability has encouraged and stimulated advances in ICT.

Activity 1.8 Business and society in the information age

Discuss and contrast the concept of the information society with the information industry and outline the main characteristics that distinguish the information society from the information industry. Then investigate whether your college or university has access to online information services. List and catalogue the services that are available.

1.10 Technology growth in the global information age

The power and processing capability of ICT grows at an ever increasing rate over time. Often hardware is advancing far more rapidly than the capability of software. In turn, both hardware and software are advancing faster than the capability of people within business organizations to understand and apply ICT to its most effective extent.

It is the case that hardware is growing exponentially compared to software growth and the inherent business organization's understanding of ICT. The relationship between hardware, software and business understanding of ICT is indicated in Figure 1.2. It is estimated that, on average, the capability (or productivity) of hardware increases ten times over a five-year period. The capability (or productivity) of software increases by a factor of two every eight years. However, the rate at which business organizations understand and apply ICT increases far more slowly. Therefore, there is an awareness in business information systems that people and organizations need to increase their knowledge and understanding of ICT and the application of ICT within the business environment. Keeping pace with advances in ICT is a constant battle for any commercial organization. Keeping pace with advances in ICT and its capabilities can only be achieved by increased ICT literacy. For organizations to be competitive they must increase the rate at which people within the organization absorb, understand and apply ICT and use their knowledge in the business environment. The challenge that business faces is to increase the capability (or productivity) of ICT understanding within the business organization domain.

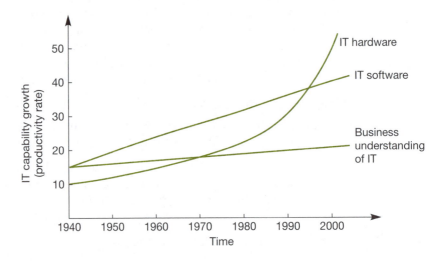

Figure 1.2 Business organization understanding of IT

1.11 Data, information, knowledge and wisdom

Earlier in this chapter information was defined as processed data. In the information age this relationship can be extended to include the concept of information for decision making. Once information has been obtained, it can be further refined to provide *knowledge* and, with advances in technology, knowledge may even provide eventual *wisdom*. Figure 1.3 shows the progression from data through to wisdom.

Considering Figure 1.3, in order to understand how information technology has impacted on the processing of data; the handling of information; the provision of knowledge for decision-making and the possibility of machine independence and responsibility for determining wisdom, a history of the evolution of electronic computers and ICT must be undertaken.

The evolution of computing technology

The evolution of computing is often categorized into generations. The generations are described by the nature and sophistication of the underlying mechanical or electronic technology. For example, the first electronic computers were produced in the 1940s and since then computing and information technology has witnessed a number of advances in the electronics field. Each step up in the power of technology leads to a new generation. The generations of computing can be classified as follows:

▶ **First generation computing (1940s and 1950s):** the earliest use of computing technology in the form of *valves* and *vacuum tubes*. Unfortunately, vacuum tubes consumed large amounts of electricity and often overheated. First generation computers were very large but limited in terms of memory and processing capacity. First generation computers were limited to number-crunching activities and, therefore, were mainly used in the mathematical disciplines of science and engineering. Normally, punch cards were used to program these computers. The computers that categorized this generation of technology were EDSAC, EDVAC, LEO and UNIVAC1.

▶ **Second generation computing (late 1950s and early 1960s):** categorized by the use of more advanced technology in the form of *transistors* that replaced valve technology. Transitors were smaller, more economical, more reliable and cheaper than vacuum tubes. Magnetic tape was normally used to store programs and data. The increases in processing power and memory capacity enabled these computers to become more useful within the business domain, for example to automate administrative tasks and calculate routine data, such as payroll and salaries. The computers that categorized this generation of technology were the LEO III, ATLAS and the IBM 7000 series.

Figure 1.3 Progression from data into wisdom

▶ **Third generation computing (late 1960s and 1970s):** used more advanced technology than first and second generation computers in the form of *integrated circuits* that allowed thousands of transistors to be etched on to silicon chips. Thus memory and processing speeds were greatly increased over previous generations of technology. This generation of computing is also categorized by smaller and more compact technology. The process of miniaturization of physical technology is known as *downsizing*. Programs for third generation technology were less mathematical and symbolic and based more on natural language. Third generation computers are categorized by the ICL 1900 series and the IBM 360 series.

▶ **Fourth generation computing (1980s and 1990s):** used more complex integrated circuits known as large-scale integration (LSI) or very large-scale integration (VLSI). This allows millions of circuits to be etched on to a chip. This generation was also characterized by the development of microprocessor technology, whereby an entire central processing unit (CPU) could be etched on to a single silicon chip. Fourth generation technology was (and is) categorized by the collateral trends of miniaturization of computer components and massive increases in technology processing power.

▶ **Fifth generation computing (post 1990s):** the development of 'thinking' machines that mimic human reasoning and intelligence with the added advantage of greater information processing ability and power. Fifth generation technology lies in the realms of artificial intelligence, expert systems, biological computing and technologies to support and mimic human decision-making capabilities.

1.12 A history of business computing

Information can be equated with 'power' to the extent that information provides the knowledge to make informed decisions. Being ICT literate is an essential skill and capability in the information age. This idea of the importance of information and knowledge can even be found in the early literature of H.G. Wells, who described in the 1930s various fictional technological trends – some of which have evolved from fiction to reality in many respects!

Did you know?

In his book *World Brain*, written in 1938, H.G. Wells wrote: 'In a few score years there will be thousands of workers at this business of ordering and digesting knowledge where you now have only one.'

The earliest *electronic computers* in the 1940s were large and relatively slow, with ponderous, unsophisticated processing power. Work on the first *digital computer* can be attributed to Howard Aitkin, a mathematician at Harvard University in the USA, in the late 1930s. His work, using electro-mechanical switches, began in 1937 and culminated in 1943 with the Mark I computer that contained 750 000 component parts and measured 15 metres long and 2.5 metres high. The

Mark I was designed as an arithmetic machine (which could add, subtract, divide and multiply) and was used by the American army during the Second World War to calculate ballistic tables for army gunners. The success of this computer led the American government to fund a team (led by J.P. Eckert and J. Mauchly) at the University of Pennsylvania to build a faster computer based on vacuum tubes rather than electro-mechanical switches. The computer was named the ENIAC (Electronic Numerical Integrator and Calculator) and its purpose was again to perform arithmetic calculations. Although the ENIAC was designed to compute routine and tedious calculations it is interesting because its designers made it programmable. The ENIAC could be set to perform a range of calculation tasks. Hence, the purpose of computation led the first machines to be named computers. The ENIAC computer was large (it covered a room area of 15×9 metres) and was a heavy consumer of electrical power.

Did you know?

The hot glowing vacuum tubes of the earliest computers attracted moths to the lights. These flying bugs often damaged the machinery and would have to be removed from the machine by technicians, a process known as debugging. The term bug in the system is now used to refer to any problem found within a computer system, but originally it referred to a real bug in the system!

In 1951 J.P. Eckert and J. Mauchly followed up the ENIAC computer with a more sophisticated computer designed for commercial applications which was known as the UNIVAC (**Univ**ersal **A**utomatic **C**omputer). The UNIVAC, which was based on vacuum tubes, was developed for the American Census Bureau and began work on the American census of 1950. The UNIVAC was significant in using peripheral devices such as magnetic tape and electronic printers. The advances made in computing through the UNIVAC project led to large organizations of the 1950s realizing the potential of commercial computing, which manifested itself in a movement into the research, design and development of computing technology.

The late 1950s saw the use of vacuum tubes replaced by transistors that were smaller and processed data faster than vacuum tube technology. In 1959 two physicists, R. Noyce and J. Hoerni, developed the first *integrated circuit*, which entailed the microscopic photo-engraving of transistors on a single chip the size of an average human thumb nail. Integrated circuitry led to the development of smaller but more powerful computers and opened up the possibility of computers becoming available to a wider audience of commercial organizations. In the 1960s International Business Machines (IBM) in the USA realized the potential of computing. The president of IBM in the 1960s, T. Watson, had the vision to appreciate the value of computers to business organizations and actively moved IBM into the development and manufacturing of mainframe computers. IBM eventually moved away from the business of manufacturing and selling business machines, such as cash registers, into computing technology. IBM first developed the 7000 series of computers. But in 1964 IBM moved into the third generation of computing technology with the development of the IBM 360 series of computers aimed at satisfying the requirements of large commercial business organizations.

IBM was so successful and dominant in the computing industry that the IBM S/360 computer became a standard business machine in the 1960s. These were supported by a number of peripheral devices, such as tape drives, printers and card readers, but were still very large and required an enormous amount of physical space within an organization. This in turn led to business organizations establishing departments that were dedicated to the function of electronic computing. These business areas became known as electronic data processing (EDP) departments and were supported by numerous computing technicians and various other staff, dedicated solely to supporting the computer technology. The IBM S/360 computers were able to process instructions at the rate of around 100 000 instructions per second. These computers were used for carrying out the mechanical and essential functional systems operations of large organizations, such as payroll, stock processing, personnel records and financial accounting. Computers improved the speed, efficiency and effectiveness of data processing within the organization. These areas were suitable for large-scale *batch processing*, which was the process of putting through the computer a mass of data and information in one computer-processing run.

The profit to be made from selling computers to business organizations led to other companies entering the computing industry, such as Burroughs, NCR (National Cash Registers), Honeywell and Hewlett-Packard. If one business organization acquired a computer, it led to other business organizations within the industry acquiring a computer in order to maintain a competitive edge over its rivals. During this period of growth within computing IBM became the business leader within the industry, to an extent whereby it dictated the standards to be matched and adhered to by other companies within the industry. In the 1970s attention turned towards the development of more sophisticated peripheral input and output devices to support mainframe computing; input terminals and output devices were consequently improved.

The 1970s saw the start of miniaturization of computing technology that is continuing today and is associated with the concept of *downsizing* in the computing and ICT domain. Downsizing allowed smaller businesses the scope to incorporate computing technology into all their organizational processes at relatively low cost. Therefore, computing was no longer the preserve of the large business organizations with vast purchasing budgets. The computing industry moved away from mainframe computers into what were known as *minicomputers*. Minicomputing introduced the concept of distributed computing whereby processing functions were distributed to terminals within various parts of a business organization – thus leading to the concept of *networking*. The stand-alone terminals (sometimes known as 'dumb' terminals) used with mainframe environments were beginning to be replaced with 'smarter' terminals and, by so doing, provided greater participation within an organization for computing operations and functions. In the 1970s (and more so in the early 1980s) many commercial organizations entered the computing industry to provide cloned IBM technology that greatly challenged the earning potential of IBM. Minicomputers, based on distributed (networked) computing, were cheaper than mainframes and became a standard within the majority of medium-size business organizations in the 1970s.

As technology, such as microchips, became cheaper and more freely available, more component manufacturers entered the computing industry, which led to the development and supply of 'off-the-shelf' computers and peripheral technology, rather than one-off computer systems for large business clients. The late 1970s saw a dramatic increase in organizations offering off-the-shelf software. Along with hardware technology, software applications for word-processing, spreadsheet modelling, graphics and database storage were developed as off-the-shelf applications for commercial business purposes. This eliminated the requirement for business organizations to employ many specialist programmers to write software applications that were specific to one application within a specific organization. The provision of off-the-shelf generic software is often known as *commodity software*. The late 1970s saw a range of off-the-shelf commercial software applications. Other companies, such as Lotus 1-2-3, also entered the computing industry during this era to provide readily available software applications for business purposes.

The late 1970s and the early 1980s witnessed computer input terminals proliferating in business organizations. Computing became cheaper and more available to all functional areas within a commercial business organization to the extent that mainframes were becoming obsolete for the majority of business organizations. The 1980s witnessed computing downsized to the extent that it pervaded all aspects of a business organization and furthermore proliferated to individuals for personal use and applications in the home. The Apple I computer was developed by Steve Jobs and Steve Wozniak in 1976. Jobs and Wozniak started their business (Apple Computers) from Job's garage. The users bought the parts for the Apple I and constructed their own computer. The sales of Apple I and Apple II computers showed the world that there was a huge market for home computing. Later, the 1980s became associated with the birth of *personal computing* as the proliferation of technology spread to individuals within society at large.

> **Did you know?**
>
> The first commercially available spreadsheet application program was written by D. Bricklin and B. Frankston and was known as VisiCalc.

Personal computing was made possible by the development of microprocessor technology on single silicon chips. The Intel Corporation produced the first available microprocessor, known as the Intel 8008, and the 1080 chip in the early 1970s and other companies followed suit with the development of other microprocessor-based technology. In the mid-1970s a company known as MITS (Micro Instrumentation and Telemetry Systems) produced a kit-form component computer known as Altair. The availability of such kit-form microprocessor chip technology allowed computer-literate individuals to produce their own customized computers, which encouraged the development of the microcomputer industry. It was also in the mid–1970s that Bill Gates and Paul Allen formed a company to market software systems that became known as Microsoft.

By the end of the 1970s it was becoming apparent that personal computers (PCs) were starting to replace mainframe computing and the peripheral technology that surrounded mainframe computing, such as 'dumb' terminals. PCs could be used not only as terminal emulators for mainframes and minicomputers but also to carry out single and stand-alone business functions involving word-processing, spreadsheet applications, database applications and graphics. PCs were more versatile to an organization operating in a dynamic and ever-changing business environment. IBM was at first slow to appreciate the growing importance of PCs to business, instead preferring to concentrate on the provision of large mainframe computers to business organizations. However, by the early 1980s IBM had moved into the PC marketplace and had set the IBM standard for PCs that were cloned by other computer manufacturers. The early IBM PCs used an 8088 processor produced by Intel in the USA and a disk operating system (DOS) that was supplied by the Microsoft corporation. The disk operating system allows the sequencing and processing of computer instructions.

The Compaq corporation and Commodore were examples of computing businesses that grew large on the profits from providing PCs to business. The increase in companies competing to sell PCs and related business software led to prices being reduced during the 1980s and 1990s to levels at which all business organizations from large to small were able to acquire useful business computing technology. Gradually, computing manufacturers of hardware and software technology moved away from competing on price, when prices fell to levels where it was difficult to generate a profit, to competing on performance and quality.

The 1990s were characterized by relatively affordable computing technology with ever-increasing performance capabilities. Business organizations cannot compete without the effective use and integration of ICT within the organization fabric. In essence, it was the PC revolution within the computing world that led to a cultural change in the way computers were integrated into the business environment, and the way job roles and responsibilities became defined within organizations. The 1990s were characterized by a large number of ICT providers (vendors), with many of the large computer mainframe vendors of the 1980s having gone out of business, merged or refocused towards selling business and personal computer software rather than hardware. Commercial business software was the largest profit earner for ICT vendors in the 1990s.

The start of the twenty-first century has seen a shift in emphasis away from fixed ICT, located in offices, towards ICT that frees up the worker to operate from any location and at any time. Wireless networks and mobile devices predominate the business systems environment. The ability to support the *mobile workforce* has become a paramount consideration in the business information systems world. Wireless *mobile computing* and mobile commerce predominate the developments in ICT. Computing is no longer the preserve of the PC but is embedded into a range of static and dynamic devices (such as in-vehicle information systems, wireless mobile phones, wireless laptops, and remote access to the mobile internet, via wireless personal digital assistants (PDAs)).

What is mobile computing?

The use of the mobile devices (e.g. mobile phones, PDAs, laptops, etc.) and wireless networking environments necessary to provide location-independent connectivity.

Activity 1.9 A history of business computing

Outline the main distinguishing features of first, second, third, fourth and fifth generation computing. Search your college or university library to find relevant information to construct a chronology of the main decade-by-decade developments within the computing and ICT industry from the 1940s to the start of the twenty-first century. Discuss the significance of these developments for business systems activity and end-user computing. What will be the consequences of *mobile computing* on the design and development of business information systems in the twenty-first century?

1.13 Business systems environments

Information systems are shaped by the aims and objectives of the business organization. However, the shape and development of business information systems are often constrained by a number of secondary considerations that are internal and external to the business organization. A constraint limits the capacity of an organization to achieve its aims and objectives. These constraining factors may be technical, economic, political, statutory, social or cultural. One or all of these factors may constrain or influence the shape and configuration of a business information system. Figure 1.4 shows the various layers of the business systems environment.

The organization is often affected by both the internal and external business environment. Figure 1.4 outlines the internal and external factors that influence and constrain a business organization. Information systems environments can be termed as either *open* or *closed*. Closed information systems are self-contained and isolated from the external constraints. An open information system is influenced and affected by the external business environment.

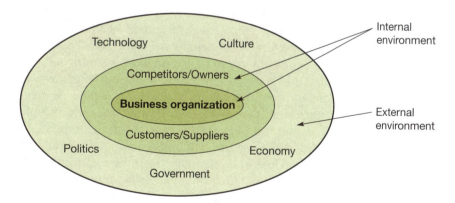

Figure 1.4 The business systems environment

The business systems environment

Divide up into pairs and describe the main constraints that might influence the shape and development of a business information system. Outline and try to categorize these constraints into internal and external business factors. Consider and explain what is meant by an open system and a closed system within the context of the business environment.

1.14 Enterprise transformation and globalization

We have seen that within any business organization there are three essential resources that have to be managed and coordinated to allow an organization to maximize its profit efficiently and effectively. These are people, technology and organization. In the information age the profit potential of a business organization is governed by the competitive nature of the global economy in which it operates – and how efficiently and effectively the organization utilizes all its resources to exploit global market advantages.

The success of a business in the twenty-first century depends upon its ability to compete in the global economy. There are two major forces that affect the way that business activity is conducted in the twenty-first century: globalization and enterprise transformation. Globalization is the term used to represent the emergence of the global economy. The products and services produced by a business organization will rarely be unique to a particular country, although the product or service can be customized to the tastes of people in certain countries. For example, motor vehicles are used and sold in nearly every country around the world. However, there are approximately only ten major mass-market vehicle manufacturers in the world. Yet these few vehicle manufacturers sell cars to many countries and compete in a global marketplace. The same is true of many other industries, such as the computer industry and mobile telecommunications. Therefore, business information systems need to be designed and built to recognize global effects and to appreciate the greater complexity of global trade.

The idea of enterprise transformation encapsulates the forces and trends that are affecting the shape and nature of business organizations. For example, organizations in the information age are not normally, or predominantly, centred on manufacturing; they have been transformed into information and knowledge-based organizations. In such organizations the most valuable asset is the knowledge and ability of the employees, rather than the value of equipment and machinery. Organizations focus on thinking up innovative ways of exploiting ICT opportunities, rather than merely focusing on buying better or more expensive ICT. Within the global economy business organizations are becoming transformed into entities with a global identity rather than a national identity. To compete in the knowledge-based global economy organizations have transformed into learning organizations that use and exploit the human resource of knowledge and experience.

The forces of globalization have led to many of these enterprise transformations. Globalization brings new threats but also new opportunities for an organization. Business systems need to be constructed to deal with these threats and opportunities. At their most basic level, business information systems need to handle the additional complexities of managing global enterprises: by dealing with differences in time, location and culture. Globalization has turned business into a 24-hour-a-day (often seven days a week) enterprise and activity. The twenty-first century is becoming dominated by the '24/7' business organization. Again, this is a significant organizational transformation.

Another major transformation in the twenty-first century is a change in organizational structures. Business enterprises no longer conform to one homogenous structure (e.g. a hierarchical management structure) but take on many different forms. These structural changes have included the movement away from centralized offices towards a more mobile workforce. Working from home (known as telecommuting) and working away from an office, but still being connected via portable wireless technologies, have made organizational structures more fluid. Global business activity needs to be supported by flexible and adaptive information systems rather than by a rigid and fixed structure associated with one particular country or market. The rise of mobility and wireless technology in the business information systems domain has led to the development of the *virtual organization*.

The development and growth of virtual organizations is described in the following extract:

> Information technology has created the global village. The business world is not as big as it used to be. Businesses can now exist in a variety of formats. The need to be physically in a particular place is no longer required. For example, a few years ago IBM decided to mobilize its sales and field support personnel. Their offices were taken away and instead they were allowed to reserve a cubicle when they needed to attach to a network or use any of the office support services. They simply plugged their laptop into the network and their phone number was forwarded to the cubicle that they reserved. We are also seeing the growth of businesses that exist totally on the public access networks [i.e. internet]. Information is bought and sold over the networks; research data is compiled and stored and available for purchase to any interested party; orders are placed, payments are made, deliveries scheduled. Business can literally be transacted anyplace, anytime and anywhere. The traditional physical boundaries are no longer a necessary part of many businesses. (Wysocki and DeMichiell, 1997, pp. 9–10)

These factors have major implications for organizational transformation and working practices. Mobility, supported by wireless connectivity and networking, has transformed the way in which information and knowledge is handled and managed in the organizational domain. Responsiveness is a key concept in virtual organizations. It represents the ability to respond to continuous change in the global economy and the delivery of mass-customized goods. Mass customization is where an organization sells a product or service to a large number of people (i.e. many hundreds of thousands) but is still able to provide a level of product or service customization to groups within the mass market. For example, computers are sold in millions around the world. However, many vendors, such as Dell Computers, allow their customers a certain level of customization in terms of memory versus processing power, or type of screen device and other peripherals. Customers can then determine a fixed price, but within that ceiling price they can trade off (or prioritize) certain aspects of the product for themselves; some customers may be interested in powerful processing capacity, while others would trade off that feature for more storage capacity.

Virtual organizations represent groups of people working together, connected by wireless and wired networks, with the aim of innovatively creating products and services untethered by traditional organizational structures. The importance of human connectivity and technology networking within the virtual organizational domain has led many to refer to such organizations as *networked enterprises*. These organizations link people, technologies and ideas together within the global economy. Highly networked virtual organizations have no defined physical (or national) boundaries. Therefore, the task of designing and developing business systems gravitates away from merely defining boundaries towards concentration on structuring and evaluating systems to support virtual working practices.

1.15 Chapter summary

Organizations that compete with each other are affected by technological change in the business environment. To be competitive, organizations must understand the nature, role and influence of ICT on business information systems performance. Technological, human and organizational change must be successfully managed in order to be competitive and generate a profit in global and dynamic business environments. ICT pervades the whole fabric of a business organization. The capability to recognize technological transformation, and develop ICT solutions to deal with such transformation, is a skill that must be acquired and constructively applied in the information age.

ICT is a global phenomenon that makes the world, in virtual terms and in real terms, a smaller place through increased speed of action and connectivity. In the information age, ICT is absorbed into everyday life to the extent that it is part of our social fabric, clothing our working lives and our social lives. The development of mobile computing has even blurred the distinction between our working life and our personal life. We have the opportunity in the information age to have a mass of information and technological resources at our fingertips; this enables us to conduct and transact business and order our social life at the same time.

Organizations recognize the opportunities that appear with ICT and the affect ICT has on business information systems activity. Organizations aim to achieve effective and efficient 'business at the speed of thought' (the title of a book by Bill Gates). The globalization of business competitiveness predominates the mindset of business information systems professionals in the twenty-first century. The imperative of handling and managing information and knowledge in the information age was emphasized by the writer John Buchan back in 1919: 'This war is a pack of surprises. Both sides are struggling for the margin, the little fraction of advantage, and between evenly matched enemies it's just the extra atom of foreknowledge that tells.'

Buchan indicates the value of information and knowledge and the need for information systems to deliver knowledge on which to base informed and intuitive decision making. The quote describes how even a little additional knowledge benefits the possessors of that knowledge and ultimately can gain them an advantage over the competition.

SHORT SELF-ASSESSMENT QUESTIONS

1.1 Outline and explain the three fundamental resources of a business organization.

1.2 Define the role and purpose of a *BIS professional* within a business organization.

1.3 Explain what is meant by *knowledge management* and explain the role of knowledge management in business.

1.4 Define the concept of *competitive advantage* and explain the type of strategy that can be employed to deliver an advantage in a competitive business environment.

1.5 Explain the term *end-user computing* as it applies within a business organization and explain the possible role of end users in information systems development.

1.6 Outline five key trends in ICT within the business systems domain and explain the significance of each issue.

1.7 Define and explain the fundamental differences and distinctions between *ICT* and *computing*.

1.8 Define the term *ICT literacy* and explain how such literacy affects the job specifications of *knowledge workers*.

1.9 Explain why it is important to understand the value of information in an organization.

1.10 Outline the three component parts of an information system in a business organization and explain the relationship between these parts.

1.11 Explain the terms *supply side technology growth* and *demand side technology growth* and provide examples of demand for information and supply of technology.

1.12 Define and explain what is meant by a *virtual organization* in the information age.

1.13 Define the terms *globalization* and *enterprise transformation* as applied to business systems in the global economy.

EXTENDED STUDENT ACTIVITIES

Individual reporting activity

By searching your university or college library for any examples of ICT used in the business environment, locate a suitable article or case study that describes the use of information systems and ICT in a particular organization. For your example:

1 Describe the information system and ICT in terms of the inputs, outputs and processing activity undertaken.

2 Describe and explain the interaction of people, technology and organization upon the information system.

3 Outline the various external and internal sources of information that impact on that information system and discuss the technology that is used to carry out the operations of the system.

4 Consider and discuss the type of training and education required to operate and implement the information system in order to achieve suitable levels of ICT literacy within the organization.

Your findings should be written up in a report to your colleagues or presented to them in the form of an oral and/or visual presentation.

Group-based activity

Divide into groups and select team leaders. Discuss how virtual organizations (or networked enterprises) affect the way that people live and work within society. In particular, consider the impact on society of mobile working practices. Explain the possible benefits and drawbacks of the mobile workforce within business and society. Write a brief report of your group discussions. The report should be exchanged with the other groups for further discussion.

REFERENCES AND FURTHER STUDY

Books and articles

Beynon-Davies, P. (2002) *Information Systems: An Introduction to Informatics in Organisations*, Palgrave, ISBN: 0333963903

Bird, P.J. (1994) LEO: *The First Business Computer*, Hasler Publishing, ISBN: 0952165104

Cho, Dong-Sung and Moon, Hwy-Chang (2000) *From Adam Smith to Michael Porter: Evolution of Competitiveness Theory*, World Scientific Publishing, ISBN: 9810244312

Davenport, T.H. and Prusak, L. (2000) *Working Knowledge: How Organizations Manage What They Know*, Harvard Business School Press, ISBN: 1578513014

Doz, Y.L., Santos, J. and Williams, P. (2001) *From Global to Metanational: How Companies Win in the Knowledge Economy*, Harvard Business School Press, ISBN: 0875848702

Duff, A.S., Craig, D. and McNeill, D.A. (1996) 'A note on the origins of the information society', *Journal of Information Science*, 22(2), pp. 117–22

Elliott, G. and Phillips, N. (2004) *Mobile Commerce and Wireless Computing Systems*, Addison-Wesley, ISBN: 0201752409

Garfield, E. (1979) '2001: an information society?', *Journal of Information Science*, 1(4), pp. 209–15

Gates, B. (2000) *Business @ the Speed of Thought: Succeeding in the Digital Age*, Penguin Books, ISBN: 0140283129

Koelsch, F. (1995) *The Infomedia Revolution*, McGraw-Hill, ISBN: 0075518473

Laudon, K.C. and Laudon, J.P. (2000) *Information Systems: A Problem Solving Approach*, Prentice Hall, ISBN: 0130156825

Laudon, K.C. and Laudon, J.P. (2002) *Management Information Systems: Managing the Digital Firm*, Pearson Education, Prentice Hall, ISBN: 0130619604

Lavington, S. (1980) *Early British Computers*, Manchester University Press, ISBN: 0719008107

Malhotra, Y. (Ed.) (2001) *Knowledge Management and Business Model Innovation Idea*, Group Publishing, ISBN: 1878289985

Nonaka, I. and Takeuchi, H. (1995) *The Knowledge Creating Company*, Oxford University Press, ISBN: 0195092694

Porter, M.E. (1998) *The Competitive Advantage: Creating and Sustaining Superior Performance*, Simon and Schuster, ISBN: 0684841460

Porter, M.E. (1998) *Competitive Strategies: Techniques for Analyzing Industries and Competitors*, Simon and Schuster, ISBN: 0684841487

Porter, M.E. (1998) *The Competitive Advantage of Nations*, Palgrave, ISBN: 0333736427

Senn, J.A. (1998) *Information Technology in Business*, Prentice Hall International Edition, ISBN: 0139064478

Slywotzky, A., Morrison, D.J. and Morrison, D. (2001) *How Digital is Your Business?* Nicholas Brealey Publishing, ISBN: 1857882903

Smith, A. (1776) (edited by K. Sunderland, 1998) *The Wealth of Nations*, Oxford Paperbacks, ISBN: 0192835467

Stewart, T.A. (2002) *The Wealth of Knowledge: Intellectual Capital and the Twenty-First Century Organization*, Nicholas Brealey Publishing, ISBN: 185788287

Thurow, L.C. (2003) *Head to Head: The Coming Economic Battle Among Japan, Europe, and America*, HarperCollins, ISBN: 006053639x

Tiwana, A. (2002) *The Knowledge Management Toolkit: Practical Techniques for Building a Knowledge Management System*, Prentice Hall, ISBN: 013009224

Wenger, E. (2002) *Cultivating Communities of Practice: A Guide to Managing Knowledge*, Harvard Business School Press, ISBN: 1578513308

Wysocki, R.K. and DeMichiell, R.L. (1997) *Managing Information Across the Enterprise*, John Wiley and Sons, ISBN: 0471127191

Web resources

Learning and Teaching Support Network for Information and Computer Sciences (UK) – promotes the use of online teaching and learning resources in ICT.
www.ics.ltsn.ac.uk

World Lecture Hall – Computer Science (USA) – contains links to university-level material in information systems and ICT.
http://wnt.cc.utexas.edu/~wlh/browse/index.cfm

Journal of Digital Information (UK) – journal on the management and presentation of digital information.
http://jodi.ecs.soton.ac.uk

MIT Laboratory for Computer Science (USA) – a research centre focusing on developments in ICT.
www.lcs.mit.edu

Association for Information Systems (global) – professional body for information systems professionals and knowledge workers.
www.aisnet.org

The history and evolution of LEO computers (UK) – the first business computer.
www.leo-computers.org.uk

Chapter 2

General systems theory

When you have studied this chapter you will be able to:

▶ describe and outline the development and philosophy of general systems theory;

▶ appreciate those who have been influential in the development of systems theory;

▶ interpret and describe the difference between physical and logical systems thinking;

▶ understand the universal principles and characteristics that define a system within the business environment;

▶ distinguish the three main organizational levels of a business and be able to describe the information systems characteristics of each level;

▶ describe the nature and characteristics of different types of business information systems found within the business environment.

2.1 Introduction to general systems theory

The world is made up of *systems* and *sub-systems*. Human beings are complex and organizing systems. Within the human system exist various sub-systems, like the brain, the blood circulation system, the body temperature system and many other physiological and biological sub-systems. Coexisting alongside human beings are various other *natural* systems, such as the climatic system (i.e. the four seasons of spring, summer, autumn and winter) and the planets in our galaxy revolving around the Sun. We may even wish to argue philosophically that the universe is a larger system made up of smaller sub-systems. In addition, systems that merely exist through human organization or influence (e.g. transportation systems, communication systems, vehicle and railroad networks etc.) are termed *human-made* systems. There is a universal understanding that the whole world is comprised of systems.

The study of systems is known as *systems science*. To appreciate *business systems*, and particularly business information systems, we must first of all understand *general systems theory*. General systems theory is a multi-disciplinary study of how things are organized and relate to one another within their environment.

Pause for thought 2.1 provides a definition of systems theory prepared for a renowned dictionary of philosophy. Study this section carefully and then read on further to discover details of all the concepts highlighted.

PAUSE FOR THOUGHT 2.1

What is systems theory?

Systems theory: The transdisciplinary study of the abstract organisation of phenomena, independent of their substance, type, or spatial or temporal scale of existence. It investigates both the principles common to all complex entities, and the (usually mathematical) models which can be used to describe them.

Systems theory was proposed in the 1940s by the biologist Ludwig von Bertalanffy (anthology: *General Systems Theory*, 1968), and furthered by Ross Ashby (*Introduction to Cybernetics*, 1956). Von Bertalanffy was both reacting against **reductionism** and attempting to revive the **unity of Science**. He emphasised that real systems are open to, and interact with, their environments, and that they can acquire qualitatively new properties through **emergence**, resulting in continual **evolution**. Rather than reducing an entity (e.g. the human body) to the properties of its parts or elements (e.g. organs or cells), systems theory focuses on the arrangement of and **relations** between the parts which connect them into a whole (**holism**). This particular **organisation** determines a **system**, which is independent of the concrete substance of the elements (e.g. particles, cells, transistors, people, etc.). Thus, the same concepts and principles of organisation underlie the different disciplines (physics, biology, technology, sociology, etc.), providing a basis for their unification. Systems concepts include: system-environment **boundary**, **input**, **output**, **process**, **state**, **hierarchy**, **goal directness** and **information**.

The developments of systems theory are diverse (G.J. Klir, *Facets of Systems Science*, 1991), including conceptual foundations and philosophy; mathematical modelling and **information theory**; and practical applications. Mathematical systems theory arose from the development of isomorphies between the models of electrical circuits and other systems. Applications include engineering, computing, ecology, management and family psychotherapy. Systems analysis, developed independently of systems theory, applies systems principles to aid a decision maker with problems of identifying, reconstructing, optimising and controlling a system (usually a socio-technical organisation), while taking into account multiple objectives, constraints and resources. It aims to specify possible courses of action, together with their risks, costs and benefits. Systems theory is closely connected to **cybernetics**, and also **system dynamics**, which models changes in a **network** of coupled variables. Related ideas are used in the emerging 'sciences of **complexity**', studying **self-organisation** and heterogeneous networks of interacting actors, and associated domains such as **far-from-equilibrium thermodynamics**, **chaotic dynamics**, **artificial life**, **artificial intelligence**, **neural networks**, and computer **modelling and simulation**.

Source: Prepared for the *Cambridge Dictionary of Philosophy* (© Cambridge University Press); reproduced by permission of Principia Cybernetica Web (http://pespmc1.vub.ac.be).

Activity 2.1 Systems theory

Briefly discuss why it is important to understand general systems theory in order to appreciate and develop information systems in business. After reading Pause for thought 2.1 look in an ordinary (or scientific) dictionary for the meaning of the following words:

▶ reductionism

▶ holistic

▶ emergence

▶ organization

▶ hierarchy

▶ cybernetics.

Study these definitions until you are clear about them, and provide general systems examples to illustrate the meaning of each conceptual word.

Systems found within the universe can be categorized into three generic types:

▶ **Natural systems**: climate, seasons, evolution, etc.

▶ **Human-made systems**: transportation, telecommunications, etc.

▶ **Social systems**: economic system, banking system, legal system, etc.

Business is considered to be a *human activity system*. Therefore, business information systems are often designed with reference to human activity, human behaviour and general social systems behaviour. Business information systems are concerned with the flows of data and information throughout an organization that are required for human decision making. It is important to note that consideration of the logical characteristics of an information system should always precede consideration of the technological aspects of the system; technology is merely a tool for enabling human-made information systems to become more efficient and effective.

Did you know?

The theoretical biologist Ludwig von Bertalanffy was one of the founding fathers of general systems theory.

2.2 General systems principles

It should now have become clear that certain general concepts and principles underpin systems theory. So what are these principles?

▶ A *system* is a set of interrelated parts, arranged into an organized whole or orderly structure. This is referred to as *holism*. Such an organized whole is arranged in such a way that it is said to be *systematic*. To be systematic is to be methodical, acting according to a plan, and not casual, sporadic or unintentional.

▶ All systems can be *decomposed*, or broken down into constituent parts. This is known as *reductionism*. Systems can be broken down into *sub-systems* that can be further reduced down until the most basic constituents of the larger system are reached. For example, a human being can be reduced down to physiological organs, which can be further broken down into cells, which can in turn be reduced down to molecules, which can be reduced into atoms, which can be further decomposed into particles (made up of neutrons and electrons). Even these neutrons and electrons can be further reduced down into trace matter known as quarks.

What is a system?

An organized set of components that interact in a regulated fashion to achieve a goal or objective. The word 'system' is derived from the Greek word *synhistanai*, meaning to place or combine together.

▶ Systems have *perspectives* and *boundaries* that establish viewpoints and set perimeters around a system. Perspectives are views of a situation or even attitudes within a systems context. Boundaries establish borders around a systems domain and can be physical or merely logical. Boundaries distinguish conscious or sub-conscious sub-system's borders. These can be real, perceptual or virtual.

▶ The behaviour or activities of systems and sub-systems can be *modelled*. A model attempts to define the activity and relationships that make up a system. In effect, a model is an abstract representation of an explicit, perceived or tacit reality. The activities within a system can be simple and structured, or complex and unstructured. Nevertheless, the activities and actions of a system can be observed and modelled.

▶ The activities and actions of a system give rise to *emergent properties*. Organisms often share some common underlying characteristics but are very different in appearance. What emerges from the basic building blocks of a system is determined by the structure, relationship and connectivity of the basic building blocks. In other words, how these building blocks are structured will determine the nature and appearance of the object. This is sometimes referred to in general systems theory literature as *emergence*. Therefore, it is often important to look at the system as a whole (i.e. take an holistic view) rather than focus on an individual component, or part, that may often be shared by a number of systems.

Did you know?

Scientists learn about the world by carrying out experiments in which they do not examine wholes but try to reduce the situation they are investigating to its simplest and most elementary form.

Living organisms such as human beings, animals, and sea life are built upon strings of DNA (deoxyribonucleic acid), which are sometimes known as the building blocks of life. DNA is the nucleic acid found in the nuclei of all cells and is considered as a gene. The shape and characteristics of life forms are determined by the nature and number of genes found within those living organisms. The sequence of bases in a gene constitutes a code that determines the nature of the quality conferred on the organism inheriting that gene. It is the structure of the genetic code that determines the nature of a life form.

2.3 Systems perspectives

In the study of general systems theory it is often not desirable to take a reductionist approach to systems analysis, by reducing systems to their component parts, because the reason they exist can only be seen through a perspective on the whole system. This perspective is known as taking a *top-down* view of a system. The opposite of studying a system by looking at it holistically is to study the system's smallest component parts without regard to what has emerged from those component parts through their interaction and relationship with one another within the larger system. This process of synthesis is known as a *bottom-up* approach. The top-down or bottom-up view of systems can influence the way information systems are analyzed, designed and evaluated. The further study of systems methodologies in subsequent chapters will reveal that systems design methodologies use various forms of the top-down or bottom-up approach to studying systems.

The sub-systems and component parts of a larger system are normally interdependent. Therefore, a change in one part of the system may often lead to positive or negative changes in other parts of the system because of sub-system *dependency*. All the parts of a working system should act together in harmony to achieve some purpose or system's goal.

It is a fundamental principle that all systems are goal seeking. The reason for a system's existence is directly related to its *purpose* or *goal*. Goal-seeking behaviour within a systems environment is a major component principle of systems theory.

Activity 2.2 General systems theory

Discuss and explain what is meant by holism in the context of general systems theory. Then, taking a holistic systems view, define the principle of emergence and explain how the composition of systems components often leads to very different emergent properties. Consider whether you think that the same system will, over time, always possess the same goals. If not, what may influence a system's goal-seeking behaviour? This should be considered in the context of explaining why goal seeking is a primary behavioural principle of all systems. Finally, discuss and indicate what goals or purpose a student might have for being at a university or college. Are these goals the same for each student? If not, discuss why these goals are different and determine whether goals can be ranked or prioritized.

2.4 Holistic systems thinking

The doctrine of general systems theory states that a *holistic system* provides greater benefit than the component parts of a system all working independently. This provides the fundamental concept that underpins systems theory: *that the whole is greater than the sum of its parts*. Thus, the component parts of a system working together within the whole system provide a greater return than the parts working independent of one another and outside an organized and structured system.

Did you know?

The systems idea that the whole is greater than the sum of its parts is not a new idea. It was believed to have been first stated and recorded by Aristotle (384–322 BC) the Greek philosopher and tutor of Alexander the Great.

The human being is an interesting example of this doctrine of the system being greater than the sum of the parts. Section 2.2 revealed how the human system can be broken down into its constituent parts, even down to atomic particles comprised of neutrons and electrons. However, the reason humans exist in the form that we understand can only be seen in the whole and not by looking at biological human parts in isolation. Humans are more than their component parts; they have a consciousness and soul that are not accounted for by merely dissecting and reducing the human body to its component parts.

A reductionist approach misses the reasons why systems exist. The nature of a system can only be seen by viewing the system as a whole – in its *holistic* context. The top-down approach views the system in the context of its overall goal or purpose. For example, the physiological organs of the body all work together to achieve the goal of sustaining life in the human body. If the parts of the human body are looked at in isolation then an understanding of the individual purpose and role of these parts will be missed. Therefore, the existence and consciousness of a human being is more than the sum of the parts; a human being has self-identity that is not observed by simply studying the individual parts of the body in total isolation. Human systems, like many other systems, are complex. Complexity can only be understood by observing connected actions within a systems whole. To observe and understand the human system, and its connection with the world at large, we must recognize the role of thinking and consciousness. This consciousness is a property that *emerges* from the complex human system that is certainly recognized if not entirely understood.

> ### Did you know?
>
> The doctrine of synergism, a theological doctrine that the human will and divine grace are two efficient agents that cooperate in human regeneration and salvation, is attributed to Philip Melanchthon (1497–1560). In modern systems terms synergy means the working together of two things to introduce effects greater than the sum of the individual effects. It is derived from the Greek word *sunergos*, meaning to work together.

A holistic view observes the whole of a system and not just the parts in isolation without any recognition of the system's purpose or goal. The additional quality, benefit or property that emerges from linking the parts together into a system is referred to as *synergy*. Synergy is the process of working together, or cooperation, for the combined good of the system. A good example of emergence and synergy can be found by looking at the qualities of carbon. The combination of carbon atoms into molecules may take on various shapes and forms, which in turn lead to entities that differ greatly in appearance and purpose. For instance, the carbon-based forms of graphite and diamond are very different. Graphite is soft, black and opaque while a diamond is hard and transparent. Nevertheless, both are made up of the same substance: carbon. The difference lies in the way in which the carbon molecules are structured and organized into a whole. Therefore, within systems theory, the organization of the component parts influences the purpose or goal of the holistic system.

> ### What is synthesis?
>
> The process of synthesis involves the building up and construction of parts into a whole. Within the process of 'thought', synthesis involves reasoning from general principles to an outcome or conclusion.

Activity 2.3 Perspectives on systems theory

Explain the fundamental difference between a bottom-up approach and a top-down approach in general systems theory. Discuss the idea of 'the whole is greater than the sum of its parts'. Provide two examples of systems in which this is the case. Explain what might be 'missing' from the whole if analysis of a human being was modelled using a bottom-up approach.

2.5 General systems thinking

The work of Ludwig von Bertalanffy (1901–72)

All systems share common underlying characteristics, whether they are natural systems, human-made systems or social systems. The concept of the existence of *universal* systems characteristics was proposed by Ludwig von Bertalanffy in a book entitled *General Systems Theory* published in 1968. This book discusses the existence of underlying systems principles to explain systematic behaviour and activity. Ludwig von Bertalanffy realized that organized processes from very different backgrounds (i.e. physiology, biology, psychology, science, etc.) seemed to share common principles governing their existence. Therefore, the question that von Bertalanffy asked was whether a system could be defined by its inherent nature and *characteristics*. For example, a human being can be defined by underlying and common characteristics, such as, normally, two eyes, two arms, two legs, hair on the top of the head and nails on the ends of the fingers. If only two characteristics such as legs and arms were used to define the human body, this would not be sufficient to define clearly, or distinguish, a human being from an object such as a chair, which also may have characteristics called arms and legs! However, if we add more and more characteristics to the distinction list of common characteristics, then a clearer definition of the form of a human being may be gained. Consequently, it is possible to define an object, and a system, by its distinguishing characteristics. Therefore, a system can be defined by its *common characteristics*.

Ludwig von Bertalanffy is a good example of the multi-disciplinary concept of general systems theory. He started his university education in Innsbruck, Austria, in 1918, by studying the history of art and philosophy. He then published books on theoretical biology in the 1920s. He studied the effect of reductionism in biology and aspects of self-organizing dynamic behaviour witnessed in many systems. He developed a kinetic theory of open systems characteristics. One of these characteristics was homogeneity (or steady-state behaviour) in biological systems. Von Bertalanffy then came into contact with a number of academics in mathematics and physics and through his multi-disciplinary approach formed a general systems theory in the 1940s. In 1949 he emigrated to Canada and concentrated on the development of general systems theory throughout the 1950s. By the 1960s he was considering the psychological and humanistic aspects of systems, such as culture, later referred to by many systems researchers as a human-based world-view.

Von Bertalanffy was a true multi-disciplinary polymath – an expert in many subjects. He found through research that systems appeared to possess common characteristics. For example, many systems appear to be self-regulating; some systems interact with their environment and to some extent get shaped by their environment; furthermore, ideas, values, culture and ideology play a role in shaping human systems. General systems theory was a way of describing, in a qualitative manner, the universal principles (and characteristics) that are true for systems in general.

The work of Sir Geoffrey Vickers (1894–1982)

Sir Geoffrey Vickers' appreciation of systems theory was based on his experiences. He served in the First World War (1914–18) and was awarded the highest military medal for distinguished military service from the British Army – the Victoria Cross. He studied classics at Oxford University and graduated in 1923. He practised law and became a distinguished civil servant in the British government. He is particularly noted for defining the idea of an *appreciative system* within general systems thinking.

The human aspects of systems are very important to an understanding of systems theory. Vickers is noted for introducing a number of terms and words into the systems dictionary. For example, *appreciative systems* is a phrase that attempts to describe human behaviour and activity in systems terms. Appreciative systems are those where human activity and interaction is determined by the person's understanding (or appreciation) of the environment in which they operate and exist. Vickers was influenced by von Bertalanffy's ideas of emergence. To some extent the emergent properties of a system depend upon a person's appreciation of the systems environment encapsulated in their actions and perceptions of people within that environment. Vickers stated that activities and actions of people within a system were constantly being observed and interpreted by other people in that system. The *meaning* of these actions varies according to the individual person observing the actions and activity. In other words meaning is based on perceptions and appreciation of people's actions. The context in which these actions take place is perceived differently by different human observers.

Within appreciative systems thinking both culture and communication are vital aspects for interpreting systems activity. Therefore, to understand and describe a number of common assumptions and standards need to be defined beforehand. These common assumptions can assist in providing a collective understanding of a system and, particularly, the actions and activities of humans within the system. These shared standards are sometimes referred to as *epistemological assumptions* (an epistemology being a theory of knowledge). These then form shared assumptions concerning a system.

In general people are influenced by their experiences, concerns and attitudes to other people, and the perceived reasons for their actions, within a systems environment. Appreciative systems thinking recognizes that these perceptions and attitudes are dynamic and can alter and change with further observation and experience of people's actions within a systems domain. Vickers outlined seven levels of shared appreciation (sometimes referred to as 'trust') within a systems domain. These levels of trust and shared appreciation are:

▶ **Violence**: erodes trust and creates responses that try to contain violence. In itself, it is a very unsophisticated form of 'communication'. Some would say it serves no communication purpose.

▶ **Threat**: depends upon the person being threatened believing that the threat is true. The idea involves carrying out a condition in order to avoid the threat and its consequences.

▶ **Bargain**: assumes greater shared understanding and appreciation than the previous two levels. Within this level of appreciation there is a shared under-standing that both parties can negotiate and come to mutually beneficial out-comes. However, it is important that both parties believe the other will honour its obligations in the negotiated bargain.

▶ **Information**: the receiver of information must trust that the sender of infor-mation is reliable and that the information is accurate. There is a shared assumption that the appreciative systems of the sender and receiver of infor-mation are the same and there is shared common meaning.

▶ **Persuasion**: one party actively tries to change the behaviour or perception of the other party. It involves encouraging one party to adopt the other party's view or perspective.

▶ **Argument**: each party is involved in persuasion. Both parties alter their view or perspectives so that at the end of the process of argument both parties have shifted their view, or perspectives, towards a common, but different, view to their original views or perspectives.

▶ **Dialogue**: sharing experiences and views in order to come to a collective per-spective or view. Each party attempts to understand and share the other party's view or perspective. All parties are open to persuasion. The outcome is that all parties can be moved towards a mutual understanding but not necessarily a shared appreciation – they have a broader knowledge of the range of perspec-tives in a system domain.

These levels define the nature and content of human communication within a system.

High quality levels of communication, such as dialogue, create an environ-ment whereby people are more likely to appreciate correctly the actions and activities of others within a systems domain. Communication is an important aspect of appreciative systems thinking. Communication is a means by which people reflect on and codify experiences, set common perceived standards and establish common understanding. In effect, Vickers views systems as merely human constructs that constitute people, organizations and norms of social behaviour.

Did you know?

The challenge [for appreciative systems] is to create appreciative environments that integrate social, psychological, physical and virtual (ICT) environments. If done well, these can facilitate negotiation, sharing of knowledge and mutual learning.
Source: Takala and Hawk, 2001.

Vickers' view of the systems world challenged the idea of reductionism and promoted the idea that systems were dependent upon human interactivity and should be viewed as a whole. He also promoted the idea that decision making within an organizational context was influenced by the way people thought. Their *world-view* of a system was influenced by values, ideas, past experiences and judgement. Vickers also noted that human interaction and interdependence (i.e. the way that people are dependent upon one another or influenced by one another) affect a system. A system, or organization, can prosper by establishing norms of appreciation within the system's domain.

> **Did you know?**
>
> The word 'system' is sometimes replaced with the word 'holon' to describe a complete system, its activity, and inherent human understanding of that system. Holon is used to describe an area of concern that requires investigating. Holon is derived from the Greek word *holos*, meaning whole, with the suffix '-on' denoting an association with subatomic particles (e.g. electron and neutron etc.).

Other systems thinkers

The work of von Bertalanffy and Vickers has influenced many other writers in the systems field. For example, Peter Checkland is famous for his work on soft systems methodology (SSM) that has been influenced by the philosophical, social and human aspects of von Bertalanffy's later work and Vickers' work on human behaviour in organizational system domains. A number of concepts developed by von Bertalanffy and Vickers were adopted by Checkland in his systems thinking and systems practice approach to the analysis of business systems problems – for example, the idea of systems being comprised of sub-systems with their own understanding in the shape of holons, and the concept of systems exhibiting goal-seeking behaviour. Checkland studied the reasons why many activities and projects within business organizations failed. His conclusions were that the human aspect to systems activity was missing from the purely technical evaluation techniques used to analyze information systems environments in business. Checkland advocated a *systemic* approach to the analysis of systems problems and problem scenarios that involved consideration of the human aspects of business systems. He promoted the idea of *weltanschauung*, which is a German word meaning world-view. In studying systems the person observing the system and the subjects of the system will already possess a preconceived world-view of that system and its operation. These are perceived realities that need to be distinguished from reality itself.

In general, these systems thinkers share certain common assumptions regarding systems activity:

▶ A pure reductionist approach cannot be applied to organizational systems analysis without losing some of the systems meaning.

▶ Systems should be viewed as open, rather than closed, because systems are affected by the environment in which they reside.

▶ Systems involve interactivity where certain emergent properties arise out of the complex interactivity of a system's component parts.

▶ Systems, particularly in business, are influenced by human activity; therefore, organizational analysis cannot ignore the human aspect in systems activity.

A number of other systems thinkers have influenced the academic discipline of information systems theory. Some of the most influential theorists in the field of systems theory are:

▶ **Russell Ackoff**: an academic and business systems thinker born in the USA. He has written a number of books on management and organizational systems.

▶ **W. Ross Ashby**: one of the founding fathers of cybernetics. He was a psychologist who developed the ideas of homeostasis, the law of requisite variety, principles of self-organization, and the law of regulating models.

▶ **Stafford Beer**: management cyberneticist. He is the creator of the viable system model (VSM) and he is famous for linking systems thinking to the management domain in organizations.

▶ **Kenneth E. Boulding**: economist and one of the founding fathers of general systems theory.

▶ **Jay Forrester**: engineer. He is the creator of system dynamics and applications for the modelling of industry development, in cities throughout the world.

▶ **George Klir**: mathematical systems theorist. He was the creator of the general systems problem solver methodology for modelling.

▶ **James Grier Miller**: biologist and the creator of living systems theory.

▶ **Howard Pattee**: theoretical biologist who studied hierarchy and semantic closure in organisms.

▶ **Claude Shannon**: founder of information theory (this theory is expanded upon in the next section).

▶ **Heinz von Foerster**: one of the founding fathers of cybernetics. He was one of the first to study self-organization, self-reference and other circularities.

▶ **John von Neumann**: mathematician and one of the founding fathers of computation. He developed theories of quantum logic, axioms of quantum mechanics, the digital computer, cellular automata and self-reproducing systems.

2.6 Information and meaning

Information is difficult to quantify and to define. Information content is determined by its meaning and message, specifically to the person receiving the information. An additional factor also concerns the manner in which information is *communicated*. The complexity of this problem has led to the study of information theory. One of the major thinkers in information theory was Claude Shannon (1916–2001) who wrote a seminal academic paper on information and communication theory in 1948. Shannon's work is a founding part of the digital revolution of the twentieth and twenty-first centuries. Information theory as defined by Shannon is concerned with the transmission of expressions. When we design and build information systems we are much more concerned with the transmission of meanings and so we analyze the semantics of the phrases in the language of a particular domain.

Communication as the transmission of meaning between different parties is what information systems designers hope to achieve. Beyond shared meaning is shared understanding – think about all those times when you thought you understood someone only to discover they meant something entirely different to what you thought they meant. At this level, meaning and understanding get bound up with intention – common purpose and coordinated action that is effective in meeting that purpose are the hallmarks of an organization with good communication. Communication between any two people (or *agents*) requires that those people share some common language. They must each be familiar with a set of expressions and ascribe similar meanings to those expressions, or communication is impossible. This set of expressions and their common meaning forms the universe of discourse between the two agents (Elliott and Phillips, 2004).

Did you know?

Claude Shannon, who died aged 84, perhaps more than anyone else laid the groundwork for today's digital revolution. His single-handed exposition of information theory, stating that all information could be represented mathematically as a succession of noughts and ones, facilitated the digital manipulation of data without which today's information society would be unthinkable. More correctly, his theory applied not only to data but also to communication of all kinds and, combined with the pulse code modulation system of digital telecommunications transmission devised in 1937 by Englishman Alec Reeves, effectively laid the foundations for today's modern digital communications and broadcasting networks, the internet and much more.

Source: A. Emerson, Obituary for Claude Shannon, *Guardian*, 8 March 2001.

The natural languages with which we are all familiar, such as English, German, Arabic, etc., are particular forms of a much larger family of languages that also includes non-natural languages used in computing and ICT (e.g. computer programming languages). Therefore, a study of languages and meaning is important for an appreciation of the definition of information. Semiotics, the study of linguistics and the philosophy of language, is a starting point for answering the question 'what is information?' Semiotics within information systems is concerned with the meaning of signs and expressions. The ability to communicate complex abstract ideas is one the major defining characteristics of humanity. Within the semiotics framework there are a number of conditions:

▶ the communication of messages will be between two agents;

▶ the intention and meaning conveyed between two agents will be encapsulated in a message;

▶ the sender and receiver of a message, via some defined medium (e.g. voice, electronic signals etc.) will understand how to interpret the expressions and signs of the message.

Did you know?

The study of natural languages is called linguistics, while the study of the set of all possible languages is called semiotics.

Therefore, human communication within systems domains is a social construct that involves interpretation of human intentions. The minimum requirement for communication to take place is that the sender and receiver of a message (i.e. the two agents) will in fact understand each other. This understanding is dependent upon the two agents clearly, and commonly, appreciating the meaning and intention of the signs and expressions of the message.

Signs can be many and various – for example, voice intonation, body language, capitalization of e-mail text and style of memorandum writing. The study of signs can be separated into four areas:

▶ **Pragmatics**: the culture and social and expected behavioural context of communication.

▶ **Semantics**: the meaning inherent in signs. People react in a particular way because of the meaning of signs and symbols (e.g. the picture of a male or female on a washroom or lavatory door, road signs, etc.).

▶ **Syntax**: the grammatical logic of expressions and sign systems (e.g. English grammar and the grammar of computer languages).

▶ **Empirics**: the type and characteristics of the medium, or channel, of communication (e.g. the channel of communication can include voice, electronic, infrared, wireless waves etc.).

Domains of discourse develop around practices and associated activities creating sub-languages where common expressions develop specialist meanings. In particular, any group of people regularly engaged in a common set of activities will develop a specialized language that compresses long descriptions into short expressions. For example, a complicated accounting procedure might be summed up as 'I'm doing form 702' and this will carry much more 'information' to people in the accounting department than a lengthy description of the actual activities will to an outsider. Being able to encode complex ideas in this way is an essential part of effective communication in business systems domains (Elliott and Phillips, 2004).

Information is a means of reducing uncertainty in the business systems domain. It should be noted that information is time, place and context dependent. The presence of information from a particular and understood source, or at a particular time, might reduce the level of uncertainty within a systems domain. The Shannon model of communication shows how there are a number of variables that need to be understood. These are diagrammatically represented in Figure 2.1. There is the information source (i.e. the originator of the message, such as a human or a computer program); the transmitting device that converts the signal from the source into a signal that can be carried by the channel; the message channel, which is a means of carrying a signal through some media (e.g. fixed wire or wireless wave channels); the receiving device that converts the signal from the channel into a form that can be understood at the destination; and the destination is the final agent that receives the message from the source. In addition, there is one other factor, that of noise. This is the term used to indicate that a message will lose some of its quality in the process of transmission (e.g. someone not fully hearing all the words in a sentence).

Flow sequence

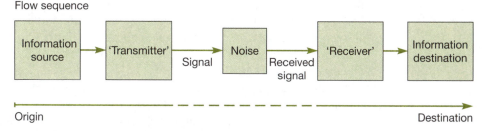

Figure 2.1 General communication system
Source: Adapted from Shannon, 1948.

Communication of information can be divided into formal and informal information. Formal information is based on facts and figures and substantiated data; informal information is the subject of conjecture and opinion. Communication itself can also be divided into two categories:

▶ **First-order communication**: the simplest form of communication. It involves simple feedback (e.g. a heating system thermostat maintains a predefined temperature by monitoring its closed systems environment).

▶ **Second-order communication**: involves more complex understanding of meaning of signs and expressions within messages. It includes language, perceptions and behaviour.

2.7 Systems characteristics

We have seen from the work of Ludwig von Bertalanffy that a system can be defined by its inherent characteristics. In general, all systems normally share five common characteristics that allow a system to be defined as a system, rather than an inanimate object. A systems framework model can be developed of the five common systems characteristics that allow a system to be more clearly defined. The five defining characteristics of a system are:

▶ inputs and outputs
▶ goals or objectives
▶ systems boundary (or environment)
▶ feedback and control
▶ interrelated parts (activity).

To be defined as a 'system', all these characteristics must be present within the domain of the system.

A system is a collection of interrelated parts, some of which may be common with other related systems. A system cannot be considered a static object, like a table, chair, pen or other inanimate entity. For a system to be a system it must assume some form of *activity*. In the case of information systems the fundamental activity is the processing of data and information to provide knowledge for subsequent decision making. For example, the arrangement of inanimate chairs and tables into rows within a room, and the numbering of tables by examination candidate number, may form parts of an examination system's process. However, the component parts of that system, such as the chairs and tables, are not in themselves a system. But the organization and activity of the component parts will comprise a system.

From the list of five characteristics it can be seen that all systems have *inputs* and *outputs*. For example, in the case of information systems the input to be processed is 'data' and the resultant output of the system is 'information'. The output of one system can often form the input for another system. Therefore, various systems can be connected by their inputs and outputs. It is possible to visualize the whole business environment as being composed of numerous systems and sub-systems. The activities and processes of a system are determined by its *goals*. For example, one of the main purposes, or goals, of ICT-based business information systems is to make the human activity of information processing more efficient and effective within an organization. The outputs from the processes of a system are directly related to the system's goal, set of goals, or objective.

To understand and recognize separate systems and sub-systems within various systems environments it is necessary to be able to define the *boundaries* of the system. This is particularly important when studying the specifics of systems in greater detail. A systems boundary (or environment) can be defined as whatever lies within the scope of the system and interacts with that system. The emphasis in establishing boundaries is to determine the specific impact of environmental considerations on a system or sub-system. If something resides outside the system's boundaries, and does not impact on the system or affect the system in any way, then this would be outside the system's immediate environment. In any study of systems activity it is important to be able to define the boundaries of a system in order to focus attention more effectively on the issues that affect that system. The shape and constituent parts of a particular system are determined by its pre-established *logical* boundary, not its physical boundary.

Activity   **2.4**   Systems characteristics

Outline and explain the types of inputs and outputs that would usually be found within the general environment of business systems. Provide an example of a human-made or natural system found in business, and the world at large, and define the boundaries of each system that you have described.

2.8 Systems control and feedback

Another major defining characteristic of systems is the existence of *control* and *feedback*. All systems have regulatory controls that allow a system to maintain or pursue its objectives and goals. The control aspect oversees the processing activities of most systems. For a system to meet its goal, or set of goals, some form of control and feedback mechanism is essential to the system's effective operation. The sub-system of control within a larger system may well have its own goals or objectives. For example, the blood temperature system of the human body is controlled by the central cortex at the back of the human brain. The goal of the body's temperature system is to maintain the human body temperature at 36°C (96.8°F). If the temperature of the human body falls or rises from its natural temperature, the body will feed back this information to the body's thermostatic system, so that physiological measures can be implemented to bring the temperature back to its natural state. For instance, if the human temperature falls below its natural level the skin starts to get cold and the body will start to shake and pump blood at a faster rate in order to heat the body back up to its natural temperature level. If the body's temperature rises above the normal level, the skin begins to perspire and give up body fluid, which has the effect of cooling the skin down and bringing the body's temperature back to its normal and natural state.

The goal of the human body is to maintain a predetermined temperature level. A system that maintains a predetermined, or steady state, is known as *homeostatic*. Homeostasis is a movement within a system towards equilibrium. Such homeostatic control systems attempt to maintain a static balance (or equilibrium) within the system. Many other control systems do not try to maintain static balance but are dynamic, ever changing, or *pursuing* target goals. Business is a human activity system that is constantly under pressure to change in the face of externalities, such as consumer demand, tastes and preferences. Therefore, control of change on a broad basis can be a specific objective of business information systems.

Systems *feedback* refers to the information that enables the system processes to modify themselves and in turn meet the system's ultimate goals. Feedback can be of two types:

▶ **Negative feedback**: the output of the control system is fed back as an input to achieve a specified or predetermined state. Examples of natural systems are the human heart, human kidneys and temperature system; human-made examples are the thermostatic temperature system of a home, a business stock system, or a manufacturing control system.

▶ **Positive feedback**: the output of the control system is fed back as an input for growth. For example, a bonfire will burn and cause increasing generation of heat, which in turn will lead to further incineration until the boundaries of the available inflammable material have been totally burnt. The bonfire positively expands and grows as it burns. In the case of business organizations, profits can be reinvested back into the organization to expand or create increased economic growth within a business. Thus, retaining profits within a business is an example of positive feedback within the business environment.

Normally, all business organizations rely on feedback and control systems. All systems have objectives and, to ensure that the system's objectives are met, it is important that control is exercised within the system's processes and activities. Control can only be achieved by accurate and effective information feedback into the system that allows changes to be made to maintain the direction of a system to achieve its goals. Figure 2.2 shows a typical feedback and control model.

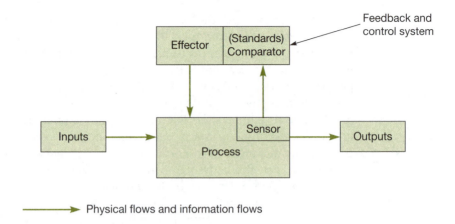

Figure 2.2 Systems feedback and control model

In Figure 2.2, information flows into a process that is monitored by a *sensor*. The sensor will often use a *comparator* mechanism to compare the inputs being processed with the system's expected *standard*. If the inputs are irregular (or non-standard) the feedback and control mechanisms will activate a change of the inputs. This will cause an action to be taken by the system. If the irregularity is brought back to the standard, then the input can be permitted to be processed and released (as output) from the main system. A feedback and control system often forms a closed loop within a system's processing activities.

The final common characteristic of systems is that they possess *interrelated parts* that work in harmony to achieve the goals of the overall system. Systems can be interrelated to one another by their inputs and outputs. Systems can also comprise component sub-systems that can be decomposed down into a *hierarchical* model, where larger systems are reduced to smaller sub-systems which are in turn reduced to even smaller sub-sub-systems. Each sub-system is itself a system with goals or objectives, inputs, outputs and processes, often with its own particular system-specific control and feedback characteristics.

When the output of one system can be the input to another system, such systems are said to be *dependent systems*. Systems that are not related to one another are termed *independent systems*. This dependence, or linkage, between systems is often termed *systems coupling*. The measurement of dependence of one system on another system is known as the *degree of coupling*. Systems that are strongly dependent upon one another are referred to as *highly coupled*.

The measurement of coupling can be determined by calculating the percentage of output of one system being used as the input for another system. The level of coupling is important in determining the extent to which one system affects another system. This is a particularly important consideration if it is the case that the failure of one system will lead directly to the failure of another system. For example, system Y may be highly coupled with system Z. If system Y fails it will also cause a failure in system Z, as a consequence of the high level of coupling between the two systems.

Coupling has consequences for the development of control mechanisms that regulate the flow of output from one system to another system. Control mechanisms must be placed between highly coupled systems to prevent one system adversely affecting another dependent system. These basic control mechanisms act as a filter, controlling the flows of physical objects, data or information between systems. To ensure that the system's objectives are met it is important that some form of control operates over the system's processing activities. The activity of separating highly coupled systems is known as systems decoupling. There are three main ways of achieving systems decoupling:

▶ building marginal capacity into the physical aspects of an information system;

▶ creating an information buffer between systems;

▶ establishing an information filter to validate and verify the data or information.

All three of these control mechanisms may be used to assess and validate output information from one system before it is permitted to be used as input information for another system. For example, the NASA (National Aeronautical and Space Administration) space shuttle is made up of many interconnected systems working in unison to achieve the goal of flight into space with the safe return of its crew to Earth, after some predefined duration. The failure of one system within the space shuttle, or its dependent systems, may result in life-threatening consequences for a space mission. Therefore, it is important that control systems are put into place to decouple the dependency of systems. The consequences may not always be life threatening within business systems, but failure to implement adequate and reliable control mechanisms within business systems may certainly threaten the economic well-being of a business.

Activity 2.5   Universal systems characteristics

Explain the five main characteristics used to define a system and discuss what is meant by a holistic approach to systems thinking. Do you consider that a personal computer or a mobile phone can be classified as a system? Explain your answer in terms of the possible goal or purpose of a computer, a mobile phone, a telecommunications network and a network of computers.

If all systems are shaped and formed by their respective goals, explain the goals or purposes of the following:

▶ a *student* at university

▶ an aircraft *autopilot*

▶ a *toilet*

▶ a *research and development* department

▶ a *marketing system*.

Systems may incorporate feedback and control mechanisms. Provide a biological, mechanical and business systems example of a negative feedback system and a positive feedback system. Discuss whether the feedback and control mechanisms of the systems you propose are related to the goal or purpose of those systems.

2.9 Deterministic and functional business systems

Systems where the inputs and outputs are defined and known with certainty are termed *deterministic systems*. Such systems are limited in scope and definition; they are often predefined before any systems processing activity has been undertaken. ICT hardware and software should be deterministic to the extent that the same inputs will always produce a finite, determined output (as long as no malfunction or error has occurred in the system). Humans and human activity on the other hand are not deterministic. Human activity changes and alters with environmental considerations. Such dynamic activity can be considered to be *adaptive* to the environment in which the system exists. Adaptive systems normally try to be suitable for a purpose, and modify (or alter) with the changing environment and over time. Humans are not static; they are adaptive, dynamic and complex systems. Human beings, and human activity systems, are always changing their behaviour patterns, unlike a passive computer and its implicit technology (i.e. deterministic working parts). Therefore, it can be said that humans are adaptive while computers are deterministic. Likewise, the pursuit of business is a human activity that is adaptive to the circumstances of the internal and external business environment. Information systems can be either deterministic or adaptive depending on the goals or purpose of the information system.

What are complex adaptive systems?

Many natural systems (e.g. brains, immune systems, ecologies, societies) and increasingly, many artificial systems (parallel and distributed computing systems, artificial intelligence systems, artificial neural networks, evolutionary programs) are characterized by apparently complex behaviours that emerge as a result of often non-linear spatio-temporal interactions among a large number of component systems at different levels of organization. Consequently, researchers in a number of disparate areas including computer science, artificial intelligence, neural networks, cognitive science, computational economics, mathematics, optimization, complexity theory, control systems, biology, neuroscience, psychology, engineering etc. have begun to address, through a combination of basic and applied theoretical as well as experimental research, analysis and synthesis of such systems.

Systems that exist to implement the routine, or day-to-day, activities of business are normally deterministic, while systems that are used for decision making, which is not prone to routine analysis, are considered to be adaptive. The extent to which a system is either deterministic or adaptive is governed by the level of information certainty within the systems environment with regard to the inputs and outputs of the system. Deterministic business systems are often known in the business world as *functional systems* because they carry out a defined function, transaction or routine business activity. For instance, all business organizations utilize common functional systems such as salaries or payroll. It is important to understand functional systems in order to understand the use and development of systems that are considered not to be deterministic. Typical of functional systems within a product *manufacturing organization* would be:

- sales order processing
- purchase order processing
- production control
- production planning
- input stock controlling (of raw materials)
- output stock controlling (of finished goods)
- goods distribution
- payroll (wages and salaries).

In addition, these functional systems would be supported by higher-level organizational systems that possess both deterministic and non-deterministic aspects, such as:

- marketing
- research and development
- customer service
- human resource management (personnel)
- financial and managerial accounting.

All these systems will share the five common defining characteristics of systems: goal seeking, possessing defined boundaries, having inputs and outputs, interrelated parts, and some form of feedback and control.

Figure 2.3 shows how all these functional systems are typically integrated. Information flows into and out of each subsystem. The linking together of systems by their respective inputs and outputs, but ignoring the internal structure and activities, is known as a *black-box* approach to information systems. What is important in this approach are the information flows between the systems. Remember, that in *systems decomposition* the outputs of one sub-system may form the inputs of another sub-system of the business organization.

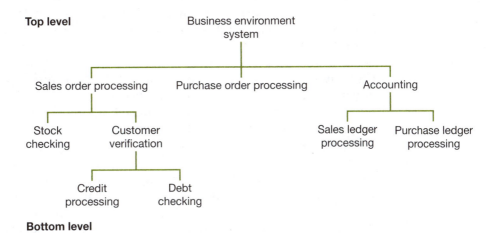

Figure 2.3 Systems decomposition

Since most sub-systems within a business organization are related to one another by their inputs and outputs, any view of the overall organization should not consider individual business components in isolation. The analysis, design, implementation and evaluation of business information systems involves taking a view of the system in its *totality*. The *total systems* approach is central to business information technology in that systems cannot be built without regard to the overall goals of the business organization. To concentrate on one specific system, in order to optimize the efficiency and effectiveness of the inputs, processes and outputs, may lead to neglect or sub-optimization in other related systems to the detriment of the overriding business goals.

Activity 2.6 Functional business systems

Discuss and explain the terms deterministic and adaptive behaviour in the context of systems theory and provide an example for each type of systems behaviour. Suggest why functional systems within the business environment are considered deterministic and suggest three possible characteristics such deterministic systems may possess.

2.10 Physical versus logical systems thinking

One of the most important concepts within information systems theory is the concept of separating logical systems thinking from physical systems thinking. Any manufacturing process requires raw materials to be manufactured into a finished product; business organizations may also buy and sell services that are more abstract and less prone to physical definition. In systems theory it is imperative to understand the logical purpose, or goal, of a system before thinking about the system in physical and technological terms. For example, the goal of a stock system in a large organization will be fundamentally the same as the goal of a stock system in a small organization; they are logically the same. The goal of a stock system, irrespective of the size of the organization and other physical characteristics, will be to monitor and ensure determined levels of stock. However, the physical aspects of a stock system in a large organization may be very different to the physical aspects of a stock system in a small organization in terms of the number of employees responsible for the system, the amount of hardware and software needed to maintain the system and the physical location in which the stock system is located. Therefore, the logical basis of the stock system will be the same for all business organizations on a global basis; however, the physical aspects of each stock system may be very different.

The logical systems process assumes activity, such as sales order processing, purchase order processing and stock controlling. 'Processing' and 'controlling' (and normally any word ending in 'ing') are verbs or action words. However, 'stock', 'employee' and 'order' are nouns, naming physical items. Physical descriptions contain nouns, while logical descriptions are verbs or action words. When studying information systems it is the logical processes that are important and not the physical environment and technology in which the system activities take place. A logical representation of physical activities and processes is the fundamental basis for designing and developing business information systems. It is imperative that the logical aspects of a system are separated out from the physical aspects of that system.

We now know from earlier studies that a system can be classified by its characteristics to determine whether it is a system or not a system. Systems can then be further identified by *type* according to their behaviour. Systems can be any of the following:

▶ goal keeping, aiming or pursuing;

▶ deterministic, adaptive, purposeful or homeostatic;

▶ possess negative feedback or positive feedback.

Business information systems provide the information needed for managers to make informed and reasoned decisions. When humans interact with a human-made system the whole system can move from deterministic to adaptive. However, some functional systems, such as stock control, are deterministic irrespective of the human element of interaction. Other systems, such as marketing, do not remain deterministic when the human aspects are added to the system equation. Whether a system is deterministic or adaptive, through the addition of human interaction, depends upon the type and level of the organizational structure in which the business system resides. This means that anyone involved in systems thinking needs to know how systems are absorbed into the fabric of a business organization. The subsequent sections will describe the typical organizational hierarchy and explain the type and role of systems at each level of the organizational hierarchy.

Activity 2.7 Physical versus logical systems thinking

A system can be classified by its defining characteristics to determine whether it is a system or not a system. Systems can be further identified by type according to their behaviour. Systems can be: (a) goal keeping, aiming or pursuing; (b) deterministic, adaptive, purposeful or homeostatic; or (c) possess negative feedback or positive feedback. Identify which of the following are systems and identify which of the above terms within (a), (b) or (c) apply, and explain your reasoning:

▶ a robot welding machine
▶ an aircraft autopilot
▶ the British national economy
▶ the human body's temperature system
▶ achieving a qualification at university
▶ selling a business product
▶ a computer
▶ a software application
▶ the weather
▶ the human body
▶ a stock control system
▶ a marketing system
▶ the universe.

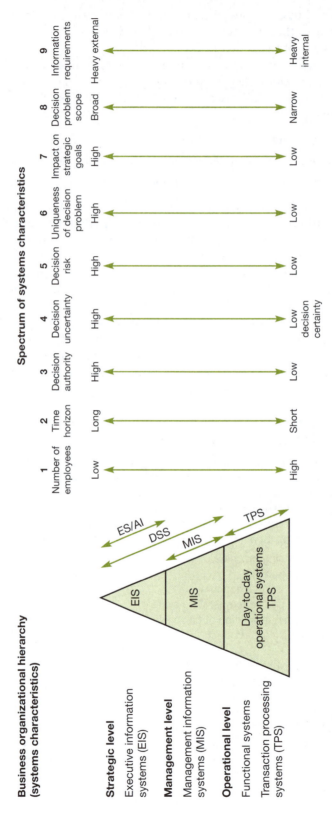

Figure 2.4 Information systems decision levels within a business organization

2.11 Decision levels of the business organization

A typical hierarchical business will have three broad levels of organizational decision-making. From top to bottom, these are:

▶ strategic (or executive)

▶ management

▶ operational.

Each organizational level exhibits different information requirement characteristics in terms of the decision timeframe, certainty, risk, responsiveness, information structure and application of technology. These decision-making levels are characterized by information systems that are different in design and composition because of the *level-specific* goals of the information systems at each level of the hierarchy. The characteristics of information systems and decision-making activity at the three levels of the organizational hierarchy can be seen in Figure 2.4. The decision-making levels are highly significant in terms of systems thinking, since the purpose of processing data is to produce information for decision making.

Within a typical hierarchical business organization the *operational systems* are responsive and deterministic to the extent that the inputs and outputs are known with certainty; such systems are mechanical in their processes and algorithmic in their decision-making functions. Operational systems play a significant part in manufacturing business environments, but are also found to varying extents in normal business environments. Operational systems are sometimes referred to in business systems literature as *transaction processing systems* (TPS). Examples of such systems within business organizations are stock control, production scheduling and payroll. By contrast, *strategic information systems* are often heuristic (random) and only as accurate as the level of certainty (or uncertainty) of the predicted probabilities and expected events of the business information environment. Within the strategic information systems environment the information is often unstructured and the decision-making activities are uncertain. This level of decision making is characterized by *executive information systems* (EIS), *decision support systems* (DSS), *expert systems* (ES) and *artificial intelligence* (AI). Within the middle level of the business are usually found *management information systems* (MIS). These are characterized by medium-term budgeting and forecasting functions, and lie somewhere on the hierarchical spectrum between strategic systems and operational systems, but normally have characteristics of both the bottom and top levels of business systems.

The *decision-making activities* at the lowest level of the organization hierarchy are usually routine and repetitive, whereas at the highest level of the organization hierarchy the decision-making activity is more one-off and user-specific in nature. Figure 2.4 highlights the roles of various information systems within the organization hierarchy. The spectrum of characteristics reveals how information systems requirements are dependent upon the nature of the environment in which the system resides.

The evolutionary trends in computing and ICT, described in Chapter 1, have been horizontally absorbed into business in general from the top to the bottom of the organization. The decision-making levels of an organization are highly significant, since the purpose of processing data is to produce good information for decision making. A specialist working within the business information technology environment therefore needs not only an understanding of computing and IT, but also a substantive understanding of the application and characteristics of information systems at each level of decision making within information-sensitive business environments.

Information is considered to be the 'life-blood' of any organization in the information and knowledge age. Information can fall into either of two categories:

▶ **Formal information**: factual and produced by standard, verifiable procedures and practices.

▶ **Informal information**: subjective and often based on opinion.

For information to be formal it must have been acquired and processed within a structured (and formalized) information systems environment. This does not necessarily mean that formal information is always more accurate than informal information, but only that the procedures used to handle the information were structured and formalized within the organizational hierarchy.

Activity 2.8   Decision characteristics within an organization hierarchy

The traditional organizational hierarchy can be segmented into three decision-making levels (*see* Figure 2.4). Discuss the various characteristics found at each organizational level and describe the type of goals a system would have at the operational, managerial and strategic levels of an organization. Notice from Figure 2.4 that there are arrows indicating the level of absorption of decision support systems (DSS), expert systems (ES) and artificial intelligence (AI) throughout the typical business hierarchy. From the following list of business environment sectors draw an organizational hierarchy indicating the level and extent of absorption of DSS, ES and AI from the top to the bottom of a typical organization:

▶ equity trading
▶ insurance and finance
▶ internet banking
▶ tourist industry.

Discuss why some areas of business activity may show a higher absorption of such systems than other sectors of business.

2.12   Decision making within the organizational hierarchy

The scope of decision-making activity within a typical organizational hierarchy is dependent upon the level and nature of the system being used. Generally, the most intensive decision-making activity occurs at the strategic level of an organization, and the least intensive decision-making activity occurs at the operational level. Operational systems include such activities as payroll, stock control and financial accounting. The activity of preparing payrolls, for example, is a vital but repetitive task that is often done by external organizations that specialize in providing such mechanical and routine services. Likewise, any manufacturing organization that maintains levels of inventory (or stock) in raw materials or finished goods needs to operate a stock control system. Inventory must be controlled to maintain the appropriate minimum stock levels across a range of goods. Inventory systems should ideally contain up-to-date information on inventory quantity levels, inventory prices, minimum inventory levels and historically recorded inventory levels. For instance, an inventory system should automatically indicate when minimum stock levels have been reached.

Inventory control systems will also generate useful supplementary reports on sales patterns, stock flow through the manufacturing process and early and late inventory orders. In manufacturing environments there are normally two types of inventory system working in harmony; one is an input (raw materials) inventory system and the other is an output (finished goods) inventory system. The main effect of an ICT-based inventory control system is that any manager can identify inventory levels and the price of any individual item instantly, often at the touch of a button.

All business organizations will have some form of management accounting and financial accounting system that will generate reports on the transactions and trading performance of the business. Financial accounting reports are produced for *external* information use and are known in the UK and the USA as a balance sheet (showing assets and liabilities), a profit and loss account (showing the gross and net profit of the business) and a source and application of funds statement, sometimes a cash-flow statement, showing the movement in liquid or cash assets between two periods. Operational systems are concerned with the recording of day-to-day transactions that occur internally and externally within the business environment. There is very little decision-making activity concerned with operational systems, other than when and how to initiate a transaction processing activity.

Activity **2.9**   Transaction processing systems

Explain why operational systems are often referred to as transaction processing systems and discuss why such systems are usually referred to as deterministic. Once you are happy with the concept of transaction processing, provide two examples of an operational system and determine who (or what) would be responsible for initiating or operating such systems.

Management Information Systems (MIS) are often characterized by a semi-structured information environment. In operational systems the whole of the decision picture is *known*. However, in a management information system only parts of the decision picture are known; and in strategic information systems large aspects of the decision picture are *unknown*. The normal aim of all information systems is to get as near to decision-making certainty as possible. Management information systems are concerned with the provision of relevant, timely and useful information for the management *control* of an organization's resources. Therefore, management information systems are not concerned with day-to-day operational decisions, but with decisions that are in the management sphere; management decisions have a longer decision timeframe than operational decisions.

What is a management information system (MIS)?

A system providing information for decision making usually intended for middle management. The information may be internal to an organization or external to an organization.

Management information systems are designed to select, analyze and produce information that is useful to the activity of management decision making. Therefore, the information systems and technology support the activity of management decision making. The primary role of management information systems is to *plan and coordinate* the resources of the business organization. Management is a human activity and management information systems must take into account the people aspect of business organizations. Successful management information systems show a due regard to human as well as technical aspects of the business organization. Management information systems are developed with regard to a range of *knowledge concepts* and techniques that are relevant to the business environment. The knowledge concepts for an understanding of management information systems are:

▶ general systems theory
▶ information and communications technology
▶ the nature of data, information and knowledge
▶ organizational structures and processes
▶ people and human behaviour
▶ planning, decision making and control techniques
▶ organizational levels and functions
▶ interpersonal management techniques.

It is the goal of a management information system to provide management with information, based on data from both *internal* and *external* sources; to enable timely and relevant decisions for planning, directing and controlling the resources of the organization. Management information systems will be tailored to the needs of specific organizations and utilize internal information sources to a greater extent than external information sources.

Did you know?

Henri Fayol (1841–1925), a famous French industrialist, is credited with laying the classical academic foundations of the theory of management. Fayol defined the process of management as follows: '*To manage is to forecast and plan, to organize, to command, to coordinate and to control.*'

If an organization operates in a stable and relatively static and unchanging business environment the management information systems of that organization will be designed to deal with relatively more structured and mechanistic planning and control of resources. However, in dynamic and volatile business environments such information systems should be adaptive and responsive to deal with change in the internal and external environment. Management information systems are usually characterized by the following factors:

▶ There is a wider span of organizational coverage and control than operational systems.

▶ Data and information is normally drawn from a wide range of internal and external sources.

▶ Decision making can be complex and uncertain and requires reasoned management judgement.

▶ Control is usually assisted by monitoring and feedback provision incorporated into the system.

▶ The use of the system is allied with reasoned and educated management judgement.

▶ Meaningful reports are generated for management decision making and personnel information.

The data used in an MIS will be drawn from internal and external sources within the business environment. Much of the input data for a management information system may originate from output data and information from other, often operational, systems, such as stock, sales order processing, purchase order processing, or even production scheduling. This type of operational information may be processed by an MIS to provide evidence on which to base management decision making.

Activity 2.10 Management information systems decision making

Discuss the primary role of management information systems within a typical business organization. You should also discuss the eight basic knowledge concepts that underpin the design and development of management information systems. Indicate who would normally be responsible for using an MIS and explain their possible role and responsibility within a business organization.

The systems to support executive or strategic decision making are known as *Executive Information Systems* (EIS). Strategic decision making is concerned with the long-term effects of decisions; and such decisions usually influence the future direction of an organization. At the strategic level, decisions have a longer timeframe than both management and operational information systems.

What is an executive information system (EIS)?

A system that provides information to senior executive managers on strategic areas of a business organization's activities to aid strategic decision making. The information may be internal to an organization or external to the organization.

Executive information systems are designed to support high-level executives, responsible for an organization's strategic policies and direction, in the process and practice of decision making. The environment in which strategic decision making is undertaken is normally characterized by high levels of uncertainty. An EIS that provides a fraction more certainty than a competitor's EIS, within the decision-making scenario, will gain a competitive advantage within the business environment. Executive information systems are designed to eliminate information overload and provide clear, summarized information that usually highlights opportunities or weaknesses for the organization. It is critical to a business to be aware of the strategic factors that may influence the direction of the organization.

The strategic direction of an organization can often be assessed by *SWOT analysis*, which represents a business organization's:

▶ Strengths: within the internal and external environment.

▶ Weaknesses: within the internal and external environment.

▶ Opportunities: for growth and profit within the business environment.

▶ Threats: from competitors, technology and other trends.

Executive information systems normally comprise powerful data storage capabilities to handle both formal and informal information, which is used and manipulated by a range of sophisticated IT-based applications for simulation and mathematical modelling. Executive information systems are normally characterized by the following factors:

▶ There is a wider span of organizational coverage and control than operational and management systems.

▶ It is concerned with new and unstructured decision-making situations and environments.

▶ Shrewd executive reasoning and judgement are used in the collection and interpretation of information.

▶ Data and information are largely drawn from sources external to the organization.

▶ Information sources are usually report-based (alphanumeric) and often semi-formal or informal.

▶ Decision making can be uncertain and has long-term significance for an organization.

▶ It relies on forecasting, prediction and trend analysis of the long-term future.

▶ The information environment is boundary-less and not confined in decision-making scope.

▶ The use of the system requires reasoning, judgement and a broad assessment of multiple variables.

▶ It is a user-specific system that is operated personally by an individual or group of individuals.

Executive information systems must be fast and easy to use by executives who will not necessarily possess a technical background or expertise in information systems and information technology. Therefore, all EIS should be characterized by ease of use through the incorporation of menu-driven, dialogue-box techniques, touch screens, graphics and easy information interchange between systems. Rapid access to data is often permitted through exploration of the data known as *drilling down the data*. Most systems provide easy-to-use and effective front-end screen applications to permit data simulation and modelling, with the incorporation of presentable report formats. Figure 2.4 shows the link between all these aspects found within an executive information systems environment.

It is essential that executive information systems, which may be user-specific, are developed with the involvement of the user (or small group of users) so that the system reflects their requirements. This is essential given the unstructured nature of the decision-making environment in which strategic decision making is undertaken; remember that executive systems are usually built to be specific to one executive or a very small group of top-level executives. Overall, executive information systems attempt to provide a broad and holistic view of the strengths and weaknesses of the business organization within the competitive business environment.

Activity 2.11 Executive information systems

Discuss and then outline the main characteristics that are significant in determining an executive information system. Explain how such strategic information systems may be designed and used to reduce the level of uncertainty found within the executive decision-making environment of a business organization.

2.13 Decision support systems

Decision support systems (DSS) are specifically used by organizations as support tools within management or strategic decision making. Decision support systems can be part of the MIS or EIS domains of the business organization. Such decision support systems are usually characterized by levels of *expert knowledge* built into the base of the system. These expert systems can give advice on areas such as whether a bank should make a loan to a customer, or assess a customer's credit worthiness and make a decision on the loan application. Banking was one of the first industries to use DSS and general information technology to enable them to increase their profits and gain a competitive advantage. Pause for thought 2.2 describes the use of a 'lending adviser' to assist bankers and managers.

PAUSE FOR THOUGHT 2.2

The use of an IT-based lending adviser to assist bank managers

A major city bank in the USA and the UK installed an ICT system in the 1990s that was called a 'lending adviser'. It is used to assist branch bank managers in determining the underlying factors affecting the decision to lend to business customers. The lending adviser system is part of the credit risk analysis process and provides a decision support tool to provide interactive and structured analysis for the modelling of likely scenarios. The system presents bank managers with a series of forms (or screen reports) to complete about a business organization. The information ranges from the finances of the business to the quality of the management and the state of the industry sector in which the business competes.

For example, when assessing the qualities of a business organization, a bank manager and the business concerned would work in consultation with the lending adviser's accumulated knowledge and the business customer's information. To assess the industry sector, the bank manager and the business organization answer questions concerning the degree of competition in the respective industry sector; whether that is changing; how cyclical is demand (sales and revenue); the possibility of product substitutes; and the various risks of trading. Once such information is input, the lending adviser produces a score for how good a risk that company is within the relevant sector. The lending adviser would also review a range of other information, including the organization's cash flow, balance sheet, size and the quality of debtors and creditors. In addition, there is a subjective assessment of the managerial structure, succession and skills. If the bank manager believes that the financial control is good, but that the financial figures are dubious, the lending adviser will ask the bank manager to review the situation again for reassurance. In addition to the information mentioned, the lending adviser asks questions related to ethics; for instance, is the organization 'law abiding', 'law bending', 'law breaking', 'unscrupulous' or 'fraudulent'? These questions rely very much on the bank manager's judgement.

After all the questions have been contemplated and answered, the scores for each screen page are aggregated in a final set that may include some of the following factors:

Key assessments:
- ▶ Industrial risk
- ▶ Financial management evaluation
- ▶ Management competence
- ▶ Projected financial condition

Key strengths and weaknesses:
- ▶ Stock quality
- ▶ Management expertise
- ▶ Industrial risk
- ▶ Operating performance

If at the end of the process the indicators are good (i.e. positive to an acceptable degree) the bank manager will begin negotiating with the business customer about credit security and rates of interest. The main aim of the lending adviser system is to improve the process of assessing lending risk. The advantage of such a system is that various variables can be altered in order to carry out 'what-if?' analysis by rerunning the lending adviser system until all facets of the lending process have been iteratively analyzed.

What is a decision support system (DSS)?

A system that supports managers and executives by modelling the decision-making process.

Decision support systems are useful in situations where there is only a semi-structured information environment. A DSS is characterized by model building, based on expert knowledge that has been automatically incorporated into the operation of the system. The emphasis of a DSS is on supporting decision making rather than an automation of the whole decision-making process. Decision support systems are usually designed for individual or small group decision making rather than for large monolithic data processing systems found at the operational levels of the business organization. The main characteristics of decision support systems are as follows:

▶ They are best suited to *semi-structured* or *unstructured* problems and within decision-making environments where computer-based analysis can aid a decision maker's judgement.

▶ They provide support for the decision-making process but do not replace the decision maker's judgement, flair and imagination in the collection and interpretation of information.

▶ They are concerned with *predicting* and *forecasting* the future in terms of trends in the internal and external environment and predicting the effects of business and technology change.

▶ They may utilize formal and informal information sources, as well as qualitative and quantitative information.

▶ The boundaries of the decision-making environment are flexible and changeable in that the DSS is not confined to a specific functional area of activity and must reflect a holistic view of the decision-making environment.

▶ The decision-making activity involves exploring alternative courses of action through the analysis and alteration of a range of information variables.

Decision support systems assist unique, non-recurring decision making in environments that are relatively unstructured. Such systems are prevalent in managerial and strategic decision-making environments where *models of reality* are built to describe decision-making environments and provide support for engaging in 'what-if' decision-making.

Related to the area of decision support systems are applications known as *expert systems* (ES) and *artificial intelligence* (AI). Normally, an expert system uses heuristic processing techniques – finding things out through deductive reasoning, based on an expert's knowledge. It can help decision makers investigate alternative courses of action and the likely effects of these different courses of action.

Did you know?

Mortgage lenders often use expert systems to carry out credit evaluation on customers seeking a loan; the system can be interrogated with a range of different variables to come up with the optimum and unique loan analysis for an individual customer's needs.

Expert systems contain the knowledge base of an expert with the ability to mimic the thought processes of that expert. An expert system can be provided with a general set of rules instructing it on how to reason and draw conclusions from the evidence and data submitted to the system. Two areas where expert systems have been operating for some time are medical diagnosis and geological prospecting. In medical diagnosis an expert system can be provided with a range of symptoms and taught how to diagnose diseases from the information on the symptoms. In geological prospecting the expert system compares the geological characteristics of an area with its memory of the corresponding characteristics in areas where there is a high probability of finding mineral deposits.

What is an expert system (ES)?

A system that acts or behaves like a human expert in a field or area, with the facility to replicate the expert's knowledge base.

Related to the area of expert systems is *artificial intelligence* (AI), which is concerned with the design of intelligent or thinking machines. AI attempts to mimic the characteristics associated with human intelligence, such as understanding natural language, problem solving, learning and human reasoning. What distinguishes an AI system from a decision support system is the ability of the AI system to learn from past experiences and be able to reapply knowledge that has been acquired from past experience and learning.

Artificial intelligence systems attempt to undertake the process of human thought by reasoning and thinking through the higher and *emergent* aspects of a decision-making problem.

What is artificial intelligence (AI)?

A form of computer systems operation that replicates the characteristics commonly associated with human intelligence (e.g. problem solving, learning and reasoning).

Activity 2.12   Decision support

Outline and discuss the six main characteristics of a decision support system and explain the consequences of using information systems in semi-structured or unstructured decision-making environments. Then consider and highlight the importance of building conceptual models for decision-making activity and indicate the types of models that may be used within a decision support systems environment.

Business information can be categorized into internal and external information, which can be further categorized according to the purpose for which the information is intended, and the organizational level at which the information is used. The underlying purpose of information within the business environment can be broadly categorized into five main areas:

▶ **Situation information**: can be operational, managerial or strategic. Its purpose is to keep operators, managers and executives informed of current situations or company policy decisions.

▶ **Status information**: can be managerial or strategic. Its purpose is to keep managers and executives informed of continuous progress targets or met objectives.

▶ **Feedback and control information**: can be operational or managerial. Its purpose is to provide the more structured and mechanical organizational decision levels with warning or alarm signals concerning occurring or impending problems.

▶ **Planning information**: can be managerial or strategic. Its purpose is to describe future events and business policy within the mid-term time-frame for management planning and the long-term time-frame for executive planning.

▶ **Environmental information**: can be used primarily for strategic decision making, but also management decision making. It is concerned with the mass of national, economic and business intelligence and information reports that are generated to provide information on performance (e.g. annual financial accounts, government reports, academic and industrial research).

Information sources are characterized by database applications and technology to store, handle and disseminate information internally and externally within the business environment. Therefore, effective and efficient information retrieval techniques and appropriate technology for information recall and retrieval are essential to support the activities of business decision making.

Activity 2.13 Information categories

Discuss the nature and type of information required at each level of decision making within a typical organizational hierarchy. Consider and suggest three possible information sources that could be used to provide data and information for decision making. What are the desired qualities of information at each level of the organizational hierarchy? Are these desirable characteristics different at each level or are there any common desirable characteristics? How would you define the importance of decision making at each level of the organizational hierarchy?

2.14 Chapter summary

A thorough knowledge and understanding of systems theory allows a business systems professional to apply general systems principles correctly and permits better information systems design, through better planning, analysis, implementation and evaluation of business systems problems. An understanding of the principles of systems theory (and practice) provides a means of building better and more appropriate systems at all levels within a business organization; as well as an understanding of the nature of general systems behaviour. Systems theory, or systems science, argues that no matter how complex or diverse the world that we experience, we will always perceive different types of organization within it, and such organization can be described by principles that are independent from the specific domain at which we are looking. Hence, if we can uncover those general laws, we can analyze and solve problems in any domain, pertaining to any type of system.

The following chapters will look in more detail at the types of systems found within the business environment, how they are developed, and how they can be made to work to the benefit of business organizations.

SHORT SELF-ASSESSMENT QUESTIONS

2.1   Explain what is meant by modelling a system through a *bottom-up* or *top-down* approach.

2.2   Outline the three main categories of system found within the world at large.

2.3   Define the term *holistic* and explain what is meant by a holistic view of systems.

2.4   Define and explain the concept of *emergence* within general systems theory.

2.5   Explain the term *homeostasis* and suggest why a system may wish to maintain a static state equilibrium.

2.6   Explain the terms *negative feedback* and *positive feedback* and provide examples of both types of feedback.

2.7   Define the term *systems decoupling* and explain why coupling is an important concept within systems theory.

2.8   Explain what is meant by a *total systems approach* and indicate why such an approach is an important consideration for business information systems analysis.

2.9   Explain the difference between a *logical system* and a *physical system* and provide an example of a business system to illustrate the difference.

2.10   Define the concept of *formal* and *informal* information and provide examples of both sorts of information.

2.11   Highlight the three decision-making levels of a hierarchical business organization and explain why the characteristics that define these systems are different at each level.

2.12   Explain the relationship between unstructured decision-making environments and uncertainty and explain how and why this relationship affects the strategic and operational levels of a business hierarchy.

2.13   Explain the main characteristics that are significant in defining a *management information system*.

2.14   Outline and explain the use of *SWOT analysis* for strategic planning, control and decision making.

2.15   Define the term *decision support system* and indicate the levels of a business organization in which you would expect to find such systems.

EXTENDED STUDENT ACTIVITIES

Individual reporting activity

One of the most important concepts in systems theory is to be able to separate a logical system from a physical system. For example, computer software (the instructions that operate a physical system) is defined in abstract terms like mathematics. Likewise, systems must be reduced from the physical to the logical. It is important that the logical processes are thought about and not the physical environment in which those logical processes operate. The following is a physical and logical description of a business system known as 'sales order processing':

> Stephanie Holloway receives a pile of sales orders each morning and sorts them into different areas before passing them to Hugh. Hugh then sorts the orders alphabetically and passes each group to one of the order processors. Each order processor takes an order and looks at the name in the electronic customer register and then inputs the customer number into the computer-based system. The computerized system tells the order processors if the customer is cleared to receive goods. If clear, then the product number is checked and entered into the computerized system, along with the quantity of the order. Once this is done the next order is processed.

1 Draw a picture, or diagram, to show the processes and information flows present in the above narrative.

2 Separate out the physical scenario from the logical scenario and sketch a diagram showing the logical system.

3 Isolate all the logical components of the system and attach a logical verb description of each process or activity.

GENERAL SYSTEMS THEORY: SEMANTICS AND PHRASES

Boundary The logical (and sometimes physical) borders of a system within its appreciated environment.

Closed system A system that is self-sufficient (i.e. its inputs and outputs are contained within the systems boundary). Such systems do not interact with, or depend upon, systems external to their environment.

Connectivity The dependence and connection between systems and sub-systems within a domain.

Coupling The level of connectivity, and the strength of connectivity, between systems or sub-systems.

Emergence The property that materializes from systems activity. The concept is linked with the idea that 'the whole is greater than the sum of its parts'.

Environment The systems domain. The term can be used to indicate both the internal and external domains of a system.

Feedback The process of systems monitoring their environment and acting on information collected from the environment. For example, a heating system thermostat monitors air temperature in order to control a heating system.

Holon The collective world-view of a systems domain, which helps to define the systems boundary. The term is used to describe an area of concern that requires investigating.

Open system A system that feeds off its external environment. The inputs and outputs are into and out of the system's boundaries.

Weltanschauung Sometimes referred to as a world-view. It indicates that a set of observers perceive the same things in a systems boundary: they all have a world-view of the system and its operation.

REFERENCES AND FURTHER STUDY

Books and articles

An asterisk (*) indicates a seminal text – a major source for later academic developments.

Ackoff, R.L. (1999) *Re-creating the Corporation: A Design for Organizations for the 21st Century*, Oxford University Press, ISBN: 0195123875

Ackoff, R.L. (1999) *Ackoff's Best: His Classic Writings on Management*, John Wiley and Sons, ISBN: 0471316342

Ashby, R. (1956) *An Introduction to Cybernetics*, John Wiley and Sons

*Betalanffy, L. von (1950) 'An outline of general systems theory', *British Journal for the Philosophy of Science*, 1, pp. 139–64

*Bertalanffy, L. von (1968) *General Systems Theory*, Braziller, ISBN: 0807604534

Bertallanfy, L. von (1971) 'Cultures as systems: toward a critique of historical reason', *Bucknell Review*, 22, pp. 151–61

Checkland, P.B. (1976) 'Science and the systems paradigm', *International Journal of General Systems*, 3(2), pp. 127–34

Checkland, P. (1980) *Systems Thinking, Systems Practice*, John Wiley and Sons, ISBN: 0471279110

Checkland, P. and Scholes, J. (1990) *Soft Systems Methodology in Practice*, John Wiley and Sons, ISBN: 0471927686

Checkland, P. and Howell, S. (1997) *Information, Systems and Information Systems: Making Sense of the Field*, John Wiley and Sons, ISBN: 0471958204

Checkland, P. and Scholes, J. (1999) *Soft Systems Methodology in Action: Includes a 30-year Retrospective*, John Wiley and Sons, ISBN: 0471986054

Elliott, G. and Phillips, N. (2004) *Mobile Commerce and Wireless Computing Systems*, Addison Wesley, ISBN: 0201752409

Klir, G.J. (1988) 'Systems profile: the emergence of systems science', *Systems Research*, 5(2), pp. 145–56

Liebenau, J. and Backhouse, J. (1990) *Understanding Information: An Introduction*, Palgrave Macmillan Publishing, ISBN: 0333536800

Mulgan, G. (1998) *Connexity: How to Live in a Connected World*, Harvard Business School Press, ISBN: 0875848508

Rosen, R. (1986) 'Some comments on systems theory', *International Journal of General Systems*, 13(1), pp. 1–3

*Shannon, C. (1948) 'A mathematical theory of communication', *The Bell Systems Technical Journal*, 27 (July, October), pp. 379–423, 623–56

Shneiderman, B. (2002) *Leonardo's Laptop: Human Needs and the New Computing Technologies*, MIT Press, ISBN: 0262692996

Takala, M. and Hawk, D. (2001) 'Transformation of corporations: towards appreciative service systems', proceedings of the 45th Annual Meeting for the System Sciences, Asilomar, California, USA, 8–13 July

Vickers, G. (1970) *Value Systems and Social Process*, Penguin Books, ISBN: 0140212159

Vickers, G. (1972) *Freedom in a Rocking Boat: Changing Values in an Unstable Society*, Penguin Books, ISBN: 0140212051

Vickers, G. (1995) *The Art of Judgement: A Study of Policy Making*, Sage Publishing (reprinted from 1965 edition), ISBN: 0803973624

Waldrop, M.M. (1992) *Complexity: The Emerging Science at the Edge of Order and Chaos*, Viking Publishing, ISBN: 0670850454

Weinberg, G.M. (2001) *An Introduction to General Systems Thinking*, Dorset House Publishing, ISBN: 0932633498

Web resources

Learning and Teaching Support Network for Information and Computer Sciences (UK) – promotes the use of online teaching and learning resources in ICT.
www.ics.ltsn.ac.uk

Systemic Business (USA/UK) – an online community with an interest in a systemic approach to business.
www.systemicbusiness.org

IBM Systems Journal (USA) – academic and industry journal in computing and information systems.
www.research.ibm.com/journal/sj

International Society for the Systems Sciences (USA) – scientists, philosophers and educators with an interest in the systems sciences.
www.isss.org

Association for Information Systems (global) – professional body for information systems professionals and knowledge workers.
www.aisnet.org

Chapter 3

Global information systems development

When you have studied this chapter you will be able to:

▶ discuss the history of information systems development within the business environment;

▶ outline the role, purpose and effectiveness of the traditional systems development life cycle (SDLC);

▶ explain the components of the four generic stages of the traditional systems development life cycle;

▶ describe the strengths and weaknesses of the various approaches to information systems development within the business environment;

▶ assess the nature and role of end-user computing within information systems development theory and practice;

▶ highlight the development and significance of outsourcing and the support of end-user systems development;

▶ discuss the significance of application service providers (ASP) and their role in information systems support;

▶ evaluate the nature and role of object-oriented systems development and applications integration.

3.1 Introduction to information systems development

Information systems do not normally appear randomly in the business environment; their development is a time-consuming and often costly experience that must only be undertaken after careful analysis and consideration of the objectives and goals of an organization. The *goals* of an information system are paramount in determining the scope, shape, content and nature of a business information system.

The traditional approach to information systems development was known as the *waterfall* approach or *systems development life cycle* approach – the SDLC approach. This technique of business information systems development was based on structured, sequential stages of development where each stage of the life cycle had to be formally completed and signed off before the systems development team could move on to the requirements of the next stage of development. This approach was prevalent in business systems development in the 1960s and

1970s and is sometimes used as an original template for systems development approaches in the twenty-first century. However, the traditional SDLC approach to systems development has evolved over the last 40 years and spawned a number of systems development approaches that have been shaped by advances in information technology, the growth of end-user computing and the development of applications software that has enabled information systems users to become involved in the information systems development process.

The ultimate goal or objective of all systems development approaches and techniques is to build business information systems that meet the requirements of the end-users and deliver optimal business benefits in competitive global trading environments.

3.2 The traditional systems development life cycle

The oldest formalized methodology for building information systems was known as the *systems development life cycle* (SDLC). This methodology pursues the development of information systems in a very deliberate, structured and methodical way, requiring each stage of the life cycle, from inception of the idea to delivery of the final system, to be carried out rigidly and sequentially. This is often known as *imperative development*, since it is imperative (or obligatory) to complete one stage before moving on to the next stage of the development cycle. The traditional systems development life cycle originated in the 1960s to develop large-scale functional business systems in an age of large industrial business conglomerates. Information systems activities revolved around heavy data processing and 'number crunching' routines. Today the SDLC approach is mainly used for very large-scale computer-based information systems development. For example, aspects of the SDLC are still employed in the telecommunications industry when it is necessary periodically to change telephone numbers and area codes. This involves a great deal of change to software code to reprogram the core backbone systems. Therefore, the SDLC is still used for code-intensive systems applications.

The SDLC also still forms the basis of a number of modern structured approaches to information systems development, such as the *structured systems analysis and design method* (SSADM), which is still used as a framework for building information systems in large government departments in the UK. Since the 1980s the traditional life cycle approach to systems development has been increasingly replaced with alternative approaches and frameworks, which attempt to overcome some of the inherent deficiencies of the traditional SDLC. A number of alternative approaches to the SDLC will be studied in more detail in Chapter 4. However, it is important to understand the traditional SDLC approach in order to be able to compare and contrast the advantages and disadvantages of modern approaches to information systems development within the global business environment.

Table 3.1 The traditional systems development life cycle (SDLC)

Stage 1 Systems analysis	
Activities	
System definition	Define and state the scope and objectives
	Investigate and identify problems and areas of concern
Feasibility study	Collect and collate information
	Assess project costs
	Consider constraints
	Assess alternatives
Requirements specification	Describe the business requirements
	Describe the systems requirements
	Integrate and detail the systems requirements
Stage 2 Systems design	
Activities	
Logical design	Create and document logical design specifications
	Model the logical design specifications
Physical design	Create and document technical design specifications
	Model the technological design specifications
	Model the ergonomic design specifications
Stage 3 Systems implementation	
Activities	
Programming	Construct and write program code (applications-based systems development)
	Integrate hardware and software applications
Installation	Implement business system
	Implement technical system
Conversion	Convert old system to new system
Documentation	Prepare systems-user documentation
Training	Initiate human training and development
Stage 4 Systems evaluation	
Activities	
Testing	Evaluate technical systems
	Evaluate business systems
	Evaluate systems and cost audit
Organization	Evaluate systems integration
	Evaluate human–technical integration
Maintenance	Undertake systems maintenance

The traditional SDLC approach to information systems development is an evolutionary life cycle that starts with the inception of the system and ends with the eventual death (or redundancy) of the system at the end of the information system's useful life. The end of a system's life cycle is indicated by it no longer being relevant or useful for the purpose for which it was initially developed. There are *four generic stages* to the systems development life cycle:

▶ systems analysis
▶ systems design
▶ systems implementation
▶ systems evaluation.

Each of the four stages of the life cycle can be broken down into *component activities*, which are illustrated in greater detail in Table 3.1. The traditional SDLC approach is known as a *waterfall* approach because each stage of the development process cascades down to the next stage and, like a waterfall, once the water is running downwards it cannot be put back up without artificial means. Within the waterfall methodology, the development process is broken down into distinct stages of analysis, design, implementation and evaluation, all of which must be completed in a formalized sequence; one stage must be undertaken and completed before moving on to the next stage of the development life cycle. For example, systems analysis (the first stage) must be completed in isolation and *signed off* as completed before proceeding to the next stage of systems design. In turn, the systems design stage will be completed in isolation and only after completion is the implementation stage begun. This rigid sequence continues until the evaluation stage has been completed and the finished information system is delivered to the end users. In this process the next stage cannot be started before the preceding stage has been formally signed off as completed. Hence, the development process being referred to as a waterfall approach, whereby the development waterfall cascades down each stage of the systems development life cycle in sequential order.

Within the SDLC approach the end users of the information system under development do not play a major role in the overall development process. The systems development process will normally be carried out by technical computing specialists and software developers, performing their traditional roles of *systems analyst* and *systems programmer*. The systems analyst would normally interact with the users to establish their requirements and the programmer would convert those requirements to computer language code and undertake the technical integration of the information system into the business environment.

The end user would effectively be redundant in the development process until the eventual system came online and was operational. By this stage the end user is faced with a *fait accompli*, in other words, an action completed and not open to argument. At this point it may be too late in the day for the information systems end user to rectify any user problems. Therefore, the traditional systems development life cycle relies on the user and system's *requirements* being clearly defined at the beginning of the systems development project. However, such levels of certainty are difficult to achieve without the involvement of end users in the design and development process.

The development of business information systems is a major undertaking that any competitive business organization cannot afford to initiate lightly. So what reasons are there for seeking to develop new information systems or replace old information systems? The fundamental reason lies in change – business is an *adaptive activity* that must constantly change or modify in order for an organization to remain competitive. The reasons for initiating the systems development process may be many and various and conditional on the sector of business in which an organization operates. Some reasons for initiating a systems development project are as follows:

▶ The current system may no longer be suitable for its purpose or the environment in which it operates. As business requirements change, so do the systems requirements. It is always valuable to assess continuously the effectiveness of information systems to establish whether they align with the current business requirements. Information systems that were established under previous business conditions may no longer be suitable for the prevailing situation. Changes in environmental constraints, such as organizational structure, human resourcing, work practices and statutory obligations, lead to information systems being reassessed.

▶ The current system may have become redundant due to technological developments. Advances in technology offer systems solutions that are often superior to the existing technology-based or manual systems. Information technology may also offer opportunities that encourage new systems to be established or previous systems to be merged and integrated. Improvements in hardware, software and telecommunications often lead to a rationalization of systems structures and domains that allows information technology to be exploited for competitive advantage in the business domain.

▶ The current systems may have become too expensive or resource intensive which may reduce an organization's ability to be flexible and competitive. One of the main reasons for building replacement information systems is to reduce costs or improve the efficiency of current resources, such as human resources, physical assets and technology. New systems can be developed either to cut costs or produce a greater return on existing resources through the focusing of business objectives.

Activity 3.1 Information systems development

Discuss and explain what is meant by the term information systems development life cycle (SDLC) and outline three main reasons why the traditional SDLC is considered to be too inflexible in the design and development of information systems for modern business.

Discuss and outline some of the consequences of lack of end-user involvement within the systems development process. Then highlight some of the reasons for initiating an information systems development project. Provide an example, from your experience or knowledge, of an information system that was developed, and explain the reasons behind its development.

PAUSE FOR THOUGHT 3.1

Farewell to waterfalls!

Within dynamic business environments very few organizations can afford to use the time-consuming waterfall model for systems development. The rigidity of the waterfall approach requires the systems development team to complete each stage before moving on to the next stage. Consequently, rapid applications development (RAD) has become very popular in the business environment. RAD is often a natural way to do things because the range of tools and techniques available to modern business systems design and implementation allows development teams to work without having to know all the details of an application.

Speed of business systems development is of paramount importance. Often, if a systems development project lasts more than six to nine months there is a higher than normal risk of loss of user's interest or a change in the essential processes of the business organization. RAD has the advantage of being an iterative approach whereby a systems development team can deliver parts of a system in an incremental manner, all the time incorporating the views and ideas of the end users themselves. The sooner that end users can see a tangible product the easier it is for them to accept a changed system. The RAD approach is an excellent way of discovering the concerns and needs of the end users. The RAD phenomenon is to some extent driven by the availability of visual programming tools and techniques that allow end users to be a working part of the systems development process. RAD incorporates tools and techniques that allow for the better design and delivery of graphical user interfaces (GUIs). Many business organizations incorporate joint applications development (JAD) into the RAD process with the development and incorporation of employee workshops into the fabric of the organization.

RAD is a useful approach for developing real-time systems such as bank loan systems and other online applications for dealing with financial transactions. Such systems can also evolve over time, with the addition of other applications as and when necessary; a particularly important consideration where user requirements are not well known or easy to define. RAD can be used for developing a decision support system (DSS) that can access data from an online transaction processing system (TPS) which might have been developed using the traditional waterfall approach. Therefore, RAD is very flexible and can be used in association with systems developed using the traditional SDLC approach.

With RAD, care must be taken with issues of standardization and systems quality; visual tools and techniques allow users to see what they need through prototypes, rather than reading

▶

through textual descriptions of the system. However, because of RAD's lack of a clear methodological framework or process, the end product is not always as inbued with quality as it should be, sometimes because RAD emphasizes front-end analysis rather than larger issues of database design and back-end processing.

Therefore, does RAD require a methodology that focuses on the mechanisms of systems development or would such a methodological constraint wipe out the creative aspects of RAD? What is not in doubt is the fact that RAD tools and techniques had a significant effect on software and systems development in the last decade of the twentieth century, with the majority of business organizations now adopting RAD approaches, rather than the SDLC approaches, to business systems development.

Did you know?

The earliest use of computers was for mathematical and scientific applications where the processing of numbers was the primary activity. When computer technology began to be absorbed into the business environment in the 1960s and 1970s, the main use of computers was for functional and operational processing systems activities.

The basic business processing activities of the 1960s and 1970s included data and information storage, retrieval, sorting, collating, analyzing, calculating and communicating (through the generation of paper-based reports). As computing and ICT became increasingly absorbed into the information systems fabric of business organizations, it became apparent that there was a need for a structured method (or methodology) to be applied to the development of information systems in business. The development of information systems had become an increasingly expensive and time-consuming activity that needed to be carried out with careful thought and planning. This was allied to the fact that information systems end users were becoming increasingly dissatisfied with the information systems that were being developed on a one-off basis, without any obvious regard to the effect on other related systems within the business organization. Over time, due to a need for increasingly efficient and effective information systems, business organizations wanted structured development approaches that expanded their brief and addressed the issues of information systems analysis, design, implementation and evaluation in global competitive environments.

In modern information systems development the methods used are not only inward looking (i.e. at the systems and procedures of the organization) but are also outward looking (i.e. they take into consideration the competitive forces that affect the business organization both nationally and internationally).

What is the difference between a method and a methodology?

A method is a way of doing something, or a procedure for doing something. A methodology is a branch of human philosophy dealing with the science of method or procedure.

3.3 The four generic stages of the systems development life cycle

Systems analysis

This stage of the information systems development process involves undertaking a *feasibility study* and *systems investigation*. At this stage the scope and objectives of the proposed system must be defined. The aim of the study is to understand the systems *problem* and determine whether it is worth solving. The feasibility study should investigate the current system (if there is one) and ascertain the problems and requirements of the old and proposed new system. The study should determine whether the proposed system is viable and workable on the grounds of legality, organizational structure, technical constraints and cost constraints.

This stage will usually result in a set of information systems alternatives within a given set of constraints. This systems investigation and feasibility will normally be delivered in the form of a report (and/or presentation) to the managerial or executive level of the business organization. Hence, anyone involved in issues relating to business information systems and technology requires good human communication and presentation skills in order to convey ideas and gain approval for the initiation of new projects. At this stage a decision is made to determine whether to progress to the subsequent stages of the development life cycle.

Systems investigation involves *fact-finding*. The investigation will normally look at the *system requirements* and *business requirements* of the existing system and the proposed new system. The facts are gathered and collated through the use of a number of tools and techniques including interviews, questionnaires, task observation and the analysis of existing systems documentation. The task of systems analysis should determine what the information system must do in order to solve an information-based problem. The result of this investigative stage will normally be delivery of a list of systems requirements and priorities, which will be laid out in what is commonly termed a *feasibility report*. Some of the issues commonly addressed in a feasibility report are:

▶ assessment of existing business systems and sub-systems
▶ purpose and goals of the system
▶ the business environment
▶ systems integration
▶ human, technical and legal constraints
▶ cost and return on investment
▶ assessment of alternative solutions.

The investigative stage of systems analysis will normally require formal documentation to capture data and information from people, technology and the organization. Current systems will have to be analyzed, assessed and evaluated. The process of systems investigation involves collecting and collating data and information from a range of sources. This can be achieved by various means such as:

▶ interviews and questionnaires from employees and other people
▶ studying business and other systems documentation
▶ data acquisition through human observation
▶ data acquisition through technical measurement.

Normally, interviews and questionnaires are an important method of getting a general feeling for a system. Interviews should be carried out with employees from the specific system and related systems to assess the effects the eventual information system might have on the operation of business. The use of interviewing techniques and questionnaires should not involve open-ended questioning. They should be carefully structured to elicit concise and detailed data or information, which in turn must be clearly documented. An example of a formal questionnaire, gathering data on ICT outsourcing, can be found in Appendix 1 at the end of this book.

All large, organized and well-managed business organizations maintain records and documentation that act as a verifiable history of business and systems processes. This documentary evidence can be *numerical* or *alphanumerical* and comes from a range of internal and external business sources. Table 3.2 outlines the possible sources of documentation available within the business environment. These have been separated into the three pillars of a business organization; people, organization and technology.

When studying a business organization's documentation it is important to consider the nature of that documentation, for instance, whether the information is in date or out of date, and the integrity (or formality) of the procedures that gave rise to the documentation. It is also important to remember that documentation is often an indication of what should be happening and not necessarily what is happening in a business organization.

Data acquisition through human observation is a direct method of analyzing systems processes and collecting information. During observation, a time and motion study can be carried out of human and systems activity. Observation is a very useful way of gathering information about how human activity interacts with technical systems activity. However, an observer should be aware that observed people tend to behave differently to their normal unobserved behav-

Table 3.2 Types of business organization documentation

People	Organization	Technology
Personnel records	Mission statement	User instruction manuals
Employment contracts	Policy documents	Systems documentation
Job descriptions	Financial statements	Telecommunications protocols
Time and motion records	Management reports	
Education and training material	Statutory regulations	
Monitoring and appraisal records	Procedures manual	

iour. This is known as the *Hawthorne effect*, whereby there is an improvement in performance resulting from the interest expressed by researchers and the knowledge of those being observed that their activity is being measured. Nevertheless, observation is a beneficial source of data and information on the interaction of the human, technical and organizational aspects of a business organization.

Data acquisition through *technical measurement* involves the use of computing and information technology to monitor and measure human and technical systems activity. Such measurement often employs the use of sensors to detect electronically human and technical systems activity. For example, the number of occasions a system is used can easily be determined by keeping an electronic record of when and how a system was activated throughout a given period of time. Technical measurement is mostly employed to gather *quantitative data* that can be statistically measured and evaluated.

Having collected and collated data and analyzed the systems environment, what factors might determine an information systems project going ahead? There are five main *feasibility factors* that might assist in determining the probability of an information systems project being undertaken. These are known by the mnemonic TELOS, which represents:

▶ **Technical feasibility**: determining the possibility and practicality of using existing and modern information technology to develop the proposed system.

▶ **Economic feasibility**: assessing the budgetary and financial constraints of the proposed information system.

▶ **Legal feasibility**: indicating the existing legal requirements on the business and determining whether any conflict exists between the proposed system and the paramount legal and statutory obligations on the organization.

▶ **Operational feasibility**: determining whether existing or proposed procedures and practices are adequate for the purposes of the proposed system. Consideration will also be given to the education, training and development required to operate the proposed information system.

▶ **Schedule feasibility**: determining the practicality and acceptability of the timeframe for development of the proposed information system.

Activity 3.2   Activities of information systems development

Explain the role and function of information systems analysis within the systems development life cycle and suggest why it is important for the feasibility of a proposed new (or replacement) information system to be investigated. The process of systems investigation involves collecting and collating data and information from various sources within the business environment: discuss advantages and disadvantages of each of the possible methods, sources and documentation used in the investigation of an information system within the business domain or any other organizational domain.

Systems design

This stage involves designing an information system to overcome a particular information-based problem and meet the end user's requirements. This stage is characterized by the separation of the *logical* design from the *physical* design process. Remember that in Chapter 2 it was essential to determine a system's logical purpose before being concerned with the system's physical design. The logical design process describes the functional requirements or *purpose* of the information system. The physical design model follows from the logical design and describes the physical and technological characteristics that the information system should possess. The logical process and physical design models indicate the inputs, outputs, processing technology and computer user interfaces necessary for the successful operation of the information system.

The logical design *conceptualizes* what the system should do to solve the problems identified through the earlier analysis stage. Logical design involves determining the purpose and other aspects of an information system independently of hardware and software considerations. Therefore, the inputs, outputs and processing activities of the system are logically described in terms of their required or desired characteristics. Then the physical design model specifies the hardware, software and human interaction required to convert the logical design into a physical system. The physical aspects of the logical design will normally involve consideration of the following tangible elements:

▶ **Hardware technology**: the input, processing and output devices and their respective performance characteristics.

▶ **Software technology**: software applications and their integration, specifications and performance within the system.

▶ **Storage media**: the type, structure and function of storage media, such as computer files, databases, CD-ROMs and other data and information storage technology.

▶ **Telecommunications technology**: the specifications, use and characteristics of the technology both internally and externally to the organization.

▶ **People and organization**: the description and remit of human interaction, plus the procedures and control aspects of the organization that impact on the system.

Activity 3.3 Systems design

Explain the role and function of information systems design within the systems development life cycle and describe the distinction between logical design and physical design. Why do you think it is important for an analyst and systems designer to possess the skills of logical systems thinking as well as physical systems thinking?

Implementation stage

This stage is concerned with building the components of an information system. This involves the installation and putting into place of a system, inclusive of all its physical aspects. It may also involve the writing of computer programs or the integration of pre-coded applications and software, which is often referred to as *applications-based development*. This stage is primarily concerned with the acquisition of hardware, software and other wired and wireless telecommunications technology necessary physically to construct and implement the system.

There should also be an element of end-user training incorporated into this stage, assisted by policy and user documentation. The implementation stage should result in the delivery of an installed and operational information system that can be tested and evaluated. The outcome of each stage is sometimes referred to in computing and IT jargon by the term *deliverable* (e.g. 'what are the deliverables of this stage?'). It is important that any new system should be run in parallel with the old system (if it exists) for a period of time to prevent any changeover or system conversion problems. Once the users are completely confident with the new system then the old system can be removed or taken 'offline'. The implementation stage will involve acquiring hardware and software technology from computer vendors, who may be an individual or other business organization.

The implementation stage normally includes the following considerations:

▶ hardware acquisition

▶ software acquisition

▶ user familiarization and training

▶ environment preparation

▶ information and data preparation.

A number of decisions need to be made, such as whether to acquire externally developed (bespoke) software, or off-the-shelf software, or in-house developed software and other applications. The hardware and software acquired need to be harmoniously integrated into the business organization.

Activity 3.4 Systems implementation

Discuss the role and purpose of implementation within the systems development life cycle (SDLC) and highlight five main considerations of this stage of information systems development. Discuss whether you think that these considerations should be undertaken in isolation from the other stages of the SDLC. State the types of computing vendor that might be contacted at the implementation stage of systems development.

Evaluation stage

This stage involves testing and appraisal to determine whether the system is meeting its requirements. An *evaluation report* should be produced to assess whether the system is meeting the requirements set out in the initial feasibility report efficiently and effectively. If the system is not meeting its requirements then the SDLC process may begin again. A number of evaluation techniques can be used to assess the merits of the final system. The following are some commonly used evaluation techniques:

▶ **User evaluation**: involves formal and informal feedback from the end users of the system to determine whether the system is efficient and effective. With user involvement in the development process this is made easier, since the

Table 3.3 Types of system costs and benefits

System costs	System benefits
System development expenses	Reduced salaries and wages
People and resourcing	Reduced environment costs
Information technology purchased	Greater efficiency and effectiveness
Licenses and other fees	New products and services
Equipment rental and leasing fees	Increased customer base
Salaries and wages	Better products and services
Heating, lighting and electricity	Better work procedures and practices
Maintenance and training	
Insurance	

users will be aware of the mutually agreed systems requirements from the start of the systems development project.

▶ **Cost–benefit analysis (CBA)**: attempts to match the aggregate of the costs against the aggregate of the benefits of the system. Hopefully, the benefits will outweigh the costs! The costs will include development and operational costs, which can be divided into fixed costs and variable costs. Table 3.3 lists the possible costs and benefits that may be considered for evaluation.

> **What are fixed and variable costs?**
> A fixed cost is a cost that is fixed and does not vary with systems activity (e.g. initial equipment purchase costs). A variable cost is a cost that increases with activity (e.g. the direct wages of an operator or the electricity consumed).

▶ **Benchmark testing**: involves comparing the actual performance of the system to the ideal standard for that system. The performance of the system is judged by whether it is below or above the standard set.

A detailed study of the tools and techniques often found and used within each generic stage is provided in Chapter 5.

Activity **3.5** Systems evaluation

Discuss in groups the main role and function of information systems evaluation within the systems development life cycle and explain what is meant by user evaluation, cost–benefit analysis and benchmarking within the evaluation process. Then outline and discuss some of the possible costs and benefits of an information systems project that you have read about or seen on the news.

3.4 Strengths and weaknesses of the traditional systems development life cycle

The traditional systems development life cycle was relevant to the needs of large-scale computer-based systems development in the 1960s and 1970s. At that time computing technology was restricted to only a small section of the business organization, often known as the *electronic data processing* (EDP) department or function. Therefore, computing and information technology did not pervade throughout the whole of the business organization. Today the situation is very different, with computing and information technology existing at every level and function of an organization. Users of information technology are expected to be responsible for using and managing various technologies without regard to a separate EDP function or department; organizations have become more dynamic in dealing with business change and competition. Nevertheless, the traditional SDLC possesses a number of strengths that sometimes make it relevant to the modern information systems environment:

▶ The SDLC is a tried and tested approach that is very suitable for the development of large-scale information systems.

▶ The traditional SDLC relies on the production of systems documentation and standards of development that can be used to guide the development of an information system and can be used as reference and training material for users.

▶ The sequential and phased nature of the SDLC allows a complex systems development problem to be broken down into manageable and understandable tasks.

▶ The SDLC relies on the use of formalized analysis and design tools and techniques that graphically show the nature of data and information flows within the system.

▶ The structured nature of the traditional SDLC allows the incorporation of formal project management techniques and tools to guide the systems development process.

The SDLC was appropriate for the systems environment that existed at the time of its development and use in the 1960s and 1970s. However, the development of information systems in modern-day business requires adopting methods of development that are more appropriate to dynamic business environments. The main weaknesses with the traditional systems development life cycle are as follows:

▶ The SDLC ignores or underplays end-user involvement in the systems development process. The end user is often faced with operating an information system that is user-unfriendly or fails to deliver the user's requirements for the system. The traditional SDLC only permits users to appreciate the system once it has been completed and installed. User dissatisfaction may lead to the user developing their own customized and informal application of the system to the detriment of the overall systems within a business organization.

▶ Over 90 per cent of IT-based systems development occurs within the business environment. The use of computing and information technology within business organizations is based on small desktop machines or personal computers, usually networked locally (in a local area network within the organization) or connected to the wider business environment (through a wide area network). The traditional SDLC is concerned with large-scale systems development and is not appropriate to PC-based and small-scale development of business information systems.

▶ The traditional SDLC is time consuming and costly in terms of human resourcing and monetary expenditure. The modern-day business requirement is for systems to be developed as quickly as is practicable and within certain budgetary constraints. Business information systems are often developed for one-off projects or for functions that are constantly evolving with business changes.

▶ The development methodology is often too rigid, sequential and inflexible to change. Time and cost savings can be achieved by developing stages of the life cycle in parallel or out of sequence. The important aim is for an eventual end user to be able to visualize the final system so that time and energy are not wasted pursuing systems development avenues that are not required by the end users. Often an inflexible development methodology, which is output driven, does not possess the scope to accommodate changes to the system's output specifications.

▶ The SDLC approach is often a slow and laborious process. This is a problem when there is a need for information systems to be developed as quickly as possible to meet the requirements of dynamic business environments. The use of the SDLC for large-scale systems projects often leads to systems development backlogs where users are forced to wait so long that the system no longer meets their requirements when it is eventually delivered.

▶ The SDLC assumes a sequential, step-by-step approach to development that ignores the possibility of testing the proposed system at an early stage of the life cycle following the discovery of new user requirements. Most human activity systems are fine-tuned through a process of *iteration* to focus an information system to meet its requirements. Iteration is the process of repeating a series of operations until an ideal solution is achieved.

▶ The traditional SDLC is particularly useful for the development of operational data processing systems where the information processing is structured and routine. However, there is an increasing need within the managerial and executive levels of most business organizations for information systems that process unstructured information and operate within uncertain decision-making environments. The traditional SDLC is not appropriate for the development of such managerial and executive decision-making systems.

▶ The traditional SDLC was originally centred on systems development problems in the UK and the USA. As ICT spreads around the world it has united weaker economies with stronger economies, so the relevance of the SDLC, and its narrow geographical parameters, has declined.

These failings of the traditional approach to systems development have led to the evolution of alternative development approaches with the aims of:

▶ reducing development time and cost of systems development;

▶ improving the delivery of system and user requirements;

▶ recognizing advances in computing and information technology;

▶ recognizing the nature of systems within modern business environments.

The alternatives are development solutions that attempt to overcome the deficiencies of the traditional systems development life cycle approach to building information systems.

Activity 3.6 Systems development

Discuss and explain the main weaknesses of the SDLC that make it no longer appropriate for many business organizations and global business environments. Outline some of the possible aims in the search for alternative development methods. For example, should an alternative development methodology try to overcome the weaknesses of the traditional SDLC? Should an ideal systems development method be applicable to any country or industry anywhere in the world? What are the global problems of applying development methods that are primarily focused on one particular country or region?

3.5 Alternative approaches to information systems development

The downsizing of physical information and communications technology within the business environment and the growth of networked desktop computing in business have seen the traditional SDLC become outdated and irrelevant in many respects. There are a number of approaches that have evolved, particularly in the 1990s, as alternatives to the traditional SDLC, some of which utilize the development life cycle approach and some of which are radical departures from the staged analysis, design, implementation and evaluation approach.

Most development approaches and methodologies are underpinned or influenced by aspects of general systems theory, which were detailed in Chapter 2, and the early developments of information systems development methods. Alternative approaches to systems development acknowledge that most business systems involve complex human activity that makes systems unpredictable. Furthermore, there is an apparent recognition that systems cannot be seen in isolation – they must be looked at in totality. Most business organizations, by their very nature of trading with the environment at large, are considered open systems. Business organizations influence, and are influenced by, the wider systems environment.

Alternative approaches to information systems development that utilize the concept of end-user computing are:

▶ rapid applications development (RAD)
▶ dynamic systems development method (DSDM)
▶ joint applications development (JAD)
▶ prototyping systems development
▶ object-oriented systems development (OOSD)
▶ business process re-engineering.

All these approaches share a common characteristic of emphasizing the importance of humans and systems users in the development process of information systems within business. Therefore, it is important in these alternative methods and approaches to be able to describe the impact and importance of the end user on information systems development.

Activity 3.7   Alternative information systems development

Search your college or university library for abstract and/or journal sources for ten articles related to rapid applications development (RAD), dynamic systems development method (DSDM) and joint applications development (JAD). Discuss whether the articles you found were from journals in the business area or the computing area or another related academic area and whether each area was addressed from a different perspective. Outline the main differences and similarities of these three aspects of the information systems development activity.

3.6 End-user information systems development

The evolution of end-user computing was outlined in Chapter 1, which described the development of information systems that utilize the knowledge and abilities of the user of the information system to create and build systems that meet the requirements of the business organization.

In historical terms the permeation of desktop computers into all hierarchical levels of a business organization meant that computer processing power could be sited wherever it was required. Desktop personal computers also ran their own applications (e.g. spreadsheets, word-processors, presentation software and operating systems software). These applications were specifically designed and written for the end users within an organization. As a consequence, end users gained experience of a number of aspects of computing and became more confident in expressing their personal requirements for the information systems that supported their activities in the organization. This higher level of involvement and confidence has also led, in many circumstances, to many end users actively writing their own programs and systems applications.

In addition, end users have been involved in advising on the integration of applications within an organizational domain. In the late 1990s the integration of these applications became increasingly networked and distributed throughout organizations with the growth and development of more robust electronic data networks. This enabled computers to communicate speedily and actively with one another, thus extending the scope of end-user computing. This trend of networking and distribution reached its climax with the extensive use of the internet as a major component of modern business systems activity.

Unlike the traditional SDLC approach, where the system user is peripheral to the development process, in end-user computing the final user of the system is central to the development process. By including end users in development it is hoped that the information system that is finally constructed and delivered will better meet the needs and business requirements of the organization, and in turn increase the potential for generating wealth for the business. The professional roles and responsibilities of the traditional systems analyst and programmer have largely become merged into one single role, that of the *systems end user*.

Who are these end users, and why are they sometimes referred to as systems *stakeholders*?

Systems stakeholders

Systems stakeholders are the users of an information system. They may be internal or external to the organization and can be individuals or groups. A stakeholder is anyone that falls within the logical boundaries of the system. Possible stakeholders in an information systems development project might include:

▶ the project management team for the systems development task;

▶ the clients of the systems project management team, who may be all the employees of an organization or merely a sub-set of individuals within an organization;

▶ the end users themselves, who may be managers, executives or functional operators within the organization;

▶ the customers of the organization who initiated the systems development project and their clients;

▶ the suppliers of the organization and various other agents (e.g. franchises and collaborating partner organizations);

▶ competitors of the organization, but obviously these are not normally involved in the systems development project;

▶ government and various other business regulators and agencies that influence the shape and nature of information systems built for organizations.

A stakeholder group can often be a conceptual construct as well as a physical group. Ideas of influence and organizational politics play a part in defining a stakeholder or group of stakeholders. However, it is clear to say that a stakeholder is anyone, or any group, that influences how an information system is designed, built and used.

End-user responsibility

Within the process of end-user information systems development, ICT tools and resources are given directly to the system end users in order for them to influence the development of specific aspects of an organizational information system. Responsibility for the success of an information systems development project is in many respects transferred to the end users rather than held with an intermediary, such as a systems analyst or a software programmer. Therefore, the end user must be aware, able and competent in deciding how to use and integrate software applications and various other ICT resources to deliver a working business system within budget and on time.

What is an end user?

A stakeholder or group of stakeholders in an organization that use an information system to carry out their roles, responsibilities and tasks.

End-user information systems development has been encouraged by the distillation and networked distribution of ICT into every level of a business organization and because of the movement away from *centralization* towards *decentralization* within the business domain.

Decentralization transfers decision-making powers to departments, or even individuals, to determine their own information systems development. Therefore, with people becoming more ICT literate there is no longer a need for the centralization of information system specialisms like programming and systems analysis. Within the business environment, the specialisms that do exist have often evolved into hardware and software maintenance and support roles within in-house ICT support centres or external *application service providers* (ASP). The concept of an information centre is to provide a support mechanism to assist end-user information systems development. In practice, to get the most out of end-user information systems development, it is necessary that:

▶ the business knows how and where to apply ICT within the organization;

▶ staff at every level of the organization need to be comfortable in using ICT;

▶ there is an awareness of the need to build information systems that adapt to change in the business environment.

 **3.8** End-user information systems development

Discuss the evolution of end-user information systems development and explain how it may affect the nature and role of systems development within the business environment. Do you think that end users require specific support and assistance in the development of information systems? If so, what type of assistance do they require and how would you suggest that the assistance is implemented within an organization?

3.7 Modern software development languages

End-user information systems development is often aided by the proliferation of user-friendly fourth generation software language environments that promote the development of business information systems with little formal assistance from technical specialists. Software refers to the programs written to run on a computer. In effect a computer program is a list of instructions in a particular language that determines the actions and operation of a computerized system. In effect a program comprises a series of instructions that controls and manages the operation of a computerized system.

The *generation* of the programming language describes the level of use of natural language that is used within the program code; a high-level language has a higher level of natural language used in the program code than a lower-level language and should consequently be more user-friendly for the information systems developer. Natural language is the language that we use to communicate with each other (e.g. English, French, Spanish, Swedish etc.). The use of natural language within the program code assists a non-technical specialist to build information systems, since they already possess a high level of understanding of

Table 3.4 Generations of programming language

First generation languages	(1GLs)	Assembly language, machine language code
Second generation languages	(2GLs)	FORTRAN, COBOL
Third generation languages	(3GLs)	BASIC, C, Pascal
Fourth generation languages	(4GLs)	Visual Basic, Visual C++, Smalltalk, Java

natural language. Table 3.4 lists examples of programming languages at each generation of language evolution.

First generation language code – machine language code – is the most elemental language of all computer systems. Machine code operates the computer processing unit (CPU) microprocessor chip in modern personal computers. Most personal computers can execute machine code at a rate of several hundred million instructions per second. Machine code performs very elemental operations (e.g. transferring a number into a byte of memory). It is, therefore, not appropriate for higher-level operations within the information systems domain. Programs written in higher-level languages, higher than machine code, cannot be readily understood by the CPU chip. Therefore, these higher-level languages need to be converted to machine language code. This is achieved through two main processes: compilation and interpretation. A compiler takes a higher-level language and converts it to machine code. These compiled programs can then be run on any machine with appropriate and compatible CPU types (i.e. a compiler for a Pentium 4 chip with another machine containing a Pentium 4 chip). An interpreter is a program that runs on a host client's computer. It executes instructions one at a time and translates each instruction to machine code before executing the instruction. Interpreter programs have an advantage over compilers in that they can be hosted on any computer and can run on any operating system platform that has the interpreter.

The first non-machine code languages were FORTRAN, BASIC and COBOL. These were structured and imperative languages. These languages were more intuitive than machine code. These were soon superseded by more procedural and functional programming languages, such as C and Pascal. These were referred to as third generation languages (3GLs). These languages allowed code developers to group program functions and, therefore, made it easier to maintain code because functions could be isolated and repaired without having to go through dense machine code. Third generation language environments, which are closely tied to programming within traditional systems development, are imperative, structured and more suitable for sequential systems development methods such as the SDLC. Third generation development environments did not have the same level of flexibility as fourth generation development environments; consequently, they were less user-friendly for the purposes of end-user development. The next significant step, after incorporating functionality into the programming domain, was embedded object orientation in fourth generation languages, such as, C++ and Java.

Within the object-oriented paradigm software programs are collections of objects with methods that act and operate on the objects. Object orientation enables code to be slotted in and out of a programming domain as and when conditions change. For example, an object dealing with suppliers can be altered without having to change all of the code within the program environment. Object code can also be collated and collected together in object libraries and used as and when required – a bit like taking a book out of a normal library and returning that book to the shelves when the subject has been studied. Object orientation within the software development world took off in the mid-1990s. Object-oriented languages allow code to be maintained more easily and also enable the code to be portable between software applications. Hence the importance of object-oriented languages for building applications-based information systems in modern information systems development environments.

> ### Did you know?
> Fourth generation programming language environments are often non-procedural and have been developed to be more user-friendly than imperative third generation language development environments.

Fourth generation languages (4GLs) are, by their nature, less structured, non-procedural, and more user-friendly for non-technical business specialists. The main advantage of 4GLs lies in permitting greater end-user involvement in the information systems development process. Fourth generation language development tools provide an opportunity for users to be directly involved in hands-on software development. Furthermore, the less structured program coding domains within 4GLs allow frequent program changes to be made with very little cost, while still maintaining the integrity of the overall information systems development process; programming changes can be made without having to go back to the start of the development life cycle. Fourth generation languages also allow working models (or prototypes) to be developed early in the development life cycle and then iteratively tested and evaluated by the information system end users. (Iteration is the process of repeated refinement and modification to achieve an optimal solution.)

In the modern information age the business information technology specialist is unlikely to work within information systems development environments or on computing applications that deal with highly structured language development tools more associated with 3GL environments. Information technology changes over the last 20 years have brought about fundamental changes in working practices within all types of business organization. Consequently, many business information systems are now built by *integrating* standard software application packages, rather than starting from scratch using Ada, Pascal, C or some other 3GL environment. The practice of using standard software packages, which are often predesigned and coded, to build information systems is known as *applications-based systems development*. Standard applications packages can be customized, and often integrated, to achieve a technical information systems solution to solve an information problem. For example, standard software applications packages within the Microsoft Office environment can be linked and integrated using 4GL environments such as Visual Basic. Therefore, there are a number of underlying advantages in using 4GL development tools:

▶ greater end-user involvement in the development process;

▶ relatively less program coding with 4GLs compared to 3GLs;

▶ user-friendly development tools and environment;

▶ less structured and more flexible design and development framework;

▶ shorter development time and faster systems delivery;

▶ end users with basic computer literacy can be involved in the analysis, design, implementation and evaluation of information systems.

What are fourth generation languages (4GLs)?

Non-procedural programming languages developed to replace third generation languages.

Within end-user information systems development, 4GLs are suitable for customizing, tailoring and integrating standard software application packages (e.g. word-processors, spreadsheets and databases) that are commonly found and used within integrated electronic office environments. In terms of information systems development, 4GL environments involve end users in all of the four generic stages of the systems development life cycle process of analysis, design, implementation and evaluation. End-user developers play a primary role in defining the information system goals and, through the building of working prototype systems, can evaluate alternative solutions to achieve optimal information system development. The main tools and techniques of fourth generation information systems development include:

▶ applications-based software development (word-processors, databases, spreadsheets, presentation packages, etc.)

▶ rapid applications development (RAD)

▶ 4GL environments and other software development tools

▶ information systems prototyping

▶ software tools:
   – software application generators
   – visual programming languages
   – standard query languages
   – graphics languages.

Although 4GLs give end users a significant role in the systems development process, they do not liberate end users from developing information systems according to professional programming, documentation and evaluation *standards*. The dominant language generations used in present-day business to build software applications for organizations are 3GLs and 4GLs. Increasingly, however, 4GLs are replacing 3GLs as the predominant business systems development language environment. The rigid nature of 3GLs, such as COBOL, C, and Pascal, and the laborious (often time-consuming) coding requirements have persuaded organizations to instigate 4GL development methods. This systems development trend has been fuelled by the rise of *client-server technology* that can make available multi-various software development tools throughout the whole business organization. Client-server technology is concerned with the networking of software applications throughout an organization and external bodies, which allows employees freedom of access to software tools and techniques that would otherwise be too specific or customized to be held by individual employee or departmental systems.

What is client-server computing?

A model of computer networking that separates the processing of tasks between the client computer and servers on a network. Each computing device is assigned the functions and tasks that it performs best.

As information systems development tools have evolved, the boundaries between each tool have become increasingly blurred as the tools become more powerful and integrate multiple development characteristics. However, despite having many benefits, 4GLs also have certain weaknesses, so a decision on the use and application of 3GLs or 4GLs should include the following factors:

▶ The laborious and time-consuming nature of coding in 3GLs is often overcome by using support tools such as CASE (computer-aided software engineering) that reduces development time by automatically generating language code. This makes programming with 3GLs rational and more productive.

▶ The detailed and transparent nature of 3GL program codes may make systems testing and maintenance more apparent, compared to 4GLs that often contain hidden pregenerated language code.

▶ Third generation languages are more appropriate for building large-scale (transactions-based), complex mainframe systems that warrant more sophisticated technical solutions. With large-scale and functional systems, such as national telephone networks and government taxation, these are still better developed and managed using traditional 3GL methods.

▶ By giving up responsibility for development to end users the business suffers the potential danger of losing control over the design and development process. Furthermore, end-user development using 4GLs may be idiosyncratic and less prone to formal business and computing standardization than 3GL systems built by trained technical specialists. Information systems that are operated and managed by multiple end users require formalized support documentation to confirm the integrity of the data and support the correct use of the system.

Within fourth generation development environments the end users are normally supported by other technical systems specialists who provide a guiding or supervisory role in the systems development process. It must be remembered that within 4GL development environments there is still a need to be rigorous in the application of verifiable standards to the analysis, design, implementation and evaluation of an information system, irrespective of whether the system being built is large or small scale.

3.8 Software-based information systems

It is software where the real end-user value is created. Usable programming languages should be unambiguous; the program command words (referred to as the program *syntax*) should have only one meaning, not multiple meanings. Software languages normally have fewer common words of meaning than natural languages. Most software language environments normally have four main types of instruction functions:

▶ **Data manipulation**: mathematical operations and functions.

▶ **Data transfer**: moving data and information between memory, screen and various storage media (e.g. CD-ROM, disk etc).

▶ **Flow control**: where inputs result in different program executions.

▶ **Input and output**: keyboard input and printing to screen.

Software can be categorized into two main types, each of which performs different functions within a computerized system:

▶ **Systems software**: operates the computers and various peripheral devices (e.g. printers, scanners and networks). Systems software carries out basic instructions for the central processor, memory boards, communication links and use of peripheral devices. Examples of systems software are Microsoft Windows 2000 and Linux.

▶ **Applications software**: programs written for users (and in some cases written by users). Microsoft Office is an example of application software. It contains a spreadsheet, word-processing package, PowerPoint presentation package and an Excel database. Applications software is primarily operated by the end users to support their job functions. Standard applications software can be customized by end users using programming languages, such as Visual Basic in the Microsoft Office environment.

Table 3.5 Categories of software

Systems software	
Back-end programs	Operating systems (e.g. Unix, Linux, MacOS) Language translators (e.g. interpreters and compilers) Utility programs (e.g. creating files, storage and running routines, communication links)
Systems programs	Manage and control the physical operation of the computers, networks and linked devices
Applications software	
Front-end programs	Programming languages (e.g. Java, C++, Visual Basic, HTML) Applications (e.g. Microsoft Office, Netscape browser, Eudora Email)
Application programs	Enable users to use tools to support their job functions

Sometimes systems software is referred to as *back-end* programming and applications software is referred to as *front-end* programming. Table 3.5 outlines some of the main characteristics of systems and applications software.

Systems software comprises three main types:

▶ operating systems software

▶ language translators

▶ utility programs.

When users interact with any computing system the interaction is controlled by the operating systems software. Users interact or, as it is referred to in computing jargon, *interface* with a computer system through a *graphical user interface* (GUI). There are other forms of interface, such as voice and sensor, but the main form of interface in the business information systems environment is the combination of a graphical screen, keyboard and mouse. The graphical user interface uses screen *pointers*, operated by a mouse, *icons*, which represent pictures to indicate applications, and *dialogue boxes*, which provide windows to interface with the computer system. (Computer users before 1985 would not have had the modern luxury of a GUI. Instead they would have used what was known as a DOS text command line interface, where commands were typed by line and fed to the computer.)

There are a number of modern operating systems. The main types of PC-based operating systems (OS) are outlined in Table 3.6, which includes some of their basic features.

Applications software is focused in the front-end, end-user domain. The goal of applications software is to support users in their various tasks. This support can be in the form of doing tasks efficiently and quickly, or in the form of enabling users to use software to support decision making or manage complex problems. There are many programming languages available to develop application soft-

Table 3.6 Popular operating systems

Operating system	First available	Features
Windows 98, Windows 2000, Windows NT	1998	32-bit OS. Good user interface and networking capabilities. Internet software.
OS/2	2000	32-bit IBM OS. Good multitasking and networking capabilities.
MacOS	2001	Macintosh computers. Later versions very robust and based on Linux.
Linux	1999	Runs on many different computers. Alternative to Windows 2000. Enables access to source code at operating systems level. Freely available.
Unix	1995*	Used for powerful PCs and networked mainframes. Enables multi-user multitasking.

*Unix was developed by Bell Laboratories in 1969. However, robust and popular PC-based versions were only available in the 1990s.

ware. Within the end-user applications software domain the objective is to understand the various strengths and weaknesses of software applications and be able to make judgements on which tools and techniques to adopt within a computerized information systems environment.

One of the first application software languages was FORTRAN (**Formula Trans**lator). It was developed in the 1950s specifically to support scientific and mathematical applications. It was a programming language that was particularly useful for processing numerical data and running mathematical formulae. The syntax used in FORTRAN was mainly numerical with few natural language words within its command list of words. The syntax structure (i.e. the way in which the command lines were written) was very strict and rigid. FORTRAN is considered to be a second generation language on the evolutionary scale of language development.

The first real business applications language was developed in the 1960s. It was called COBOL (**Common Business Oriented Language**). It was used to program and automate a number of early business domain applications and functions. It was able to handle and process large data files of both text and numbers (i.e. both numerical and alphanumerical data). COBOL was specifically developed to automate a number of clerical and administrative functions in business. Therefore, it can be said to be the first real applications software for the business information systems domain. Another, and equally important, third generation programming language was BASIC (**Beginners All-purpose Symbolic Instructions Code**). It was the first programming language that was used specifically to teach programming in schools and colleges. BASIC was developed in 1964 for the purposes of teaching programming to students. In many ways it was the precursor to many later languages that encourage end users to get involved in the activity of systems programming.

In the late 1960s another applications software language was developed called Pascal. It was named after Blaise Pascal, a famous seventeenth-century European mathematician. The Pascal programming language was developed in Switzerland specifically to teach logical programming to computing students. In the 1970s a language called C was developed that could be used in both business and education. It was developed by Bell Laboratories in the USA. It could be used on PCs and was transferable between PCs with different microprocessors. Therefore, it was a useful and important language in an era that was witnessing a growth in PCs within the business systems environment. C could also be used to create both operating systems software (e.g. Unix) and applications software. It is a language that is still in use today. However, later versions of C are called C++ and incorporate object-oriented ideas into the original language domain. C++ is particularly useful for building modern, object-based, business information systems applications.

Fourth generation languages are characterized by a greater level of natural language in their command syntax and are in many respects non-imperative (referred to as non-procedural in computing terms). As a consequence, users do not require the same level of training and logical and mathematical skills as were necessary with second and third generation languages. The advantage of non-procedural languages is that normally a programmer needs to use fewer lines of code to accomplish a given task. This fact, allied with the incorporation of natural language words in the command syntax, makes fourth generation languages a very useful tool for end-user involvement in the business information systems development process. Fourth generation languages can be separated into a number of categories:

▶ **Query languages**: used primarily in the data handling and database domains of business systems. Query languages are used to interrogate and retrieve information from large databases.

▶ **Productivity tools and software**: come in many forms, such as applications generators and computer-assisted software engineering (CASE). These applications speed up the production of code by automating the development of code. For example, a user can indicate a basic requirement and the applications-generating software produces the code and application. Some of these productivity tools are so advanced that they enable whole applications, such as company websites, to be built in an afternoon.

▶ **Graphics languages**: predominately found where data is being analyzed and a visual feel for the results is necessary. Examples include displaying statistical data in the form of charts, or scanning students' work for plagiarism and producing a colour picture of matching text indicating areas of high and low match, rather than a mere percentage number indicating matching text.

▶ **Very high level programming (VHLP) languages**: mainly used by professional programmers to speed up the production of software applications.

▶ **Application software packages**: pre-built applications that are used on a daily basis in business and education. Examples include word-processors, spreadsheets, e-mail packages, web browsers, PC video-conferencing, databases, database management application packages and groupware. Groupware is a particularly important application in the modern information systems domain, since it allows information sharing, real-time communication and meetings to take place in a virtual networked environment where the issue of geographical distance between employees and workers is eliminated. Lotus Notes was one of the first groupware applications. A number of packages, such as Netscape Communicator and FirstClass, offer groupware-based collaborative facilities.

Modern software development languages and applications are predominantly object-oriented. The main object-oriented programming languages used in the business systems domain at the start of the twenty-first century are Java, HTML (**H**yper**T**ext **M**ark-up **L**anguage) and XML (e**X**tensible **M**ark-up **L**anguage).

Object-oriented programming languages, unlike third generation languages, are characterized by combining into one object the data and procedures (or *methods*) that operate on the data and translate it into one object. Programming languages that are not object-oriented treat data and procedures as independent activities and components. The objects can be transferred between different systems and reused. The concept of reusability is a powerful aspect of object-oriented languages. Objects can be used in different systems without changing the code. Reusability reduces the time needed to write program code and thus speeds up the time it takes to build business information systems. Furthermore, libraries of reusable objects can be collated and then used to make different systems. The analogy used is with toy building bricks that can be put together in different ways to make different things, using the same number and size of objects. Object-oriented programming is based on *classes* and *inheritance*. A class is a set of code for a particular purpose. Objects can belong to certain classes; objects belonging to a certain class should normally possess all the features of that class. Classes of objects can inherit the features of a more general class, thus leading to less need to rewrite or reprogram a class.

One of the commonest object-oriented programming languages used in the modern information systems development domain is Java. The Java language allows programs to be built and run on different computer systems irrespective of the type of microprocessor or operating system software being used by the information system. This interoperability allows for the creation of portable programs that can be used in any systems environment, architecture or operating platform. The idea is that a program can be written and then used extensively on any platform. The code only needs to be written once. Java possesses high data integrity and is a robust programming environment. Java is used extensively in website design and development: it can be used to provide web pages with multimedia, dynamic capabilities; for example, Java Applets (objects) can be used to handle video, sound and movement in web pages.

Did you know?

The Java programming language was developed by Sun Microsystems and was developed for interoperability to run on any computer regardless of its operating system or make of microprocessor.

The HTML language is a modern and popular language that was created specifically for web page development. A mark-up language is a description language that states how a page should be displayed in a web browser. HTML uses commands called *tags* that mark up how a page should operate. There are a number of productivity tools that automatically generate HTML to create web pages. A relative of HTML, called xHTML, is used to create web pages for hand-held devices, such as mobile phones and wireless personal digital assistants (PDAs). A modern extended development of HTML is XML, which not only describes how web pages should be marked up but also describes how data is handled in the documents and pages. The ability to handle and describe data makes XML a serious and important software applications language, particularly for web-based business information systems. xHTML uses both HTML and XML concepts. It is used on the web to create HTML pages with data and document type definitions, enabling data-based applications to be created, written and run on different platforms using the interface of the web.

Activity 3.9 Language development environments

Fourth generation information systems development provides end users with more control over the definition of system requirements and the overall development process. You are required to give a five minute presentation, following these instructions:

▶ State and describe what tools and techniques are employed by end-user information systems developers within fourth generation development environments.

▶ Outline and describe the use of applications-based systems development and the consequences of using pre-built software.

▶ Summarize the main advantages and disadvantages of fourth generation information systems development to a business organization.

▶ Outline the types of software applications used to support computerized information systems environments.

3.9 Information systems support centres

One of the major ways adopted by large business organizations to manage fourth generation development and to maximize the return from end-user development is through information systems support centres. These are sometimes referred to as *ICT support centres*. Such support centres provide a facility for guidance, training and support for end-user systems development. They may be operated by one individual, or a group of individuals, depending on the nature of the organization within the business environment. The depth of ICT support will depend upon the inherent technical abilities of the end users. However, one of the major tasks of an ICT support centre is software and systems maintenance. The support centre may also provide the software, hardware and other applications tools needed for end-user development, or it may only provide training and guidance in fourth generation development tools and techniques. ICT support facilities can be used to coordinate and manage the development of end-user systems development within a business organization. The ICT support centre can also be responsible for some of the practical systems development in terms of suggesting development approaches, or assisting the building of systems prototypes for evaluation purposes.

Some of the services that may be provided by an ICT support centre are:

▶ training and advising business specialists on existing hardware and software applications that may be useful to their respective job functions;

▶ advising on the appropriate use of various development methodologies that can be used to solve particular information systems problems;

▶ building working prototypes of particular information systems that can be used and iteratively tested by end users;

▶ providing reference and other documentation on hardware, software, ICT integration and methodologies for the benefit of end-user systems development;

▶ keeping up to date with current and new ICT tools and evaluating hardware and software applications;

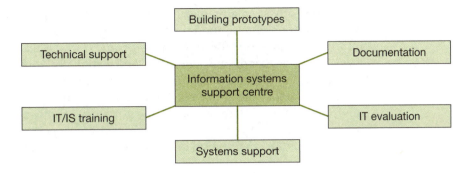

Figure 3.1 ICT support centre

▶ providing a physical resource of hardware and software for end users to use at will and providing access to communications links to remote information sources.

Figure 3.1 outlines some typical activities undertaken by ICT support centres. The ICT support centre can be used to benefit the employees of a business organization in terms of the spread of ICT literacy throughout the whole organization. Such support activities may also lead to increased job productivity among employees through the more efficient and effective use of ICT applications. Some of the advantages of an ICT support centre are:

▶ establishing and promoting consistent information technology standards throughout the business organization;

▶ improving communications between technical and business specialists and so reducing the culture gap that exists in many business organizations;

▶ advising executive management on appropriate hardware and software to be used within the business organization.

A business organization must be able to appraise the cost and benefit of providing an ICT support centre to assist end-user information systems development, exploring the possible alternative policy of employing external technical specialists with a single brief to develop business information systems independently. The alternative policy may lead to an organization becoming dependent upon the expertise of outside bodies, with the detrimental effect of loss of control over ICT strategy within the business organization.

Activity 3.10   ICT support centres

Discuss the concept of the ICT support centre and outline the main use and purpose of an ICT support centre in a business organization. Describe the possible costs and benefits to an organization of an ICT support centre. Do you think that the growth of ICT support centres has been encouraged by the evolution of end-user information systems development? Do you think that ICT support centres could engage in aspects of systems software maintenance?

Systems software maintenance, of both operating systems software and applications software, is an important aspect in maintaining the health of a business information system. Software needs to be updated and maintained regularly to meet changing conditions internally and externally within an organization. Therefore, in designing and constructing business information systems, a number of factors need to be taken into consideration, such as the compatibility of software across systems domains, the efficiency of software in terms of rewriting and adding software code, and the ease of support and maintenance by employees of the organization or by outside companies that provide systems and software development skills.

A big area of the computing systems industry in the twenty-first century is the provision of software applications support and services for organizations. The companies that provide these support services and software applications are called *applications software providers* (ASPs). These companies operate, provide and maintain many aspects of an organization's information systems infrastructure. Many of these companies provide access to applications remotely and online, offering organizations access to sophisticated software systems applications without the need to purchase and maintain expensive in-house information systems. With the growth and spread of the web nearly all business organizations can access software systems online via a web portal. The typical model of an ASP is where software systems and individual applications are managed remotely and offered to multiple business users or organizations. Rather than purchase software applications, organizations can purchase access time to applications over the web. These applications can be customized by the ASP for the specific requirements of an client organization.

The ASP takes responsibility for maintaining and upgrading software applications. It also provides specialist technical support and client organizations can rent applications and services as and when they need them. The advantage to the client organization is that it has one portal to access software applications and does not have to worry about software systems incompatibility or systems maintenance. In essence, the ASP is a software applications host, offering applications to client customers. The clients of ASPs are mainly small and medium-size companies, which do not have the ability to invest heavily in computer hardware and computerized systems infrastructures.

Activity 3.11 End users and ICT support centres

Information technology support within an organization can be internal or external to the business organization. ICT centres are a solution to some of the problems of end-user information systems development, such as a lack of consistency and application of common standards in the development process or method.

Prepare a summary handbook of rules and regulations that outlines the relationship between an information centre and the end users within a business organization. Suggest whether systems are best maintained in-house or by a specialist software systems support company outside an organization.

3.10 Chapter summary

This chapter set out to explain the nature and characteristics of the traditional systems development life cycle. This traditional approach to information systems development has been influenced and shaped by the evolution of end-user computing and the development of user-friendly software development tools and techniques. These trends have encouraged end-user participation in the systems development life cycle. Such participation makes it more likely that the user requirements of an information system will be met when the system is designed and implemented.

When deciding how to integrate software into the information systems environment there are thirteen factors that need to be taken into consideration (Aron and Sampler, 2003). These factors determine to a large extent the objectives of a software-based information system. The thirteen factors are:

1 **Functionality**: the software should efficiently perform routine operations and effectively carry out the functional requirements of a business organization.

2 **Cost**: the cost of the ICT solution should not outweigh the benefits of the software-based systems solution.

3 **Performance**: the processing speed, reliability and accuracy of the software-based systems solution.

4 **Usability**: the user-friendliness of the system. A system can be technically efficient, but it also has to be user-efficient and user-friendly.

5 **Integrity**: the data and information within the system must be accurate and users must have confidence that the data is secure and always available (i.e. there are adequate security gateways and adequate back-up of data).

6 **Security**: the users of a system must feel that the system is confidential and secure when transferring data and information around the system.

7 **Speed**: the systems development process, the speed of the system itself and the maintenance times for a system must be quick and efficient. The longer the time to develop or upgrade a system, or receive information, the less use it will be to the users.

8 **Maintainability**: all systems need to be maintained and upgraded on a regular basis. Maintenance must be effected quickly and with the minimum of disruption to the system's users.

9 **Flexibility**: systems should be flexible enough to be altered and realigned to unexpected market conditions. The system should be flexible enough to change with the needs and requirements of an organization.

10 **Extensibility**: a system should be able to be extended in terms of software and systems requirements. Software systems should possess the capability to expand and grow without losing their inherent effectiveness to the organization.

11 **Scalability**: the ease with which systems performance can be increased. Systems need to be extended in size (i.e. adding more computers to a network or adding another computer server).

12 **Robustness**: the ability of the software system to work continually and be available to users. Systems should be able to be used without any significant failure.

13 **Portability**: the ability of the software and the system itself to be carried to other technology platforms and still remain operational.

The next chapter will extend the discussion of systems development in a more detailed study of a range of alternative approaches to business information systems development.

CASE STUDY

An audit of end-user computing

Corporate overview

Burlington Northern Railroad (BNRR) merged with the Atchison, Topeka and Santa Fe Railway in September 1995 to form The Burlington Northern and Santa Fe Railway Company. BNRR was one of the largest railroads in North America. Annual gross revenue was approximately US$4.5 billion. Total employees numbered approximately 32 000. BNRR operated over 60 000 rail cars and 2500 locomotives on a system composed of over 25 000 miles of track in 25 states and two Canadian provinces. BNRR's headquarters were in Fort Worth, Texas, and it had major offices in St Paul, Minnesota; Overland Park, Kansas; and Denver, Colorado.

Internal audit

The internal audit department was located in St Paul, Minnesota. It was composed of approximately 30 professional staff including an assistant vice president and three managers. The department adopted an 'integrated' approach to information systems (IS) audits and did not contain a specific sub-set of IS auditors. It did, however, have a number of auditors with IS backgrounds who were used on technical audits.

Philosophically, in addition to its role as a reviewer of internal controls, the internal audit department was viewed as a training ground by BNRR management. Auditors were typically promoted to positions in accounting and marketing after spending three to five years in audit.

Information systems

The information systems department (ISD) at BNRR included over 400 personnel. The hardware used to support the company consisted primarily of four IBM-compatible mainframes and a number of Wang and DEC minicomputers. A large network of Zerox workstations was also used. The mainframes processed about 75 per cent of the production volume, with the other systems processing the remaining 25 per cent.

Role of end-user and departmental computing

Many of the production applications in use at BNRR had been developed by end users. The use of PCs, however, was relatively light. The emphasis on end-user computing (EUC) had been to encourage users to develop applications on the mainframe using fourth generation languages, such as FOCUS and SAS and TSO. RACF was used to control access to the system and individual datasets.

Departmental computing also played a large role at BNRR. Historically, individual departments had been free to buy their own hardware and hire specialists to design and program production systems to be used to make the departments more efficient. These departmental systems were typically networked with the ISD mainframe systems to allow the transfer of data between them. ISD technical personnel provided some support for these systems (e.g. systems programming and maintenance), but the systems were considered the property of the department that acquired them. A large number of production applications that were not developed by the central ISD programming staff ran on these departmental machines.

EUC support organization

Within ISD, a division called client services was established. It contained 35 people spread among the corporate locations in St Paul, Fort Worth, Overland Park, and Denver. The primary roles of this group were as follows:

▶ educating users on how to use and manage the technology available to them;
▶ consulting with the users on the best approach to solving problems using technology;
▶ developing systems in partnership with users, when the users required a good example to follow.

In addition to the 35 people performing the above functions, another 25 support personnel were used by client services to staff user help lines, develop EUC education courses and test new EUC products that might have been recommended to users.

The client services group had been working to develop a list of recommended practices to be followed by end users. It had organized these practices into an end-user computing manual. The manual had been distributed to users after they attended training sessions, presented by client services personnel, on how to control and manage end-user applications. These sessions were typically presented on a departmental basis, and attendance was required by senior management for implementors and managers of EUC. The manual covered a wide variety of topics, including:

▶ defining business needs
▶ evaluating EUC versus ISD development alternatives
▶ categorizing the application by risk and complexity
▶ developing the EUC application
▶ following documentation standards and naming conventions.

One of the biggest roles played by client services in the past several years had been to establish departmental libraries for EUC applications. This served to consolidate all EUC applications developed for use within an individual department into a single library. As well as making it easier to manage EUC production applications from a security and back-up perspective, it gave client services the ability to better control and manage the quality of EUC applications.

Client services controled the migration of applications from the users' individual libraries into the departmental libraries. Before migration, the user had to show proof of adequate documentation, compliance with dataset naming conventions, consideration of data security, etc. Basically, users had to comply with the recommended practices outlined in the EUC manual. The advantages to users who moved their production applications to the departmental library included the ability to have the job automatically executed by placing it on the job scheduling system (if it was to be run on a regular basis), automatic back-up on a daily basis, and the ability of others to use it in their absence.

▶

Internal audit role in EUC

Internal audit viewed EUC as an integral part of production systems. As such, it devoted a portion of the annual audit budget to reviewing EUC data centres and significant application systems.

A variety of approaches was used to identify EUC applications. General EUC controls were reviewed during the course of departmental reviews. Significant applications supporting the department were identified and reviewed if appropriate. Departmental data centres also underwent periodic general controls reviews.

In the past, internal audit also attempted to perform an annual inventory of major EUC applications at all the company's major operating locations. A risk analysis was then performed and the most critical or high-risk applications were scheduled for review within the current audit year. The inventory process had been necessary because of the autonomy of each department with regard to equipment acquisition and system development. No one individual or group within the company was aware of all major EUC activity at the various company locations.

The emergence of the client services group over the past few years changed this situation. This group developed a listing of all production applications that resided in the departmental libraries across all company locations.

Internal audit planned to interact closely with client services to keep abreast of significant development activity in the future. Client services, in turn, planned to rely on internal audit to enforce compliance with its recommended practices.

Representative EUC audit

In the course of a departmental audit, internal audit identified a new EUC application that was being used to support the capital projects budgeting and monitoring process. Due to the impact capital projects had on the profitability of the business, internal audit determined that the system should be reviewed more closely. The system had been developed in FOCUS and was executed on the IBM mainframe. It was designed to add functionality by interfacing with the older system master files and adding some additional data and processing options. The entire new system had been created mainly by a single end user and consisted of over 100 FOCUS programs.

As a result of the audit, internal audit noted the following problems:

▶ *Redundant data*: multiple files contained the same information.
▶ *Inaccurate data*: updates to one file could be made without corresponding updates being made to related files. This situation led to out-of-balance conditions.
▶ *Inadequate audit trails*: audit trails did not exist for all changes to master file data.
▶ *Inadequate documentation*: little or no documentation existed for the EUC system.

The audit summarized a number of shortcomings, of which many users had been aware for some period of time. Ultimately, the management of the user department responsible for the system and the client services group decided that the entire system should be redesigned. As an interim step, management assigned the resources to remedy the most critical weaknesses within the system.

Conclusion

BNRR is a good example of a company that came to grips with the issues associated with controlling EUC. Its approach to controlling EUC encompassed:

▶ dedicated personnel in the client services department
▶ internal audit awareness and proactive audit steps (periodic inventory)
▶ published standards and procedures

▶ user education
▶ support by upper management of EUC control policies.

BNRR acknowledged that it still had a way to go before it was completely satisfied with controls over the entire EUC environment, but it had laid a solid foundation on which to build the remaining control structure.

Source: Based on www.bnsf.com

Major programmes of the Institute of Internal Auditors Research Foundation

Academic programmes

The Institute of Internal Auditors Research Foundation plays a key role in helping internal auditors keep up with the trends in their profession. In today's competitive global marketplace, education is an integral part of becoming and staying marketable to an employer. The Institute of Internal Auditors (IIA), aided by the Foundation, has supported a programme to build knowledge and aware-ness of internal auditing in college and university classrooms. Through supportive professors and university curricula, internal auditing is presented to future practitioners, managers and public accountants.

In 1986 the Foundation began funding IIA-endorsed programmes in internal auditing, modelled after a pilot programme developed by the Department of Accounting at Louisiana State University. The objective is to add internal auditing curricula and to encourage internal auditing research at colleges and universities. In 1992 the Foundation board of trustees committed $250 000 to support IIA-endorsed programmes in internal auditing over the ensuing five years. The IIA-endorsed school grant programme represented an opportunity to develop and experiment with internal auditing educational programmes and to demonstrate to other schools that such programmes are viable and worth the resource commitment. In 1994 the Foundation completed its 1992 commitment of $250 000 to the IIA's endorsed internal auditing programme, with the funding of programmes at the University of Texas at Austin and the University of Tennessee at Knoxville.

Internal auditing educator's symposiums

The Foundation sponsors internal auditing educator's symposiums to discuss the best methods for teaching internal auditing in colleges and universities. Discussions centre on internal auditing topics, including analytical auditing procedures, internal controls, operational auditing, evidence, auditing programmes, technology auditing and sampling. Course materials are provided, as well as numer-ous publications and other handouts from the IIA.

Foundation forums

The Foundation sponsors advanced technology forums at two-year intervals. These forums are designed to bring together recognized experts and specialists in specific areas of interest to internal auditors. They provide an intensive and innovative arena for discussion of technology issues. Forum proceedings are published and distributed to internal auditing professionals who want to stay up to date with new developments in technology and auditing, control, and security.

Source: © Institute of Internal Auditors Research Foundation: *Systems Auditability and Control, Module 7: End-User and Departmental Computing*, pp. 7–77 and 7–80.

SHORT SELF-ASSESSMENT QUESTIONS

3.1 Define the four generic stages of the traditional SDLC and outline the nature and purpose of each stage.

3.2 Explain why the traditional SDLC is also called a *waterfall* approach to information systems development.

3.3 Explain what is involved in a *feasibility study* and outline what would normally be found in a *feasibility report*.

3.4 Highlight and explain the five main feasibility factors (known by the mnemonic TELOS) which assist in determining the probability of an information systems project being undertaken.

3.5 Explain what is meant by the term *computing vendor* and indicate three possible main concerns in dealing with a computing vendor.

3.6 Outline and explain the main strengths and weaknesses of the traditional systems development life cycle.

3.7 Define and explain what is meant by the term *fourth generation language (4GL) development environment* within business information systems.

3.8 Outline the main software tools and applications used by end users within fourth generation development environments and explain some of the reasons for using each of the tools and applications.

3.9 Contrast and explain the differences between a fourth generation language and a third generation language in terms of their respective nature and characteristics.

3.10 Explain why fourth generation tools and techniques have assisted the rise of end-user computing and end-user involvement in the information systems development process.

3.11 Define the term *client-server computing* and explain the relationship between client-server computing and end-user information systems development.

3.12 Outline the four main types of instruction functions found within software language environments.

3.13 Explain the main underlying differences between *operating systems* software and *applications* software.

3.14 Explain the two main benefits of using an *object-oriented programming language*, such as Java, and outline why Java is a useful tool in website design and development.

3.15 Outline the role of *application service providers* (ASPs) and explain the benefits of employing an ASP.

EXTENDED STUDENT ACTIVITIES

Individual reporting activity

TopSat Corporation is an international business organization trading in the sale and distribution of satellite technology around the world. The chief executive officer (CEO) has engaged your services to advise on the development of a marketing and sales information system to replace the system currently in operation. The CEO requires a 500-word summary, in which you should:

1 Indicate what tasks are to be performed in the various stages of the systems development process.

2 State the milestones and deadlines to be completed at each stage of the information systems development process.

3 Advise on whether employees should be involved in the development process and state the advantages and disadvantages of involving end users.

4 State the possible reasons why this information systems project should be initiated and advise on the benefits of defining the requirements of a proposed new information system.

5 Outline the costs and possible benefits of undertaking the systems development project and indicate and describe the possible tools and techniques to be used in the systems development project.

Group-based activity

Discuss the advantages and the disadvantages of using the traditional systems development life cycle for constructing business information systems. Provide a reasoned argument to determine whether the following statement is true or false: '*It is impossible to develop a good information systems solution and design the first time around.*'

Your reasoned argument should be incorporated into a presentation of a maximum of four overheads. You will be assessed on the originality of your argument, and your appropriate reasoning as a group.

REFERENCES AND FURTHER STUDY

Books and articles

Aron, D. and Sampler, J.L. (2003) *Understanding IT – A Manager's Guide*, FT Prentice Hall, ISBN: 0273682083

Avison, D.E. and Fitzgerald, G. (2002) *Information Systems Development: Methodologies, Techniques and Tools (Information Systems Series)*, McGraw-Hill, ISBN: 0077096266

Cadle, J. and Yeates, D. (2001) *Project Management for Information Systems*, FT Prentice Hall, ISBN: 0273651455

Chaffey, D., Bocij, P., Greasley, A. and Hickie, S. (2002) *Business Information Systems: Technology Development and Management in the E-business*, FT Prentice Hall, ISBN: 027365540x

Curtis, G. and Cobham, D. (2001) *Business Information Systems,* 4th edition, FT Prentice Hall, ISBN: 0273651307

Daniels, A. and Yeates D.A. (1971) *Basic Training in Systems Analysis*, 2nd edition, Pitman, ISBN: 0273316567

Elliott, G. (1997) '2001 a systems odyssey: is rapid applications development a method or madness of the information age?', proceedings of the 4th International Conference on Financial Information Systems, Sheffield Hallam University, 2–3 July

Factor, A. (2001) *Analyzing Application Service Providers*, Prentice Hall PTR, ISBN: 0130894257

Gane, C. and Sarson, T. (1979) *Structured Systems Analysis*, Prentice Hall, ISBN: 0138545472

Harney, J. (2001) *Application Service Providers (ASPs)*, Addison-Wesley, ISBN: 0201726599

Hoffer, J.A., George, J.F. and Valacich, J.S. (2001) *Modern Systems Analysis and Design*, 3rd edition, Prentice Hall, ISBN: 0130339903

Linthicum, D.S. (1995) 'The end of programming', *BYTE*, August, pp. 69–72

Linthicum, D.S. (2000) 'EAI application integration exposed', *Software Magazine*, February/March

Lucas, H.C. (1992) *The Analysis, Design, Implementation of Information Systems*, 4th edition, McGraw-Hill, ISBN: 0071126864

Richardson, M. (1995) '4GL database tools – what's happening?', *CMA Magazine*, December/January, pp. 23–6

Satzinger, J.W. and Olfman, L. (1998) 'User interface consistency across applications', *Journal of Management Information Systems* 14(4), Spring

Shah, H.U. and Avison, D.E. (1997) *Information Systems Development Cycle*, McGraw-Hill, ISBN: 0077092449

Yongbeom, K. and Stohr, E.A. (1998) 'Software Reuse', *Journal of Management Information Systems*, 14(4), Spring

Journals

Communications of the ACM
European Journal of Information Systems
Journal of Management Information Systems
Journal of Information Technology

Web resources

Learning and Teaching Support Network for Information and Computer Sciences (UK) – promotes the use of online teaching and learning resources in ICT.
www.ics.ltsn.ac.uk

World Lecture Hall – Computer Science (USA) – access to online materials in ICT and computing.
http://wnt.cc.utexas.edu/~wlh/browse/index.cfm

Java Programming (USA/global) – the Sun Microsystems Java site.
http://java.sun.com

Linux Online Site (global) – information and resources on Linux.
www.linux.org

XML.com Site (global) – information and resources on XML.
www.xml.com

Chapter 4

Rapid applications development in dynamic global business environments

earning outcomes   When you have studied this chapter you will be able to:

▶ evaluate the history, evolution and context of rapid applications development (RAD) within business information systems development;

▶ describe the role of user participation in the information systems development process through the use of joint applications development (JAD);

▶ understand the characteristics and explain the function of rapid applications development tools and techniques within information systems development;

▶ evaluate the importance of formalized methods, such as the dynamic systems development method (DSDM);

▶ outline and understand the use of alternative approaches to the traditional systems development life cycle that fall under the rapid applications development umbrella;

▶ understand and describe the strengths, weaknesses and circumstances for adopting various alternative approaches to information systems development.

4.1 Introduction to rapid applications development

The previous chapter looked at the traditional systems development life cycle (SDLC) and the role of end-user participation within the process of business information systems development. The traditional waterfall approach to systems development is prone to a number of weaknesses, outlined in the previous chapter, which have led to the use of alternative systems development methods, many of which are more appropriate for information systems development in global, dynamic and competitive business environments.

The choice of systems development method, and the approach used, is an important business decision; remember that the process of information systems development can be time consuming and costly. Therefore, the decision to invest in information systems infrastructures should only be undertaken after careful analysis and full consideration of all the business objectives of the organization. The predominant aim of business systems development is to construct quickly and effectively information systems that meet the requirements of business end users.

Before progressing further, it is important to be clear about the inherent failings of the traditional approach to systems development, particularly with respect to modern and global business systems environments. Modern business considerations have in many ways led to the evolution of alternative information systems development approaches, with the aims of:

▶ reducing the time and cost of systems development;
▶ improving the delivery of system and user requirements;
▶ incorporating advances in computing and information technology;
▶ recognizing the nature of information systems within dynamic and global business environments.

The alternative information systems development methods that have evolved are an attempt to overcome the shortcomings of the traditional SDLC approach to building systems within competitive business environments.

4.2 Alternative approaches to information systems development

There are a number of approaches that have evolved as alternatives to the traditional SDLC, some of which utilize the development life-cycle approach and some that are radical departures from the sequential waterfall approach. Most development approaches and methodologies are influenced by a number of fundamental principles of general systems theory. Most acknowledge the fact that business systems involve human activity; this makes the systems development process less predictable. Furthermore, there is a growing recognition that systems cannot be seen in isolation within an organization, but must be seen as an integrated logical and physical concept. Most organizations, by their nature of trading with the global business environment at large, are considered open systems. Therefore, organizations influence, and are influenced by, the wider business environment in which they operate.

Alternative approaches to information systems development, which use the concepts of rapid systems development and end-user applications computing within the systems development process, are:

▶ rapid applications development (RAD)
▶ joint applications development (JAD)
▶ prototyping systems development
▶ object-oriented systems development (OOSD)
▶ dynamic systems development method (DSDM)
▶ business process re-engineering (BPR)
▶ strategic information systems development.

All these approaches share a common characteristic of emphasizing the importance of end users within the process of information systems development. The last approach to systems development, strategic information systems development, emphasizes the strategic nature and effect of information systems.

Approaches to information systems development

Search your college or university's online library facilities for journal articles and other academic sources to find one article on each of the following areas:

▶ prototyping systems development

▶ object-oriented development (OOD)

▶ business process re-engineering (BPR)

▶ rapid applications development (RAD).

Use one of your articles as a case study to form the basis of an assignment on alternative approaches to systems development. The title of your assignment is 'What contribution does this alternative systems development method, or approach, make to the science of information systems development?'

4.3 Rapid applications development

The term *rapid applications development* (RAD) is an umbrella reference to the use of various fourth generation methods, tools and techniques integrated to achieve fast, rapid information systems development within the business environment. The emphasis within RAD is on the *synergy* created by the effective deployment of these various tools and techniques to achieve delivery of an information system solution in the shortest possible time. Synergy refers to the combined actions of two or more activities, or objects, that lead to a greater outcome than the objects working in isolation. Therefore, RAD applies one of the main principles of systems theory – that the sum is greater than its parts – to the process of developing business information systems. The RAD approach is complemented by the cooperation of technical specialists with business specialists using various participative frameworks, such as *joint applications development* (JAD) to enhance user participation and speed up the development process.

What is rapid applications development (RAD)?

An umbrella term that uses a number of tools and techniques to enable user participation and speed up the information systems development process. Speed of business information systems development is of the essence to a competitive organization.

The increasing need to develop information systems as rapidly as possible has been driven by the need for organizations to compete effectively in a constantly changing global business environment. Organizations have become more customer oriented as they have become more competitive. Business organizations must now compete with other organizations in other countries and on other continents on a *global* scale. This type of competition is characterized by continuous *change*. Change management and systems change management are very important concepts in such dynamic and competitive business environments. It is imperative that information systems within a business organization are flexible and responsive enough to change continuously in line with changes in the over-all business environment.

Therefore, speed of business information systems development is of the essence to a competitive organization. The slow, and often laborious, nature of the traditional SDLC approach to building information systems makes it an inherently inefficient development method for most organizations competing in dynamic business environments. Consequently, business organizations are turning to the more attractive alternative frameworks within the general rapid applications development domain. In the late 1990s a consortium of business organizations came together to try to structure and formalize the RAD approach. They developed a conceptual model and approach known as the *dynamic systems development method* (DSDM). This model of information systems development will be looked at in more detail later on in this chapter.

Did you know?

Rapid applications development (RAD) is a concept that encompasses a number of methods, tools and techniques that speed up the information systems development process. Although the method is not attributed to a particular individual, it is associated to a certain degree with a systems specialist named James Martin, author of *Rapid Applications Development*, published in 1991.

The principles of rapid applications development are based on the premise that fast, effective and efficient information systems can only be developed by the careful alignment of specific development methods with suitable software application tools. There are four main principles within the RAD framework:

▶ improving the speed of systems development by using tools and techniques appropriate to the business organization and its competitive environment;

▶ using an iterative prototyping approach to development, rather than the traditional systems development life cycle;

▶ emphasizing concentrated end-user participation and involvement in the whole development process via workshops and group meetings, deliberately trying to fulfil end-user requirements;

▶ using a number of known modelling tools and techniques that are collated together in the form of a resource toolbox.

The use of RAD techniques encourages efficiency in the systems development process. It is claimed (*see* Pause for thought 4.1 on Norwich Union) that RAD can produce information systems applications much faster than conventional methods; this is particularly important for organizations that face customer pressure to provide products and services at ever increasing rates of service and quality. Information systems must often be developed rapidly to allow the business to support its existing customers or extend its customer base within the business environment in which it operates. Systems development is usually measured in *function points*, which indicate a specific feature of a software product or application to be delivered. Pause for thought 4.1 shows how by using RAD techniques efficiently and effectively it is possible to increase the delivery of function points by a factor of eight.

Did you know?

The head of RAD development at Norwich Union in the UK asserts that it averaged 64 function points per person per month compared with an average of only eight function points per person per month for the insurance industry as a whole in the 1990s.

The problem with the traditional waterfall approach of the SDLC is that what emerges from the development process often is not what end users need from the information system. In the traditional systems approach, development success is measured against how close the finished system is to the original specification, even if the original specification turns out to fall short of the user's requirements. However, RAD concentrates on measuring the effectiveness of an information system by how well it matches the *business specifications* of the organization and how well it delivers business benefits of that specification.

However, the RAD framework is no less rigorous than the traditional SDLC. The tools, techniques and methods that fall under the umbrella term RAD are increasingly referred to as the dynamic systems development method (DSDM), which implies that there is a methodological basis to using RAD. To support this idea, and to ensure recognition of alternative methods, tools and techniques for information systems development, a dynamic systems development method consortium, including many large and reputable companies, was set up in the UK in the mid-1990s. The remit of the consortium was to promote RAD methods within the business environment and ensure development framework standards.

RAD is a group-based, participative activity, relying on business specialists and technical specialists working together in teams and through workshops to analyze, design and formulate information systems solutions. The use and application of RAD methods should never be a solitary activity within an organization. In many ways RAD, and its associated tools and techniques, has had an effect on the structural nature of business organizations in promoting group-based work activities. Within this participative environment decision-making is devolved to the business specialists, in discussion with the technical specialists, who make decisions in groups, or through structured workshops, and often by consensus. Therefore, for the development process to work, it is important to get the correct and most suitable mix of people involved in the group-based systems development activities.

Along with greater involvement comes greater responsibility, which should often lead to higher levels of commitment and demand on the participant's energies. Such participation is known to be challenging, so it is often imperative to employ a group selection criterion that helps to formulate cooperative and effective project groups. For example, the TOBI method can be used for selecting compatible individuals for group-based development activities. The TOBI method allows the profiling of individuals on the basis of whether they show an aptitude for being a *leader*, *administrator*, *scheduler* or *maintainer*. Groups can then be more professionally established, and include individuals with expertise in one of the four areas mentioned.

PAUSE FOR THOUGHT 4.1

The development of RAD as an alternative for building effective and efficient systems

Norwich Union

Norwich Union is a general insurance business in the UK. Between 1994 and 1996 the Norwich Union built and delivered over 20 systems using the RAD appoach to information and software-based systems development. Norwich Union has witnessed high increases in systems development productivity by using RAD. In contrast to traditional waterfall methods, where eventual systems quality is measured by how close the finished product is to the specification (regardless of whether the initial specification was correct in the first place), in RAD quality is measured against business benefits. By using RAD the Norwich Union has admitted that systems development effectiveness and efficiency has in combination increased eightfold since 1994.

The Co-operative Bank

The Co-operative Bank, located in the UK, first used RAD tools and techniques when it needed to replace an existing centralized and computer-based application that processed customer application forms. Within the Co-operative Bank existed a range of conventional, mainframe-based, legacy software from the 1960s, 1970s and 1980s. The organization wished to re-engineer its fundamental processes and procedures and such a significant leap could only be achieved by using a RAD approach.

The systems development project was broken into phases because the system that the Co-operative Bank was looking to replace was a fundamental and major system of the business. The phases involved determining user requirements, through the use of workshops and prototyping. The workshops were a critical key to success; it was determined that everyone involved would be allowed to make decisions on the spot as and when necessary. The RAD approach was used to create a sense of trust and empowerment within the workforce and the system's end users.

The application of RAD was a huge success, with the head of technical systems at the bank declaring in 1995 that because of prototyping and the high level of involvement of business people in the design stage, what emerged was just what was required for the business. This was achieved without providing any formal training and despite the presence of a steep learning curve.

BUPA

BUPA is a private medical insurance business operating in the UK. When BUPA required a care management system to supervise its new Healthmanager product there appeared to be nothing on the market to match its requirements, so it was recommended that the organization use a RAD approach because of the time constraints and the dynamic nature of its changing requirements. BUPA formed a joint development team with another consultancy organization to deliver the required care management system. The aim of the system was to log all contacts, appointments and hospital stays. Before the new system was developed, BUPA used a range of small systems, including manual paper-based systems, to administrate the Healthmanager product. The old system had become unmanageable because the system was expected to manage over 34 000 incidents of treatment, with each incident report containing an average of 18 separate contacts.

By using RAD, the first phase of the system was delivered in August 1995 after only an 11-week systems development cycle. A senior project manager at BUPA claimed that had it used traditional systems development methods it would have taken over six months. However, by using RAD tools and techniques the system at BUPA was delivered in the timescale required and with substantial cost savings.

Activity 4.2 Rapid applications development

Discuss and explain what is meant by rapid applications development (RAD) and suggest two reasons for its existence as an alternative approach to the SDLC. Explain why speed of applications and systems development is so important to a competitive business organization, particularly to organizations competing on a global scale where the sophistication of information technology varies.

The RAD approach to systems development has four main phases (not sequential stages), which are set out in Table 4.1.

Requirements planning

Emphasis in this phase is placed on the early stages of planning, when it is important to establish the correct end-user and business requirements. The two techniques used at this stage for facilitating this process are *joint requirements planning* (JRP) and *joint applications development* (JAD); often these two

Table 4.1 The four phases of rapid applications development (RAD)

Phase 1	Requirements planning	
	Technique:	joint requirements planning (JRP)
	Technique:	joint applications development (JAD)
Phase 2	**User design**	
	Technique:	joint applications development (JAD)
	Tool:	prototyping
	Tool:	computer-aided software engineering (CASE)
Phase 3	**Construction**	
	Tool:	prototyping
	Tool:	computer-aided software engineering (CASE)
Phase 4	**Cutover**	
	Tool:	testing and evaluation
	Tool:	user training

techniques are used interchangeably. Both techniques attempt to establish an appropriate arena in which all users meet and define the system's requirements. This phase is characterized by structured meetings and intensive brainstorming and group workshop sessions. Full participation by technical and business specialists is essential. The role of JRP is to establish the requirements of the business at the strategic, managerial and functional levels of the organization. Therefore, the executive level of the business organization and the management level is required to participate in the systems development process, which was not necessarily the case with the traditional SDLC. The structured meetings and workshops within the JRP framework are used to identify the *goals* of the information system under investigation, with a view to achieving a consensus agreement on the priorities and direction of systems development. It is important for the strategic level of an organization to be included in the systems development process because it is at this level that decisions can rapidly be made without regard to a lower, and longer, chain of command.

User design

The main technique used in this phase is joint applications development (JAD). This phase is characterized by full end-user participation in the *analysis* and *design* of the information system. It is essential for the right team of users to be put together in the most suitable environment to participate in the JAD process, to achieve the fulfilment of the end users' requirements. This phase normally uses *diagramming* tools and techniques to explore the proposed systems processes and user interfaces. The diagrammed prototyping can be used to investigate particular areas of the proposed system, which may be contentious, or the system as a whole. The end-user design is developed by using tools such as functional decomposition, entity modelling and data flow diagrams (all these design tools will be looked at in detail in Chapter 5). The results of the end-user design are often represented using computer-aided software design and development tools.

Construction

This phase involves converting the user design into a more detailed design, then implementing that design by the development of working *prototypes* that can be evaluated by end users. This phase is mostly given over to technical specialists to build any software-based applications that are required. The process of prototype evaluation by users is brought forward, compared to the SDLC approach, because of the involvement of end users in the analysis and design aspects of the proposed information system. Then the technical specialists, responsible for the physical construction of the system, use techniques such as implementing reusable designs and program codes to build the system. Normally, only a small team of technical specialists are used in the construction process in order to avoid any developmental overlap or confusion of responsibilities.

Cutover

This phase is concerned with the conversion of the old system to the new system (if an old system is being replaced) and the application of thorough systems testing and evaluation. It is common practice that the old (or in-place) system should be run in parallel with the new system until total reliability and confidence is established in the new system. Training is then given to users, although such training will be limited by the fact that users are already familiar with the system from participation in the development process and testing of prototypes, thus reducing training costs for the business organization.

PAUSE FOR THOUGHT 4.2

Rapid applications development

Rapid applications development (RAD) comprises a set of tools and techniques for designing and developing information systems in the information age. One of the major benefits of the RAD approach is the incorporation of user-friendly programming languages that allow less formalized and detailed computer programming to be carried out within an information systems development project. The RAD approach offers the possibility of a shorter and more flexible systems development life cycle, because of the use of techniques such as prototyping. Another advantage lies in the use of fourth generation programming languages that permit deeper and more effective participation of end users in the programming process of the systems development project. Therefore, with RAD the amount of time allocated to pure computer programming can be reduced significantly.

Many of the tools and techniques found under the RAD umbrella were used well before the issues of rapid application development became so important. For example, prototyping is a valuable technique in the design stage because it allows the end users and the development team, in cooperation, to determine the look and nature of an information system more rapidly, which can lead to an early creation of a prototype that looks and acts like the intended system. However, RAD extends the capabilities of prototyping by providing systems developers with everything they need to build a prototype, as well as turning the prototype into a fully functional set of processes and software applications. In other words, the prototype does not have to be converted to a particular computer language once the development team is happy with the system because the program coding is already implicit in the working prototype.

Within the RAD framework developers build systems applications primarily by designing the interfaces of the system. An interface determines how a user interacts with a system. The development team will primarily develop interface components such as menus, windows, buttons and even dialogue boxes that work in a WIMP environment (WIMP is an acronym for windows, icons, menus and pointers). The development team should be more concerned with what a systems application does rather than how it does it.

Prototyping also allows for a system to be iteratively tested by users in what is often called spiral development, which implies a development process of 'getting it wrong' many times before 'getting it right' for the final delivered system. However, care must be taken to ensure that the final system is appropriate and acceptable within the integrated business systems environment. The fixing and refining of a system after it has been delivered wastes money and may lead to user dissatisfaction, which is sometimes referred to as the 'prototyping death

▶

spiral'. Therefore, a holistic view of a system within the wider system environment is an important and necessary characteristic of RAD.

Another major technique of RAD is the use of object-oriented development, which allows sets of code or parts of various software applications (objects) to be put together like building blocks. Rather than programming from scratch, a system can be developed by building objects to the specification of the users of the system. For example, Borland's Delphi is a RAD tool that allows developers to assemble software applications from pre-built components. Delphi uses an object-oriented variant of the Pascal programming language for development and links to most major database servers. With advances in information technology, particularly the internet, objects can be located and found across global networks and not just localized business environments. The development team also has wider access to 'good development practice' in other business systems environments.

Most RAD tools provide facilities for component reuse. Often simple components are built and reused throughout the various applications of an information system. This process can be assisted by the reuse capabilities of most RAD tools to build ready-made object code libraries of applications. Furthermore, RAD tools largely incorporate visual programming languages (like Visual Basic and IBM's VisualAge), which make the programming aspect of systems development more apparent to the ordinary (or less program-oriented) systems user. Other technological tools and techniques used in RAD include object-oriented analysis and design methods and CASE (computer-assisted software engineering) tools.

RAD does not totally 'eRADicate' the need for programming but it does, by the use of various modern programming tools and techniques (known as the programming environment), allow for a reduction in the programming task that was so time consuming in the traditional systems development life cycle. RAD projects promote development speed but they do not eliminate the requirement for considered analysis and design, nor the need for skilful development through the use of programming tools and techniques. An advantage of RAD is that it encourages systems participation by allowing end users to become part of the development process and part of a systems development team. However, with speed of development predominating a systems development project, there is often a danger of the issues of development consistency, systems standardization and software maintainability becoming secondary unless they become subsumed into the fabric of the development process. Nonetheless, RAD offers speed of systems development and the possibility of competitive advantage to any organization that depends upon fast and effective information systems development.

Activity 4.3 Rapid applications development within the business environment

Write a brief one-page report outlining the reasons why a business organization may use rapid applications development to develop information systems and, within the report, provide five reasons why RAD tools and techniques may be effective in maximizing the productivity of the systems development process.

Before investigating joint applications development in the next section, discuss the possible human and technical problems of implementing a RAD approach to information systems development within business organizations. For example, how do you get people to participate collectively in systems development discussions and activities?

4.4 Joint applications development

Joint applications development (JAD) is a useful technique for establishing an information system's overall business requirements. JAD can be used in a number of business environments in place of traditional data collection and requirements analysis procedures. JAD involves group meetings between end users, technical specialists, business specialists and other systems stakeholders, all working together to analyze existing systems, propose possible solutions and define the system's requirements. The concept emphasizes the word 'joint' to refer to the close working relationship of business specialists and technical specialists. JAD uses *structured meetings* and workshops to bring technical specialists and business specialists together to agree the system's requirements. Therefore, it requires the right people being brought together within the most suitable working environment.

> ### What is joint applications development (JAD)?
>
> Joint applications development (JAD) is a group-based approach to end-user participation in information systems development. It provides a framework for more concentrated and enhanced end-user involvement in the systems development process. The technique was originally conceptualized by IBM Canada in the 1970s. It was later developed by James Martin & Associates of the USA, a notable information systems consultancy.

The technical specialist and the business specialist bring two types of mental model to the JAD process. These mental models are acquired separately by the specialists over time and are normally based on the baggage of past experience, expertise and knowledge. The fundamental purpose of JAD is to design a *conceptual model* of the proposed information system that exactly matches the mental design models envisaged by both the technical specialist and the business specialist. The two mental models can only come together into a mutually acceptable *conceptual design model* by a process of continuous iteration, within the modelling process, to break down the differences between the contrasting conceptual models. This can only be facilitated as part of an interactive group-based brainstorming process that airs all preconceived views and overcomes areas of technical and business ignorance. Figure 4.1 shows a typical layout for a JAD meeting or workshop. Within this environment one person acts as *facilitator* to encourage and guide the brainstorming process of the workshop environment.

There are three main principles to the JAD participative framework:

▶ **An intensive brainstorming meeting**: involving all relevant technical and business users of the information system. These meetings must be structured with an agenda, a set of objectives and a code of conduct between the participants. There should ideally be no more than 15 participants involved in the JAD meetings. The role of the business specialists is usually to decide on end-user requirements, while the role of the technical specialists is to advise on the technical constraints and implications of the ideas being proposed.

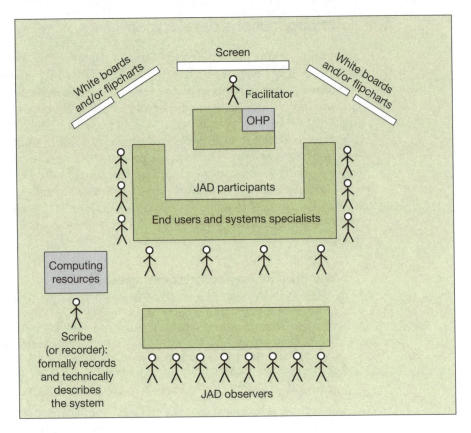

The JAD environment does not contain:

Telephones   Pagers/beepers   Mobile phones

Rank/position
(the relationship of participants is not based on outside rank or position)

Figure 4.1 JAD meeting (or workshop) environment

▶ **A structured meeting room environment**: as shown in Figure 4.1. The layout of the room and the positioning of the participants is vital to the creative process. Many tools, such as white boards and flipcharts, are used to encourage the brainstorming exercise. It is advised that the length of the meeting be determined in advance, with attendance from start to finish of the meeting. The meeting should also be held away from any of the possible interruptions that are usually found within the business environment. Therefore the JAD environment should be isolated from the outside world, apart from a possible telecommunications link to or from the scribe's computing resources.

▶ **A facilitator**: the person who manages and guides the JAD process. This person performs a task over and above that of the chair of the meeting. The facilitator should be independent of the participants and should be an expert in group dynamics and group behaviour. The facilitator is responsible for controlling the participants and guiding the creative process of the meeting to achieve the stated objectives. The process is also assisted by a person who acts as a *scribe*, translating the requirements of users into systems designs. This person is responsible for transcribing and documenting the JAD process. This person may also be responsible for guiding the use of various tools and techniques essential for establishing prototypes.

This process of JAD can also be used in environments beyond systems development where there is a need to establish general business organization requirements.

There are a number of advantages of the JAD participative process:

▶ It encourages participants to focus on systems problems and solutions without interruption. This speeds the process of analysis and design. JAD avoids the lengthy process of constructing questionnaires and setting up individual meetings with users. All decisions are agreed and accepted by all participants at the JAD meetings.

▶ It brings together all stakeholders in the system such as the managers, technical specialists and business end users. Decisions can be made without going through the more usual and formal communications channels of the business organization.

▶ It enfranchises participants in the decision-making process so that they are better able to achieve a universal commitment to the systems development process. When individuals feel they are part of the decision-making process they are less likely to create resistance to the development of a system.

▶ It employs an independent facilitator who understands group dynamics. This person is neutral within the JAD process and can arbitrate and overcome many of the internal organizational politics that may compromise the development of an ideal information system.

PAUSE FOR THOUGHT 4.3

Joint applications development techniques

Today's business organizations have to cope with shorter product life cycles and demands for higher customer service levels. Firms that take too long to deliver products or provide products of unacceptable quality are doomed to failure.

Corporate information services (IS) departments are businesses too. Many of them are in trouble because they are unable to respond quickly to senior executives' needs for applications and information. Companies have automated many manual processes over the years to increase efficiency. However, these systems only support the routine operational needs of the company. Now, companies need applications that cross functional boundaries and provide higher-level management information and decision support to senior executives who need help to respond to new customer demands.

Progressive organizations are looking beyond simply patching up the way they do business. They are re-engineering their business processes to change dramatically the way they operate and the products they provide. Progressive IS departments are also changing by taking advantage of new tools and new techniques to re-engineer the way they build systems.

▶

Development life cycle

As a business, the IS department's primary function is to manufacture and support products called information systems for its customers called users. The manufacturing process, planning, analysis, design, development, and maintenance, traditionally has been called the 'systems development life cycle'.

The classical systems development life cycle specifies the sequence of activities required to take an IS application concept through design and development to successful deployment. This is a sequence of steps and procedures that we all learned about years ago. I imagine that we all feel pretty guilty that we've not followed this life cycle as well as we should have. But we will, on our very next development project, if we have the time.

Missing the mark

Unfortunately, pure development projects are few and far between these days. In most of our shops, up to 90% of our time is spent in maintenance of existing applications. We spend more time patching new functionality into old systems than we do designing new systems to replace the old ones.

So where has this classical systems development life cycle gotten us? Let's review some industry statistics:

60% of large systems projects have significant cost overruns,

75% of completed systems are in need of constant maintenance,

60% to 80% of errors originate in the user requirements and functional specifications.

A survey conducted by the Index Group of Cambridge Massachusetts in early 1990 concluded that 'Systems developers are operating amid turf battles, historical bickering, low credibility and the difficulty in pinning down ever-changing systems requirements.' Their survey of 95 systems development directors found that:

64% say that they cannot get users in different departments to cooperate in cross-functional systems projects,

78% say that coordinating efforts between end user developers and professional systems developers is a major challenge even though the number of end users developing their own systems is on the rise,

less than 29% say they have any long-range plans for retiring obsolete systems.

These statistics reflect the 'state of the art' in software systems development in large organizations today. We might be tempted to say that it's different in small organizations. Yes, it probably is different, but likely no better. The information needs of large organizations have hit smaller companies as well. For example:

▶ We've all got a need to develop strategic systems that support users in multiple functions.

▶ The need for cross-functional strategic applications makes it more difficult to get users to agree to and sign off on system specifications. At the same time, tools are maturing that can help us develop and implement applications faster than ever before.

In 'real life' systems development, time and effort are heavily skewed towards coding. We feel the need to get started writing the code so we can get it done in time to allow us to debug the system before we implement it.

This often results in poor planning, feeding inadequate design that does not meet business needs and requires major revisions and difficult maintenance over the life of the system. To complicate matters, we've got application systems that have been in production, in some cases, for over 15 years. Each year those creaky old systems get harder and harder to maintain and modify.

Today's environment

Computer-aided software engineering (CASE) tools are available today to help us develop applications very quickly. Along with the tools, the industry has evolved new views of the traditional systems development life cycle.

The information engineering proponents have redefined and simplified the life cycle to four phases: planning, analysis, design, and construction. Other methodologies have defined similar phases.

The one thing all of today's development methodologies agree upon is that we need to improve the quality of the input – the user requirements. Requirements must be defined and specified in a consistent, repeatable, and structured way.

Consequently, the heart of the IS business has moved up the life cycle. Today we must focus more on analysis and design and less on the traditional 'nuts and bolts', the coding and the implementation tools.

That means to develop effective information systems today we must take the time to integrate the technical aspects of information technology and the social aspects of the organization.

To determine user requirements today, we must adopt more effective techniques that recognize both the differences in communications styles of our colleagues in the company and the differences in application requirements of the business functions that we serve. One such technique is joint application design (JAD).

What is JAD?

Joint application design is a management process – a people process – which allows IS to work more effectively with users in a shorter time frame. Since the late seventies, JAD has proven to be an effective technique for building user commitment to the success of application systems through their active participation in the analysis of requirements and the specification of the system design.

The facilitated JAD workshop brings key users (stakeholders) and systems professionals together to resolve their differences in a neutral, non-hostile atmosphere. Key to the workshop is a specially trained, unbiased facilitator who is not a member of the project team and therefore has no political stake in the outcome of the workshop. The workshop will build a team that will stay together, psychologically at least, for the life of the project.

The power of JAD is in the integration of behavioural and group dynamics techniques within the structure of a soundly engineered methodology. What does that mean? It means that a JAD workshop is not just a nice meeting.

The workshop has a highly structured agenda with clear objectives including a mechanism for resolving open issues that often bog down the design process. The deliverables are clearly defined during the pre-workshop activities so that there can be a smooth and successful transition to the next phase in the life cycle – application design or acquisition.

Workshops are effective at all levels: enterprise, business area, application, and implementation project management. Facilitated workshops can be used whenever a group of diverse individuals needs to reach a workable consensus. Today, workshops are commonly used for strategic business planning, strategic IS plans, IS architecture definition, re-engineering business processes, detailed system design, process and data modelling, and project management.

▶

This positive, team-building environment gives people a chance to learn from each other and to understand each other's needs and concerns. The participants will develop a common view of the project and a common language to discuss the project issues.

A common language

We need a common language so that we can understand each other's concerns – not the broad issues that are obvious to everyone, but the subtleties that give individual business functions that extra edge.

Users know what they want but they don't have a way to articulate the subtleties of their business needs so that IS can understand them and build working systems to support them effectively.

Different functional units have different ways of operating, of making decisions, and of analyzing what's going on around them. Finance and accounting people, for instance, tend to be very 'cut and dried' or mechanistic in the way they analyze a problem and judge the merits of a proposed solution. For an accountant, 2 plus 2 is always 4. A lot of systems people think like accountants. We like to work towards that one right answer.

Marketing people, on the other hand, are more willing to work with abstractions and uncertainties. Consequently, they can be more frustrating for IS to deal with. They tend to see many shades of gray. What's 2 plus 2 in the marketing department? 'Well, it depends, are we buying or are we selling.'

Today we need applications that cross functional boundaries and provide high-level management information and decision support to all of our top executives, to help them respond to the changing business environment.

However, as we move up the corporate ladder, there is a greater tendency towards a more open, organic, and adaptive view. That means that there may not be one right answer. Instead, we may need to choose among a group of not wrong answers to find the one that best fits the organization's culture, business, and marketplace. That means it's harder to get upper management to express their needs in terms that systems people can understand.

The common language developed in the facilitated JAD workshop helps all the participants communicate and understand each other's needs so that IS can build systems that more effectively support the company's higher-level information needs.

Pre-workshop activities

Good preparation is key to success. There is between one and three weeks of work required to prepare for a workshop. That preparation is required to:

Identify project objectives and limitations

It is vital to have clear objectives for the workshop and for the project as a whole. The pre-workshop activities, the planning and scoping, set the expectations of the workshop sponsors and participants.

Scoping identifies the business functions that are within the scope of the project. It also tries to assess both the project design and implementation complexity.

The political sensitivity of the project should be assessed. Has this been tried in the past? How many false starts were there? How many implementation failures were there?

Sizing is important. For best results, systems projects should be sized so that a complete design – right down to screens and menus – can be designed in eight to ten workshop days.

Identify critical success factors

It is important to identify the critical success factors for both the development project and the business function being studied. How will we know that the planned changes have been effective? How will success be measured? Planning for outcomes assessment helps us judge the effectiveness and the quality of the implemented system over its entire operational life.

Define project deliverables

In general, the deliverables from a workshop are documentation and a design. It is important to define the form and level of detail of the workshop documentation. What types of diagrams will be provided? What type or form of narrative will be supplied?

It is a good idea to start using a CASE tool for diagramming support right from the start. Most of the available tools have good to great diagramming capabilities but their narrative support is generally weak. The narrative is best produced with your standard word processing software.

Define the schedule of workshop activities

Workshops vary in length from one to five days. The initial workshop for a project should not be less than three days. It takes the participants most of the first day to get comfortable with their roles, with each other, and with the environment. The second day is spent learning to understand each other and developing a common language with which to communicate issues and concerns. By the third day, everyone is working together on the problem and real productivity is achieved.

After the initial workshop, the team-building has been done. Shorter workshops can be scheduled for subsequent phases of the project, for instance to verify a prototype. However, it will take the participants from one to three hours to re-establish the team psychology of the initial workshop.

Select the participants

These are the business users, the IS professionals, and the outside experts that will be needed for a successful workshop.

Prepare the workshop material

Before the workshop, the project manager and the facilitator perform an analysis and build a preliminary design or straw man to focus the workshop. The workshop material consists of documentation, worksheets, diagrams, and even props that will help the participants understand the business function under investigation.

Organize workshop activities and exercises

The facilitator must design workshop exercises and activities to provide interim deliverables that build towards the final output of the workshop. The pre-workshop activities help design those workshop exercises. For example, for a business area analysis, what's in it? A decomposition diagram? A high-level entity-relationship diagram? A normalized data model? A state transition diagram? A dependency diagram? All of the above? None of the above? It is important to define the level of technical diagramming that is appropriate to the environment. The most important thing about a diagram is that it must be understood by the users.

Once the diagram choice is made, the facilitator designs exercises into the workshop agenda to get the group to develop those diagrams.

A workshop combines exercises that are serially oriented to build on one another, and parallel exercises, with each sub-team working on a piece of the problem or working on the same thing for a different functional area.

High-intensity exercises led by the facilitator energize the group and direct it towards a specific goal. Low-intensity exercises allow for detailed discussions before decisions. The discussions can involve the total group or teams can work out the issues and present a limited number of suggestions for the whole group to consider.

To integrate the participants, the facilitator can match people with similar expertise from different departments. To help participants learn from each other, he can mix the expertise. It's up to the facilitator to mix and match the sub-team members to accomplish the organizational, cultural, and political objectives of the workshop.

A workshop operates on both the technical level and the political level. It is the facilitator's job to build consensus and communications, to force issues out early in the process. There is no need to worry about the technical implementation of a system if the underlying business issues cannot be resolved.

Prepare, inform, educate the workshop participants

All of the participants in the workshop must be made aware of the objectives and limitations of the project and the expected deliverables of the workshop.

Briefing of participants should take place one to five days before the workshop. This briefing may be teleconferenced if participants are widely dispersed.

The briefing document might be called the Familiarization Guide, Briefing Guide, Project Scope Definition, or the Management Definition Guide – or anything else that seems appropriate. It is a document of eight to twelve pages, and it provides a clear definition of the scope of the project for the participants.

The briefing itself lasts two to four hours. It provides the psychological preparation everyone needs to move forward into the workshop.

Coordinate workshop logistics

Workshops should be held off-site to avoid interruptions. Projectors, screens, PCs, tables, markers, masking tape, Post-It notes, and lots of other props should be prepared.

What specific facilities and props are needed is up to the facilitator. They can vary from simple flip charts to electronic white boards. In any case, the layout of the room must promote the communication and interaction of the participants.

The key players

The facilitator

The facilitator is in charge of the workshop – the guardian of the process. It is the facilitator's responsibility to ensure that the expected workshop deliverables are produced and the expected consensus is achieved. The facilitator is an unbiased leader who has no ties to the project. He can come from some other department or from outside the company. Some companies are training facilitators who work out of a facilitation center attached to the human resources department.

The ideal facilitator is an individual who is excited by working with people. That would include only between 10% and 15% of senior systems analysts. Good facilitators often come from non-computer science fields such as teaching or sales. In addition to an aptitude for working with people, the facilitator must have the skills required to achieve the level of analysis detail expected from the workshop. That means training in the following areas: the methodology (such as information engineering) that will be used in development, group dynamics, basic selling skills, issue recognition, and listening skills. Good facilitators listen, recognize issues as they arise, and provide the leadership and direction to help people come together.

The facilitator is responsible for ensuring that each person is heard and has an equal opportunity to influence the decision. The facilitator is also responsible for ensuring that the participants in the workshop construct a solution that everyone can live with.

Documentation expert

This individual has to document the decisions and the issues in the workshop – to act as a scribe.

The executive sponsor

This is the executive who charters the project – the system owner. The sponsor must be high enough in the organization to be able to clear the calendars of the people required in the workshop. The sponsor provides motivation for commitment through a short speech at the opening of the workshop and has to be available for strategic direction and scoping information during the pre-workshop phase. During the workshop, the executive sponsor must be available for policy decisions appropriate for his level of authority.

Without the executive sponsor's commitment, people do not show up for workshops on time or sometimes at all. Schedules change and projects are delayed. In short, without an executive sponsor, there is no project!

The project manager

This is the person responsible for the project who will work closely with the facilitator. The project manager, as the client of the workshop process, receives the deliverables.

Business users

These are the intended users of the system being designed. They are in the workshop because of their business expertise. Business users fall into two categories: real end users – the people who are actually going the have to use the screens and reports to do their jobs; and representative end users – the people who think they know what's going on in the field. They are responsible for standards and methodology for the business functions they represent.

It is important to get both types of users into the workshop. If the workshop consists of only representative users, then we get a good theoretical model – how things should be – but the theories may not work in practice. If we have only real end users, then we get a good system for today but it might not work next year or two years down the road.

Systems experts

The workshop is trying to establish rapport and communications among stakeholders – including IS. Systems people need to be there to know the constraints so they can advise the business people regarding hardware and software under discussion. A good rule of thumb is one systems person for every four users.

Outside experts

Outside experts are business consultants or technology consultants who can provide the expertise that may not be available in-house. For example, the workshop may need support from outside consultants for manufacturing, distribution, marketing, prototyping, organizational dynamics, and change management.

Observers

Observers are not allowed to participate in the workshop in any way. They may observe to gain some insight into the business area under investigation or to become familiar with the workshop process.

Post-workshop activities

After the workshop, it is important to address and resolve the open issues generated by the workshop. A three-day workshop typically generates about 20 open issues, most of which are business issues. It is critical to get these issues out on the table for discussion and resolution before any code gets written.

The facilitator and the documentation expert work together to finalize the workshop documentation. The project manager is the client who receives the deliverables.

The documentation moves forward through the organization to continue to enroll support and approvals for the development project if necessary.

▶

The design moves forward either for inclusion in a request for proposal for application software acquisition or towards a prototype or a code generation phase. It may contain details such as screen layouts and menus. The data model will contain volumes and capacities. The process model will specify transaction volumes.

If the design is taken into a prototype, there should be a series of half-day or one-day workshops to evaluate and validate the prototype.

Workshop benefits

Builds consensus and ownership
The workshop approach will quickly achieve consensus and commitment among users – the customers of the IS function.

Improves design quality
The workshop improves the quality of the deliverable of the design phase because it forces a definition of that deliverable in advance. During the workshop the participants are all focused on a common goal. Users in the workshop will have a better understanding of the business issues, the systems issues, and the volume of work to be done.

Project teams get focused and stay focused
In the workshop, the participants will build a common view of the project and a common language to discuss the issues. These elements will stay with the team for the life of the project.

A natural partnership with modern development tools
JAD helps realize the full potential of today's powerful development tools by providing high-quality input requirements quickly.

20% reduction in overall life cycle costs
In 1989, computer industry productivity expert, Capers Jones, studied 60 development projects and found:

▶ Without JAD, 35% of the functionality was missed and that had an impact on at least 50% of the code – core functionality was missed.

▶ With JAD, less than 10% of the functionality was missed and that had a minimal impact on the code – indicating that the core functionality was good but refinement was going on. JAD doesn't stop refinement – it helps manage it better. Those projects that used JAD combined with prototyping did even better!

Conclusion

The information needs of our top executives are not well defined. The business climate is uncertain and changing. There is no single right answer, there is no single right system.

Progressive systems departments are taking advantage of new tools and new techniques to re-engineer the way they build systems. There are new development tools, new methodologies and supporting techniques such as joint application design for developing the requirements specifications for the systems our users need.

To develop effective information systems today we must take the time to integrate the technical aspects of information technology and the social aspects of the organization. That's what facilitated workshop requirements analysis is all about!

Source: Bill Jennerich, 'Joint application design: business requirements analysis for successful re-engineering', © Blubird Enterprises Inc. website (www.bluebirdenterprises.com), August 2003.

4.4 Joint applications development

Discuss with and advise your colleagues on the use and role of joint applications development (JAD) workshops within a RAD environment. Then explain the reasons behind including all stakeholders in meetings concerned with defining the requirements of the information systems under consideration. Describe the possible strengths and weaknesses of the JAD approach to problem solving and suggest possible effects the approach has on the overall timeframe for delivery of a business information system.

4.5 Prototyping

A *prototype* is a working and representative model of a system or sub-system, the purpose of which is to permit systems end users to be involved in the design and development process through the activity of testing and evaluation of the working prototype. Prototyping allows an information system to be tested and evaluated earlier in the overall development process than is the case with a traditional systems development life cycle. Prototyping uses a process of *iteration* to refine the system to an ideal; iteration is the process of repeating a series of operations until the desired solution is achieved. The iterative aspect of prototyping provides greater scope for testing alternatives and building an information system more quickly and at less cost. Ideally, when end users work with a prototype they develop a more focused and discerning idea of the delivery of business system requirements in practice. The prototype also puts a greater emphasis on the development of the *front-end interface* between the user and the system's technology. Systems users, through working and interacting with the prototype, often demand a higher level of user-friendly IS/IT interface design.

What is a prototype?

A representative and working model of an information system or entity, designed to be tested and evaluated by the ultimate end users.

Prototyping places great emphasis on participative end-user involvement at the start of the systems design process, which includes describing the proposed outcome of the information systems development project. However, end users often have limited training in traditional tools of systems analysis and design so have to rely on transcribing the system requirements in terms of symbols, pictures and narrative illustration. This is a technique known as *story-boarding*, which uses rough drawings to describe the requirements of the information system. Such informal analysis, using symbols, icons and a limited amount of narrative, permits a non-technical end user to describe and communicate a proposed information system to any technical specialist.

The outcome of producing a drawing, with symbols and limited wording, is known as a *rich picture*. The rich picture should act as a graphical representation of the information system's user requirements. Such rich pictures can be developed individually or in groups in workshops to provide an analytical view of

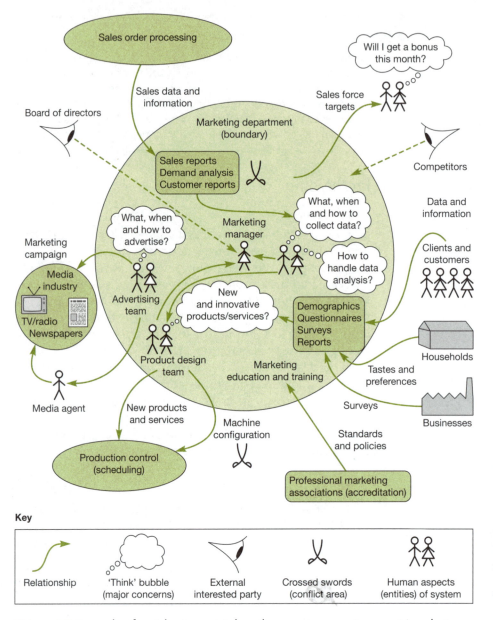

Figure 4.2 Example of a rich picture to describe a systems environment (marketing function)

the system's requirements and specifications. Examples of the technique and the use of rich pictures within soft systems development methodologies will be discussed at length in Chapter 5. Figure 4.2 provides a typical example of a rich picture using pictures and icons to represent the marketing systems environment. Furthermore, there are a number of software applications that accommodate the development of user story-boarding for defining an information system.

There are a number of strengths inherent in the prototyping approach:

▶ It overcomes many of the problems of the traditional systems development life cycle, in terms of inadequate requirements definition, by involving end users in the systems development process.

▶ It can be developed using fourth generation tools and techniques, which are inherently more user-friendly than third generation computing tools and techniques.

▶ It allows the end user to work with more pre-coded software applications (e.g. spreadsheets, databases, graphics packages), which can be integrated to build business-specific information systems (this is known as applications-based development).

▶ It places a greater emphasis on input and output forms and human–computer interface design. It also improves the process of systems investigation and analysis.

▶ It involves business specialists in the system problem-solving process to an extent that is not practical with the traditional systems development life cycle. This overcomes the problem of inadequate communication between technical specialists and non-technical end users.

▶ It is a useful tool when the applications area is poorly defined or 'fuzzy', or where a business organization is unfamiliar with the information technology aspect of the proposed information system.

A prototype is normally built by using special tools and techniques to speed up the process of requirements analysis and design of human–computer interfaces. Examples of PC-based tools and techniques include Microsoft Access (for database development) and Visual Basic (for various applications integration and development). For instance, Visual Basic can be used to enhance the power, capability and integration of software applications by using user-friendly programming to empower pre-built applications software (e.g. spreadsheets), or to integrate software, such as linking a database to a spreadsheet.

A prototype model can also be used as a tool for *organizational learning*, as well as supporting the systems development process. In prototyping practice, the business specialists will define and illustrate the requirements of the information system, followed by the development of a working prototype built with the cooperation and guidance of technical specialists. Therefore, the business interests predominate in ensuring that the *business* requirements and the *system* requirements are promoted and aligned in harmony. There are five steps to the incorporation of a prototype into the information systems development process:

▶ identify and define business and system requirements;

▶ develop a full working prototype;

▶ ask end users to test and evaluate the prototype;

▶ refine and enhance the prototype through iteration;

▶ document and deliver the optimum information system.

Prototyping is most effective for the development of information systems for decision making in environments that are characterized by uncertainty and subject to dynamic market forces. A prototype can be particularly useful where the decision-making requirements are unclear, or where there is a need to clarify the problem-solving process to deliver a more effective and useful information system's solution. However, this is qualified by the fact that prototyping is most effective for smaller, PC-based information systems development. Prototyping is often not appropriate for large, mainframe-based development with incumbent complex and large-scale data processing requirements. Furthermore, there is a need for any finalized information system to include aspects of *data security* and user *documentation*. However, these aspects often do not fall within the scope of the prototype development framework.

Activity 4.5 Systems prototyping

Discuss what is meant by the term prototyping as used in information systems development environments and explain the importance of iteration to the process of prototyping within systems development.

Normally a university or college will operate a system of student admissions to coordinate, control and manage the process of offering places on courses, and the eventual enrolment of students on to those various courses. Investigate the role and nature of university and college admissions and produce a rich picture of the systems environment. Note that you will first have to define the boundaries of the system that is under consideration and then describe the environment with the use of pictures and a minimal amount of wording.

4.6 Object-oriented systems development

The growth of graphical interfaces, the spread of internet browser technology and the increasing use of client-server networking have stimulated an interest in object-oriented systems development. Object-oriented development (OOD) involves the linking together of *objects* to create specific systems applications. These objects may consist of a set of computer codes or an encapsulated collection of data and operations performed on that data. These objects can be interchanged between applications, allowing a systems builder to obtain objects of code and applications from an *object library*. The various objects can be assembled, like building blocks, into a systems application for any business organization or its particular trading environment. The OOD concept is important in that it treats data and procedures within one defined object.

Did you know?

The concepts and theory of object-oriented development (OOD) originated in the 1970s. However, OOD lay on the margins of information systems and computer programming until the late 1980s and early 1990s, when it re-emerged as a systems development framework rejuvenated by advances in information technology.

The advantage of object-oriented systems design lies in the reusability of computer codes, whereby processing routines and data can be built into objects which can be used in a number of systems software applications. However, it is still a skill to be able to analyze business functions correctly so that they can be encapsulated into an object. Objects possess *classes* and component *members*. For example, a plant may be a class of object with leaves and stem as component members. The importance of OOD is that an organization can build up a *library* of object classes that deals with all the systems functions of the business organization. Systems development, involving software applications development, becomes a task of selecting and connecting existing classes of objects into a systems application. This will normally speed along the process of overall systems development.

What is object-oriented development (OOD)?

A software development method that combines data and the associated instructions for that data into one object or entity that can be used interchangeably and built into other systems' software applications.

Activity 4.6 Object-oriented development

Discuss and explain the term object-oriented development and suggest why there has been a resurgence of interest in a technique that dates back to the 1970s. Describe what is meant by objects and explain the possible use, role and function of object libraries in applications and systems development within business organizations. Then suggest three possible advantages of using pre-coded or pre-formed objects to build different information systems within one organization.

4.7 Dynamic systems development method

The dynamic systems development method (DSDM) was proposed in the mid-1990s as a way of formalizing the RAD approach to building modern information systems in ever-changing business environments. A consortium of companies came together in the mid-1990s to develop the DSDM framework. In 2000–2001 the use of DSDM became international with the establishment of an International DSDM Consortium based in North America, comprising Canada, the USA, and Mexico. The overall mission of the consortium is to sustain, promote and continually evolve the RAD approach.

What is dynamic systems development method (DSDM)?

A formalized approach to business sytems development in RAD environments that utilizes a number of proprietary and non-proprietary tools and techniques to deliver fast and effective information systems.

The DSDM framework for building applications-based information systems was a de facto standard in the UK and Europe in the late 1990s. It then became a popular systems development framework in North America at the start of the twenty-first century. One of the aims of the DSDM Consortium is to develop a global network of information systems practitioners that utilize DSDM and its associated rapid applications development tools and techniques. The modern idea of DSDM is to try to deliver accelerated business solutions in the internet age.

The DSDM Consortium has detailed its history and development, as follows:

In the early part of the 1990s a new term 'rapid application development' (or RAD) was launched upon an unsuspecting IT industry. RAD was intended to be different from the classical sequential (or 'waterfall') methods for application development. Indeed its origins sprang from the frustrations of users and IT alike with methods that were seen as inappropriate for a fast-moving business environment, forced users to fix their requirements in concrete early in the cycle and did not allow for rapid iterative delivery.

However, RAD grew as a movement in a very unstructured way; there was no commonly agreed definition of a RAD process, and many different vendors and consultants came up with their own interpretation and approach.

By 1993 there was momentum in the marketplace with a growing number of tools for RAD and vendors developing or repositioning their products to meet a growing demand from their customers for RAD technology. But still there was a piece missing . . . for every customer that needed RAD tools to improve their development capability, there was a customer who needed to change the development process. It was out of this recognition in the marketplace for an industry standard RAD framework that the DSDM Consortium was born.

The founding members of the DSDM Consortium met for the first time in January 1994. The organizations had the single objective of jointly developing and promoting an independent framework. At a meeting in February, it was agreed that a high-level framework should be produced in time for the next full meeting in March. At the March meeting of the Consortium, the high-level framework was approved by the 36 members unanimously. The basic concepts have remained in place since that time, but the framework has been developed and refined over the life of the Consortium. It has been found to be applicable in nearly every technical and business environment where systems are needed quickly.

Version 1 was completed on time, agreed unanimously by all members of the Consortium in January 1995 and published in February 1995. Alongside the publication of the framework, the Consortium put in place a training scheme, with accredited training organizations and examination procedures for DSDM practitioners, trainers and examiners to gain certification. In January 1997, a workshop was held to decide what changes may be needed to the framework. There was increasing use of DSDM in business process change projects, whereas the previous focus had been on purely application development. This was felt to be a major shift that should be reflected in the framework and Task Groups were set up to consider its implications. Version 3 was published in October 1997. The current version in use is version 4.2 [in 2003].

The beginnings of DSDM were focused around RAD and IT; however, today DSDM is used, across a variety of industries, as a framework to deliver on time solutions, which meet the needs of businesses. (DSDM Consortium website, September 2003)

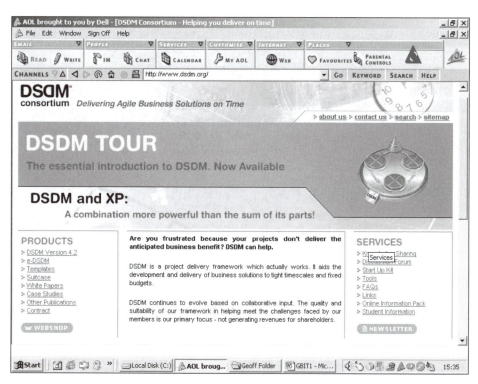

Figure 4.3 The DSDM Consortium website

Source: Frame from AOL; screenshot from DSDM Consortium website (www.dsdm.org).

The DSDM approach uses time-boxing, facilitated workshops, incremental and iterative delivery, and object reuse, as some of its techniques for reducing systems development uncertainty in quick turnaround systems development environments. The aim is to achieve 'rapid and right' systems development. In many ways DSDM is different to the traditional waterfall approach to systems development. In traditional approaches the focus is mainly on satisfying the contents of a requirements document and conforming to previous deliverables, even though the requirements are often inaccurate, the previous deliverables may be flawed and the business needs may have changed since the start of the project. In addition, time and resources are often allowed to vary during development. In DSDM, the exact opposite is true: time is fixed for the life of a project, and resources are fixed as far as possible. This means that the requirements that will be satisfied are allowed to change.

In the early part of the twenty-first century (2000–4) DSDM evolved to take into account new ideas and concepts in software development, referred to generically as *agile software development methods*. DSDM has become associated with a range of tools and techniques, such as extreme programming (XP), feature driven development and adaptive software development. Throughout the DSDM process the aim is to align systems development with the requirements of the users, and their changing needs, by using a phased approach to the development life cycle. The overarching aim is to shorten the 'time-to-market' period for systems development projects.

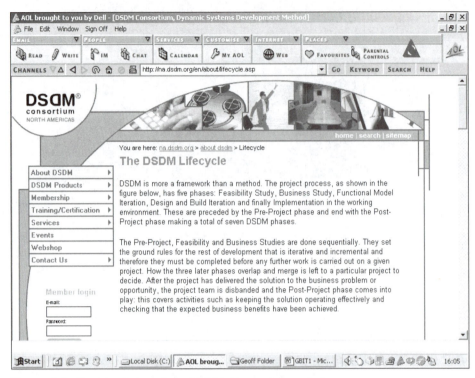

Figure 4.4 The North American DSDM Consortium website

Source: Frame from AOL; screenshot from DSBM consortium website (www.dsdm.org).

The DSDM framework has many supporters in the systems development domain. Many surveys have been carried out to assess the effectiveness of DSDM. For example, a study commissioned in 2002 by Xansa, an international supplier of application management services in the UK, shows that by using DSDM companies can achieve 200 per cent increases in return on investment. The study compared DSDM to traditional systems development approaches over a seven-year period (from 1994 to 2001), focusing on systems development productivity (i.e. how quickly a system could be developed that met the user's requirements).

There are a number of benefits of using DSDM:

▶ It uses the prototyping technique of iterative development. If the project is large, then DSDM breaks the problem down into smaller components, either for incremental delivery or for development by parallel teams.

▶ It uses ideas of user participation and involves the users throughout the systems development project life cycle. Therefore, the users are more likely to claim ownership of the system; the risk of building the wrong system is greatly reduced; the final system is more likely to meet the users' real business requirements; and the end users will be better trained as their representatives will define and coordinate the training required.

▶ It develops strategies and implements techniques that enable the systems developers and end users to communicate ideas and requirements, with the minimum of misunderstanding. For example, the communication between systems developers and end users is facilitated by having *ambassador-users*.

These are knowledgeable user representatives who can participate throughout the project life cycle and provide coverage of the views of all the users, defined by *user-class*.

▶ It has small development teams, which allow communication and understanding of the systems development problem to be better defined.

▶ It does not ignore the importance of establishing and publishing systems documentation – an advantage over earlier RAD frameworks.

Within the conceptual sphere of any information systems development project are three main factors:

▶ **Functionality**: what the system should be able to do.

▶ **Time**: the period of time needed to complete the project.

▶ **Resources**: i.e. the physical and logical objects available to complete the project.

Within the traditional systems development life cycle approach the functionality is fixed but the time and resources are free to vary. Hence, projects can run over time and exceed their budgets. However, with the DSDM approach the resources and time are fixed, but the functionality is free to vary throughout the iterative process of development. This concept is illustrated in Figure 4.5 which shows the differences between DSDM and the traditional SDLC approach to systems development.

There are nine principles that underpin the use of DSDM as a systems development approach:

▶ **Active end-user involvement**: active and hands-on user participation is included in the development process.

▶ **Project team empowerment**: the users and technical systems developers must have the authority to take decisions and actions.

▶ **Focus on the delivery of functions and objects**: the approach must be flexible enough to deliver functions and objects frequently and on time.

▶ **Fitness for purpose**: deliverables must be fit for their purpose and fit the business requirements accurately.

▶ **Concentration on iterative and incremental development**: prototyping is

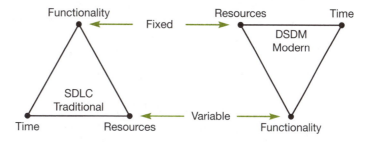

Figure 4.5 The difference between DSDM and the SDLC approach

Source: DSDM Consortium website (www.dsdm.org).

used to enable end-user feedback to be iteratively employed to find optimal solutions.

▶ **Non-sequential and non-rigid development**: the process should be flexible enough to enable project teams to go back as well as forwards in phased development.

▶ **Requirements established at a high level**: the purpose and scope of the systems development project is established and bounded at the highest logical level, thus establishing the overarching goal of the systems project.

▶ **Testing integrated throughout the life cycle**: the system is incrementally developed through user feedback and testing.

▶ **Full collaboration and cooperation between all the stakeholders**: good communication is required between users and technical specialists, as are clear high level aims and goals.

These principles need to be accepted by all the stakeholders (i.e. technical software and systems developers, end users, managers, and all the associated agents of the information system being developed. Once this has occurred, then the systems development project can be undertaken. It is important to note a couple of semantic imperatives in the DSDM approach:

▶ those that employ DSDM refer to the approach as a *framework* rather than a pure methodology;

▶ the activities within the DSDM framework are referred to as phases, or even activities, rather than stages, because stages imply that the development process is rigid and sequential, which this is not the case with DSDM.

There are a number of activities in the DSDM approach:

▶ **Pre-project**: establishing whether there are funds and structures in place to initiate a systems development project. Questions that may be asked are: 'Is the time right?' and 'Do we have the strategic go-ahead?'

▶ **Feasibility study**: defining the problem along with the costs and assessment of the systems approach. This phase is normally a short activity lasting a few weeks.

▶ **Business study**: analyzing business processes and business systems requirements. This is a collaborative phase, using a series of facilitated workshops attended by knowledgeable and empowered staff who can set priorities and establish business systems objectives. The result of this phase will be a *business area definition* that identifies the business processes and the classes (i.e. types of users) who will be affected by the introduction of the system.

▶ **Functional model iteration**: trying to prototype and refine the business objectives through iterative testing and evaluation. The iterative process involves identifying what is to be produced; agreeing how to produce it; creating prototypes; and providing feedback through the testing and evaluation of logical and sometimes physical prototypes.

▶ **Design and build iteration**: extending the previous phase. The systems should be at a level of refinement so that all end users can test the suitability and robustness of the system. This phase tests the strength of the system, whereas the functional model iteration concentrates mainly on testing the functional parameters of the system.

▶ **Implementation**: moving from the development environment to the operational environment. This activity is often referred to by systems developers as the *cutover phase*. Normally, an *increment review document* is available at this phase. This summarizes what the project has achieved in terms of short-term objectives. It outlines whether all, or some, of the requirements have been completed. It also outlines where additional functionality has been discovered but not yet addressed in the incremental development, so that the additional functionality can be incorporated into the original business study.

▶ **Post-project**: ensuring that the systems solution operates efficiently and effectively. Ideally, the system is maintained and users are knowledgeable and empowered to employ the system to support their job functions.

The DSDM methodology is flexible, reliable and now well established as a business systems development framework. There are educational courses in DSDM and many companies encourage their systems development employees to become members of the DSDM Consortium. The global nature of DSDM makes it a useful international systems development framework. In recent years, the usefulness of DSDM has been augmented by developments in object-oriented software development and what have become known as agile software development techniques (or *agile methods*). These agile methods involve quick and rapid software development as their underlying principle. Therefore, these methods ally themselves very neatly with RAD tools and techniques and the DSDM framework. The next section focuses on software approaches and software applications within the RAD domain.

4.8 Applications-based systems development

Agile software development methods within the RAD domain are characterized by a number of principles:

▶ They are referred to as *extreme programming* (XP) or even adaptive software development methods because they aim to develop software quickly, to build software that can adapt to user requirements and to base software development on functionality and objects.

▶ They are designed to meet changing user requirements, working closely and collaboratively with systems end users.

▶ They encourage face-to-face contact between software developers and the end users, along with a continual regard for technical excellence and good design characteristics.

▶ They enable software changes to be achieved through iterative processes, using tools and techniques to reflect and adjust software according to user requirements.

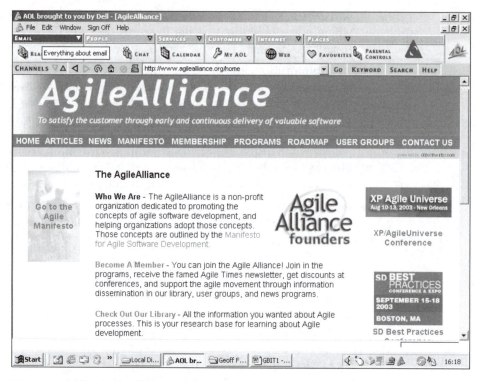

Figure 4.6 The Agile Alliance website

Source: Frame from AOL; screenshot from Agile Alliance website (www.agilealliance.org).

As well as software methods that support RAD there are other types of software tools and applications that are objects in their own right. For example, software applications and packages (i.e. databases, spreadsheets, word-processors, presentation packages, e-mail packages, etc.) are normally pre-coded and commercially available programs. This eliminates the requirement for writing additional software code each time the software application is required by an organization. Software applications packages perform many tasks and functions and can be divided into the following generic areas within the business environment:

▶ database applications

▶ modelling and spreadsheet applications

▶ word-processing applications

▶ desktop publishing (DTP) applications

▶ graphics and multimedia applications

▶ e-mail and communications software applications

▶ group and collaborative meetings software

▶ operating system (OS) utilities.

Many small-scale information systems can now be built using pre-coded software applications packages. These form the objects that can be put together (i.e. like building blocks) to construct small systems effectively and quickly. This is a process normally referred to as *applications-based systems development*. This activity reduces the time needed within the traditional systems development life cycle for program coding. In particular, small-scale, desktop-based, networked ICT projects lend themselves well to applications-based information systems development. There are a number of advantages of applications-based systems development:

▶ It allows end users to build systems that meet their individual requirements within the business organization.

▶ It reduces the need for large numbers of in-house technical specialists and encourages employees to become more IT literate.

▶ Most commercial software applications come with user support (or online help facilities) that lower the in-house costs associated with systems development.

▶ Many package environments allow various applications to be integrated so that systems can be built with harmony. For example, the Microsoft Corporation encourages user integration of its suite of office applications through the use of the programming language called Visual Basic that can be used to extend the capabilities of basic packages, such as Microsoft Word and Microsoft Excel.

Applications-based development does not negate the need to undertake the phases of systems analysis, design, implementation and evaluation. It is particularly suitable for developing prototypes for information systems used in the managerial and executive levels of a business organization, where systems applications are specific to individual needs and small team requirements. However, one of the main disadvantages of applications-based development lies in the fact that idiosyncratic systems may be developed without regard to consistent and commonly practised standards of systems development throughout the whole organization.

Activity 4.7   Applications-based systems development

Explain the term applications-based systems development and suggest why it has arisen as a fast method of developing software-based information systems within the business environment. Then outline and discuss all the possible advantages and disadvantages of using 'off-the-shelf', pre-coded software for the purposes of applications-based information systems development. Also outline the use and importance of agile software development methods within the system development process.

What issues of standardization and development consistency do you think need to be addressed when customizing software applications for specific business systems within an organization?

4.9 Outsourcing of information systems development

The outsourcing of information systems development activities is the practice of employing an external company to service a business organization's in-house ICT needs. This concept can also extend to the hiring of outside companies, or personnel, to design and develop an organization's internal information systems. With outsourcing, many of a business organization's ICT responsibilities are given over to outside control. For example, it is common practice for many smaller business organizations to outsource the operational functions of salaries (or payroll) and stock control. Some of the services and facilities offered by outsourcing agents include:

▶ staffing and managing a business organization's ICT centre;

▶ advising on, or designing, a business organization's information systems;

▶ developing business-specific applications for an organization;

▶ undertaking all a business organization's functional systems (e.g. stock control, payroll, sales order processing and purchase order processing).

Outsourcing should not be undertaken lightly by any business: choosing an outsourcing company requires care and consideration. Special attention must be paid to the contractual obligations incumbent upon both parties involved in any legal agreement. There are a number of reasons for initiating an outsourcing agreement:

▶ **Financial**: to reduce costs, improve cost control or make cost centres more effective and efficient.

▶ **Organizational**: to achieve organizational change, to facilitate mergers and acquisitions, or to devolve and restructure.

▶ **Strategy**: to facilitate strategic aims, to enable the business to focus on other core aims or to utilize an outsourcer's expertise.

▶ **Technical**: to improve access to technical resources, to gain technical expertise or to keep up to date with technological change.

There are several advantages of outsourcing:

▶ Fixed price contracts can be negotiated, which enable a level of predictability for organizations to plan more effectively.

▶ The variable costs inherent in any technology (i.e. overruns and over-budget increases) can be controlled by the conversion of these variable costs to a fixed cost contract.

▶ An organization has access to the latest ICT tools and techniques and can better compete with other organizations, irrespective of organizational size or influence.

▶ Human resources can be freed up to concentrate on the core activities of the business organization: people and employees can be focused on business activity rather than systems activity.

However, these advantages have to be weighed against the disadvantage of potential loss of control through outsourcing. An organization may become reliant on the outsourcer and therefore become dependent upon all conditions that may be set later on in the outsourcing contract. The main danger is being tied to an outsourcer with concurrent loss of control of the business resources of the organization. This is where shrewd contract negotiation is of paramount importance. Most organizations need to factor into their plans the legal costs of establishing an outsourcing relationship.

Activity 4.8 ## Outsourcing information systems development

Discuss what is meant by the term outsourcing as applied to information systems development within the business environment and explain the main advantages and disadvantages of outsourcing.

From your knowledge or experience, indicate aspects of outsourcing that may remove information systems control from a business organization. Create a mock pro forma (or outline agreement) between a business organization and an outsourcing agent that indicates the main activities of ICT outsourcing. How formal do you think this agreement should be in reality?

4.10 Business process re-engineering

So far in this chapter the approaches to business information systems development have deliberately not included issues relevant to the strategic level of a business organization. However, *business process re-engineering* (BPR) is a concept that addresses the overall strategic nature of ICT within a business organization and looks at business systems issues in the context of the overall strategic direction of the business. Therefore, BPR does not merely look at the functionality of individual information systems but looks at the purpose, objectives and assumptions of ICT to gauge whether the existing business systems are still appropriate to the organization's fundamental strategic objectives. BPR is a concept, rather than a rigid methodology. It attempts to re-engineer business processes that are underperforming, or no longer relevant, in the prevailing business conditions. One of the main principles of BPR is that re-engineering of processes is made possible and practicable by advances in information and communication technology.

BPR was very popular as a process for initiating systems change in the 1980s. It became somewhat discredited in the 1990s when it was associated with organizational downsizing. However, the late 1990s witnessed a reappraisal of BPR and its role in informing system development methods.

What is business process re-engineering (BPR)?

The process of fundamental and radical redesign of business systems' processes and practices to achieve dramatic improvements in critical, contemporary measures of performance, such as cost, quality, service and speed.

Source: Hammer and Champy, 2001.

The original drive within BPR was 'radical change' (i.e. radically changing the way a business organization perceived the role and purpose of its business activities). The emphasis was on what should be done to improve business performance, rather than what was done in the past (i.e. the systems' tendency to maintain the status quo). Therefore, BPR proposed that there was a need for business organizations to 're-invent' themselves by determining what they should be doing and how they should be achieving it. BPR became a high-risk systems activity that entailed an organization looking at the fundamental nature of its business activities, processes and purpose. Ultimately, the task of BPR was to find innovative ways to improve overall performance within the business environment.

BPR considered that organizations may attempt to re-engineer themselves for a number of reasons that flow from the belief that an organization may be underperforming. Reasons for initiating BPR include:

▶ The organization is facing the prospect of going out of business and has no alternative but to look at the very nature of its business activities and the information systems that support those activities.

▶ Competitive forces and change within the business environment may require a business organization to rethink the way information systems support the strategic objectives of the organization.

▶ The business organization may wish to establish a competitive edge over other organizations within its trading environment.

BPR was not a methodology that required incremental change; it required *fundamental* organizational change to the core business activities of the organization. With the advantage of hindsight, it is clear that BPR often led to major organizational upheaval. BPR required competent management of change measures being employed. BPR was fundamentally linked to improving overall business performance, therefore a business organization needed to establish a set of *performance criteria* to judge or evaluate whether improvements in business performance had been achieved through BPR. The use of performance criteria to judge the success of any form of ICT engineering was an important contribution to the theory and practice of information systems development. Performance criteria may include:

▶ end-user or customer satisfaction surveys;

▶ reduced systems variable and fixed costs across the whole business;

▶ increased systems productivity or efficiency as gauged by income and expenditure;

▶ increased human effectiveness and efficiency as gauged by productivity;

▶ increased overall business profit as gauged by return on resources employed.

Within the strategic domain the performance of information systems can be further assessed by the use of systems metrics (i.e. groups of measurement criteria) or even a systems audit grid. Figure 4.7 shows a common systems audit grid, used here to evaluate the usefulness of ICT to a business organization. The systems audit grid evaluates the strengths and weaknesses of ICT provision on the basis of *business contribution* and *technical quality*. If a system falls within the upper left-hand quadrant it indicates that the system is of low technical quality and low business contribution. Therefore, the business organization would get rid of (or divest) its ICT-based system and replace it with alternative systems.

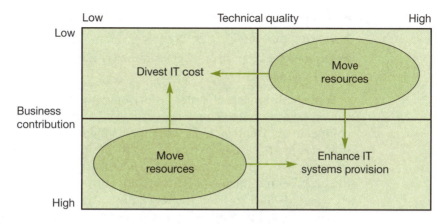

Figure 4.7 IT systems audit grid
Source: Earl, 1989.

However, if the system falls within the lower right-hand quadrant this indicates that both the technical quality and the business contribution of the system are high. Therefore, the system should be enhanced, with resources moved to support the enhancement.

This type of evaluation model can also be used to identify ICT opportunities that can be aligned within the overall strategy of a business organization. Nevertheless, there are a number of studies that indicate there is often an inherent reluctance among managers and executives in business organizations to undertake such a radical reappraisal of business processes. One of the major issues with any business systems development project is managing and controlling change – and eliminating the fear of unnecessary change and upheaval within the business environment.

Activity 4.9   Business process re-engineering

Discuss with your fellow students some of the possible effects of implementing BPR on the organizational structure of a business organization. Describe a set of five performance indicators that could be used to evaluate whether improvements in business performance have been achieved. Then explain the relationship between BPR and the attempt to align ICT with the strategic top-level of a business organization. Do you think that there is a role for business executives in deciding on information systems change?

4.11 Strategic information systems development

Strategic information systems development is not a self-contained methodology but an umbrella term for approaches to systems development that take into account the strategic nature and effects of business information systems change. The strategic area is particularly concerned with how ICT can be used to:

▶ achieve a competitive advantage within the business environment;

▶ improve overall business performance within an organization;

▶ develop new products or services;

▶ improve the relationship between the business organization and its customers and suppliers.

Strategic information systems development is concerned with finding innovative ways of undertaking business activity and increasing profit. Using ICT for competitive advantage is an attempt to increase income opportunities rather than merely try to reduce costs. Reducing business costs is an attempt to improve *efficiency*, while increasing income is an attempt to improve *effectiveness*. Many of the ideas behind the use of ICT for competitive advantage evolve out of work by Professor Michael Porter of Harvard University, which was mentioned in Chapter 1 of this book. He identified five main competitive forces found within the business environment (Porter, 1998). These forces are:

▶ the threat of new entrants;

▶ the threat of substitute services or products;

▶ the competition and rivalry between business organizations;

▶ the bargaining power of suppliers;

▶ the bargaining power of customers.

The premise of *competitive strategy* is that a business organization can achieve a competitive advantage within the business environment by dealing with one or all of the competitive forces more successfully than the other business organizations within that environment. For example, it may avoid the threat of new entrants, or even reduce the bargaining power of suppliers and customers within the business environment. The work of Professor Porter provides a framework for strategic information systems development in that it highlights a model for decision making with regard to strategic systems thinking. Porter's work was augmented by Professor Michael Earl in the late 1980s and 1990s, which highlighted the strategic role of ICT within the business environment. Earl set out a framework that indicated how ICT can be used to deal with Porter's five strategic forces. For example, ICT can be used to establish barriers to new entrants; ICT can be used to reduce the influence of customers and suppliers; and ICT can be used to add value to existing products and services or to create innovative new products and services.

This leads to the conceptual idea that business organizations need to formulate an *ICT strategy*. A superior ICT strategy can provide a competitive advantage in its own right. An ICT strategy should include an analysis of:

▶ the strategic aims and objectives of the organization;

▶ current business processes and ICT infrastructures;

▶ the use and application of ICT within the organization;

▶ the use and application of ICT for global competitive advantage.

These four aspects form the basis upon which an ICT strategy can be constructed, with each aspect being determined by using various tools and techniques. For example, the aims and objectives of a business organization can be elucidated by SWOT analysis, JAD meetings, or ascertaining the critical success factors inherent to the organization. SWOT analysis is used extensively in the business environment. SWOT analysis would include:

▶ Strengths: within the systems domain.

▶ Weaknesses: within the systems domain.

▶ Opportunities: offered by reconfiguring business systems.

▶ Threats: from competitors and from ineffective use of business systems.

The second aspect of ICT strategy – the analysis of current ICT configuration – can be supported by the use of performance criteria to determine the efficiency and effectiveness of the current information systems (i.e. their fitness for purpose). The third aspect of the ICT strategy will attempt to find possible opportunities provided by ICT, which requires a review of current and future systems and technologies. The fourth aspect of ICT strategy should consider the global ramifications of systems change on how the organization operates both nationally and internationally.

Care must be taken to avoid merely trying to match the ICT configuration of competitor organizations; instead, the investigation should establish how ICT should be better used to enhance the inherent strengths of a business organization to provide it with a competitive *edge* in the global business environment.

Activity 4.10 Strategic information systems development

Discuss what is meant by the term strategic information systems development and indicate why it is important to consider the strategic level of a business organization within systems development thinking.

Outline four main forces that impact upon the strategic nature of information systems within a business organization and compare them to Michael Porter's forces of competitive strategy.

Discuss with your fellow students the following: Do you believe that there are any further forces that can be added to Porter's list within competitive strategy? What factors influence strategic thinking at the executive level of a business organization?

4.12 Chapter summary

You will by this point have reviewed a number of alternative approaches to the traditional systems development life cycle. Predominant among these is the umbrella approach known as rapid applications development (RAD) that embraces a number of tools and techniques to hasten the process of information systems development within the business environment. The aims of any information systems development methodology are to:

▶ improve the process of information systems development;

▶ permit the effective monitoring of IS development;

▶ achieve accurate analysis of requirements;

▶ permit accurate documentation of the design process;

▶ allow IS to be delivered within a required time limit;

▶ ensure that the benefits outweigh the cost;

▶ ensure that the needs of the users are fully satisfied.

In turn, the reasons for using strategic information systems development techniques are to:

▶ achieve a competitive advantage;

▶ improve overall business performance;

▶ develop new products or services;

▶ improve the relationship between customers and suppliers;

▶ align the strategic aims and objectives of the organization;

▶ analyze current business processes and ICT;

▶ analyze ICT within the organization.

Within the RAD umbrella the DSDM framework has become a de facto worldwide standard for developing business systems solutions within tight time frames. Modern DSDM has incorporated a number of tools and techniques, particularly in software development, such as agile programming methods that combine extreme programming (XP) with the fundamental software project management techniques inherent in DSDM. With agile programming methods all the main effort is in the design because the construction and building of software code is almost costless. Therefore, the rapid and flexible nature of agile methods is closely allied to the principles of flexible systems development in DSDM. For example, agile methods are focused on meeting customer and end-user needs and are people-centred rather than process-oriented.

It is important to recognize that information systems development is not a prescriptive exercise, but rather it can be a flexible activity, where the scope of the system development process is shaped and determined by the specific dynamics and nature of the business environment in which an organization operates. User-focused systems development flexibility is of paramount importance to business organizations in the twenty-first century.

SHORT SELF-ASSESSMENT QUESTIONS

4.1 Explain why most business organizations are considered to be open systems within the business environment.

4.2 Indicate and explain why a knowledge of human activity systems is important to systems development within business organizations.

4.3 Outline and describe the four main principles of *rapid applications development* (RAD) for information systems development within the business environment.

4.4 Describe why systems development productivity is measured in *function points* and explain how RAD may increase the productivity of function points in systems development.

4.5 Explain the reasons why group-based activity is important to the philosophy of RAD and indicate why the use of the TOBI method encourages good group composition.

4.6 Outline and explain the four phases of rapid applications development and describe which particular tools and techniques are appropriate in each phase.

4.7 Explain why speed of applications and systems development is so important to a competitive business organization.

4.8 Define the term *joint applications development* (JAD) and explain the main emphasis within this approach to systems problem solving.

4.9 Outline and explain the three main principles behind JAD and describe the role and function of the independent *facilitator*.

4.10 Describe the function and use of the techniques of *story-boarding* and *rich pictures* to describe a system's overall environment.

4.11 List and explain the main advantages of using *prototyping* and suggest possible disadvantages in relation to end-user information systems development.

4.12 Outline and explain the five main steps of prototyping and suggest how these steps differ from the stages of the traditional systems development life cycle approach.

4.13 Outline and describe six generic areas where software applications are found within the business environment.

4.14 Describe the main advantages and disadvantages of using *pre-coded software application packages* in the building of business information systems.

4.15 Explain why one of the main weaknesses of *applications-based development* lies in the fact of idiosyncratic systems being developed without regard to commonly practised standards.

4.16 Define and explain what is meant by the term *business process re-engineering* (BPR) as used in business systems development.

4.17 Provide three main reasons why competitive organizations may wish to undertake the upheaval of business process re-engineering.

4.18 Explain how the formulation of an information systems and information technology *strategy* can provide a competitive advantage to a business organization.

4.19 Outline and describe the purpose and role of the nine main principles underlying the DSDM approach to building business systems.

4.20 Explain the meaning of the term *agile methods* and describe the main features of agile methods in relation to DSDM.

EXTENDED STUDENT ACTIVITIES

Individual reporting activity

Activity 4.1 at the beginning of this chapter required you to search your college or University online library facilities for any journal articles and other academic sources, with an aim of finding an article on one of the following areas:

▶ prototyping systems development

▶ object-oriented development

▶ business process re-engineering

▶ rapid applications development.

Use the article that you found as a case study to write a brief 500-word executive report that includes the following:

1 An explanation of how end-user information systems development impacts on the role of the traditional systems development life cycle (SDLC). Make sure you augment your explanation and argument by reference to your chosen case study.

2 An evaluation criteria model for assessing the costs and benefits of end-user development. Figure 4.7 shows an ICT systems audit grid, developed by Michael Earl, which can be used as a basis for developing a criteria model for assessing the value of ICT.

3 Advice on the creation of end-user guidelines for an employee of a business organization engaged in information systems development, to ensure common standards and consistency of systems development across the organization.

Group-based activity 1

Outline all the possible advantages and disadvantages of outsourcing the function of information systems development. Then discuss whether giving up the information systems development function to an outside agent may lead to a loss of control within a business organization of its ICT functions.

Study the following hypothetical quote:

> Applications software can be rented, leased or purchased outright from a software applications vendor, who may develop generic application programs that are sold to many business organizations. Such software applications are often known as 'off-the-shelf' programs; many business organizations use off-the-shelf software applications to support various business processes and systems.

Outline all the possible advantages and disadvantages of using off-the-shelf software for the purposes of applications-based information systems development. Then discuss the issues that need to be addressed when customizing software applications for specific business processes and systems within a business organization.

Discuss some of the possible problems of standardization of information systems development when using applications-based development to build business information systems.

REFERENCES AND FURTHER STUDY

Books and articles

An asterisk (*) indicates a seminal text – a major source for later academic developments.

Ambler, S.W. (2002) *Agile Modelling: Effective Practices for Extreme Programming and the Unified Process*, John Wiley and Sons, ISBN: 0471202827

Bell, S. and Wood-Harper, T. (1998) *Rapid Information Systems Development: Systems Analysis and Systems Design in an Imperfect World*, McGraw-Hill Education, ISBN: 0077094271

Bennett, S., McRobb, S. and Farmer, R. (2001) *Object Oriented Systems Analysis and Design (using UML)*, McGraw-Hill Education, ISBN: 0077098641

Beynon-Davies, P., Mackay, H., Slack, R. and Tudhope, D. (1996) 'Rapid applications development: the future of business systems development?', 6th Annual Business Information Technology Conference, Manchester Metropolitan University, UK, 7 November, pp. 133–43

Champy, J. (2002) *X-engineering the Corporation*, Holder and Stoughton, ISBN: 0887308805

Cockburn, A. (2002) *Agile Software Development: Software Through People*, Addison-Wesley, ISBN: 0201699699

Earl, M.J. (1989) *Management Strategies for Information Technology*, Prentice-Hall, ISBN: 0135516560

Elliott, G. (1997) 'Rapid applications development (RAD): an odyssey of information systems methods, tools and techniques?', *Electronic Journal of Financial Information Systems*, www.shu.ac.uk/schools/fsl/fisjnl/vol1996/pprs1997/gelliot/fis97.htm

Fitzgerald, B., Russo, N. and Stolterman, E. (2002) *Information Systems Development: Methods in Action*, Osborne McGraw-Hill, ISBN: 0077098366

Grahan, I. (1999) *Requirements Engineering and Rapid Development: An Object Oriented Approach*, Addison-Wesley, ISBN: 0201360470

Hammer, M. and Champy, J. (1993) *Re-engineering the Corporation: A Manifesto for Business Revolution*, HarperCollins, ISBN: 0887306403

Hammer, M. and Champy, J. (2001) *Re-engineering the Corporation: A Manifesto for Business Revolution*, Nicholas Brealey Publishing, ISBN: 1857880978

Hughes, C. and Hughes, T. (2000) *Linux Rapid Applications Development*, John Wiley and Sons, ISBN: 0764547402

*Martin, J. (1990) *Rapid Applications Development*, Macmillan USA, ISBN: 0023767758

Palmer, S and Felsing, M. (2002) *Practical Guide to Feature-Driven Development*, Prentice Hall PTR, ISBN: 0130676152

Porter, M.E. (1998) *Competitive Strategies: Techniques for Analyzing Industries and Competitors*, Simon and Schuster, ISBN: 0684841487

Stapleton, J. (1997) *Dynamic Systems Development Method: The Method in Practice*, Addison-Wesley, ISBN: 0201178893

Stapleton, J. (2003) DSDM: *A Framework for Business Centred Development (The Agile Software Development Series)*, Addison-Wesley, ISBN: 0321112245

Journals

Communications of the ACM
European Journal of Information Systems
Information Systems Journal

Web resources

Dynamic Systems Development Method Consortium (UK/North America/global) – promotes the use of DSDM as a de facto global systems development framework.
www.dsdm.org   www.na.dsdm.org

Agile Alliance (USA) – access to information and discussion material on agile methods, extreme programming and DSDM.
www.agilealliance.com

New Software Development and Systems Development Methods (USA/global) – a resource of papers by Martin Fowler, consultant and software engineer.
www.martinfowler.com/articles/newMethodology.html

Rapid Development (global) – academic papers on Rapid Application Development by various authors.
www.processimprovement.com/resources/rapid.htm

Chapter 5

Information systems modelling

When you have studied this chapter you will be able to:

▶ contrast and explain the difference between process modelling and data modelling within information systems development;

▶ indicate and describe the use and application of tools and techniques for modelling information systems within the business environment;

▶ understand and explain the difference between hard and soft tools and techniques for building effective business information systems;

▶ evaluate and explain the advantages and disadvantages of the various tools and techniques for process modelling and data modelling;

▶ describe the characteristics and usability of the various tools and techniques for analysis, design, implementation and evaluation of information systems;

▶ understand the importance of prototype modelling within the business information systems domain.

5.1 Introduction to information systems modelling

This chapter will introduce a range of business information technology tools and techniques used to assist the development and delivery of a systems development project. A number of traditional and modern tools and techniques are explored, putting into context the historical and current approaches to designing, modelling and building information systems. Any systems that incorporate human activity interacting with technology will by their very nature be considered *complex systems*. Therefore, to understand the systems environment a number of tools and techniques need to be utilized to model information systems behaviour.

The process of modelling information systems behaviour is a fundamental part of the activity of information systems development. Systems behaviour can be modelled graphically (i.e. using pictures, icons and diagramming techniques) to reveal data and information flows and systems connectivity. However, before explaining the role, use and nature of each systems modelling tool and technique, it is important to understand the difference between *process modelling* and *data modelling*. Each of these modelling techniques requires the use of a range of different tools and techniques.

What are tools and techniques?

A tool is anything that is used to assist a person in their activities; a technique is the body of procedures and methods of a science, art or activity.

Source: Webster's Encyclopedic Dictionary

A central theme of systems development is modelling the information systems environment. A *model* can be described as an abstract representation of the real world. The analysis and design stages of the information systems development process use modelling techniques to describe aspects of the proposed information system; a model is a useful way of describing and understanding how an information system will operate in reality. Modelling can provide flexibility, in that it allows various *parameters* (or constant variables) to be altered at will to analyze what factors might impact on the proposed information system.

What is a model?

A representation of the facts, factors and influences of an object or real world situation.

In the context of information systems development, the modelling process is concerned with studying the functions and activities of information systems in operation. A *process* is a progressive series of activities, or changes, that carry through the stages or phases of the development process. The systems analysis and systems design aspects of information systems development rely on a number of tools and techniques for describing business systems activity. This activity can be separated into three business processes as follows:

▶ decision-making processes
▶ information-based processes
▶ functional processes.

These various processes must be decomposed into their *logical* parts so that a *conceptual model* of the information system (or sub-system components) can be constructed. The development aspects of systems analysis and systems design are concerned with two primary activities:

▶ **Process modelling**: representing the various processes that are found within an information systems domain.
▶ **Data modelling**: understanding and documenting data that forms the body and content of an information system.

More recently, there has been a resurgence of interest in object-oriented development and evolutionary prototyping, which attempts to include processes and data within one model (as mentioned in Chapter 4).

Within the information systems modelling domain a model is developed to provide a medium of communication between the users and stakeholders within the information systems environment being studied. Some of these stakeholders may be technical experts, while others may not possess a technical (or ICT) background. Therefore, the modelling techniques used need to be equally obvious to both technical users and non-technical stakeholders. The purpose of the model is to:

▶ communicate an idea or message that can be discussed and refined;

▶ represent an abstraction of reality – an *abstract* is a summary, or simplification, of a more complex real-world situation.

To be successful, the modelling technique requires:

▶ a common understanding of the model's components and elements – these are often referred to as the model's *constructs*;

▶ a commonly accepted and understood *notation* whereby a systems situation can be described and annotated with pictures, symbols and icons that are familiar to all those involved in systems modelling;

▶ a set of commonly shared *rules* that determine the way that a model is developed and presented.

Business is a human activity system. Therefore, the modelling of business information systems not only involves understanding data and information flows, but also involves understanding human interaction and behaviour within a systems environment. Most information systems modelling activity involves developing a high-level *conceptual model* that represents an overall understanding of the system's domain. This is then augmented at a lower level with an analysis of the logical and structural aspects of the model and the physical components of the model.

The study of systems behaviour can be separated into two parts:

▶ human behaviour and interaction within a systems domain

▶ data behaviour and interaction within a systems domain.

Data and information are fundamental components within information systems. In modelling data and data transformation, there are four main components:

▶ **Agent/node/connector**: the receiver or originator of data within an information systems domain.

▶ **Data flow**: the direction of data flowing within and between the agents and nodes of an information system.

▶ **Data store**: the location where the data is stored. Within a data repository the data can be structurally modelled using entity-relationship-attribute diagramming techniques.

▶ **Process**: the activity that transforms data within the systems environment.

These four components can be graphically represented. The agent/node/connector is often graphically represented as a circle. The data flow is represented by an arrow or a multidirectional arrow. The data store is often represented by a rectangular box, often with the right-hand side open. The process is often graphically represented by a rectangular box with all sides closed. However, there are a number of different diagramming techniques that also employ similar and extended diagramming symbols.

5.2 Process modelling

Process modelling is concerned with identifying and analyzing the various processes of an information system. This technique attempts to decompose the range of processes and functions found within an information systems domain into more manageable and understandable parts. For example, a complex system can be decomposed down from the highest level into greater levels of detail, which is normally known as *functional decomposition*. A systems process will usually have one (or more) of the following characteristics:

▶ inputs, outputs and information flows

▶ control and management of an organization

▶ decision making.

The technique of decomposition will normally continue until the most elementary processes are identified. Figure 5.1 shows an example of a business area known as Business Area 1 decomposed into three processes, known as A, B and C. Process C is further decomposed into elementary processes known as D, E and F. Figure 5.2 shows the activities of a finished goods stock control system, which has been hierarchically decomposed into various sub-processes. Process modelling is normally performed in a structured and disciplined fashion and will continue until the most elementary processes are identified within the overall information system. The symbols used are shown in greater detail in Figure 5.7 later on in this chapter.

It must be remembered that the *logical* aspects of the information system are being modelled and not the *physical* aspects of that system. Therefore, for analysis and design purposes, the logical must be separated from the physical within systems development thinking. To do this, the first task of process modelling is to define the boundaries of the system under analysis, then the main subsequent

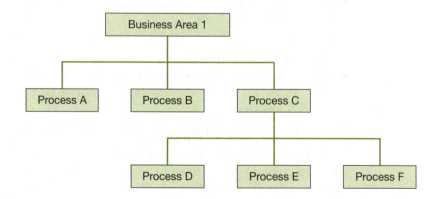

Figure 5.1 Process decomposition

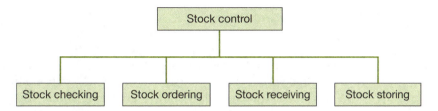

Figure 5.2 Stock control system decomposition

task is to decompose higher-level processes into lower-level constituent processes. Decomposition is a *top-down* approach to the analysis of business systems processes. All systems *processes* should be defined as verbs (or action words), such as recording, handling or processing, and there will usually be an *object* of the process, which should be defined as a noun (or naming word), such as stock, product or department. For example, within the process of handling stock, handling is the (action) verb and stock is the (object) noun. It should be noticed that the processes often end in 'ing', as in handling and recording, which indicates activity, which is an underlying principle in defining a system from an inanimate object.

> **Did you know?**
>
> Conceptual modelling requires an understanding of grammatical language in order to separate the logical thinking from physical thinking in the analysis and design of information systems. A verb is an action or doing word (e.g. talking, computing, processing). An adverb is a word that modifies an adjective or verb and expresses a relation of place, time or manner (e.g. gently, very, now, where). An adjective is an attribute added to the name of something to describe it more fully, and a noun is a word used to name a person, place, thing, state or quality (e.g. Edward, London, chair, beauty).

It is during the activity of *process analysis* that the major group interaction often occurs between business specialists and technical specialists. Therefore, it is important that all the identifiable systems processes are mutually agreed and confirmed by both the parties involved in the systems development project. Process modelling assists the activity of analyzing and designing an information system by using structured tools and techniques that bring the technical specialist and user views of the system into line; this is particularly useful in the designing of systems that do not stand alone, but are integrated with other systems within the business environment.

Activity 5.1   Process modelling

Discuss and outline the main characteristics of process modelling and explain what is meant by functional decomposition. Then explain why process analysis should describe business systems processes as verbs (or action words), which imply an activity within the business environment. Discuss the meaning and nature of a conceptual model. Why is a conceptual model so important in defining the boundaries of an information system?

5.3 Data modelling

Data modelling is concerned with data structures and the *elements* of data, rather than information systems processes that are the preserve of process modelling. Data modelling is strongly related to aspects of *data storage* and *data structuring*; it is concerned with understanding, analyzing and documenting data and information that forms the body of an information system. As with process analysis, it is important to separate out the physical data model from the logical data model. The aim is for the data model to be implementation-independent – in other words, it should not matter whether the technology used is IT-based (such as a relational database), or even manual (such as a card file), as long as the logical model is correct. Therefore, the logical model will not be dependent upon the prevailing technology and should not be affected by technological change in the business environment; consequently a *logical data model* can be transcribed across a range of different information technologies and business environments.

Data modelling should systematically attempt to identify the data in a business environment and the relationship between data elements within the organization. This analysis of the relationship between data elements is known as *data structuring* and the objective is to identify the data elements and analyze their structure and meaning within a business organization. This data analysis activity relies on the gathering of data and information from the employees of a business organization and other related sources. This can be done through observation of work tasks, interviews, analyzing formal output documentation from various processes, and other human and electronic data-capturing techniques. Once the data is collected and collated it can be modelled.

The data model is produced by using a number of tools and techniques. One particularly important technique is *entity modelling*, which aims to establish the relationship between data elements within a business organization – an entity can be described as a body or object such as customer, supplier, or employee. Techniques and tools used in the data modelling activity of information systems development include:

▶ entity-relationship diagrams (ERDs)

▶ entity life histories

▶ normalization.

Since data and information are the lifeblood of most business organizations, data modelling is an important activity in the analysis and design of information systems. Data modelling has a number of benefits:

▶ It describes logical data relationships and not physical data relationships. This makes data modelling a stable activity even in environments of technological change. Therefore, data modelling is technology independent.

▶ It can be used by both technical specialists and business specialists. It can also be used to establish and confirm the user's data requirements of an information system.

▶ It is usually deterministic and rule-based, which permits it to be understood across systems and organizations. Therefore, data modelling is not specific to any one business organization and it can be readily translated into a computerized database model.

Data modelling

Explain what is meant by the terms data structuring and entity modelling and explain the various ways by which data may be captured and recorded within a business organization. (Clue: data capture can be carried out by investigating existing business documentation, or by a range of other means such as observation of employees and work practices, interviews and questionnaires.) List and explain ten methods of capturing and recording data: five must be electronic (or IT-based) methods and five must be human-based methods (or a mixture of both). For example, lorries that deliver building-site raw materials for construction purposes are often electronically weighed on a platform sensor that automatically calculates the weight of raw materials being carried by the lorry. (Clue: think of the retail and banking sector and how data is captured and recorded.)

5.4 Tools and techniques of process modelling

There are a number of tools and techniques used to document the analysis and design activities of information systems development. The most widely used tools within process modelling are:

- ▶ flowcharting
- ▶ data flow diagrams (DFDs)
- ▶ decision tables
- ▶ structured English.

Flowcharting

One of the underlying problems with agreeing a logical (or conceptual) model of processes within a system is the fact that people will generally describe work processes in physical terms. For example, the recording of accounting data may be described as 'I sit at a computer and type in various numbers each morning' or the handling of stock may be described as 'I move this box from the stock room to the distribution department each Tuesday afternoon'. The latter description may be indicating the logical activity of handling stock but this is not apparent from this physical description. Therefore, it is imperative to convert physical activity to logical processes by using a structured framework of systems tools and techniques. The tools mentioned above help to ease the task of converting the physical description of existing activities into a logical process model.

Before a logical model can be constructed there is a need to document the processes in some form of descriptive language. Flowcharts show the relationship between systems (or applications) within a business organization; such flowcharts can exist in two main forms as follows:

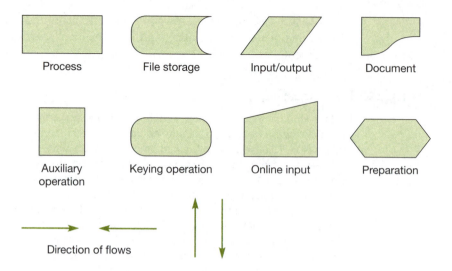

Figure 5.3 Basic systems flowcharting symbols

▶ **Systems flowcharts**: describing an entire information system. Figure 5.3 shows a set of basic systems flowcharting symbols. Notice that the central symbol is a rectangular box that represents the systems process.

▶ **Program flowcharts**: describing the steps that are followed in a specific computer program. Figure 5.4 shows a set of basic program flowcharting symbols.

Systems flowcharting can be further divided into:

▶ **Simplified systems flowcharts**: showing the relationship between various systems processes within a business organization. For example, Figure 5.5 shows the simplified relationship between three systems processes of sales order processing, finished goods stock control and accounting.

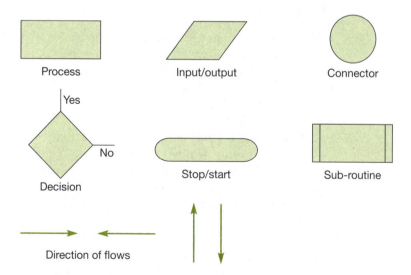

Figure 5.4 Basic program flowcharting symbols

Figure 5.5 Simplified systems flowchart

▶ **Detailed systems flowcharts**: showing all the various documents, files and activities that impact on a particular systems process. Figure 5.6 shows a detailed systems flowchart for a typical accounting system process.

Program flowcharts are drawn using three control structures for executing instructions:

▶ **Sequence structure**: a series of statements that are executed in the order in which they appear. For example, statement B will follow statement A.

▶ **Selection structure**: a series of statements that test a condition, such as true or false, yes or no, off or on, 1 or 0. Depending upon whether the results of the test are true or false, one of two alternative instructions will be executed.

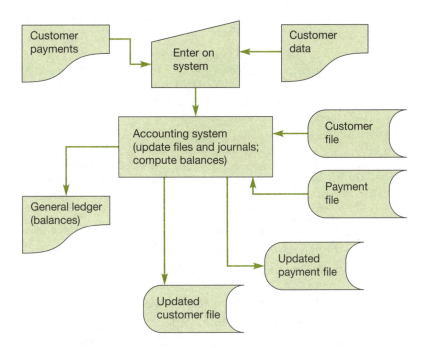

Figure 5.6 Detailed systems flowchart

▶ **Iteration structure**: a series of statements that repeats an instruction as long as the results of the condition are true. For example, statement B will be executed as long as condition X is always satisfied.

Systems flowcharts document the sequence and integration of processes that occur within an information system, and data and information input and output are of paramount importance. Flowcharts use formalized symbols (see Figures 5.3 and 5.4) to represent information flows and the related processing activities. Systems flowcharts depict the flow of documentation (and records) as inputs and outputs in an information system. The wider the symbol vocabulary, the more articulate can be the analysis. Therefore, flowcharting is a graphic form of representing information flows within a business organization.

Flowcharts have a number of advantages in assisting in process analysis and the development of a process model:

▶ Program flowcharts provide a structured framework for designing logical software programs that abide by certain design principles.

▶ Flowcharts are a useful representation of a process that graphically shows the technical specialist and the business specialist the correctness and suitability of the process design.

▶ They can be incorporated into any systems or end-user documentation as instructional or reference material for continued systems maintenance.

Activity 5.3 Flowcharting

Discuss the difference between systems flowcharting and program flowcharting and describe why such graphical flowcharting techniques are important in the activity of information systems analysis and design.

To build effective information systems, we need to be able to understand the operation of logical model building applying flowcharting techniques. Read carefully the following narrative which describes decision-making activities in both physical and logical terms (remember you will need to separate out the logical aspects of the narrative in order to build a logical conceptual model):

> Gillian Baker met Steve Jones a few days ago, when Steve had said he would meet Gillian at the Abbey Conference meeting room on Friday afternoon at 3.00 pm. Gillian wanted to attend the meeting but was not sure if Steve was going to chair the meeting or whether it would be chaired by an outsider (in which case she would not attend). Anyway, Gillian was not sure whether she would be busy Friday afternoon and she certainly was not going to go along to the meeting if no one else was attending from her department.

1 Separate out the logical from the physical aspects of Gillian's job.

2 Break down the decisions into their component parts within the system.

3 Identify the decisions and label them 1 or 0 depending on whether the decision is yes or no.

4 Identify what action will be undertaken to acquire any further information for each decision in the decision chain.

5 Draw a flowchart to describe the decision-making activities of Gillian Baker.

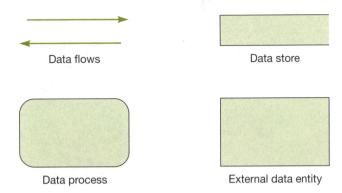

Figure 5.7 Symbols used for data flow diagramming

Data flow diagrams (DFDs)

Data flow diagrams (DFDs) emphasize the structured nature of data processes. They assist in the construction of a logical system model, unlike flowcharts, which often describe a system in terms of the physical files and documentation and storage mediums. Data flow diagrams graphically show flows of data within an information system and the various processes that act upon (and transform) that data. DFDs are very important for defining the logical design of an information system. Data flows through a system can be manual or automated and involve human interaction; however, DFDs do not make any distinction because it is the logical aspects of the system that are investigated: there exists logical and physical independence. Data flow diagramming is a graphical technique that can be used as documentation of an information system or a communications tool between the technical and business specialists of a business organization. Data flow diagrams use a restricted set of symbols, which are shown in Figure 5.7.

> **Did you know?**
>
> DFDs are a widely used technique within the structured systems analysis and design method (SSADM), which is a development methodology much in use in government departments in the UK and many large North American organizations.

It can be seen that data flow diagrams can be constructed by using just four graphical symbols:

▶ **Data flow**: represented by an arrow that points into or out of a data process; it indicates that data is moving from one process to another process and the direction of the flow. The nature of the data flow is uniquely labelled as it passes through the system. Data flows can be single data elements or multiple data elements. Data flows may consist of computer files, reports or other data representations.

▶ **Data process**: represented by a round-edged box or sometimes a straight-edged and closed rectangle. The process is an activity that transforms or alters the data in some way. For example, the data may be sorted, merged or verified. The

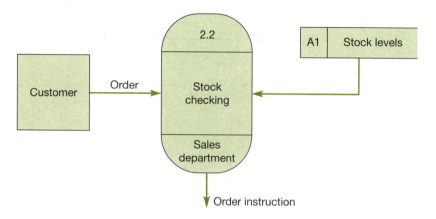

Figure 5.8 DFD symbols (process of stock checking)

round-edged box symbol usually has three compartments at the top, middle and bottom of the box. The top compartment contains a reference number for the process. The middle compartment contains the description of the process. The bottom compartment contains information on the location where the process occurs (*see* Figure 5.8). The data process box should usually have a data flow into the box and a data outflow from the box.

▶ **Data stores**: represented by an open-ended rectangle that is uniquely labelled. Data stores are where data flows finally stop. A data store contains data from a process or stored data for retrieval to a process. Unlike flowcharts, a data store symbol within a DFD does not indicate the type of storage media used; it can be an electronic file or even a manual handwritten list. The data store has two compartments: one for a reference code and the other indicating the name of the data store (*see* Figure 5.8).

▶ **External data entity**: represented by a rectangle or square. This is the external source or destination of data (*see* Figure 5.8) – where data may finally stop. External data entities may be external to the business organization, such as customers or suppliers. They may also be another separate system within the business organization. These external data entities are often referred to as data *sources* or data *sinks*. A source indicates data coming into a business organization and a sink indicates data leaving an organization and being received by an external entity.

The advantage of DFDs is that they use only four symbols and they are independent of the method of processing, so they can be used to describe either IT-based or manual systems. Figure 5.8 shows the DFD symbols being used for a typical business process known as sales order processing, which has been the example used previously to describe flowcharting. Within sales order processing there is an activity known as stock checking to determine whether a business organization holds sufficient stock to meet a customer order.

Data flow diagrams are constructed to visualize an information system at various decomposed levels of detail. The top level of detail can be broken down into deeper and deeper layers of detail. The very top level of symbolic representation

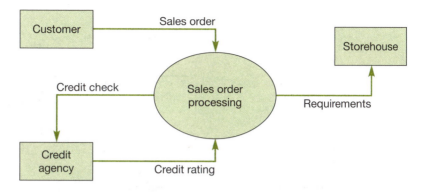

Figure 5.9 Context diagram (level 0) for a sales order processing system

is known as a *context diagram*. This is a general and broad representation of an information system. This context diagram can be broken into successive layers of detail. Therefore, the levels of a DFD are constructed using a top-down approach that begins with a context diagram and is broken down into level 1, level 2, level 3 and so on until the absolute level of detail is reached. The top-level context diagram consists of the overall system being represented as a single process box, which alludes to the external entities. The data flows to and from the external data entities are represented by labelled arrows. The decomposition of the context diagram into further levels provides greater detail of the system being studied. This process of decomposition in the context of DFDs is known as *levelling*.

Figure 5.9 shows the top level, or context diagram, for a sales order processing system. The system is represented by as a single process circle (or 'black-box') which alludes to the external entities of customer, storehouse and credit agency. This can be ascribed as level 0.

The level 0 diagram is known as the context diagram because it shows the extent of the system boundaries. In Figure 5.9 the system's boundaries are shown

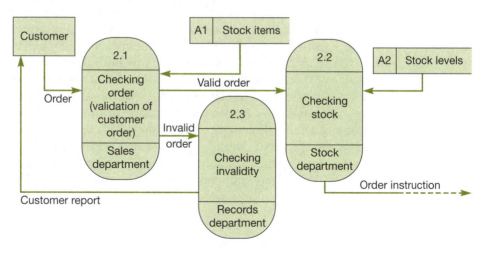

Figure 5.10 Level 1 diagram for a sales order processing system (checking order)

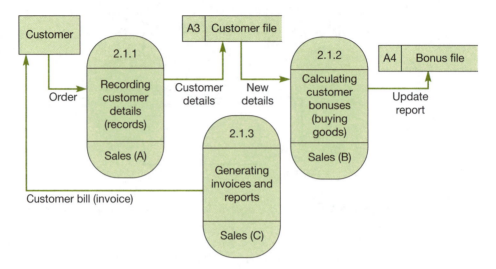

Figure 5.11 Level 2 diagram for a sales order processing system (checking order)

by a circle bounding the system; in this case the sales order processing system. The level 0 context diagram should also normally show all the external entities (indicated by square boxes), and the inputs and outputs (indicated by narrated arrows). Figure 5.10 shows this context diagram broken down to level 1, giving more detail of the processes of the sales order processing system. Within sales order processing there is a sub-process known as stock checking where a customer's order is checked against existing stock items held by the organization. If these are available, items of finished stock will be dispatched to the customer, after all other checks (such as the customer's credit rating) have been made relating to the order. Figure 5.10 shows the process of *checking order* and its related level 1 processes and data storage.

Within data flow diagramming the processes can be 'exploded' into greater levels of detail. Figure 5.11 shows a level 2 diagram revealing flows that exist within the process, known as checking order. The process of checking order has been exploded down to three sub-processes of recording customer details, calculating customer bonuses, and generating invoices and reports.

The DFDs can be refined and agreed by both the business specialists and the technical specialists until both are satisfied that the system has been correctly documented. The advantage of DFDs is that they are usually understood by business systems end users with relatively little instruction. Alongside the activity of levelling will be the activity of collecting details of each piece of data used in the DFDs. Details about each piece of data used in the data flows is contained in a *data dictionary* which contains information about the data flows and data stores in the DFDs. Data dictionaries provide information on all the data elements within an information system.

Activity 5.4   Data flow diagrams

Discuss the role, purpose and function of data flow diagrams (DFDs) within process modelling and describe how DFDs are broken down into lower and lower levels of detail. Then explain what is meant by a context diagram and draw and annotate a context diagram to represent level 0 for a purchase order processing system.

Decision tables

Another tool that can be used to document the logic of process modelling is the *decision table*. This is a tool that facilitates the documentation of logical process modelling. The processes that are identified in DFDs are often described in written narrative, but sometimes this is not adequate for the purpose of describing complex actions within a data process. What is required is a decision table to describe what is taking place in the process by defining the *conditions* and *actions* of the process. Decision tables are a tabular representation of complex conditions and actions that cannot easily be documented in written form. Decision tables can be separated into four separate quadrants:

Condition stub	Condition rules
Action stub	Action entries

The top line lists the conditions to be tested, whereas the bottom line lists the range of possible actions to be undertaken. Each decision table contains:

▶ **Condition stub**: listing all the possible conditions that can arise during a process.

▶ **Action stub**: listing all the possible actions that can occur within a process.

▶ **Condition rules**: containing a binary entry for each possible combination of conditions, for example, 'yes' or 'no', 'on' or 'off', '1' or '0'.

▶ **Action entries**: indicating the action to be performed under specific and unique conditions.

Decision tables are a way of representing the logic of a complex process where a number of actions can be undertaken given a finite set of conditions. For example, consider a process within sales order processing known as *validating customer order*. This process checks if a customer has a satisfactory credit rating or is an acceptable person to trade with for a business organization. If the customer has a satisfactory credit rating, or is a regular cash payer, the order will be approved for goods to be sent to the customer. If the customer does not have a satisfactory credit rating, or is not a regular cash payer, the order will be rejected. Therefore, the two conditions are credit satisfactory or cash payer. Each condition will have an action entry of either 'yes' or 'no'. The two actions will be either

Table 5.1 Decision table for validating a customer order

	1	2	3	4
Credit satisfactory	Y	Y	N	N
Cash payer	Y	N	Y	N
Approve order	x	x	x	
Reject order				x

approve order or reject order. The decision table is represented in Table 5.1. There are obviously only four possible permutations for the conditions of credit satisfactory and cash payer (i.e. YY, YN, NY, NN).

Activity 5.5 Decision tables

To determine price reductions (rebates) for buying in bulk, the business organization Norman Payne Enterprises divides customers into two categories: those who buy 500 or more units of a product at one time and those who buy less than 500 units at one time. If the number of units bought is equal to 500, or more than 500, the overall price is reduced by 15 per cent. If the number of units sold is 500 or more and the customer has a Payne Enterprises Charge Card, the overall price is reduced by 25 per cent. Using this example:

1 Discuss why a business organization would wish to charge customers a different price according to the amount bought and having a charge card.

2 Draw a flowchart to represent the decisions that need to be made regarding the different delivery charges.

3 Draw a decision table to reflect the conditions and actions to determine the different delivery charges according to sales region code.

Structured English

In addition to flowcharting, data flow diagramming and decision tables, another technique used to represent processes is *structured English*, which is a precise approach to process or procedure design that uses a restricted sub-set of the natural English language. It uses plain English statements rather than graphic symbols to describe the processing stages and logic of the information systems activities. This is sometimes referred to as *pseudo-code*. There are a number of rules that underpin the use of structured English:

▶ complex sentences and grammatical structures are broken down into logical parts;

▶ statements contain a precise verb and object (e.g. compute tax);

▶ adjectives, adverbs and other words of vague meaning are avoided;

▶ words and sentences that are irrelevant to the process are ignored;

▶ unique terms are used to identify items of data within the process;

▶ data terms found within DFDs and associated data dictionaries are consistently used.

What decision tables, logic flowcharting and structured English provide is a structured approach analyzing processes that may assist the eventual technical systems programming or applications-based development. However, there is an obvious trade-off between wishing to maintain the user-friendliness of the graphical approach and the need to encourage structured program design and construction.

Activity 5.6

Structured English

Define the term structured English as used in the context of business information systems development and indicate its usefulness to the activity of process modelling. Then describe the rules that underpin the use of structured English and explain why the technique is sometimes referred to as pseudo-code.

5.5 Tools and techniques of data modelling

The development of database technology and database management systems (DBMS) has led to a greater emphasis within the modelling of business information systems on data and data structures. Data analysis techniques were initially developed to assist the construction and implementation of database systems. Therefore, this area is strongly related to issues of data storage and database structuring. However, data modelling is also a useful and general technique used to analyze any data structure found within the business information systems environment. The main technique used in data modelling is known as *entity-attribute modelling*. The essence of entity-attribute modelling is to establish the *relationship* between data elements within a business organization. An entity can be defined as a body or object such as a customer, supplier, employee or any other noun that is of interest to the business organization.

The data structures of an organization can be graphically represented through the use of *entity-relationship diagrams* (ERDs), a design tool that represents all of the information requirements of a system. Entity-relationship diagrams use just three component objects to model data relationships within an information system. These components can be used to construct a model that reveals the data configuration and structures of an information system. The three component objects of the ERD are as follows:

▶ **Entity**: an object or thing of interest that needs to be stored as data.

▶ **Attribute**: the property of some given entity.

▶ **Relationship**: the association and interrelationship between two or more entities.

The *entity-attribute-relationship model*, shown in Figure 5.12, is sometimes known by the initials EAR, or sometimes the E-R model for short. An *entity* is something about which data is to be stored. The key characteristic of an entity is that it is capable of independent existence within an organization. For example, a customer, supplier, employee or product might be entities about which a business may wish to store information. These objects are of interest to the business organization. Entities are usually represented as rectangles. An *attribute* is a fact

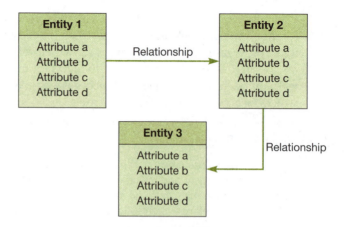

Figure 5.12 The entity-attribute-relationship model

that needs to be stored about an entity. For example, the attributes of the entity of customer may be name, address, unique customer identification number and credit status. Another example may be the entity of employee, which may have the attributes name, address, data of birth, employee number, and department name. Attributes can be considered properties of an entity. Within database construction an attribute is known as a field. Each entity should possess a unique attribute that is often known as the *key attribute*. The key attribute is a separate and unique characteristic that is not duplicated within the overall data structure of an information system. For example, a unique customer number could be a key attribute of the entity of customer. If this was the case, a unique customer number should identify only one customer of the business organization and not multiple customers.

Entity types within a business organization may bear some *relationship* to one another within that business organization. For example, there may be a relationship between the entities of customer and order, or between the entities of employee and department. However, it may be the case that not all entities will bear relationships to all other entities within the business organization. The relationship between entities is shown in an EAR by lines between the rectangular boxes. The relationship between entities is of particular importance to data modelling. The relationship between two entities will be addressed with some form of descriptive term that defines the relationship between the two entities. For example, within the relationship 'customer places order', the 'customer' and the 'order' are entities and the descriptive relationship name is 'places'. Another example might be the relationship between 'customer returns product', where 'customer' and 'product' are entities and 'returns' is the descriptive relationship term.

For example, in a typical business organization the first task of data modelling would be to identify the entities of the organization. Figure 5.13 shows four identified entities of employee, department, management staff and technical staff. It can be seen that there is a relationship between the employee and the department and employee and management staff (which might indicate the

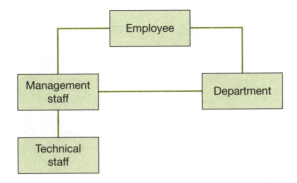

Figure 5.13 Entity modelling

employee's line manager). However, no attributes have been defined for the entities in Figure 5.13. Figure 5.14 shows the same entity relationships with information on the attributes of each entity (the verbs between the boxes). The attributes should define the properties of the entity.

Notice that an employee may only have one department, but a department entity may have many employees. Also, each department appears to have many managers. What has been revealed is the fact that there may be multiple relationships between entities. Data modelling using ERDs gives rise to three generic relationships:

▶ one-to-one (denoted by the symbolic ratio of 1:1)

▶ one-to-many (denoted by the symbolic ratio of 1:m)

▶ many-to-many (denoted by the symbolic ratio of m:m)

These relationships are graphically shown in Figure 5.15. It shows a one-to-one relationship between the two entities of man and woman. The descriptive relationship term is known as marries. This one-to-one relationship will occur if one man is allowed to marry only one woman. If one man is allowed to marry many women, then the relationship will be described as one-to-many. The diagram also shows a one-to-many relationship, as when a customer places an order. The many-to-many relationship is represented by many customers buying many products (or many products delivered to many customers).

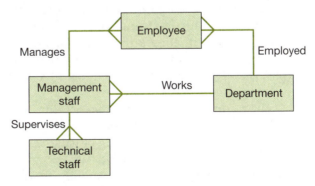

Figure 5.14 Entity modelling with relationships

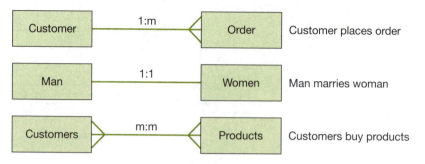

Figure 5.15 Entity relationships

There are four main stages to *entity analysis* within data modelling:

▶ define and set the boundaries for analysis;
▶ define the entities and establish the relationships between entities;
▶ establish the attributes and key attribute for each entity;
▶ normalize all the entities.

Activity 5.7 Entity-relationship diagramming

Define and explain the technique of entity-relationship diagramming to analyze a business information system, then create an E-R diagram to show the relationships between the entities of supplier and order, and between product and order part.

Entity-relationship diagrams can be converted to a physical database, where each of the entities will become a table (sometimes known as a record) and each attribute will become a field on a table. To find the most effective database design, a technique known as *normalization* is used. This is the process of creating the most effective design for the data model. Normalization aims to improve the logical design of an entity-relationship diagram by making it free of redundant data, so that each fact is only recorded in one place, and by making it flexible enough to allow future additions of entities, attributes and relationships without producing anomalies within the data model. Normalization is a formalized technique for ensuring organization within data structuring, so that updating a piece of data should only require adjustment in one place and deleting a piece of data should not lead to loss of other data. Normalization can be used in its own right to structure any form of data in a business organization, but commonly it is done prior to the development of a computerized database system.

The technique of normalization developed as a response to the development of integrated database technology that shared common data files. The issue of insertion, deletion and updating of data becomes more significant if many files are affected on an integrated database system. Normalization attempts to rationalize data storage in order to simplify the process of insertion, deletion and updating data. For example, Table 5.2 shows a sales–order relationship as a table.

Table 5.2 Sales–order relationship (three attributes)

Customer name	Product code	Quantity ordered
Khan	C443185	35
Morris	F429008	13
Smith	C329859	8

In Table 5.2, customer name, product code and quantity ordered are attributes of the entity of sales–order. This is a simple form of entity-relationship model. Each row in a relation table is called a *tuple*. No two tuples should be identical in the entity-relationship model. In Table 5.2 the key attribute is customer name. However, in reality there may be more than one customer with the same name, so a unique customer number attribute would be more appropriate. This is shown in Table 5.3.

In Table 5.3 the key attribute is customer number. This table with the four attributes of customer number, customer name, product code and quantity ordered (with the key attribute of customer number) can be expressed in short-hand notation as: sales–order (number, name, code, quantity).

The theory of normalization was pioneered by an academic named Ted Codd in 1970. He suggested that the practice of normalization had three sequential levels:

▶ **First normal form (1NF):** all the attributes are established at their most basic level and each attribute should have only one possible value. The aim of first normal form is to remove all the repeated occurrences of attributes in the logical design, thus eliminating redundant data.

▶ **Second normal form (2NF):** all the attributes that are not key attributes should be functionally *dependent* upon the key attribute. Therefore, all non-key attributes must be dependent on the key attribute. To convert to second normal form, any attribute that is not dependent upon a key attribute must be removed and placed in a different table along with the key attribute on which it is dependent.

▶ **Third normal form (3NF):** all the non-key attributes should be functionally independent of each other attribute. Therefore, the aim is that there are no non-key attributes that are dependent upon any other non-key attributes. Once this level of normalization is complete, the tables are referred to as fully normalized.

Later writers on normalization have suggested that up to five levels of normalization can be achieved. Under the original academic theory, achieving third

Table 5.3 Sales–order relationship (four attributes)

Customer number	Customer name	Product code	Quantity ordered
3456	Khan	C443185	35
4469	Morris	F429008	13
8995	Smith	C329859	8

normal form is considered satisfactory in practice and forms the basis of most data models.

The aim is to make all the attributes in a relation table dependent upon the key attribute and nothing but the key attribute. For example, the key attribute of customer number (in Table 5.3) will probably have functionally dependent attributes of customer name and customer address. The customer name and customer address attributes should not be found anywhere else other than 'attached' and dependent upon the key attribute of customer number.

Activity 5.8 Data normalization

Define the term normalization and explain why the process of normalization is so important to the construction of physical databases. Then explain and describe the steps involved in first normal form, second normal form and third normal form. Indicate the significance of functional dependency, whereby non-key attributes are dependent upon a key attribute.

5.6 Soft systems tools and techniques

Many of the techniques and tools discussed so far originate out of the traditional systems development life cycle and other structured methods used to assist information systems development. However, when an information system is being developed at the management and executive levels of a business organization the systems environment is often unclear or 'fuzzy'. In such environments it is suggested that less structured tools and techniques should be used. This is often known as a *soft systems approach*. The soft systems approach uses its own tools and techniques for analyzing and designing the information systems environment. Three of the main techniques used are:

▶ rich pictures
▶ root definitions
▶ conceptual modelling.

All these three techniques assist the analysis of information systems within the business environment. They originate from the *soft systems methodology* (SSM) of Checkland (1980) and Checkland and Scholes (1990). The soft systems methodology will be studied in greater detail in the next chapter.

A *rich picture* uses graphics and symbols to express all the issues related to the system's environment and boundaries. It should address people, organization, technology and internal and external political issues. The rich picture may also include social roles and human behaviour present within the systems environment. The rich picture attempts explicitly to highlight conflicts of interest that are not considered, to the same extent, by other tools and techniques. It should be a *holistic* view of the role and purpose of the systems within a business organization.

A rich picture should include both hard (objective) facts and soft (subjective) information about the business organization. Since business is a human activity

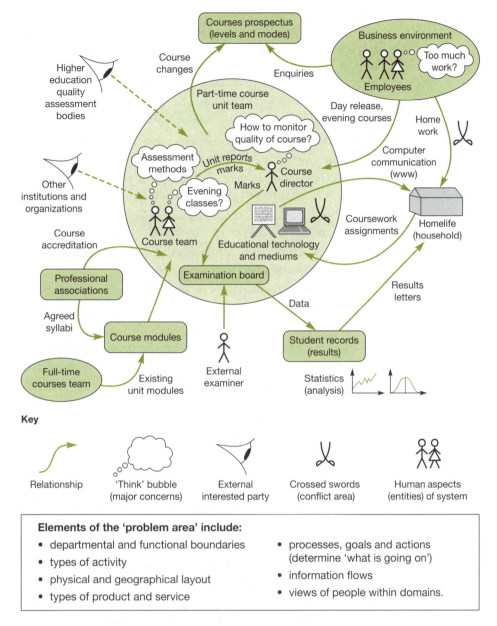

Key

| Relationship | 'Think' bubble (major concerns) | External interested party | Crossed swords (conflict area) | Human aspects (entities) of system |

Elements of the 'problem area' include:

- departmental and functional boundaries
- types of activity
- physical and geographical layout
- types of product and service
- processes, goals and actions (determine 'what is going on')
- information flows
- views of people within domains.

Figure 5.16 Rich picture (a university part-time course unit)

system, the rich picture technique is a useful way of analyzing human to technical systems interaction. It is essential that the rich picture is easily understood and requires little or no explanation. It can then be used as a communications tool to encourage users and systems participants to reveal their particular view of the system's environment.

A rich picture should set out to establish the elements of the system and then to look at the processes that are evident between the elements. The rich picture uses sketched objects that are linked by lines and arrows to indicate a relationship between elements. There is no universal set of symbols; any symbols or pictures that seem appropriate can be used. However, two symbols that appear to be used as standards within rich pictures are crossed swords and 'think' bubbles. A crossed sword indicates some form of conflict and the 'think' bubbles indicate the concerns of the participants within the system. Figure 5.16 is an example of a rich picture.

There are five main advantages in using rich pictures as follows:

▶ The act of putting pen to paper focuses all participants in the process of defining the systems environment.

▶ Visual images are a more direct way of eliciting the issues of an information system than words or lengthy narrative.

▶ It incorporates human, social and political issues to a greater extent than other tools and techniques of systems development.

▶ It can be used as a communications tool between technical specialists and business specialists.

▶ It encourages participation in the analysis and design of information systems by the end users.

The rich picture should aim to highlight the primary purposes of the business organization at the highest level. The secondary purpose is to identify the issues that matter and are of concern in the development of an efficient and effective information system. However, the technique does require a high level of individual freedom to allow political and human issues to be debated by all participants, irrespective of their level and role within the business organization.

Activity 5.9 Rich pictures

Discuss and explain the technique of rich pictures and indicate why it is referred to as a soft systems approach to information systems analysis and design. Draw a rich picture to describe the systems environment of a mail-order business – remember to highlight conflicts of interest.

Activity 5.10 A rich picture of the University of the World

The following is a scenario of a university work placement and internship placement system as described by one of the senior management team of the university:

The University of the World is based in North America. It is an inner city university providing courses in the academic areas of engineering, computing, business studies and teacher training. The university has 18,000 students on two campus sites. These are 3 km apart.

The university central administration office currently finds work placements and various internships for approximately 2,000 students. The engineering, computing and business studies programmes encourage students to undertake work-based placements and internships after the second year of the course, although the work placement is not mandatory. The students on the business studies and the computing courses normally take a full one-year placement or internship.

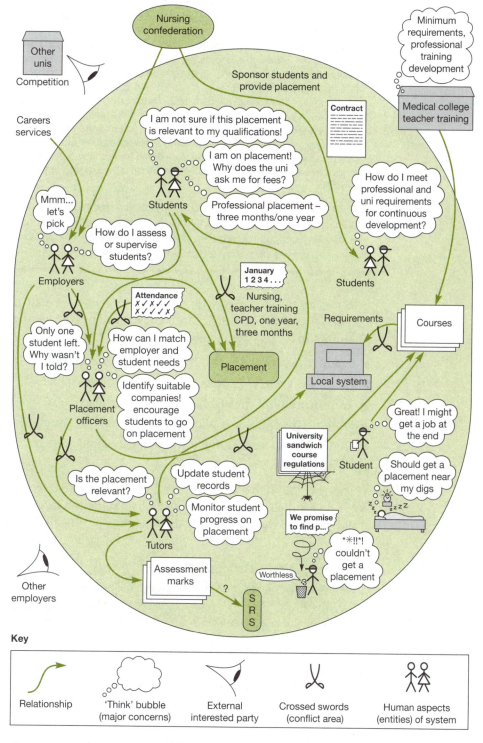

Figure 5.17 The University of the World

Source: Dr Shushma Patel, London South Bank University.

The role of the placement and internship officers is to ensure that the work opportunities provided are appropriate to the courses that students are studying. The officers liaise with the course leaders to ensure relevancy of the placement. It is the placement officer's responsibility to find suitable placement and internship opportunities, although students are also encourged to find their own placement opportunities and internships. A student on a placement or internship is required to inform the placements officer of progress and problems. The students are normally visited at work by their placement officer whilst they are working with companies and organizations. At the end of the internship or placement the students are required to submit a report on their activities and development during the internship or placement.

The university is currently purchasing a new computerized student record system (SRS) and wants to rationalize its procedures for managing placements and internships. It sees the new SRS as a centralized resource for managing student records and profiles.

Look at the rich picture in Figure 5.17, which is a graphical representation of the University of the World problem situation. Discuss whether you believe that it adequately describes the problem scenario. Then discuss what is missing from the rich picture and draw a rich picture that better describes the situation.

A *root definition* is a concise description of the essential nature of an information system. The root definition is developed by considering six characteristics of an information system, which are known by the mnemonic CATWOE:

▶ **Client**: the person affected by the information system.

▶ **Actor**: the agent of process transformation and change.

▶ **Transformation**: the change that is taking place.

▶ **Weltanschauung**: the established world view of assumptions.

▶ **Owner**: the sponsor of the information system.

▶ **Environment**: the wider system.

The use of CATWOE is a way of getting all participants in the system to agree and focus on a suitable root definition. By its nature, the formulation of a root definition is a good way of exposing the different views of all the system participants.

What is *Weltanschauung*?

A German word that refers to the idea that people and organizations are bound by a cultural, political and social view of ideas and attitudes.

A *conceptual model* shows how the various processes or activities of an information system are related and logically connected. It is vital to the design of an information system in that it establishes the foundations for the implementation of the information system. The conceptual model should ideally be understood and agreed by the business specialists and the technical specialists and should take its essential form from the root definition. The conceptual model should be sketched through a number of levels, with each level describing the actions of a particular process or sub-system.

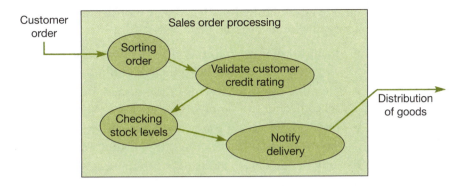

Figure 5.18 Level 1 conceptual model

The conceptual model is an attempt to do things better and recognizes that there may be more than one way to achieve a particular systems solution. The conceptual model can be compared with reality and is particularly useful in highlighting informal information flows within a business organization (this is also true of rich pictures, which look at both formal and informal information flows). It also serves as a:

▶ tool for analysis and design
▶ medium of communication between the designers and client end users
▶ set of instructions for the implementation of the information system.

Figure 5.18 shows an example of a conceptual model sketch for a sales order processing system at one level of detail. Figure 5.19 shows the same conceptual model detailed down to level 2.

The conceptual model will be derived and drawn from the root definition. The root definition will form the overall mission statement for the business organization, which will determine the shape and character of the required information systems. The conceptual model should illustrate what ought to be happening within the information systems environment; it attempts to achieve the

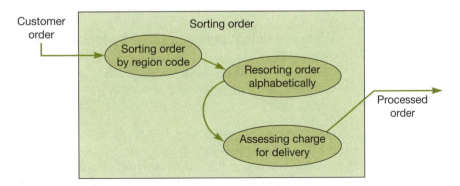

Figure 5.19 Level 2 conceptual model

objectives established in the overall root definition. The steps to forming the conceptual model should be:

▶ establish a holistic impression of the system as based on the root definition using verbs to describe the activities within the boundaries of the system;

▶ determine the requirements of the system and outline aspects of monitoring and control of the various aspect of the system;

▶ group together generic activities and logically connect each of these activities with arrows to indicate various flows of information;

▶ verify the model by comparing it to the real world problem situation.

5.7 Data and information management systems

Many software applications exist to provide data management. These are collectively referred to as *database management systems* (DBMS). These software applications enable data to be structured into *data elements* that constitute a set of related data items or values. Each data item has an associated *data type* classification.

Modern DBMS enable images and graphics to be stored and managed as well as alphanumeric data. For example, pictures, images, video and text can be stored, hosted on an integrated network and accessed by a data management system.

Database management systems perform four main functions:

▶ **Data organization**: structures are maintained that enable data to be easily accessed, maintained and updated.

▶ **Data administration**: access to data and its use in the organization is monitored and tracked, thus preserving its integrity.

▶ **Data networking**: data is fully integrated into the organizational domain and accessible over an internal network, within given security walls.

▶ **Data targeting**: the system should be sophisticated enough to target specific data to different types of users as and when they require that data, and in a format that is suitable to their needs.

What is a database management system (DBMS)?

A software-based systems environment that enables an organization to store and handle efficiently the transmission of data to various user groups. A DBMS acts as an interface between the data and the various user groups.

The desirable properties of a DBMS are that data should be available to be shared by more than one person, or group of users, at the same time. Organizations try to manage data carefully so that it can be assessed and used by executives, managers and many other stakeholder groups across the organization. That means that the data should be reliable and secure. This is referred to as the data's *integrity*: an important aspect when the data is being used to inform decision making within an organization. The data should be secure both at the storage level and the transmission (or electronic communication) level. The data should have adequate security and protection to deter and prevent unauthorized access or unauthorized communication over a computer network.

Data and information support decision making. Therefore, a DBMS needs to respond to the needs of decision makers as quickly as possible. The response time of a DBMS is an important consideration. *Data warehousing* is the term used to describe modern database systems that are specifically designed to support decision-making needs. However, a data warehouse is not merely a database. It is a large electronic repository, or computerized storage area (often up to 500 Gbytes), where data has been extracted from a range of applications, both internally and externally. Therefore, *data integration* is a very important aspect of a data management system.

A DBMS normally has three inherent software parts and functions:

▶ **Data definition language**: the software language used to specify the content and structure of the data.

▶ **Data manipulation language**: a high-level programming environment, using third and fourth generation software to enable users to manipulate data in the data repository. (One of the most popular in modern DBMS is the Structured Query Language, or SQL.)

▶ **Data dictionary**: providing definitions for data elements and data characteristics, such as ownership of data, data authorization authority and updating authority.

Database management systems are usually relational. Data is represented in two-dimensional tables where a record in a relation is referred to as a tuple. The concept of a tuple was described earlier in this chapter. Many modern DBMS applications are object-oriented, thus enabling more complex data such as graphics and pictures to be associated into objects of data and procedures that can be retrieved and shared. Object-oriented database management systems are popular in organizations because they enable the handling and management of multimedia elements, and object-orientation is particularly useful in association with web-based applications.

Normally, data is centralized for security purposes and ease of management, sometimes secured on a single security fire-walled computer server. However, the data access needs to be distributed around the organization. Since it is not always possible, or desirable, to store data in one location, a distributed database may be established where the data is distributed to more than one physical location. There are therefore two main types of distributed database:

▶ **Centralization**: multiple access points (or computers) are distributed around the organization and its clients.

▶ **Decentralization**: the data itself is located and distributed around the organization as well as the access points.

Activity 5.11 Database management systems

Discuss the importance of database management systems within business organizations. What is the main role and purpose of a DBMS? Describe why an integrated DBMS is important for organizational decision making. What is the importance of a distributed database management system? Once you have answered these questions, investigate whether your college or university has a DBMS. If it does, what data manipulation languages are used to manipulate data and interact with data?

5.8 Data warehousing and data mining

The traditional alphanumeric database is not on its own useful in the modern business systems environment. Modern business information systems are object-oriented, multidimensional and inherently web-based. Decision making in an organization requires accessing multimedia data and information in different forms. Therefore, databases and database management systems need to be sophisticated enough to cope with the demands of decision makers. In addition, a database management system needs to be accessible on a global scale with access via the interface of the web. Multidimensional database applications often have a temporal aspect (i.e. the time of access and location of data at a given moment in time are of critical importance). For example, the buying and selling of stocks and equities is time-critical. A multidimensional database may also include location and type of data (e.g. a geographic dimension and the dimension of type of multimedia).

What is a data warehouse?

A very large database application with associated report and query language tools that can extract current and historical operational data for management decision making.

Organizations need to analyze multidimensional data for such processes as:

▶ tracking prices in relation to regions and countries;

▶ tracking and monitoring past performance of products and services;

▶ predicting future pricing policies based on historical data;

▶ comparing performance across a range of performance indicators.

This is often referred to as *online analytical processing* (OLAP). This type of temporal online data processing is only possible with sophisticated database management systems.

Data warehouses are very large databases that store vast amounts of data from the operational systems of a business. Most data warehousing applications also have associated manipulation languages that enable users to 'query' and interrogate the database (*see* Figure 5.20). The data is extracted in various reporting formats and is used for business decision making. The data in the data warehouse originates from the various operational systems located within the fabric of the

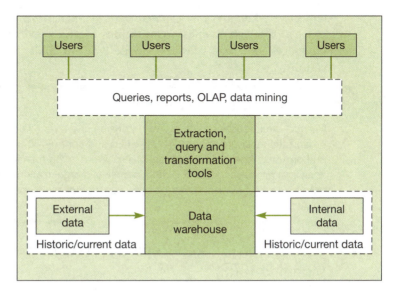

Figure 5.20 Data warehousing

organization and consists of both internal and external data. Many modern integrated data warehousing applications use web front-end applications to interface with the data. The data warehouses need to be flexible enough to accommodate different types of data from relational and non-relational databases and from the web. The data from operational systems is usually captured on a regular basis; for example, each day, or each hour, a copy of the data being generated by operational systems is captured and copied to the data warehouse. Therefore, users can access the most recent data available. To be useful to an organization the data warehouse needs to be an enterprise-wide application. Therefore, the integration of data collection systems and sub-systems is of paramount importance to a modern business organization.

Data mining is a concept closely associated with data warehousing; in data mining the data of a data warehouse is studied and analyzed in order to find patterns and rules that can be used to assist and guide the decision-making process. Data mining software tools are used to query the data in a data warehouse to determine the characteristics of past and present business behaviour and to predict future business behaviour. Data mining can be used to discover cause-and-effect relationships in customer behaviour. It can also be used to analyze customer and client behaviour through an analysis of their use and access of business websites. Some companies use sophisticated modern data mining techniques to analyze customer preferences, using historical data of their purchasing patterns, and can then determine how to best sell those customers future products and services.

With the development of a web-based interface to data, data mining is also able to analyze and determine the preferences and activities of customers who go online and access company websites. Linking databases to the web so that they may be accessed and queried via a web browser is a fact of business life in many modern business organizations. This is an area of information systems collectively known as *web database design and development*. Linking internal databases to the web enables organizations to utilize existing software, such as web languages and web browsers, to design and build data-based business applications.

Activity 5.12   Data warehousing and data mining

Discuss the importance of data warehousing and data mining in the context of organizational coordination, management and control. What are the main advantages and disadvantages of data warehousing? What is the role and function of online analytical processing (OLAP) within a business organization? Describe the importance of the web as a front-end technology enabling access to centralized database applications.

5.9 Business process conceptualization and enterprise resource planning (ERP)

Processes are critical to the concept of business systems. Systems are a collection of business processes. These processes handle data and information for business decision making. Therefore, the correct analysis of business processes is an important activity of business systems design and development. Central to the concept of processes is the idea that they have inputs, outputs and activity (as studied in Chapter 2). One of the most detailed academic studies of business processes was by Professor Michael Porter, whose study of competitive advantage termed the interrelationship of business processes as a *value chain*. In essence, processes are linked together within an organization. The business processes start with the suppliers, and other business agents, and end with the customers: the value chain provides value to the business and its customers.

> **What is a value chain?**
> A set of linked processes within an organization, each of which provides value to a business organization's products and services.

Within Porter's idea of value chains each process can be categorized into primary and secondary processes or activities:

▶ **Primary activities**: the core backbone processes without which the business organization would fail.

▶ **Secondary activities**: the processes that support the core business processes.

Porter's concept of the value chain is illustrated in Figure 5.21. The primary activities of Porter's value chain are inbound logistics, operations, outbound logistics, marketing and sales and after sales service. The secondary activities and processes are business/enterprise infrastructure, human resource management, technology development, and procurement.

The value chain of processes, residing within an organization, can provide an organization with a competitive advantage over other organizations in the busi-

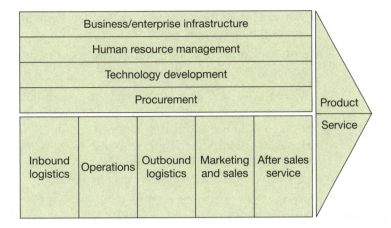

Figure 5.21 Porter's value chain

ness environment: Porter's concept assumes that business organizations are competing with one another for customers and business opportunities.

A competitive business organization is composed of a series of value chains that comprise the total *value system*. The aim of any competitive organization is to extract as much value as possible from the value chains in order to compete with other organizations. The two main value chains within a competitive organization are the supply chain and the customer chain. In this context, the suppliers and the customers are the external entities.

To determine process value a range of benchmarks need to be established. These benchmarks can act as gauges of business performance. Processes can be compared to benchmarks to ascertain whether they fall above or below the benchmark standard set by the management of an organization. All this activity requires a high level of process and systems integration within an organization. The need to handle and manage large data applications has led to the concept of *enterprise resource planning* (ERP).

An ERP system is a large integrated business system that handles and manages business processes and databases across a range of business units and business functions. There are many outsourcing companies that provide ERP systems to large and medium-size organizations. Predominant among these in the early part of the twenty-first century is a company called SAP AG, which is one of the most important providers of ERP systems in the world. SAP provides an enterprise resource planning electronic business systems platform known as mySAP. The importance of ERP lies in the fact that collections of business processes (value chains) can be integrated and managed in order to achieve increased business benefits. Typical ERP activities include product planning, stock and inventory management, customer and supply chain management, and logistics. These are many of the primary and secondary activities outlined in Porter's value chain.

Some of the benefits of an ERP system are:

▶ **Process standardization**: within data-distributed global organizational environments.

▶ **Systems integration**: combining the management of multiple processes under one umbrella system.

▶ **Systems control**: authorizing access, security and maintenance of business systems and their inherent processes.

A key feature of ERP systems is the ability to link and integrate areas of a business that are globally distributed. An ERP system can improve data and information communication within an organization and thus lead to better decision making. Standardization of processes also leads to greater benefits in terms of systems maintenance and system integration – data integration is a major concern of modern information systems development.

Activity 5.13 Enterprise resource planning (ERP)

Discuss the importance of enterprise resource planning (ERP) within a business organization. What are the main advantages and disadvantages of ERP, particularly for integrating organizations that have business units spread across the world? What is the role and function of ERP within the management of an organization? Search the web for references to ERP and list the three main ICT vendors supplying ERP systems in the world today.

5.10 Chapter summary

Process modelling assists the activity of designing and constructing information systems by using structured tools and techniques that bring the views of the technical specialist and end user into line. Process modelling is particularly useful to the design of systems that are not stand-alone, but are integrated with other systems, within a business organization. The analysis of business processes can be categorized into value chains. In support of process modelling is data modelling that concentrates on establishing the relationships between components of data, which is a useful prerequisite technique for creating physical database systems. Both process modelling and data modelling require a range of different tools and techniques. These tools and techniques are used within the information systems development process to assist the analysis and design of processes.

It should be evident from this chapter that a fundamental theme of systems development is modelling information systems processes and activities. The modelling activity relies on a number of tools, techniques and approaches for describing business systems activity, which can be separated into decision-making processes, information-based processes and functional processes. A thorough knowledge of an organization's processes establishes a picture of how an organization operates internally, and competes with other organizations externally.

Knowledge of business systems processes enables systems to be redesigned in a more organized manner. A knowledge of business processes also enables good practice to be spread across an organization, and it allows new processes to be added that enhance the competitiveness of the organization as an integrated whole. The following chapter will study how the tools, techniques and approaches are integrated into the fabric of various information systems development methodologies.

SHORT SELF-ASSESSMENT QUESTIONS

5.1   Briefly explain the difference between *process modelling* and *data modelling* within information systems development.

5.2   Define and explain the terms *tool* and *technique* and define the term *modelling* as applied in information systems.

5.3   Define and explain what is meant by the term *data modelling* and why such modelling is important to a business organization.

5.4   Explain why the use of *flowcharting* may assist the analysis of decision making within a business organization.

5.5   Outline the main advantages and disadvantages of using flowcharting within an information systems development project.

5.6   Outline three main advantages of using *data flow diagrams* and compare the usefulness of DFDs with other flowcharting techniques.

5.7   Define and explain when it is appropriate to use *decision tables* to describe and model processes within an information system.

5.8   Explain and describe the four quadrants of a decision table for recruiting part-time staff to a business organization. (Remember you must identify your conditions and actions in order to complete the decision table.)

5.9   Explain the terms of *entity, relationship* and *attribute* and provide three examples to describe a one-to-one, many-to-many and one-to-many relationship.

5.10   Outline the main advantages of using *rich pictures* and indicate why it is important to have a holistic view of a business organization and its systems.

5.11   Describe the role and function of *data warehousing* within a business organization and outline the main advantages of data warehousing for decision making.

5.12   Describe the role and function of *data mining* and outline the nature and purpose of *OLAP* for business decision-making.

5.13   What are the primary and secondary activities and processes in Michael Porter's *value chain*?

5.14   Discuss why business process modelling is so important for business information systems design and development.

5.15   Describe the role and purpose of an *enterprise resource planning* (ERP) system within a business organization and describe how such a system enables data integration.

EXTENDED STUDENT ACTIVITIES

Individual reporting activity 1

Outline and discuss the possible tools, techniques and approaches that could be used in process modelling and data modelling. Evaluate any four techniques that might be used to analyze an information system and describe the use of such tools and techniques for gathering data concerning an existing system.

Write a 500-word report for a potential customer outlining the main differences between process modelling and data modelling. Clearly indicate how and why data and process modelling should be used to analyze and design effective information systems.

Individual reporting activity 2

Most manufacturing organizations that produce goods will distribute those goods to customers for an additional delivery charge. The charge will often depend upon the location of the customer and the type of goods being delivered. The following is an example of a process for determining delivery charges for goods:

> For the purposes of determining delivery charges for the Fast-Goods Corporation, customers are divided into two categories, those whose sales region code is 50 or above and those whose sales region code is less than 50. If the sales region code is less than 50 and the sales invoice amount less than £1,000, a £30 delivery charge is added to the sales invoice total. If the invoice value is greater than or equal to £1,000, the delivery charge is £15. However, if the sales region code is greater than or equal to 50 and the sales invoice amount less than £1,000, the delivery charge is £40. If the sales invoice value is greater than or equal to £1,000, the charge is £20.

1 Draw a flowchart to determine an algorithm for computing the delivery charge.

2 Construct a decision table to determine the delivery charge under the various conditions.

Individual reporting activity 3

You have been asked by your line manager to prepare a 10-minute presentation to the chief executive officer (CEO) to explain the advantages and disadvantages of using soft systems tools and techniques for analyzing and designing a new customer relations information system. The CEO believes that a soft systems approach might be beneficial because the end users are integrated into the development process. Your task is to convince the CEO by clearly indicating the benefits to the business organization and by describing the use of rich picture diagramming techniques within the soft systems approach to process analysis. The CEO is particularly interested in discovering the role and purpose of root definitions and conceptual modelling within the soft systems framework.

Group-based activity 1

Discuss with colleagues the role and function of data flow diagrams (DFD) within the context of systems development tools and techniques. Then, as a group, outline the symbols used in data flow diagramming and suggest whether these symbols are appropriate and sufficient to describe an information systems problem within the business environment.

Group-based activity 2

Divide up into groups. In each group:

1 Choose a single tool and technique for analyzing the timetabling system for your university or college.

2 Present to the other groups your findings in terms of ease of information acquisition and information presentation.

3 Outline three main advantages and disadvantages using the tool or technique you chose when dealing with the end users of the timetabling system.

REFERENCES AND FURTHER STUDY

Books and articles

An asterisk (*) indicates a seminal text – a major source for later academic developments.

Avison, D. and Cuthbertson, C. (2002) *A Management Approach to Database Applications*, McGraw-Hill Education, ISBN: 0077097823

Becker, J., Kugeler, M. and Rosemann, M. (2002) *Process Management: A Guide for the Design of Business Processes*, Springer-Verlag, ISBN: 3540434992

Brady, J. and Monk, E. (2001) *Concepts in Enterprise Resource Planning*, Thomson Course Technology, ISBN: 0619015934

Checkland, P. (1980) *Systems Thinking, Systems Practice*, John Wiley and Sons, ISBN: 0471279110

Checkland, P. and Scholes, J. (1990) *Soft Systems Methodology in Practice*, John Wiley and Sons, ISBN: 0471927686

*Codd, E.F. (1970) 'A relational model of data for large shared data banks', *Communications of the ACM*, (13)6

Date, C.J. (2003) *An Introduction to Database Systems: An International Edition*, Addison-Wesley, ISBN: 0321189566

Hand, D., Mannila, H. and Smyth, P. (2001) *Principles of Data Mining*, MIT Press, ISBN: 026208290x

Hoffer, J. (2003) *Modern Systems Analysis and Design Casebook*, Prentice Hall, ISBN: 0130605301

McDonald, K. et al. (2002) *Mastering the SAP Business Information Warehouse*, John Wiley and Sons, ISBN: 0471219711

McKeown, P. (2003) *Information Technology and the Networked Economy*, 2nd edition, Thomson Publishing, ISBN: 003034851x

Moeller, R. (2000) *Distributed Data Warehousing Using Web Technology: How to Build a more Cost Effective and Flexible Warehouse*, Amacom Publishing, ISBN: 0814405886

Porter, M.E. (1998) *The Competitive Advantage: Creating and Sustaining Superior Performance*, Simon and Schuster, ISBN: 0684841460

Roiger, R. and Geatz, M. (2002) *Data Mining: A Tutorial Based Primer*, Addison-Wesley, ISBN: 0201741288

Thomsen, E. (2002) *OLAP Solutions: Building Multi-dimensional Information Systems*, John Wiley and Sons, ISBN: 0471400300

Yeates, D., Shields, M. and Helmj, D. (1994) *Systems Analysis and Design*, FT Prentice Hall, ISBN: 0273600664

Web resources   **Journal of Digital Information (UK)** – journal on the management and presentation of digital information.
http://jodi.ecs.soton.ac.uk

Association for Information Systems (global) – professional body for information systems professionals and knowledge workers.
www.aisnet.org

Chapter 6

Information systems methodologies

When you have studied this chapter you will be able to:

▶ describe the role and function of various information systems development methodologies within the business environment;

▶ evaluate the characteristics of a methodology and compare the appropriateness of using different methodologies for systems development;

▶ differentiate between hard and soft methodologies and be able to determine which approach best fits the systems development problem;

▶ apply and contrast the relevant tools and techniques that are appropriate within the context of the various methodologies;

▶ discuss and explain the development of a methodological framework for analyzing and developing information systems;

▶ describe and evaluate modern approaches to system development, such as SSADM and UML;

▶ describe the importance of a methodological approach to systems development and the chronology of systems development methods.

6.1 Introduction to information systems methodologies

The development of systems within business organizations requires a framework, or methodology, to guide and control the information systems development process. A number of information systems methodologies have been proposed and published since the early 1970s, designed to organize and coordinate the development of information systems within the business environment. Often a methodology is named after the individual, or group of individuals, that proposed or developed the methodology – these are often referred to as *proprietary methodologies*. For example, the Jackson systems development approach is named after a software and systems developer called Michael Jackson (not the famous pop singer!). Obviously, not all methodologies are the same and it is a general principle that methodologies can be categorized as either *soft* or *hard*. A hard methodology will incorporate a greater amount of formalization of procedures and development structure within the approach to systems development. Soft methodologies are as rigorous as hard methodologies, but they are not as formally structured as the hard approaches to information systems development.

Information systems development methods did not become a major academic research discipline until the late 1960s. Previous to this time, information systems were developed without the guidance of explicit methodologies. This was due to the nature of computing and computing technology at that time, which was largely concerned with imperative programming, and the fact that computing services within a business organization were often the sole preserve of specific and isolated corporate departments with their own trained systems analysts. Therefore, information systems were often developed ad hoc and determined by the abilities of a computer programmer or analyst in the computing department. However, with the pervasion of ICT throughout the whole business environment, there is now a need for information systems developers not only to be technically competent but also to possess good human communication skills. ICT is now subsumed within all aspects of our lives. Information systems development is a process that benefits from a rounded education, which includes the capability to communicate hard and soft systems problems to all stakeholders involved in the business systems environment. A well-educated systems developer requires the skills of communication, an understanding of systems methods, and a good technical understanding of modern ICT and its use and application in the business domain.

There are a number of reasons why a methodology is a requirement for information systems development within business organizations:

▶ Information systems can be used to provide a competitive advantage to most business organizations.

▶ Systems should go through the process of rigorous planning, analysis and design and implementation, as is the case with other major business projects.

▶ Most business organizations need an integrated approach to systems development rather than an ad hoc approach to the problem.

The aims (or objectives) of any information systems development methodology should be to:

▶ improve the process of information systems development;

▶ permit the effective monitoring of the development process;

▶ achieve accurate analysis of business and systems requirements;

▶ permit the accurate documentation of the analysis and design process;

▶ allow information systems to be delivered within a required time limit;

▶ ensure that the benefits outweigh the cost of using the methodology;

▶ improve the efficiency and effectiveness of the business organization;

▶ improve the delivery or achievement of business organization objectives;

▶ ensure that the needs of the users are fully satisfied.

An information systems methodology is usually based on a *philosophical view* of the development process, which in turn leads to the use of specific tools and techniques that are deemed appropriate within a specific business domain. Some methodologies are very structured and inflexible, while others are more expedient and often place emphasis on the human aspect of end-user involvement in

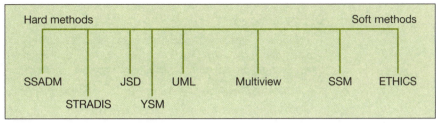

Key

SSADM	Soft systems analysis and design method
STRADIS	Structured analysis and design of information systems
JSD	Jackson systems development
YSM	Yourdon systems method
UML	Unified Modeling Language™
SSM	Soft systems methodology
ETHICS	Effective technical and human implementation of computer-based systems

Figure 6.1 Spectrum of information systems methodologies

the process of systems development. A number of development methodologies will be studied in this chapter, which span the spectrum from hard to soft development approaches, as shown in Figure 6.1.

Activity 6.1 Systems methodologies

Discuss the difference between soft systems methodologies and hard systems methodologies within the information systems development context, then explain why a systems methodology is usually based on a philosophical view of the development process, which leads to the establishment of the tools and techniques of the various methodologies. Then search your college or university library for journal or magazine articles on hard and soft information systems methodologies. Construct a definition for both hard and soft approaches. Form into groups of five people and spend 20 minutes discussing with your colleagues the definitions you have constructed. At the end of the session, elect a spokesperson to deliver your group-based definitions of hard and soft systems methodologies. Did your individual definitions change as a result of the group discussion?

6.2 Structured analysis and design of information systems

Structured analysis and design of information systems (STRADIS) is a highly structured approach to information systems development originated by Chris Gane and Trish Sarson in the late 1970s. It is sometimes referred to as the 'Gane and Sarson approach'. STRADIS is a *process-oriented* methodology that emphasizes such tools and techniques as functional decomposition, data flow diagramming, decision tables and structured English. (All these tools and techniques were covered in detail in Chapter 5.) The methodology was proposed in 1979 and encapsulated various work at that time into structured design processes and their application to information systems.

Did you know?

The Gane and Sarson approach to the analysis and design of information systems concentrates more on the tools and techniques for a structured design, rather than attempting the development of an all-encompassing methodology.

The STRADIS approach emphasizes the importance of decomposing systems functions and it also formalizes the use of data flow diagrams to structure the information systems problem. The approach does not restrict itself to large or small systems development projects. The approach proposes a number of detailed stages to systems development:

▶ **Initial study** (or feasibility study): making a decision as to whether the benefits outweigh the costs of the proposed information systems project.

▶ **Detailed study**: including, for example, determining the potential uses and users of the system under investigation. It is at this stage that the potential users of the system are interviewed through formal questionnaires and other structured data collection techniques. Logical data flow diagrams (DFDs) are then drafted that structure and determine the systems boundaries under consideration. The STRADIS approach necessitates detailed data flow diagramming of the problem, which is then broken down into many sub-levels. The detailed study would normally include:
  – a definition of the uses and users of the system
  – a logical model of the current or proposed system
  – a detailed statement of the costs and revenues accruing to the proposed system.

▶ **Defining and designing alternatives to the proposed system**: matching the business organization's objectives with the proposed information system's objectives – the two should be aligned for optimal business performance. It is at this stage that the proposed information system could be refined.

▶ **Physical design**: converting the refined proposal to a physical design, based on the current nature of ICT. This final stage also tries to ensure that the systems environment is satisfactory to users, in terms of the end-user interfaces and the application of information technology to business processes.

Activity 6.2 STRADIS

Discuss with your colleagues why STRADIS is considered a process-oriented methodology and describe the types of tools and techniques that would be used within the STRADIS approach. Then construct a one-page executive statement for distribution to all employees in an organization indicating the resources and time required to implement STRADIS in terms of questionnaires, interviews, and the use of various professional systems development tools and techniques. How would you justify time spent to build an information system with the benefits of that information system?

6.3 The Yourdon systems method

The *Yourdon systems method* (YSM) is another structured approach that is similar to STRADIS. It emphasizes functional decomposition, which is inherently a top-down approach to systems development. The Yourdon systems method was first proposed in the early 1980s and has undergone a number of version changes over time. This methodology uses most of the formal tools and techniques for documenting and describing an information system and considers both the systems requirements and the business organization's requirements. For example, an entity-relationship diagram may be constructed for a section or department within an organization, but only part of it may be appropriate for the proposed system. Emphasis is placed on modelling both the business organization and the system at the same time.

In modern information systems development practice the activity of modelling the systems environment has become of paramount importance. Modern systems development approaches, such as the Unified Modelling Language (UML), which was developed in the late 1990s, emphasize the importance of software systems modelling. Within UML the modelling activity is concerned with the designing of software applications before coding. A model plays the same role in software and systems development that blueprints and construction plans play in the building of a block of apartments. The modelling process is undertaken to ensure that business functionality is established and the objectives of end users are suitably addressed.

> **Did you know?**
> The Yourdon systems method (YSM) is named after its developer, Edward Yourdon, and as such can be labelled a proprietary methodology. Many of the structured features of YSM are shared by the Gane and Sarson STRADIS approach, and at one time in the 1970s Gane and Sarson were colleagues of Yourdon.

There are three main stages within the Yourdon systems method:

▶ **Feasibility study**: examining the current system and the information systems environment.

▶ **Essential model**: outlining the requirements of the proposed system. However, at this stage the Yourdon method does not consider any cost or technological constraints; it assumes unlimited resources and an absence of environmental constraints. The essential model is a representation of what is needed to satisfy the user's requirements and the modelling exercise involves:
  – constructing an environmental model consisting of a statement of purpose, a context diagram and an event list of things to which the system must respond;
  – constructing a behavioural model, consisting of data flow diagrams, entity-relationship diagrams, data dictionaries and process specifications, such as structured English or decision tables.

The role of the environmental model is to define the boundaries of the system, taking into account the data flowing in and out of the system, whereas the role of the behavioural model is to indicate how the system behaves or deals with its environment over time, and can be equated to an entity life cycle.

▶ **Implementation model**: activating the systems design process. It is at this stage that the ideal model developed at the second stage is refined with regard to the limitations and constraints present in the environment. Such constraints include the performance and availability of information technology that may modify the essential model.

It is interesting to note that Yourdon introduced the notion of modelling into the information systems environment. The allusion to modelling distinguishe the Yourdon approach from the earlier Gane and Sarson approach to building effective information systems. Later approaches to systems development have encompassed the idea of software and systems modelling and allied it with ideas of object orientation, which entered systems development thinking in the early 1990s.

Activity 6.3 Yourdon systems method

Outline and discuss the three main stages of systems development within the Yourdon systems method and suggest why the second stage does not consider any cost or technological constraints. Then describe the essential modelling exercise of YSM and explain the use and purpose of each category of model used within the method. Do you think that the activity of modelling is a useful exercise within business information systems development? If so, outline the main advantages to modelling within the analysis and design phases of information systems development.

6.4 Information engineering

Care should be used when referring to *information engineering* (IE) as there does not appear to be a standard information engineering methodology, but rather a generic class of IE methodologies. Information engineering is a *data-oriented* systems approach, rather than a process-oriented approach, which emphasizes the nature and structure of data found within an organization. It identifies data as being more stable than the processes that act upon the data. The IE approach uses diagramming to enable all stakeholders involved in the information system to understand the nature and role of the system. This approach, along with the STRADIS and Yourden approaches, uses standard and formal symbols for diagramming. Later methodologies, such as soft systems thinking, moved away from formalized symbols and towards diagramming symbols that were more obvious to all end users. Soft systems approaches use storyboards and cartoon diagrams to analyze and eventually design the systems environment.

What is information engineering (IE)?

A methodology that was collated and expanded upon by Clive Finkelstein and James Martin, two eminent thinkers on systems development, in 1981, in a two-volume book entitled *Information Engineering*.

The primary information engineering model consists of three components:

▶ data
▶ activity
▶ interaction (of the data and activities).

The IE approach usually utilizes *computer-aided software engineering* (CASE) tools. The IE methodology can be separated into four layers:

▶ **Information strategy planning**: constructing an information strategy, or information architecture, that supports the overall and high-level require-ments of the business organization. The information strategy plan should con-sider the following four issues:
  - situation analysis of the business strengths, weaknesses, opportunities and threats
  - executive and managerial requirements analysis by individual or department
  - information and technical architecture definition of the system
  - information strategy plan that emphasizes information priorities.

▶ **Business area analysis**: involving the end users of the system and dealing with the business areas identified in the information strategy plan. The business area analysis should consider the following five issues:
  - analysis of entities and functions
  - analysis of interactions between data and functions
  - analysis of the current system
  - verification and checking of results
  - definition of the design areas for consideration.

▶ **Systems planning and design**: the internal and external design of business systems and the technical design. This layer involves the following aspects:
  - data structure design
  - system structure design
  - procedure design
  - verification and checking
  - technical design plan
  - data design
  - software design
  - conversion design
  - security and operations design
  - systems testing
  - planning for the implementation.

▶ **Implementation and cutover from old system**: the physical construction of the information system, including:
  - construction of the IT environment
  - systems verification and testing
  - preparation for changeover
  - installation and conversion to new system
  - checking consistency of systems use
  - evaluation of system
  - systems maintenance.

It should be noted that these four layers can often be undertaken in parallel and not necessarily in rigid sequential stages. Hence the term of layers is used rather than stages of development in the IE approach to systems development.

Did you know?

James Martin, one of the founders of the IE approach, has set up a number of business enterprises to develop CASE tools to implement the IE approach. One of the best known CASE tools to support the methodology is known as the Information Engineering Facility (IEF), which James Martin built in cooperation with Texas Instruments in the 1980s.

Activity 6.4 Information engineering

Explain the significance of information strategy planning and business area analysis within the domain of information systems methods. Then indicate why the various components of IE are known as layers and not stages and describe some of the consequences of undertaking the development of various layers in parallel. Discuss whether the IE approach is a formalized approach or a non-formalized approach to systems development. Do you believe that data-oriented approaches are more important than process-oriented approaches to information systems development?

6.5 Structured systems analysis and design method

Structured systems analysis and design method (SSADM) is, as its name suggests, a highly structured approach used primarily to develop large-scale information systems for government departments in the UK. It is also used in a number of organizations in North America, Australia and New Zealand. The approach was first used in the UK in 1981. It is still used today, although it has gone through a number of evolutionary developments (and versions) since the early 1980s. SSADM is primarily a *data-oriented* methodology that emphasizes data modelling tools and techniques. The manuals and documentation for SSADM run into a number of thick volumes, each one prescriptively outlining how the methodology should be applied. Because of its prominence within the business environment, SSADM is probably the best-known structured systems development approach. However, its predominance is being challenged by a number of proprietary methods and approaches, such as the Open Management Group's UML approach and the Jacobson object-oriented software engineering approach to systems and software development.

Did you know?

The structured systems analysis and design method (SSADM) was developed by Learmouth and Burchett Management Systems and the Central Computer Telecommunications Agency (CCTA) in the UK in the early 1980s. It is still used today as a major structured approach to information systems development in business.

In the early days of large-scale information systems development in the 1970s many organizations used the programming language COBOL to build functional systems, such as payroll, stock control and customer order processing. Information systems development was traditionally characterized at this time by limited user involvement, inadequate requirements elicitation, time-consuming use of 3GL tools and inflexibility of method and approach. Frequently the results satisfied the technical requirements, but did not satisfy the business requirements. In addition, the users felt a lack of ownership in the systems development process because of low user involvement and because there was no way of altering systems requirements once the process of systems development was under way. It was apparent in the late 1970s and the early 1980s that there did not exist any adequate analysis and design tools and techniques. The response of the information systems community to these problems was the development of structured methodologies in the early 1980s. The aim of this formalization was to structure the analysis of systems and introduce systems development techniques to support the analysis and design activities of systems development. The earliest version of SSADM, in common with other structured methodologies at the time, adopted a prescriptive approach to information systems development. It specified stages and activities to be undertaken. Early versions of SSADM adopted the waterfall approach to systems development, where each stage of the development process needed to be agreed and signed off before moving on to the next stage.

However, since the early 1980s the SSADM approach has been refined through a number of versions. Version 4, launched in 1990, was different to earlier versions in that it recognized the importance of user involvement in the design and development of information systems in organizations. Today SSADM is an open standard (i.e. it is freely available for use in industry and the business environment at large).

SSADM version 4.0 lists seven stages to the development process (labelled 0 through to 6), which are outlined in Table 6.1.

Each stage of the SSADM life cycle is strictly defined along with the outcomes of each stage; these outcomes are often referred to as *deliverables* within systems vocabulary. SSADM uses its own symbol terminology for data flow diagramming, which is referred to as data flow modelling. Figure 6.2 shows the stages of the SSADM life cycle.

The main activities of each stage of the SSADM life cycle, outlined in detail in Table 6.1 are:

▶ **Feasibility stage**: using such techniques as interviews, questionnaires and data flow models of the flow of information documentation.

▶ **Investigation of the current systems environment stage**: expanding upon the feasibility stage by adding detail to the feasibility study.

▶ **Business systems options stage**: carrying out a cost–benefit analysis. Only those systems options that show greater benefit to cost ratio will be continued and carried forward to the next stage.

▶ **Definition of requirements stage**: establishing the full requirements specification and determining the following design stage. This stage is important in

Table 6.1 The seven stages of SSADM

Stage 0	**Feasibility study**
	Activities: Decide whether the project should go ahead
	– Define the problem and select options
	– Create feasibility report
Stage 1	**Requirements analysis: investigate current systems environment**
	Activities: Draw data flow diagrams (DFDs) and a logical data model (LDM) – which are similar to entity-relationship diagrams – to establish and understand the boundaries and content of the current system
	– Establish analysis framework
	– Investigate and define requirements
	– Investigate current processing
	– Investigate current data
	– Derive logical view of current services
	– Assemble investigation results
Stage 2	**Requirements analysis: business system options (BSOs)**
	Activities: Describe the new system's functionality using words and DFDs to establish business system options
	– Define business system options
	– Select business system options
	– Define requirements
Stage 3	**Requirements specification: definition of requirements**
	Activities: Model how the new system will respond to events – a process known as entity behaviour modelling, using entity life histories (ELHs)
	– Define required system processing
	– Develop required data model
	– Derive system functions
	– Enhance required data model
	– Develop specification prototypes
	– Develop processing specification
	– Confirm system objectives
	– Assemble and construct requirements specification
Stage 4	**Logical systems specification: technical systems options (TSOs)**
	Activities: Describe the costs and benefits, and the various constraints, of implementing the new system's specification
	– Define technical systems options
	– Select technical systems options
	– Define physical design modules
Stage 5	**Logical systems specification: logical design**
	Activities: Define data processing and update ELHs with indications of state and processing
	– Define user dialogues
	– Define update processes
	– Define enquiry processes
	– Assemble and construct logical design
Stage 6	**Physical design**
	Activities: Construct the physical aspects of the new system (e.g. the user interfaces) and implement the new system's processes
	– Prepare for physical design
	– Create physical data design
	– Create function component implementation map
	– Optimize physical data design
	– Complete function specification
	– Consolidate process data interface
	– Assemble and construct physical design

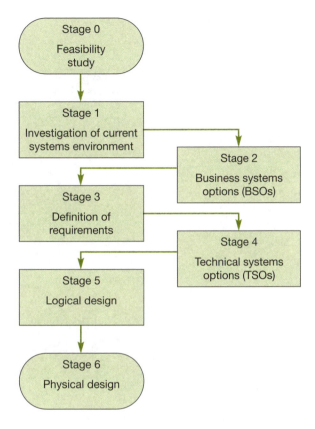

Figure 6.2 The SSADM life cycle

replacing investigation and analysis with specification and design. The question that needs to be asked is 'What will be the requirements of the new or proposed system?' This stage will normally involve entity modelling and normalization of data relationships. Currently, within this stage in version 4.0 is a definition of user roles within the system. In addition, SSADM version 4.0 permits some element of *prototyping* to be carried out to assess the accuracy of user requirements, particularly in terms of user interface design.

▶ **Technical systems options stage**: determining the software and hardware configuration of the IT to be applied to the information system; consideration is also given to the technical *constraints* that will impact on the final systems configuration. This stage is usually carried out in parallel with the logical design stage. (Remember that Chapter 2 outlined the importance of separating the logical from the physical systems model in order to ascertain the correct purpose and nature of the information system under development.)

▶ **Logical design stage**: incorporating user views of the proposed system in order to establish the logical requirements of the system.

▶ **Physical design stage**: converting the logical design into a physical ICT environment. The main objective of this stage should be to establish a physical configuration that meets the user's requirements.

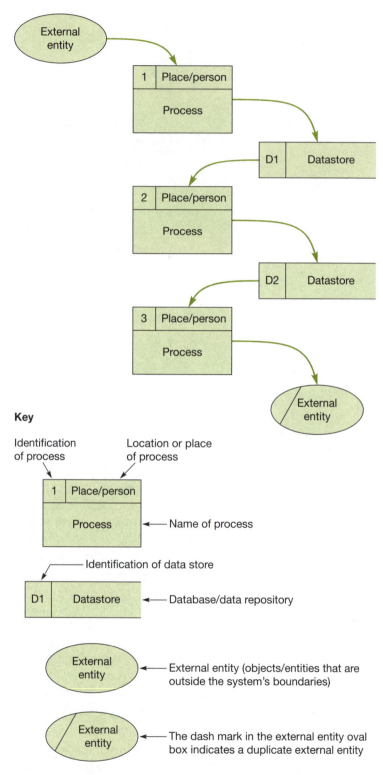

Figure 6.3 Data flow diagram (DFD) notation within SSADM

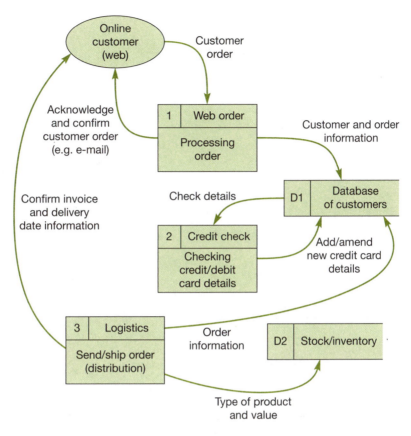

Figure 6.4 Example of a DFD for an online ordering system

The SSADM approach to systems development uses various diagramming techniques. These diagramming techniques have their origins in a number of earlier diagramming models used in structured systems analysis and design. The SSADM approach normally uses data flow diagrams (DFDs), logical data models (LDMs), entity life histories (ELH) and effective correspondence diagrams (ECDs) to describe the old and new system's environment. Figures 6.3 and 6.4 show examples of data flow diagrams. The role of *data flow diagramming* is to reveal the data processing relationships apparent in the systems domain. DFDs show how data is processed by the system. Figure 6.4 shows an example of a DFD for an online ordering system that is common in many web-based electronic commerce (e-commerce) systems.

Figure 6.5 shows a *logical data model* (LDM) and describes the entity relationships in the systems domain.

Figure 6.6 reveals the relationship of entities and events, called *entity life histories* (ELHs), as they occur in the life of a system. The diagrams are drawn as a hierarchical set of entities, known as *top-down decomposition*. Each ELH represents the life of a single entity from its beginning, or creation, to its deletion, revealing all the changes that affect the entity (i.e. additions or deletions to data stored in the entity). For example, Figure 6.6 shows the ELH for a student at college or

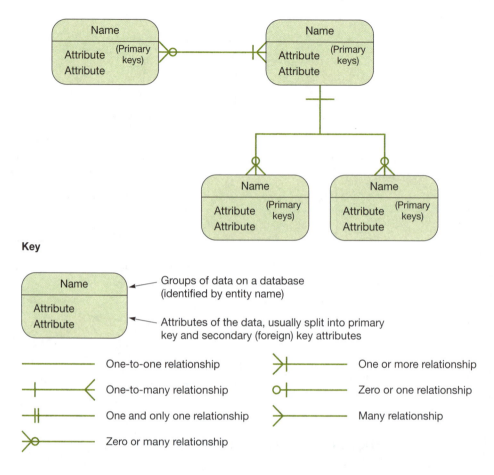

Key

Name | Groups of data on a database (identified by entity name)

Attribute
Attribute | Attributes of the data, usually split into primary key and secondary (foreign) key attributes

———————— One-to-one relationship   ≻— One or more relationship

—+—≺ One-to-many relationship   o+— Zero or one relationship

—‖— One and only one relationship   ≻— Many relationship

≻o— Zero or many relationship

Note: Sometimes LDMs contain 'C' or 'R's. The 'C' indicates that all child entities are cleared if the parent entity is deleted. The 'R' indicates that the parent entity may not be cleared (i.e. it must not be retained) if the child entity still exists.

Figure 6.5 Logical data modelling (LDM) notation within SSADM

university. The student would normally enrol on a course, may at some time change their details (e.g. address, results, etc.), and could transfer or withdraw from their course. The events in the life of the entity (labelled 'student') are shown in Figure 6.6 as a hierarchical diagram, with events placed in order from left to right (for example, 'change of student details' precedes 'transfer course'.

Finally, within SSADM diagramming, Figure 6.7 shows the *effect correspondence diagram* (ECD) notation that occurs in entity life history diagrams.

The rigour and structure of SSADM has enabled the methodology to become established in the information systems development arena. This has been assisted by the fact that SSADM, as a formal systems technique, is taught in many university departments, from business studies to computing, around the world. Within general data flow diagramming the diagrams can be shown in various

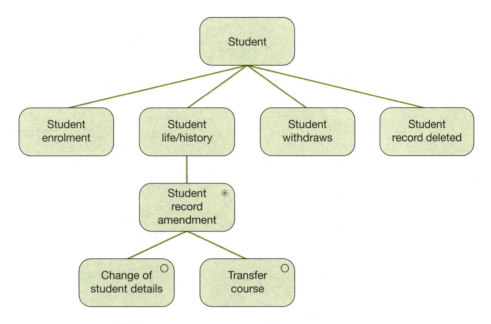

Figure 6.6 Entity life history (ELH) notation within SSADM

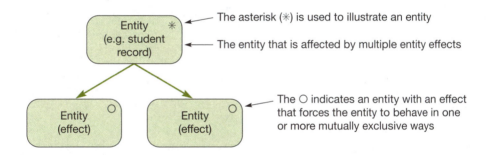

Figure 6.7 Effect correspondence diagram (ECD) notation within SSADM

levels of decomposition. A level 1 DFD can be refined down to a level 2 diagram that in turn can be refined down to a level 3 diagram. Figure 6.8 shows a typical student enrolment system at a college or university. The level 1 diagram has three processes: 'recruit student', 'receive acceptance confirmation' and then 'enrol student'. The 'recruit student' process can then be broken down (or decomposed) into a more detailed DFD for that process at level 2. A data dictionary would be used to record information about all the data used in the system with regard to data flows and database stores (or repositories) in the data flow diagrams.

The use of DFDs is important because they:

▶ represent flows of data to and from data stores;

▶ can be used to identify internal and external entities;

▶ act as a means of communication that facilitate an understanding of the information systems domain.

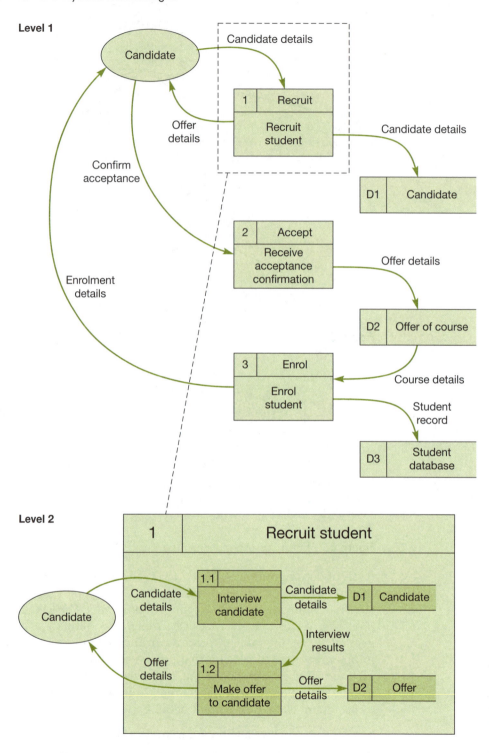

Figure 6.8 Levelling within data flow diagramming

SSADM

Describe the systems development approach known as SSADM and outline the main difference of version 4.0 to previous versions of the method. Then define the term deliverable and outline the deliverables of each stage of the SSADM approach to building information systems. Suggest some of the main advantages and disadvantages to a business organization of using the SSADM approach to information systems development.

Do you think that the methodology is appropriate to large-scale or small-scale information systems development projects? Discuss reasons why the use of SSADM may be highly inappropriate for certain sizes of business organizations.

Outline the importance of data flow diagramming within SSADM and suggest three reasons why DFDs are important for understanding a systems environment within an organization.

6.6 Jackson systems development

The *Jackson systems development* (JSD) approach is the last structured and 'hard' systems development methodology that will be reviewed. The methodology is named after Michael Jackson and is, therefore, another proprietary systems methodology. This methodology associates information systems development with the same techniques used for computer program language design: the information systems project is effectively seen as a large computer program. Therefore, the methodology is useful in the development of large-scale software-based systems where the emphasis is on software rather than other issues of the organization's overall strategic *business* requirements.

> ### Did you know?
> The JSD approach was developed by Michael Jackson, an eminent systems developer, in the early 1980s, and results from earlier work that was referred to as Jackson structured programming (JSP). Jackson systems development is still used today.

The JSD approach attempts to overcome the 'hidden path' problems between the initial specification and the final implementation by using what are termed *process scheduling* and *real-world modelling*. The three generic stages of the JSD approach are:

▶ **Modelling stage**: identifying entities and events and creating dynamic entity life cycles. The emphasis is as far as possible on modelling the 'real world'. An entity structure is then imposed and represented as a hierarchical JSD structure diagram that shows the sequence within the system's processes. Within this structure the timing and sequence of systems activities is considered; the *entity structure diagrams* represent a sequence of activities that are ordered in time from the beginning of an entity's life until its termination.

▶ **Network stage**: encompassing:

- An initial model step that is a simulation of the real world. For example, for each defined entity a sequential process is defined in the model to simulate the activities of the entity. This sequential process should be correspondingly implementable on a computer in the form of a program – this is referred to in JSD as structure text.
- A function step that ensures that the required outputs are produced as a consequence of the occurrence of events.
- System timing which is concerned with the speed of execution of processes and their timing. There is a need to determine the lag times between receiving inputs to the various parts of the system and the timing of the resultant outputs. This timing information concerning the various parts of the proposed system are analyzed in JSD by time markers, which provide information on the timing and execution of processes.

▶ **Implementation stage**: examining the physical systems specification, assisted by the use of systems implementation diagrams that hierarchically show the scheduling of processes.

The advantages of JSD reside in its attempt to model dynamic real-world situations and, in order to achieve this end, JSD emphasizes the importance of timing and scheduling considerations. The overall approach is process-oriented rather than static data-oriented.

Activity 6.6 Jackson systems development (JSD)

Briefly discuss and explain the relationship between computer program code structure and the JSD methodology and suggest two possible advantages of applying the structured technique of programming to information systems development.

Suggest three advantages and disadvantages of using JSD to develop information systems within the business environment. Do you think that such software-oriented systems development techniques are appropriate for analyzing and developing business information systems in the twenty-first century?

6.7 Effective technical and human implementation of computer-based systems

Effective technical and human implementation of computer-based systems (ETHICS) lies at the soft end of the methodological spectrum of systems development. The philosophy of ETHICS encompasses a *socio-technical* view of the systems development process. It is essential in this methodology for the technology to align closely with the social and organizational factors present within a business organization. The human approach must consider such factors as the job satisfaction and quality of life of the human users of the system. The interests of the human users are paramount in the ETHICS methodology. The socio-technical view is based on a recognition of the interaction between technology, people and the organization. The ETHICS approach is represented by two fundamental philosophical strands:

What is ETHICS?

A methodology proposed by Enid Mumford, at the Manchester Business School in the UK. It is a socio-technical development methodology that is based on end-user participation within the systems development process. The methodology stresses the importance of the social and ethical aspects of information systems, as well as the economic and technical aspects of information systems incorporated into the business environment.

▶ **Job satisfaction**: an information system will only be efficient and effective if it allows the system's end user to have job satisfaction. To achieve satisfaction requires the system aligning the employee's aspirations and expectations of the job with what is required of the job by the system, which is known as organizational 'goodness of fit'. Job satisfaction can be achieved in a number of ways, for example, by increasing task variety, by job enrichment, through greater responsibility, and by job development through end-user suggested improvements to current methods.

▶ **End-user participation**: the involvement of users in the decision-making exercises of the systems development process. The ETHICS definition of end users is sufficiently broad to encompass direct and indirect users, such as managers, employees, suppliers and even customers. The decision making will often include hard and soft technical decisions motivated by the drive to use information technology to improve job satisfaction within the system's environment.

The *management of change* is a constant theme in the ETHICS approach, along with the collateral drive to manage organizational conflict. Involvement has a purpose in that the end users are often the most knowledgeable concerning their current job specifications and requirements. There is also a far greater likelihood of a system being accepted by the users if they were involved in decision making than if they were not involved in the decision-making process. The aim of the ETHICS approach is to ensure that the users are satisfied that their requirements are met by the information system. User involvement must be engaged at all stages of the generic development process – from analysis and design through to implementation and evaluation.

Participation by end users in the decision-making process of systems development possesses a number of benefits. It:

▶ overcomes human resentment of the information system, thus reducing the risk of individuals working against the system or blaming the system for unjustified problems;

▶ can reduce the cost of training or retraining in the use of the system because of the fact that the end users already possess significant levels of knowledge from the development process;

▶ increases the level of communication between employees at all levels of the organization and, in doing so, publicizes the overall strategic goals of the business organization;

▶ encourages and improves human–computer interface design (the quality of computer interfaces is measured in terms of visibility, simplicity, consistency and flexibility in meeting the end user's needs);

▶ engenders a feeling of empowerment within users that can lead to increased job satisfaction.

Participation must be real: a genuine collaboration between the users and the technical specialists. Within this scenario the role of the technical specialist is one of *facilitator,* ensuring the implementation of the user's requirements. The facilitator can be internal or external to the business organization. Enid Mumford (1995) has suggested three levels of possible participation by the users:

▶ **Consultative participation**: the weakest and lowest form of participation, where users are merely consulted about change within the business organization. This level of consultation may only take the form of user questionnaires and interviews.

▶ **Representative participation**: a higher form of participation than consultative participation. In this scenario the users and the technical specialists form a team, with users and technical specialists having an equal contribution within the decision-making process.

▶ **Consensus participation**: the most significant level of participation, with users driving the systems development process. Here, the end users, rather than the technical specialists, are paramount in the design and development process.

With the evolution of end-user systems development the issue of participation is becoming commonly accepted within competitive business organizations. However, participation can be restricted to a predefined boundary, with the role and remit of participation being stated at the outset. To build effective and efficient business information systems the participants should ideally possess equal knowledge. However, this may not always be possible, particularly where there are technical and non-technical specialists in a team with different experiences. Nevertheless, this team is often referred to as the *design group*.

There are effectively 13 generic stages to the ETHICS design and development process. However, these stages have never been formalized within the ETHICS approach and, therefore, the number of steps can vary from 13 through to 25 steps. The 13 steps below are a generic collation of the main principles of the design and development process:

1 **Discussion of change:**
   – reasons for change
   – SWOT analysis of change.

2 Identification of systems boundaries:
- establish systems boundaries
- assess impact on business activities
- assess impact on business organization.

3 Description of existing system:
- establish current system operation
- input-activity-output analysis
- describe the design area activities.

4 Establishment of the key objectives, outcomes and tasks:
- define the role and purpose of systems areas
- define the functions of systems areas
- define the variance between the current and proposed system.

5 Diagnosis of variances:
- analyze the systemic variances
- analyze the operational variances
- analyze deviations from required standards.

6 Measurement of job satisfaction needs:
- conduct ETHICS questionnaire
- formulate improvements to system.

7 Identification of future changes:
- analyze future system needs
- build flexible margins into the system.

8 Balancing systems efficiency with job satisfaction:
- rank the objectives
- establish priority objectives.

9 Organizational design:
- specify organizational changes
- establish criteria for meeting the job satisfaction objectives
- assess the organizational objectives.

10 Technical design:
- specify technical hardware and software
- merge the organizational and technical design options.

11 Detailed design:
- define data flows and other relationships
- confirm design with objectives and requirements.

12 Implementation:
- implement the detailed design
- coordinate the strategy for training and education
- convert the old to the new system.

13 Evaluation:
- check and test the system.

The ETHICS approach can be used to design small or large-scale business systems projects and the methodology is particularly useful in analyzing and establishing the requirements of a business information system.

Activity   **6.7 ETHICS**

Discuss and describe the main benefits of end-user participation within the ETHICS methodology and explain the general importance of user participation in human–computer interface design. Discuss the importance of a facilitator within the ETHICS approach when creating a suitable environment in which technical and non-technical users can equally participate in the systems development process.

Describe the three levels of possible participation by end users within the ETHICS systems development process and explain what is meant by the term design group. What do you think the problems might be in selecting a design group of systems users?

6.8 Soft systems methodology

The *soft systems methodology* (SSM) uses many of the principles of general systems theory discussed in Chapter 2, and incorporates them into a practical methodology for business organizations. The SSM approach argues that business is often a complex human activity system where the individual components of a business system may react differently when examined individually than when those parts are seen in the context of the whole business system.

One of the problems with traditional scientific analysis of systems is the insistence on decomposing a complex problem into its constituent parts by a process of decomposition to the lowest common denominator. The SSM approach states that only the application of a soft systems methodology can provide the correct *insight* into business systems and human processes; in turn, this may lead to a better chance of achieving the most appropriate systems solution in the long term. SSM is the opposite of the structured and hard methodologies in that SSM argues that complex systems problems cannot be solved with rigid and deterministic methods.

> **Did you know?**
>
> The soft systems methodology (SSM) was developed by Peter Checkland, at Lancaster University in the UK, as a more appropriate and applicable method for developing information systems than the hard and structured methodologies that were in use in the early 1980s. Checkland's original ideas were published in 1981; since that time a range of research papers have been published on the theory and practice of the soft systems methodology.

The SSM approach also implies that in addition to systems having goals they may more appropriately have *purposes* and *missions* that are not as simplistic as systems goals. The soft systems approach brings people together to determine the nature of a problem situation and attempts to search for a set of agreed *views* concerning the problem situation; this is referred to within the method by the German word *Weltanschauung* which loosely translates as 'world-view'. This world-view establishes a set of beliefs and assumptions with regard to the system and its requirements. The world-view sometimes materializes as a *mission statement* of the overall purpose of the system. For example, a university may have a world-view that it should 'seek to provide the highest standard of education'. A business organization may hold a world-view that seeks 'to maximize revenue from overseas operations'.

The principles that underpin the soft systems approach can be distilled into the following:

▶ Any system should be seen in its holistic systems context.

▶ Business systems problems are often unstructured and are not deterministic.

▶ Information systems problems are usually specific to a business organization (such systems are normally not prone to the application of a single methodology).

▶ Normally business systems are complex and involve human activity components.

▶ Business systems problems are usually ill-defined or considered 'fuzzy' (these are sometimes referred to as soft problem situations).

▶ It is important to recognize the various forms of organization within business.

▶ Human activity is unpredictable within systems environments.

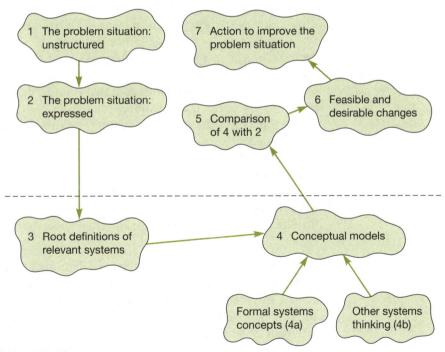

Figure 6.9 SSM in action

Source: Checkland, 1981.

All the ideas of the soft systems methodology are incorporated in two books by Peter Checkland: *Systems Thinking, Systems Practice* (1981) and, with Scholes, *Soft Systems Methodology in Action* (1990).

There are seven stages to the SSM approach, some of which are referred to as *real-world activities* and some of which are referred to as contemplation and *thinking stages*. Checkland stresses that the stages need not be taken in sequence; he argues that a number of stages can be undertaken simultaneously and often stages will need to be revisited. Figure 6.9 indicates the framework necessary for applying SSM.

1 **The problem situation: unstructured**: gaining an unstructured view of the problem situation. The term 'problem situation' is used by Checkland in preference to other terms that specifically relate to systems requirements. This stage involves participation by all those concerned with the system under observation and investigation, where the various views of the problem situation are gathered and acknowledged. This stage is undertaken to ascertain the channels of formal and informal communication within the system: SSM also looks at informal communications channels that fall outside the formal organizational structure of the business corporation.

2 **The problem situation: expressed**: taking the informal and unstructured picture of the problem situation, gathered in stage 1, and expressing the problem in a more formal and structured way. One of the tools used to achieve this is the creation of a *rich picture* of the problem situation. A rich picture uses visual symbols, pictures and drawings (with a minimum of text) to describe the problem situation (*see* Figure 5.16). The rich picture should pictorially show the processes, actors and interaction of processes within the problem situation; it can be a useful tool for communication between the technical specialists and the non-technical specialists, and other users, of the system. A rich picture should:
   - use the terminology and vocabulary that is understood in the environment of the system under investigation and analysis;
   - reveal problems and sources of conflict within the information systems environment;
   - serve as a tool of communication between the technical and non-technical system specialists;
   - be used to identify problems and themes present within the systems environment;
   - include the users, tasks, processes, internal and external agents affecting the system.

3 **The root definitions of relevant systems**: defining and naming relevant systems. Often a number of options will be proposed and these will need to be evaluated to determine the most appropriate solution to the problem situation. The main activity of this stage is the formulation of a *root definition* for the relevant system. The root definition defines the problems and the system. The root definition should be a concise, tightly constructed description of a human activity system which states and defines the nature of the system. The

root definition is created using a CATWOE technique that is a mnemonic for:

Client: the person affected by the information system.
Actor: the agent of change who carries out the transformation process.
Transformation: the change itself.
Weltanschauung: the world-view assumptions.
Owner: the answerable authority.
Environment: the wider holistic system.

Root definitions are a useful tool for clarifying the problems of a system and for exposing different viewpoints.

4 **Conceptual models**: building conceptual models, or diagrammatic representations of the activities and purpose of the system. This stage is undertaken when the participants in the system are satisfied that they have established a solid root definition. The conceptual models should give rise to debate in order to evaluate their application to the real world. A conceptual model should be drawn for each root definition and the models can be altered by a process of iterative changes, resulting from debate, by the participants using the methodology.

5 **Comparing the conceptual models with reality**: comparing the rich pictures of the problem situation with the conceptual models. This stage should ideally lead to the formulation of recommendations of the necessary changes within the systems environment.

6 **Feasibility and desirable changes**: analyzing the recommended changes from stage 5 to ascertain which changes are feasible and desirable.

7 **Action to improve the problem situation**: recommending actions for a solution to the initial problem situation that gave rise to the activity of systems analysis and design.

Overall, the strength of SSM resides in providing a framework for understanding a problem situation. However, a weakness is the fact that it is short on aspects related to implementation and evaluation of information systems. Significantly, SSM is different to hard methodologies because it studies the softer human activity present within systems environments. Therefore, the SSM approach is often seen as an excellent method for *analyzing* systems problems before adopting harder approaches for *implementing* a solution. In reality, the majority of systems development projects within the business environment often assume a hybrid approach to solving systems problems, which may lead to adoption of tools, techniques and ideas from a range of development methodologies.

The underlying strength of SSM lies in the fact that it tries to describe an organization's key activities and processes, and identify the main stakeholders and end users in the processes. The aim is to elicit a world-view of belief systems within the organizational domain, thus making it easier to design and develop systems that fit the organization and its collection of human activity.

6.8 Soft systems methodology

Outline and then discuss the main principles that underpin SSM and explain the problems of analyzing 'fuzzy' systems within the business environment. Think about and discuss the term *Weltanschauung*, which loosely translates as 'world-view', and indicate how this world-view may constrain or influence the shape and form of information systems within a business organization. Describe the process of developing a conceptual model and explain whether the use of conceptual models is a beneficial and appropriate way of defining the problem situation facing a business organization. Find a problem situation that occurs within business and use the soft systems method to analyze and solve the problem situation. Then prepare a report to your colleagues making recommendations regarding the problem situation and the required information systems solution.

6.9 Multiview

Multiview is a systems development methodology that is a hybrid of a number of other methodologies and adopts various tools and techniques that are appropriate to the systems situation. It was particularly popular in the 1990s. Multiview is a soft systems development approach that borrows many of the ideas of SSM and ETHICS, but incorporates harder tools and techniques as necessary. It is a flexible approach that is often used for small-scale project development and to assist applications-based development. Multiview is a methodology that, as its name implies, takes a multiple view (or perspective) of a system's environment; it takes a view of the human, technical and organizational aspects of information systems.

The five stages of multiview are:

1 **Analysis of human activity:**
   – establish a *Weltanschauung*
   – describe the systems requirements using rich pictures
   – establish root definitions
   – establish a conceptual model of activities
   – compare the conceptual model with the rich pictures
   – implement any changes through a process of iteration.

2 **Information modelling:**
   – develop a functional model
   – develop an entity model.

3 **Analysis and design of socio-technical aspects:**
   – establish human requirements
   – establish organizational requirements
   – establish socio-technical goodness of fit
   – assess future socio-technical environment.

4 **Design of the human–computer interface:**
   – develop the technical design of the human–computer interface
   – establish the design of input and output mediums.

5 **Design of technical aspects:**
   - design technical environment
   - implement a technical solution
   - test and evaluate the system
   - maintain ongoing systems evaluation.

> ### What is multiview?
>
> An exploration in information systems development. The main premise of the approach is that only particular systems techniques will be appropriate to certain business organizations; therefore a business should adopt different aspects of the various available methodologies as thought appropriate within its own systems environment.

It should be recognized that the analysis of human activity stage is closely related to the SSM approach to analyzing problem situations. Stage 2 involves information modelling to analyze the entities and functions of the system; this is done through the development of a functional model that decomposes the functions down to understandable levels. Data flow diagrams can also be used to show the sequence of events. These can then be augmented with the development of an entity model through the use of data modelling techniques. The third stage involves the analysis and design of the socio-technical aspects of the system. This stage is influenced by the ETHICS approach to information systems development, particularly through user participation and systems stakeholder involvement in the development process; this stage assesses the socio-technical systems alternatives. The fourth stage – the design of the human–computer interface – is often one of the primary concerns of most systems users. The fifth stage involves the design of the technical aspects of the system; this stage uses the entity models from stage 2 and the technical requirements from stage 4 to establish a technical design to implement, test and evaluate the system on a continuous basis.

Activity 6.9 Multiview

Discuss the role and purpose of information modelling within the multiview approach and suggest how this methodology might assist the design of human-to-technology aspects of business information systems. List and describe four main advantages and disadvantages of using a methodology that is a hybrid of a number of other methodologies. Discuss the importance of multiview in modern information systems development.

6.10 Unified Modeling Language (UML)

The Unified Modeling Language (UML) was developed by the Object Management Group in the late 1990s. UML is concerned with enabling core business applications to be built successfully. UML is an open standard programming language for specifying, visualizing, constructing and documenting all the artefacts (i.e. applications and objects) of a software system. The themes of UML are scalability, security, and robust execution under stressful conditions. The object orientation idea is extended within UML to enable systems to be built and updated quickly, and to enable easier maintenance. Modelling the software systems environment is of paramount importance. UML tries to ensure software reliability within the systems domain, so emphasizes modelling the system, visualizing the design, and checking it against requirements before program coding begins. In some ways the UML approach is allied to *extreme programming* – the technique of flexible and quick software development that meets changing end-user requirements.

Open, cross-platform compatibility is fundamental to UML. It is claimed – and there is supporting evidence from its use in business – that UML should be able to be used across any application, running on any type and combination of hardware, operating system, programming language or network. The idea behind UML is that it is a realistic software systems development approach. Therefore, it is aimed at addressing real-world business problems and tries to be more flexible than previous structured software systems approaches. Since it is based on object-oriented ideas, it fits well with modern object-oriented tools and techniques found in modern systems development domains. It is an approach that is compatible with a range of modern object-oriented programming environments, such as C++ and Java. However, it can also be used with other programming environments, such as Visual Basic (VB).

What is the Unified Modeling Language?

A proprietary systems development method developed by Grady Brooch, Ivar Jacobson and James Rumbaugh. It was developed by the Object Management Group in the late 1990s and incorporates object-oriented techniques into the systems and software development activity.

One of the fundamental aspects of UML is good software systems design that meets end-user requirements. The emphasis is on structured modelling and design, but at the same time being flexible enough to adapt to changing user needs. UML has been called *evolutionary systems development* because information systems can be updated and refined in the light of changing business conditions or changing user requirements. Another characteristic of UML is that it is methodology-independent. The idea is to choose a methodology then map the UML approach on to it, specifically dealing with software-based systems development. UML also tries to emphasize code reuse within its object-oriented framework. Organizations can build up libraries of object code that constitute systems and sub-systems. Then information systems domains can be quickly customized and updated from existing libraries of coded applications (or objects).

UML defines 12 types of diagrams, divided into three categories:

▶ **Structural diagrams**: including class diagrams, object diagrams, component diagrams and deployment diagrams. These represent static application structure.

▶ **Behaviour diagrams**: including case diagrams, sequence diagrams, activity diagrams, collaboration diagrams and state-chart diagrams. These represent different aspects of dynamic behaviour.

▶ **Model management diagrams**: including packages, sub-systems and models. These represent the organization and management of applications and objects.

This set of static and dynamic diagrams represents the systems and business functions of an ICT architecture and how these functions relate to one another. The diagrams produce a 'blueprint' plan that systems developers can use to build and maintain ICT infrastructures and software. The main UML specification (and documentation) is available from the Object Management Group (OMG) website.

Activity 6.10   UML

Discuss the role and purpose of UML within software systems development. Outline the main characteristics of UML. Suggest why UML has become so popular in the systems development domain since the late 1990s. Discuss whether UML is a more globally accepted systems approach than SSADM. What are the main differences between SSADM and UML? Discuss the importance of UML in modern information systems development theory and practice.

PAUSE FOR THOUGHT 6.1

Modelling modern business information systems

Like it or not, modeling has become an essential way for agencies to handle the complexities of contemporary software and systems design. Developers can use modeling tools to graphically depict the parts of a proposed system and then use the models to guide their work.

Government business processes are also getting more complicated, as technology enables new forms of collaboration and information sharing within and between agencies. To assist in these activities, agencies are increasingly using modeling as a tool to develop and depict information technology enterprise architectures, which resemble blueprints that show the relationship between agency business processes and their supporting IT systems. Decision makers use these blueprints to help plan future IT investments.

Unified Modeling Language (UML), which was first released by the Object Management Group (OMG) in 1997, is one of the more important standards in the field. It's already the basis for most object-oriented software design, and it's becoming a standard for describing business processes.

Numerous companies that offer software development tools, called integrated development environments, have recently added or soon will add direct support for UML. The addition is expected to boost developers' productivity while allowing them to crank out software applications that better reflect the business processes that they automate.

But many see the potential for collaboration between end users and system developers as UML's most important advantage. Both groups are major stakeholders in an application development project, but they often struggle to talk to one another.

Proponents believe UML can help because it is an accessible, visual way of presenting

▶

software design elements and business processes to software engineers and business executives.

'Diagrams produced using UML are easily understood both by software and systems people and by normal people,' said Terry Quatrani, a self-described UML evangelist for software tools vendor Rational Software. The company is one of the original developers of UML and now part of IBM Corp.'s software group.

Before UML's existence, companies such as Rational toiled to clearly present complicated flow diagrams to customers 'who were not plugged into the geeky stuff,' she said. 'So UML definitely helps with that,' she said. 'It helps our customers to understand the intentions of the software that's been developed.'

'It is the same for groups within end-user organizations,' said Regina Gonzales, principal member of the technical staff at Sandia National Laboratories. Her group is using UML in business process re-engineering to formalize Sandia's technical business and the transfer and implementation of information. UML is also assisting in the development of an enterprise architecture to model the labs' business side and the IT side's execution of business processes.

'Even though the two groups may have a different way of looking at things, they are still reasoning about the same concepts,' she said. 'The nice thing about UML is that it creates positives for even those people who don't use a model-based approach and where there is a huge transition in translating things from a business to an IT-based perspective.'

In that sense, using UML 'really helps to get over that hump in communication,' she said. UML will also be a key factor in the development of web services because it lets people develop services in a language-neutral way. 'Architects and software designers can focus on what applications need to do without worrying about how they will be implemented,' said John Magee, vice president for Oracle9i JDeveloper at Oracle Corporation. That's particularly valuable in organizations that might have many different platforms and people who need to collaborate without breaking down the code.

'Another trend is how UML will affect the way applications developers work,' he said.

'Traditionally, the business analysts have made their models and then taken their requirements and "thrown them over the wall" to the developers and told them to go develop,' Magee said. 'Not surprisingly, the model has tended to sit on a shelf while the developers go about doing things their way.'

'But there's a need now for increased integration of the business and developer worlds,' he said. UML can link the business models and the code so that the models are updated automatically.

New software development tools incorporate this dynamic two-way interaction. Compuware Corp.'s OptimalJ, for example, is designed to speed the development of Java applications by generating working applications directly from visual models.

Modeling in the past was the domain of 'ivory tower businesspeople,' said Greg Keller, director of design and modeling solutions for Embarcadero Technologies Inc. They tended to forget about code developers when deadlines got tight, and higher-level requirements would be discarded, which complicated later changes. 'With UML, the developers no longer have an excuse not to be tied closely to the business requirements,' he said. 'UML has been wonderfully adopted by the high end of the analysts, and now we need to see how to make UML meaningful to coders so they don't have to stop modeling.'

'One benefit is making coding easier,' said Glenn Cammarata, a computer engineer working on flight software for the James Webb Space Telescope at NASA's Goddard Space Flight Center. 'Just by itself, UML doesn't give you any real bang for your buck,' he said. 'The other major thing it provides is automated generation of code.'

Cammarata uses a real-time variant of IBM's Rational Rose RealTime, one of the major UML-based development tools. It provides automatic generation of code from models, 'so once the code is generated,' he said, 'you don't have to touch it.' 'Producing code is around a quarter of our total development costs, so just in this one area we can see a 40 to 60 percent gain in savings,' he said. Saying you are using UML is not enough, however, 'because it's just a language, after all,' said Jan Popkin, founder and chief executive officer of Popkin Software. You also need a process to put the diagrams that UML creates into context to produce a coherent model. 'And that's probably the bigger challenge,' he said. 'To use UML effectively, an agency needs the expertise to be able to fit it into the bigger picture.' 'Also,' he said, 'UML describes many things well but not everything.' When describing data, for example, there are other standards that do a better job, so users should always be aware that they will probably need to use other standards or models with UML.

'You also don't have to learn everything that is included with UML,' said Rob Byrd, chief operational architect for SI International, an IT services contractor that is doing extensive work on the Defense Department's Architecture Framework.

But he feels the time is past when people could choose to bypass UML and modeling completely. 'The traditional ways are not working anymore,' he said. 'They did when things were simple, but IT systems are now so overwhelmingly complex that you simply have to work in a different way.'

Source: Brian Robinson, 'Dynamic duo: business modelling and software tools find common ground', *Federal Computer Week*, 21 July 2003, © www.fcw.com.

6.11 An odyssey of information systems methods

Within Greek mythology, Odysseus was the king of the Ithaca renowned for his courage and resourcefulness. The *Odyssey* is an epic Greek poem in 24 books, attributed to the ancient Greek poet and author Homer (eighth century BC), that relates the adventures of Odysseus, known to the Romans as Ulysses, in his attempts to return home following the siege of Troy. Odysseus wanders on a long and adventurous journey for ten years until he finally returns home to the island kingdom of Ithaca. Odysseus is also credited with involvement in the idea of the wooden horse that finally led to the defeat of Troy.

In many ways the evolution of information systems is like a wandering odyssey from the 1960s until the early twenty-first century. Information systems methods and approaches have evolved and matured over time as information and communication technology, and business organizational structures, have evolved. Business is a human, dynamic and adaptive systems activity. In turn, methods and approaches to systems development in business have adapted and evolved to deal with the changing requirements of business systems.

One of the most important aspects of modern information systems development methods is the need to build information systems quickly to meet business requirements in competitive trading environments. All modern information systems development methods and approaches stress the imperative of rapid applications development. It can be said that 'information is power' in the modern business systems domain. Yet this is not a new concept: John Buchan's novel *Mr Steadfast* was written during the First World War (1914–18) and first published in 1919; in it he wrote: 'This war is a pack of surprises. Both sides are struggling for the margin, the little fraction of advantage, and between evenly matched enemies it's just the extra atom of fore-knowledge that tells.' Within this quote are found the conceptual ideas of competitive advantage, through the possession of information before a competitor, and the fact that systems are unpredictable (i.e. uncertain and dynamic) and full of surprises (i.e. business and environmental uncertainty). Therefore, modern information systems development methods enable easier maintenance and upgrading, and are inherently object based to enable reassembly to meet changing business conditions.

Over time the tools and techniques used in the systems development domain have become more sophisticated. These tools and techniques (e.g. diagramming tools, and object-oriented techniques and ideas) have also evolved. These various tools and techniques have through a serendipitous odyssey come together to provide the essence of modern rapid, object-oriented, information systems development. The journey of these tools and techniques from their inception in the 1960s and 1970s through to the twenty-first century has been long, winding and adventurous, particularly to those with a love of the information systems field.

6.12 Global information systems development methods

With advances in information and communications technology, particularly the web, object-oriented tools and techniques have become significant within the systems development process. In the networked and distributed business systems domain, systems objects can be located and found across global networks, rather than being restricted to localized business systems environments in any one geographical location, as was the case before advanced and accessible global networking. In addition, systems development teams, through technological advances in ICT, have wider access to good development practice within other business systems development environments.

One of the major changes in modern systems development practice has been the incorporation of end users into the systems development domain, thus allowing previously unachievable participation by end users in the systems development process. Advances in information and communication technology (both wired and wireless) and general end-user ICT literacy have created a global business environment that has enabled a range of tools and techniques to be used in harmony to achieve better systems development processes. What were formerly disparate and unrelated tools, techniques and methods have now, through an Odysseus-like journey from many locations of time and space, converged into a range of global methodologies for building information systems.

Many systems development methods in the early 1990s were specific to one particular country. However, as the 1990s progressed many of these methodologies merged and became global rather than country specific. For example, the STRADIS methodology developed in the early 1970s stressed the importance of DFDs and top-down problem decomposition. These tools and techniques are still used today in different forms in modern systems development approaches, such as UML and SSADM. In turn, SSADM has become a globally accepted structured methodology for building information systems. Later on in the 1990s the

Yourdon systems method (YSM) used functional decomposition and emphasized the importance of data structures. These ideas were taken up later, and in many ways UML is a product of 30 years of systems thinking and systems practice.

In the early 1990s a development methodology known as MERISE was used in France, Spain and Switzerland and was based on a life cycle approach to systems development. MERISE consisted of three development cycles, the decision cycle, the life cycle and the abstraction cycle. The abstraction cycle was the key: in this cycle both data and processes are viewed firstly at the conceptual level, then the logical or organizational level and finally at the physical or operational level. Some of these conceptual modelling ideas have found their way, both consciously and sub-consciously, into other development methodologies, such as UML that uses a range of modelling and diagramming technique cycles.

In modern systems development environments the DSDM Consortium represents a global approach to systems development. It is a consortium of some of the world's largest and most influential corporations, all propounding a common approach to rapid information systems development known as the dynamic systems development method. In many ways a methodology can be said to be a set of tools and techniques underpinned by a philosophy. Typically, a methodology adopts a set of integrated techniques, such as entity-relationship modelling and data flow modelling. The model being developed is the basis of the methodology's 'view of the world'. That world in business systems terms is now a lot smaller because of the development of globally integrated business information systems.

6.13   Chapter summary

Information systems methodologies come in many forms, some relying on hard tools and techniques and others on softer approaches to information system development. Therefore, there is no single universally adopted methodology for building business information systems. However, the aim of all systems methodologies is to develop the most efficient and effective information system for decision making within the business environment as is practicable and possible, given the environmental system's constraints.

A methodology formally defines the processes used to gather business and end-user requirements, analyzes them, and designs an application that meets those requirements. There are many reasons why one methodology may be better than another for a particular business domain. For example, some are better suited for large enterprise applications while others are built to design small-scale systems that can be regularly upgraded and altered (in an object-oriented manner) to meet changing business environment conditions.

What is a methodology?

A recommended collection of philosophies, phrases, procedures, rules, techniques, tools, documentation, management and training for the development of information systems.

Source: The British Computer Society Working Group

It is essential for any student who studies information systems within the business environment to be aware of the scope and flexibility inherent within the spectrum of information systems development methodologies. It is often the case that information systems environments that are difficult to define call for a softer approach to the analysis and design of a business systems solution. On the other hand, many harder methodologies are based on more formal tools and techniques.

In the final analysis the adoption of a methodological framework should depend upon the nature of the organization and its global environment. It should always be recognized that human interaction within the systems environment is a significant factor that must be successfully addressed in order to achieve effective and efficient business information systems development. The eventual adoption of a methodology often depends upon the systems philosophy prevailing within the organization and the design team and the effect of the ethos, or personality, of that business organization.

SHORT SELF-ASSESSMENT QUESTIONS

6.1 List and explain the main reasons why a *methodology* is a requirement for information systems development within the business environment.

6.2 Describe the ideal *aims* or objectives that any information systems development methodology should encompass.

6.3 Define the methodology known as *structured systems analysis and design of information systems* (STRADIS) and explain its evolution as a systems development method.

6.4 Suggest some of the possible benefits to a business organization of using a structured approach to information systems design and development.

6.5 Outline the four main stages of information systems development within STRADIS and explain the significance of each stage and its relationship to the traditional SDLC.

6.6 Define the *Yourdon systems method* (YSM) and describe the tools and techniques that would be used within the Yourdon method.

6.7 Define the *information engineering* (IE) method for developing information systems and describe the tools and techniques that would be used within the IE method.

6.8 Describe the four layers of IE and explain the purpose and function of each layer within the IE methodology.

6.9 Outline and explain the seven main stages of information systems development within *SSADM*.

6.10 Define *Jackson systems development* (JSD) and describe the main tools and techniques used within the JSD methodology.

6.11 Outline the three generic stages to systems development within the JSD methodology and explain the importance of *modelling* within the scope and remit of the JSD approach.

6.12   Define *effective technical and human implementation of computer-based systems* (ETHICS) and describe the two main *philosophical* strands present within the ETHICS approach to systems development.

6.13   Outline and describe the importance of user involvement in the ETHICS methodology and explain why job satisfaction and job enrichment are important aspects within its methodological framework.

6.14   Outline the 13 generic stages to ETHICS design and development and indicate the main principles of the development process.

6.15   Define *soft systems methodology* (SSM) and explain the use of the term 'soft' to describe the nature of an information systems development framework.

6.16   Outline and describe the seven stages to systems building using SSM and explain the difference between the *real-world activities* and the *thinking* stages.

6.17   Describe the use of *rich pictures* at stage 2 of SSM and outline the main advantages and disadvantages of using rich pictures to communicate the problem situation.

6.18   Explain the purpose and role of the *root definition* at stage 3 and describe the mnemonic CATWOE in defining a root definition.

6.19   Explain how *multiview* combines various systems ideas, tools and techniques into a holistic approach to systems development.

6.20   Describe the five stages of multiview and indicate the role of user participation within each stage of the systems development process.

6.21   Outline the main characteristics of the *Unified Modeling Language* (UML) and explain the significance of UML in the modern information systems development domain.

EXTENDED STUDENT ACTIVITIES

Individual reporting activity   Compile a list of ten points outlining the benefits of using a known systems development methodology as a framework for building effective and efficient information systems. Discuss how a methodological framework can be used as a problem-solving tool for analyzing and designing effective business information systems. Discuss what you believe to be the roles and responsibilities of the business end user and the technical systems specialist in the analysis, design, implementation and evaluation of information systems.

Group-based activity   Effective technical and human implementation of computer-based systems (ETHICS) lies at the soft end of the systems development methodology spectrum. It is a people-oriented systems development methodology that is based on user participation within the development process. The philosophy of ETHICS encompasses a socio-technical view of systems development. Discuss with your colleagues the merits of basing a systems development methodology on the two aspects of:

▶ job satisfaction

▶ user involvement in the system development process.

Create a user guide for systems development that explains the level and function of user participation in the information systems development process. Your user guide should be precise – no longer than three pages in length. The guide should include rules, policy guidelines and explain the role of user participants, such as the facilitator.

REFERENCES AND FURTHER STUDY

Books and articles

An asterisk (*) indicates a seminal text – a major source for later academic developments.

Avison, D.E. and Fitzgerald, D. (2002) *Information Systems Development: Methodologies, Techniques and Tools*, McGraw-Hill Education, ISBN: 0077096266

Avison, D.E. and Wood-Harper, A.T. (1990) *Multiview: An Exploration in Information Systems Development*, McGraw-Hill, ISBN: 0632630267

Bell, G.A. et al. (2002) 'The Holon framework and software process improvement: a radiotherapy project case study', *Software Process Improvement and Practice*, 7, pp. 57–70

Bennett, S., McRobb, S. and Farmer, R. (2001) *Object Oriented Systems Analysis and Design Using UML*, McGraw-Hill Education, ISBN: 0077098641

*Checkland, P. (1981) *Systems Thinking, Systems Practice*, John Wiley and Sons, ISBN: 0471279110

Checkland, P. and Scholes, J. (1990) *Soft Systems Methodology in Action*, John Wiley and Sons, ISBN: 0471927686

Checkland, P. and Scholes, J. (1999) *Soft Systems Methodology in Action: Includes a 30-year Retrospective*, John Wiley and Sons, ISBN: 0471986054

Conallen, J. (2002) *Building Web Applications with UML*, Addison-Wesley, ISBN: 0201730383

DeMarco, T. (1979) *Structured Analysis and System Specification*, Prentice Hall, ISBN: 0138543801

Fowler, M. and Scott, K. (1999) *UML Distilled: A Brief Guide to the Standard Object Modelling Language*, Addison-Wesley, ISBN: 020165783x

*Gane, C. and Sarson, T. (1979) *Structured Systems Analysis: Tools and Techniques*, Prentice Hall, ISBN: 0138545472

Goodland, M. and Slater, C. (1995) *SSADM Version 4*, McGraw-Hill Education, ISBN: 007709073x

Jackson, M.C. (2000) *Systems Approaches to Management*, Kluwer Academic, ISBN: 030646506x

Maciaszek, L. (2001) *Requirements Analysis and Systems Design: Developing Information Systems with UML*, Addison-Wesley, ISBN: 0201709449

Mumford, E. (1995) *Effective Systems Design and Requirements Analysis: The ETHICS Approach*, Palgrave Macmillan, ISBN: 0333639081

Mumford, E. (1998) *Systems Design: Ethical Tools for Ethical Change*, Palgrave Macmillan, ISBN: 0333669290

Mumford, E. (2000) *Redesigning Human Systems*, Idea Group Inc, ISBN: 1931777888

Sutcliffe, A. (1988) *Jackson Systems Development*, Prentice Hall, ISBN: 013308136x

Tardieu, H. et al. (1991) *MERISE in Practice*, Palgrave Macmillan, ISBN: 033355020x

Weaver, P.L. (1998) *Practical SSADM Version 4+*, FT Prentice Hall, ISBN: 0273626752

Weaver, P.L. et al. (2002) *Practical Business Systems Development Using SSADM: A Complete Tutorial Guide*, FT Prentice Hall, ISBN: 0273655752

Wieringa, R.J. (2003) *Design Methods for Reactive Systems: Yourdon, Statemate and the UML*, Morgan Kaufmann, ISBN: 1558607552

Yourdon, E. (1993) *Yourdon Systems Method: Model Driven Systems Development*, Yourdon Press, ISBN: 0130451622

Yourdon, E. (1993) *The Decline and Fall of the American Programmer*, Prentice Hall PTR, ISBN: 0132036703

Yourdon, E. (1993) *The Rise and Resurrection of the American Programmer*, Prentice Hall PTR, ISBN: 013121831x

Journals   *European Journal of Information Systems*
Information Systems Journal

Web resources   **Dynamic Systems Development Method Consortium (UK/North America/global)** – promotes the use of DSDM as a de facto global systems development framework.
www.dsdm.org   www.na.dssm.org

Agile Alliance (USA) – access to information and discussion material on agile methods, extreme programming and DSDM.
www.agilealliance.com

Object Management Group (USA) – access to information and discussion material on UML.
www.omg.com

PART **2**

The application of information and communication technology (ICT)

Chapter 7

Business systems activity

When you have studied this chapter you will be able to:

▶ define the role and purpose of planning, decision making and control within the business systems environment;

▶ describe the environmental differences between the various systems processes found at each level of decision making within the business environment;

▶ evaluate the nature of decision making within the business systems environment and understand how ICT is incorporated into the decision-making processes of business activity;

▶ distinguish the characteristics and role of operational systems, management systems and strategic systems within the business environment;

▶ understand the relationship and integration of transaction processing systems within the business environment.

7.1 Introduction to business systems activity

The activity of *decision making* within the business systems environment involves undertaking two prerequisite activities of *planning* and *control*. The sequence of activity follows the path of:

▶ **Planning**: deciding, in advance, *what* is to be done, *how* it is to be carried out, *when* it is to be achieved and *who* (or what) is to achieve it. Therefore, planning is heavily dependent upon accurate data and information generated from reliable information systems. This type of data is often referred to as *intelligence* within the decision-making process. Planning is a means of providing a guiding steering mechanism for decision making.

▶ **Decision making**: directing an organization down a particular, desirable and chosen path. Decision making involves deciding on appropriate and suitable action in given situations. To take appropriate business decisions requires information. Solid, reliable, accurate and factual information is critical for decision making.

▶ **Control**: monitoring and ensuring that the plans of the organization are being implemented and are on schedule, within a given timescale.

The activity of planning, decision making and control occurs throughout all decision-making levels of a business organization. Chapter 2 examined the nature and role of the three main generic decision-making levels of a typical hierarchical business organization: the operational (or transactional), managerial and strategic (or executive) levels. At the bottom level of the decision-making hierarchy *transaction processing systems* (TPS) are concerned with short-term planning and systems control; at the middle of the organizational hierarchy *management information systems* (MIS) are concerned with medium-term planning, decision making and control; and at the top of the organizational hierarchy, at and near the organizational apex, *executive information systems* (EIS) are concerned with long-term strategic planning, decision making and control.

A large amount of academic study since the 1960s has been directed at defining the process of decision making within the business contest. Much of this work derives from the seminal work of Simon in 1960. It is generally accepted that there are a number of generic stages in the decision-making process, as follows:

▶ **Input**: gathering and collecting data.

▶ **Intelligence**: scrutinizing and examining the data.

▶ **Design**: formulating the problem and testing solutions.

▶ **Choice**: making a selection from a number of options.

▶ **Implementation**: choosing and implementing the choice option.

▶ **Output**: the decision.

Decision making can be divided into *rational* and *non-rational* decision making. Rational decision making is based on substantiated facts and data. Non-rational decision making is largely based on opinion, feelings or instinctive judgement. Within business both rational and non-rational types of decision making occur. However, it is generally accepted that rational decision making, based on facts and gathered data, is more certain than non-rational decision making. In reality, most decision making in the business domain is based on imperfect knowledge and data. Decisions are often made on the basis of incomplete data and information. This obviously reduces the level of certainty within the decision-making domain. The three main problems causing the level of certainty to fall are:

▶ limited time available to make a decision;

▶ limited information and data, providing an incomplete picture of the problem;

▶ ineffective systems for processing data and information for the purpose of decision making.

Accurate and timely information reduces uncertainty in the decision-making environment. Information is the lifeblood of decision making. Rational decision making involves making decisions on the basis of guidelines and rules – this is often known as *objective* decision making. Non-rational decision making takes place without relying on rules, guidelines or substantiated data and is often considered to be *subjective* (i.e. based on feeling and intuition rather than facts and figures).

The process of planning, decision making and control normally relies on the activity of information modelling. Models can be graphical, numerical, symbolic, mathematical or algorithmic. Modelling assists the planning, decision-making and control process by allowing variables and alternative courses of action to be studied and manipulated at controllable organizational cost and with minimal business risk. The successful process of planning, decision making and control enables the activity of decision making on a daily, weekly, monthly and yearly basis.

The process of decision making involves selecting an approach and taking action on a preferred plan. There are four main systems modelling phases in the decision-making process:

▶ investigating the occasions and conditions for decision-making activity;

▶ looking at and analyzing a range of alternative courses of action;

▶ choosing and selecting a course of action and implementing the decision;

▶ evaluating and reviewing past decision choices and actions.

Like planning, the activity of recurring decision making is dependent upon reliable and accurate information that needs to be fed back into the decision-making systems environment from the established systems control mechanisms. Planning, decision making and control is a *life cycle*. The output is fed back into the life cycle so that future decisions are based on previous experience. Remember Chapter 2 outlined the theory and practice of feedback and control models within information systems. The various decision-making levels of a business organization exhibit different feedback and control timeframes. Decision making at the strategic level of an organization will have a long time lag between the decision being made and the availability of feedback information to evaluate the initial decision. Such strategic decision making will also rely on a high level of human judgement that implies that the strategic decision-making activity is prone to high levels of uncertainty and, therefore, correlated risk. However, at the transaction processing level of business, at the bottom of the typical organizational hierarchy, the decision-making activity will have an immediate timescale between a decision being made and the availability of feedback information to evaluate that decision. Such operational decision making is made on a day-to-day, or ephemeral, basis and is characterized by structured and deterministic systems environments, with minimal human judgement or discretion involved in the decision-making activity.

Within the decision-making and information feedback scenario the activity of control is concerned with the use of techniques and procedures to ensure that the decisions made, at each level of the organization hierarchy, are implemented as required and according to the plan.

Activity 7.1 Planning, decision making and control

Write a 500-word executive report to explain what is meant by the planning, decision-making and control life cycle. Explain why these business systems activities are intrinsically related and suggest in the report whether there are any known phases or stages to the planning, decision-making and control life cycle. Then, outline seven reasons why the process of planning is considered difficult. Do you believe that a business organization should invest human and technological resources in the activity and process of planning?

Outline the main activities involved in the decision-making process of a business organization and explain some of the different characteristics of decision making within the three main organizational levels of a typical decision-making hierarchy. Suggest why the process of control is a vital part of the planning, decision-making and control life cycle and state the intended aim of management control within a typical business organization.

7.2 Real-world decision making

Decision making in the real world is subject to varying levels of uncertainty. The reason for this is because time is limited when making decisions. If too long is taken to make a decision then there is a danger that the conditions that under-pin the decision-making environment will change and, therefore, the facts and figures presented are no longer relevant. It is also essential to have complete and unabridged information. The more complete the information picture the more certain the decision-making environment. The way that information is processed in an organization is also critical. It is not enough to have accurate information, it must also be reliable and reliability depends on the accuracy of processing within an information systems environment.

The planning, decision-making and control life cycle has the following steps:

▶ objectives setting
▶ planning strategies
▶ decision making
▶ directing and executing tasks
▶ obtaining feedback
▶ monitoring and control.

Information systems are essential in assisting the activities and processes of planning, decision making and control; they are part of the decision-making infrastructure and can also assist the decision-making process by providing infor-mation and support where and when required. In this chapter we will investigate the nature of the business systems environment and the types of information system used to support the planning, decision-making and control activities found within the three generic levels of a hierarchical organization.

The information systems at each generic level of an organization display a con-tinuum of different characteristics that determine the goals and nature of each individual system used for decision making. We discovered in Chapter 2 that operational systems operate under conditions of certainty and are deterministic to the extent that the inputs and outputs are known with certainty. The nature of the management information systems environment is different to that of the operational systems environment in that such systems operate under higher levels of uncertainty. The main goal of most managerial systems is to assist managers in their decision-making activities. Strategic information systems operate under business environment conditions of greater uncertainty than managerial systems, with the purpose of strategic information systems being to assist senior executives in making decisions that affect the long-term strategic direction of the overall business organization.

At the operational level of the business systems environment routine decisions are made on a day-to-day basis, where much decision making is undertaken by computerized transaction processing systems. Management information systems aim to provide information for managers to take decisions regarding the allocation of resources, both human and technological, within the bounds of the organization. Therefore, managers carry out the plans of senior executives by supervising, managing and coordinating the resources of the business organization and thereby fulfilling a role within the control systems of an organization. Executive information systems aim to assist the senior executives in their task of guiding the long-term future direction of the business organization. Executive decision making is characterized by decision-making creativity and judgement

Did you know?

Operational systems such as inventory (or stock) control can be computerized automatically to reorder stocks of raw materials for the manufacturing process when the minimum stock levels have been reached. When stock levels are low, the computer automatically sends an electronic message or signal to the suppliers' computer system to place a reorder of stock; the suppliers' system actions the request and automatically generates a decision for goods to be supplied to its customer.

and unstructured problems which are infrequent and difficult to define, often in environments exhibiting high levels of uncertainty.

The quality of decision making will affect the performance of a business organization. Therefore, planning, decision making and control are activities and processes that must be carried out thoroughly with regard to all relevant environmental factors. An information system used to assist decision making, particularly at the management and executive levels of an organization, should:

▶ consider the full range of factors affecting the decision, both formal and informal;

▶ explore all the alternative courses of action available within the decision-making environment;

▶ assimilate all the possible information related to the decision-making environment;

▶ evaluate the risks, costs and benefits of a range of courses of action;

▶ make detailed plans for implementing the various and available courses of action;

▶ review the effectiveness of past decisions to assess the impact on current decisions.

The overall objective of the planning, decision-making and control life cycle is to achieve the business goals and objectives of the organization, and information systems are established in business organizations to support this activity.

Activity 7.2 The Campari model

The creative use of business plans can determine whether an individual or business organization receives any monetary backing for business ventures and projects. One method used by banks to judge the merits of a plan is known as the Campari model (see Pause for thought 7.1). It stands for:

character
ability
margin
purpose
amount
repayment
insurance.

Write a brief 500-word management report on the main strengths and weaknesses of the Campari method for evaluating business plans and indicate other aspects that would need to be considered for the purposes of planning, decision making and control.

PAUSE FOR THOUGHT 7.1

Creative use of plans can bring in funds

Creative use of business plans for ongoing monitoring of a firm's performance is one thing banks look for when assessing whether to give backing, according to David Lavarack, head of small business services at Barclays Bank.

He gave some tips on how to secure bank finance – including matching up to what is known as the Campari test – to an Institute of Directors' conference on financing company growth.

What worries Mr Lavarack is a lack of essential commercial skills among British managers in running their own businesses, underlined by some Barclays research. This showed only 54 per cent of businesses drew up a formal business plan, covering cash flow, budgeting, sales and marketing, production targets and staffing.

Only one in five understand that a business plan should be used as a living document to measure ongoing commercial performance. This is because most businesses see writing a business plan primarily as a means of obtaining finance.

Two-thirds of businesses plan only a month ahead, with less than a quarter taking a one-year view.

Mr Lavarack said that, increasingly, Barclays bases its criteria for funding small businesses on evidence of thorough planning and sound commercial acumen. Barclays has found nearly 40 per cent of plans contain no detailed marketing and sales estimates. With nearly two-thirds of businesses not fully understanding their costs, they underestimate the value of products and charge less than customers are prepared to pay.

A fifth of businesses without a plan have a deliberate policy of undercutting the competition, whereas only 4 per cent of those with a plan adopt this policy.

The Campari test covers assessments for character (of those running the business), ability (business skills levels), margin (the interest rate to be struck in relation to risk), purpose (the precise use of a bank loan which should be stuck to), amount (lending too little can be wrong), repayment, and insurance (in the sense of security for a loan).

Source: Derek Harris, *Guardian*, November 1993.

7.3 The classic approach to decision making

The process of planning, decision making and control is a major activity for business managers. The role of a manager is to plan, coordinate, organize, then decide on various courses of action, and control costs and budgets. In modern business systems domains the manager is also required to be a trainer and motivator of staff. All these activities of managers are referred to as the *behavioural model* of management. Within modern business environments a manager utilizes formal methods and non-formal methods of decision-making behaviour. Managers are often reactive to situations, but in some circumstances can be proactive. Management is very much a human systems activity. It requires knowledge of human behaviour as well as systems behaviour.

In the 1970s Henry Mintzberg studied the behaviour of managers, mainly through observational studies of managers going about their everyday jobs. Mintzberg classified managerial roles into three categories:

▶ **Interpersonal**: the manager acts as a figurehead in the organization. The figurehead is a symbolic position that represents the organization and its employees. The role involves acting as a leader, supporter and motivator of staff and involves liaison between the three main levels of the organizational hierarchy: the manager sits at the middle level of the hierarchy acting as a conduit between the lowest level and the highest level of the organization. Thus the role is one of facilitating interpersonal relationships within the organization.

▶ **Informational**: the manager acts as an information repository. The manager distributes information to employees that require that information – thus the manager becomes an information communicator and information facilitator.

▶ **Decisional**: the manager takes responsibility for day-to-day decision making. The manager is seen as the person responsible for making decisions, negotiating solutions to problems and 'fire-fighting' the problems that occur between employees and employees and systems. The manager takes the initiative to solve problems through incisive decision making. The role also involves allocating resources to employees to enable their job functions.

However, managers do not often work in isolation – they often work within collaborative networks of managers. An effective manager will understand the organization, its structures and political motivations. Within *bureaucratic models* of decision making the reduction of uncertainty is a paramount consideration. The aim of a bureaucratic organization is self-preservation. Bureaucratic models of organizational structure are slow to change: the emphasis is on controlling uncertainty and attempting either incremental growth or self-sustainment. Such organizations are structurally rigid and based on documented and standard operating system procedures. Government departments are often referred to as bureaucratic organizations because they identify closely with these characteristics.

The bureaucratic model of organizational decision making can be compared with the *political model* of decision making. These organizations are less rigid in terms of structures and procedures. Solutions to problems are worked out on an ad hoc basis. There is no formal reliance on structured standard operating system procedures. Decisions are taken quickly through bargaining and political negotiation between employees and departments in an organization. The models of responsibility and authority are less defined in political models of decision making than in bureaucratic models of decision making.

Within any organizational setting there are four main psychological types of decision maker:

▶ **Intuitive decision maker**: leads and makes decisions by holistic judgment. Intuitive decision makers are more likely to want to see the larger picture of the problem environment – they are not concerned with the details, but with the 'bigger issues'.

▶ **Thinking decision maker**: is analytical, logical and takes their time to work through the details of the problem. These people tend to rely on facts and figures and underplay aspects of intuition and feelings.

▶ **Feeling decision maker**: is aware of the effect of decisions on employees and others in the organization. These people follow their own feelings, and loyalties to people, and are primarily concerned with buttressing the feelings of others.

▶ **Sensing decision maker**: reacts to the environment around them. They make decisions based on the current facts and data. They try to contextualize problems and to be very aware of current trends and objectives within an organization.

Business is a human systems activity. It relies on people and so needs to deal with the individuality of people. People possess different cognitive styles. In addition, the behaviour of human beings is often adaptive and non-deterministic. However, people interact with computerized ICT systems that by their vary nature are deterministic. So how do systems developers build systems to meet the needs of human decision makers? The primary objective of any information system is to support the process of planning, decision making and control. Systems therefore need to be flexible and, if possible, adaptive. The systems should be capable of supporting different human cognitive styles and they should be designed to align with the nature of an organization (i.e. either a bureaucratic or political organizational structure).

The following sections of this chapter outline some of the main functional and managerial systems used within business organizations to collate information to support decision making.

7.4 Transaction processing systems

Operational systems within the business environment are normally referred to as *functional systems* or *transaction processing systems* (TPS) because they carry out the basic day-to-day activities, transactions and functions of an organization. Irrespective of whether a business organization sells products or services, it will rely on a range of operational systems. The following is a list of the common transaction processing systems found within the operational level of a typical business organization:

- sales order processing
- purchase order processing
- receiving and distribution
- payroll (wages and salaries)
- accounting (financial accounting and management accounting)
- production planning
- production control
- inventory (or stock) control.

These operational systems are usually found within organizations that manufacture or produce products. However, many of these operational systems are also found within the systems environments of organizations that only sell or market services. Other information systems that are commonly found at the operational level and also at higher levels of an organization are:

- marketing
- customer service (or after-sales customer support)
- research and development
- personnel (or human resources).

Transactions between a business organization and its customers give rise to an exchange of money, therefore operational systems are essential to overall business prosperity in that they directly interact with an organization's customers and suppliers.

What is the difference between a supplier and a customer?

In the context of the business systems environment, a supplier is an individual or organization that provides goods or services to a business organization; these may be either finished products or raw materials. A customer is an individual or organization that purchases a product or service from a business organization. The customer and the supplier are sometimes referred to as the 'external entities' of a business organization.

A typical transaction processing system is characterized by the processing of large amounts of numeric and alphanumeric data. Normally a transaction processing system will have four main components:

▶ **Data input**: keyboard, data scanner, voice input, data downloading, biometric input, etc.

▶ **Data processing**: mainframe, server, PC or networked server environment, etc.

▶ **Data and information output**: computer screen, file transfer, reports, electronic data interchange (EDI), etc.

▶ **Data storage**: computer disk, CD-ROM, mainframe storage, DVD-RW, etc.

Transaction processing systems are typified by a number of characteristics that are indicative of the routine and deterministic nature of operational systems activity within a business systems environment:

▶ large-scale alphanumeric data processing activities

▶ heavy data storage requirements

▶ high level of routine and repetitive processing

▶ reliance on deterministic computation and mathematical algorithms

▶ frequent and routine operation on a regular day-to-day basis.

Transaction processing activities

Transaction processing systems usually involve the following activities:

▶ **Data collection**: collecting and collating all the data necessary for the transaction processing system. This data can be collected in a number of ways, such as electronic or paper-based invoices, bar code readers, scanners and electronic point-of-sale (EPOS) terminals, or even biometric identification.

▶ **Data manipulation**: transforming data by performing calculations, and operations, on that data. This process may involve sorting, aggregating, classifying, summarizing or calculation of the data.

▶ **Data storage**: placing data in the correct and appropriate storage area once it has been through the process of data manipulation.

▶ **Data or information generation**: outputting information in a form that can be used for immediate decision making or which can be used as the data input source of another related information system within the business systems environment.

▶ **Output**: a computer screen or hardcopy report, or a data file that can be input into a related system via *electronic data interchange* (EDI), which is concerned with the electronic transfer of data and information from one computer-based system to another computer-based system via a computer network. The network could be a *local area network* (LAN) within a building or department or it could be a *wide area network* (WAN) that extends beyond the physical boundaries of an organization.

Transaction processing methods

When automated computerization first impacted upon transaction processing systems in the 1960s and 1970s there was only one method available for data processing, known as *batch processing*. Data was collated or grouped into batches that were processed together in one processing run. However, as information and communications technology improved it was possible to achieve a more efficient method of processing known as online or *real-time processing*. Such transaction processing involves dealing with transactions and processing transactions immediately, as and when they occur. An airline booking system is an example of a real-time transaction system, where flight reservations are made online and the system immediately records and updates the central booking and reservation system. The majority of information systems within business are now real-time systems. However, the payroll function (i.e. salaries and wages), within many organizations is still dealt with by batch processing methods, particularly when the payroll system has been outsourced to an external company.

Transaction processing architectures

Transaction processing systems integrate a number of applications, the nature of which is dependent upon the type of operational system that is being used. Many traditional operational systems included a master file and a transactions file: the master file represented a permanent storage of data (or information) on a storage medium such as a computer disk, CD-ROM or DVD. Examples of master (or core data) files are customer data files, supplier data files, or employee files. The data on the master files often remained locked in time until the file was updated. Related to such files were transaction files that contained activities or transactions that affected the master file. Most modern-day systems processing architectures utilize more sophisticated technologies that allow the automatic separation of master file and transaction file components.

The pervasion of computing and ICT on the operational functions within the business systems environment has improved the efficiency and effectiveness of these systems by:

▶ ensuring a high level of accuracy;
▶ allowing security of data entry and output;
▶ increasing the speed and productivity of operational functions;
▶ encouraging alignment and integration of operational functions.

Did you know?

An area of business that relies on large data storage and manipulation capacities is the trading and equities exchanges, such as the London Stock Exchange, the New York Stock Exchange and the Frankfurt Stock Exchange in Germany.

Among the first business functions to be affected by computerization and the proliferation of ICT within the business systems environment were the activities of sales order processing and purchase order processing. The following sections provide greater detail concerning the 12 functional systems outlined earlier in this section.

7.3 Transaction processing systems

Describe the main characteristics of a TPS and discuss why the payroll function of business organizations is considered an operational system. Explain what is meant by transaction processing activities and transaction processing method, and provide two examples of a transaction processing method. Discuss why transaction processing systems are so important to the financial health of a business organization.

7.5 The sales order processing system

Sales order processing activity involves collecting and collating orders from a business organization's customers. Customers usually place orders using a variety of communications mediums, including telephone orders, fax orders, e-mail orders, and orders communicated directly from one business organization's computer network to another organization's computer network – known as electronic data interchange (EDI). With wired or wireless electronic data interchange a customer or client can place orders directly from their transaction processing system into the transaction order processing system of another organization.

Within the framework of electronic data exchange there are no constraints on the time that orders can be placed, since they can be efficiently and effectively placed any time of the day or night, with the advantage of immediate electronic acknowledgment of receipt of the order by the order processing system.

Order processing systems can be either real-time or batch processed. They normally generate the following *output* information:

▶ daily sales journal (used as input to the accounting system);
▶ customer invoices (sent to the customer who placed the order);
▶ stock order notes (sent to the output stock system);
▶ sales reports (used by the marketing system).

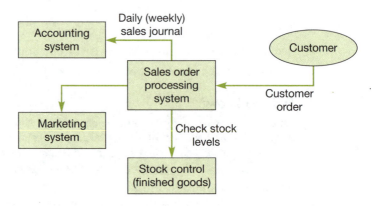

Figure 7.1 Sales order processing system

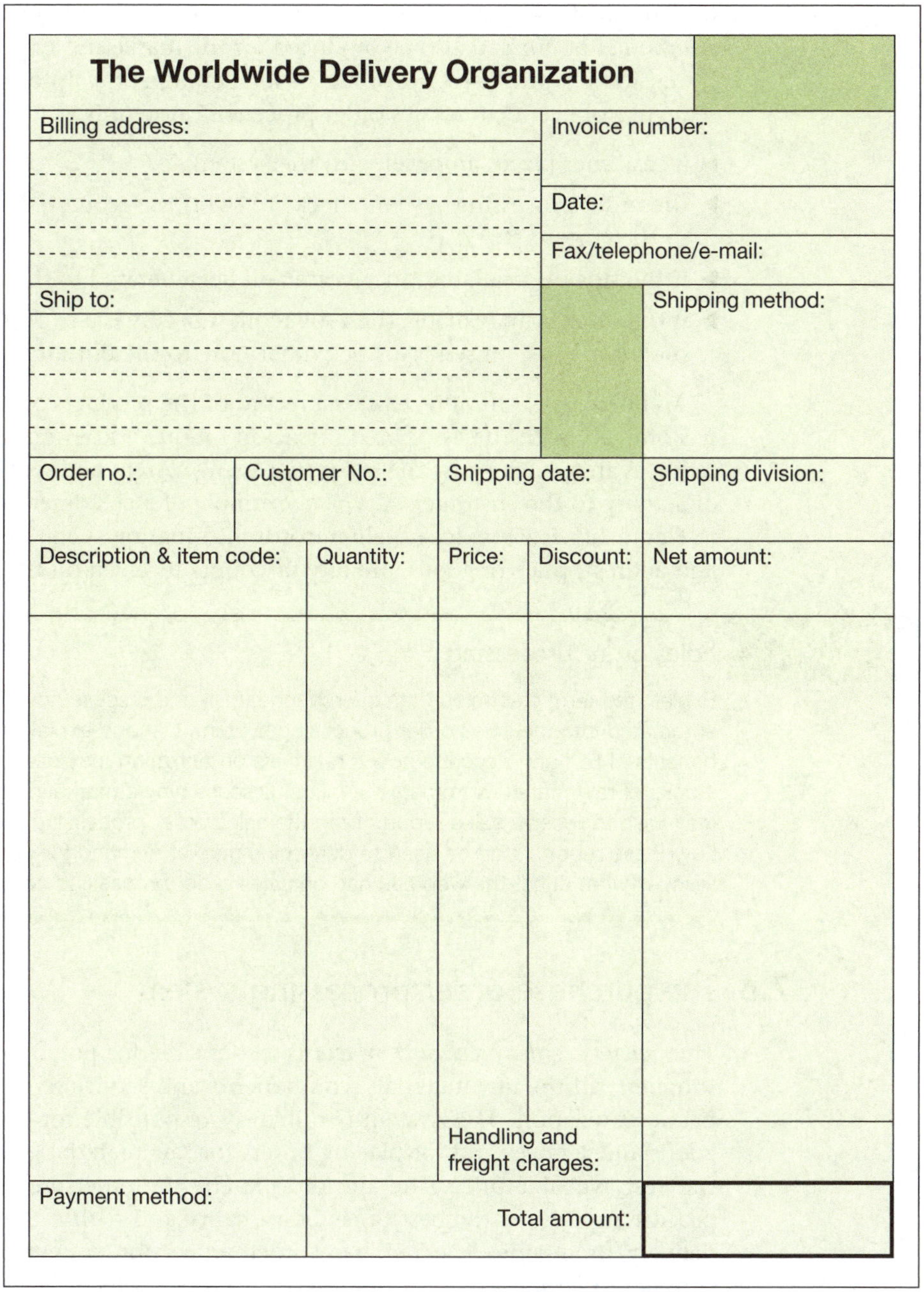

The Worldwide Delivery Organization

Billing address:	Invoice number:
	Date:
	Fax/telephone/e-mail:
Ship to:	Shipping method:

Order no.:	Customer No.:	Shipping date:	Shipping division:
Description & item code:	Quantity:	Price:	Discount:	Net amount:

			Handling and freight charges:	
Payment method:			Total amount:	

Figure 7.2 Example of an invoice

The connection between the sales order processing system and related systems is illustrated in Figure 7.1.

The *sales journal* information, which is sent to the accounting system as input data, usually includes customer information, products ordered (with product codes), discounts offered and price information. The *stock order notes* are sent to the output stock system if there is a requirement for further stock to be accumulated. *Sales reports* can also be produced for the marketing system, analyzing sales by customer, product line or by other demographic information. The usual sequence of events in a sales order processing system is as follows:

▶ a customer places an order with the system;
▶ the order processing system checks to see if the requested items are available in the current stock;
▶ if the stock is available, an invoice will be generated to the customer;
▶ if the stock is unavailable then the request becomes a back order and the order processing system sends a stock order note to the output stock system.

An *invoice* (i.e. bill or receipt) is a record of the products or services a customer has ordered, with the associated price and unique and associated product codes. Invoices are generated by the order processing system and sent as a factual record of activity to the customer. A typical example of a customer invoice can be seen in Figure 7.2. The invoice usually records information such as the customer name and address, price of goods and any discounts received on the goods.

Activity 7.4 Sales order processing

Explain the term electronic data interchange (EDI) and discuss how EDI may be automated into the sales order processing system. List and explain three possible benefits of EDI and describe how a business organization may use EDI to reorder stocks of raw materials from its suppliers. Discuss why a marketing information system may wish to receive sales reports from the sales order processing system and indicate how these reports may be used to determine market demand for goods and services. Discuss what effect the web has had on sales order processing activity.

7.6 The purchase order processing system

The *purchase order processing system* is responsible for purchasing, from external suppliers, all the raw materials, components and service requirements of a business organization. This system is primarily responsible for contract bidding for goods and services and for placing orders for raw material goods and services at the best available price. The aim of a purchasing order processing system is to procure supplies at the best price, best quality and within the most appropriate delivery timeframe. The purchase order processing system places orders with external organizations in a number of ways, such as by telephone, fax, e-mail or EDI. Purchasing order processing also has the aim of maintaining a good relationship with suppliers in order to secure competitive prices from them in the future.

The purchase order processing system usually generates the following *output* data and information:

▶ daily purchases journal (used as input to the accounting system);
▶ supplier orders (sent to the relevant supplier).

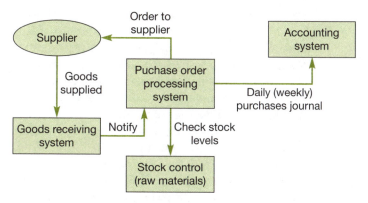

Figure 7.3 Purchase order processing system

The connection between the purchase order processing system and related systems is illustrated in Figure 7.3. The main activities of purchasing are to administer the purchasing of raw materials and equipment, maintain good contact with suppliers, keep track of new product developments, and negotiate suitable supplier contracts. The usual sequence of events in a purchase order processing system is as follows:

▶ a purchase order note is received from the input stock system;

▶ the purchase order processing system checks to see which suppliers need to be contacted for the requested items;

▶ a supplier order is generated and placed with the supplier;

▶ the purchase order system receives a supplier invoice.

Every business organization will have its own policies, practices and procedures for the purchasing of raw materials and other equipment from suppliers. The purchase order processing system will usually possess vast stores of data and information on suppliers' goods and services. Purchasing is a major activity that can often absorb up to 75 per cent of the earned income of a large manufacturing organization. Therefore, any cost savings can have a great effect on the overall profitability of a business organization.

Did you know?

The aim of purchasing (which is sometimes known as procurement or buying) is to buy the right material at the right quantity, in the right quality, at the right price, from the right supplier, with the right delivery arrangements, at the right delivery time and at the right payment terms.

The increased use of information and communication technology within business has given the purchasing function a broader and deeper access to information. For example, the internet and online electronic consumer databases have allowed purchasing managers to compare products and prices more efficiently and effectively than was the case previously. Furthermore, a business organization's computerized purchase order processing system can be directly linked to the computer systems of its suppliers, to reorder supplies automatically. This has allowed business organizations to maintain low (yet adequate) raw material stock levels that in turn can provide reduced purchasing costs and a saving of time. The efficiencies that have evolved from the purchasing of supplies and raw materials has led to the development of processes known as *just-in-time* systems. For example, the immediate delivery of raw materials to a manufacturing line, just when the minimum level is reached is referred to as *just-in-time manufacturing*. This enables an organization to maintain lower levels of physical raw material inventory on-site.

The *minimum stock level* for manufactured goods is determined by the volume of sales (or customer demand) for those products. Stock levels are monitored and compared with the minimum stock level required for an individual raw material to determine when to buy raw materials and components for the manufacturing process. Therefore, although they are separate systems within a business organization, sales order processing, purchase order processing and stock control are closely linked and related.

Activity 7.5 Purchase order processing systems

Discuss how electronic data interchange (EDI) is automated into the purchase order processing system and describe how it benefits the relationship between a business organization and its suppliers. Outline and explain the main aims and activities of the purchasing function of a business organization and indicate the possible relationship of the goods receiving system and the stock control system within the overall purchase order processing system. Discuss what effect the web has had on purchase order processing systems activity.

7.7 The goods receiving system and goods distribution system

The *goods receiving system* is usually responsible for physically taking possession of all the raw material goods coming into the business organization. The receiving system is also responsible for inspecting the supplied goods and routing them to the input stock system. The receiving system should notify the purchase order processing system when items have been received (*see* Figure 7.3). The inspection process may take many forms, but it is primarily responsible for ensuring an acceptable level of *quality control*.

Inspection procedures, and automated practices, can be established to monitor the quality of incoming raw materials and other equipment; any goods that fail the inspection can be sent back to the suppliers. The goods are usually delivered internally to the input stock system with a *stock received note*. Often, not all supplied goods are inspected, but rather a random sample of supplied goods are quality-checked on delivery. The goods receiving system often uses automated *sensors* and other control mechanisms to monitor the quality of goods incoming from suppliers.

The *goods distribution system* is responsible for shipping and delivering finished goods to the customer. The distribution system is responsible for implementing the most effective and efficient method of delivering goods to the customer. The system is also known as *logistics*. The distribution function, or logistical process, is usually given the responsibility for physically packaging and delivering all products to customers. The delivery method can include mail service, truck and rail distribution or aeroplane distribution. For example, the sale of books and other products through Amazon.com relies on a sophisticated logistical distribution network across the globe.

Physical goods are usually accompanied by a *stock delivery note*. Many distribution systems are also responsible for keeping track of the location of goods during delivery. For example, many parcel delivery companies enable their customers to track their parcels via a web interface. The customer logs into the parcel delivery system and is able to determine when a parcel is likely to be delivered: this is achieved by various systems scanning the parcel and automatically identifying the parcel as it goes through periodic scanning and identification processes during its journey to its final destination.

The function of getting goods from a business organization to its customers is known as *logistical planning*. Many software applications packages are available to assist in the logistical planning and coordination of the delivery of goods. Another application that is found within the distribution function is quality control of goods being dispatched to the customer.

Many online distribution systems allow customers and clients to ascertain the status of their orders and products as they are in transit from the business organization to the customer. Pause for thought 7.2 provides an example of a worldwide parcel delivery distribution system.

Activity 7.6   The goods receiving system and goods distribution system

Discuss and describe the role that quality control plays within the two systems of goods receiving and goods distribution and suggest how information technology has affected these two business functions. Then describe the data and documentation that are inputs and outputs of the goods receiving and goods distribution systems.

PAUSE FOR THOUGHT 7.2

A worldwide parcel and package delivery system

To meet the demands of efficiency and effectiveness, courier and package delivery organizations such as Federal Express, DHL and United Parcel Service (UPS) have invested millions of pounds in information technology. Such investment is being used in two major ways:

▶ The global parcel and package delivery operators transact business on a global scale and the operational efficiencies of operating in many different countries are dependent upon increasingly sophisticated IT-based networks to hold them together.
▶ IT can enhance the relationship of the organization with customers, and can, by doing so, provide a competitive advantage in a very profitable sector of the business environment.

The courier package and parcel delivery sector has changed from one based on mere transportation to one that is critically dependent upon information technology. Today, IT-based systems are used to schedule vehicle (and other types of transportation) fleets and to help plan and control the most efficient routes to delivery destinations. Global parcel and package delivery operators are faced each day with demands from customers to provide them with package and parcel tracking services, which entail the storage and retrieval of vast amounts of information, as and when required. Much of this information is gathered and transmitted to the customer organizations to augment their internal management information systems. For example, a business that has been given responsibility for conveying a very valuable package or consignment will need to know at all stages its delivery status, from leaving until its arrival at its destination. Fast reporting of management information is vital to the reputation of a parcel and package delivery business.

Consider the case of UPS, a long-standing delivery business, which in the early 1980s operated a manual package handling system. Although this system was efficient, to a certain extent, it could not match Federal Express in terms of information technology provision and use, both internally and externally to the organization. It was apparent to UPS that the leader in information management would be the eventual leader in package and parcel distribution and logistics. Therefore, UPS embarked on a heavy and directed programme of investment in information technlogy. It spent $50 million on a global IT-based information network; $100 million for a data centre to manage its data and information handling requirements; and $350 million for a delivery information acquisition system to track package and parcel consignments anywhere in the world. This major scale of IT investment was accompanied with investment among the workforce in terms of computerizing their job tasks. For instance, hand-held computer facilities are installed into all forms of transportation for the drivers and operators; and throughout the processes of the delivery machine readable bar codes are used for tagging packages, in an effort to reduce reliance on paper-based information sources that are more vulnerable to error.

The delivery information acquisition system used by UPS allows two-way, and multiple, communication between drivers, operators and the source and destination depots. The system is used to collect details and to provide proof that deliveries have been made or where they are in transit around the world or nationally. The cost of packages and parcels going astray, or being lost, has dramatically decreased, because a parcel can be tracked from sending to receipt, whether by land, sea or air. UPS handles around 1 million to 2 million parcels per day on a global scale, a feat that would not be efficiently or effectively possible without investment in information technology in the requisite areas of the business. The technological investment has also led to competitive advantages in that UPS can additionally now offer a full 'business logistics service' that transcends national boundaries. For example, a manufacturing organization based in Germany or France that needs to be supplied with a network of material components from other business organizations from around the world (including any forms of trans-border authorization or documentation) can outsource the logistical headache to an external delivery services business without the worry or cost involved in one-off, or specific, logistical projects.

7.8 The payroll system

The *payroll system*, sometimes known as the salaries and wages system, was one of the first transaction processing systems to be computerized within the business systems environment back in the 1970s. Most payroll systems are still run through batch mode processing and payroll systems usually generate the following *output* data and information:

▶ wages or salary statement (sent to employees as a record of work);
▶ payroll journal (sent to the accounting system).

The *wages or salary statement* is sent to employees as a factual record of work activity. The statement usually contains information such as the employee name, department or location, the time period worked, tax and various other deductions. A typical example of a salary statement can be seen in Figure 7.4. Payroll systems are required to handle such variables as normal and overtime hours worked, holiday pay, national and local taxation and deductions, productivity and internal incentive bonuses. Most payroll systems have EDI applications and interfaces that permit money to be electronically transferred from one business organization's bank account to the individual accounts of its employees and various other agents.

What is the difference between salary and wages?

Traditionally, the term salary was applied to an employee payment made every month, whereas the term wages implied a payment made to employees on a weekly basis.

Most payroll systems also produce a *payroll journal* that is used by the accounting system of a business organization. The payroll journal usually records such information as employee names, departments where employees work, the total salary or wage paid to each employee by department, various deductions and other net pay calculations. The payroll journal can be used by the accounting system to produce a figure for total wages paid in any given period of trading operations. The aggregated wages information can be used as part of the auditing and information reporting processes of an organization. Such data enables the accounting system to produce an organization's *trading and profit and loss statement* and *balance sheet* which are published in the annual accounts of every business organization. This is a legal requirement of commercial organizations around the globe – all trading nations have legislation that requires commercial organizations to produce annual company data for general publication.

Many payroll systems are tailor-made for specific industries. Normally, payroll data is collected and collated using a range of sources and technologies, including time-cards, productivity measures and industrial sensors. Payroll systems can

Activity 7.7 The payroll system

Explain the role of a wages or salary statement and describe the type of data and information included in such a statement. Indicate the types of data and information produced by the payroll system and suggest which other systems within a business organization use payroll data as information inputs. Most employee pay statements are in paper form; what do you think of the idea of sending employees an electronic statement of their monthly pay? Is this a practicable and sensible idea? Discuss the systems necessary to support such an electronic process of pay statement distribution.

Organization name:			Period No.:	Department:	Employee code:	Employee name:
National insurance code:	Tax code: 375L	Period:	Taxable pay:	Division:	Pay location:	
Code & payments:	Hours:	Rate:	Period:	Code & deductions:	Period:	Balance:	Net pay:
Total payments:				Total deductions:			Amount payable:

Figure 7.4 Example of a salary statement

handle overtime, holiday pay, variable and multirate salary structures, incentive schemes and commissions. The aggregated payroll amounts will appear in the *general ledger* of the accounting system.

7.9 The accounting system

The *accounting system* is responsible for the collection and collation of financial data and information relating to all transactions that are internal and external to the business organization.

> **What is an accounting system?**
> The process of identifying, measuring and communicating economic information to permit informed judgements and decisions by the users of the information.
> *Source*: American Accounting Association.

The accounting system can be separated into the two distinct functions:

▶ **Financial accounting**: information is produced for individuals and other organizations that are external to the business (e.g. shareholders, stock holders, investors). Such information is contained in the annual accounts, or *annual report*, that all business organizations are required by law to produce for public scrutiny.

▶ **Management accounting**: information is produced for internal management consumption in order to organize, control and direct more efficiently and effectively the internal human and technology resources of a business organization (e.g. production costs and monthly budgets).

There are three essential applications within any accounting system:

▶ **Accounts receivable**: usually takes the form of a statement of payment sent to the customer for goods (or services) previously supplied and invoiced to that customer. The bill sent to the customer usually includes information such as the customer's name and address, date of the order, product codes and description, allowances and returns, monetary amounts paid to date and monetary amounts receivable. It is this business function that receives money payment from customers for goods and services previously supplied. The accounts receivable data can be aggregated to determine total sales (or demand) for a given period of business activity.

Most business organizations can handle the payment for goods and services in a number of forms, including cash, bank cheques, credit card payment, or direct electronic funds transfer (EFT). The accounts receivable application of an accounting system allows a business organization to collect money efficiently from customers. It also enables a business organization to minimize losses by quickly identifying 'bad debt' customers. Such information can be transmitted to the order processing system to highlight bad debt customers and prevent them from ordering further goods until the bad debts are paid. The computerization of the accounts receivable application has in most cases allowed business organizations to achieve better cash flows.

▶ **Accounts payable:** aims to manage and control the outflow of money to the business organization's suppliers. The activity involves issuing cheques to suppliers for materials and services purchased by the business organization with the aim of providing control over the purchasing activity of the business organization. The accounts payable activity checks that bills received are accurate and that the goods or services covered by the bill have been satisfactorily delivered. A typical report produced by the accounts payable activity is a *purchases journal* that summarizes the business organization's bill paying activities. Such information is important for a business to control its cash flows. This is also known as *liquidity control*.

▶ **General ledger:** a large and aggregated list of all the transactions and internal business activities of the organization. A computerized general ledger allows automated financial reporting and data entry. The reports that are generated include:
  – trading and profit and loss statements
  – balance sheets.

Examples of these statements are illustrated in Figures 7.5 and 7.6. All business organizations will have an accounting system that will generate reports on the trading performance of that business. The reports are known in the UK as a balance sheet (showing assets and liabilities), a profit and loss account (showing the gross and net profit of the business) and cash flow statements (showing the movement in liquid or cash assets between two periods).

Historical data can also be compiled from previous accounting periods in order to carry out an analysis of demand and supply trends for the organization over time. In statistics a technique known as *time-series analysis* is used to compare data between years. For example, the net profit of a business can be compared over time (e.g. 2003 the net profit was 2 million dollars, in 2004 it was 3.5 million dollars). Another statistical technique is *panel data* whereby a data item is compared between companies. For example, the net profit of nine organizations could be compared in any given year. It is a same-year comparison that looks at individual performance of indicators, such as net profit or expanses.

Figure 7.7 shows the integration of sales order processing, purchase order processing and their relationship to the accounting system.

Activity **7.8** The accounting system

Discuss and explain the three essential applications present within an accounting system and describe the function of each application. List two other business systems that supply information to the accounting system and describe how this information is incorporated into the general ledger application.

Elephant and Castle Inc.
Trading and profit and loss account for the year ending 31.12.04

	($000s)	($000s)
Sales (revenue)		500
Less: Cost of sales		
Opening stock	50	
Stock purchases	300	
Less: closing stock	(150)	200
Gross profit		300
Period expenses:		
Rent	50	
Wages	85	
Electricity	35	
Professional fees	25	
Depreciation	20	
Bad debts	15	(230)
Net profit		70

Figure 7.5 Example of a profit and loss statement

Elephant and Castle Inc.
Balance sheet as at 31.12.04

	($000s)	($000s)
Fixed assets		
Freehold buildings	100	
Plant and machinery	75	
Motor vehicles	75	250
Current assets		
Stock	75	
Trade debtors	50	
Cash in hand	25	
	150	
Less: current liabilities		
Trade creditors	(40)	
Bank overdraft	(25)	
	(65)	
Net current assets		85
		335
Capital and reserves		
Share capital	255	
Retained profits	70	325

Figure 7.6 Example of a balance sheet (vertical format)

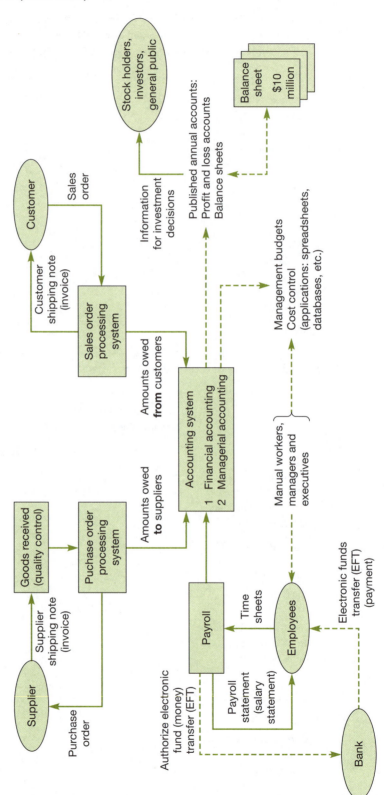

Figure 7.7 Integration of purchases, sales and accounting

7.10 The production planning and production control systems

An organization that relies on manufacturing as the basis of its business activities will require two particular systems to deal with the manufacturing or production processes:

▶ **Production planning**: planning when to make a product. The role of production planning is to produce a *production schedule* that is used by the production control system in manufacturing to determine the next week, next month, or any other time period's production activity.

▶ **Production control**: managing and coordinating production resources, and configuring manufacturing machinery to carry out the instructions implicit in the production schedule. The aim is to produce finished goods through the most efficient and effective configuration of production resources; these resources being people, organization and information technology.

Manufacturing organizations produce products that require the use of raw materials, or other part-made components, as inputs to the manufacturing process. For example, a computer consists of microchips, disk drives and peripheral casing; often, smaller clone-machine manufacturers assemble various parts and produce their own branded computers. Normally the most expensive part of any manufacturing organization is the manufacturing process, which requires heavy investment in a location for production, employees, machinery and other peripheral equipment to carry out the manufacturing operation. Within ICT-based manufacturing environments much of the manufacturing process is often automated, with robots and other cybernetic technology undertaking the production control process.

Quality control checks are essential to the manufacturing process. These checks can be made for all items that come off the production process or just for a random selection of finished goods. The inventory system within the manufacturing process relies upon an *input stock system*, an *output stock system* and a

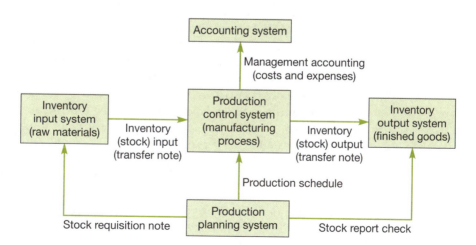

Figure 7.8 The related systems of the production process

production planning system. The relationship between these three systems is illustrated in Figure 7.8.

The systems processes of *input stock control* and *output stock control* are essential to the overall manufacturing process. Raw material stock must be kept at exactly the right levels. Too little stock would hold up the manufacturing process and too much stock would incur additional and unwanted costs of storage. It is essential for stock to be delivered into the manufacturing process at the exact time required and in the exact amounts, which, as we mentioned earlier, is referred to as just-in-time'(JIT) manufacturing.

The consumer food retail industry is a prime example of a business area that relies on an efficient and effective stock control system to increase profits and maintain a competitive edge over rivals. Within stock control systems technology, particularly within the consumer food retail sector, the use of *laser tills* has increased the efficiency of stock handling. A laser till uses a laser to scan bar codes on products or items of stock. The laser till is linked to a computer that recognizes the product being scanned and carries out a number of data recording, updating and checking activities. The computer system also sends back a description of the item being purchased and its price to the terminal, which is in turn then printed on to the customer's (or client's) receipt.

A key function of electronic laser till technology is to capture retail sales data, update stock information and generate management reports on retail store performance. The particular functions of laser technology are to read bar codes, update stock positions by product category, analyze sales demand by product category, calculate and monitor money through the till. In addition to laser technology in retailing, it is also possible to use wireless tracking by 'tagging' products before sale. Most of the large food retailers in the world have used information and communication technology for many years for competitive advantage. Such technology allows managers to know which products are selling and how many are being sold, which provides an indication of product demand. If this information is not quickly and accurately available, the products will go out of stock and sales may be lost.

Most products that are sold in shops and malls now have a bar code that details information concerning that product. Inventory (or stock) systems technology also uses bar codes extensively. Most bar code numbers used in the UK, for example, are administered by the Article Numbering Association that uses unique numbers for individual products. Figure 7.9 is an example of a product bar code. The digits at the bottom of the bar code correspond to items of information about the product. Under the Article Numbering Association system, the first two digits identify the number bank that issued the number. The next five digits are allocated to the company marketing or manufacturing the product. The following five digits are allocated to the particular size or variation of that product. The last digit is a computer check digit to make sure the bar code is correctly composed.

Laser check-out technology used in retailing is normally referred to as *electronic point of sale* (EPOS) technology.

5   0 1 2 3 4 5   9 4 6 7 8 9

Figure 7.9 Example of a product bar code

Using EPOS technology benefits the retail sector because it encourages:

▶ increased checkout accuracy and more efficient checkout operation;
▶ individual cashier performance assessment and customer analysis of buying habits;
▶ efficient service, including itemized receipts and bills;
▶ efficient and effective stock-level monitoring and marketing report analysis;
▶ increases in the product range held and reduced out-of-stock items;
▶ improvements in store layouts and reduced stock storage areas.

> ### Did you know?
> Laser till technology was first used in the early 1980s in the food retail sector; Sainsbury's became the first business organization in the UK to link weighing scales to scanning terminals. In modern information systems retail organizations with global reach – i.e. with shops located around the world – use integrated systems to access the performance of stores and shops in various countries.

Related to EPOS is a technology known as *electronic funds transfer at point of sale* (EFTPOS), which allows money to be immediately transferred electronically from a customer's bank account into that of the business organization's bank account. In the retail sector, an EPOS terminal can also incorporate EFTPOS technology to cover electronic payment methods. The electronic transfer of funds between accounts is made through the use of a customer's *bank debit card*. In the USA, and in many other parts of the world, the system is known as Maestro. In the UK the system is called *switch*. For example, when a cashier at an EFTPOS till has produced the bill (or receipt) for goods or services the customer may hand the cashier their debit card. The card is scanned through a reader, which interprets the customer's details from the magnetic strip on the back of the switch card; the total value of the transaction is entered into the EFTPOS terminal and monetary funds can then be transferred electronically immediately.

Unlike a credit card, the debit card transaction does not provide periods of credit. This approach to payment has the advantage of being an immediate and direct payment method, straight from the user's bank account, eliminating the need to carry cash. A significant advantage of EPOS and EFTPOS technology is witnessed in various productivity improvements in retail store layout and

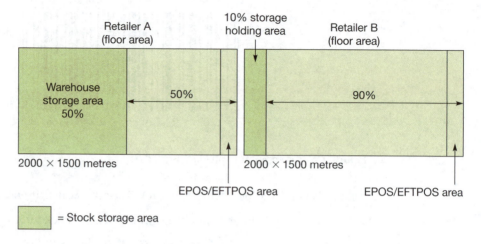

Figure 7.10 Example of retail storage areas

reduced storage areas needed physically to contain stock. The food retail sector is a good example of an area of business that has benefited from reduced inventory storage areas within its stores.

Traditionally, the area within a shop set aside for inventory storage was a wasted resource. The area given over to storage is unproductive related to the area that is set aside for products on display for customers to select and purchase. Ideally, stores wish to maximize the floor area available for displaying and selling goods and products. Figure 7.10 provides an example of two food retailers: retailer A dedicates half the available shop area (50 per cent) to holding inventory, while retailer B has eliminated much of the inventory holding area to make the product display and purchasing area larger, and so just 10 per cent of the shop area is dedicated to inventory storage. It is assumed that retailer B has a holding area for inventory palettes, unloaded from lorries and awaiting stacking on shop shelves. By having inventory palettes delivered 'just in time', as and when required, the store need not maintain large areas of its shop dedicated to warehouse storage.

From the example in Figure 7.10 it can be seen that retail store A has a storage area of 50 per cent and retail store B a storage area of 10 per cent. Assuming that each square metre of store area generates on average $5 income, then the following calculations can be made:

	Retail store A	*Retail Store B*
Total floor space	3000 square metres	3000 square metres
Earning area	50%	90%
Earnings per store	50% × 3000 × $5	90% × 3000 × $5
	= $7500	= $13 500

Therefore, by dedicating a smaller area to inventory warehousing, retail store B has earned an income of $6000 more than retail store A. This is only possible if a retail shop receives inventory 'just in time', as and when requested. Having the right, and appropriate, inventory levels is based on a number of simple rules related to maintaining minimum inventory (stock) levels. A detailed study of the *inventory* (or *stock*) *control system* of a business organization is given in the next section.

Activity **7.9** Production planning and production control

Discuss the importance of an input stock system and an output inventory (stock) system to the production control system and indicate why it is necessary to have raw material received 'just in time', as and when requested.

Explain the role and function of laser till technology (and other related technologies) for handling inventory and product identification in the retail industry. Outline four possible events that may halt the manufacturing process and indicate what the consequences are of having either too much stock or not enough inventory of raw materials passing into the manufacturing process.

7.11 The inventory (or stock) control system

Any manufacturing organization that keeps stocks of raw materials or finished goods needs to operate a *stock control system*. Normally, stock must be controlled and coordinated to maintain the appropriate *minimum inventory (stock) levels* across a range of goods. Inventory systems should contain up-to-date information on quantity levels, product prices, minimum inventory levels and reorder levels. An efficient and effective inventory system should automatically indicate when minimum inventory levels have been reached. Inventory (or stock) control systems will also usually generate useful reports on sales patterns, stock flow through the manufacturing process, and early and late inventory orders. The main effects of an automated inventory control system are that a manager can quickly identify inventory levels and the price of any individual item at any given time, usually at the touch of a button.

Inventory refers either to the physical goods and raw materials that are bought in for the manufacturing process of the business organization or to finished goods that are produced and waiting to be sold on to customers. The central aim of an inventory control system is to monitor and control the flow of inventory into and out of the production process. Therefore, inventory systems can be divided into:

▶ **Input inventory (stock) system**: dealing with the raw materials that have been bought into an organization; these raw materials are held in inventory holding areas until they are required to be used in the manufacturing process. The goal of the input inventory (stock) system is to make the production activity more efficient and effective by placing just the right amount of raw material stock into the production control process.

▶ **Output inventory (stock) system**: dealing with finished goods that are stored and waiting to be distributed to the customer. It should be remembered that the logical inventory system should not be equated to the physical environment in which inventory is stored. A warehouse for goods is merely the physical evidence of an inventory system. The goal of the output inventory (stock) system is to maintain and control the flow of inventory from the manufacturing process out to the customer.

Various reports are produced by the inventory system, including *inventory status reports* that indicate the levels of inventory held in stores. These are used by the production planning system to determine which particular set of goods or products need to be manufactured in a given production planning period. The inventory status reports assist the production planning activity to determine a *production schedule* for the manufacturing and production control system.

Minimum inventory (stock) levels

Having the right inventory level is based on some simple rules. Inventory levels are dependent upon the movement of inventory coming into or out of the warehouse storage area. The balance is calculated by the number in store, which is constantly checked against the minimum inventory level. The minimum inventory level is calculated in the following way:

Minimum inventory (stock) level = (lead time × rate of use) + safety margin

The *lead time* indicates the lag time required for raw materials or inventory to be reordered and delivered; the *rate of use* refers to the rate at which inventory is consumed; the *safety margin* refers to the level of inventory held in case of unforeseen circumstances and other contingencies. For example, if the demand (sales) for product A is 1000 units per day, the lead time is 5 days and the safety margin is 500 units, then the minimum stock level will be as follows:

Minimum inventory (stock) level:
= 1000 (units per day) × 5 (days) + 500 (units)
= 5500 (units)

Therefore, the minimum inventory level is 5500 units. The lead times, rate of use and safety margins will be determined by the nature of the individual product and in turn the nature of a product may be determined by product *trend analysis*. For example, a supermarket store may perform a trend analysis on every product line in its stores, taking into account changes in seasonal demand, marketing campaigns and special offers.

The complexity of the inventory control system will depend upon the nature and range of products manufactured by a business organization. Minimum inventory (stock) levels can be affected by what is called *shelf-life*, which is the time it takes products to deteriorate or spoil; any unused or soiled goods will be wasted after their shelf-life. This can constitute a significant cost to an organization and is, therefore, of significance to the inventory control system. In a manufacturing organization the production planning system is activated by *finished goods* levels. The decision-making activity is revealed in Figure 7.11. The production planning system will make decisions on how many units to produce, the order in which they are to be made and the timeframe necessary for production. This information is contained in a production schedule that is passed to the production control system. The aim of the production planning function is to achieve the goal of maintaining stock to meet demand at the lowest possible cost.

Did you know?

The production schedule must indicate what is to be made, how it is to be made and when it is to be made. This is true for any manufacturing organization anywhere in the world.

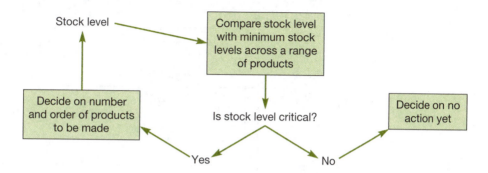

Figure 7.11 Production planning and decision making

Activity 7.10 The inventory (stock) control system

Discuss what information is required in order for the production planning system to produce a production schedule for the production control system. Explain the decision-making process necessary in determining the production schedule for a given time period and state the main aim of the production planning manager.

Now, assume that you have been appointed the production planning manager of a jam-making business known as PL Jams Incorporated. The inventory (stock) control system maintains a record of what is in storage and the minimum inventory levels required. Below is a pro forma production schedule for raw materials delivered to the business organization. The information you have is that the supplier delivers 3000 units of raw materials on 21 March; the manufacturing process then draws 500 units on 28 March, 2000 units on 2 April, and a further 800 units are drawn on 7 April.

Date	Stock in	Stock out	Stock balance	Minimum stock level
2 March	2000	0	2000	1200
8 March	0	700	1300	1200
15 March	0	300	1000	1200
21 March	?	0	?	1200
28 March	?	?	?	1200
2 April	?	?	?	1200
7 April	?	?	?	1200

Fill in the gaps indicated by the question mark symbol, using the above information on delivery and drawing of stock. Indicate at what point the stock became critical, which means it fell below the minimum inventory (stock) level.

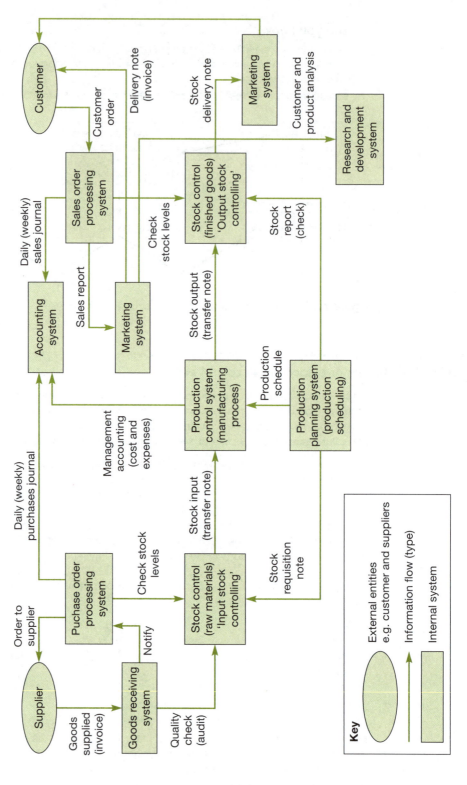

Figure 7.12 Integrated systems within a business organization

Figure 7.12 is an integrated illustration of the relationship between various functions within the business systems environment.

7.12 Management decision systems

So far this chapter has addressed operational systems within the business environment that rely on deterministic and routine transactions. The management information systems environment, in contrast, normally deals with data and information that is both objective and subjective to varying degrees.

Four particular systems that fall within the management information systems sphere are marketing systems, customer support systems, research and development and personnel systems (sometimes referred to as human resource systems). The goal of all management information systems is to provide managers with information that allows them to plan, control and organize more effectively and efficiently the finite resources of a business organization.

Did you know?

The aim of management information systems is to provide the right information to the right person in the right format at the right time. Implicit in this function are the activities of planning, decision making and control of human, technological and other resources to achieve the aims and objectives of the organization.

Managers rely on formal reports generated by the various information systems within an organization. These reports focus on a number of internal activities such as resource scheduling, product demand and supply, and resource allocation. Such information is used by managers to control the medium-term direction of a business organization and to keep it progressing in the appropriate and required direction, dictated by the strategic level of the organization.

The information generated from internal information systems is normally internally produced evidence of the functioning of the business organization; external information usually forms only a minor part of the decision-making activity within the management information systems function. Therefore, management information is usually derived from internal data generated within a business organization. Most management information systems' reports rely on using past (i.e. historic) and present information that can be used to extrapolate, or forecast, the activities of a business for the next month, year or any time period between these two timeframes.

Marketing information system

This system falls within the management information sphere and is concerned with supporting managerial activity in the area of product development, customer distribution methods, pricing, promotion, advertising, and sales demand forecasting. There are two main functions within a marketing system:

▶ data and information collection and collation

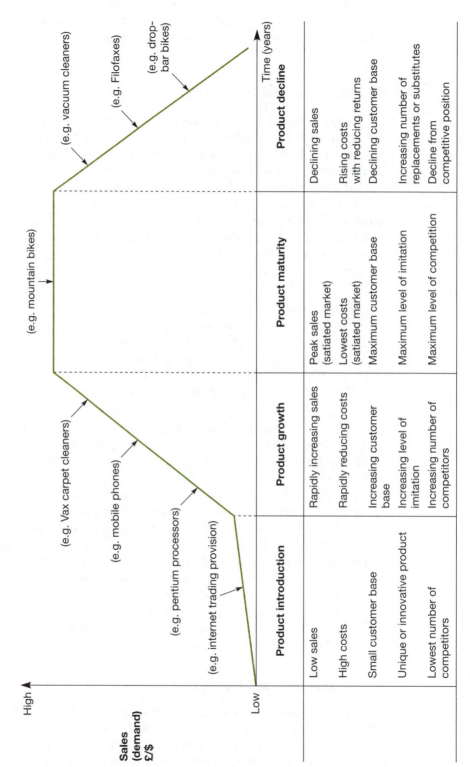

Figure 7.13 The product life cycle

▶ advertising and promotion.

Often the two activities are confused within the umbrella term of marketing. It is commonly, but wrongly, assumed that marketing represents advertising. Marketing, more than most systems, relies on a significant amount of external as well as internal information. The marketing activities are usually determined by the overall strategic plan of a business organization, which may set sales targets that are influenced by the marketing activities of data collection and promotional advertising.

Types of input into a marketing system include:

▶ **Sales reports**: information about customer demand for goods and services, which can be used to forecast future sales activity or indicate areas of growth and decline in demand. Sales reports are generated by the order processing system.

▶ **Competition analysis**: information on competitor organizations such as new products being developed, pricing policies and advertising strategies.

▶ **Customer analysis**: information from customers in various forms, including questionnaires, interviews, customer surveys and information collated by the customer support system.

▶ **Advertising**: information and feedback from advertising campaigns, which can be used to produce different products or services or to modify the marketing strategy of an organization.

The underlying premise of marketing is that long-term business growth can only be achieved if the needs of the customer are identified, anticipated and fulfilled. Therefore, the marketing system can provide a business with a competitive edge, since marketing is concerned with the relationship between a business organization and its external environment. Various models have been developed to make the activities of the marketing system more effective in achieving its goals. One of these is known as the *4 P Model*, which represents:

▶ product
▶ promotion
▶ price
▶ place.

For a business organization to be successful it must have the right product, with the right promotion, at the right price and placed in the right market area.

The role of the market research function is to reduce uncertainty in decision making within the business environment. All products and services have a life cycle, from being born into a market place until they expire – due to changing tastes or the rise of more appealing substitute products. Figure 7.13 illustrates a typical product life cycle and indicates the characteristics and significance of each stage of the cycle.

Activity 7.11   Management decision systems – types of approach

Provide four examples of the types of decision making undertaken by managers and describe the information requirements of a typical management information system. Explain four types of information inputs to a marketing system and then discuss why it is important for a marketing system to appreciate the position and status of a product on the product life cycle.

Customer support system

Customer support systems are vital in maintaining a good working relationship between a business organization and its customers. This area is closely related to after-sales care and after-sales service, with the aim being to create a good and *continuous* working relationship between a business organization and its customers; this will often encourage customer loyalty to a particular product or business organization. The customer support system usually gathers information from customers, in the form of questionnaires and surveys, which can be used by either the marketing system or the research and development system. The marketing system can use customer information to focus advertising and promotion campaigns. The research and development system can incorporate customer views and preferences into the development of products that will appeal to customer tastes.

Customers often interact with organizations in a number of different ways. It is particularly important for organizations that frequently trade with the same customers to maintain a good relationship with those customers. A significant aspect of sales is encouraging customers to come back and purchase further goods and services. In modern information systems this is referred to as *customer relationship management* (CRM). The underlying philosophy of CRM is maintaining good relationships with customers and meeting their individual needs. Often *mass-customization* (the idea that a manufacturing process is flexible enough to provide customized products to specific groups of consumers in a mass market) is used to ensure that groups of customers can receive products and services tailored to their needs. CRM tries to ensure that customer needs are fulfilled. Normally, CRM systems track the interaction of customers within a business organization (i.e. through orders made and after-sales services provided to customers).

Research and development system

This type of system usually concerns itself with researching the nature of products and attempting to develop new products that will be attractive to the customers of the business in the future. Therefore, product research is a valuable exercise in identifying the features that customers desire in a product or service. For example, size, colour, composition, appearance, compatibility and suitability can be investigated to develop products and services that will be demanded by customers. *Focus groups* are often set up to collate opinions and evidence of preferences. The input data and information for research and development comes from the marketing system in the form of market research data and market reports generated from marketing analysis.

The human resources system

The human resources system is concerned with contractual matters relating to the personnel (employees) of an organization. People are the most valuable resource of most organizations and as such need to be coordinated and guided by managers. The main activities of the human resources system include employee hiring, employee contracts, maintaining employee records, performance analysis and employee performance evaluation. Often human resources managers need a good legal background to deal with employee legislation and law on employment and contracts.

Inputs into the human resources system include payroll information, employee appraisal reports, personal employee data and employee work and employment status. The main activity of human resources is controlling the contractual obligations between the employee and the organization that are usually determined on being hired by the business organization. Most business organizations have computerized human resources information systems to store employee data. These systems can often be used to match the skills of employees to particular projects and activities that arise on an intermittent basis. Output reports from the human resources system include human resource planning and coordination, job application review profiles, employee skills analysis and salary surveys.

Effective human resources planning requires forecasting future demand for employees, matched by related skills, and anticipating future supply of skilled and able employees. Human resourcing systems usually include the following main activities:

▶ employee selection and recruitment administration and profiling;

▶ maintainence of employee records related to skills, training and employee development;

▶ employee scheduling, placement and team composition profiling;

▶ wages and salaries administration and related salary surveys.

The human resources system allows a business organization to coordinate and direct human activity efficiently in order to achieve the overall strategic goals of an organization. This area is generically referred to as *human resource management* (HRM).

Activity 7.12 | Management decision systems – HRM systems

Discuss the main information inputs and outputs of a typical human resources information system and explain the four main activities of a human resources system. Describe how a human resources system may be used to formulate working groups based on employee profiling.

7.13 Executive decision systems

Strategic decision making endeavours to predict the nature of business and the direction of the organization into the distant future; the timeframes for strategic decision making may vary from one to 20 years. Such far-sighted decision making is not functional, nor deterministic, and normally relies on the marginal accuracy of various decision support applications used to assist the decision-making judgement of a high-level business executive. *Executive decision support systems* share a number of desirable characteristics, which enable them to:

▶ handle vast amounts of alphanumeric, textual, graphical and other multimedia information;

▶ handle, process and interpret data and information from very different sources, using different presentational formats;

▶ provide report and presentational flexibility, which can be integrated into different output media;

▶ manipulate and analyze data and information through modelling and simulation and other *what-if* analysis.

Executive decision support systems are used by business organizations as a guidance tool for strategic decision making. Therefore, financial modelling and statistical software application packages are often considered part of the available set of decision support tools and techniques. Decision support systems can also cross over into the domain of expert systems that attempt to replicate the knowledge and decision-making ability of a professional expert in various areas. Executive decision support systems are characterized by user-friendly interfaces that are customized to an individual chief executive officer or select set of individuals at the executive level of a business organization. The systems are usually tailored to the particular requirements of the executive level of a business organization.

There are four main models produced by executive decision support systems:

▶ **Financial**: analyzing and predicting the financial operations of the organization, including cash flow analysis, investment analysis and rates of return analysis.

▶ **Statistical analysis**: providing statistics, trend analysis, statistical and econometric testing over a range of different variables.

▶ **Graphical**: providing a visual picture of the underlying data and information held within the decision-making environment.

▶ **Management**: controlling and predicting the management structure of an organization and guiding any form of required project management to deliver the strategic aims of the business organization.

Figure 7.14 illustrates the components that would be expected to be present within an executive decision support systems environment.

Executive decision support environments that assist strategic decision making have a number of characteristics:

▶ There is access to a wide variety of information sources.

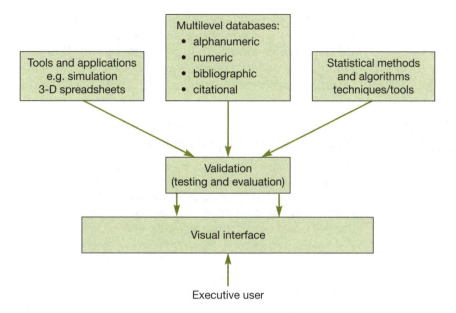

Figure 7.14 Components of an executive decision support systems environment

▶ The decision-making environment is usually complex and highly uncertain.

▶ Strategic decision support systems are used to assist the evaluation of long-term decision making.

▶ Strategic information systems are end-user driven and customized to meet the needs of specific executive strategists.

▶ Strategic information systems are usually *multi-layered* and three-dimensional (e.g. possessing three-dimensional modelling applications).

▶ Strategic information systems are usually *multi-faceted*, with an interface masking a relational database, modelling tools, decision simulation rules and algorithms.

Along with these characteristics there are usually a number of corresponding problems that need to be addressed when using executive decision support systems:

▶ Strategic decision making takes place in *dynamic* environments where information tends to be more subjective than objective.

▶ Strategic decision making relies on numeric as well as non-numeric (sometimes bibliographical) data and information (e.g. socio-economic reports).

▶ There is commonly an absence of information and *data validation*. Therefore, there is often an absence of data source testing and evaluation.

▶ Strategic decision systems often fail to test information and data sources, for example in terms of the statistical characteristics of distribution (range and skewedness) inherent in data sets.

▶ There is often a failure to recognize or test for user-executive *risk psychology* (e.g. whether the executive user is risk neutral or a risk taker).

The strategic decision systems environment includes the hardware, software, procedures and support personnel required to assist the decision-making activities of the executive board of a business organization. Ultimately, the strategic information systems environment must possess the capability to support strategic planning, control and decision making with regard to the whole organization's resources.

Activity 7.13 Executive decision support environments

Provide four examples of the types of decision making undertaken by executives at the strategic levels of a business organization. Describe the four main models produced by executive decision support systems and explain how the information produced by these models would be used within the business environment. Discuss the main components that you would expect to find within the strategic information systems environment.

7.14 Chapter summary

We have seen from the evidence of this chapter that the operational systems of a business organization perform the day-to-day activities of recording, processing and disseminating data-based transactions. These systems normally operate within information environments of absolute certainty. The data that is produced by operational systems is often used at other decision-making levels of an organization, for example, at the managerial or strategic levels. Management information systems are designed to select, analyze and produce useful information to enable managers to make decisions regarding the allocation of business resources. At the top decision making level of the organizational hierarchy are systems to support executive or strategic decision making. These systems normally integrate various modelling facilities in order to predict or forecast the long-term effects of decisions that may influence the future direction of an organization.

The following chapters will study the role of specific technologies and their respective environments. In particular, aspects of integrated office systems technology will be covered in terms of the range of methods, and procedures, for using information and communications technology to improve the efficiency and effectiveness of business of global and integrated business processes.

SHORT SELF-ASSESSMENT QUESTIONS

7.1   Define the concept of the *planning, decision-making and control life cycle* and provide an example of the life cycle within any level of the organizational hierarchy.

7.2   Define and explain the term *transaction processing system* (TPS) and provide four examples of such systems within the business environment.

7.3   Define and explain the system known as *sales order processing* and indicate the sort of data that is input and output to the system.

7.4   Define and explain the system known as *purchase order processing* and indicate the sort of data that is input and output to the system.

7.5   Describe the systems known as *goods receiving* and *goods distribution* within the business systems environment.

7.6   Outline and explain the main functions and objectives of the goods receiving and goods distribution systems.

7.7   Define the system known as *payroll* and suggest why this business function was the first to be automated within most business organizations.

7.8   Outline the function of the *payroll journal* and describe the type of information typically included in the payroll journal.

7.9   Explain the role and function of the *accounting system* within a business organization.

7.10   Describe the two main reports incorporated into the *annual accounts* of a business organization, which can be produced from the general ledger application.

7.11   Define and explain the terms *production planning system* and *production control system* within business organizations.

7.12   Describe the physical and information inputs and outputs of a manufacturing process and indicate which business systems are directly related to the production control system.

7.13   Define the two information technologies known as EPOS and EFTPOS and outline five main advantages of using EFTPOS technology.

7.14   Explain the system known as *inventory (stock) control* and describe the difference between an *input inventory (stock) system* and an *output inventory (stock) system* within a manufacturing organization.

7.15   Explain the role and function of maintaining *minimum inventory levels* and describe the elements that are required in order to calculate the minimum inventory level.

7.16   Describe a *marketing information system* and indicate the two main functions of marketing within the business environment.

7.17   Explain the function and role of the systems known as *customer support*, *research and development*, and *human resources*.

7.18   Describe the concept of *strategic decision support* and outline the main characteristics of such a strategic level system.

7.19   Outline the main components of a *strategic (or executive) information system* and suggest how such systems support the decision making of chief executive officers (CEOs).

EXTENDED STUDENT ACTIVITIES

Individual reporting activity 1

Business organizations are formed with the goal of making money by providing a service or by manufacturing a product. Outline in one or two sentences the goals of the following business systems:

▶ input inventory (stock) control

▶ output inventory (stock) control

▶ production planning

▶ production control

▶ sales order processing

▶ purchase order processing.

Outline the types of information flows between the various operational systems within a business organization engaged in manufacturing. Explain how and why the information flows are used as inputs or outputs to the various business information systems.

Individual reporting activity 2

Inventory reports provide evidence of the level of finished goods in storage. For example, in the case of the Lillington Jam Boiling Factory these are needed to decide on how much jam the factory should produce. The decision on quantity to produce is carried out by the manager in charge of the production planning system.

The Lillington Jam Boiling Factory operates a machine known as a jam boiler that reduces down the ingredients needed to make a range of tasty jams and conserves. The jam boiler can make a maximum of 1000 kg of jam and each boiling process takes one hour, with only six hours of boiling time available per working day (assuming five working days per week of production).

The following is an inventory report for the Lillington Jam Boiling Factory for last week.

Jam type	Stock balance	Minimum stock level (kg)	Weekly rate of sales (demand)	Daily rate of sales
Apricot	2000	2600	3200	?
Cherry	3000	2100	2000	?
Mixed fruit	2700	2500	3200	?
Plum	3500	2000	2200	?
Raspberry/ Apple	1200	1800	2000	?
Raspberry	4000	3500	4200	?
Strawberry	4800	5000	6500	?

1 Fill in the gaps indicated by the question mark symbol by providing the daily rate of sales figures.

2 Acting as a production planning manager, indicate which jams should be made and in which order of boiling.

3 Jam is produced in boilers that can make 1000 kg per batch. Indicate why the production planning system might not want to make less than a full batch.

4 The production planning system is also concerned with reducing non-productive time. Suggest what form this may take with a jam boiler.

5 ICT-based systems monitor the state of production planning in the production control system and know who and which machinery is doing what at any time. Suggest what form monitoring should take in such an environment.

6 Suggest what additional information can be derived from the production control process.

Group-based activity

This task should be undertaken in groups of two or three students. Prepare a presentation of 10 minutes duration to explain the development of technology to bring about a 'cashless' or paperless society where money is replaced with transaction systems that electronically transfer money from one source to another within the business environment. Your presentation should explain the use and development of retail technology such as EPOS terminals, laser tills and EFTPOS. Explain how such technology generates operational information that can be used by managers and executives to monitor and control the activities of a business organization.

REFERENCES AND FURTHER STUDY

Books and articles

An asterisk (*) indicates a seminal text – a major source for later academic developments.

Beer, S. (1994) *Diagnosing the Systems for Organizations*, John Wiley and Sons, ISBN: 0471951316

Chaffey, D. (2002) *Business Information Systems: Technology Development and Management in the E-business,* FT Prentice Hall, ISBN: 027365540x

Elliott, G. (1995) 'Applying statistical evaluation techniques in information retrieval to a company's business information systems to analyze performance and decision-making', Bulletin of the International Statistical Institute's 50th session, Beijing, China, pp. 320–1

LaMoreaux, R.D. (1995) *Bar Codes and Other Automated Identification Systems*, Pira International, ISBN: 1858020956

Laudon, K.C. and Laudon, J.P. (2002) *Management Information Systems (Managing the Digital Firm)*, Prentice Hall, ISBN: 0130619604

*Mintzberg, H. (1973) *The Nature of Managerial Work*, Harper and Row, ISBN: 0060445556

Mintzberg, H. et al. (2001) *Strategic Safari: The Complete Guide Through the Wilds of Strategic Management*, FT Prentice Hall, ISBN: 0273656368

Mintzberg, H. et al. (2003) *The Strategy Process*, international edition, Prentice Hall, ISBN: 0131227904

Parkan, C. (1994) 'Decision making under partial probability information', *European Journal of Operational Research*, 79, pp. 115–22

Popper, K.C. (translated by P. Camiller) (2001) *All Life is Problem Solving*, Routledge, ISBN: 0415249929

Robson, W. (1997) *Strategic Management and Information Systems*, FT Prentice Hall, ISBN: 0273615912

*Simon, H. (1960) *The New Science of Management Decisions*, Harper and Row, ISBN: 0060360003

Stair, R. and Reynolds, G. (2003) *Principles of Information Systems*, Course Technology, ISBN: 0619064897

Turban, E. (2000) *Decision Support Systems and Intelligent Systems*, US Imports and PHIPES, ISBN: 0130327239

Turban, E. et al. (2001) *IT for Management: Making Connections for Strategic Advantage*, John Wiley and Sons, ISBN: 0471389196

Ward, J. and Peppard, J. (2002) *Strategic Management for Information Systems*, John Wiley and Sons, ISBN: 0470841478

Watson, H. (1997) *Building Executive Information Systems with DSS, AI and Groupware SW*, John Wiley and Sons, ISBN: 0471173188

Web resources

Customer Relationship Management Forum (UK/global) – promotes the use of CRM and acts as a network for CRM managers.
www.crm-forum.com

Association for Information Systems (USA/global) – professional body for information systems professionals and knowledge workers.
www.aisnet.org

Chapter 8

The global business environment

When you have studied this chapter you will be able to:

▶ describe the nature of the business environment and the forces that impact, shape and constrain a business organization;

▶ evaluate and contrast the legal, economic, cultural and technological environments in which business organizations operate;

▶ explain the implications of Data Protection and Freedom of Information Acts in the design of business information systems;

▶ evaluate and describe the role and function of information and communications technology within the business environment;

▶ contrast and describe the impact of ICT on various trading sectors of the business environment.

8.1 Introduction to the business environment

A business organization can be considered to be a *human activity system* that deals with, and is affected by, the *internal* and *external* forces found within the business environment. Therefore, an organization is in many ways an *open system* that builds information systems processes to deal with these internal and external forces. Internal to any business organization are its employees. External to any organization are its customers, clients, suppliers, national government agencies and international agencies. The nature of a business organization's systems is shaped and governed by five main forces present within the modern business systems environment. These component forces are:

▶ the legal and political environment

▶ the economic environment

▶ the cultural and global environment

▶ the wireless mobile environment

▶ the technological environment.

Business is not an independent or solitary activity; the success of a business organization will depend upon how well it integrates its systems and processes into the internal and external environment. This is made up of:

▶ **The legal and political environment**: government laws, business legislation and other directives that influence the activities of an organization and dictate the manner in which data is handled, stored and disseminated.

▶ **The economic environment**: the performance of national economies and international money markets that in turn affect taxation levels, trading quotas, inflation rates and national economic growth rates.

▶ **The cultural and global environment**: the way in which people relate to business activity and their conceptual ideas of business practice. Cultural factors are influenced by fashions, tastes, cultural behaviour and various other environmental and ethical considerations within the business environment.

▶ **The technological environment**: the way that information and communications technology influences the competitive nature of all business organizations.

 8.1 The business environment

Search your college or university library for magazine or journal articles on the use of information and communications technology in the banking or finance sectors of the business environment. The article you select will be used as a unique case study and will form the basis for answering a range of questions in the individual reporting activities at the end of this chapter.

8.2 The legal and political environment

The legal and political environment in which business operates will vary according to the country in which the organization is located. This is known as the organization's *domicile* and is an important consideration as it determines where a company is located for corporate taxation purposes. Many countries and regions show a liberal attitude to business that encourages free market competition (known as *laissez-faire*), while other countries prefer to impose particular guidelines and constraints on business activity. The most direct way in which a country politically controls business activity is through taxation. Most countries also have laws that influence the way business activity is conducted and impose rules on the way that business activity is reported within the internal and external environment. In the UK, the USA and Europe the way companies collect, collate and disseminate information is governed by specific legislation that is normally updated every few years.

The government of a country, state or region can influence business activity in a number of ways:

▶ direct state intervention through government agencies that control business activity;

▶ economic and fiscal policy to control inflation rates and economic growth;

▶ legislation affecting company law, contract law and employment law.

Legislation comes in a number of forms. The primary form of legislation dictates how a business organization should present its data and information to the outside world. In effect this legislation determines how a business organization 'discloses' information to the general public in terms of the format, style and content of that information. Many countries also determine how such corporate information is disseminated to the general public. For example, in the UK, USA and Europe various corporate and companies legislation (sometimes referred to as Company Acts) define forms of business structure, or *forms of incorporation*, and prescribe the documentation that must be produced. Often legislation is very prescriptive and provides very little flexibility in how and when data and information must be disclosed to the general public. Normally, such legislation will determine the format requirements for presenting net and gross profit and statements on assets and liabilities (known as *balance sheets*).

In addition to company legislation, many countries also establish *contract laws* that govern the use and nature of contracts between individuals and between individuals and business organizations. A legal contract is an agreement between two parties (or agents) that is enforceable under the laws and legislation of a country. Normally, business activity relies on formal and informal contracts between customers, suppliers and the organizations to which they relate. As well as contract law, many countries also have *employment laws* concerned with protecting employee rights in their relationship with business organizations. Such legislation relates to matters of health and safety and the conditions under which employees and employers work within the general business environment.

8.3 International data protection legislation

Information is often equated in people's minds to 'power and influence'. Therefore, any country or society should have a number of legal and statutory checks and balances in place to prevent the misuse of information. With vast amounts of information being publicly available and communicated around the world, there are ethical issues in ensuring the correct ownership of information and the proper use of information. A major consequence of the use of information and communications technology is the growth of information gathered on employees, customers, suppliers and other individuals in the business environment. Often this information is of a personal and private nature and the individual, or organization, is often reluctant for such information to be made available to the general public or other information agencies without their permission, knowledge or control. The main areas of primary concern on privacy and data protection are that:

▶ data and information should be secure;

▶ any private, personal or other data should be accurate;

▶ any data stored should not be misused.

The concern and fear that private and personal information could be used for purposes other than that for which it was intended, and by people without the authority to use that information, has led to the introduction and development of policies and legislation to protect data and information from misuse. The main national and international legislation in this area is:

▶ Data Protection Act (UK)

▶ European Parliament Directive on Privacy and Electronic Communication (EC)

▶ Freedom of Information Act (UK)

▶ Freedom of Information Act (USA).

It should be noted that the emphasis in this legislation is on data protection, within information systems, and freedom of information in terms of enabling the subject of information to have access to information held on them. The above legislation is by no means the whole picture. Most countries that rely on trade and business activity produce their own specific legislation. For example, similar legislation is available in Australia, Canada and New Zealand. The content of legislation on data protection and privacy is much the same in each of these countries. The main differences lie in how the legislation is implemented in a specific country. Therefore, the study of data protection and privacy in one country is of use to a student in any other country that possesses legislation in this area.

A study of the main data protection legislation in the UK will provide a picture of the nature and orientation of such legislation. In the UK the *Data Protection Act* was first introduced in 1984. The latest version was enacted in 1998. The purpose of the Act is to provide greater legal protection for data held on individuals by organizations. The Data Protection Act set out to regulate the use of automatically processed information relating to individuals, and the provision of services in respect of such information. It requires that all holders of computer-based records must register their databases with the Data Protection Registrar. The Act refers to individuals as the *data subject* and defines personal data as being data related to identifiable living individuals. Individuals also have the right not to have any information they supply to organizations kept in computer-based formats; individuals can opt to have the information kept in manual form. Most large organizations are required to employ a person in the role of a data protection officer, or data controller, whose responsibility it is to deal with matters related to the Data Protection Act.

The Data Protection Act (1998) lays out eight main principles concerning data protection, which can also be considered as general data protection principles, as follows:

1 The data held for processing must have been obtained fairly and legally and it must be processed fairly and lawfully.

2 The data held must only be used for the specific purpose for which it was intended (i.e. it must be processed for limited purposes).

3 The data held must not be excessive but should be adequate and relevant for the purpose for which it was intended (i.e. it must be adequate, relevant and not excessive).

4 The data held must be accurate and up to date.

5 The data held must not be kept longer than is necessary for the specified purpose.

6 The data must be protected and held securely against unauthorized access, alteration or disclosure.

7 The data must be available to the data subject on request and the individual data subject has the right to have the data corrected and/or erased (i.e. the data must be processed in accordance with the data subject's rights).

8 The data must not be transferred to countries without adequate protection.

The first five principles of the Data Protection Act establish general standards of data quality. The sixth principle requires that there are adequate security precautions in place to prevent the loss, destruction or unauthorized disclosure of the data. The seventh principle says that the data should be processed in accordance with the rights of data subjects under the Act. This means that individuals have the right to be informed upon request of all the information held about them by a particular data controller; to prevent the processing of their data for the purposes of direct marketing; to seek compensation if they can show that they have been caused damage by any contravention of the Act; and to demand the removal or correction of any inaccurate data about them. The eighth principle requires organizations not to transfer data outside the European Union unless they are satisfied that the country in question can provide an adequate level of security for that data. However, a European business organization may always transfer data outside the European Union boundaries where it has the data subject's consent.

Anyone processing personal data must comply with the eight enforceable principles of good practice. Personal data covers both facts and opinions about the individual. It also includes information regarding the intentions of the data controller towards the individual, although in some limited circumstances exemptions will apply. With processing, the definition is far wider than before. For example, the website of the Information Commissioner (responsible for enforcing the Data Protection Act) maintains that processing personal data incorporates the concepts of 'obtaining', holding' and 'disclosing'.

Certain categories of data are exempt from the Data Protection Act. The main categories of data that are exempt are:

▶ data held for national security
▶ medical and social service records and information
▶ data held by Customs and Excise and the Inland Revenue
▶ data held by the police for the detection and prevention of crime
▶ data held for personal, family or household use.

For example, data held by the Inland Revenue (the body responsible for taxation in the UK) , which is used for the purposes of collecting taxation, is exempt. Also exempt is information held by the police for the specific purposes of preventing crime and prosecuting criminals. These types of exemptions are also found in the data protection legislation of many other countries.

> ### Did you know?
>
> It is the responsibility of the Information Commissioner's office to consider complaints against data users and to determine whether there has been any infringement of the principles of the Data Protection Act in the UK.

The Data Protection Act attempts to give protection to individuals against personal information being misused or inaccurately recorded. The Act requires anyone who intends to keep information about individuals on a computer to be listed in a register. Business organizations, or other organizations (or individuals), that wish to keep information about people are known as *data users*. This register is open to public inspection and data users must only operate within the limits of the entry in the register. Even if someone is exempt from the data protection legislation, they are still required to comply with the eight data protection principles. The principles are rules of good information handling practice. Essentially, the principles must be applied to individual situations by individual data controllers and the onus is on the data controller to ensure that organizational use of data does not breach these principles.

PAUSE FOR THOUGHT 8.1

Data Protection Act 1998: small business information – compliance advice

As an owner or manager of a small business you may view Data Protection as just another legal requirement to be 'dealt with' in the course of carrying out your business. Unfortunately, the Act as it stands makes no particular allowance for the existence of 'small businesses' and contains no special provisions for those who run them. Legally it requires you to comply with the Act in exactly the same way as if you were a large corporation. Under the Data Protection Act 1998 the size of your business is actually immaterial. What is important is the personal information you hold in relation to your business activities.

With the maximum penalty for failing to notify the Information Commissioner of your processing now at a level of a £5000 fine plus costs in the Magistrates' Courts, or an unlimited fine in the Higher Courts, it is not a subject you can afford to disregard. However, what we do recognize is that those running small businesses work under a great deal of pressure, facing a great many time-consuming administrative demands.

It may be at present you consider the requirements of the Data Protection Act 1998 to be nothing more than a bureaucratic burden. What you will find however is that by following the good information-handling practices contained within the Act, you will be establishing a good set of operating practices which will be of considerable benefit to your business generally.

Data protection – what's it all about?

The Data Protection Act 1998 came into effect on 1 March 2000. The Act regulates the use of personal data and gives effect in UK law to the European Directive on Data Protection. The Act is concerned with 'personal data'.

Personal data is information about living, identifiable individuals. This need not be particularly sensitive information and can be as little as a name and address. The Act works in two ways –

giving individuals (data subjects) certain rights whilst requiring those who record and use personal information (data controllers) to be open about their use of that information and to follow sound and proper practices (the Data Protection Principles). Data controllers are those who control the purpose for which and the manner in which personal data is processed. This can be any type of company or organization, large or small, within the public or private sector. A data controller can also be a sole trader, partnership, or an individual. A data controller need not necessarily own a computer. Data subjects are the individuals to whom the personal data relate.

The Information Commissioner is responsible for administering and enforcing the Data Protection Act. Companies are required to deal with the Notification Department or the Compliance Department which deals with the private sector.

Who needs to notify?

This is the question which interests small business people most. The answer is fairly straightforward: if you hold personal information about living individuals on computer or have such information processed on computer by others (for example, a computer bureau or your accountant), yes – you may well need to notify under the Data Protection Act 1998.

There are a number of exemptions from notification under the requirements of the Act for individuals and organizations that make only limited use of personal data. There is no procedure for officially claiming an exemption, and data controllers are not obliged to inform the Commissioner that they are relying on one. However, you should be aware that you may need to defend your decision to rely on an exemption in the criminal or civil courts. There are currently two ways to make an application to notify: by internet or by telephone. When an organization receives notification it is added to the register. The Data Protection Register is published on the internet. Any business organization that possesses personal data on computer may well need to notify under the Data Protection Act 1998.

Source: Based on 'Data Protection Act 1998: small business information – compliance advice', Information Commissioner's website (www.informationcommissioner.gov.uk), 2003.

Activity 8.2 Data and information protection

Discuss the role of the Data Protection Act (1998) and provide two examples of how the Act can protect the privacy and interests of consumers, or other individuals, with regard to personal information held on information systems. Select a banking application (e.g. loans, mortgages, electronic funds transfer, share and stock dealing, etc.) and explain, in the form of a report, the following:

▶ the purpose and nature of the application you have chosen;

▶ the advantages of ICT to the application;

▶ three pieces of personal customer information that may be stored by the bank;

▶ the methods used to ensure data security;

▶ two examples of data that are exempt from the Data Protection Act.

8.4 Principles of data protection and information privacy

Data protection legislation affects the way that information systems are designed and developed. Most data protection legislation dictates that business information systems should process data 'fairly'. That is to say that data on individuals should be accurate and transparent and it should be clear why the data has been gathered. Only legitimately collected data should be processed. Any business organization collecting data has an obligation to inform people what the data on them is going to be used for and to whom the data is going to be disclosed. The data subjects should always be informed of how and why data is being collected and collated. Every data subject has the right not to provide information to business organizations or to opt out from being asked for information (i.e. marketing mailing lists etc.). Organizations that keep data on data subjects should ensure that the amount of data held is not excessive, out of date or inaccurate. Data subjects have a right to know what data is held on them by various organizations.

Above all else, information systems should be developed with security measures in place. It is the role of organizational data controllers to ensure that there is adequate data security in the systems environment to prevent unauthorized access to personal data or accidental loss of personal data. A system of passwords should be in use to ensure that only authorized staff can gain access to personal data. Business organizations should have established, documented procedures that set out access authority within the systems domain. Many information systems are distributed and 'mobile' (i.e. many workers use laptops and mobile phones to record and disseminate data). In such systems environments it is essential that laptop users have sophisticated security software and organizational procedures in place to avoid data loss or unauthorized access. Organizations should also give due regard to the possibility of laptop and mobile phone theft.

It is a requirement that information systems are built to ensure that there is adequate security in place to protect sensitive data. The Data Protection Act defines eight categories of sensitive personal data, of data subjects':

▶ racial or ethnic origin
▶ political opinions
▶ religious beliefs or other beliefs of a similar nature
▶ membership of trade unions
▶ physical or mental health or condition
▶ sexual orientation and activities
▶ previous criminal records or court proceedings.

Trans-border data transfer is a particularly important factor in the modern business systems domain. The majority of modern business information systems are networked and integrated over a large geographical area. Most large corporations that trade internationally have information systems that integrate offices around the world. Data security across borders becomes a significant consideration within such systems environments. Most data protection legislation requires organizations to take extra care in building systems that require data to be sent across national or state borders by establishing adequate protection for the data in the receiving and sending country, or obtaining the consent of the data subject to enable the transfer of data in an insecure manner if necessary.

The issue of trans-border information flows has become so significant within global information systems that many countries, states and regions have enacted legislation to deal with it. For example, the European Union published a Directive of the European Parliament in July 2002 covering the privacy of electronic communications (Directive 2002/58/EC). The directive is concerned with the processing of personal data and the protection of privacy in electronic communications across borders. The Directive states, in paragraph 5, that:

> New advanced digital technologies are currently being introduced in public communications networks in the community, which give rise to specific requirements concerning the protection of personal data and privacy of the user. The development of the information society is characterized by the introduction of new electronic communications services. Access to digital mobile networks has become available and affordable for a large public. These digital networks have large capacities and possibilities for processing personal data. The successful cross-border development of these services is partly dependent on the confidence of users that their privacy will not be at risk.

Clearly, trans-border electronic data communication is an important feature of modern business information systems. The Directive goes on to state in paragraph 7 that:

> In the case of public communications networks, specific legal, regulatory and technical provisions should be made in order to protect fundamental rights and freedoms of natural persons and legitimate interests of legal persons, in particular with regard to the increasing capacity for automated storage and processing of data relating to subscribers and users.

These measures highlight the changes to data protection law needed to protect consumers' privacy where e-mail, mobile text messages and other forms of electronic communications are used within a distributed and networked business information systems domain. Data protection laws around the world are constantly being updated to keep pace with the latest information and communications technology.

8.5 Freedom of information

In addition to data protection, all organizations are required to give regard to *freedom of information*. The USA was one of the first countries to define the role and purpose of freedom of information. Many other countries, such as the UK and Canada, have followed suit.

Did you know?

In early 1975 the FBI assigned a handful of employees the task of handling an anticipated influx of Freedom of Information Act requests due to new legislation. Although the Freedom of Information Act had been in effect since 1967, it did not apply to investigatory files compiled for law enforcement purposes, thus generally exempting FBI files from public access. By the end of 1975, amendments to the Freedom of Information Act had become effective and the Privacy Act of 1974 also became effective. The passage of these laws provided for broad access to FBI records which previously had been severely limited.

Source: Based on Federal Bureau of Investigation (FBI) website, (www.fbi.gov), 2003.

In the UK the *Freedom of Information Act (2000)* was passed in November 2000. Both the Freedom of Information Act and the Data Protection Act relate to information handling. The underpinning reason for the Freedom of Information Act in the UK is to provide general access rights to all types of information held by public authorities, government agencies, and other bodies on individuals in the general public. The Act attempts to give people a general right of access to data held on them, particularly public bodies. It is public bodies (i.e. hospitals, doctor's surgeries, dentists, pharmacists, universities, colleges, the police and other government agencies) that are the main concern of the Freedom of Information Act in the UK. The legislation provides a duty on these public bodies to publish a guide to the information they hold on people, which is publicly available, and to deal effectively with individual requests by people to access information held on them by these public bodies. All public authorities in the UK are required to deal with individual requests for information from 1 January 2005, when the general right of access to information held by public authorities is fully in force.

The Freedom of Information Act extends the right of individuals under the Data Protection Act to empower and allow access to all the types of information held on people, whether personal or non-personal. Anyone will be able make a request for information, although the request must be made in writing, which includes e-mails. The request must contain details of the applicant and the information sought. The Act gives applicants two related rights:

▶ to be told whether any information is held by a public authority on them;

▶ to receive the information in the manner requested by the person.

Some of the information held by a public authority may be regarded as exempt information and there are 23 such exemptions relating to information held for a variety of functions: these include national security, law enforcement, commercial interests, and personal data. Before relying on an exemption, a public authority will usually be obliged to consider two further points:

▶ Some of the exemptions can only be claimed if the release of the information would prejudice the purpose to which the exemption relates. Hence, information held in connection with law enforcement can only be withheld if its release would, for example, prejudice the prevention or the detection of a crime.

▶ Some of the exemptions also require the public authority to apply the *public interest* test before making a final decision as to whether or not to release the information. The public interest test requires a public authority to consider whether the public interest in withholding the exempt information outweighs the public interest in releasing it (Information Commissioner's website, 2003).

The Freedom of Information Act in the USA has been in effect since the 1960s. Freedom of information legislation in many other countries has been influenced by the Freedom of Information Act in the USA. The USA legislation was updated and amended in 1996 by the *Electronic Freedom of Information Act Amendments* (1996). The legislation states (reproduced here in abridged form to provide a flavour of the statute):

▶ Each agency shall separately state and currently publish in the Federal Register for the guidance of the public – descriptions of its central and field organiz-ation and the established places at which the employees (and, in the case of a uniformed service, the members) from whom, and the methods whereby, the public may obtain information, make submittals or requests, or obtain decisions; statements of the general course and method by which its functions are channeled and determined, including the nature and requirements of all formal and informal procedures available; rules of procedure, descriptions of forms available or the places at which forms may be obtained, and instructions as to the scope and contents of all papers, reports, or examinations; substan-tive rules of general applicability adopted as authorized by law, and statements of general policy or interpretations of general applicability formulated and adopted by the agency; and each amendment, revision, or repeal of the fore-going.

▶ Each agency, in accordance with published rules, shall make available for public inspection and copying – final opinions, including concurring and dis-senting opinions, as well as orders, made in the adjudication of cases; those statements of policy and interpretations which have been adopted by the agency and are not published in the Federal Register; administrative staff man-uals and instructions to staff that affect a member of the public; copies of all records, regardless of form or format, which have been released to any person under and which, because of the nature of their subject matter, the agency determines have become or are likely to become the subject of subsequent requests for substantially the same records.

The importance of the Electronic Freedom of Information Act Amendments can be gauged from Pause for thought 8.2, by the ex-President of the USA, Bill Clinton.

PAUSE FOR THOUGHT 8.2

Clinton signs the Electronic Freedom of Information Act Amendments

I am pleased to sign into law today H.R. 3802, the Electronic Freedom of Information Act Amendments of 1996. This bill represents the culmination of several years of leadership by Senator Patrick Leahy to bring this important law up to date.

Enacted in 1966, the Freedom of Information Act (FOIA) was the first law to establish an effective legal right of access to government information, underscoring the crucial need in a democracy for open access to government information by citizens. In the last 30 years, citizens, scholars, and reporters have used FOIA to obtain vital and valuable government information.

Since 1966, the world has changed a great deal. Records are no longer principally maintained in paper format. Now, they are maintained in a variety of technologies, including CD-ROM and computer tapes and diskettes, making it easier to put more information online.

My Administration has launched numerous initiatives to bring more government information to the public. We have established World Wide Web pages, which identify and link information resources throughout the Federal Government. An enormous range of documents and data, including the Federal budget, is now available online or in electronic format, making government more accessible than ever. And in the last year, we have declassified unprecedented amounts of national security material, including information on nuclear testing.

The legislation I sign today brings FOIA into the information and electronic age by clarifying that it applies to records maintained in electronic format. This law also broadens public access to government information by placing more material online and expanding the role of the agency reading room. As the Government actively disseminates more information, I hope that there will be less need to use FOIA to obtain government information.

This legislation not only affirms the importance, but also the challenge of maintaining openness in government. In a period of government downsizing, the numbers of requests continue to rise. In addition, growing numbers of requests are for information that must be reviewed for declassification, or in which there is a proprietary interest or a privacy concern. The result in many agencies is huge backlogs of requests.

In this Act, the Congress recognized that with today's limited resources, it is frequently difficult to respond to a FOIA request within the 10 days formerly required in the law. This legislation extends the legal response period to 20 days.

More importantly, it recognizes that many FOIA requests are so broad and complex that they cannot possibly be completed even within this longer period, and the time spent processing them only delays other requests. Accordingly, H.R. 3802 establishes procedures for an agency to discuss with requesters ways of tailoring large requests to improve responsiveness. This approach explicitly recognizes that FOIA works best when agencies and requesters work together.

Our country was founded on democratic principles of openness and accountability, and for 30 years FOIA has supported these principles. Today, the Electronic Freedom of Information Act Amendments of 1996 re-forges an important link between the United States Government and the American people.

Source: Statement issued by President Clinton upon signing the 1996 FOIA Amendments into law on 2 October 1996, US Department of State website (www.state.gov), 2003.

The use of freedom of information legislation within trading nations significantly influences how data is handled, stored and distributed. It puts obligations on business organizations to be aware of the general public in the environment in which organizations operate. Therefore, information systems cannot be developed in isolation, or without any regard to the laws and statutes of countries in which the organizations are domiciled.

Activity 8.3 Freedom of information

Discuss the role of freedom of information legislation and provide three examples of how such legislation can protect the privacy and interests of people. What effect does such legislation have on the way that information systems are constructed? Why is it important for people to have access to information held on them in both business organizations and public bodies? What procedures and guidelines would you put into place to ensure that personal data is kept and maintained properly in both business organizations and public bodies?

8.6 The economic environment

The fundamental aim of all business activity is to make money. The economic environment can be divided into:

▶ **Micro-economics**: the nature of individual business organizations and their activities, such as pricing, cost evaluation and competitive business behaviour.

▶ **Macro-economics**: the aggregated effects of individual business activity on the national, regional or state economy. Macro-economics is primarily concerned with national growth rates, inflation rates, the cost of government borrowing, international trade balances and the value of national currencies.

Figure 8.1 outlines some of the economic variables of the business environment. The business environment is shaped, affected and influenced by the national economy and the internationalization of the economy, in terms of global trade and the development of economic communities, such as the European Union (EU).

The major economic impact of information and communication technology on society has been on labour force working patterns that have affected the type of work available in society and the *nature* of working practices and conditions. In economic terms, technology has caused the creation of jobs in many new areas, but at the same time the collateral loss of some jobs. The nature of work, as a consequence, has also changed over time, along with the nature of general working patterns and expectations.

The rapid pace of change in information and communication technology affects the skills requirement of society and means that workers and employees have to be trained and re-educated more frequently than ever before during their working life, particularly as the jobs they previously did are superseded or replaced by other working practices, or altered by advances in ICT. The economic cost of technological training and retraining has become a major expense to

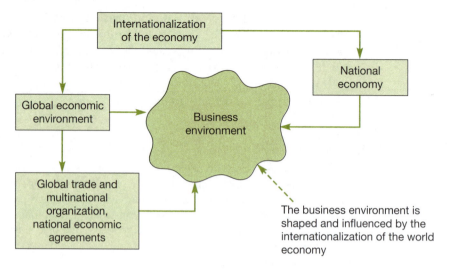

Key

National economy:
- gross domestic product (GDP)
- growth rate
- annual inflation rate
- government deficit/surplus
- external government dept
- balance of payments
- foreign trade
- unemployment rate

Internationalization of the economy:
- trade (percentage of GDP)
- currency controls
- cross-border economic agreements
- global trade
- cross-national business organization (e.g. global multinational companies)

Figure 8.1 The internationalization of the business environment

many competitive business organizations. ICT training and consultancy is a major industry in its own right. Many graduates in ICT end up as corporate training managers responsible for re-educating company employees in the ways and methods of modern ICT.

The highest incidence of job losses in modern information societies has occurred in the production and manufacturing sectors, where human labour has been replaced with computer-aided manufacturing and computer-based production robotics. However, it is often the pace of change and not technology itself that leads to job losses. For example, if new information and communication technology is incorporated into society at business organizational level at a steady and manageable rate then there is adequate assimilation time available to deal with labour force retraining or redeployment. Under such circumstances, job losses can often be managed by workforce contraction due to natural employee wastage (e.g. retirements and normal movements of labour between jobs). It is the impact of instant, or sudden change, in the application of new information technology that leads to job losses, as a mismatch develops between the availability of new jobs in information and communications technology and the available pool of retrained or re-educated workers.

Did you know?

Studies have shown that in the long term more jobs are created than lost by the introduction and use of information and communications technology, which can often lead to new business opportunities in terms of products or services. For example, certain parcel courier services, who deliver business packages between clients, use internal ICT for 'tracking' the location of a parcel from leaving one client to receipt by another client. This internal tracking service, provided by ICT, is sold on to the clients at an additional cost so that the client organization can keep track of its own set of parcels being delivered around the world. This is referred to as a value-added service to customers.

In economic terms ICT is adopted because it provides benefits to an individual or a collective group of individuals within a business organization. ICT may also enable an organization to achieve a higher profit return than by operating manual systems – due merely to the extraction of efficiencies within the business systems environment. If this potential increase in profit is multiplied across all organizations in an economy the national increase in economic wealth can be significant. It is claimed that one of the reasons for Japan's great economic success in the second half of the twentieth century was the development and adoption of all forms of information and communications technology on a national scale within the business environment. Japan and other technologically advanced countries and regions use ICT to increase the general per capita (per person) wealth of the nation. Ultimately, the bulk of jobs created in technological economies are in areas related to information and communications technology.

Activity **8.4** The economic environment

Discuss what is meant by micro-economics and macro-economics and suggest how each economic force influences the nature of business activity. Provide two examples of jobs that have disappeared and two examples of jobs that have been created as a result of the growth of information and communications technology. Then investigate sources of published business information and list all the possible users and uses of the various business information sources. Analyze and describe whether the sources of business information you have found are required, or influenced, by legislation or more general government policy.

8.7 The cultural and global environment

The cultural environment is influenced by people's views and beliefs and the way in which people relate to one another to conduct business activity. The cultural environment in which business activity takes place is shaped and influenced by the views, beliefs and expectations of customers, suppliers, employees, the general public, politicians, shareholders and many other stakeholders who collectively make up an economy. All business activity relies on individuals acting as customers, suppliers and employees. The cultural environment is also affected by fashions and trends, influenced and encouraged by mass beliefs and practices that constitute a collective set of beliefs and guidelines.

All business systems activity is influenced by environmental, social and ethical considerations; for example, the way in which business organizations treat their employees and the way in which an organization demonstrates a concern for others in society in terms of dealing with waste and pollution. Many organizations attract customers by offering socially conscious investment opportunities, known as *green investment*, or by ensuring that the production of goods and services does not result in the exploitation of its workforce. *Ethical business behaviour* is a concern of the modern business environment. Companies that fail in their ethical duties to employees, suppliers and customers risk losing their reputation and ability to trade.

Did you know?

As health and welfare continually improves and the death rate decreases, so the world population continues to grow and live longer. Modern consumer societies are becoming older thus changing the nature of products and services offered by business organizations. The world population was estimated to be approximately 300 million in AD 1000. But by the end of AD 2000 it was over 6000 million (or 6 billion).

One of the major cultural changes within business activity has been the growth of *telecommuting* (i.e. working from home) and *mobile working* patterns, facilitated by wireless telecommunications and the development of portable mobile computing devices. Telecommuting involves an employee being set up at home with all the facilities of the traditional integrated office environment: the facilities of the office environment are mirrored in the home environment. Mobile working involves using different types of computing devices to support mobile workers, such as sales people and other transient workers. For example, a wired or wireless networked computer with electronic mail (e-mail) and internet facilities, all linked to a wired or wireless modem, can permit certain categories of employee to carry out their work as efficiently and effectively as being located physically within the office environment. The concept of mobile working is often referred to as *m-work* or *m-business*.

Telecommuting can remove the need for physical attendance in the office environment for many types of workers. It can also often lead to more productive work patterns because employees do not have to commute regularly into work at the same time or to the same place each day. Mobile working offers flexibility: it enables workers to complement their social activities (e.g. collecting children from school and dealing with maintenance problems in the home). Telecommuting and mobile working may also result in reducing sickness rates through 'commuting stress', which may in turn lead to an increase in employee morale. ICT often improves mobile worker productivity, which in turn leads to a broader mobility pattern and, therefore, more mobile working.

The main disadvantage of telecommuting or mobile working is the loss of personal contact between people in an office environment, thus leading to a loss of social contact and the informal business networking activity that is common in office environments. Some employees may also find it difficult to separate the work role and home role, instead favouring a two-site approach to their life.

The social effects of the application of information and communications technology have been widespread throughout the business environment. Many types of manual jobs have been eliminated or automated, thus reducing the need for human labour. Therefore, the development of *intellectual labour*, rather than manual labour, has become a predominant pursuit of many modern business organizations. However, a significant advantage of the application of ICT in the business environment has been the elimination of many unpleasant and dangerous jobs that can now be carried out by robotics and computer automation. Whatever the role and remit of information technology, it is indisputable that it has altered the workplace environment. Many laborious and deterministic tasks are now carried out more quickly and more efficiently than ever was the case before.

However, workers that interact with ICT often have other problems. They are often required to spend long hours sitting in front of computer screens or other peripheral technology that can cause a number of health problems: for example, poor posture, eye-strain and the possible health consequences of using mobile phones. Some of these problems are being overcome by greater research into *ergonomics* (the study of the interaction of human to machine relationships, often known as human computer interaction or HCI) and wireless technology health and safety.

Did you know?

Research commissioned by LogicaCMG, a global solutions company providing management and IT consultancy, systems integration and outsourcing services, revealed that the majority of European executives were in favour of mobile working. The one notable exception was France, where there was opposition to technology that would allow staff to work while out of the office. The survey focused on employees of large enterprises in the UK, France, Germany and the Netherlands and found that 96 per cent consider mobility as a positive way to improve job flexibility.

Source: Based on LogicaCMG, 2003.

The growing sophistication of wireless telecommunications technology permits people to meet and interact in forms not previously possible. For example, mobile workers can *teleconference* or exchange data remotely. Teleconferencing is an electronic form of meeting that enables a number of people to confer using telephone, e-mail and other types of groupware-based conferencing applications. This enables geographically dispersed people to meet and communicate as if in the same physical location. Another technology is *videoconferencing*, which is a form of teleconferencing with the addition of video links between people. Videoconferencing is standard practice in many business systems environments.

Both teleconferencing and videoconferencing enable people to communicate ideas and thoughts within a meeting forum without the cost and time involved in transporting people from one physical location to another. This is a significant consideration for organizations that do business on a global scale. There is an additional benefit in that such technology enables ideas and attitudes to flourish within the global business environment.

Activity 8.5 The cultural and global environment

Describe what is meant by cultural environment and explain how attitudes and beliefs (i.e. *weltanschauung*) affect business activity and business systems thinking. Discuss all the possible categories of people who might interact with the internal and external environment of a business organization and explain how people influence the nature of business activity systems. Now read Pause for thought 8.3 and outline ten significant aspects of telecommuting within the business environment. Write a report discussing whether the trend of telecommuting is likely to increase in the future and what implications there are on the contractual obligations between an employee and a business organization. Discuss the ways in which telecommuting affects the nature of interaction between humans, technology and the organization.

PAUSE FOR THOUGHT 8.3

The advantages and disadvantages of working from home

The information age will reach most individuals and organizations through the internet, electronic commerce and various other forms of information technology. Households can now conduct business, purchase goods, play computer games and keep in contact with agencies, organizations and individuals through electronic mail. A natural consequence of this information technology is the ability to work from home because the technology allows an individual to work unrestricted by geographical or physical location.

Business organizations are constantly seeking access to information technology that will help employees to complete their jobs more effectively and efficiently. With the development of 'knowledge working' within the business environment, telecommuting (or working from home) seems to fit the knowledge worker model of activity. Knowledge workers develop and exchange information to complete their job functions. However, the need for information is not limited to the physical confines of a corporate headquarters or regional office. Even when away from a physical office, home workers can access data, information and software applications as and when they need these resources.

So, what are the benefits and drawbacks of telecommuting? Employees will often view telecommuting as a convenient, flexible aspect of an otherwise rigid environment, such as being confined for 35 hours per week in a particular office location. Business organizations believe that telecommuting is a clever way of extending the working week at no extra cost, while reducing overhead costs such as rent, lighting, heating and electricity in one physical office location. Telecommuting may also attract strong and able staff by providing a flexible and independent working environment. Often telecommuting is the only viable alternative for sole traders or small businesses that cannot afford luxury office space.

Many companies do not have defined policies towards telecommuting and many are still psychologically unfavourable towards the concept, believing that it may lead to a loss of organizational control over employees. Many regions of the world, particularly in the USA, have legislation (such as Clean Air Acts) that encourage telecommuting. To effectively deal with telecommuting, many business organizations are going through the difficult process of evolving policies and organizational structures to deal with the issues it raises.

One major drawback of telecommuting is often the lack of the correct and appropriate computing infrastructures to support a teleworker's demands. For example, many telecommunications networks are often slow or difficult to access, which may lead to a loss of time and revenue. Also, there is a need for a good local area network to be available in the home to deal with peripheral equipment such as scanners, printers and telecommunications modems. Other drawbacks include the loss of personal contact between individuals, which may lead to a feeling of social isolation.

Whatever the advantages and disadvantages of telecommuting, it is often the case that telecommuting can provide tangible benefits to a competitive business organization – as long as the prerequisites of a suitable contract and appropriate environment are present within a business organization.

8.8 Wireless-enabled mobile working

The development of mobile working patterns and wireless mobile technologies has led to the development and sale of mobile products and services. Users of mobile phones and wireless personal digital assistants (PDAs), in addition to purchasing digital products, can also use commercial digital services, such as:

▶ travel (e.g. booking online or checking availability)

▶ ticketing and billing (e.g. booking online and new vending and payment types)

▶ banking (e.g. checking statements online and transferring money between accounts)

▶ news and sport bulletins (e.g. paying a premium rate to receive tailored news bulletins)

▶ gambling (e.g. holding an online account to transact bets and check prices)

▶ purchasing goods and services (e.g. e-vending machines and indirect online buying and selling)

▶ business services (e.g. checking stocks and shares and company reports).

One of the most successful online applications and services is the capability to check the availability of planes, trains and other forms of travel. For example, various web travel sites enable the user to check flights and destinations and to book flights online. Many of these services are available over what is known as the *mobile internet* or *wireless internet*. This is where web-based products and services can be accessed on the move from laptops (with wireless modems), wireless PDAs or sophisticated and smart mobile phones. *Fixed-wired internet access* through a PC requires the user always to access the internet from the same location, using a static applications environment, usually for a routine purpose. In contrast, wireless internet users normally initiate mobile internet access on impulse or dependent upon their location. Access to the wireless mobile internet is normally triggered by four connected aspects:

▶ situation (i.e. flying, driving, walking, working etc.)

▶ location (i.e. town, country, home or abroad)

▶ mission (i.e. purpose or objective)

▶ time (i.e. a transient one-off occurrence).

Location and mobility are the two greatest assets of the wireless mobile internet. The early business adopters of mobile technology acquired the technology, but did not always link the technology to their business systems thinking. For example, the advantages of mobile technology for mobile working are significant in terms of the flexibility the technology can offer and the cost reductions that can be achieved. Later adopters of mobile technology began to link the technology to their overall business systems architectures. Hence mobile information systems thinking became part of overall business thinking. The adoption of wireless mobile technology then became a systems issue rather than merely a procurement of technology issue. The two main issues with mobile technology are the same as the adoption of normal business information technology: security issues and technical support costs.

Modern business systems thinking requires understanding both fixed applications and mobile applications in the business environment. In mobile systems systems thinking the concept of wireless is differentiated from the concepts of mobility. For instance, fixed computer systems can still utilize wireless technology even if they are fixed in the same building, because they can communicate by wireless signals through *wireless local area networks* (WLANs). However, the usual systems thinking involves the engagement of mobile devices (e.g. PDAs) with immobile devices (e.g. PCs or household appliances), using the medium of wireless communication.

Most mobile business systems thinking tries to extract, or *leverage*, value from various wireless mobile technologies. The integration of mobile and wireless technologies into efficient, effective and holistic structures is the aim of business systems thinking in the world of the mWorker.

Leveraging value from mobile technologies requires an understanding of the three main advantages of mobile devices and applications, which are:

▶ mobility

▶ portability

▶ wireless connectivity.

These advantages can be integrated by information systems developers into business applications that meet mWorker needs. In general there are three types of mobile systems environments:

▶ **Static mobile environments**: people working away from their office (e.g. in a roadside diner) but at the same time still accessing the applications that would be in their office. Examples include using a laptop (with wireless modem rather than their wired office PC, and using a mobile phone rather than their office land-line telephone. The laptop user has full and normal access to the databases and network servers that they would use while sitting at their office computer.

▶ **Location-response mobile environments**: more sophisticated environments utilizing mobile phones, PDAs, laptops and various other wireless devices to receive and send data that checks, monitors or responds to the location of a user. An example is a parcel delivery person requiring an electronic signature on a mobile wireless keypad – this data is only sent back to headquarters on receipt of the customer's signature on delivery. The delivery person can also be monitored to determine their location and data can be transmitted to the delivery person regarding their remaining delivery schedule. For example, a mobile worker may be remotely located by the signal emitting from their mobile device and data specifically targeted to the device, or they can be automatically alerted to relevant information, based on their location.

▶ **Dedicated-embedded mobile environments**: the most sophisticated of mobile business environments, characterized by devices with embedded technologies that interact with a user who happens to come within the device's wireless reception area. Examples include a wireless local area computer network recognizing a user's PDA as the user approaches the network, or devices that activate only when a user is within range (e.g. security doors opening on recognizing the security signals of the user's mobile device).

Within wireless mobile systems environments the objective is to push and pull data to where it is needed. The value of data is not based on quantity but rather on quality and pertinence to the situation, location or business environment. In the mobile world, data is moved to different places at different times based on location and environment. Wireless business systems thinking usually focuses on issues of business systems connectivity. For example, they explore how mWorkers can use wireless PDAs to access data on inventory levels, customer

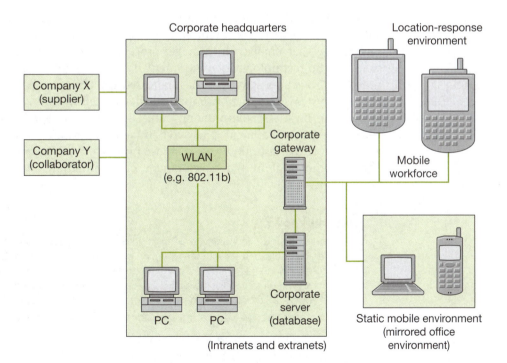

Figure 8.2 Mobile wireless systems environments

profiles, pricing and various policies on maintaining customer relationships. Mobile workers can also access corporate intranets and extranets that have been extended to the wireless systems domain.

Figure 8.2 provides an example of mobile workers interacting with information systems within a business organization. For example, at corporate headquarters a client-server architecture exists in both fixed wire and wireless modes (via a wireless LAN). The corporate gateway provides a window of contact with the external environment. It connects the corporate headquarters with the mobile workers in the field. This mobile workforce can exist within either in a static environment or a dynamic location-response environment. The corporate databases and servers are accessible by the mobile workforce and data can be pulled (downloaded) and pushed (uploaded) from the servers, following the necessary systems security and access checks.

Activity 8.6 The wireless mobile environment

Describe the three types of wireless mobile systems environments. Why does wireless business systems thinking usually focus on issues of connectivity? Why do the types of software applications in use depend upon the nature of the business system and its goals? What are the benefits of mobility to workers and organizations? Why are mWorkers so important in the modern business systems environment?

8.9 The technological environment

Information and communications technology is an integral part of everyday life. Information is considered an important business and human asset – and so is the technology that enables the storage, processing and communication of information. The technological environment has greatly influenced the nature and practice of business activity. It has increased the efficiency and effectiveness of business systems and in turn improved the way business organizations operate within the business environment. Table 8.1 outlines some of the important technological developments that have influenced business activity and business systems over the last 200 years. It shows how many people and countries have been instrumental in the development of information and communication technology.

Did you know?

The development of technology to perform automatically specific tasks can be traced as far back as 1804 with the invention of the Jacquard card-controlled loom. Joseph Marie Jacquard was a French textile manufacturer who used a punch card system to control the weaved pattern on a loom. Jacquard's loom allowed complicated patterns to be woven automatically.

The incorporation of technology into the business environment is not a new concept. In 1890 Herman Hollerith, who worked for the Census Bureau in the USA, invented an automated punch card machine known as a Pantograph Punch

Table 8.1 Historical developments affecting business systems and technology

BC	
c. 2000	The Senkereh Tablet found near Babylon lists numbers in cuneiform writing.
c. 650	An Indian Hindu named Brahmagupta invents decimal numbers.
c. 500	The Egyptians and Greeks use a simple abacus to record financial information.

AD	
c. 876	Indians use zero as a place holder in written numbers.
c. 1000	The Arabic decimal notation makes its way to Europe (Arabic or Hindu-Arabic numerals).
c. 1300	Early evidence of business systems and record keeping by an Italian business organization trading in Provence.
1492	An Italian named Pelacci claims to have invented the decimal point.
1494	A Franciscan friar named Luca Pacioli produces the first textbook on accounting systems called *Summa de Arithmetica, Geometrica, Proportioni et Proportionalita*.
1694	Leibnitz (German philosopher and mathematician) produces a calculating machine to perform multiplication.
1725	A Frenchman named Bouchon in Lyons uses a silk loom controlled by the positions of holes in a paper roll.
1804	A Frenchman named Joseph Jacquard uses a fully automatic loom where the pattern is controlled by punch cards.
1814	George Stephenson (British engineer) constructs the first successful steam locomotive.
1822	A Briton named Charles Babbage demonstrated a Difference Engine.
1825	The first passenger railway between Stockton and Darlington (in England) was opened.
1833	Charles Babbage begins work on an Analytical Engine (unfortunately the project ran out of funding before being built).
1842	Lady Lovelace writes punch-card programs for Babbage's Analytical Engine.
1850	An American named Parmalee patented a calculator with numbered keys.
1877	Thomas Edison (US physicist) invents the phonograph and contributes to the development of the electric lamp and other electrical devices.
1890	Herman Hollerith of the USA invents a series of machines to process census data.
1911	Punch card technology is used in the British census.
1920	A British company invents a machine that prints alphabetic data from punch cards.
1936	Alan Turing (British academic) proposes the concept of the digital computer.
1945	Von Neumann of the USA writes a report detailing the characteristics of computer processing.

and Electrical Tabulator. This mechanical device was invented to allow quicker and more accurate processing of census results through punch-card technology. The handwritten data obtained from printed census forms was transferred on to punched cards that were placed through a tabulator that sorted and processed the information more rapidly than previous manual methods. Hollerith's automated machine allowed the 1890 census to be completed in only three years, compared to the seven years it took to complete the 1880 census. In 1911 punch cards were used in the British census for the first time. In the USA tabulators were used up until the 1960s, when advances in electronics and computer technology allowed smaller, cheaper and more reliable machines to be built.

Did you know?

Herman Hollerith, who used punch cards to input census data into a tabulation machine in the 1890s, went on to become one of the founders of the business organization known today as IBM, which originally started out in the corporate world as International Business Machines (IBM).

Information and communications technology has had a significant impact on society as a whole because of the rapid developments since the 1940s in electronics, integrated circuitry, semiconductors, silicon microchip technology and telecommunications. Information and communications technology has had an impact on individuals, business organizations and society. By far the biggest impact of information and communications technology has been seen within the business environment. Some of the earliest applications were focused on the accurate processing of clerical or operational business data, for payroll and stock control. Such operational systems have been described previously in Chapter 7. Information and communications technology then gravitated into the management sphere and is today mainly used to assist management and executive decision making.

In the manufacturing sector information technology tools and techniques, such as computer-aided design (CAD), computer-aided manufacture (CAM), robotics and artificial intelligence, are used to improve products and manufacturing performance. Such technology is particularly prevalent in the research and development operations of the business environment. *Computer-aided design* allows design models to be created on a computer screen; the structure of the designs can normally be easily altered and simulated to achieve different design concepts. One of the advantages of CAD is that it saves time over manual methods; ideas can be sketched on a computer screen and can be saved, recalled or modified. The sketches are usually three-dimensional and can be tilted, rotated and reshaped as required. CAD is used in the design of large structures such as cars, ships, buildings, and small structures such as microprocessor circuits and electronic items. CAD systems usually allow simulation criteria such as stresses and forces on buildings to be tested and compared safely in the design department.

Information and communication technology applications in production and manufacturing often take the form of factory automation. *Computer-aided manufacturing* techniques are used to replace human intervention in the factory assembly line process. Technology is used to control intricate or precision machine tools. Industrial components can be cut and shaped to higher standards of accuracy and consistency than through manual control processes. Such systems are appropriate for repetitive, precision tasks. The actions of the machine tools are determined by comparison with a design pattern (of size and shape specifications) stored in the computer. The CAM system can be alerted to any variations or deviations from the computer design pattern and the system will often adjust as appropriate. This is known as *computer-aided quality assessment.*

The other main area of CAM is the application of industrial *robots* that replace human activity within the manufacturing process. An industrial robot often consists of manipulative arms with articulated joints to allow flexible movement. The manipulative actions of a robot are determined by pre-coded computer programs. Robots sometimes operate within certain bounds of sensitivity, and are often fitted with sensors that detect the immediate environment around the robot. For example, robots can be programmed to detect and differentiate between shapes and sizes, whereby the robotics may be programmed to pick up only certain shapes or sizes that fall between two bounds (e.g. to retrieve particular shapes measuring between 20 cm and 45 cm). The increased use of robots has led to the decrease in manual work by employees and the increase in supervision and control of technology.

Usually information and communications technology will be adopted where there is a need to improve the efficiency and effectiveness of a process or work task. For instance, technology may allow some tasks to be carried out that would be impossible to do manually. In the nuclear industry radioactive materials in the centre of atomic reactors are handled remotely by machinery, such as robotic arms, controlled by workers sitting at computer terminals.

Activity 8.7 **The technological environment**

Discuss the concept of the 'technological environment' and outline the significant technological developments over the past 200 years that have most affected the business environment. Define the concepts of computer-aided design and computer-aided manufacturing and describe three possible uses of robotics within the manufacturing systems process. What is the role and purpose of robots in the business environment?

8.10 International banking environment

Information and communications technology has had a significant impact on the way in which an organization relates to its customers, clients and suppliers, which can loosely be classified as the *consumer environment.* Technology in the consumer environment is most obvious in the retailing and banking sectors of society. In recent years the use of cheques, as a medium of payment, has been largely replaced by the use of credit card and debit card payments and other forms of electronic funds transfer and payment. A *credit card* allows a customer to buy goods and pay for them later after a period of time. Credit cards offer credit to a pre-set limit and each month the cardholder receives a statement listing the outstanding balance and the transactions for that month. No interest is normally charged if the cardholder settles the full amount of the balance. However, a cardholder need not settle the full amount but may pay off a proportion of the outstanding balance; there is usually a minimum amount that has to be paid each month. Alternatively, a *debit card* automatically transfers money out of a customer's bank account to another bank account when the card has been processed through an appropriate *electronic funds transfer at point of sale* (EFTPOS) terminal.

Many of the large retail food distributors use information and communications technology within their business operations and activities. All large supermarkets and malls have cash tills that are connected to bar code optical laser scanners and other detection technologies. Such technology automatically decodes and registers information on a central computerized system. The information is used to reconcile the items sold with the money spent on the items and to update the stock records to reorder items that have been consumed down to their minimum stock requirement levels. This type of technology is also used to analyze individual cashier, or teller, performance and provide sales analysis reports for managers.

Many advanced societies are effectively *cashless societies*. One of the advantages of a cashless society is the elimination of the need to withdraw large sums of money from the bank whenever a person needs to make an expensive purchase of goods. (However, people in many countries do still rely on cash as the main medium of exchange for goods and services.) One disadvantage of the cashless society is that people become dependent upon credit rather than paying for goods immediately. One of the consequences of a cashless society is the requirement for tight data accuracy and data security controls to prevent fraudulent misuse of funds.

Banking was one of the first industry sectors to make use of information and communications technology to assist in dealing with their customers and, particularly, in the use of communications technology to exchange money between customers both nationally and internationally. Banks have used ICT as a competitive weapon to gain an advantage over their banking rivals to the extent that banks are always looking for information technology to provide new services for customers and to increase employee productivity.

In the 1980s banks introduced *automated teller machines* (ATMs) as an important customer service. ATMs are cash service points that are usually situated outside banks and in other areas of high population movement, such as airports and shopping malls. ATMs allow customers to draw out money, check their bank balance, or order statements of credit. The advantage of ATMs are ubiquity of access, as they are normally available 24 hours a day and seven days a week – provided the money in the tills has not run out! – and the fact that ATMs are located all around the world. Maestro debit cards can be used to withdraw cash from ATMs in any country that displays the Maestro symbol. ATMs are normally networked to a central computer system where any cash withdrawals or transactions are recorded and individual customer accounts are adjusted.

Data and information accuracy is therefore of paramount importance within the business environment. Business organizations rely on data being accurate in order to carry out appropriate and correct decision making. Organizations often model data to present a range of decision-making scenarios. The best option will then be selected by the company after consideration and deliberation of each option. If the information is inaccurate then the business organization is prevented from choosing an optimum decision scenario and may lose potential income. Therefore, data accuracy is essential to the smooth application and working of information technology in the business environment. For instance, ATMs dispense money to account customers when the correct PIN (*personal identification number*) is keyed in on the ATM machine. The system will compare the keyed number with the one that has been allocated to the card. If the keyed number is inaccurate the user will have a further two opportunities to enter the correct PIN number. If, after three attempts, the inaccurate number, or numbers, is persistently keyed in then the card will be retained by the machine. It is essential in order to achieve the confidence of the consumer that information technology treats data and information with integrity. Correctly built information systems in banking usually incorporate checking routines to detect data input and output errors. These systems should include safeguards to prevent data being corrupted by unforeseen faults.

Modern banking practices also use information and communications technology to transfer money from one place to another, a process known as *electronic funds transfer* (EFT). The electronic processing of cheques and money transfers saves time and paperwork. International banks use EFT to transfer funds from one country to another country where the funds will earn the highest international interest rate. In 1971 a system known as the *Society for Worldwide Interbank Financial Telecommunications* (SWIFT) was established to provide secure and reliable international communications between European and American banks. SWIFT is based in the Belgian capital of Brussels and is essentially a message-switching system where the messages contain instructions and advice about funds transfer, although the system does not actually move money into and out of bank accounts.

Most countries operate national banks that handle the accounts of government and ensure international trade: for example, the Bank of England in the UK, or the Federal Reserve System, which acts as the central banking system of the USA. The Federal Reserve System was founded by Congress in 1913 to provide the USA with a safer, more flexible and more stable monetary and financial system. Today the Federal Reserve's duties fall into four general areas:

▶ conducting the nation's monetary policy;
▶ supervising and regulating banking institutions and protecting the credit rights of consumers;
▶ maintaining the stability of the financial system;
▶ providing certain financial services to the US government, the public, financial institutions, and foreign official institutions.

The Federal Reserve System is composed of a central, governmental agency (the Board of Governors) in Washington, DC, and 12 regional Federal Reserve Banks located in major cities throughout the USA. The seven members of the Board of Governors of the Federal Reserve System are nominated by the President of the

USA and confirmed by the US Senate. Other countries have similar central banks to handle similar business: for example, the Deutsche Bundesbank in Germany, the Banque de France and the Bank of Japan.

Activity 8.8 The banking environment

Discuss how advances in information and communications technology are used by banks across the world to gain a competitive advantage over their rivals. Then choose a bank that operates over the web and discuss how the bank uses information and communications technology to support its customers and operations. Write a report on your findings. Your headings should include:

▶ background intelligence on the bank from newspaper sources and web references;

▶ how online and web-based banks are different to other banks;

▶ the use of ICT to support banking functions, such as customer payments, savings and investments, and funds transfer.

PAUSE FOR THOUGHT 8.4

Information and communications technology in national banks

The Bank of England, founded in 1694, is the central bank for the UK. It plays a very similar role to other national banks, such as the Federal Reserve System in the USA, the Deutsche Bundesbank in Germany, the Banque de France and the Bank of Japan.

These banks make extensive use of information and communications technology (ICT) in all aspects of banking business. For example, the Bank of England was using punch-card systems in the 1930s for handling data input and these were replaced by the first modern computer systems in the 1960s. Today, the use of information and communications technology is regarded as a normal and accepted part of the Bank's day-to-day activities. The Bank's ICT-based development is linked closely with that of other financial institutions, both British and international. This kind of systems interconnectivity requires close cooperation between a number of financial organizations to plan and develop new and improved ways of taking advantage of ICT.

One of the earliest ICT-based systems initiatives was called CHAPS (Clearing House Automated Payments System) which conveys guaranteed payments between banks. This was followed by the CGO (Central Gilts Office) which is a transfer and settlement system for gilt-edged securities. More recently this has been augmented with the CMO (Central Moneymakers Office) and the ESO (European Moneymarkets Office), which deal with certificates of deposit. This systems interconnectivity has led to the development of various communications systems linking all the European central banks. Such interconnectivity relies on efficient and effective systems and telecommunications networks.

The Bank of England keeps a constant watch on developments in IT. Throughout the 1970s and 1980s many services were provided through centrally operated mainframe computers, with most of the systems being operated and developed by the Bank's own in-house ICT staff. However, by the late 1980s and early 1990s responsibility for the development and operation of some ICT-based systems started to be devolved to end users and specific business areas, with central ICT resources only providing support. This trend was fuelled by the introduction of an increasing number of personal computers into the fabric of the Bank's operations. By the mid-1990s there was a deliberate strategy by the Bank of England to move away from centralized, shared services, towards distributed processing. This led to separate ICT programmes being pursued in different areas of the Bank, as appropriate to the localized needs of areas and users. A greater reliance was placed on the use of standard commercial applications software, accompanied by some degree of localized development and tailoring of applications package software.

The Bank of England's business is conducted from a number of separate sites, including London, Gloucester, Birmingham, Bristol and Leeds. The main site is in the City of London (in Threadneedle Street) and most of the Bank of England's ICT activities take place in the London premises. For commercial operations the Bank used a number of platforms such as Unix and PC environments in the late 1990s. Systems such as CMO, CGO and CHAPS, which serve the financial markets, and for which system failure is unacceptable, operate on fault-tolerant processors. These systems were and are supported by 'stand by' systems in case of major disasters. An integrated office system is prevalent throughout the Bank of England with extensive use of electronic mail (e-mail) using LANs supported by the various modern ICT platforms.

The Bank of England, despite its long history and tradition, uses ICT as comprehensively as any other modern banking institution: behind its traditional facade in Threadneedle Street in London lies an organization with its feet firmly in the information age.

8.11 Expert systems within the business environment

An *expert system* (ES) mimics the expertise and knowledge base of a human expert by using a process of heuristic, or random, induction to arrive at findings and conclusions. Expert systems are in use in a wide range of business environments to assist business activity and decision making. For example, many banking and financial institutions use expert systems to assist managers in the critical decision of whether or not to make financial loans to customers. Expert systems are often used to assist human decision-making processes and as such fall into the realm of decision support systems.

An expert system is usually comprised of three main components:

▶ **Knowledge base**: represented by deterministic rules and semantic networks. It is also concerned with knowledge structures and the information relationships that exist in specific knowledge fields. The knowledge base captures and stores the knowledge, experience and reasoning of an expert. A knowledge base is usually assembled by establishing the range and boundaries of knowledge of groups of experts in a particular subject domain. However, the obvious problem here is that some experts are more knowledgeable than others. The relationship between information and knowledge in an expert system is referred to as the *semantic network*. The semantic network is concerned with the way in which knowledge, or information objects, are stored and related in a particular knowledge field. Semantic networks, or *semantic nets* as they are commonly called, are logical hierarchical relationships between information objects that are based on inherited characteristics.

▶ **Inference engine**: aims to seek information and understand relationships from the knowledge base to provide answers to enquiries. The inference engine attempts to find the correct and logical information, rules and interpretations from a knowledge base in order to deliver a correct answer to an enquiry.

▶ **User interface**: allows the system to be interrogated by a human user. The role of the user interface is to be as user-friendly as possible and permit a free and easy interrelationship between the user and the expert system. The emphasis is on creating a clear communications channel between the human user and the technology of the expert system.

Expert systems possess a number of advantages that benefit their use in the business environment:

▶ They provide decision-making support that allows an individual to call on the knowledge and experience of an expert, as and when required, without the constraints of time and availability of the comparable human expert.

▶ They can be used at the highest levels of the decision-making hierarchy within a business organization. Strategic goal setting through the life cycle of planning, decision making and control can be assisted with reference to an expert system or set of expert systems.

▶ They are useful when knowledge is required in a number of different locations (e.g. branches of a bank or global offices in a multinational organization), where it would normally be too costly to place multiple human experts because of the demographics of the branch region.

Some of the disadvantages of expert systems revolve around the issue of a knowledge base being only as good as the experience and knowledge of the human expertise underpinning the system.

Expert systems are normally developed in cooperation between the three individuals:

▶ Field expert: an individual, or group of individuals, with an expertise that needs to be captured within an expert system.

▶ Knowledge engineer: the individual that has the responsibility for analysis, design, implementation and maintenance of the expert system.

▶ End user: the individual, or select group of individuals, who use and benefit from the expert system.

Traditionally, expert systems were developed by technical specialists. However, ICT advanced to a stage whereby it is now possible and practicable for expert systems to be developed by cooperation between the field expert and the end users. This has been made possible by *expert system shells* and other products available within the business environment that remove much of the program coding burden and allow end users to develop their own expert systems relatively easily.

An expert system shell is a collection of software tools and techniques that permit end users to analyze, design, develop and maintain an expert system. A number of pre-designed and pre-built expert shells can be purchased commercially from software vendors. For example, a financial adviser shell can be used to analyze financial investment in a business's fixed assets, such as the purchasing of factories, machinery and other major equipment.

Did you know?

Knowledgepro was a commercially available expert system shell that allowed the integration of other software applications, such as databases and spreadsheets, to allow organizations to build expert systems using existing datasets and modelling applications.

The advantages of using expert system shells are that they:

▶ are normally user-friendly and utilize high-level programming environment tools and techniques;

▶ comprise established rules and knowledge matrices that can readily be applied to a knowledge field;

▶ can be used by field experts and end users to build systems, rather than relying on a knowledge engineer to convert an understanding of the problem into program code.

Expert systems can be used for a number of purposes, from providing services to business planning, quality control and business diagnosis. Table 8.2 outlines a brief catalogue of expert systems and applications. Expert systems applications are continuously evolving and moving into every area of the business environment. There are also now a number of software tools available on the internet to help systems developers build expert systems.

Table 8.2 A brief catalogue of expert systems application areas

MYCIN	Medical expert system used to diagnose diseases
ACE	An expert system used to manage and maintain telephone networks
CLUES	Loan underwriting expert system to determine credit worthiness
CARGEX	An expert system used for logistical management and goods distribution
ExpertTax	Tax profiling expert system for optimal tax evaluation

Activity 8.9 Expert systems in the business environment

Discuss the use of expert systems in the business environment. What are the main components of an expert system? What are the advantages and disadvantages of using expert systems in the business environment? What the the main advantages of using expert system shells? Investigate the types of expert systems used in an organization with which you are familiar and discuss how these expert systems are used in practice.

8.12 Artificial intelligence within the business environment

Closely allied to the design and use of expert systems is the use of *artificial intelligence* (AI) in the business environment. Artificial intelligence systems do not necessarily possess a knowledge base, but they do possess the capability of mimicking human thought processes, particularly human reasoning and learning from past experience. The most advanced chess computers are a good example of the differences between artificial intelligence and expert systems. The most sophisticated chess computers use both expert system and artificial intelligence techniques. A chess computer possesses a knowledge base in order to understand the moves and rules of chess. However, the most advanced chess computers have the additional capability to apply human reasoning to a given situation; with the ability to learn from past mistakes and experience by adding knowledge and experience to their internal memory and knowledge base.

What is artificial intelligence (AI)?

The study of how computer systems can simulate intelligent processes such as learning, reasoning and understanding symbolic information in context. AI is inherently a multidisciplinary field. Although it is most commonly viewed as a sub-field of computer science, and draws upon work in algorithms, databases and theoretical computer science, AI also has close connections to the neurosciences, cognitive science and cognitive psychology, mathematical logic and engineering.

Source: Based on IBM Think Research website (www.research.ibm.com/thinkresearch).

The applications of artificial intelligence are many and varied, as demonstrated by the following comments of the President of the American Association for Artificial Intelligence (AAAI):

Ever since computers were invented, it has been natural to wonder whether they might be able to learn. Imagine computers learning from medical records to discover emerging trends in the spread and treatment of new diseases, houses learning from experience to optimize energy costs based on the particular usage patterns of their occupants, or personal software assistants learning the evolving interests of their users to highlight especially relevant stories from the online morning newspaper. (AAAI website)

The AAAI defines artificial intelligence as 'the scientific understanding of the mechanisms underlying thought and intelligent behavior and their embodiment in machines'. Artificial intelligence is found in many areas of the business environment, from manufacturing robotics through to various business decision-making environments. The following is a list of just some of the aspects of AI found within business organizations:

▶ **Robotics**: replacing human activity in mechanical and other manufacturing processes, such as manufacturing and production assembly lines and quality control systems that utilize computer-aided manufacturing techniques.

▶ **Sensor and perception systems**: providing systems with an ability to sense the immediate environment, for example mimicking human vision and hearing. This is particularly useful for systems that need to recognize patterns of size and shape of manufacturing components.

▶ **Neural networks**: building computer systems that are modelled on the neural processes of the human brain. The goals are to understand and develop systems that possess human 'thinking', although what is human thinking is still a much researched and debated problem.

▶ **Intelligent agent software**: developing software to act on behalf of a human user to search for information and assist humans to define their individual information needs. For example, the internet can utilize intelligent agent software to search for information sources and define information requirements by automatically and routinely searching the internet. Such software acts like an employed agent on behalf of a human user of a system.

Intelligent agents are becoming increasingly important in the business environment. An agent is someone who acts on someone else's behalf. Computerized intelligent agents, normally operating in web-based internet environments, do the same thing in that they work on behalf of a computer user. Intelligent agents come in many forms, and carry out many functions. For example, collaborative agents are agents that cooperate, personal agents are agents with user profiles determining their activities and remits, information agents are agents that retrieve information, and mobile agents are agents that move around computer networks. Intelligent agents are essentially programs that carry out a task unsupervised and apply some degree of intelligence to the task. The intelligence may be pretty minimal but will often include some degree of learning from past experience. Some intelligent agents can also interact with one another. There is considerable ongoing research in this field, with many exciting possibilities for autonomous intelligent agent activity on the internet.

Intelligence is an essential asset for organizations, whether it is human or artificial. Most intelligent agents operate in conjunction with the internet: the internet utilizes intelligent agents to find and process information and disseminate it to humans and, increasingly, to other agents. However, human intelligence is still the most important and sophisticated form of intelligence in the environment at large.

Activity 8.10   Artificial intelligence in the business environment

Discuss the role and function of artificial intelligence systems within business organizations and outline five application areas of the business environment that utilize the tools and technology of artificial intelligence. What are the main characteristics of artificial intelligence and how do these compare to expert systems? What business functions benefit from the application of artificial intelligence? What is the role of intelligent agents in business and computing?

PAUSE FOR THOUGHT 8.5

Artificial intelligence and systems security

Expert systems and artificial intelligence add intrinsic value to a business organization. Artificial intelligence is used in many areas of the business environment. One particularly interesting application is the use of AI in fraud detection by studying the habits of business customers and users. For example, one of the largest threats to the stability of the banking industry is credit card fraud. Banks and other financial institutions spend a great deal of time, effort and expense on finding innovative ways to combat financial fraud. A typical fraud may involve a credit card being stolen and used to buy goods up to the card's credit limit. Most credit card providers receive information reports on card transactions up to two or three days following the transaction. These usage reports are not timely enough to detect immediately fraudulent card usage. Often a credit card provider is only aware of a problem when a card is reported stolen by a customer.

However, expert systems and artificial intelligence can be used to detect and combat fraudulent credit card usage by profiling customers and applying many hundreds of rules to credit patterns and credit transactions. The system analyzes transaction patterns related to particular categories of customer and provides a warning of unusual or suspicious credit card usage. Such an expert system is usually programmed to retrieve credit card transaction data from a central data bank source – for example, on a daily or hourly basis – and automatically search for variations and deviations from standard customer profiles.

For example, a customer profile that indicates a rare dependence on drawing cash on the credit card would automatically be alerted to a transaction that withdrew a large amount of cash from an ATM. The expert system assigns a 'fraud likelihood score' to each transaction and alerts either the credit card provider or credit card customer to determine the legitimacy of the unusual transaction. This form of expert system has saved credit card providers a large amount of money by detecting irregularities and fraud.

Did you know?

Alan Turing (1912–54) was a mathematician and philosopher who was one of the founding fathers of computer science and artificial intelligence. He is the man behind the Turing Test of computer intelligence. In 1950 he published a paper entitled 'Computing machinery and intelligence' in which he asked the question 'can a machine think?' and 'if a computer could think, how could we tell?'. The Turing Test proposed that if the responses from the computer were indistinguishable from that of a human, then the computer could be said to be 'thinking'.

Artificial intelligence and intelligent agents are often referred to as *mind tools*. One of the first people to try to investigate human intelligence with regard to computers was Alan Turing, who established a test of machine intelligence in 1950 that is still referred to as the Turing Test of machine intelligence. Other important people in the development of the theoretical field of artificial intelligence were Allen Newell (1927–92) and Herbert A. Simon (1916–2001). Newell's work involved using computer simulation as the key research tool for understanding and modelling the human mind. He, along with J.C. Shaw and H.A. Simon, developed one of the first chess computer programs in the 1950s.

Simon is another significant person in the development of artificial intelligence theory and practice. He predicted in 1957 that computers would one day compose music, solve mathematical theorems and even beat a world chess champion – all events that have proved to be true with the passage of time. He was an economist, psychologist and computer scientist who was fascinated by human decision making and problem solving. In many ways he saw artificial intelligence in computing as a part of the solution to complex problem solving.

8.13 Internet-based integrated office environments

Information and communications technology is common in nearly all areas of the business environment. Integrated office systems encompass applications, architectures, systems methods and data processing techniques. An integrated office system aims primarily to automate office methods and procedures, to make them more efficient, and on a secondary basis to provide tools to assist human decision-making activity.

The types of applications found are many and various. For example, applications such as spreadsheets, word-processors, presentation packages (e.g. PowerPoint), databases and diary tools are commonplace in the integrated office environment. More sophisticated applications include groupware, internet messaging, conferencing software, internet notice boards, and electronic mail (e-mail). These applications, used daily in the business environment, are underpinned by computer architectures that are networked both internally and externally in the integrated office environment. The overall aim is to improve efficiency and effectiveness of administrative office practices. However, do these applications and their inherent use remove the need for paper? The paperless office is an aim of many organizations. Yet, applications such as e-mail often lead to greater paper production in the office environment than traditional paper-based administrative methods. However, what is certain is that the use of e-mail, often in conjunction with the internet and access to the *information highway*, has changed the nature and pattern of communication within many organizations.

What is the internet?

A network of tens of thousands of computer networks that allows computers to communicate with one another on a global scale. The internet connects computers and people together to permit the sharing of resources and information, irrespective of the nature of software and hardware underpinning an integrated office system.

The uses of the internet by business organizations are many and varied, including:

▶ **E-mail**: sending and receiving e-mail along internet pathways to users in other business organizations. This is the largest use of the internet.

▶ **Transferring information between networked systems**: using the internet as an electronic library where information can be accessed, stored or retrieved without leaving the safe confines of the user's computer system.

▶ **Searching and accessing information sources**: using commercially available software applications to browse the information on the internet.

▶ **Groupware and multi-user participation**: communicating with other interested groups and individuals by leaving messages on bulletin boards or developing direct contacts through e-mail and real-time internet messaging.

▶ **Real-time video and voice connection**: accessing data and information in multimedia form (i.e. pictures, sounds, video, movies, etc.).

Typical integrated office applications, used in conjunction with the internet as a front-end technology, include:

▶ Software applications for word-processing, database management, spreadsheet applications, presentations and multimedia information support.

▶ Input and output technology in the form of CD-ROMs, DVDs, optical scanning and document production.

▶ Communications technology, such as e-mail, group conferencing (e.g. FirstClass), wireless and wired modems and networking (e.g. wireless LANs and wide area networks – WANs).

▶ Digital electronic (wired and wireless) data interchange using terrestrial (i.e. wire or fibre optics) or extra-terrestrial (i.e. radio and microwave) technology to transmit electronically and receive data and information between computer systems.

▶ Multimedia technology supported by high-storage memory devices such as CD-ROM, DVD and internet databases.

▶ Teleconferencing and more sophisticated videoconferencing technology which allows numerous people to be connected simultaneously in vision and sound, even though they may be in remote locations and many hundreds or thousands of kilometres apart.

Activity 8.11 The internet-based integrated office environment

Discuss the concept of the internet-based integrated office environment and indicate the main role and responsibility of such systems within business organizations. Explain four possible uses of the internet within business and suggest the various categories of information an organization may wish to send and receive. Indicate the advantages and disadvantages of using e-mail and internet messaging as compared to non-electronic means of communication, such as face-to-face contact.

8.14 Chapter summary

The use and application of information and communication technology pervades the whole of the business environment. The legal, economic, cultural and technological forces that impact on business must be appreciated in order to understand their effect on the building of information systems within the business environment. The use of ICT within office environments can be at a low level (i.e. used for purely routine administrative tasks) or it can be used at a higher level of the business organization to support managerial or executive decision making. Therefore, an understanding of expert systems and artificial intelligence and their support in the process of decision making is fundamental in appreciating the use and integration of such technology within the business environment.

The following chapter will study various information and communication technology applications and architectures, so developing further our understanding of the integration of ICT applications within the business environment.

SHORT SELF-ASSESSMENT QUESTIONS

8.1 Outline and explain the four main component forces of the business environment.

8.2 Explain why *legal* and *technological* factors may affect the way information systems are designed and operated within the business environment.

8.3 Define and describe the *political* environment and explain how national legislation affects business practices and working patterns.

8.4 Describe three ways in which the government of a country can influence business activity within the business environment.

8.5 Explain the term *telecommuting* and suggest three possible advantages and disadvantages of telecommuting from the point of view of the individual employee and the business organization.

8.6 Identify two types of job that could be done by telecommuting and discuss the attributes that make telecommuting appropriate to certain jobs.

8.7 Define the term *ergonomics* and explain the significance of ergonomics to the design of human–computer interfaces.

8.8 Suggest some of the main health hazards that can arise when ICT is badly configured, with little regard to human considerations present within human–computer interaction.

8.9 Describe the gravitation of information technology from operational systems into management and executive information systems within the business environment.

8.10 Describe the *consumer environment* and explain how consumers transact their business in the modern business environment.

8.11 Explain the significance of ICT to the retailing and banking industries in your country and provide two examples of technologies that have altered the way customers interact with shops and banks.

8.12 Describe ways in which ICT has enabled banks to offer services on a 24-7 basis.

8.13 Explain the main areas of primary concern on privacy and data protection within the business environment.

8.14 Outline and explain the significance of *data protection legislation* in terms of its main principles and discuss why such legislation is so important in your country, region or state.

8.15 Describe ways in which data protection and privacy is protected in many business organizations.

8.16 Describe the use and importance of *secure transaction* in the retail and banking sectors of the business environment.

8.17 Suggest three security techniques that may reduce the possibility of data and information being wrongly accessed or incorrectly recorded.

8.18 Define the terms *expert system* and *artificial intelligence* and contrast the differences between the two definitions as found within the business environment.

8.19 Explain the relationship between the *field expert*, the *knowledge engineer* and the *end user* in the development of expert systems within the business environment.

EXTENDED STUDENT ACTIVITIES

Individual reporting activity 1

You were required in Activity 8.1 to search your college or university library for a magazine or journal article on the use of information technology in the banking or finance sectors of the business environment. The article you selected should be used as a unique case study and the basis for answering the following questions:

1 Explain why banks are leaders in the use and application of information and communications technology and suggest five possible advantages that banks gain by successfully implementing IT-based systems.

2 From your understanding, explain the use and categorization of information and communications technology for customers of banks. How do customers interact with ICT in banks and other financial institutions?

3 Discuss how reliant the banks should be on outsourced ICT functions in terms of developing expert systems that handle sensitive and private data on customers.

Individual reporting activity 2

Construct a questionnaire for a survey of customers that shop at a large store or mall to find out whether the customers pay for the goods by cash, credit card, debit card or electronic funds transfer. Use this to carry out a survey of people who shop at a local shop or mall. From the findings in your questionnaire write a brief report outlining the ICT implications of each service provided by the shop or the mall and whether any of the services could be better provided by the use of applications such as expert systems and artificial intelligence. Then discuss some of the security aspects of customer data and information of various technologies found in stores and malls.

Individual reporting activity 3

Many business organizations collect, collate and store data about customers and suppliers, which is held on ICT-based information systems.

1 Name three business organizations known to you that store data and information about customers and suppliers in electronic form and suggest the types of information that is appropriate and inappropriate to be stored.

2   Provide two arguments for why there might be concern in the business environment about the use of ICT to handle and store personal information.

3   Describe two of the measures provided by data protection and freedom of information legislation that are intended to reduce misuse of personal data and information held within the business environment.

4   Suggest, with reasoned arguments, two ways in which a business organization may try to overcome the concerns of internal and external stakeholders with regard to the handling of personal data within its information systems.

The productivity of employees is often monitored to provide valuable management information for decision making. Such monitoring is undertaken by using various ICT tools and techniques.

1   State some advantages and disadvantages of using such information for management decision making and control.

2   How could these productivity and other activity statistics be used for management decision making? Indicate how and why such information may be incorporated into an expert system.

Group-based activity

Form into groups of three or four students. Discuss what you consider to be the main characteristics of human intelligence. Discuss the problems of capturing knowledge from a human expert and suggest whether there are any ethical, political, cultural or legal issues that need to be addressed in the development of expert systems within the business environment.

Select a job activity found within the business environment where the decision-making activity could be captured by an expert system. Each member of the group should adopt the role of either knowledge engineer or end user. Interview the expert and attempt to capture that expert's knowledge and decision-making capabilities by establishing a set of rules and guidelines that can be converted into a program to determine answers to questions in the expert's knowledge field.

REFERENCES AND FURTHER STUDY

Books and articles

An asterisk (*) indicates a seminal text – a major source for later academic developments.

Callan, R. (1998) *The Essence of Neural Networks (Essence of Computing)*, Prentice Hall, ISBN: 013908732X

Cawsey, A. (1998) *Essence of Artificial Intelligence (Essence of Computing)*, Prentice Hall, ISBN: 0135717795

Cheeseman, H.R. (2001) *The Legal and Regulatory Environment of Business: Contemporary Perspectives in Business*, Prentice Hall, ISBN: 0130330264

Clark, A. (2002) *Organizations, Competition and the Business Environment*, FT Prentice Hall, ISBN: 0201619083

Darlington, K.W. (1999) *The Essence of Expert Systems (ESE)*, Prentice Hall, ISBN: 0130227749

Elliott, G. and Phillips, N. (2004) *Mobile Commerce and Wireless Computing Systems*, Addison-Wesley, ISBN: 0201752409

Faulkner, C. (1998) *The Essence of Human-Computer Interaction (Essence of Computing)*, Prentice Hall, ISBN: 0137519753

Giarratano, J. (1998) *Expert Systems: Principles and Programming*, PWS Publishing, ISBN: 0534950531

Jackson, P. (1999) *Introduction to Expert Systems*, Addison-Wesley, ISBN: 0201876868

Leondes, C.T. (ed.) (1998) *Fuzzy Logic and Expert Systems Applications*, Academic Press, ISBN: 0124438660

Luger, G.F. (2001) *Artificial Intelligence: Structures and Strategies for Complex Problem Solving*, Addison Wesley, ISBN: 0201648660

Mockler, R. (1992) *Developing Knowledge Based Systems Using an Expert Systems Shell*, Macmillan, ISBN: 0023818751

Morrison, J. (2002) *The International Business Environment: Diversity and the Global Economy*, Palgrave Macmillan, ISBN: 0333921453

Negnevitsky, M. (2001) *Artificial Intelligence: A Guide to Intelligent Systems*, Addison Wesley, ISBN: 0201711591

Newell, A. (1994) *Unified Theories of Cognition (William James Lectures)*, Harvard University Press, ISBN: 0674921011

Newell, A., Shaw, J.C. and Simon, H.A. (1958) 'Chess-playing programs and the problem of complexity', *IBM Journal of Research and Development*, 2, pp. 320–5

*Turing, A.M. (1950) 'Computing machinery and intelligence', *Mind*, 59, pp. 433–60

Yoon, Y., Guimaraes, T. and O'Neal, Q. (1995) 'Exploring the factors associated with expert system success', *MIS Quarterly*, 19(1)

Zuboff, S. and Maxim, J. (2003) *The Support Economy: Why Corporations Are Failing Individuals and the Next Episode of Capitalism*, Allen Lane, ISBN: 0713993200

Journals   *Journal of AI Research*

Journal of Biorobotics

Web resources   **Artificial Intelligence Center (USA/global)** – provides a centre for research into artificial intelligence.
www.ai.sri.com

American Association for Artificial Intelligence (USA/global) – organization for academics specializing in artificial intelligence.
www.aaai.org

Information Commissioner (UK) – information about the Information Commissioner.
www.informationcommissioner.gov.uk

Bureau of Economic Analysis (USA) – an American government site with economic statistics and economic analysis.
www.bea.doc.gov

MobileWorking.com (USA/global) – website for mobile professionals in business.
www.MobileWorking.com

chapter 9

Applications for handling data and information modelling

When you have studied this chapter you will be able to:

▶ define and describe the nature, function and role of software applications within the business environment;

▶ evaluate the integration of software applications within the business systems environment;

▶ compare and contrast a range of applications, tools and techniques for data and information modelling;

▶ describe the use and integration of various applications to model the decision-making environment within a business organization;

▶ advise on presentational methods and mediums for conveying information within the business systems environment.

9.1 Introduction to information modelling

Chapter 5 introduced the concepts of data modelling and process modelling. This chapter will look in further detail at information modelling in terms of the applications software available to handle data storage and model the information environment. The aim of data handling and information modelling is to deliver information to users for the purposes of decision making.

Software applications can be categorized into seven broad areas:

▶ word-processing

▶ spreadsheet modelling

▶ desktop publishing

▶ databases

▶ programming

▶ multimedia and presentation

▶ electronic communication.

Information modelling is concerned with the output from an information system and the use of that information output for the purposes of business decision making. Therefore, this chapter is less concerned with the structuring of data but more concerned with the modelling style and delivery of information for decision making within the business environment.

9.2 Modelling information within the business systems environment

Decision making involves the handling of data and the conversion of data into usable information; such usable information will often be the basis on which a business makes critical organizational decisions. Therefore, how this data is collected, collated and presented is of paramount importance within the business systems environment. The need for information has existed since the creation of human beings; and need for systematic handling of facts and figures has evolved as human beings have developed more sophisticated ways of living and interacting with one another. The development of interwoven societies, trade and commerce has led to an increased need for information to be handled and processed efficiently and effectively.

Today the amount of information in general circulation in the world grows ever more each year. Applications and infrastructures like the web enable people to have access to vast stores of data and information. We read in Chapter 1 that this deluge of information and the need for knowledge has led to the twenty-first century being referred to as the information age. Information provides a person with knowledge, and knowledge in turn empowers a person to take *optimal* decisions. However, as human decision makers, we do not have the individual capacity to cope with the deluge of information that is available within the business environment; so we depend upon ICT and its inherent capacity to handle data and information on our behalf.

Did you know?

The ancient Egyptians over 4000 years ago kept information and records on the building of the pyramids for the Pharaohs. Evidence exists that the Egyptians kept records on the division of labour and the number of workers required to construct the pyramids. They also kept two-column hieroglyphic records on income and expenditure, similar to the double-entry accounting technique used by modern business.

The modern process of business information modelling can be traced through a number of routes to the American space programme of the 1960s. In that decade the National Aeronautics and Space Administration (NASA) mission, outlined by President John F. Kennedy in 1961, was to put a man on the Moon by the end of the decade. On 25 May 1961, before a joint session of Congress in the USA, President Kennedy said:

I believe that this nation should commit itself to achieving the goal, before this decade is out, of landing a man on the Moon and returning him safely to Earth. No single space project in this period will be more impressive to mankind, or more important for the long-range exploration of space; and none will be so difficult or expensive to accomplish.

On 20 July 1969 this vision was fulfilled when astronaut Neil Armstrong stepped on to the Moon's surface. (The last Moon-walk by an astronaut was in December 1972.) This feat to land a man on the Moon required vast amounts of information to be collected, processed and stored. New information and communication technologies were required to accomplish this feat. For instance, the need to handle data and information effectively led NASA scientists to develop the first computerized data storage systems known as *databases* to manage and coordinate vast banks of information.

Did you know?

It is from the work by NASA into database techniques that the first commercially available business database applications package was developed, known as R:Base. Much of the theory and practice of data modelling theory and database management practice owes its origins to the NASA space programme of the 1960s.

However, before information can be modelled, data must first be selected, obtained and structured. This process can be sequentially separated into ten stages of development from converting raw data into information. These ten stages of data acquisition, handling and delivery are:

1 Selecting the data (data selection).
2 Collecting the data (data capture).
3 Organizing the data (data structure).
4 Inputting the data (input method).
5 Searching the data (data interrogation).
6 Manipulating the data (data management).
7 Retrieving the data (output method).
8 Delivering the data (communications medium).
9 Presenting the data (data format).
10 Information for decision making.

Activity 9.1 Modelling information within the business environment

Discuss the main role and function of data and information modelling within a business organization. Explain why modelling is such an important exercise within the business environment. Why is it important to be able to handle efficiently the storage of data within an organization?

9.3 Data and information capture

Before any form of business data processing can occur, the data (or pre-processed information) must first of all be selected and obtained. Initial data selection involves searching and finding data that is relevant and suitable to

Lillington's Video/DVD Hire Club – Leeds Branch		
APPLICATION FORM FOR MEMBERSHIP		
Membership number:		(Form: A4New)
SURNAME:		VIDEO CATEGORY
FIRST NAMES:		PREFERENCE
		(Please tick box)
Address: -------------------------------------		Adventure	
-------------------------------------		Comedy	
-------------------------------------		Drama	
-------------------------------------		Horror	
Postcode: -------------------------------------		Thriller	
Telephone (home):		Science fiction	
Telephone (work):		Chidren's	
Comments:		Other (specify)	
Type of proof of identity shown:		
Date of application:		
Signature of applicant:		
Signature of branch manager:		

Figure 9.1 Example of a data capture form

the requirements of the business user and appropriate to the decision-making environment. There are many and various sources of business data and other information. Information can be obtained in computer-readable format, such as from the internet or a database in the corporate environment. It can be obtained locally via CD-ROM or electronic mail attachments. It can even be obtained from hardcopy formats that can be scanned, or digitized, into formats for use with various software applications.

Another method of obtaining data is by the use of *data sensors* that monitor and collect information automatically and remotely. An example of data sensoring is the scanning of bar codes on products sold in shops: a laser-scanning device reads the bar code and records the item and the price of the item within its computerized system. The data is then recorded and stored for future reference. The data acquired from sensors can be stored and maybe at a later stage input into a database application in the required organizational format.

A popular method of information acquisition is through the design and use of *data capture forms* that can either be paper-based or in electronic format, such as web page forms that ask for a user's information. For example, if a new DVD or video hire club opens, it will need to have data capture forms to be completed by all applicants wishing to become a member of the video club. Figure 9.1 shows a typical data capture form for a DVD/video hire club, which could also be used as an online web data capture form.

9.2 Information and data capture

Discuss the main role and function of data capture techniques and suggest three types of data capture format found within the business environment. Outline four methods of capturing data and indicate types of data that would be collected and the use of such data to a decision maker within the business environment. Why might the method of data capture be so important? Are there any ethical issues with collecting data automatically and remotely without the user's knowledge?

9.4 Data and information structuring

Before the evolution of computerized database technology and database management systems, a business organization stored its captured data in paper-based filing systems that were structured into a number of files. Each file contained a collection of records, and each record was composed of a number of fields that in turn referred to the basic facts being stored. The terms *record* and *field* still exist in the computerized database domain.

A *database* is a repository for large, structured data sets. A simple database might be a single file containing many records, each of which contains the same set of fields where each field is a certain fixed length of characters (i.e. text and numbers). In modern systems terms a database is merely one component of a *database management system* (DBMS). This is a suite of computer programs that typically manages large structured sets of data. A database management system offers the capability of 'search and find' queries. A *query* is a search question for a database. The system normally accepts requests for data from the application program and instructs the operating system to transfer the appropriate data from its repository. Database management systems can be simple or complex, depending on the nature and extent of the data being stored. Text and numbers are the easiest data to store, whereas pictures, sounds and images in graphical databases are complex to store and arrange.

What is a database management system (DBMS)?

A suite of computer programs that manages large structured sets of data. A database management system offers the users the capability of 'search and find' queries to locate and retrieve data from its data repository.

Normally, database management systems control the organization, structure, storage and retrieval of data (i.e. fields, records and files) in a database. Most database management systems offer additional security features, such as passwords and identification codes to control access to data. New categories of data can be added or deleted within the database only by authorized users. Data security prevents unauthorized users from viewing or updating the database. Furthermore, a DBMS enables an organization to control who can and who cannot change data within its information environment.

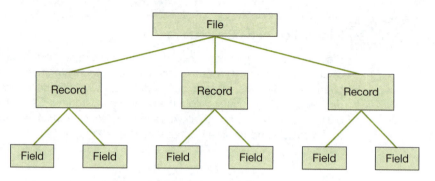

Figure 9.2 Traditional hierarchical data organization

The traditional form of *hierarchical* data organization is shown in Figure 9.2. The process of data structuring is similar to entity-relationship diagrams (ERDs) discussed in Chapter 5. Remember that ERDs were composed of the three elements of entity, attribute and relationship. Therefore, ERDs can be used as a tool and technique for data modelling within the business environment.

Within a hierarchical data structure, a *file* refers to the overall subject of the data to be stored; a file is defined as a collection of related records of data. For example, a file might be concerned with personnel information in a human resources system or market research data within a marketing information system. Each file would consist of a collection of *records* that contain a sub-division categorization of data within the file. A record is divided into a number of *fields*, each of which relates to an item of information found within the record. A field is often referred to as an *attribute* and a record as an *entity*. Records may contain as many fields as required by the user of the information. The sub-division of files into records and the sub-division of records into fields can clearly be seen from Figure 9.2. In the video/DVD hire club example of a data capture form (Figure 9.1), if this was to be transferred to a hierarchical database structure then the file would be all the members of the video hire club. Each member would have their own personal record and the fields would comprise the information contained in the data capture form (e.g. membership number, surname, first names, postcode, telephone number).

Records in a file can have fields of either fixed or variable length. The length refers to the number of alphanumeric character positions allocated to a field. (The combination of letters of the alphabet and numerals is known by the term *alphanumeric*, and a particular combination of letters and numbers is known as an *alphanumeric string* – e.g. ABC123.) If the fields are of fixed length then each field has a maximum set number of character positions. If the fields are of variable length then the number of characters in each field will not be the same for every record. Again, referring to the example of the video/DVD hire club in Figure 9.1, an example of a fixed length field would be the postcode, since this is of a specified length determined by the Post Office. The format of these postcodes or zip codes are a maximum of four characters followed by three characters (e.g. SE34 5XD). This is also an example of an alphanumeric field. The surname field could be of fixed or variable length. For example, a maximum length of 30 char-

Table 9.1 Example of data structuring

Employee no.	Employee name	Gender	Department	Age	Grade	Salary($)
9056497	Smith G.R.	M	Sales	54	2	31 000
9315649	Jones M.T.A.	M	Accounts	23	5	12 000
9543287	Evans W.	F	Accounts	29	4	15 000
9567845	Khan C.	M	Marketing	31	4	15 000
9647825	Davies F.	F	Personnel	43	3	21 000

acters could be used to hold the surname. However, since most surnames are considerably shorter than this, it would be a waste of storage space to use a fixed length field.

How would the structuring of data occur in business practice? Table 9.1 illustrates a typical structure of a company personnel database, as may be found within an application of a business organization's payroll system. The personnel data shows a record for each employee; each record has seven fields (or attributes), reading across the page from employee name to salary. For example, the record for Davies shows fields for employee number, employee name, gender, department, age, grade and salary.

Each record within a file will always have a field that uniquely identifies that record. This type of field is often referred to as the *primary key*. In the personnel database in Table 9.1, it might be assumed that a specific record could be identified and located by the employee's name. However, this is not possible if employees have the same surname. In reality, some personnel files contain multiple employees with the same name; to ensure that a record can be uniquely identified each employee must be assigned a primary key field that is unique to that employee's personnel record. In this example, the primary key field is employee number. However, if it is only necessary to retrieve a group of records that fulfil a wider search criteria then *secondary keys* may be used. For example, a company may wish to retrieve all the records related to grade-2 employees, in order to establish salary differences at that grade. The secondary key of grade would then be used to search and retrieve all the records that matched 2 in the field (or attribute) of grade.

There are a number of problems and disadvantages associated with the traditional hierarchical file system approach:

▶ **Data redundancy**: the traditional file system encourages duplicate files to be kept because separate applications may use the same categories of data across a business organization.

▶ **Data inconsistency**: the same data may occur on many files but be updated at different times which causes reduced control over the data and reduced data accuracy at a given time point.

Overcoming data redundancy and data inconsistency was covered in detail in Chapter 5 with an analysis and discussion of data *normalization*. Advances in ICT have enabled data to be stored in more user-friendly structures and environments. A database is an organized collection of data that can be accessed by many users and for many purposes. Database management systems provide a means to interactively enter and update data and information, as well as interrogate it. Most systems also provide the capability to track data changes and deletions. Therefore, an audit trail of data changes can be maintained. Most business information systems are made up of subjects (i.e. customers, suppliers, employees, agents, etc.) and activities (i.e. orders, payments, purchases, stock updating, etc.). Database design is the process of deciding how to organize this data into record types and how the record types will relate to each other. A database management system should mirror an organization's data structures and processes.

There are three main types of database structure found within the business environment:

▶ hierarchical

▶ relational

▶ network.

The most suitable structure depends on an organization's data handling requirements and on the transaction rate. Commercial *relational* database applications have become the norm in most business organizations (e.g. Microsoft Access).

There are a number of advantages of database management systems over traditional digital data file storage systems:

▶ A reduction in wasted storage capacity and reduced data redundancy: database is controlled and structured to avoid data duplication and wasted capacity.

▶ A database encourages data standardization and security by maintaining unique standards of data structuring, storage and user access within a database environment.

▶ Databases are easier to maintain and expand than traditional computerized file systems.

The coordination and control of a set of databases is usually assisted by a database management system that carries out the functions of storing, searching, retrieving, maintaining security and information integrity, and providing facilities for the manipulation of data within the database framework. In many ways a database management system acts as a user-friendly front-end interface tool between the end user and the data store or repository. The ultimate aim of database structuring is normally to organize, control and make data accessible to the systems end user so that reliable, accurate and timely information is available for business decision making.

Integrated and networked databases enable organizations to handle data processing across a distributed business environment, where an organization has offices and companies around the world. Since the world of information is made up of data, text, pictures, images and audio, it is now becoming common for databases to store and handle all types of multimedia data and information. The advantage of modern database management systems is that they are often linked to web-based data resources that are inherently multimedia-based. Web databases are becoming the norm in many business organizations in the twenty-first century.

9.3 Information and data structuring

Describe the main disadvantages associated with the traditional hierarchical file system approach and outline the main advantages of relational database systems within the business organization. Discuss the relationship between the files, records and fields of traditional hierarchical file design and the use of entity-relationship diagrams (ERDs) as a tool for structuring data. Describe the advantages of using networked web databases rather than traditional stand-alone databases.

9.5 Data input methods and data modelling

Once the data within a business environment has a logical structure, it then has to be input into a relevant database application. The most common method of *data input* is by using a normal qwerty keyboard connected to a computer or data storage device (e.g. DVD or CD-ROM). Inputting can also take a range of other forms, such as voice recognition input, scanning text and pictures, and electronic downloading and uploading of computer files from other local or remote online applications. With the growth of multimedia technology and the internet, pictures, graphs, sounds and movies may also now form part of a database application.

> ### Did you know?
> The term qwerty arises from the first five letters on a standard keyboard. The qwerty configuration was originally designed to slow down the typist to prevent the hammers of the old manual typewriter from jamming. Today, research is being carried out to find a more efficient and appropriate configuration of letters for quicker and more effective data and information input.

Once data is stored in a database application it may be interrogated and edited:

▶ **Database editing and data maintenance**: adding deleting data within a database application. For example, if an employee moves home, then their new home address would have to be changed in their individual personnel record within an application of the human resources system.

▶ **Database interrogation**: accessing a record to validate the information contained in a particular record, but not to alter the record. For example, the personnel record of an employee may be referenced to check the age of that employee and their current salary level.

Data and information are structured and modelled within a database environment. Models allow complex and data-intensive systems to be understood and their behaviour predicted. A model may be used as the basis for data mining and data simulation.

9.6 Information output and search patterns

Databases can be sorted, merged and integrated with other applications across a range of systems within the business environment; this area is often known as *data manipulation*. For example, data can be sorted into ascending or descending order, as required by an end user, or merged by interleaving the data from two or more files to produce one large database application. Table 9.2 illustrates a worked example of database sorting and merging techniques. In this example there are two files in a database, labelled File A and File B. File A contains five records and File B contains seven records. Both files have records with the same number and type of fields (or attributes).

Table 9.2 Data and information manipulation

File A

Record no.	Name	Department	Age	Salary($)
20543	Davies T.	Sales	54	28 500
25765	Evans G.D.	Accounts	23	14 000
22359	Francis P.A.	Accounts	29	15 500
31527	Evans C.	Marketing	31	18 000
25980	Jones D.F.	Personnel	43	21 500

File B

Record no.	Name	Department	Age	Salary($)
21337	Ghandi A.G.	Accounts	24	14 000
29879	Evans D.A.	Sales	24	14 000
22341	Smith C.	Sales	37	20 000
23336	White G.D.	Personnel	21	13 500
27614	Jones S.B.	Buying	47	24 000
25601	Brown C.	Accounts	58	30 500
25753	Carter V.M.	Marketing	32	23 500

If File A and File B are sorted by the primary key field of record number in ascending order, then two new sorted listings would occur (see Tables 9.3 and 9.4):

Table 9.3 File A (sorted by record number)

Record no.	Name	Department	Age	Salary($)
20543	Davies T.	Sales	54	28 500
22359	Francis P.A.	Accounts	29	15 500
25765	Evans G.D.	Accounts	23	14 000
25980	Jones D.F.	Personnel	43	21 500
31527	Evans C.	Marketing	31	18 000

Table 9.4 File B (sorted by record number)

Record no.	Name	Department	Age	Salary($)
21337	Ghandi A.G.	Accounts	24	14 000
22341	Smith C.	Sales	37	20 000
23336	White G.D.	Personnel	21	13 500
25601	Brown C.	Accounts	58	30 500
25753	Carter V.M.	Marketing	32	23 500
27614	Jones S.B.	Buying	47	24 000
29879	Evans D.A.	Sales	24	14 000

If File A was *merged* with File B and sorted by the field of record number, then File C would occur (see Table 9.5):

Table 9.5 File C (Files A and B merged and sorted by record number)

Record no.	Name	Department	Age	Salary($)
20543	Davies T.	Sales	54	28 500
21337	Ghandi A.G.	Accounts	24	14 000
22341	Smith C.	Sales	37	20 000
22359	Francis P.A.	Accounts	29	15 500
23336	White G.D.	Personnel	21	13 500
25601	Brown C.	Accounts	58	30 500
25753	Carter V.M.	Marketing	32	23 500
25765	Evans G.D.	Accounts	23	14 000
25980	Jones D.F.	Personnel	43	21 500
27614	Jones S.B.	Buying	47	24 000
29879	Evans D.A.	Sales	24	14 000
31527	Evans C.	Marketing	31	18 000

Finally, File A can be merged with File B (to create File C) and sorted alphabetically by the field name (see Table 9.6):

Table 9.6 File C (Files A and B merged and sorted alphabetically by name)

Record no.	Name	Department	Age	Salary($)
25601	Brown C.	Accounts	58	30 500
25753	Carter V.M.	Marketing	32	23 500
20543	Davies T.	Sales	54	28 500
31527	Evans C.	Marketing	31	18 000
29879	Evans D.A.	Sales	24	14 000
25765	Evans G.D.	Accounts	23	14 000
22359	Francis P.A.	Accounts	29	15 500
21337	Ghandi A.G.	Accounts	24	14 000
25980	Jones D.F.	Personnel	43	21 500
27614	Jones S.B.	Buying	47	24 000
22341	Smith C.	Sales	37	20 000
23336	White G.D.	Personnel	21	13 500

In many circumstances the users of data files require the information listed and printed out in formats similar to those for File C. Databases can be searched and data ordered into various output formats, which in turn can be downloaded to other applications within the business environment.

Databases can be searched using search-term alphanumeric strings or by using *Boolean logic*. Boolean logic operators are 'and', 'or' and 'not'. By using such operators a subject or topic area can be searched and the relevant records retrieved from the database. For example, a manager of a business organization may wish to retrieve all the records in a database system relating to employees on grade 3 or 4. Then the *search pattern* may be as follows: 'employee and (grade 3 or 4)'. Note that in Boolean logic the terms in the brackets will usually be linked and the operation carried out before other terms in the search pattern.

One of the ways of presenting data is in the form of *reports* to be read by a manager or executive, or to be presented to a manager or executive of a business organization. The report will need to be annotated with headings and titles and presented neatly for the report end user. The content and the report itself should be clear, visual and purposeful.

Activity 9.4 Information output and search patterns

Norman Payne Enterprises operates a purchase order processing system. The company requires you to advise and recommend improvements to the current system. Using a database application of your choice, set up a database to manage and coordinate the ordering of raw materials from various suppliers. (Remember Chapter 7 outlined the role and purpose of a purchase order processing system.) The record structure should include such data and information as the supplier's name and address, product category, and supplier product codes and descriptions. Indicate the data and information requirements of the purchase order processing system for Norman Payne Enterprises.

Design a suitable data capture format to record the above information required for the system and state whether it is numeric, alphabetical or alphanumeric. Then, advise the business organization on the implications of too much or too little data handling within a business information system.

9.7 Spreadsheet modelling

One of the most popular applications used to model data is an electronic spreadsheet. A spreadsheet is an application program that lays out an analysis sheet of rows and columns. The spreadsheet is based on the traditional accountant's lined analysis sheet, used for financial calculations for determining profit and loss, and assets and liabilities. In an electronic spreadsheet the rows and columns make up a matrix of *cells* that can be uniquely identified by a number (row) and letter (column). Text, numbers or formulae can be entered into the cells of the spreadsheet and each cell will have a unique alphanumeric code. For example, the first cell in the top left-hand corner of a spreadsheet is identified as A1. (Most elec-

Summary cash budget for a six-month period
(Example of management planning and control)

	Jan (£)	Feb (£)	Mar (£)	Apr (£)	May (£)	Jun (£)	Six-month total
Opening bank balance	3435	4685	4935	4585	3085	1535	
Total receipts	3900	3000	2500	1450	1500	3000	£15 350
Less: total payments	2650	2750	2850	2950	3050	3150	£17 400
Net receipts	1250	250	−350	−1500	−1550	−150	−£12 050
Balance carried forward	4685	4935	4585	3085	1535	1385	
Bank overdraft limit	1500	1500	1500	1500	1500	1500	£9 000
Overdraft margin	3185	3435	3085	1585	35	−115	

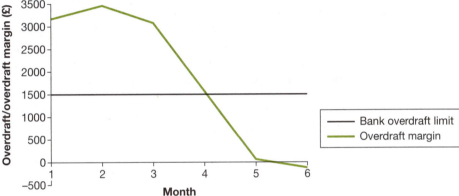

Chart of overdraft limit against overdraft margin

Figure 9.3 Example of a cash flow budget modelled in a spreadsheet application

tronic spreadsheets have at least 63 columns and 254 rows, making 16 002 available cells!)

The power of the spreadsheet within the business domain lies in the ability not only to do calculations in single cells, but also to be able to recalculate the whole spreadsheet each time one or more changes are made to any individual cell. The recalculations can be performed almost instantaneously. Thus, spreadsheets lead to a reduction in clerical effort and an increase in data modelling efficiency. Figure 9.3 illustrates an example of a spreadsheet application showing a summary cash budget and its corresponding graphical presentation.

Electronic spreadsheets were originally designed for use by accountants. However, an electronic spreadsheet can be used in any subject area where there is a need to model and manipulate information. The uses of the spreadsheet are limited only by the imagination of the modeller. While a basic spreadsheet manipulates string data in rows and columns of cells, some spreadsheets support three-dimensional matrices and iterative calculation and recalculation. An essential feature of a spreadsheet is the capability to undertake 'what-if?' analysis. The user gives desired conditions and parameters and assigns several input cells to be varied automatically as a consequence of changing the conditions and parameters. An area of the spreadsheet is assigned to show the results. Cells may be either absolute or relative in either their horizontal or vertical aspects. All copies of an absolute reference will refer to the same row, column or cell, whereas a relative reference refers to a cell with a given offset from the current cell. Modern spreadsheets usually incorporate a macro language (e.g. Microsoft Excel has a Visual Basic language interface) so that a spreadsheet can be associated with other applications, such as word-processors and databases. Macros can be written to input data from a database, manipulate that data in the spreadsheet environment, and output the data to suitable formats.

In the late 1970s a calculation program called VisiCalc was introduced by VisiCorp Inc. to the business environment. It was the first commercial spreadsheet program. It was soon followed by a number of other programs in the 1980s and 1990s (e.g. Lotus 1-2-3 in the 1980s and Microsoft Excel in the 1990s). VisiCalc was first conceived by a man named Dan Bricklin while he was an MBA student at Harvard Business School in the USA. He was later helped on the development of VisiCalc by Bob Frankston. Bricklin set out to design an electronic application that would combine the intuitiveness of pencil and paper calculations with the power of a programmable calculator. VisiCalc is widely credited with creating much of the demand for desktop computers in business in the 1980s, because companies saw the advantage of electronic spreadsheets (and word-processors). In many ways VisiCalc could be said to be one of the first 'killer-apps' within the business environment. (A 'killer-app' is a software application that has a dramatic effect on the way in which people do things in the business domain.) In the modern business systems environment Microsoft Excel is probably the most widely used spreadsheet in the world today.

Did you know?

The Microsoft Corporation is the largest supplier of business software applications in the world. It supplies PC-operating systems, business applications (e.g. Microsoft Office) and various networking and web-browser applications. Microsoft was founded in 1975 by Bill Gates and his high school friend Paul Allen. One of their first software products was a version of the computer language BASIC for the Altair computer.

Spreadsheet methods

Spreadsheets recognize and manipulate four types of data or information:

- ▶ **Text**: often used for column or row headings.
- ▶ **Numbers**: used for the calculations.
- ▶ **Formulae**: used to calculate results in certain cells from information contained or referenced in other cells.
- ▶ **Operators**: arithmetic signs, usually + for addition, − for subtraction, * for multiplication, / for division, and ^ for raising to a power.

Spreadsheet layout

Spreadsheets can be *formatted* so that column sizes can be altered and the data within cells justified to the left or right or centred, and they have the facility to add or delete columns from the worksheet. A *worksheet* is the name given to the area of rows and columns that are being used to store and record numbers, text or formulae. A user can move around the spreadsheet, from cell to cell, by using the cursor (or arrow) keys (< >) located on the keyboard and the mouse. The cursor is often indicated on the spreadsheet by a flashing line or by one cell being highlighted more than the other cells. Commonly used spreadsheet terms include:

▶ **Active cell**: the cell that is currently waiting to receive data. It is indicated on the screen by the cursor.

▶ **Cell**: identified by a column number and a row letter (e.g. A1). A cell is empty until it receives some type of data.

▶ **Command bar**: appears either at the top or the bottom of the worksheet. It indicates the options available to the user.

▶ **Display window**: what is actually seen on the screen. It may only be a portion of a large worksheet.

▶ **Entry line**: can appear either at the top of the screen or the bottom of the screen. It is used to input and display the commands or data to be placed into a cell.

▶ **Scrolling**: moving around the worksheet over a number of cells.

▶ **Status bar**: appears either at the top or bottom of the screen. It keeps the user informed of each cell's status (e.g. text, numbers or formulae).

All spreadsheet applications have a command menu bar that appears at the top or the bottom of the spreadsheet screen, which provides useful general command options for the user, such as saving a worksheet, loading a worksheet, inserting or deleting rows or columns, and creating pictorial displays of data such as graphs, charts and diagrams. Many spreadsheets are far too large to be viewed on a single screen and so a portion of the worksheet must be chosen for viewing at any one time. The computer screen may be regarded as a *window* that can be used to view any portion of the spreadsheet.

Spreadsheet functions

One of the advantages of spreadsheets is that formulae may be entered and stored in cells. The mathematical formula allows a cell to be recalculated if a number is changed in a related cell; a related cell is one that is affected by the formula. A formula can be either simple or complex, depending on the situation and what is being modelled. Most spreadsheet applications have *formulae functions* built into the spreadsheet applications package. A function is a special kind of formula that has been prepared in advance to perform a variety of chores. Most functions carry out some action on a cell value or group of cell values in order to produce another value. A simple example is the function known as SUM, which is a frequently used function to total rows and columns. For example, the function formula SUM(C3-C9) is informing the spreadsheet to add together all the values in cells C3 to C9. The form and sequence of alphanumeric characters, or the syntax, of the command formulae may vary slightly from package to package. Common functions that are built into spreadsheet applications include:

▶ **AVERAGE**: finds the average of a row or column.

▶ **IF**: tests the value of a cell and does one thing if the test is positive (true) or another thing if the test is negative (false).

▶ **MIN**: reveals the lowest number in the selected cells.

▶ **MAX**: reveals the highest number in the selected cells.

▶ **PI**: provides the number for pi (3.1415926536).

▶ **SUM**: finds the total in a row or column.

▶ **SQRT**: finds the mathematical square root of a number.

Activity 9.5 Spreadsheet modelling

Discuss the role and function of spreadsheet applications for the modelling of decisions within the business environment. Provide examples of the use of spreadsheet modelling of accounting applications and information modelling within a marketing information system. Describe the information requirements for a decision regarding the purchase of an additional factory to support a business organization's manufacturing process and discuss the way you would go about building a spreadsheet model of the decision-making environment.

9.8 Modelling techniques

Modelling is at the heart of problem solving and eventual decision making within the business environment. A model is a representation of some aspect of reality. Models attempt to recreate in a controlled manner the *systems* that exist in reality. Within the activity of modelling, the term system is used to mean all the features of reality the model is attempting to explain.

Models can be categorized into three types:

1 **Physical** models
2 **Logical** (mathematical) models
3 **Mixed** logical and physical models.

▶ **Physical models**: for example, the use of wind tunnels to model the effects of wind patterns and vortices of air flowing over the frame of an airplane or even a racing car. The wind tunnel model would be physically built to be as realistic as possible. Physical models such as this are built and tested because it would be too expensive, and often too dangerous, to build and test a full-size airplane or racing car. Another example of a physical model is the building of small engineering models of tall buildings to test the stresses and other forces exerted on the frames and main supports of the building. Such modelling is essential within the construction sector of the business environment. Again, a model would be built because it would be too costly in time and money to build an untested actual-size building.

▶ **Logical models**: theoretical models that are made up of statements of principles, logical assumptions and numerical calculations. The process of logical modelling is the forming of concepts about everyday reality within domains of the business environment. Such models are appropriately designed using data analysis and logical analysis techniques. Logical and mathematical models lend themselves easily to computer-based analysis and implementation. A spreadsheet applications package is ideal for building logical models because the logical assumptions and numerical calculations can be readily structured, and usually such packages are supplied with in-built mathematical functions. For example, a model can be built using logical assumptions of demand and supply to extrapolate or predict the sales of products and services. Other statistical analysis and modelling packages may be used as appropriate (e.g. Genesis Model Building or Witness). By using a business information technology (BIT) modelling application a user may analyze, experiment and test any model of business systems reality.

▶ **Mixed logical and physical models**: logical modelling techniques that are applied to a built physical model. For example, a flight simulator program run on an ordinary home computer allows the user (or player!) to simulate the flying of an airplane. The flight simulator computer program is designed and written using theoretical, logical and mathematical principles of flight; the user is able to interact physically (by using the joy-stick) to fly the airplane. An ideal mixed modelling system is the commercial flight simulators built and designed to train commercial airline pilots. The simulator box is a physical model and all movement and flight is attained by computer programs using logical (and mathematical) modelling. Another example of a mixed logical and physical model is where customer telephone calls are monitored and distributed to help-desk operators. Commercial applications can be used to model customer or client calls coming through a telephone switchboard to analyze the number and type of calls made and related user-support activity resulting from these calls. The idea is to build the most efficient telephone user-support system to deal with client enquiries.

What is a software application?

A self-contained program that performs a specific task (e.g. spreadsheet, word-processor, database, presentation package etc.) and is used on a daily or routine basis. Software applications (or 'apps') are used by end users and are referred to as front-end applications, whereas operating systems software is referred to as back-end applications software.

The bounds of what can be modelled within the business environment is only limited by the imagination, or inspiration, of the modeller. Most models are based on theoretical principles and logical assumptions. It would be very rare to find a model that perfectly represented reality. However, the role of a model is to represent, as far as possible, some degree of reality. A model enables a user to predict, test or explain a representation of reality. Often no two managers or executives will carry out a model-building exercise in the same way; there is plenty of scope in modelling for individuality of thought and approach. However, within modelling there are standard concepts and guidelines on development stages to assist the model builder. Any model should be developed methodically and systematically. There are eight generic stages in the process of designing and developing a model for the business environment:

1 Determine which system of reality is to be modelled.
2 Formalize the specifications of the model.
3 Establish the assumptions and variables of the model.
4 Prepare a proposal for the building of the model.
5 Carry out data collection and data modelling.
6 Create user documentation for the model.
7 Carry out a validation of the model.
8 Put the model into use and update the model as required.

Stage 1 of any model building exercise begins with the establishment of which *system* of reality is to be modelled. Once an area of interest has been established by the model builder, then, in stage 2, the *specifications* of the model should be formally laid out. These indicate the bounds of the modelling environment. The specification indicates which particular aspects of reality are to be modelled; it defines the *boundary* of the model system. Stage 3 of the model-building exercise requires the establishment and description of the model's *assumptions* and *variables*. The assumptions of any model summarize the simplifications and limiting principles made in identifying the system to be analyzed; the assumptions also state and describe the relationship between components of the system. The variables of the system identify the quantifiable components, also referred to as the *entities*, of the system. The model builder should always list and describe all the variables in the system model and the relationship between the variables. This relationship between variables can often be reflected in simple or complex numerical formulae. In any model there is usually one or more *decision variable* in the list of total variables. A decision variable is controlled by the modeller and is fundamental to the modelling exercise. These control variables are sometimes referred to as the control *parameters* of the model.

The fourth stage of the model-building exercise is to prepare a *proposal* for the building of the model. The proposal should determine how the model is to be built, what is to be used, and whether it is to be a physical, logical or mixed model. The proposal should also indicate the type of information technology to be used to construct the model or assist in the modelling exercise. The fifth stage of *data collection* and *data modelling* is central to the model-building exercise. Once the assumptions and variables have been determined, then the data to be analyzed needs to be collected and quantified. It is at this stage that the data can be modelled, based on the assumptions and relationships between variables established in previous stages. In logical models the modelling will involve establishing mathematical formulae for the relationship between variables.

The sixth stage of the modelling exercise is to *document* the model to explain the purpose and function of the model. The documentation should also be written to explain to new users how to operate the model. It is often the case that a model may be developed by one person then updated and used in the future by another person. The seventh stage of the modelling process is *model validation*. This is an important part of the modelling process. The model is tested to verify that it is true and accurate. Models can often be validated by testing them against known or observed systems behaviour. Validation involves determining the accuracy of the model within certain predefined modelling parameters. For example, a model that determines the required braking distance for a vehicle at various speeds could be validated by setting up a practical experiment with vehicles braking at certain speeds then recording the data. The real data recorded for braking distances can then be matched against the braking distances established by the model.

The final process of the modelling exercise is to put the model into *use* and to *update* the model in the future to incorporate any changes in the model's constraints. For example, a spreadsheet model could be set up to determine the amount of monthly interest received by an investor who deposited money in a bank at the existing interest rate. The spreadsheet would likely include a column recording the 12 months of the year, a column for the interest payment and a column for the resulting amount including interest. If the interest rate changed in the future, then the new rate could be input into the model and the new amount of interest payable could then be ascertained.

An explanation of all the concepts found in the development stages of modelling can be found in the following example of a spreadsheet application, Table 9.7, modelling the number of products sold by Miss Coady, a sales agent for Norman Payne Enterprises.

In the spreadsheet in Table 9.7 the *system* being modelled is Miss Coady's monthly salary and bonus for working as a sales agent. The bonus is related to the number of products sold each calendar month. The *variables* of the model are Miss Coady's bonus, the number of products sold, the month of the year and

Table 9.7 Spreadsheet application example – Miss Coady (sales agent)

	A	B	C	D
	Month	**Products sold**	**Salary($)**	**Bonus($)**
1				
2	Jan	42	84.70	21
3	Feb	27	79.45	13.5
4	March	34	81.90	17
5	April	19	80.15	14.5
6	May	23	78.05	11.5
7	June	40	84.00	20
8	July	31	80.85	15.5
9	Aug	17	75.95	8.5
10	Sept	33	81.55	16.5
11	Oct	32	81.20	16
12	Nov	18	76.30	9
13	Dec	54	88.90	27

Miss Coady's monthly pay (salary). The *relationship* between variables is embedded in the column formulae of the worksheet. Miss Coady's bonus recorded in column D is calculated by the formula (B2*0.5). This indicates that for every product sold, Miss Coady receives 50 cents as a bonus. Therefore, there is a relationship between column B and column D. Miss Coady's monthly salary is calculated by the formula (($100+D2)*(0.7)). This indicates that Miss Coady receives a fixed salary of $100 plus the bonus precalculated in column D. This total is then multiplied by 0.7 (or 70 per cent) to work out the salary after taxation. This makes the *assumption* that the taxation rate is 30 per cent. Obviously, this assumption can be varied to model the effects of any taxation rate.

What makes this example a model, and not just a representation of a situation, is the existence of *decision variables*. In this example the decision variables are the bonus rate (e.g. 50 cents), the basic salary of $100 and the taxation rate (e.g. 30 per cent). A decision variable is a variable that is controlled by the model user and forms the basis of any experimentation carried out on the model. The variables are sometimes referred to as the parameters of a model. Certain parameters can be fixed in order to establish a *sensitivity analysis* of the altered variables. For example, the bonus rate of 50 cents per product could be changed to 60 cents per product. The model user would merely have to change the formula in column D to indicate 0.6 rather than 0.5 and the whole spreadsheet could be recalculated to ascertain Miss Coady's new salary situation. The model could be used to predict what salary Miss Coady may receive in the future or what Miss Coady's salary would have been had the bonus been 60 cents and not 50 cents. The worksheet would be established by *data gathering* of information on the number of products sold by Miss Coady. This could be done by looking through sales order invoices processed by the sales order processing system. Therefore, data gathering is an essential exercise in the model-building process.

It can be seen from Miss Coady's model that it is important to *document* the model in some way. For example, a new user would have no idea of the origin of the percentage rates used for the bonus in column D (e.g. 0.5) or the origin of the after-taxation rate used in column C (e.g. 0.7). Any documentation of the model should include the basis of the technique used for data gathering and the items of any formulae used or embedded into the model. Finally, the model should be *validated* by testing the worksheet to determine if the variables are being calculated and processed correctly. The spreadsheet can also be *updated* and used in the future to incorporate any changes, such as Miss Coady receiving additional bonuses for selling other products.

Sophisticated calculations can be performed in spreadsheet applications by writing program *macros* to perform certain operations. A macro is a complex set of formulae that is like a short computer program. Macros allow laborious spreadsheet operations to be undertaken methodically and to a more sophisticated extent than is possible by merely using inbuilt functions. The term macro originated in the early days of computer technology and referred to 'macro assemblers'. In modern systems terminology macro is used to describe the language code that is used within an applications environment, specifically to enhance the basic capabilities of a software application, such as a spreadsheet or database. Macros can be written to link different applications together within the business systems domain. For example, Microsoft Visual Basic is a useful fourth generation language programming tool for empowering and integrating applications within Microsoft Office's overall suite of software applications. It allows data from a database to be automatically transferred into a spreadsheet and then automatically output to a graphical package to produce useful reports. This level of package *empowerment* can only be achieved by writing macros to perform and implement various operations.

Activity 9.6   Spreadsheet modelling practice

Provide a definition for three categories of model and explain the characteristics, function and purpose of each category of model. Describe the role and function of macros in empowering software applications and outline three benefits of using fourth generation programming languages to integrate software applications within a business organization. Then consider the following scenario:

A photographic shop charges $250 for taking pictures at weddings. It also charges $12.50 for each film of 24 exposures that it uses. Reprints are charged at $3.50 for a 15 × 10 cm photograph, $3.70 for a 18 × 13 cm photograph, $4.00 for a 23 × 15 cm photograph, $5.50 for a 30 × 20 cm photograph and $15 for a 60 × 40 cm photograph.

Create a spreadsheet model for the business organization so that the number of reprints of each size of photograph and the number of films used, once entered, creates a breakdown of the total cost, which can be presented to the customer as an indication of the estimated cost.

9.9   Information communication and presentation

Word-processing is one of the most widely used software applications in the business systems domain, particularly in integrated office systems. Word-processing can be used to communicate and present information that has previously been modelled using database and spreadsheet applications. Word-processing can be defined as the 'automatic manipulation of natural language text'. The modern day computer-based word-processing technology is a direct descendant of the earliest manual typewriters that emerged over 125 years ago. Progressive improvements have been incorporated over the years: from the days of heavy manual typewriters through to fast and light electronic typewriters, which allowed limited levels of text manipulation, to today's highly manipulative computer-based word-processing applications.

Did you know?

In the UK, one of the first mechanical typewriting tools was patented by Henry Mill in 1714. Commercial typewriters were first manufactured on a large scale in the 1870s and the first semi-automatic typewriters, which used punched paper rolls as input, were manufactured in the early 1930s. The first machines to incorporate facilities to manipulate text were produced in the 1940s.

In 1943 the International Business Machines Corporation, now known as IBM, won a contract from the government of the USA to produce an automatic machine to produce personalized letters to be sent to the next of kin of war casualties. The contract required the machine to be capable of inserting sections into, or omitting sections from, a standard text prepared on paper tape. In the 1960s IBM produced a commercial typewriter called the Selectric that was known as a golf-ball typewriter and enabled a typist to manipulate the golf-ball to achieve different type styles on the same machine. Rather than keys, the Selectric had a golf-ball-shaped printing device that was more efficient in printing individual letters. Further advances in the 1960s included the capability for text justification, high quality printing and typewriters with magnetic memory features. All these advances were incorporated into the fast and lightweight electronic typewriters of the 1970s and 1980s. However, electronic typewriters were soon overtaken by the expansion of computer-based word-processing packages in the 1990s. It is now vary rare to see a typewriter in use in the business systems environment!

Word-processing applications allow text to be corrected and modified more easily so that letters or documents do not have to be rewritten each time an alteration is required. Word-processing applications can be integrated with other applications such as databases and spreadsheets. Using word-processing, letters and documents can be personalized, edited, stored and eventually printed to specific formats. However, a distinction must be made between *text-processing* and *word-processing*. Text-processing is primarily concerned with presentation, while word-processing is concerned with the mechanics of communicating a message. However, with advances in applications software the limits of these two areas are becoming blurred; often it is the case that word-processing applications contain extensive *desktop publishing* (DTP) features to incorporate the handling of both text-processing (i.e. style and layout) and word-processing (i.e. text content).

Certain features of word-processing have not changed with the process of technological advancement. The standard qwerty keyboard used today to input alphanumeric data has changed relatively little over time. However, increasingly popular forms of data input are through *voice recognition* software applications. These applications enable people to speak text into a computer at a rate of data inputting that matches how quickly someone speaks (although these applications have to be 'trained' beforehand by the user speaking words into the application's memory so that the application can understand the nuances of the user's voice).

9.10 Principles of information presentation

Word-processing applications allow alphanumeric text and numbers to be input, edited, manipulated, stored in memory, and eventually printed to a computer screen or paper printer, or downloaded to another software application. Word-processing improves the efficiency and effectiveness of people who undertake the task of producing high-quality text documents. Above all word-processing applications save time and reduce the repetitive nature of letter writing and document preparation. Word-processing application packages can be either menu driven or

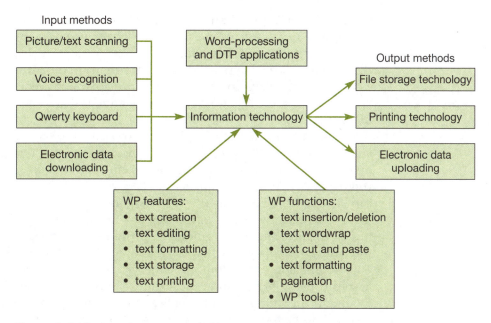

Figure 9.4 The word-processing/DTP environment

command driven. Menu-driven applications allow the user to select functions and features, such as page set-up and printing, by selecting a particular menu option and sub-option. With command-driven applications the user must remember the commands that are required for a particular function. Most word-processing applications have additional tools such as a spell checker, grammar checker, thesaurus (to enable the user to search for synonyms or words with similar meanings), word counter and general help facilities. Figure 9.4 illustrates the usual features and functions of a word-processing/DTP application found within the business environment.

The most popular word-processing application in the world is Microsoft Word. Most word-processing packages are WYSIWYG ('what you see is what you get'). Text and numbers are input through a keyboard and the text appears on the screen. Any changes to the text are seen on the screen as they are made. The alterations to text can be made by using various keys on the keyboard or highlighting the particular areas of text using a hand-held mouse and on-screen pointer. A common term for such graphical user interfaces is WIMP, which represents windows, icons, mouse and pointer. Microsoft Windows (2000 and NT) is among the most popular WIMP operating systems environments in the world. A *windows environment* uses dialogue boxes to highlight files and applications, and icons and buttons to represent application areas and applications functions. Other windows operating systems include Apple Macintosh, Unix and Linux.

The origin of WIMP systems application environments for business applications was in the 1970s. The Xerox PARC team established the WIMP concept that appeared commercially in the Xerox 8010 systems in the early 1980s. In the late 1980s a team of software application developers, led by Jeff Raskin and the Apple Computers team (including former members of the Xerox PARC team) further developed the WIMP environment for operation on its Apple computer in the mid-1980s. Microsoft later modelled its first windows-based operating system on the Apple Mac operating system. However, it should be noted that there is some dispute over who 'owned' the rights to the windows idea and concept. In the late 1980s Apple Computers sued Microsoft over infringement of the look-and-feel of the Apple Macintosh operating system – the court case ran for many years.

The main user interaction within windows-based operating systems is mouse and screen pointer. By using the cursor keys or a mouse, the pages of text can be moved into view or out of view on the screen, which is known as *scrolling*. When completed, letters and documents can be given a name and saved to a file that can be recalled to screen as and when required. The functions of entering, editing, formatting, saving and outputting text files are usually performed by marking (or highlighting) the beginning and end of the particular block of text and then using the various function commands to carry out the command operation. These commands can be initiated either by using a combination of keys on the keyboard or by highlighting the menu option if the system is attached to a mouse. Most word-processing applications enable graphics, pictures, text and diagrams to be imported into the current document. Using computers for text layout and graphics for printing in magazines, newsletters and brochures is commonly referred to as *desk-top publishing* (DTP).

Many word-processing applications have a facility known as *mail merge* that enables a user to import data from another file into the current document file. For example, a typical letter file may be merged with a file containing data such as names and addresses of the customers of a business organization. The two files can be combined so that standard letters can be personalized with different names and addresses.

The common *functions* of word-processing (e.g. pagination, justification, text size, text status, tabulation, etc.) can be used to emphasize certain aspects of the text document. Usually, most of these functions, related to formatting of text, can be carried out by using page set-up commands. Most systems are set up with default (existing) parameters, such as margin size and text font, which can be altered by the user to suit their requirements.

Printers (and peripherals)

Once the text document has been formatted it can be saved to an electronic file either on the hard disk of the computer or to a read-write CD-ROM, data storage pen, or even a 'floppy disk'. The document can then be sent to a printing device or downloaded to another application within the business systems environment. The main types of printer in use today are dot-matrix printers, laser printers and ink-jet printers, although dot-matrix printers are now becoming very rare. Dot-matrix printers were quick, but did not give high-quality printouts. The best output results are achieved by using laser printers that provide greater text resolution – over 300 dpi (dots per inch) – and a greater range of fonts than dot-matrix printers. A laser printer works by scanning a laser beam across a charged xerographical drum to build up an electrostatic image of the text. High-quality photocopying paper is then passed over the surface of the drum and the toner is transferred to the paper. Ink-jet printers transfer text to paper by spraying a series of precision ink dots.

Did you know?

From as early as AD 600–700 the Chinese were using porcelain character blocks to reproduce images on paper. By the eleventh century AD the Chinese were using movable character printing blocks that could be assembled and reassembled for different printing tasks. In Europe in the 1450s a German goldsmith named Johann Gutenberg pioneered the development of movable type made from cast metal characters. The print characters were arranged in wooden trays, inked, then paper was placed on top and pressed using a hand-operated press.

Desktop publishing (DTP)

Text-processing is concerned with the presentation of a document and not merely with the production of short documents such as letters. This area of word-processing is referred to as desktop publishing (DTP). It has become more afford-able to all types of business organization and is no longer the exclusive domain of professional typesetters. DTP can be used to produce newsletters, in-house magazines, publicity materials, business forms, presentation materials and a range of other applications where good design and layout are essential. A desk-top publishing application enables the incorporation of text, pictures, graphs, tables and diagrams into a unified form that allows more complex and visually meaningful information to be produced. Most modern Microsoft Word appli-cations enable a very high degree of DTP facilities. In many ways word-process-ing and text-processing have become indistinguishable within the word-processing environment.

Did you know?

In Europe in the Middle Ages much copying out of written work was done by monks, usually in the Latin or Greek language, on calfskin or sheepskin called vellum. The people who copied out written works were known as scribes. The books produced were beautiful and decorative examples of typography; the works were embellished with flowing capital letters and decorated borders.

Desktop publishing has its roots in the art of typography and printing. In the Middle Ages, chronicles and written works were laboriously done by hand-crafted penmanship. Those with the ability to read and write were few. Usually they were members of religious orders or the nobility. In 1884 Ottmar Mergenthaler from the USA invented a machine called the linograph that enabled a complete line of text to be cast at one time. In the 1980s typesetting ideas, along with graphics, were introduced to DTP technology. Advances in information technology have led to DTP becoming more commonly available within the business environ-ment at an affordable cost within standard word-processing and presentation applications (e.g. PowerPoint).

Usually, DTP makes extensive use of WIMP technology. A window is viewed on the monitor and a user can put a number of windows on the monitor's screen at the same time. An icon is a small picture that represents a facility (e.g. an application package, or a wastepaper basket to represent a bin for deleting files).

A desktop publishing system ideally includes the following facilities:

▶ computer with DTP applications

▶ large high-resolution colour screen monitor

▶ high-quality laser or ink-jet printer

▶ text and image scanner

▶ computer-aided design (CAD) tablet and pen.

When undertaking a DTP project there are a number of initial technical considerations that have to be addressed and understood. First, what sort of text layout will be adopted? Second, what sort of typesetting will be adopted? Text may be displayed on a document in block format or in *snaking columns* where the text flows from the bottom of one column to the top of the next until the page is filled, then it flows on to the next page. Multiple columns can be used to create a number of effects to achieve a more informative appearance.

There are also many thousands of different *typefaces* in professional and general use with DTP systems. Each typeface has its own characteristics of design and form. Typefaces can be divided into two broad groups:

▶ **Serif typefaces**: have a fine line either at the top or bottom of a text character and make sentences easier to read because they make the eyes flow over the line of print. Serif typefaces are often used when typesetting books and newspapers.

▶ **Sans serif typefaces**: have no serifs and are more modern and functional in visual appearance.

What typefaces does your word-processor possess? A font is a complete set of typefaces of a particular size and design: have a look at the available fonts in your word-processing application.

Did you know?

A typically used example of a serif typeface is Times, not surprisingly used on *The Times* newspaper! A typical example of a sans serif typeface is Helvetica, which is a Swiss-designed typefont, the name coming from the Latin name for Switzerland.

The sort of font adopted will depend upon the purpose of the material produced on a DTP system. The font that is used must be appropriate for its intended purpose. For example, the font used on business conference material may be produced to look elegant and eye-catching. However, the font used for motorway signs should not be decorative, but instead should be clear, informative and functional. Often the range of fonts available will be determined by the capability of the application package. Additional fonts may be downloaded from the web and stored on word-processing and presentation applications. Common fonts include

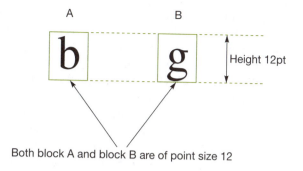

Both block A and block B are of point size 12

Figure 9.5 Point size type measurement

Arial, Bookman old style, **Comic Sans MS**, Courier, Palatino, Times New Roman, and Verdana.

The size of each font can be adjusted to a different point size, which is the basic unit of measurement in typesetting. A point is normally 0.3759mm (1/72nd of an inch) and is used for measuring spaces as well as fonts. The decisions related to spacing and point size are as important in DTP as selecting the appropriate font: the appearance of a font may vary greatly depending on the size of font adopted. The point size of a font is the distance between the base line of a line of text and the base line of the line of text directly below. Traditionally the point size was based on the size of the metal body on which the character was cast for printing purposes. Figure 9.5 shows an example of point size measurement. The character 'b' has an ascender that goes to the top of the block and the character 'g' has a descender that goes to the bottom of the block.

Some fonts are used only for specific purposes. For example, Symbol is a special font that is used for creating scientific or mathematical documents where Greek letters and mathematical characters are required to produce formulae. Symbol characters from a to z are:

$$a\,b\,c\,d\,e\,f\,g\,h\,i\,j\,k\,l\,m\,n\,o\,p\,q\,r\,s\,t\,u\,v\,w\,x\,y\,z$$
$$\alpha\,\beta\,\chi\,\delta\,\varepsilon\,\phi\,\gamma\,\eta\,\iota\,\varphi\,\kappa\,\lambda\,\mu\,\nu\,o\,\pi\,\theta\,\rho\,\sigma\,\tau\,\upsilon\,\varpi\,\omega\,\xi\,\psi\,\zeta$$

Spacing is another very important aspect of DTP. Spacing can be used not only between words and lines, but also between characters of a word. The spaces between characters in a word are often closed up to achieve more pleasing and visually consistent letter spacing. This process is called *kerning*.

An important factor in the preparation of documents with multiple pages is the use of *pagination*, which is concerned with the setting of page lengths. If a document has multiple pages then the page breaks must be set to ensure that there are no awkward breaks in the body of the text. For example, it would look untidy if a sub-heading for a paragraph lay isolated at the bottom of a page; the separation of a sub-header from its text or images is a bad page break. It would be preferable to set the page break above the sub-heading, thus carrying the sub-heading forward to the next page. The terms *widow* and *orphan* are used to refer to loose items of text that get detached from the main body of a paragraph when the text is carried across a page break. The orphan is the text that gets left behind at the bottom of the page when the main body text is carried over to the next page. The widow refers to single words or part of a sentence that are carried over to the next page. However, what is considered a good page break may be a matter of visual perception and judgement by the page designer!

There are numerous *graphics* application packages available that enable illustrations and artwork to be prepared for importing into a WP/DTP system. Also available are clipart and icon libraries of ready-made images that can be customized and imported into a DTP system for graphical illustration of text. Graphical application packages usually incorporate *painting* and *drawing* facilities. Painting packages allow the user to produce bit-mapped images in black and white or colour. Drawing packages usually have additional facilities for producing geometrical shapes and lines used in technical drawing. Most packages allow the designer to use paint-and-draw facilities.

9.11   Electronic communication applications

One of the most popular (and often over-used) business applications is electronic mail (e-mail). There are a number of software applications dedicated to electronic communication, both from a PC or a hand-held PDA. Many of these are free, or commercially available; for example, Pegasus, Netscape Mail, Microsoft Outlook and Eudora. These applications are sometimes referred to as *e-mail user agents*. An e-mail message is usually handled by a program known as a *message transfer agent*, which is responsible for delivering the message locally, within its systems environment, or externally passing the e-mail message to another host computer. The message transfer agents on a computer network often communicate using a Simple Mail Transfer Protocol (SMTP).

E-mail user agent applications work by pulling mail from an e-mail computer server. An e-mail server can be a centralized computer, such as a Unix server, that stores incoming e-mail and processes outgoing e-mail. The e-mail message is normally delivered to the recipient's *mailbox* (i.e. a computer file on a server) from where the recipient can read it using a mail agent application. The e-mail user agent software application on a recipient's PC merely acts as a user-friendly application to enable users to handle e-mail in a windows environment. E-mail messages automatically pass from one computer user to another over a computer network, via modems, hardwired connections or telephone lines. Most e-mail messages have header information, such as the sender's e-mail address, the receiver's e-mail address, the nature of the content and whether there are any attachments. The MIME standard (which stands for multipurpose internet mail extensions) enables the body of the e-mail message to contain attachments.

E-mail messages pass through the conceptual layers of a computer network. These are as follows:

▶ **Network applications layer**: applications such as web browsers, HTML and e-mail (operating within or over a computer network).

▶ **Session management layer**: managing the network session, e.g. sending an e-mail using packets (includes protocols such as HyperText Transfer Protocol – HTTP, File Transfer Protocol – FTP, and Simple Mail Transfer Protocol – SMTP)

▶ **Packets and address layer**: network addressing functions (includes Transmission Control Protocol/Internet Protocol – TCP/IP, and Domain Name Service – DNS)

▶ **Physical Layer**: the physical network connections (ethernet, hubs, switches, routers, modems, and the Integrated Services Digital Network – ISDN).

E-mail has become such an important means of communication in the business domain that e-mail messages are considered to be as legally binding as normal business correspondence. Use e-mail wisely and it becomes a useful business tool. However, use it recklessly and it becomes a burden both in terms of time spent replying and in terms of e-mail abuse.

9.12 Chapter summary

Information empowers systems end users to make informed judgements and reasoned decisions upon that information. For information to be useful to the end user's needs, it must possess the good qualities and characteristics that were outlined at the beginning of this book. The availability of systems to be modelled in the business environment is only limited by the imagination of the model builder. Models can be set up using various data-gathering techniques. The operation of modelling itself can also take many forms, from robotics modelling to data modelling using spreadsheets. However, a good model should be appropriate to the circumstances of the problem situation and should reveal a breadth of understanding of the problem scenario.

The emphasis within the business systems environment is on integrating applications into a configuration that allows modelling activities to be undertaken. This will normally require a high level of understanding of software applications environments, to the extent of using languages (such as Visual Basic and C++) to script macros to integrate and extend the capability and usefulness of a software applications package environment. For example, the Microsoft Office suite of applications (normally comprising a spreadsheet, presentation package, database and word-processing application) can be empowered, customized and integrated with other Microsoft applications through the use of program macros. The Microsoft Office suite of applications offers a ready-made and integrated applications environment within the business domain.

SHORT SELF-ASSESSMENT QUESTIONS

9.1 Outline the ten generic stages of data acquisition, handling and delivery, and indicate the importance of these stages to data and information modelling.

9.2 Explain the main role and function of *data structuring* techniques and suggest why it is important to impose organization on business data and information.

9.3 Outline the three main facets of traditional *data file design* and suggest why this approach has largely been replaced by *relational database* technology.

9.4 Define the term *database management system* (DBMS) and explain the main role and function of a database management system.

9.5 Describe and explain the use of *Boolean logic* for information retrieval in the business environment.

9.6 Outline and describe three types of report formats and explain how and why such report formats would be used within a business organization.

9.7 Explain the process of sorting and merging files within a database application and provide an example of such *data manipulation* within a marketing information system.

9.8 Describe the role of *spreadsheet functions* in the construction of decision-making models and provide an example of the use of logical and mathematical functions.

9.9 Explain eight generic stages in the process of designing and developing a model for the business environment.

9.10 What is an *integrated software applications environment* and what is the significance of Microsoft Office's integrated applications environment?

EXTENDED STUDENT ACTIVITIES

Individual reporting activity 1

Market research about the television viewing habits of a large cross-section of the population can offer an insight into the success and market share of television programmes. The results are analyzed using various software tools and techniques, which enable the collection, processing and communication of information on personal viewing habits.

To predict viewing habits, information is required on a range of factors, for example, a person's occupation, gender, age, family composition, number of television sets owned, location of television sets, how much television is watched per week, etc.

1 Design a suitable data capture form (i.e. questionnaire) to record information on each person (as outlined above). Collect information from around 20 people using your data capture form. Are there any further data requirements?

2 Once the data has been effectively collected and collated, transfer the information to a database of your choice. Describe the problems and solutions involved in the process of structuring the data in the database. (Note: if you have designed the data capture criteria and form correctly then there should be no obstacles to transferring data to a database.)

3 Use your established data and information sources to find the following information and put it into an output format suitable for presentation to a senior manager:
  - the total number of television sets owned by the 20 people you interviewed;
  - the average number of television hours watched per week;
  - the age composition of individuals watching at particular times of the day and night.

4 Discuss the set of information requirements needed by a marketing research function of a business organization investigating viewing habits. Suggest reasons why such information would be of particular interest to business organizations wishing to advertise on television to particular sectors of the population.

5 Discuss the ways in which data and information can be automatically input and output from one application to another application. What methods can be employed to capture data and information from viewers and how can this be automatically input into a database application? (For example, data sensors and data scanning activities are often used for this purpose.)

Individual reporting activity 2

Hill Motor Vehicles and Finance Inc. is a company engaged in a range of activities from buying and selling cars to loans and financing. The chief executive officer in charge of the garage operations division has received the following report from a time-and-motion study of garage car maintenance practice and procedures.

The report lists the average charge for new parts, per vehicle, and the average number of hours worked on each type of vehicle:

	New parts	Hours
Buick	$35	2
Jaguar	$40	2.5
Dodge	$30	2
BMW	$30	2
Jeep	$50	3

The garage overheads are $15.50 per vehicle (for the use of the garage, petrol, oil etc.). The business organization also charges $25.00 per hour for labour. You are required to set up a model using a spreadsheet of your choice, and show the following:

1 Adjust your model to incorporate customer price and profit per vehicle. If since the model was set up the parts have gone up by 5 per cent, show the effect on customer price.

2 The increase in parts makes service too expensive, so the company reduces the profit margin by 10 per cent. Show the effect of this change in policy.

3 To meet a contract for extra work the company will have to take on more staff. (The current rate is $2 per person per vehicle.) Incorporate a range of other variables into your model that would produce a more accurate picture of reality.

Discuss how spreadsheet applications can be used to model data and information within the business environment. Suggest and recommend ways in which information could be uploaded and downloaded from a spreadsheet into other applications within the business environment.

Could information modelled in one application be used across a company to service a number of business functions, such as sales, purchasing, inventory control and research and development?

REFERENCES AND FURTHER STUDY

Books Becker, S.A. (2002) *Data Warehousing and Web Engineering*, The Idea Group Inc, ISBN: 1931777020

Date, C.J. (2003) *An Introduction to Database Systems*, Addison-Wesley, ISBN: 0321189566

Flynn, N. and Kahn, R. (2003) *E-mail Rules: A Business Guide to Managing Policies, Security and Legal Issues for E-mail and Digital Communication*, Amacom, ISBN: 0814471889

Halvorson, M. and Young, M.J. (2001) *Microsoft Office XP Inside Out*, Microsoft Press International, ISBN: 0735612773

Holden, P. (2002) *Spreadsheet Modeling in Corporate Finance*, Prentice Hall, ISBN: 0130499056

Murphy, S. and Holden, P. (2002) *ECDL Advanced Spreadsheets*, Prentice Hall, ISBN: 0130989835

Render, B. et al. (2002) *Managerial Decision Modeling and Spreadsheets,* Prentice Hall, ISBN: 0130783811

Stutely, R. (2003) *The Definitive Guide to Managing the Numbers: The Executive's Fast-track to Mastering Spreadsheets, Budgets, Forecasts, and Investment Metrics*, FT Prentice Hall, ISBN: 0273661035

Williams, H.E. and Lane, D. (2002) *Web Database Applications with PHP and MySQL*, O'Reilly Publishing, ISBN: 0596000413

Journal *Journal of Financial Research*

Web resources **Spreadsheet Modeling – How to Build Financial Models in Excel (USA/global)** – online Excel spreadsheet resources by Richard R. Brinckman.
www.spreadsheetmodeling.com

NASA and the development of computing (USA/global) – NASA research in computing.
www.nas.nasa.gov

Telecommunications, operating systems and computer networks

When you have studied this chapter you will be able to:

▶ define the nature and role of telecommunications networks found within the business environment;

▶ evaluate the most appropriate configuration of telecommunications technology to meet the requirements of a business organization;

▶ describe technological advances in terrestrial and extra-terrestrial communications and understand the characteristics and function of local and wide area networks;

▶ explain the range of communications software, hardware and operating systems requirements for networked business;

▶ evaluate the effectiveness of integrated ICT and the consequences of integration on business activity;

▶ formulate strategies for supporting both wired and wireless communications requirements within the business environment.

10.1 Introduction to telecommunications

The previous chapter described how various software applications can be used to model the information requirements of an organization. This chapter expands the study of software applications to incorporate operating systems and telecommunications. Information and communication technology is often categorized into *front-end* systems (i.e. the software applications used by people to support their job activities) and *back-end* systems (i.e. the operating systems software and telecommunication protocols necessary to enable networked computing).

The term information and communication technology assumes not only the presence of computing technology but also the systematic organization of information systems into integrated computer networks that communicate internally and externally within the business environment. In many ways it is the development of sophisticated wired and wireless telecommunications technology that has led to the creation of information superhighways across the globe.

Wired and wireless telecommunications technology is concerned with the transmission of data and information between computer systems over *local* or *remote* networks via *terrestrial* or *extra-terrestrial* (satellite) communications channels. Telecommunications systems can transmit numeric or alphanumeric text along with graphics, voice or video information. This is generally referred to as *multimedia* information. The next chapter will further discuss the internet and its role and utilization within the business environment.

An understanding of telecommunication is important within a general understanding of business information systems. The use of telecommunications to link computer networks across the world is colloquially known as the *information superhighway*. The race to service, own or dominate the worldwide business telecommunications sector is one of the most competitive of the twenty-first century. Telephone and telecommunications utilities, such as British Telecom in the UK, Vodafone in Europe and North Africa, and AT&T in the USA, are competing to build and control a vast web of electronic networks delivering information for business, education and individuals. These networks form an information highway as influential to business organizations as the first railways were to business activity at the start of the nineteenth century.

What is telecommunication?

An electronic means for sending and receiving data and information over a geographical distance.

Telephone and telecommunications utilities are able to exploit the information superhighway because they already have in place an extensive global network of *wire-based* and *wireless* telephone communications channels. These channels are now being used to communicate multimedia data and information from network to network across the globe. Wireless and wired telecommunications utilities have invested heavily in research and development. Consequently, these utilities now provide communications channels and services that can allow some or all of the following tasks:

▶ transmission of pictures, images and videos
▶ transmission of facsimile text, graphics and sound
▶ provision of teleconferencing and videoconferencing facilities
▶ provision of home–office and telecommuting facilities
▶ provision of online business (e.g. banking, shopping and trading)
▶ provision of wireless tracking and location services.

To provide these services it is essential that telecommunications utilities continuously strive to increase the transmission capacity of their telecommunications channel technology. This can be achieved by applying either of the following two approaches:

▶ Improving the efficiency of existing communications channels: by physically enhancing wired or wireless networks – replacing *coaxial wire* channels with improved materials, such as *fibre optic* cables.
▶ Installing additional communications capacity: by utilities acquiring smaller telecommunications companies or merging with other telecommunications

Figure 10.1 Fibre optic cable

Source: Science Photo Library Ltd.

utilities. The development of joint ventures in the telecommunications industry is a key feature of twenty-first century global telecommunications provision. The information superhighway not only connects business organizations, but also connects business organizations to universities, research institutions and various other profit making and non-profit making organizations.

Twisted wire transmission is a relatively unsophisticated and slow transmission medium that is often prone to communications interference. However, *coaxial cables* consist of thickly insulated copper wire that allow for faster and more reliable data communications; interference is greatly reduced because of the plastic insulation surrounding the wire. *Fibre optic* technology has superseded wire-based communications channels. Fibre optics are strands of glass fibres fitted together into cables; the cables transmit pulses of laser light rather than electronic pulses. The laser light pulses represent data signals that can be transmitted at much faster rates than conventional electronic pulses. However, fibre optic cables are less robust than wire-based cables and require correspondingly more care in installation (*see* Figure 10.1). Table 10.1 describes some of the available

Table 10.1 Telecommunication channel hardware

Terrestrial transmission	
Twisted wire cables	Capacity of 10 megabytes per second
Coaxial cables	Capacity of 200 megabytes per second
Fibre optics	Capacity of up to 10 gigabytes per second
Extra-terrestrial transmission	
Microwaves	Capacity of 100 megabytes per second
Satellites	Capacity of 100 megabytes per second

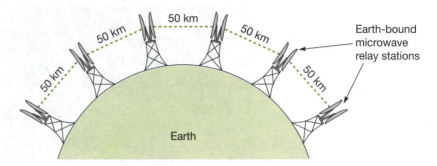

Figure 10.2 Terrestrial transmission

telecommunications hardware found within the business environment and the telecommunications capacity of each form of *communications medium.*

All of the telecommunications channels so far described are tangible and terrestrial. However, there are other forms of telecommunications channels that transmit data signals through the atmosphere. For instance, *microwave* communication methods transmit high-frequency radio signals through the air with no need for physical cabling. Mobile cell phones work on radio wave and microwave communication.

Microwaves can be transmitted using terrestrial stations or communications satellites. However, with terrestrial relay the Earth-bound relay stations can only be approximately 50 km apart to send and rebroadcast signals (*see* Figure 10.2). This is because microwaves travel in straight lines and the 'line-of sight' between the transmitter and receiver must be unobstructed. Therefore, microwave relay stations are usually located on the tops of high-rise buildings in urban areas, or at the peaks of hills and mountains in more rural areas. Microwaves can carry thousands of channels at the same time.

The preferred method of microwave transmission, where data and information is required to be sent over large unobstructed distances, is satellite transmission. A satellite is fundamentally a microwave relay station located in outer space. The satellite orbits the Earth, normally at approximately 35 000 km above the Earth. The communications satellite acts as a relay station that receives signals from one relay station on Earth and rebroadcasts that signal to another Earth-bound relay station (*see* Figure 10.3).

The advantage of satellite technology is in globalizing data communications between computer networks that span the Earth. The disadvantage of satellite technology is the time delays present in transmitting data signals thousands of kilometres into space and back again to Earth. Therefore, satellite-communicated global conferencing facilities are often prone to voice and visual time delays. For example, this is why people experience delays on long-distance videoconferencing calls.

Within extra-terrestrial transmission, a satellite is any small body that orbits a larger one, either natural or artificial. A natural satellite is the Moon that orbits the Earth. The first artificial satellite was launched into orbit around the Earth by Russia in 1957: it was called Sputnik1. Artificial satellites perform four main purposes:

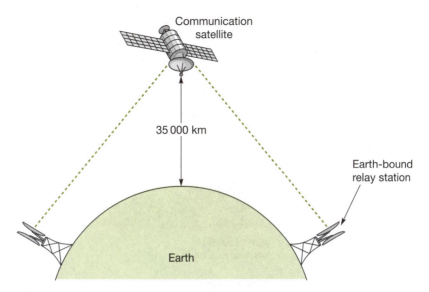

Figure 10.3 Satellite transmission

▶ scientific research
▶ weather forecasting
▶ military applications
▶ global communications.

In the modern business systems environment many organizations use their own dedicated satellites for internal telecommunications. Of growing importance are VSATs (*very small aperture terminals*), which are part of the networking infrastructures of an increasing number of organizations. A VSAT is a relatively inexpensive satellite Earth station with an antenna, normally with a diameter of under 1 metre. VSATs can be mobile and located in remote areas (*see* Figure 10.4).

Did you know?

Parcel and package delivery businesses equip their trucks with VSATs. These receivers allow the business and its drivers to be in constant contact anywhere, any place and any time.

When deciding an appropriate telecommunications medium, consideration must be given to the relationship between cost and performance. For example, satellite communications can cost more than other mediums, but the flexibility and global nature of the medium may outweigh the costs for a globally trading business organization. In many developing countries wireless telecommunication is the only possible form of communication platform available, due to the geographical terrain. For example, Egypt has more cell phones (i.e. mobile phones) than land-based telephones. This is due to the fact that much of the country is desert and unpopulated, so wireless communication has become the more effective means of communication.

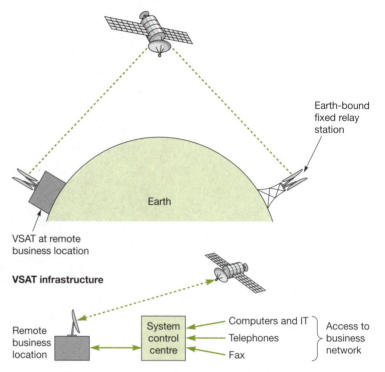

Figure 10.4 VSAT satellite communication system

Telecommunications networks

Search your college or university library for journal or magazine articles on terrestrial and extra-terrestrial communications technology. Prepare a business presentation, as if to the chief executive officer (CEO) of a business organization, to advise on the advantages and disadvantages of terrestrial and extra-terrestrial communications. Emphasize especially the effect on data security of each form of telecommunications. Then proceed to explain why and how telephone and telecommunications utilities are able to exploit the information superhighway. Discuss the advantages and disadvantages of using satellite technology to communicate data and information across the global business environment.

10.2 Pervasive computing

The term *pervasive computing* (a term often used interchangeably with *ubiquitous computing*) suggests that computing power is all around us, freed from the hard-wire confines of the desktop, and that computing involves embedded immobile devices and technologies that communicate with one another via wireless telecommunications networks. In many cases these devices are stealthily embedded to such an extent that we are unaware of them until a device is activated by its relative location to another device. The underlying attraction of pervasive computing is that it can exist around us without anyone realizing it is there, in either dynamic (i.e. active) or static (i.e. inactive) forms.

What is pervasive computing?

The emerging systems trend towards numerous, casually accessible, often invisible computing devices, frequently mobile and embedded in the environment, connected to an increasingly ubiquitous network infrastructure composed of wired and wireless elements.

Source: National Institute of Standards and Technology website (www.nist.gov).

Computerized technology is embedded in most appliances we use on an everyday basis and in many other devices we take for granted in our everyday lives. The generic term used to explain the concept of embedded computerized devices is *information appliances*. Embedded devices are normally automated and triggered by the user interacting with the computerized device. Examples include a refrigerator that monitors its own product contents and signals when product content levels are falling, or an elevator that can remotely inform a centralized maintenance computer that there is a fault that needs attention or servicing. Embedded devices monitor and control the transmission of data and information dependent upon the trigger signal from a user or an associated device. The most profound technologies are those that 'disappear': they weave themselves into the fabric of everyday life until they are indistinguishable from it (Weiser, 1991).

What is embedded computing?

The process of including, subsuming and engendering objects and devices with computerized technology.

What is ubiquitous computing?

The existence of computerized technology everywhere, and all around the world.

10.3 Computer components

The term *computer network* is used in this chapter to describe the interconnection of computers and both fixed and mobile devices by communications channels. Computer *hardware* refers to the physical parts and electronic components of a computer or computerized device. Computer *software* refers to the programs, instructions and applications that are utilized by a computer or computerized device. It should be noted that 'computer' and 'computerized device' are often used synonymously. This is because the main components of a computer can also be found in a number of not so obvious computerized devices, such as televisions, stereos, motor vehicles, refrigerators and numerous other household devices. In the modern information age computer technology *pervades* the world around us.

Within a computerized systems domain there are a number of common components. The main components are:

▶ computer hardware
▶ computer software
▶ input devices
▶ output devices
▶ computerized storage
▶ data communications.

Computing is no longer solely concerned with the defined technology of the computer or even the central processing unit (CPU). Today the computer is a component of integrated information systems and the computer exists alongside other equally sophisticated telecommunications systems, tools and techniques. Nevertheless, an understanding of the components of computing technology is essential for an understanding of how to configure and incorporate ICT-based telecommunications systems within the business environment.

A telecommunications system will normally have three main components:

▶ **Computer hardware**:
  – computer servers, mainframes and PCs (central or distributed processing units)
  – input and output devices (scanners, printers, voice recognition, keyboard, etc.)

▶ **Computer software**:
  – programs and instruction code (control input and output communications activity.)

▶ **Communication technology**:
  – communication channels (wired, wireless, fibre optic or coaxial cables, satellite, etc.)
  – communications processors (wired and wireless modems, front-end processors, multiplexers).

The most important element of a computer, or computerized system, is the central processing unit (CPU). Within this unit are three main elements:

▶ the control unit
▶ the arithmetic logic unit (ALU)
▶ the memory.

The CPU is the brains of the computer. It is sometimes referred to as merely the *processor*. The CPU is where most of the numeric calculations and operations calculations take place. On large computers, the CPU requires one or more printed circuit boards, while on smaller personal computers and laptops the CPU is housed in a single *silicon chip* called a microprocessor. A computer can be defined as a device that operates under the control of software programs that automatically input and process data to produce information as an output. The CPU manipulates inputted data (numeric, alphanumeric and symbolic) into more useful forms and controls other aspects of computer technology.

Within the CPU is the *arithmetic logic unit* (ALU), which carries out the necessary arithmetic and logical instructions upon the data. The two are not physically

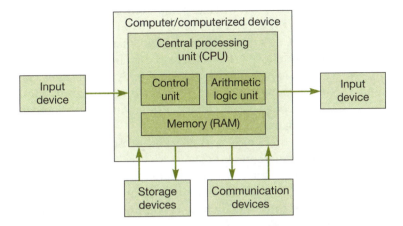

Figure 10.5 Elements of a computer system

separated, but the functions are different. The arithmetic logic unit (ALU) performs arithmetic and logical operations, while the *control unit* extracts instructions from memory and decodes and executes them, calling on the ALU when necessary. The main *memory* holds the programs and data currently being processed by the computer, or computerized device. Commonly, this memory store is known as random access memory (RAM). Figure 10.5 shows the relationship between these elements of a computer system.

A proprietary example of a CPU is the Intel Pentium processor. The CPU is often contained on an individual semiconductor silicon chip. A silicon chip allows millions of circuit elements to be etched (or embedded) into its surface, without significant error or redundancy. The silicon chip is a component of information technology largely responsible for the miniaturization of hardware found internally within a computer.

What is silicon?

The basic material used to make a computer chip. Silicon is a nonmetallic chemical element in the carbon family of elements. Silicon (atomic symbol: Si) is the second most abundant element in the Earth's crust, surpassed only by oxygen. Silicon does not occur uncombined in nature. Sand and almost all rocks contain silicon combined with oxygen, forming silica. When silicon combines with other elements, such as iron, aluminum or potassium, a silicate is formed. Compounds of silicon also occur in the atmosphere, natural waters, many plants and in the bodies of some animals.

Source: Based on www.webopedia.com.

10.4 Computer storage and computing capacity

Primary storage (or main memory storage) stores primary instructions and the related data for instructions to be carried out. Computers are data-centric devices. In modern computer systems environments data is stored in digital format. All data is stored as discrete values. The underpinning of all discrete computing data is *binary* (i.e. ones and zeros, 1101001001). Computing is all about 1 and 0, yes and no, off and on. These are known as *dichotomous states* (i.e. there can only ever be two states). A single piece of digital data (e.g. 1 or 0 is called a *bit* (**bi**nary digi**t**). Binary logic is the fundamental basis of electronic communication and computing. Groups of 8 bits are termed a *byte*. Alphanumeric characters (e.g. abc123) can be encoded into binary using American Standard Code for Information Interchange (ASCII).

Whether computers are used in isolation or coupled together to form a network they represent data in what is known as *binary data form*. Information and data is normally communicated across networks in binary format. All symbols, words, pictures and other data forms can be converted into binary digits. Within the electronic circuitry of a computer the binary state is represented by electronic charges being on or off. A conducting (charged) state in a semiconductor circuit represents 1, while a non-conducting state represents 0. Magnetic storage media works on the same binary principles. A magnetic field can be positively charged or negatively charged, the direction of the field representing either 1 or 0. Even within the human body the genetic coding for human characteristics, such as eye colour, hair colour and other features, are determined by 'switches' being either on or off within a strand of DNA (deoxyribonucleic acid).

Within binary logic the position of the 1 and 0 is significant. For computing purposes, binary coding schemes must be able to represent not only numbers, but also letters of the alphabet and symbols (for example %, $, £, &). The two most common binary coding systems are Extended Binary Coded Decimal Interchange Code (EBCDIC) and American Standard Code for Information Interchange (ASCII). EBCDIC is an 8-bit coding scheme, whereas ASCII has an 8-bit version and a 7-bit version. Each byte represents a single and unique letter, symbol or number. For example, the letter C within the ASCII coding system is represented by the 8-bit string of code 0100 0011.

Whenever data or program instructions are placed in primary storage (i.e. memory) they are assigned to bytes. A byte will possess a unique address so that is can be located when necessary. Therefore, *primary storage* consists of data and instructions held until they are required. The instructions dictate actions to be taken on the data. The results of the action will then be held (stored) until needed for output. *Secondary storage* (which is often referred to as backing storage) is used to assist primary storage in storing data and instructions (e.g. CD-ROM, magnetic disks, read and write DVD, or compact flash cards, etc.).

What is DNA (deoxyribonucleic acid)?

The nucleic acid found in the nuclei of all cells. It is considered as a gene. The chemical structure of DNA is characterized by sequences of four nitrogen bases (known as adenine, thymine, guanine and cytosine). The sequence of bases on a gene constitutes a code that determines the nature of characteristics conferred on a living organism.

Each physical computer will have a *control function* that retrieves instructions from the primary storage and interprets the instructions. The control function issues the necessary instructions to the components comprising the computer. The control function is responsible for directing the hardware operations of the computer by reading stored program instructions, usually sequentially, and directing the computer to perform certain tasks and operations. Information between functions and devices is transferred by means of *buses*. The CPU requests instructions by putting its address into memory on the *address bus*. The memory receives the request and places the instruction on the *data bus*. The CPU then receives and executes the instruction.

Storage and speed of processing are major considerations of using computers within networked architectures. A key activity of the CPU is to execute programs in *machine code*. This is the language of the silicon chip. Most CPUs have their own specific types of machine code. The operations of a computer are synchronized to a clock that determines *computing cycles*. For example, a 2.3-gigahertz (Ghz) processor indicates that the computer runs at a speed of 2.3 billion cycles per second. Computer processing consists of two types of machine cycle:

▶ **Instruction cycle**: an instruction is received from primary storage and decoded.

▶ **Execution cycle**: a data address is located, an instruction executed and the results of the execution are stored locally or remotely. During processing the computer mechanically reads a computer program and carries out operations, many of which are transferred to storage.

Storage capacity is of essential importance to computing. Memory storage capacity can be of two main types:

▶ **RAM (random access memory)**: used for short-term storage of data or program instructions. The contents of RAM can be read and changed when necessary.

▶ **ROM (read only memory)**: permanent storage of program instructions.

The storage capacity of a computer can be determined by the extent of RAM available on the computer system. Computer network storage capacity uses the following terminology:

▶ **Kilobyte**: approximately one thousand bytes (1000 storage positions).

▶ **Megabyte**: approximately one million bytes (1 000 000 storage positions).

▶ **Gigabyte**: approximately one billion bytes (1 000 000 000 storage positions).

▶ **Terabyte**: approximately one trillion bytes (1 000 000 000 000 storage positions).

Did you know?

Storage capacity is measured in bytes where the base measure is the kilobyte which equals 1024 (or 2*10) bytes.

Processing speed can be similarly determined to judge the time it would take to implement instructions, across a network, in terms of machine cycle time. The benchmark of judging the performance of processing speed is in millions of instructions per second (MIPS). The terminology used to classify levels of processing capacity is as follows:

▶ **Millisecond**: one thousandth of a second (1/1 000 second).

▶ **Microsecond**: one millionth of a second (1/1 000 000 second).

▶ **Nanosecond**: one billionth of a second (1/1 000 000 000 second).

▶ **Picosecond**: one trillionth of a second (1/1 000 000 000 000 second).

10.5 Computer systems architecture and performance

Computer systems performance is dependent upon the speed and capacity of the microprocessor technology employed within the network architecture. The three major aspects microprocessor architecture are:

▶ **Word length**: the number of bits that may be processed together as a block. Words may be subdivided into bytes, which normally correspond to the storage capacity of a single character. A byte is normally taken to be equal to 8 bits. For example, a 16-bit chip can process 16 bits in a single machine cycle (or operation), compared to an 8 bit chip which can only process 8 bits in a single machine cycle. A 32-bit chip will be faster than an 8-bit chip because it takes fewer machine cycles to transfer data between storage and the processor. A 32-bit machine can transfer four 8-bit characters in a single machine cycle, compared to an 8-bit machine that can only transfer one set of 8-bit characters. Therefore, a 32-bit machine can be said to be four times faster than an 8-bit machine.

▶ **Bus width**: the number of bits that can be transferred in a single operation between the central processing unit, primary storage and other devices within the computer. Buses within computing are physical connections that allow the transfer of data within a networked system. Buses can be of various widths. A 32-bit machine with only an 8-bit internal bus would have its performance reduced by the fact that data would be processed in 32-bit blocks, but would only be able to be transferred in 8-bit blocks between the central processing unit, main storage and external devices. There are three kinds of buses that connect the CPU, primary storage and other devices of the computer:

   – *Address bus*: carries signals used to locate a given address in primary storage.

   – *Data bus*: carries data to and from primary storage.

   – *Control bus*: carries signals indicating the read/write commands for changing specified addresses in primary storage or peripheral devices.

▶ **Clock speed**: the rate at which the processor receives pulses from a special digital clock built into the computer. Clock speed is a measure of machine cycle time, which in turn is concerned with the speed at which a processor transfers data to and from main storage. The clock speed governs the pacing of machine cycles by emitting millions of pulses per second that are received by the processor. Clock speed is measured in megahertz (MHz) and gigahertz (Ghz), which represent one million cycles per second and one billion cycles per second.

The speed and efficiency of microprocessing within networked architectures can be increased by the incorporation of advanced processor chips that allow *reduced instruction set computing* (RISC). The microprocessor chips used in RISC have only the most frequently used instructions embedded within them, rather than ordinary processors that have infrequently used instructions embedded within the chips. This makes processing more efficient and increases the speed of the networked system.

The efficiency of the network can also be improved by techniques of *parallel processing*, which is the activity of processing more than one instruction at the same time, within the physical domain of a computer. The instruction set is divided up into sub-instructions that are sent to separate processors that simultaneously tackle the problem. This is often made possible by networking computing systems. Parallel processing can be achieved by linking multiple computers together via a communications network so that the processing activities can be divided up between mainframes and microcomputers, which undertake the processing of activities cooperatively.

Activity 10.2 Networked systems performance

Discuss how binary data representation affects the computing environment and explain the two main systems used for binary coding. Describe the three major aspects of microprocessor technology (word length, bus width and clock speed) and explain the relationship of the three for gauging networked systems performance. Explain how the speed and efficiency of networked systems can be increased by the incorporation of advanced processor chips that allow reduced instruction set computing (RISC).

10.6 Communication systems and technologies

Telecommunications technology can be divided into an analysis of *communication channels*, which is concerned with the physical technology required to transmit data and information, and *communications processors*, which are responsible for providing support functions for data and information transmission.

Communication channels

Communication channels are the links via which information is transmitted between sending and receiving devices within a telecommunications network. These communications channels can be either tangible, such as wire-based, fibre optic or coaxial wire cables, or intangible, such as satellite, microwave or wireless-based communication. Communications channels act as conduits for various types of voice, sound, picture, graphics, video, numerical or text-based information being transferred between receiving and sending devices. For example, a telephone network is a system by which voice information may be transferred between human beings. However, a telephone network may also be used to communicate data or information via wire-based or wireless-based communication; to do so requires a *communications processor* such as a *modem*.

A key component of a networked computer is a modem. A modem is a device that allows a telephone channel to be connected to a computer or network of computers to transfer various types of information. A modem controls and handles the process of transmitting data across a wired or wireless telephone network. Modems come in two forms: wired or wireless modems. The main use of a modem is to provide a channel of connection to the internet, to an in-company network, or to enable e-mail to be sent or received. Often, networked computers in a local area will have network cards that act in a similar way to modems, enabling computers to communicate with one another over a computer network. Modems enable wide area network connection via telephone lines: normally an integrated services digital network (ISDN) and an asynchronous digital subscriber line (ADSL), which is a high-speed digital communications protocol. Modems act as translators for digital signals.

> ### What is a modem?
>
> A device used to translate digital signals into analogue signals and vice versa. Modem is a shortened combination word for modulator and demodulator.

Communication processors

Communication processors provide support for data or information transmission activities across a network. The modem acts as an agent technology allowing an existing telephone network to be connected to a networked telecommunications system. A modem is a simple gateway connection between networked systems. However, there is often a requirement to dedicate a single central processing unit (or separate computer) to the function of communications management. This is known as a *front-end processor* because a dedicated processing function is acting as a networked front-end interface support to a host computer. A front-end processor removes most, if not all, of the burden for management of communications from the main computer system within a network. A *multiplexer* is a communications tool that transmits data from multiple sources through a single communications channel. This performs the function of controlling the flows of information within a networked information system. A *concentrator* performs a similar communications management function by storing data messages to be forwarded together as a set, at times that allow optimal communications efficiency.

Processing hardware is supported by *telecommunications software* that performs the following four main functions within a networked information system:

▶ network management
▶ transmission control and access
▶ error detection and correction
▶ data integrity and security.

The physical hardware used for transmitting data across telecommunications channels may determine the speed, efficiency and performance of data communication. Telecommunications performance is measured in bits per second (bps). This measure is often referred to as the *baud rate* and represents an electrical charge of either positive or negative energy through the communications channel.

Activity 10.3 **Telecommunications components**

Describe the components of a telecommunications system and indicate the two main categories of communications technology. Define the term telecommunications software and describe the four main functions performed by telecommunications software within a networked information system.

10.7 Networked computing and telecommunications

A computer network is a collection of *transceiver nodes* connected by one or more communications channels. Two nodes are part of the same network if they can each send and receive signals from the other. A communications network enables many agents to 'talk' (i.e. send and receive messages in different formats) to each other simultaneously on a one-to-one or a one-to-many basis. This communication can be either *synchronous* (i.e. existing or occurring at the same time) or *asynchronous* (i.e. not existing or occurring at the same time). The most basic networked computer systems allow one user to run one application, or operation, at one time. However, most networked computer systems, particularly modern ones that are inherently windows-based, permit the user to run or activate more than one job or application at a time. Networked computer systems have advanced to a high level of sophistication, permitting more than one user to activate applications at the same time – this was traditionally referred to as a *multi-user system*.

There are a number of advantages of networking technology:

▶ Data and information can be shared by various computers within a local or remote geographical location.

▶ A more equitable distribution of computing operations, task allocation and processing activities is made possible.

▶ More rapid and effective communication of data and information for decision making is available.

▶ Peripherals (e.g. printers, scanners and storage) can be shared.

▶ Communication such as e-mail and group conferencing, is made possible.

▶ User activity can be monitored and there is better access and security control to a system.

All computer networks rely on supportive telecommunications systems. A telecommunications system consists of communications media technology and collateral software required to connect together two or more computer systems. Computer networks may be restricted to the local confines of a room or building or can span the entire globe, as with the internet. Networks that are confined to a room or single physical environment are referred to as *local area networks* (LANs) and networks that are not physically confined are referred to as *wide area networks* (WANs). Computer networks can in turn be connected to other computer networks, creating a global web of information flows.

At LAN level, networks can be used to share hardware, such as servers, scanners, printers, and software applications. LANs connect a number of computers and devices within an office building. LANs are reliable, robust and enable fairly fast data transmission, providing data transmission at speeds up to 100 megabits per second (Mbps). One of the most common standards of LAN is the Ethernet. A WAN is a collection of LANs connected together across a large geographical area (i.e. either across a country or even globally). For example, a multinational company could have offices around the country or abroad. It could network all the LANs in each office building together to form a WAN. The LANs are connected together with *routers*, communications links and data transmission protocols. LANs can exist within either a wired infrastructure or a wireless infrastructure sometimes referred to as wireless local area networks (WLANs). For example some coffee houses allow customers to connect to the internet from a wireless PDA or wireless laptop while they are sitting down in the coffee shop. At WAN level the technology can be used to direct the international operations of a globally trading business organization. However, it should be noted that LANs and WANs are bound by the physical and logical boundaries of an organization. The largest and most common type of wide area network is the internet. The internet can be connected to via an internet service provider (ISP).

What is a telecommunications system?

An organized collection of people, procedures and devices used to share and transmit information.

Networked computer systems are essential to support modern business information systems activity. In addition, there is a type of network known as a *personal area network* (PAN). These are a relatively new networks typically found within wireless domains. They enable the connection of various devices, such as personal digital assistants (PDAs), mobile phones and wireless laptops, to central computing resources. Two technologies predominate this area, known as Bluetooth and WiFi (IEEE802.11b), which enable devices to communicate with one another over a limited distance using wireless communications channels. For example, a PDA could be used to connect to the internet as long as a compatible mobile phone was alive within a reception distance. The PDA uses the mobile phone to dial up a connection to the internet. Bluetooth technology was conceived and developed by the Swedish mobile phone manafacturer Ericsson. Bluetooth enables mobile device-to-device communication. It allows for short range, but high-speed, wireless radio frequency (RF) communication for both voice (i.e. telephony) and data. Bluetooth enables communication at rates of

1 megabyte per second (MBps) within a range of separation of 100 metres. Bluetooth technology enables the 'wireless office', whereby mobile cell phones, wireless PDAs, wireless laptop computers and other computing hardware (e.g. printers, keyboards and mice, etc.) can be connected via a wireless local area network (WLAN). Within a Bluetooth environment a PAN is sometimes referred to as a *Piconet* (i.e. maybe one person or user). The collective interaction of Piconets is referred to as a *Scatternet*.

Wireless networks are attractive for a number of reasons, as follows:

▶ They get rid of the need for wires and physical links within a networked environment.

▶ They enable devices to become mobile and portable (e.g. wireless PDAs and 'smart' mobile phones can be carried in a person's pocket or briefcase).

▶ Wireless technology can be embedded in various static devices (e.g. doors, entrances, home appliances, airport departure halls, etc.) and enable people to be constantly in touch with data and data networks.

▶ Wireless technology enables workers to be active in the field with the full support of software applications and information resources (e.g. a sales team can operate at the same level of efficiency whether it is in the office or out on the road).

▶ Wireless devices are often light to carry and portable, providing freedom of movement within a wireless office environment or out-of-the-office environment, at home or sitting in a café (e.g. a number of restaurants and coffee houses enable people to connect to wireless networks while they are eating or drinking).

Did you know?

The name Bluetooth derives from the tenth-century Danish King called Harald Blatand (or 'Bluetooth' in English). He was famous for uniting Denmark and Norway and bringing Christianity to Scandinavia.

Most data and telecommunications networks have both wired and wireless infrastructures. Traditional wired networks, such as the national and international telephone networks, often include many wireless channels, such as microwave and satellite relays. Telecommunications networks are normally managed by *communications software* that forms the instructional base for data and information transmission. The rules that dictate the methods and procedures used in transmitting data and information over a network are known as protocols. The software and protocol requirements of a networked computer system are usually handled and managed by a *network control program* (NCP). Communications software performs a number of functions including:

▶ interconnection between various computers and computer systems

▶ coordination of hardware devices

▶ error checking and security control

▶ monitoring of network use and applications activities.

In addition to communications software, *network operating systems software* enables computers, and other hardware devices, to be connected in a network with telecommunications devices. Such networked computing systems software controls the computers and peripheral devices on a network and allows the various devices to communicate. A network operating system normally performs the same types of function for the network as operating systems software does for an individual computer. Examples of network operating systems software for PC-based networked environments are NetWare and WindowsNT. One of the main local area technologies is known as the Ethernet. Other software tools and utilities act as *network management software* that assists the monitoring of computers and peripheral devices on a network, scans for viruses, and ensures compliance with software licenses and company policy. Network management software usually provides functions to establish fault logging and evaluation of network systems performance, analysis of usage by node and type of data traffic, passwords and access control.

What is network management software?

Software that allows a manager on a network desktop computer to monitor the use of individual computers and shared hardware and other peripheral devices.

The rules by which one networked system sends and receives data signals with another networked system are known as *protocols*, which determine the underpinning rules of communication and indicate how one networked system 'handshakes' with another networked system. Protocols perform the actions of identifying, verifying and checking data message transmissions between computer systems and related peripheral input and output devices. The protocols act as standards for communications among networks that use different technology bases and platforms. In the 1970s the US government pioneered the development of the Transmission Control Protocol/Internet Protocol (TCP/IP) to connect its defence research departments. This is still used but has been largely been replaced with the Open Systems Interconnection (OSI) standard. In addition, the X.400, X.500 and X.25 protocols are still in use within many business organizations.

Most networked computing environments distribute activities to various computers and computer servers. Distributed networked computing comes in two types:

▶ **Peer-to-peer processing**: shares activity between servers. Activities are synchronized between servers using standards such as the Common Object Request Broker Architecture (CORBA).

▶ **Client-server processing**: distributes some of the processing activity to client computers, thus offsetting the need for servers to run everything. In client-server environments there is normally a computer server and a number of client users. These users may be using PCs or they may be using other devices, such as PDAs or a number of other embedded devices. Computers are connected to one another through *circuit-switched* networks or *packet-switched* networks.

Telecommunications systems management

Discuss the use, role and function of network management software and suggest three possible advantages to a business organization of using networked management software to control its information resources. Define the term communications protocol and outline the types of communications protocols in use within the business environment.

10.8 Network topologies

As with the building of information systems, the construction of computer networks requires at first *logical* design and then *physical* design. There are several ways of logically arranging computers and devices within a network; this is often referred to as connecting the *nodes* on a network. In essence, a node is a point of connection on a computer system or device on a network. The arrangement of nodes is referred to as the *network topology* and five main logical topologies are used to describe how networks are organized in terms of the connectivity of computers. These topologies are illustrated in Figure 10.6.

> **What is a network topology?**
> The network structure, configuration and the way in which telecommunications devices are organized into an interrelated network of components.

The five topologies are:

▶ **Ring network** (or loop network): computers and other peripheral devices placed in a logical ring or circle. The connecting metallic wire, coaxial cable or fibre optics form a closed loop that permits each computer to communicate directly with another computer in the network. Data and information is passed along the ring in one direction only, passing from one computer to another, but each computer processes its own applications independently of the other computers. Therefore, there is no central or main computer and information flows around the ring with equality of participation within the overall network.

▶ **Bus network**: is a metallic wire, coaxial cable or fibre optics cable with computers and devices attached to it. This type of network architecture connects the computers and other peripheral devices through a single communications channel. Therefore, the network consists of computers and other devices attached on a single line. All communications messages are transmitted to the entire network and messages can flow in both directions along the cable line. Each device can communicate directly with all other devices on the network. If one computer on the network fails, it does not affect the other devices, and so the configuration is far less vulnerable to total network failure. Therefore, this is a robust form of architecture because the various devices on the network are independent and are unaffected by single computers or devices failing on the network. However, the configuration is slow for data-intensive appli-

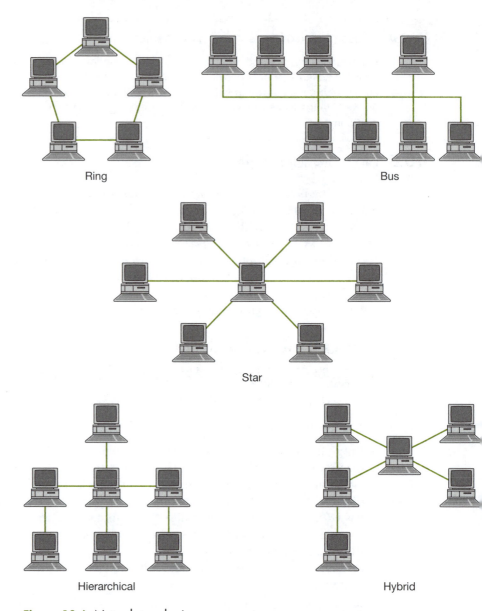

Figure 10.6 Netwok topologies

cations, particularly when a large amount of data traffic is being handled
However, the bus network operates best for applications such as e-mail and the
sharing of resources such as printers and scanners.

▶ **Star network**: a central host computer connected to a number of smaller computers and other peripheral devices such as printers. It is the central host computer that controls and coordinates the messages through the network. This
form of architecture is useful when there is a requirement to centralize
many aspects of the system. All communications are required to be relayed
through the host computer. However, a failure of the central host computer

will automatically close down the entire network. Therefore, it is more vulnerable than other forms of network topology. The star network topology is useful for organizations that wish to maintain some form of centralized control over data and information. It allows master files stored on the host computer to be downloaded to local computers for processing, but with the necessity of uploading back to the central host computer when the task has been completed.

▶ **Hierarchical network**: a tree-like configuration in which the data and information messages are passed from the top computer down through the connecting branches to the relevant computer or other device. A hierarchical network does not require a centralized host computer to control the communications of the network. Total network failure is less likely because a failure of one branch of the network will not automatically affect the whole network. Overall, a hierarchical network forms a system in which control and processing functions are allocated hierarchically and often by means of supervisory responsibility.

▶ **Hybrid network**: a combination of one or more of the topological configurations described above. The topology adopted by an organization will be dependent upon that organization's needs and network objectives on a local and wider geographical scale.

The above descriptions of network architectures used the terminology of computers, terminals and peripheral devices. Sometimes terminals are referred to as being *dumb* terminals or *intelligent* terminals. The difference lies in whether or not the computer terminal possesses its own microprocessing capability. Today, microcomputers with very effective processors pervade the whole of business; therefore, most network computer components contain powerful, independent-processing capabilities. It is becoming increasingly rare to find networks comprised of only dumb terminals without any local processing capability.

Computer networks can be further distinguished between intranets and extranets. An *intranet* is a web-based system that is only accessible by the employees of an organization. *Extranets* are used to enable employees to access internal data and information (and intranets) from outside the organization. In effect an extranet allows secure access to intranet information. Intranets and extranets use web technologies (i.e. web page formatting, web browsers, etc.) to connect to data and information. The internet is the largest network on the planet. However, it is public and open and can be accessed by anyone with a suitable computer, PDA or other device running browser applications. Secure access to an intranet is normally achieved through the use of technologies called virtual private networks (VPNs).

Activity 10.5   Network topologies

Explain the five main logical topologies used to describe how networks are organized and structured within a business environment. Contrast the five main types of network topology and suggest which type of configuration is most suitable to small desktop computer-based environments. Why are companies using web technologies within the networked computing domain?

10.9 Local area networks (LANs)

A local area network (LAN) connects computers and devices together, usually in a single building, or in a departmental floor or office suite within a building. The classification for local is dependent upon the physical distance between nodes on the network. The networked devices are normally connected together by copper, metal or fibre optic cabling. A local area network is usually characterized by a ring, bus, star, hierarchical or hybrid topology. LANs are normally used to link desktop computers and other peripheral devices together so that they can share data and information. The local area network is a popular network-based solution for many business organizations because it can be built independently of a central computing system. It is also suitable for numerous server-based applications within the business environment.

LANs are also used to enable desktop computers to share information and have access to expensive peripheral devices, such as laser printers, image/text scanners and central servers. A central *computer server* is usually a powerful computer, with large memory storage capacity, that is used to store operating programs and software applications and to provide access to peripheral devices that are available to all microcomputers on the local area network. A computer server allows other computers and devices to share files and programs. The server will transfer the necessary programs, data and other applications to the user's computer. The file server often contains the software programs used to drive and manage the LAN. Local area networks are sometimes connected to other external networks through a *network gateway* that may connect a LAN to the telephone network or other networks across the globe. A network gateway connects the LAN to public networks, such as the internet in the external environment.

In the history of computer networking a number of computer companies have been involved in developing networking software and applications. These applications include the Ethernet (developed by Xerox, DEC and Intel); AppleTalk (developed by Apple Computers); Token Ring (developed by IBM and Texas Instruments); and Arcnet (developed by Datapoint). One of the creators of the Ethernet, Bob Metcalfe, once said that the value of a network is proportional to the square of the number of nodes on a network. This has become known as 'Metcalfe's law'. By far the most common LAN technology in modern computing is the Ethernet.

Local area networks can be built around desktop computers or mainframe computers running on, for example, VAX/VMS or Unix. When a desktop computer is connected to a local area network, a network interface card is usually required to be placed in the computer's expansion slot to enable it to communicate within the network. For example, an Ethernet card must be placed in a microcomputer to enable it to communicate over the Ethernet. The Ethernet standard is adopted for LANs that use a bus topology that allows users to connect to a common communications line to share network facilities and other resources. A LAN can also be represented within a ring topology, which is often used for e-mail and the sharing of online BIT (business information technology)

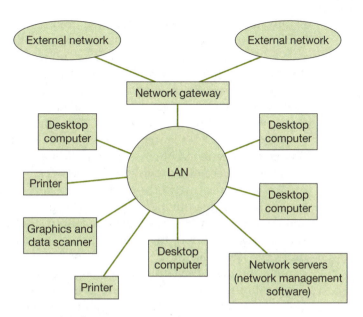

Figure 10.7 Example of a LAN ring topology

software applications. Figure 10.7 shows a typical example of a ring topology for a LAN, with associated peripheral devices.

The capability of a LAN is determined by the network operating system that is employed. The network operating system can reside on every computer on the network or it can reside on a single designated computer that acts as a server for all devices on the network. There are a number of commercially available LAN management software programs. There are also a number of other communications channel technologies in what is a competitive network software market.

Local area network technology offers three main advantages:

▶ **Resource sharing**: hardware and software can be shared by many devices and from many locations, so making a LAN economical. Expensive hardware and software applications can be purchased with the cost evened out over the total number of users on the network.

▶ **Organization**: greater organization, standardization and consistency is possible in a network within the business environment.

▶ **Integration**: disparate components and resources of a business organization can be administered and managed with greater control.

10.10 Wide area networks (WANs)

A wide area network (WAN) usually spans a broad geographical domain on a national or global scale. Such distances are usually covered using radio wave, microwave and satellite transmission or standard ISDN (integrated service digital network) telephone lines. Wide area networks, both wired and wireless, are usually provided by what are known as *common carriers*, which in the main refer to private or government-owned telephone and telecommunications utilities. The common telecommunications carriers typically determine the transmission rates and the connection between users and nodes. WANs normally require the process of communications *switching*, which involves routing messages through a range of network architecture gateways and transmission mediums. At each gateway the data message may be decoded and made more appropriate before being switched through the network. Data messages are often transmitted over networks in bundles that require coding and decoding at each gateway connection between systems, which is often known as *packet switching*.

Networks that link systems together between countries are sometimes referred to as international networks or *global area networks* (GANs). International networks give rise to a number of problems concerning trans-border data flow and and information access. Many governments restrict the ability of their citizens to access certain sites and information on the internet. Many countries also have restrictive laws governing the movement of information and data across international borders. Nevertheless, for large multinational international business organizations the use of WANs and GANs are essential for the coordination of global enterprise. WANs can be supported by either fixed-bandwidth channels, available from telecommunications carriers and utilities, or dedicated corporate virtual private networks (VPNs).

> ## What is a wide area network?
> A telecommunications network that links geographically dispersed users across the globe.

The largest WAN today is the internet, which connects millions of individual networks across the globe. The internet comprises a network of networks. The internet was originally conceived to transfer academic papers between scientists who were working on different computers using different software. The internet is a very large and extensive client-server network. Internet users are the clients, using various types of computer and computer software (e.g. Microsoft-based PCs, Apple Macintosh, Unix-based computers, Linux, etc.). The servers are host computers that are set up to store and process applications. These host computer servers are often referred to as *web servers*. In addition, the main physical components of a network, such as the internet, are controlled by:

▶ **Hubs**: enable nodes (i.e. computers and users) to communicate with one another across a network. A hub enables users to connect via an Ethernet. A hub is a multipoint repeater that forms the centre of a star network topology. Each node (or agent) is connected to the hub by a single cable.

▶ **Switches**: more sophisticated hubs. They process and filter data traffic across a computer network, making for more efficient communication of data traffic between nodes and devices.

▶ **Routers**: enable LAN (e.g. Ethernet) traffic to convert to wider area network environments. For example, they enable company LANs to connect to the internet via an internet service provider (ISP). In effect, routers connect different LANs together to form an intranet or connect a LAN to a WAN, such as the internet.

Most corporate networks provide for security *firewalls* to protect LANs from attack from computers outside its borders.

A *value added network* (VAN) is an alternative way for business organizations to manage their own networks. A value added network is a multi-path data-only network that is normally managed by a private company that operates the network on behalf of other organizations for a fee. Individual companies pay a fee to be permitted access to the network. The fee can be in the form of a rental charge or a network connection charge. For example, a company may control a particular network that uses ISDN telephone lines, or microwave and satellite technology, which a small organization is unable to afford outright. Such telecommunications technology can be made available to that organization for a fee; this allows the small organization access to advanced technology that it could otherwise not afford through its own hardware investment. The advantage of VANs is that client users do not have to invest in expensive network equipment or provide internal technical support for managing the network. The costs of using the network are usually shared among many users, so resulting in economies of scale.

Activity 10.6   Wide and local area networks

Define the term local area network (LAN) and describe the role and use of computer servers and network gateways within a LAN environment. Define the term wide area network (WAN) and describe the role and use of WANs in the business environment. Describe the use of wired and wireless LANs in business. Discuss the main advantages of wireless local area network technology within a business organization and suggest some of the possible costs and benefits of operating a WLAN. Describe the use and function of communications switching to transfer data between networks within the business environment. What are the risks of operating closed networks and open networks that connect to the internet?

10.11 Client-server computing

The sophisticated developments in network hardware and software architectures have led to a new model of networked computing known as *client-server computing*, which divides processing tasks according to whether they are appropriate to the client or server functions of a network. Client-server computing has evolved because of the increasing performance of desktop computers that have replaced dumb terminals within networked computing environments. Within the client-server model some tasks are processed by the computer server, while other tasks are processed by the connected computers that act as clients to the main computer server. Each function within the network is assigned on the basis of efficiency to optimize network resources. Therefore, computers on the network are assigned tasks that they are capable of performing to reduce some of the burden on the main computer file server. This model of networking, where the client computer takes responsibility for certain tasks, is only possible if the client hardware has the capability to process tasks independently within the overall network. The client computer may store independent user-interfaces, applications and instructions, while the main file server has the task of implementing large data storage or processing functions. The client machine often appears to be independent but empowered by increased applications handling and processing capabilities.

Most client-server networks encompass communication facilities that permit messages and data to be transferred between microcomputer users through host computer servers and across networks. The advantages of client-server technology over former network architectures are that it is:

▶ less expensive than traditional and centralized mainframe computing for many network functions;

▶ more flexible than traditional mainframe computing in terms of network architecture;

▶ more appropriate in distributed business computing environments.

The disadvantages of client-server technology are that:

▶ it may require higher end-user involvement and training;

▶ some client-server architectures are not as reliable as mainframe computers and are prone to outside breaches;

▶ there is a need for increased standardization of use and configuration.

Client-server architectures fall into two categories:

▶ **Thin clients**: run basic applications and perform very little heavy-duty processing.

▶ **Fat clients**: require client computers to run larger applications and take on many aspects of central host CPU operations for the network.

Each device on a client-server network is assigned appropriate and suitable functions, within the configuration of the network. Therefore, different hardware devices can operate on the same problem. In the client-server model some processing tasks are handled by the host computer server, while others are handled by the client computers. The aim is to apportion the functions to the computers and devices that are best at performing that function. Client-server technology allows greater end-user systems participation within the business environment by allowing user-friendly access to databases and software applications, along with the ability to download data and information to be used on the client computer.

Activity 10.7 Client-server technology

Discuss how client-server computing shares characteristics with the ideas of a mainframe computer linked to a number of terminals and suggest reasons why advances in ICT have allowed client-server technology to flourish in the business environment. Then write a résumé indicating how client-server technology has affected the way information resources are dealt with in a business organization. Prepare a five-minute presentation to communicate when and why it may be appropriate or inappropriate to use the client-server model within a networked business environment.

10.12 Open systems standardization

It is often the case that computer networks are required to connect to dissimilar networks. Therefore, there is a need for rules of engagement between networked systems. These rules were described earlier in this chapter as network protocols. Such protocols will only be effective if there is *standardization* among computer network architectures and communication channels. Standardization is an issue that is closely related to *open systems connectivity*. There are a number of standards that influence network communications and architectures. For instance, standardization within international and national telephone networks has existed for some time and has been produced by the Consultative Committee for International Telephone and Telegraphy (CCITT). This body has produced a number of standards for telecommunications, ranging from series X1 to X25, which have influenced data communications.

Governments, industries and commercial organizations with vested interests are constantly meeting to create standardization within networking and telecommunications. However, because of the rapid change in information and communications technology, and the large amounts of money invested in certain technologies, it has often been difficult to agree on common standards. The following three standards are important for a knowledge and understanding of networked environments:

▶ open systems interconnection (OSI) reference model

▶ Transmission Control Protocol/Internet Protocol (TCP/IP)

▶ integrated services digital network (ISDN).

The *open systems interconnection* (OSI) reference model was formulated by the International Standards Organization (ISO) in 1978 and has formed the basis for standardizing functional layers of control within networked systems architectures. The intention was to permit any computer on a network to be able to communicate with another computer on any other network, irrespective of the vendor-specific hardware and software being employed. The OSI reference model established seven layers to a networked architecture, whereby a data message sent from one networked system would be required to progress sequentially down the seven layers on being received by another networked system. The seven layers of communications architecture are:

1 **Physical control layer**: responsible for electronic signal transmission of data in raw binary form. It defines how 1s and 0s are processed and passed between nodes on a network. The physical layer interacts with technology platforms such as ISDN and ADSL.

2 **Data link layer**: where data is transferred in packets with control protocols to check correct transmission. This layer contains protocols for 'packaging' the data message, preparing it for transmission across a network. It provides for packet addressing. (Packet-switching' breaks a message up into short segments called 'packets'. Each packet is individually addressed.)

3 **Network layer**: routes and relays data packets over a wide area network. This

layer is concerned with getting messages received from the transport layer to their final destination.

4 **Transport layer**: checks and ensures correct end-to-end delivery between host computers. This layer undertakes packet acknowledgement, flow control and end-to-end error checking.

5 **Session layer**: establishes connections and manages dialogue between host computers. This layer is concerned with establishing, maintaining and terminating connections between networked devices.

6 **Presentation layer**: provides data transmission formats and layouts. This layer deals with any differences between applications on the two connecting devices, providing translation services where necessary. Functions include text compression, reformatting and encryption.

7 **Application layer**: provides services to applications running on a computer or other device that requires access to the network. It provides an interface between the applications and the services provided by the various protocols further down the stack. Applications concerned are web browsers and e-mail servers.

The user on one networked computer system would begin the activity of sending a data message at the seventh layer: the *application layer*. This would be fed down to the *presentation layer* that would convert the data message into a format suitable for transmission. The *session layer* then initiates communication between hosts before the data message is passed to the *transport layer* to be addressed. The data message is then passed on to the *network layer* to be split into appropriate data packets for transmission. These data packets are then checked and corrected through protocols at the *data link layer* and the data messages are then finally sent through the *physical control layer* in raw data form over suitable transmission channels.

The *Transmission Control Protocol/Internet Protocol* (TCP/IP) is a model that divides the telecommunications process into four generic stages that perform similar functions to the OSI model. The TCP/IP suite was first developed by the Advanced Research Project Agency (ARPA) that was a part of the USA's Department of Defense in 1957. This led to the development of the ARPANet that was the predecessor to the modern internet. The TCP/IP model is part of a suite of protocols used on the internet. These protocols deal with data transfer and reside at the network and transport layers of the OSI model. The TCP/IP model is public domain software (i.e. non-proprietary and free). The TCP/IP model is prevalent within certain operating systems environments such as Unix and has become an industry standard that is widely used in many network settings, particularly in the context of the internet.

The TCP/IP suite has the following four generic layers:

▶ link layer
▶ internet layer
▶ transport layer
▶ application and services layer.

The TCP/IP suite of protocols is not managed or developed by any of the traditional computing standards bodies, such as the ISO, but is publicly developed over the internet by anyone who cares to contribute to the Internet Engineering Task Force (IETF). The comparison between the OSI model and the TCP/IP model is only approximate. However, the TCP/IP model does supply the two most common protocols for modem and direct connections, these being the Point-to-Point Protocol (PPP) and the Serial Line Internet Protocol (SLIP). A key aspect of the Internet Protocol (IP) is the fact that it assigns a unique address to every computer connected to the network.

Telephone communication and standardization

The *integrated services digital network* (ISDN) is a common standard for communications through national telephone networks. ISDN permits the communication of digital data, voice and video information from computer to computer through standard telephone networks. In a similar way, the asynchronous transfer mode (ATM) permits video, voice, text and other data, which come from different technological backgrounds, to be integrated into commonly acceptable packets of information. Despite the various standards for layering networked systems architecture and for standardizing communications processes, the first interface between the user and the networked system is at the applications human end-user interface layer. The terms *baseband* and *broadband* distinguish between types of channel. In baseband networks there is a single channel that must be shared by each agent on the network. In broadband networks the cable carries multiple channels simultaneously. Cable Television is an example of a broadband system.

Data and information can be transferred through the physical paths of networks in many and various ways. Consideration must be given to the preparation mode of data transmission, and the coordination of transmissions to make the most efficient use of pathways through networks. The main forms of transfer modes within the business environment include:

▶ **Packet switching**: the data message is grouped and transmitted in manageable segments called packets. This allows data messages to be broken up into packets and sent along a number of communications pathways, rather than transmitting the data message in total over one pathway. This method of message transmission makes more effective use of available channels, thus enabling better balance of network loading. Network routers, which determine the flow of messages between computers, will normally transfer the data packets from the sending computer to the receiving computer, which reassembles all the packets into the original data message. *Code division multiple access* (CDMA) is an example of a type of wireless cellular network channel where calls are split into packets.

▶ **Circuit switching**: a continuous path is first established by switching (i.e. making connections) and is then used for the duration of the transmissions. Circuit switching is used in telephone networks and a number of digital data networks. In a circuit switching network, every time a user device attempts to connect to another device on the network the network must establish a circuit between the two devices: this role is normally performed by an exchange (e.g. telephone exchange).

▶ **Frame relay:** a faster and more economical form of transmission that uses wideband communications to transmit data messages over networks. Frame relay involves packet switching, but without the requirement for the packets to be held up for routing information and error-checking routines to be performed. Frame relay packets already include routing information that increases the speed of transmission.

▶ **Asynchronous transfer mode** (**ATM**): a high-speed transmission technology that provides for multimedia data and information in the form of voice, sound, graphics and video to be transferred through the same communications channel. ATM uses wideband communications media to speed data transfer. ATM uses cells to carry digital signals; each cell is 53 bytes. By using a standard size cell ATM can switch data using only hardware, rather than resorting to software to implement the routines of switching. This speeds transmission and allows many types of data, in various multimedia forms, to be switched between users over a network. The majority of common carrier telephone operators use the integrated services digital network (ISDN) that has become an international standard; because ISDN is used by the major telephone utilities, it comprises a ready-made network for communications.

Activity 10.8 Open systems standardization

Discuss the term open systems standardization and explain why open systems are important for efficient and effective data and information communication within the business environment. Explain what is meant by the open systems interconnection (OSI) reference model and outline the seven OSI layers to a networked architecture in a networked computing environment.

10.13 Networking principles

There are a number of network principles to consider when deciding on the network topology, type, and transfer mode to be adopted by the business organization. The network adopted must support the business organization's goals. Therefore, any organization needs to consider the following principles:

▶ **Reliability:** the performance of a business organization will depend upon the reliability of the network adopted; above average failure will adversely affect business performance. Reliability may be related to the complexity of the network design.

▶ **Security and data integrity:** the network must be protected from illegal or improper use. Users will often wish to maintain private files of information and the network manager may have to impose varying levels of privilege on access to individual data files and other applications. It is essential for data to be protected from corruption through multiple use and access to information files.

▶ **Performance**: this can be measured in terms of response time to transmit and receive data messages. The actual performance of a network will depend upon a number of connected factors, including speed and capability of computers and other devices, the network controllers that govern the coordination of devices, and the amount of data traffic the network is required to carry.

▶ **Vendor support**: appropriate vendor support is necessary to overcome problems quickly and effectively; it is important that the vendor has a track record of service and delivery. This can only be gauged by looking at the previous history of the vendor in supplying networks to other business organizations.

▶ **Flexibility and compatibility**: the network should be flexible enough to cope with changes and adjustments; it should also be expandable enough to cope with the inclusion of additional computers and devices. The network should be expected to meet current and future standards for information technology hardware and software; it should also meet all expected telecommunications standards.

▶ **Privacy and ethical factors**: privacy and control of data is important in networked business environments where there is shared access to information. Freedom of information must be balanced with the need to protect data and information from improper use and communication.

▶ **Technological infrastructure**: a network must fit into a business organization's technical infrastructure. Having to upgrade the physical environment of a business organization may increase the cost of establishing a network; this is particularly true if a network adopts fibre optic technology rather than more robust coaxial cable and wire technology.

It is important for a business organization to weigh up the factors involved in establishing a network. It should be a business requirement to create a *network plan* before embarking on the purchase of information technology to establish a telecommunications network.

Activity 10.9 Networking principles

Discuss the various networking principles that a business organization will need to consider when adopting a networked information system to support the business organization's goals. Outline the importance of a network plan before embarking on the purchase of information technology to establish a networked computing environment within a business organization.

10.14 Cellular communications networks

In 1897 Guglielmo Marconi demonstrated, for the first time, the ability to provide continuous wireless (voice) contact with ships sailing off the coast of the UK through radio wave communication. Since then, mobile wireless communications have evolved from relatively simple first generation (1G) *analogue* technologies to current third generation (3G) *digital* and broadband technologies. First generation cellular wireless communications devices evolved slowly and only became generally used in the business information systems domain in the 1980s. The 1980s witnessed the birth of wireless mobile telecommunications companies that are now amongst the most influential in the wireless world, such as Nokia in Finland, Ericsson in Sweden and Motorola in the USA. Furthermore, the 1980s saw the simultaneous development of different mobile network analogue standards for wireless telecommunications.

The popularity of wireless telecommunications increased in the late 1980s and early 1990s. But there was an increasing recognition that 1G systems were becoming unworkable because of expanded demand for network capacity, a lack of security features and the proliferation of different wireless network standards. These problems led to the development of second generation (2G) wireless systems, based on digital (rather than analogue) technology. As well as voice communication, 2G mobile phones can send and receive limited amounts of data in the form of services, such as text messaging, via the short messaging service (SMS), and wireless mobile internet browsing via the *Wireless Applications Protocol* (WAP). However, one significant drawback to 2G networks is the fact that they are primarily voice-centric telecommunication networks with only limited data transmission characteristics. Therefore, a range of enhanced 2G mobile phones were developed in the late 1990s and early 2000s to offer extended data capabilities, such as higher transmission rates and always-on connectivity via the general packet radio service (GPRS) (Elliott and Phillips, 2004). These enhanced second generation services were normally referred to as 2.5G technologies (i.e. enhanced transitional technologies between the second and third generation of wireless systems development).

Third generation wireless technologies enable users to transfer any form of multimedia data and information between remote locations, unconnected by physical wires. Its wide variety of services and capabilities includes video steaming, video telephony, and full unabridged internet access. 3G mobile cell phones normally have colour display screens and provide high-speed data transfer and always-on connectivity. 3G mobile phones are designed to support large numbers of users more efficiently than 2G networks and allow for future expansion in user capacity. The emphasis is on providing data-centric services, such as the mobile internet, with enhanced voice and multimedia capabilities. In the main, 3G networks are supported by the *universal mobile telephone system* (UMTS). Enhancements in 3G over 2G technology include broadband data transmission at rates of 2 Mbps compared to the previous *global system for mobile communication* (GSM) narrow bandwidth transmission speeds of 9.6 Kbps. 3G wireless systems also offer enhanced security and encryption features, and improvements in integrated circuitry and general battery life for mobile cell phones and devices.

One of the more interesting applications of G3 is the capability to connect to location-specific information. This is information that is provided on a geographical location (e.g. calling up a directory of restaurants in a specific location or requesting the location of bank cash machines in the local vicinity), via a mobile cell phone or other mobile device. Mobile cell phones can also be used to track individual users (via their mobile cell phone) to determine their specific geographical location anywhere in the world. Location-tracking services are encouraged by both businesses and national governments. For example, in the late

1990s the Federal Communications Commission in the USA encouraged mobile phone networks to implement location technology in order to determine the geographical location of a mobile phone user calling up an emergency service number (i.e. the emergency 911 number in the USA or 999 in the UK). The caller's location can be used to coordinate and direct emergency services to that location.

Wireless radio wave messages can be sent, and received, via static or mobile antennas or satellites. Antennas are normally Earth-bound devices, whilst satellites orbit the Earth in either stationary or non-stationary orbits. Communication satellites consist of large transponders that listen to a particular radio frequency, amplify the signal, and then rebroadcast it at another frequency. Wireless radio wave networks are normally divided up into *cells*: hence, the word cellular when describing wireless mobile phone networks. Each cell is serviced by one or more radio *transceivers* (i.e. transmitters and receivers of radio waves). The cells are arranged so that each one uses a different radio frequency from its immediate neighbour. As a mobile device user moves around from one cell to another, the call message is passed on to the frequency of the new cell. A cellular network topology enables frequency reuse by allowing related cells to reuse the same frequencies, which enables the efficient usage of limited radio resources.

Wireless mobile networks and technologies will dominate the business information systems environment of the twenty-first century. The successful adoption of wireless technology encourages business organizations to incorporate wireless technologies into their own business systems domains. Wireless networks offer connectivity, with the additional asset of location independence and mobility, within the working environment.

10.15 Chapter summary

A core strand of the study of business information systems involves a comprehensive understanding of networked computing and telecommunications environments. The successful integration of business information systems through the use of wired and wireless telecommunications can enhance the performance of a company in meeting its overall goals and objectives. Information systems integration requires an understanding of networking standards and procedures. It also requires a higher strategic understanding of the role, nature and effects of networking within the business environment.

Networked computer systems allow levels of homogeneity across markets and products that were not previously possible. For example, in the early 1990s the Ford Motor Company made a strategic decision no longer to operate business enterprises that designed and built vehicles for specific geographical markets. Previously, Ford Motors in the USA designed and built vehicles for the American market and Ford Motors in Europe designed and built vehicles for the European market. The business recognized that there was an overlap of the design, building and other business functions on a global scale. Ford Motors' solution was to isolate business functions to unique geographical areas based on functional specialization. The centralization of functions, such as design, by global region is only possible if there exist appropriate networking and telecommunications technologies to overcome distances and to make these functions appear part of the physical fabric of a business organization's domain, irrespective of its geographical location.

SHORT SELF-ASSESSMENT QUESTIONS

10.1 Define the term *telecommunications* and explain the difference between terrestrial and extra-terrestrial communications channels.

10.2 Describe the difference between *wire-based* and *wireless* communications channels and suggest five possible services offered to a typical business organization via these communications channels.

10.3 Outline two ways in which telephone and telecommunications organizations can increase the transmission capacity of their telecommunications technology.

10.4 Describe the types of physical hardware used for transmitting data across telecommunications channels and indicate the benefits and drawbacks of coaxial and fibre optic communications hardware.

10.5 Define the term *networking* and suggest three possible benefits of a communications network for a business organization.

10.6 Explain the difference between *local area networks* (LANs) and *wide area networks* (WANs) within networked computing environments.

10.7 Outline the possible advantages of *networked computer environments* for business organizations that carry out business activity on a global scale.

10.8 Explain the main functions of *communications software* and describe the role and purpose of a *network operating system* within a business organization.

10.9 Define the term *network topology* and explain the meaning of connecting nodes on a telecommunications network.

10.10 Outline the main advantages of wide area networks (WANs) within the business environment and suggest some of the possible costs and benefits of operating a WAN.

10.11 Define the term *value added network* (VAN) and describe the use and benefits of such value added networking to a typical business organization.

10.12 Define the term *client-server computing* and describe the main characteristics and differences of the client-server configuration as compared to other forms of networked environment.

10.13 Outline the main advantages and disadvantages of the client-server model of networking within the business environment.

10.14 Explain how client-server computing allows greater end-user participation within a business organization.

10.15 Discuss why the asynchronous transfer mode (ATM) is so important to the communication of multimedia data and information in the business environment.

10.16 Discuss why one of the most important layers to the end user is the human-computer interface layer within a protocol stack.

10.17 Describe the four main forms of *data transfer modes* found within the business environment.

10.18 Explain the reasons why the *integrated services digital network* (ISDN) used by common carriers has become an international standard.

10.19 Outline the significance and importance of *wireless networks* for business systems activity.

10.20 What are the main advantages and disadvantages of wireless networking within office environments?

EXTENDED STUDENT ACTIVITIES

Individual reporting activity 1

Wide area networks (WANs) are often called global area networks (GANs) in relation to global business activity. Global area networks give rise to a number of problems concerning trans-border data and information flows. Many countries have restrictive laws governing the movement of information and data across international borders. Write a 500-word business intelligence report indicating four possible problems associated with trans-border data flow between multinational business organizations.

Individual reporting activity 2

Explain why ICT and telecommunications are an essential aspect of global business information systems. Outline the various ways in which business organizations benefit from efficient and effective wired and wireless telecommunications networks. Describe why the selection and implementation of a suitable and appropriate telecommunications medium is essential in planning and implementing a networked environment. Prepare a five-minute presentation outlining the advantages and disadvantages of the following telecommunications hardware mediums:

▶ co-axial cable – wired

▶ twisted wire – wired

▶ fibre optics – wired

▶ microwaves – wireless

▶ radio waves – wireless.

Your presentation should include a review and ranking of each medium in terms of robustness, speed of data transfer and capacity of transfer.

Group-based activity 1

Divide into groups of two, three or four students. Your task is to describe the main components of a computer and describe how data storage capacity and telecommunications speed is gauged. Each group must find a commercial computer magazine that contains product evaluations and technology reviews. Select an advert or review relating to a piece of networked computing technology and write a technology evaluation report for the chief executive officer (CEO) of a business organization indicating the characteristics of the computer system in terms of capacity, speed and compatibility with other computer technology.

Your report should emphasize information such as the storage capacity, processing speed and compatibility of the technology you have selected, and the methods and criteria used to gauge the effectiveness and efficiency of the technology under review.

Group-based activity 2   Divide into groups of four students. Nominate group members to undertake the following roles:

▶ spokesperson

▶ facilitator: to encourage ideas

▶ recorder: to take minutes

▶ prosecutor: to outline the problems and possible solutions.

Discuss the ways in which ICT and telecommunications networks are used, and could be used, for competitive advantage in global business trading. Separate your analysis into factors that affect internal business information systems and factors that affect external business activity.

REFERENCES AND FURTHER STUDY

Books and articles   Burkhardt, J. et al. (2002) *Pervasive Computing: Technology and Architecture of Mobile Internet Applications*, Addison-Wesley, ISBN: 0201722151

Bussey, G. (2000) *Marconi's Atlantic Leap*, Marconi Communications, ISBN: 0953896706

Comer, D. and Droms, R. (2001) *Computer Networks and the Internet*, Prentice Hall, ISBN: 0130914495

Dodd, A.Z. (2001) *The Essential Guide to Telecommunications*, Prentice Hall, ISBN: 0130649074

Elliott, G. and Phillips, N. (2004) *Mobile Commerce and Wireless Computing Systems*, Addison-Wesley, ISBN: 0201752409

Johnson, E. (2001) *The Complete Guide to Client-Server Computing*, Prentice Hall, ISBN: 013087213X

Messerschmitt, D.G. (1999) *Networked Applications – A Guide to the New Computing Infrastructure*, Morgan-Kaufman Publishing, ISBN: 1558605363

Stallings, W. (2001) *Operating Systems*, Prentice Hall, ISBN: 013032986x

Tanenbaum, A.S. (2002) *Computer Networks*, Prentice Hall, ISBN: 0130384887

Weiser, M. (1991) 'The Computer for the 21st century', *Scientific American*, 265(3), September, pp. 94–104

Williams, R. (2000) *Computer Systems Architecture: A Networking Approach*, Addison Wesley, ISBN: 0201648598

Web resources for students   **International Standards Organization (global)** – telecommunications and network standards.
http://www.iso.org

Internet Engineering Task Force (global) – internet protocols and internet systems.
http://www.ietf.org

Wireless LAN Alliance (global) – wireless local area networks.
http://www.wlana.org

The internet and electronic business (e-business)

When you have studied this chapter you will be able to:

▶ understand the history and development of the internet and its commercial impact on the business environment;

▶ describe the nature and use of software applications for browsing and searching the internet and the use of such front-end technology within business;

▶ explain the nature of the World Wide Web (WWW) as a tool for transacting commercial ventures and business activity;

▶ understand the advantages and disadvantages of using the web within the integrated business systems environment;

▶ contrast the use and application of the internet as a medium for business activity with traditional business practices;

▶ understand the importance of electronic commerce (e-commerce) within the business systems domain;

▶ evaluate the importance and development of the wireless mobile internet within the business systems domain.

11.1 Introduction to the internet

The internet has emerged from the academic research world to become one of the most significant driving forces behind business change and innovation in the twenty-first century. The internet offers individual people, households and business organizations access to an unimaginably vast global information network of networks. The internet and the interface of World Wide Web (WWW) applications and technologies continue to inspire entrepreneurs despite the dot-com stock collapse of the late 1990s. The importance of the internet to electronic business practice can be gauged by the following quote that predicted the importance of electronic commerce (e-commerce) in the mid-1990s: 'The real promise of the Internet for entrepreneurs and consumers alike lies in its potential for electronic commerce: transaction conducted through computer networks' (*Financial Times* a–z of the Internet, 1996).

The internet provides consumers and business organizations with a global communications network that acts as a vehicle for electronic commercial transactions. The use of the internet in business has been assisted by the development of various user-friendly software applications (e.g. browsers and search agents) for searching the internet's enormous information resources. The *World Wide Web*, more colloquially referred to as merely the 'web', is the front-end aspect of the internet. The web sits on top of the internet, which is merely a vast, global network of networks. The main applications of the internet are e-mail, file transfer and web information hosting and access. The last of these applications is by far the largest use of the internet.

The web enables information to be viewed in a natural and user-friendly manner. When a browser, such as Netscape or internet Explorer, is used to access web pages of information held on the internet, the web browser opens the HyperText Transfer Protocol (HTTP) to open and create an internet session. The HTTP manages web page requests over the internet. For instance, if someone uses a web browser to call up a website they will normally type in a unique address for the site, referred to as the *universal resource locator* (URL). This uniquely identifies a web page on the internet. The act of searching or browsing the internet is often referred to as *surfing* the net. It is an appropriate analogy, given the vast ocean of information that is available for anyone with a suitable search engine (or 'surf board'!). The web page that is displayed is created from a coding language called the HyperText Mark-up Language (HTML). The mark-up language determines how the web page will look when called up in a browser. A list at the end of this chapter includes some of the main HTML command words, known as *tags*. The tags are instructions to a browser application on how to display and format text and graphics on a computer or hand-held device, such as a PDA.

11.2 What is the internet?

The internet is a global network of millions of smaller computer networks linked by terrestrial and extra-terrestrial communications channels. The most popular business use of the internet is for sending and receiving e-mail and accessing corporate web pages. The cost of e-mail is independent of how far the message travels, so this can mean a significant cost saving to an organization that relies on global communication between individuals and corporations. The internet (which is often referred to by the shortened term 'net') can also provide an important facility for cheaper videoconferencing, telephony (through the Voice Over internet Protocol – VOIP) and other interactive telecommunications. However, the most significant business feature of the internet lies in its use for global electronic commerce in the shape of transactions conducted through the millions of computer networks that make up the internet. The consumer market for a business organization's products and services is potentially vast when consumer demand is factored on a global rather than national scale. The internet is a relatively inexpensive business resource that permits small organizations to compete with larger commercial organizations because of the absence of any major entry costs or competition constraints of using the technology of the web.

The first organizations to benefit from the growth of the internet were the providers of software and telecommunications hardware used to access and handle the facilities of the web. Microsoft is the leading supplier of internet-based software applications, such as browsers and networking applications. However, other computer companies, such as Sun Microsystems (a manufacturer of powerful desktop computers) and other Unix-based computer suppliers have witnessed their profits grow through the manufacture and provision of *computer servers* used to handle the telecommunications infrastructure needed to interact with internet. Likewise, Cisco Systems and Bay Networks have earned significant profits throughout the 1990s through the provision of network architecture, such as *routers* that enable data and information traffic to be directed across the internet.

However, it is the suppliers of web and internet *software*, for searching and browsing the web, that have been the beneficiaries of the most dramatic increases in profit achieved by providing internet facilities. In the history of the web and internet, two companies benefited significantly from the provision of software for searching the internet. These were Yahoo! in the mid-1990s and Netscape Communications in the late 1990s. The profits of Yahoo! rose very quickly: after only two years of business activity, in 1996, the company was quoted on the US equity market (the Dow Jones). Netscape Communications marketed a software browser called Netscape Navigator/Communicator that was a commercial development of an earlier net browser known as Mosaic. The strength of Netscape Navigator, when it entered the internet market in the early 1990s, was its capability to handle e-mail and various associated multimedia applications written in the Java programming language developed by Sun Microsystems. The Netscape Navigator browser became the internet standard for a long time in the late 1990s. In the early part of the twenty-first century a number of law suits over the use and marketing of browser technology, and the slight widening of the marketplace, have led to the development of other browser applications, such as Internet Explorer.

Did you know?

Marc Andreessen, the co-founder of Netscape Communications with Jim Clark in April 1994, was a multimillionaire at the age of 24, when the business was placed on the US stock market in August 1995.

The widespread dissemination of marketing information and advertising across the web is the most obvious sign of the commercialization of the internet. To meet this advertising growth, a number of business organizations offer services in the creation of websites and internet-specific advertising. The provision of website development and management services is an industry in its own right. A website is a set of linked information pages that form a unique home location for a user on the internet. Individuals and organizations can create their own websites to reflect their own business needs and requirements.

Advertising on the internet not only provides a source of information, equipping consumers with knowledge to make informed decisions, but also offers the possibility of allowing consumers to interact with the product or service in the same way that a user interacts with a computer game or a real product in a shop or mall. Although advertising is extensively available on the net, consumers are largely in control of the nature and extent to which they interact with the adver tising; in contrast, with other forms of advertising, such as on television or radio it is the advertiser who is in control of the advertising message and its delivery to the consumer. By interacting with the web the consumer has more control over the nature and content of web advertising. This forces organizations to become more competitive and creative in the way they try to market and sell products and services to consumers over the internet.

Did you know?

Yahoo! was founded in 1994 and became one of the spectacular share issues of the financial year of 1996, when its value doubled in the first three hours of trading on the over-the-counter shares market in New York: the shares rose from an opening price of $13 to $26. The issue made instant multimillionaires of its two founders, Jerry Yang and David Filo. Their holdings at the end of the first day of trading were worth $140 million each.

Another significant use of the internet is the provision of online shopping retailing and banking from the comfort of a consumer's own home (or armchair). Home retailing through the internet is one of the most generally accepted com mercial activities of the web. Many electronic shopping malls and online bank enable consumers to have some level of choice as to how they transact business either in face-to-face form, in traditional retailing, or remotely and virtually (i.e without any face-to-face contact). The one major obstacle is the perceived inse curity of paying for goods and services online using credit or debit cards However, internet security has now reached a level of sophistication where the fear of insecure transactions is more perceived than real.

This has caused criminals to move to other forms of crime, such as stealing user identities in order to use other people's credit card details. When interne banking and retailing exploded in the late 1990s the three major credit card companies (MasterCard, Visa International and American Express) agreed to col laborate to establish a standard method of *encrypting* credit card data and trans mission over the internet. Encryption is the activity of coding data to protect its privacy, particularly when being transmitted over networked telecommunication links. Traditional encryption techniques use a secret *key* to encode data that i privileged only to the sending and receiving systems. The method and permuta tion of encoding is held within a *cipher*. As long as the key to the cipher remains secret then the code will remain secure and enable relatively risk-free telecommu nications. Commercial ciphers normally rely on a two-key system: one is a public key that is available to anybody and the second is a private (secure) key known only to the recipient. The development of advanced encryption technology wa essential in alleviating the fear of consumers in communicating personal and pri vate data, such as credit or debit card details. Confidential data transfer over the internet is a prerequisite for creating consumer confidence in electronic com merce (e-commerce).

11.1   The growth of the commercial internet in the 1990s

Discuss why advertising on the internet not only equips consumers with the knowledge to make informed decisions, but also offers the possibility of allowing consumers to interact with the product or service in the same way that a user interacts with a computer game or a real product in a shop. In terms of trading on the internet, outline the various business functions, such as marketing, sales and distribution, that could benefit. Then read through Pause for thought 11.1 and discuss some of the advantages and disadvantages of marketing products and services over the internet.

PAUSE FOR THOUGHT 11.1

The internet and the competitive environment of business

The explosion of the internet has brought online information services to millions of businesses and customers around the world. The internet has changed the way that businesses communicate with their customers, suppliers, employees and agents within their own organizations. For many commercial activities the internet equates to profit-making opportunities.

Businesses can benefit from the internet, but may also be victims of the internet. For example, paper-based publishers of academic journals may be affected by libraries and colleges opting to find research papers through the internet, rather than subscribe to paper-based journals. Likewise, businesses involved in telecommunications may be challenged by wireless internet-based communications using voice communications software. The attitude of 'back-bone' telecommunications providers is to join the internet revolution, rather than be left behind or be competitively challenged by the technology. For instance, internet users normally pay local call rates, irrespective of the call distance. This is a challenge to the price-per-distance approach used by telephone providers. The development of the Voice Over internet Protocol (VOIP) has had an impact on traditional telecommunications utilities.

A significant advantage of the internet is that it enables small organizations to compete effectively with larger organizations because the cost of entry to the technology is relatively low. For instance, the internet allows a business organization to provide a cut-price commercial transactions mechanism that new entrants can use without building a tangible infrastructure of high street branches, thus reducing the overhead costs associated with starting a new business. In such a dynamic competitive environment, banks and financial institutions were wise to get involved in the internet in the 1990s. In 1995 the Security First network bank, a US-based savings and loan group, was the first financial institution to offer online banking over the internet. There is now a vast range of other banks that offer internet-based products and services. Similarly, the traditional equity brokering areas of advanced commercial societies are developing online securities trading services. One of the first was the US-based E*Trade Securities, which offered share trading online in the late 1990s.

Often, business success goes to organizations that recognize consumer trends and have a knowledge of the technology required to satisfy demands. For example, the Lotus organization, which provided groupware applications in the mid-1990s before the company was acquired, entered the internet market to protect its Lotus Notes groupware from the competitive pressure of using the technology of the internet as an intranet within business organizations. (Intranets are internal corporate networks use similar software technology and communications standards

▶

as the internet, but restrict who can access the information and data.)

Many paper-based national newspapers offer online, web-based, electronic formats. Some are available free, while others are available through subscription. Advertising revenue through online newspapers has benefited the news and media sector of the business environment. Many organizations market and sell their products and services online as a standard feature of their business plan and strategy. For example, Amazon.com is said to be the largest online book shop in the world, although there are competitors all around the globe. Amazon.com can offer books at reduced costs because it can buy directly from publishers and does not have the large overhead costs of staffing and running shops in high streets. In a similar way, E-bookers, an online travel agent, is able to undercut other travel agents by offering to sell tickets and holidays without the cost overheads of traditional travel agents.

The internet offers the opportunity to challenge existing thinking on how, when and what to sell. The internet has challenged traditional models of interaction between individuals and business organizations. Therefore, creativity of business practices, using the internet, offers many business organizations new opportunities within competitive global business environments.

11.3 History of the internet and web

The web is a global collection of pages and sites on the internet. It encompasse advanced information and communication technologies that make it a user friendly way of storing, handling and accessing information on the internet Individuals and organizations can create their own unique set of information pages, colloquially known as a website, with each page being uniquely identifiee to a user or location by a URL web address. The web was originally conceived a a way of sharing documents and linking them with *hypertext links* (or *hyperlinks*)

There are many software applications available to deal with many aspects o the web, including:

▶ web page languages and applications (e.g. Java, JavaScript, HTML, Frontpage)
▶ web server programming (e.g. PHP, CGI, ASP, JSP)
▶ multimedia applications (e.g. Real Audio, Real Video, Flash)
▶ search applications (e.g. Internet Explorer, Netscape)
▶ Software applets (e.g. Cookies, Java Applets).

The web was first conceived and developed by the Conseil Européen pour le Recherche Nucléaire (CERN) – the European Council for Nuclear Research' European Laboratory for Particle Physics. CERN is located near Geneva ir Switzerland. It attracts and employs some of the best academics, physicists, math ematicians and computer scientists from around the world. The main activity a CERN is to implement experiments into sub-atomic matter using atomic particle accelerators. Such leading-edge scientific research requires extensive use anc application of computing and information technology. The web was first devel oped as an academic publishing tool to enable scientists to distribute academic papers to fellow colleagues. To achieve this, the web was conceived as a commor communications facility to deal with the different hardware platforms and soft ware languages being used by the geographically disparate research staff connected to CERN. The web was developed through the leadership of Berners Lee and a team of associated researchers at CERN.

The main advantage of the web is that it provided a common front-end interface that could be used on different hardware platforms and ICT environments. A further advantage of the web is that it offers interactive multimedia features such as graphics, icons, sound, movies and video, which can be incorporated and embedded into textual web pages. Additionally, there are the advantages of hypertext tools and techniques that allow the contents of a document to be linked and cross-referenced by embedding a unique web address into pages of information, which can in turn be called up by someone browsing the information.

Did you know?

The original internet was developed by the US Defense Department's Advanced Research Projects Agency (ARPA) (later called the Defense Advanced Research Projects Agency). It was established in 1957 by President Dwight D. Eisenhower and was originally called ARPANET.

The internet itself, the backbone network infrastructure of the web, had its origins in the 1950s (see page 390). The original internet was developed by the US Defense Department's Advanced Research Projects Agency (ARPA), which was established in 1957 by President Dwight D. Eisenhower soon after Russia launched its Sputnik satellite – the beginning of the technological competition between the USA and Russia (the former Soviet Union). ARPA set up a number of outreach research establishments that needed to be connected. So ARPA decided to investigate ways to design and build an electronic digital network to connect geographically distributed computers. ARPA put out to tender for the development of a digital network called the Advanced Research Projects Agency Network (ARPANET). The tender to build the network came from a company called Bolt, Baranek and Newman (BBN). The resulting network was able to handle e-mail by the end of the 1960s. By the 1970s the ARPANET team of research institutes included researchers from around the world. The further development of the ARPANET was encouraged by the development of digital networks and digital telephony in Europe and the USA throughout the 1970s and 1980s. In 1983 a derivative of ARPANET was established for the military in the USA and called MILNET, which controlled a network of military establishment computers.

Did you know?

Tim Berners-Lee is one of the founding fathers of the World Wide Web. He developed hyperlink techniques and applications that made user-friendly mass access to the internet a possibility in the 1990s. Berners-Lee enabled open access to the internet.

The internet works by having computers linked in digital electronic networks where specific computers (i.e. computer servers) are dedicated to providing the gateway access to individual computer networks. In 1977 a demonstration of the use of telephone networks to carry data messages was undertaken when a data message was sent from San Francisco in the USA, to University College London in the UK, and back to the University of Southern California in the USA, using telephone lines.

In the mid-1980s the internet was mainly used by academics in universities and research establishments. However, in the late 1980s Tim Berners-Lee published a research paper on the use of hypertext links to enable access to information across the internet. By the early 1990s the system that we know as the World Wide Web (the 'web') was developed, along with elementary browser applications. The first mass-usage browser in the early 1990s was called Mosaic, developed by Marc Andreessen and Eric Bina. They went on to set up the company called Netscape. To achieve the hypertext and multimedia context of the web, the scientists at CERN developed two specialist software language appli-

What is hypertext?

Hypertext is the term used to describe the technique of linking electronic multimedia documents together over a network. Key words, images or icons within one document can be highlighted and linked to other documents and information sources. These can be used by a human browser to retrieve linked pages and the information contained on these pages, which may in turn be linked to other related information pages. Theoretically, there is no end to the linkage possible, which may even be infinite based on the fact that pages of information are continuously being added globally by the second!

cations known as the *HyperText Mark-up Language* (HTML) and *HyperText Transfer Protocol* (HTTP).

HTML permits users to design web pages and other documents with hypertext links to other pages and documents. The links can be initiated locally or over global networks. The linked documents are retrieved and sent in plain text format to speed the transmission process and the browser software program interprets the HTML on to the user's screen. The HTTP application deals with the transmission of documents and overcomes the need for a user to link to other networked computer systems in order to achieve communication with another network.

Did you know?

Ted Nelson, a computer scientist, is reputed to have originated the term hypertext in 1972. He wrote a book entitled *Dream Machines* in 1974, which conceived the idea of a global hypertext network. He called the theoretical network Xanadu.

The tools and techniques of hypertext allow a web user to travel across a global array of networks connected through a set of visually obvious, but not technologically obvious, links on a web page. The user-friendly nature of browser applications has persuaded some organizations to replicate and incorporate the wider techniques of browser technology into the internal information systems of the business domain – an intranet. For instance, the visually attractive and user-friendly front-end interfaces of browsing software can be duplicated to access the integrated Information systems that are internal to a business organization. The scope of the technology is restricted to the physical and logical systems confines of a business organization; hence intranet systems offer the flexibility of browser applications technology with the additional advantage of security.

Activity 11.2 The World Wide Web

Discuss with your colleagues the benefits and drawbacks of hypertext links (often referred to as hyperlinks) and suggest whether there is any danger of loss of control of information if it is possible for a linked website to be outside the control of other websites to which it is linked or associated. Discuss whether you consider that the internet should be regulated to restrict certain information being publicly available on the web. Locate a newspaper article that refers to any form of regulation on the internet and use it as the basis of an argument for or against regulation of the internet.

PAUSE FOR THOUGHT 11.2

Equity and stock dealing on the internet

A number of electronic online equity and stock dealing services are available that exploit the flexibility of the internet. One of the earliest and best known in the USA was E*Trade Securities (etrade.com). It allowed customers to buy and sell equities and stocks (securities) over the internet. Normally, the dealing costs per transaction are lower with online share trading. All that is needed is a home computer, suitable modem and access to an online share dealing service. The costs of trading are lower because, unlike traditional stock brokers, the electronic brokers do not require expensive office buildings and numerous staff.

There are additional online services that provide financial information for investors in equities, stocks and shares. For example, a potential investor may use an online newsgroup where knowledge about businesses can be exchanged. To deal in shares with an online broker, an investor needs an account with an online brokering business. Normally, no money changes hands over the internet: only the share trades are recorded over the open lines. However, much online equity dealing is now through banks, who allow customers to transfer funds electronically into and out of accounts. In order to trade a customer must first of all open an account, often with cash or some other form of securities (like an existing portfolio of shares). Most internet brokers allow customers to monitor their 'positions' or their own portfolios and retrieve up-to-date market information. The transactions with online brokers are normally on an execution basis only: i.e. there is no brokering advice attached to a share deal. The customer is on their own and largely responsible for their own actions. Online share and equity brokers do not normally specialize in advice and personal service.

With the proliferation of such electronic commerce, national governments are often concerned to legislate against misuse of the internet. If financial institutions are to remain competitive they must embrace all the regulatory uncertainties that go along with the internet.

▶

One of the main problems is maintaining a balance between protecting investors and protecting the interests of financial institutions. In the UK, in the mid-1990s the Centre for the Study of Financial Innovation set up eight working groups to assess the implications of the internet for the financial sector. The groups covered regulation, crime, security, personal finance, retail banking, equity (share) trading, payment and settlement systems, and insurance. Ideally, a website provider should have to comply with all systems of law worldwide. For instance, should there be laws to prevent an overseas business setting up websites that comply with their own domestic laws but not with the laws of other countries?

It is important for any business organization looking to set up a website to ensure that all possible steps have been taken to protect against foreign enforcement action or to block access to anyone without an authorized password. An organization should ensure that its website complies with commonly agreed standards of fairness and accuracy, as well as with the laws of the countries towards which the website is aimed. Many countries, such as Malaysia, are reluctant to regulate the internet (beyond ordering the blocking of some websites) because they believe that their commercial future hangs on internet technology. For example, in 1996 the Malaysian government launched a scheme to attract foreign media, software, information technology and manufacturing organizations to a 'Multimedia Supercorridor' in an area of 750 square km near the Malaysian capital, Kuala Lumpur.

Business success relies on a suitable balance between national regulation, to protect investors and users of the internet, and freedom to exploit the internet to its full advantage within the global business environment.

11.4 Web applications and technologies

The web is a ubiquitous and pervasive technology. The internet is the largest public domain computer network on the planet. Most modern business information systems are built around the web and its back-end internet architecture. In other words most business systems architectures are web-based. The web is a very powerful multimedia information systems environment. Web browsers offer flexibility to search for information and content on either the global internet or within a corporate intranet. Web applications can be accessed from any location with a wired or wireless connection. The commonest web applications are browsing, e-mail, instant messaging, and groupware. *Instant messaging* (IM), for example, is a form of electronic communication that can be used on PCs or wireless mobile devices. It is a real-time alternative to e-mail that can be used in conjunction with groupware applications to encourage collaborative working practices. Instant messaging provides employees with the capability to maintain conversations with more than one person at the same time.

Did you know?

Instant messaging (IM) uses the internet as a backbone technology to host real-time communications, allowing people to send text messages in real time, as if conducting a normal conversation.

Most instant messaging services are offered as value-added services by internet service providers (ISPs), such as AOL. Instant messaging adds a real-time dimension to collaborative business projects.

Most web-based applications are *dynamic*: they enable sounds, movies and multimedia. For example, dynamic HTML and JavaScript are interpreted languages that sit within normal HTML providing for the development of dynamic multimedia web pages. Most web browsers, such as Internet Explorer and Netscape Navigator support dynamic HTML and JavaScript. An advantage of web pages is that they can be customized to individual needs or corporate needs. *Cascading style sheets* (CSS) are used to apply consistent formatting style sheets to web pages within a website. Data can also be customized with the use of the eXtensible Mark-up Language (XML) and its associated eXtensible Style Sheet Language (XSL) technologies. XML enables web pages to accommodate specific data needs.

The web is an *object-oriented* technology. It enables websites to be built by connecting together applications and content. Applications, applets and content can be downloaded and reconstructed, like building bricks, into a new web-based system. Web systems are also *client-server* based. Various computer server applications can be used in conjunction with HTTP communication. HTTP manages online requests for web pages and establishes communication sessions. For example, the common gateway interface (CGI) allows language scripts in the Perl language to be invoked by HTTP requests. In addition, Active Server Pages (ASP) and Java Server Pages (JSP) enable computer web servers to invoke program routines and database functions, such as capturing and storing data on a website.

Did you know?

The Standard Generalized Mark-up Language (SGML) is a generic mark-up language for representing documents. SGML allows document-based information to be shared and reused across applications and computer types in an open and non-proprietory format. The eXtensible Mark-up Language (XML) is an initiative from the World Wide Web Consortium (W3C) that defines an extremely simple dialect of SGML suitable for use on the web.

Most web applications and protocols are open standards that enable them to be used freely. However, a number of organizations exist to act as consortia for developments on the web. Two important organizations are the internet Engineering Task Force (IETF) and the World Wide Web Consortium (W3C). In particular, the W3C develops interoperable technologies, specifications and guidelines to develop the full potential of the web. The W3C was founded by Tim Berners-Lee in 1994 at the Massachusetts Institute of Technology Laboratory for Computer Science, with support from DARPA and the European Commission. The website of W3C provides a fascinating resource of material on the development of the web, and its founder, Tim Berners-Lee (*see* Figure 11.1).

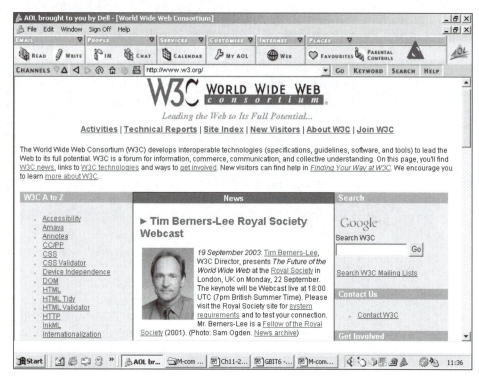

Figure 11.1 The W3C website

Source: Frame from AOL; screenshot from World Wide Web Consortium (W3C) website (www.w3.org).

11.5 Electronic business (e-business) on the web

The internet offers small business organizations the opportunity to trade alongside large business organizations on an international scale that is not possible through conventional business trading mediums based on traditional financial muscle. The potential growth of all forms of electronic commerce (e-commerce) and electronic business (e-business) is enormous and only limited by the imagination and creativity of people. For instance, electronic data interchange over the internet is on average half as costly as traditional data interchange mediums. The internet allows individual customers to interact personally with a business organization and to select aspects of information relating to that organization that are specific to the user's enquiry. Despite the problems of security, standardization and consistency of approach, the financial services domain is a major business sector that appreciates the importance of the internet. Nearly all financial services organizations around the world have their own tailored web products and services relating to loans, mortgages, pensions, online investments, savings accounts and other personal investment plans, which can be tailored by the customer to their specific needs.

However, the inter-networking of systems using different communications protocols does present a problem in terms of consistency of network performance and mechanisms to guarantee delivery of commercial transactions. For example, international commodities trading is only possible with consistency of telecommunications and the avoidance of time-lags in the trading process, which may jeopardize the operation of perfect market environments.

Despite some perceived issues of insecurity of payment through the web, the use of online electronic purchasing and payment is gaining significant popularity in the e-business domain. Online shopping, enhanced by the visual nature of the web that permits a customer to view the goods on offer in addition to a textual description, is a primary medium of purchase for many people today. In addition, general research into online shopping suggests that it encourages impulse buying. A customer can browse virtual stores to purchase goods and services such as flowers, books, records, clothes, electrical goods, food and various other products. The goods can be paid for online and delivered to an address specified by the buyer.

The banking sector is another area of e-business that benefits greatly from the sale of online financial products and services. Many banks were established in the late 1990s as internet-only banks. They had only a 'virtual presence' rather than a 'bricks-and-mortar' existence. However, many of these internet-only banks suffered as customers moved back to traditional banks with city branches in the early part of the twenty-first century.

Did you know?

One of the first specialist internet banks was First Network Bank, which was established in 1995 and originally offered basic personal banking services to customers.

In general the internet offers all organizations the opportunity to trade online. The web also enables truly global alliances to be established. For example, an electronics product (e.g. PDA or laptop computer) can be purchased from an online supplier in the USA; the product itself may have been manufactured in Japan or China; the product may be stored in Malaysia; and a logistical distribution company, perhaps based in the UK, could coordinate the delivery of the product from Malaysia to its destination at the customer's door in France. The web enables global business activity to become a reality.

Global connectivity enables global e-business. The impact of products and services is dependent upon their uniqueness, originality and appropriateness for online retail. How do organizations work out what to sell and how to sell on the internet? Traditional approaches, such as the Ansoff Matrix, can still apply in the online retail world as they do in the traditional retail world. In the 1980s Ansoff suggested four different approaches to product innovation:

1 establishing and consolidating existing products in existing markets;
2 developing new products for existing markets;
3 introducing existing products to new markets;
4 developing new products for new markets.

Clearly, the online retailing environment has been affected by the third and fourth approaches. The e-business environment attempts to introduce existing products into new markets, the virtual online market, and also tries to develop new products specifically for online consumers.

The internet has effectively created a global economy. People trade as one block, irrespective of nation or state. Therefore, e-business is sometimes referred to as 'business without borders'. However, e-business can be categorized into a number of areas, as follows:

▶ **Business-to-business (B2B) transactions**: where business organizations routinely trade with one another electronically or possess connected information systems that automatically communicate with each other (e.g. an inventory system that automatically signals a supplier's computer system when a minimum inventory level has been reached).

▶ **Business-to-consumer (B2C) transactions**: where companies communicate directly with customers over the web (e.g. online flight booking, online retailing, and online customer relationship management).

▶ **Consumer-to-consumer (C2C) activity**: where consumers and user groups meet in a virtual environment to share knowledge and information (e.g. online auctions, product and service evaluation and 'virtual societies').

The great advantage of the internet is its creation of a virtual 'global village' where people can communicate with one another, exchange ideas and engage in trade. Communication and the exchange of goods and services can occur without any time or location restrictions.

Did you know?

One of the wealthiest people in the world is Bill Gates, the founder and chief executive officer (CEO) of Microsoft Corporation. The wealth of the corporation is founded upon the development and sale of personal productivity tools and commercial software, particularly within the internet computing domain.

Activity 11.3 Business activity on the web

Using a web browser, search the internet for 'shopping mall' websites. Write a review of the website you have found, highlighting the following:

▶ ease of use and relationship between the related web pages

▶ logical and physical design characteristics

▶ payment medium process and characteristics

▶ advantages and disadvantages of shopping on the internet

▶ security measures employed to guarantee the integrity of using credit and debit cards.

Discuss the social and economic consequences of shopping from the comfort of a consumer's home or office and suggest how virtual shopping on the web is different to shopping in a city mall.

11.6 Registering a website

There are many millions of pages of information on the web. Individuals and business organizations can register a website at any time. Commercial websites range from simple product lists to elaborate multimedia presentations incorporating three-dimensional (3-D) data – images, pictures, sounds and movies. For a business to utilize the advantages of the web it must first register a website *domain name*. A number of internet service providers (ISPs) and other organizations have arisen to deal with applications from companies and individuals to establish commercial or non-commercial websites.

There are four main stages to establishing a website. First, the organization must register a domain name for its site. In the USA business domain names end with the extension '.com' indicating that the site address belongs to a company. (In the UK the domain name ends in the extension '.co.uk'). Certain non-commercial organizations often use the suffix '.org' instead of '.com'. The last letters normally indicate the country that registered the site. For example, '.uk' indicates the UK and '.au' indicates Australia. The domain name is in effect the address of the website. The following list includes a number of domain site names for various organizations:

www.amazon.com	Amazon (in the USA)
www.amazon.co.uk	Amazon (in the UK)
www.darpa.mil	DARPA
www.timeinc.com	*Time* magazine
www.oracle.com	Oracle Corporation
www.microsoft.com	Microsoft
www.ibm.com	IBM
www.apple.com	Apple Macintosh Computers
www.nbc.com	NBC
www.bbc.co.uk	BBC
www.whitehouse.gov	The White House Presidential site

The second stage to establishing a website involves deciding between having the site based in-house or serviced externally by an outside supplier or web provider. This choice may be dependent upon the size of the organization and the availability of web-literate staff in the organization. This stage will determine whether the web pages are developed internally or externally. There are a number of web service providers who will use their specialist expertise to design and create an organization's website. One of the considerations at this stage is the ease of maintainability of the site by the organization, because it is normally an ongoing requirement for business organizations to update their web pages on a regular basis, particularly to meet the changing requirements of dynamic business environments.

The third stage involves selecting a *scripting language* to construct the web pages for the site. The commonest form of scripting language application is HTML, which is simply a tool for creating web pages, with the advantage of being accessible to the majority of browsers. However, a number of other more user-friendly web publishing tools exist to ease the process of establishing a set of web pages for a website, for example Frontpage, which automates much of the process of converting content for publication and use on the web.

The fourth stage determines the *logical* relationship of the site to the customers and competitors. The decision to be made here is the purpose for which the site will be used. For example, the website can be used merely as an information board or for more sophisticated commercial activity involving levels of interaction with the user, client or customer. The logical purpose of a website will determine the design nature and complexity of the web pages and their associated hypertext links to other sites. Any form of business or commercial activity through a website will inevitably necessitate the purchase of encryption software to secure and protect customer details within the working environment of the website.

Activity 11.4 Registering a website

Evaluate, through discussion with your friends and colleagues, the significance of electronic business using the internet and explain some of the benefits and drawbacks of using electronic data interchange to pass data over the internet.

Provide examples of two sectors of the business environment that benefit from using the internet for electronic commerce (e-commerce) and electronic business (e-business). Discuss and record some of the problems of creating a website that has links to other websites within the internet domain. For example, are there any issues with the currency of information on websites?

11.7 The Java language environment and the internet

Java is a programming language developed by Sun Microsystems. In the 1990s Java became a standard dynamic language for the internet, largely because it is a cross-platform language, which means that it can be used with a variety of operating systems, from windows-operating systems to Unix, and across a range of computer platforms, from Apples to Microsoft-compatible PCs. The advantage of Java lies in the fact that it is a dynamic rather than static language, so it can extend the scope of the internet beyond its use as a mere information retrieval system. A business that records and handles information on the web usually describes it in static form. Therefore, every time the information changes the web must be updated manually. However, within the Java language environment the information changes can be extracted from a normal database; the web pages will reflect the database files and change as and when the database files change. Hence, Java permits information on websites to be dynamic rather than static.

Activity 11.5 The Java language environment and the web

Explain the significance of the Java language and its use within the environment of the internet and outline three main advantages of using the Java language environment in connection with the internet. Suggest and describe some of the ideal characteristics a programming environment should possess to be beneficial and appropriate for use on the internet. Search the web for references to Java and explain the use of JavaScript within the web domain.

11.8 Networking on the internet

The internet has liberated the stand-alone PC from its existence as a very local-ized business support tool into an exciting interface to the external business environment. The internet is largely a network of computer networks linked by telephone connections. internet communications are conveyed by backbone telecommunications carriers, such as BT in the UK, or AT&T in the USA, and a number of smaller relay carriers of data traffic. For example, in the 1990s in the USA the internet comprised five main communications traffic carriers that nor-mally used communications systems constructed by fibre optics; these were NSFnet, Alternet, AT&T, Sprintlink and PSINet. These utilities are referred to as *network service providers*. Most of these providers have invested in the develop-ment of broadband technologies for dedicated internet traffic. For example, dig-ital subscriber lines (DSLs) are dedicated internet-traffic-carrying cables and connections. In Europe most countries rely on national telephone and telecom-munications networks to convey data and information across the internet. However, these are largely linked by a European-wide system known as E-bone. It should also be noted that there are other carriers that control wireless data traf-fic and use other protocols, such as the Wireless Applications Protocol (WAP) for carrying internet content to mobile phones.

The internet telecommunications system is characterized by transmission management systems known as *hubs*, *routers* and *servers*. A hub is a computer system that deals with local services. For example, a hub can be used to connect several Ethernet strands over a local area network. internet routers provide a means of data traffic control. The aim of routers is to direct data traffic along the most efficient and effective telecommunications path in a network. The rules of transmission are governed by the Transmission Control Protocol/internet Protocol (TCP/IP), studied in the previous chapter. This protocol allows different computer hardware systems to communicate with each other, or to 'handshake' between different systems. Computer servers are computers dedicated to specific communications and internet management tasks. An e-mail message sent across the internet would leave the originator's PC, then proceed to a local computer server, then through a local hub and on through the communication channels of a backbone carrier, such as AT&T. The message would then go through the hub closest to the receiver of the e-mail message, on to the receiver's computer server, and then on through to the PC of the person receiving the e-mail message.

All computers on the internet have an Internet Protocol (IP) address. What is the IP address of your PC? E-mail communication has its own additional proto-cols, such as the Post Office Protocol (POP) or the Simple Mail Transfer Protocol (SMTP).

Within the internet communications architecture, servers act as a storage area for information and software. Such computer servers supply documents and web pages for users and some carry vital search engines that allow users to access and retrieve information. In addition, *search agents* are used to automate the process of searching information on behalf of users.

Many business organizations integrate telephony software into their internet systems, known as Voice Over the Internet Protocol (VOIP). Telephony applications can often include audioconferencing and videoconferencing capabilities. The main advantage of telephony, using transmission paths over the internet, is the relative cost reduction in making international calls, because the callers in a conversation are only charged for connection to the local internet site, irrespective of the distance of the call. However, a disadvantage lies in the fact that there is often a voice time delay that to some extent makes internet telephony inferior to normal telephone connections.

Activity 11.6 Networking and communications on the internet

Describe the role and purpose of internet transmission management systems known as routers, hubs and servers. Explain the benefits of multimedia transmission using asynchronous transfer mode (ATM) technology, which combines voice data and video data on the same transmission path. What advantages and disadvantages are present in VOIP?

11.9 Ethics and etiquette on the internet

The internet is still a relatively unregulated environment that has remained unconstrained by most national and international legislation. There are four main issues related to ethics and etiquette on the internet as follows:

▶ security of data and information flow
▶ privacy of the individual and organization user
▶ censorship and free speech
▶ ethical obligations of users.

Many of the *security* issues have been dealt with in earlier references to encryption software with regard to business and commercial activity over the internet. Most organizations spend a lot of money ensuring that their computer systems are safe and secure from hackers and from those that seek to infect computer systems with computer viruses. Current legislation by national governments has mainly concentrated on dealing with possible breaches of decency over the internet. However, the level and form of national legislation varies from country to country. Most internet access providers police their own affairs by providing *filtering software* to prevent access to sites deemed unsuitable. For example, in July 1996 the government of Singapore ordered internet access providers to block out sexually oriented and other forms of sensitive material. In Singapore the government is firm in regulating web pages and controlling access to users based in foreign countries that might undermine public morals, political stability or religious harmony. However, with such national legislation there is often much debate concerning decency versus freedom of information. Other governments have also been instrumental in restricting communications access within and beyond their national borders and jurisdiction. In most internet-literate countries there have been two main schools of thought – one favours consistent regulation and the other favours total freedom without government influence or regulation.

One fact that is clear to all users of the internet is that it is one of the largest participatory forms of free speech yet developed and as such requires ethical consideration. For example, in February 1996 the government of the USA introduced the Communications Decency Act to deal with online, offensive and indecent material. However, in June 1996 the new law was mitigated by a federal judicial ruling that declared the law unconstitutional as it did not recognize the First Amendment of the US Constitution that guarantees free speech. The ruling declared the internet: 'A medium of historic importance, a profoundly democratic channel for communication that should be nurtured, not stifled' (*Time*, 24 June 1996). The ruling continued that 'the internet deserves the highest protection from government intrusion'. What is apparent is that legislation varies from country to country.

One of the significant ethical issues involves dealing with users who use the internet to defame or smear the reputation of individuals and business organizations. An organization that strives hard to maintain a competitive reputation must ensure that no other internet user can lay claim to that reputation or attempt to besmirch that organization's reputation.

The following code of etiquette (or *netiquette*) lays out some standards of courteous behaviour that are commonly accepted on the internet:

▶ Never send any electronic message or commercial transaction that you would not want publicized or used in the public domain. The rule to remember is that what you would put on a postcard you would not mind being seen in the public domain.

▶ Never engage in the sending of abusive, threatening, harassing or bigoted electronic messages or creating web pages that threaten another individual or organization.

▶ Avoid smearing the reputation of others and avoid the creation of shadow identities on the internet that besmirch the reputation of an individual or business organization. Such shadow identities can misinform and mislead the internet user.

▶ On a technical level, try to avoid creating web pages that require an enormous amount of memory space to run. This will slow down the transmission rate and may prevent users with inferior technology being able to access the relevant websites.

Activity 11.7   Ethics and etiquette on the internet

Explain the four main issues related to use, ethics and etiquette on the internet and suggest aspects of internet use that are of particular importance to business organizations. Provide four reasons why national governments may wish to monitor or control the use of the internet by individuals and business organizations. What are the consequences of such controls for free speech?

11.10 Business communications technology

In 1991 the Commercial Internet Exchange was established to help business organizations to connect to the internet. Since then, various organizations have adopted the internet with the purpose of meeting their respective business needs. The internet is used for many purposes, ranging from sending and receiving business orders and e-mail correspondence, to information storage and retrieval. Business applications of the internet are only limited by the imagination of the organization. Some of the commonest business uses of the internet are:

▶ storing and retrieving information through the establishment of web pages and using internet search engines (e.g. browsers, XML, CGI – Common Gateway Interface, etc.);

▶ sending, receiving and distribution of e-mail messages to individuals and groups of individuals, internal and external to the business organization (and the creation of virtual communities);

▶ sending and receiving of documents around the globe and responding to suppliers and customers through EDI links;

▶ acquiring business intelligence to keep an organization abreast of competition and social, political and economic developments on a global scale;

▶ collecting and collating market research information and publishing tenders for contracts and other competitive bid work;

▶ keeping up to date in current research and development through the publication and dissemination of research articles via the areas of government, business and academia;

▶ acquiring and downloading commercial software applications that are relevant to the business environment, and the interrogation of various help and assistance sites.

Rapid, reliable and effective telecommunications are essential for competitive business. Organizations that trade over a wide geographical area or across continents need robust and clear telecommunications. Business organizations have access to a number of communications applications that speed the transmission of information. For example, *voice mail* is a system where a spoken message is digitized and transmitted over a telecommunications network to be stored for later retrieval. The message is then converted to audio and listened to by the recipient. Voice mail allows users to leave, receive and store verbal messages from anyone connected to the system across the globe. Voice mail facilities also allow the sender of a voice mail message to send the message to a single recipient or to multiple recipients. For example, the manager of a sales team that is dispersed around the world can leave a voice mail message and, through the attachment of a code to the message, have it copied to all personnel in the sales team. The advantage of voice mail lies in the fact that it does not involve typing text, as is the case with e-mail, and so can incorporates more meaning in the tone and modulation of the sender's voice.

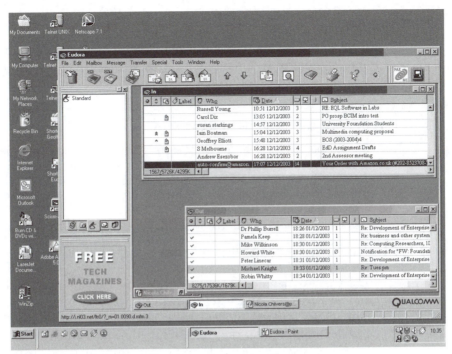

Figure 11.2 Eudora working in a windows environment

Source: Frame reprinted by permission from Microsoft Corporation; screenshot from Eudora (www.eudora.com).

E-mail is a cost-effective alternative to using the standard telephone for business communications. E-mail makes it possible for text-based messages to be sent from one computer to another connected (and networked) computer system. The receiving computer is informed that there is a message waiting and this can be accessed through windows-based (or other) communications software on the recipient's computer. There are a number of windows-based communications software programs for sending and receiving e-mail. Popular programs include Eudora, Outlook Express, Netscape Mail and PopMail. Figure 11.2 shows a typical screen image of the Eudora e-mail program being run within a windows environment.

E-mail has many advantages in terms of speed, accuracy and the ability to send, receive or forward messages to individuals or groups. However, within written language it is often difficult to interpret the sender's mood and accent on certain pieces of text. For example, should the text be read as a joke, sarcasm or a serious unembellished remark? To add tone to e-mail, a special set of symbols has become standard in the conveyance of mood and meaning. These are often referred to as *emoticons* (a play on the words 'emotion' and 'icon') or 'smileys'. Look at the following emoticons at a sideways angle and you will perceive the visual meaning:

:-)	happy	:-0	amazed!
:-(	sad	:-P	poking out tongue
;-)	wink	:->	sarcastic remark
:-||	angry	:-I	indifferent

Emoticons indicate emotions within the body of a message. It is important that electronic communication, such as e-mail, should be clear and concise and eliminate any misunderstanding. Good communication avoids misunderstanding and any tool or technique that assists in that pursuit is important within the domain of information technology in the business environment.

Activity 11.8 Business communications technology

Provide four reasons why the acquisition of business intelligence allows a business organization to keep abreast of its competition and social, political and economic developments in the global business environment. Discuss the effectiveness of voice mail and e-mail as communications mediums in the business environment. Why use emoticons in e-mail communication?

11.11 The wireless mobile internet

The wireless mobile internet describes the process of accessing web content and web pages from a wireless mobile device, such as a personal digital assistant (PDA), wireless modem in a laptop, or a mobile phone. Sophisticated mobile phones that can handle multimedia content and applications are known as *smart phones*. The content on the internet can be accessed in two varieties:

▶ on PDAs (and other hand-held organizers) and smart phones, which access and view normal (but smaller) versions of PC-type web pages;

▶ on traditional mobile phones through the Wireless Applications Protocol (WAP).

It should be noted that WAP has largely been replaced in the twenty-first century with technologies and devices that can access web pages in formats similar to PC-based access. WAP is a technical wireless telecommunications standard that is specifically designed to enable internet pages, designed in mark-up languages, such as the Wireless Mark-up Language (WML), to be viewed on the small screens of mobile cell phones. The goal of WAP was to enable portable mobile phone users to access data and information from the internet.

The wireless mobile internet is sometimes referred to as merely the *wireless internet*. When a smart mobile phone is connected to the internet (or a mobile phone and PDA are connected together, often via infrared data transfer) the user can access the internet and also send and receive e-mails anywhere and at any time. The mobile phone, on instruction, dials up a *wireless internet service provider* (WISP) and delivers content to the smart phone or wireless PDA. However, without an internet-compatible PDA, direct access to the internet via a mobile phone is only possible via a *WAP portal provider* over a telecommunications *network operator* (e.g. BT in the UK, AT&T in the USA and J-Phone in Japan). A wireless portal provider is a company that provides access to the content of the mobile internet. It effectively provides a window (or portal) on the Mobile internet.

A *wireless portal* is a doorway, or entrance, on to the internet. The portal acts as a window on to websites on the internet. Some portals are *garden walled*, whilst others allow free access to any point of information on the internet. The process of garden walling is implemented by some wireless portal providers in order to provide access only to certain commercial sites. In effect certain company web-sites are garden walled so the person accessing the portal only has access to specific products and services from authorized companies and providers. Wireless portal providers give access to wireless web services, such as browsing infor-mation content, e-mail, and *text messaging* (known as the short messaging serv-ice, or SMS). Most wireless portals are commercial ventures, but many others are merely value-added services provided to existing PC-based customers and clients. Many wireless portals are created by companies solely for their employees. These are known as *enterprise wireless portals* and form an extension to existing intranet systems within a company's computerized network.

Did you know?

A smart phone combines the functions of a mobile phone and a PDA. It normally integrates access to information sources, such as the internet. A number of smart phone devices also integrate interface expansion slots to extend the memory of the device or to make other applications available, such as games, audio clips and office applications (e.g. word-processing and database applications). The extra memory can support an electronic book (e-book) or even movies.

In the USA the American Wireless Internet Service Providers Association (WISPA) provides a list of wireless ISP directories for 39 states. WISPA outlines its mission as follows:

> The Wireless Internet Service Provider Association is a non-profit organization and co-operative, formed to serve the interests of WISPs and ISPs worldwide. Our purpose is to unite wireless ISPs in a borderless association; determine member needs and interests; develop programs and services to meet those needs and interests. We will strive to help create the standard skills, knowledge, and ethics required to continue to have a hand in the evolution of our industry ... we will steer this organization in the direction of becoming the leading professional association of the wireless internet delivery industry. (WISPA website: www.wispa.org)

Wireless portals provide a means of advertising and encourage wireless mobile internet users to engage with the internet, from 'any place, anywhere and at any time'. Each wireless service provider tries to offer unique customer services and products to its clients, such as the capability to sent text messages to other mobile phone users free of charge from a PC or the creation of customer e-mail accounts. Most wireless internet service providers also have various business links and busi-ness partnerships with retailers, banks and other business services, for example buying and selling stocks and shares, or placing a bet on a sporting event.

The development of the wireless mobile internet has encouraged business organizations to explore more innovative ways and means of reaching their customers. This form of wireless product and service provision is known as busi-ness-to-customer (B2C) trading. Customers can be targeted in a more focused manner with specific products and services. Wireless internet service providers are constantly looking for better technologies to encourage greater use of the mobile internet. For many wireless internet service providers, making the mobile internet attractive to customers is a primary business objective. The aim of wireless providers is to offer mobile internet services that are equally as good as, or better than, wired internet services, based on 'location-specific' information and products.

The wireless mobile internet has been made possible by third generation (3G) technology aimed at providing a wide variety of services and capabilities in addition to voice communication, including multimedia data transfer, videostreaming, video telephony, and full unabridged internet access. 3G technologies were first introduced to Japan in 2001 and spread to Europe and the USA in 2003. The emphasis with 3G technology is on providing data centric services (such as the wireless mobile internet) with enhanced voice and multimedia capabilities. To support 3G technology, a network service was developed in the early twenty-first century called the universal mobile telephone system (UMTS). Improvements in 3G technology over previous second generation technology, available in the 1990s, include:

▶ broadband data transmission (at rates of 2 MBps compared to second generation narrow bandwidth transmission speeds of 9.6Kbps);

▶ enhanced security and encryption features;

▶ improvements in integrated circuitry and general battery life for mobile devices;

▶ improvements in screen displays and the ability to handle multimedia data (i.e. videostreaming and graphics).

As with the wired internet in the 1990s, when there were a number of e-business opportunities for those who were the first into the commercial domain with a 'dot-com' idea, so similar opportunities exist in mobile commerce (m-commerce) using the wireless mobile internet in the twenty-first century.

11.12 Chapter summary

Effective communication is essential for business activity. Information is only a powerful resource if its communication is timely and accurate and conveyed through an appropriate telecommunications medium. The internet offers all business organizations, both large and small, the opportunity to compete globally and on equal terms, irrespective of the size and nature of the organization. Once the current barriers of perceived insecurity of data transfer are overcome, then the internet becomes a significant medium for business activity. Unlike many business opportunities in the past, the financial barriers to entry do not exist in any significant form on the internet: to establish a web presence is a relatively cheap exercise. Business organizations are likely to become more competitive and to rely on the knowledge, wisdom and creativity of people and project teams to extract value from the internet. The intelligence and creativity of such internet professionals provides competitive advantage in the world of the 'global internet village'.

SHORT SELF-ASSESSMENT QUESTIONS

11.1 Define the term *internet* and suggest three possible commercial uses of the internet for business activity.

11.2 Explain why a major obstacle to mass electronic shopping is the insecurity of paying for goods online using credit or debit mediums.

11.3 Describe the techniques used by business organizations to try to ensure the security of data when customers purchase goods using a credit or debit card.

11.4 Define the term *web* and explain why and how the web was developed as a useful communications tool.

11.5 Explain the significance and function of *hypertext* in providing *hyperlinks* to other documents and areas on the web.

11.6 Define the term *multimedia* and describe the characteristics and possible use of multimedia information in the business environment.

11.7 Evaluate the differences between the internet and the *intranet* and suggest four advantages to a business organization of operating an intranet user interface.

11.8 Describe the role and function of the *HyperText Mark-up Language* (HTML) and *HyperText Transmission Protocols* (HTTP) within the internet domain.

11.9 Outline the role and purpose of legislation and statutes related to information and content on the internet.

11.10 Explain why in order for a business to take advantage of using the web it must register a website *domain name* and describe the four main stages to establishing a *website*.

11.11 Explain why electronic commerce and electronic business prospers when *encryption* is widespread and reliable.

11.12 Evaluate the significance of traditional encryption techniques using a secret key to encode data that is privileged, and describe the method and use of *ciphers*.

11.13 Describe the commonest medium used to transmit data and information traffic over the internet.

11.14 Explain how *filtering* software may prevent breaches of decency occurring over the internet.

11.15 Define the term *netiquette* and outline the main points of etiquette that should be present when using the internet.

11.16 Define the role of *e-mail* in business and suggest three possible advantages and disadvantages of using e-mail.

11.17 Outline three main business uses of the internet and describe why these uses may be essential for business activity in the twenty-first century.

11.18 Define the term *emoticon* and describe how emoticons may reduce misunderstanding that often occurs within e-mail messages.

11.19 What is the business significance of the *wireless mobile internet* in business and how does the mobile internet differ to the PC-based internet?

11.20 Why is the mobile internet considered to be as important as PC-based internet access in the twenty-first century?

EXTENDED STUDENT ACTIVITIES

Individual reporting activity 1

Governments are continuously passing legislation to try to ensure correct and appropriate use of the internet. Outline the main problems associated with abuse of the internet and draw up policy guidelines for a business organization that indicate how the internet should be used. Then, provide a list of recommendations to encourage business organizations to make appropriate commercial use of the internet.

Using the available internet technology at your university or college, locate your university or college's home page. Write an evaluation report describing the presentation and ease of use of the home page. Discuss the information requirements for a university or college home page. If possible, interview the designers and creators of the home page and determine how they undertook the analysis, design and implementation of information requirements and screen user-interface design.

Individual reporting activity 2

Suggest how the widespread use of global networks might raise ethical and social questions for business information systems. For example, electronic networks can be used to monitor and check systems and individual use of a system. Write a report, for the chief executive officer (CEO) of a business organization, outlining some of the ethical, social, legal and related issues that may be faced by companies that use the internet. Outline the ethical arguments for and against monitoring employees on a networked business information system. Discuss whether e-mail by employees of a company should be monitored, and, if so, what should be monitored? Discuss what actions should be taken against misuse of the internet within business organizations.

Group based activity

Choose a real or virtual organization and plan a website for the organization:

1 Define the information requirements of the organization.

2 Sketch a design of the home page for the organization, indicating the hyperlinks that are necessary to link to other internal and external information.

3 Describe the problems and possible solutions facing an organization when it attempts to design and formulate a web page presence on the internet.

Discuss the problems that you may encounter designing your own web pages and websites and suggest how you might overcome these problems.

CHRONOLOGY OF THE INTERNET AND THE WORLD WIDE WEB

1835   Samuel Morse develops the prototype of the telegraph, which used magnetic transmitters and receivers to send a pattern of signals across a wire. He later developed Morse code.

1844   USA sanctions the first long-distance telegraph line, strung between posts from Baltimore, Maryland to Washington, DC (a distance of 60km). On 24 May 1884 the first telegraph message was successfully sent and received along the first telegraph wire system.

1858   The Atlantic cable is laid to carry communications across the ocean. It was initially a failure and remained in service only a short time.

1866   Sub-Atlantic cables are successfully laid for the first time to carry telegraph traffic from the UK to the USA.

1957   USSR launches Sputnik, the first artificial Earth satellite.

1958   USA forms the Advanced Research Projects Agency (ARPA).

1963   Doug Engelbart prototypes an oNLine System (NLS) which enables hypertext browsing editing, e-mail, and so on. He invents the mouse for this purpose.

1965   Ted Nelson coins the word hypertext in *A File Structure for the Complex, the Changing, and the Indeterminate,* New York, USA.

1966   Lawrence G. Roberts of MIT in the USA publishes a paper entitled 'Towards a cooperative network of time-shared computers' that constituted the first ARPANET plan.

1967   National Physical Laboratory (NPL) in Middlesex, UK develops NPL Data Network under Donald Watts Davies, who coined the term packet. ARPANET design discussions held by Larry Roberts at ARPA.

1968   Packet-switching network presented to the Advanced Research Projects Agency (ARPA). Tenders for proposals for the ARPANET.

1970   ARPANET hosts start using Network Control Protocol (NCP), the first host-to-host protocol.

1971   Ray Tomlinson of BBN invents e-mail program to send messages across a distributed network. The original program was derived from two others, an intra-machine e-mail program (SENDMSG) and an experimental file transfer program (CPYNET).

1972   International Conference on Computer Communications (ICCC) at the Washington DC Hilton demonstrates ARPANET between 40 machines, organized by Bob Kahn: the first public demonstration of the ARPANET.

1973   First international connections to the ARPANET. Vinton Cerf outlines the idea for 'gateway' architecture.

1974   Vinton Cerf and Bob Kahn publish an article entitled 'A protocol for packet network interconnection' that specifies the design of a Transmission Control Program (TCP).

1978   TCP split into TCP and Internet Protocol (IP).

1980   While consulting for CERN, June–December 1980, Tim Berners-Lee writes a notebook program, Enquire-Within-Upon-Everything, which allows links to be made between arbitrary nodes.

1982   ARPA establishes the Transmission Control Protocol (TCP) and Internet Protocol (IP) as the protocol suite, commonly known as TCP/IP, for ARPANET.

1983   ARPANET split into ARPANET and MILNET.

1984   Domain name system (DNS) introduced to the internet.

1986   Internet Engineering Task Force (IETF) and Internet Research Task Force (IRTF) come into existence.

1988   CERFnet (California Education and Research Federation network) founded by Susan Estrada.

1989   Tim Berners-Lee writes an article for circulation at CERN entitled 'Information management: a proposal'. A paper 'HyperText and CERN' was produced as background.

1990   Tim Berners-Lee starts work on a hypertext GUI browser and editor using the NeXTStep development environment. He makes up 'World Wide Web' as a name for the program.

1993   Release of the first alpha version of Marc Andreessen's Mosaic browser. Mosaic is discussed in general newspaper articles. A declaration is made by CERN that WWW technology would be freely usable by anyone, with no fees being payable to CERN. US Presidential White House comes online at www.whitehouse.gov

1994   Marc Andreessen and colleagues form Mosaic Communications Corporation, later renamed Netscape. The First International WWW Conference, hosted by CERN in Geneva, is held in May. Japanese Prime Minister goes online at www.kantei.go.jp

1995   CERN holds a two-day seminar for the European press, radio and TV, attended by 250 reporters, to show off the WWW. It is demonstrated on 60 machines, with 30 pupils from the local international high school helping the reporters 'surf the web'. Netscape is listed on the Dow Jones equity exchange.

1999   Growth of countries registering domain names. Formation of the Internet Societal Task Force (ISTF); Vinton Cerf serves as its first chair.

2003   Public Interest Registry (PIR) takes over as '.org' registry operator. By giving up '.org' VeriSign is able to retain control over '.com' domains. Largest ever worldwide virus attack (to date) on the internet by SoBig.F virus. The first official Swiss online election takes place in Anières.

Sources: The W3C website (www.w3.org); Hobbes' internet Timeline, 1993–2003 (www.zakon.org/robert/internet/timeline), Robert H. Zakon.

INTERNET TERMINOLOGY

Attachment	Text or other file that is attached to an e-mail message.
Bookmark	Means of marking a user's location on the web.
Browser	A software program displaying images and text that provides an interface to internet documents.
Cybernaut	A person who actively browses and searches the internet.
Download	To transfer data from a remote site to a user's computer.
E-mail	An electronic message that is sent between users on a network.
Emoticon	Character graphics used in e-mail messages that represent emotions.
Eudora	A windows-based e-mail management program.
FAQ	Shorthand term for 'frequently asked questions'.
FTP	File Transfer Protocol for transferring messages and files across the internet.
GIF	Graphic interchange format file extension that indicates the file contains a graphics image.
Home page	The first or main index page of a user or location, linking and pointing to a series of other pages.
Hyperlink	Hypertext link marked by the highlighting of a key word, which when clicked on with a mouse will link to a related document.
Internet service provider (ISP)	An organization that provides access services to the internet.
Netiquette	A code of conduct for users of the internet.
Netscape	A hypertext-based browser program used for locating web information.
Outlook Express	A menu-based e-mail management program.
Portal	A web page window on to other related links and sites.
Protocols	The rules that govern how software and hardware communicate on a network.
Telnet	A program for connecting and logging on to computer systems on a network.
Upload	To transfer a data file from a user's computer system to a remote system on a network.
URL	Shorthand for uniform resource locator, which identifies network locations and enables navigation on the internet.
Web address	Unique identification of user or location on the internet.
Web page	Single screen page on the web.
Website	Unique location for a user on the internet.
WWW	World Wide Web – a global collection of pages and sites on the internet.
XML	eXtensible Mark-up Language – a data-based web applications language and web-based environment.

COMMON HTML TAGS (version 4.0)

HTML was created by the World Wide Web Consortium (W3C).

(Please note this list is not definitive of all HTML tags.)

Tags to establish an HTML document

<html> </html>   The beginning and the end of an HTML document

<head> </head>   Create the Web page title and other information that will not be displayed on the Web page

<body> </body>   Establishes the visible portion of the Web page document

<title> </title>   Establishes the name of the document in the title bar

Tags to refine an HTML document

< body bgcolor=>   Sets the background color, using name or hex value (e.g. Blue)

<bodytext=>   Sets the color, using name or hex value

<body link=>   Sets the color of links, using name or hex value

<body alink=>   Sets the color of hypertext links

<font size=>**</font>**   Sets font size

Tags to format an HTML document

<ht> *text* **</hl> or <h6>** *text* **</h6>**   Creates the size of text

**** *text* ****   Embolden text

<i> *text* **</i>**   Italicize text

<p> *text* **</p>**   Creates a new paragraph

<p align=>   Aligns a paragraph to the left, right, or centre

<ol> *text* **</ol>**   Creates a numbered list

<li> *text* **</li>**   Precedes each list item, and adds a number

<ul> *text* **</ul>**   Creates a bullet list

<hr>   Inserts a horizontal rule across the web page

<hr width=>   Sets width of rule, in percentage or absolute value

Tags to create HTML tables

<table> </table>   Creates a table in the web document

<tr></tr>   Sets off each row in a table

<td></td>   Sets each cell in a row

<table border=>   Sets width or border around table cells

<table cellspacing=>   Sets amount of space between table cells

\<table cellpadding=>   Sets amount of space between a cell's border and its contents

\<tr align=> or \<td align=>   Sets alignment for cells – left, centre, or right

\<table width=# or %>   Sets width of a table

Tags to establish frames

\<frameset>\</frameset>   Establishes the framesets

\<frameset rows= "value, value">   Defines the rows with in a frameset, using number in pixels, or percentage of width

\<frameset cols= "value, value">   Defines the columns within a frameset, using number in pixels, or percentage of width

Tags to establish HTML forms

\<form>\</form>   Creates a form

\<select name="NAME">\</select>   Creates a pull-down menu dialogue box

\<select multiple name="NAME" size=>\</select>   Creates a scrolling menu

\<option>   Sets off each menu item

\<input type="checkbox" name="NAME">   Creates a checkbox

\<input type="radio" name="NAME" value="y">   Creates a radio button

\<input type="submit" value="NAME">   Creates a submit button

\<input type="reset">   Creates a reset button

Tags to establish Hypertext Links

\<a href="http://www.amazon.com">*link*\</a>   Creates a hyperlink in a Web document to a URL

\<a href="mailto: test@aol.com">\</a>   Creats a mailto: link

\<a name="NAME">\</a>   Creates a target location within a document

\<a href="#NAME">\</a>   Links to that target location from elsewhere in the document

\<img src="name">   Adds an image link to the Web document

\<img src="name" align=>   Aligns an image: left, right, centre; bottom, top, middle

\<img src="name" border=>   Establishes size of border around an image

REFERENCES AND FURTHER STUDY

Books   Anderson-Freed, S. (2001) *Weaving a Website: Programming in HTML, JavaScript, Perl and Java*, Prentice Hall, ISBN: 0130282200

Ansoff, I. (1986) *Corporate Strategy (The Library of Management Classics)*, Sidgwick & Jackson, ISBN: 0283993545

Ansoff, I. (1990) *Implanting Strategic Management*, FT Prentice Hall, ISBN: 0134518810

Applequist, D. (2001) *XML and SQL: Developing Powerful Internet Applications*, Addison-Wesley, ISBN: 0201657961

Aron, D. and Sampler, J.L. (2003) *Understanding IT – A Manager's Guide*, FT Prentice Hall, ISBN: 0273682083

Berners-Lee, T. (2000) *Weaving the Web: The Original Design and Ultimate Destiny of the World Wide Web by its Inventor*, Texere Publishing, ISBN: 1587990180

Bray, J. (2002) *Innovation and the Communications Revolution: From the Victorian Pioneers to Broadband Internet*, Institution of Electrical Engineers, ISBN: 0852962185

Cassidy, J. (2003) *Dot.con: The Real Story of Why the Internet Bubble Burst*, Penguin Books, ISBN: 0141006668

Cronin, M.J. (1997) *Banking and Finance on the Internet (Internet Management Series)*, John Wiley and Sons, ISBN: 0471292192

Deitel, H.M. et al. (2001) *Internet and the World Wide Web – How to Program*, Prentice Hall, ISBN: 0130308978

Elliott, G. and Phillips N. (2004) *Mobile Commerce and Wireless Computing Systems*, Addison-Wesley, ISBN: 0201752409

Geer, S. (2003) *Essential Internet (The Economist Series)*, Economist Books, ISBN: 1861975406

Gillies, J. and Cailliau, R. (2000) *How the Web Was Born: The Story of the World Wide Web (Popular Science)*, Oxford Paperbacks, ISBN: 0192862073

Hafner, K. and Lyon, M. (1998) *Where Wizards Stay Up Late: The Origins of the Internet*, Simon & Schuster, ISBN: 0684832674

Hall, E. (2000) *Internet Core Protocols: The Definitive Guide*, O'Reilly Publishing, ISBN: 1565925726

Kahn, D. (1997) *The Codebreakers: The Comprehensive History of Secret Communication from Ancient Times to the Internet*, Simon & Schuster, ISBN: 0684831309

Keen, P.G.W. and Mackintosh, R. (2001) *Freedom Economy: Gaining the M-Commerce Edge in the Era of the Wireless Internet*, Osborne McGraw-Hill, ISBN: 0072133678

Naughton, J. (2000) *A Brief History of the Future: The Origins of the Internet*, Phoenix, ISBN: 075381093X

Negroponte, N. (1996) *Being Digital*, Coronet, ISBN: 0340649305

Nelson, T. (1965) *A File Structure for the Complex, the Changing, and the Indeterminate*, proceedings of the 20th National ACM conference, Cleveland, Ohio

Nelson, T. (1974) *Computer Lib/Dream Machines*, ISBN: 0914845497

Nelson, T. (1988) *Computer Lib/Dream Machines*, Microsoft Press International

Standage, T (1999) *The Victorian Internet: The Remarkable Story of the Telegraph and the Nineteenth Century's Online Pioneers*, Phoenix, ISBN: 0753807033

Web resources **Defense Advanced Research Projects Agency (USA)** – government department that was originally responsible for the development of the internet.
www.darpa.mil

Internet Engineering Task Force (global) – internet protocols and internet systems.
www.ietf.org

World Wide Web (W3C) Consortium (global) – web and internet consortium founded by Tim Berners-Lee.
www.w3.org

Mobile computing security and biometrics

When you have studied this chapter you will be able to:

▶ define the nature and role of mobile computing in the business systems domain;

▶ describe the devices, networks and technologies that can be aligned to form wireless computing environments;

▶ outline the business applications of mobile and pervasive computing within the business environment;

▶ understand the concepts of computer security and security management within wired and wireless systems environments;

▶ outline the main forms of biometric identification and describe their use in systems access and security;

▶ describe the various security standards that underpin the development and use of computer security protocols;

▶ describe various aspects of computer systems misuse and fraudulent activity over the internet;

▶ understand and be able to categorize various forms of cyber-crime perpetrated on networked computer systems and the internet.

12.1 Introduction to mobile computing

Mobile computing refers to the use of mobile devices to access information through wired or wireless connection from 'any location, anywhere and at any time'. Mobile devices include personal digital assistants (PDAs), operating either Palm operating systems (OS) software or Microsoft Windows OS software for small, handheld portable devices; mobile phones and 'smart' phones, with sophisticated multimedia applications; and wireless laptops (using wireless modems to connect to the internet and corporate intranets). PDAs normally have a range of functions to support 'mobile working', including address book applications, office applications such as Word, Access, Excel spreadsheets, and e-mail. The PDA acts as a digital *personal information manager* (PIM).

What is mobile computing?

The use of mobile devices and technologies to access data and information through wired or wireless connections from 'any location, anywhere and at any time'.

One of the biggest areas of mobile computing is accessing the wireless mobile internet from smart phones and wireless PDAs. It has been predicted by many technology commentators that the number of mobile cell phones connected to the wireless mobile internet will exceed the number of internet-connected personal computers (PCs) before 2010. If this is the case then the mobile phone will become the most prevalent device for accessing the internet in the twenty-first century.

The telegraph in the 1890s, like the internet in the 1990s, was a revolutionary communications technology that transformed both the social and business aspects of human life. For example, Harrods department store in London transacted comparatively more business over the telegraph in the last decade of the 1890s than it did over the internet in the last decade of the twentieth century. The development of the telephone (known originally as the speaking telegraph) transformed telegraphic communication by making it increasingly available to non-specialists. In a similar manner, the wireless mobile internet, accessible by an internet-enabled mobile device, will do for the internet what the telephone did for the telegraph (*The Economist*, 13 October 2001).

The use of the telegraph to transmit and receive messages in Morse code in the nineteenth century, and the extended use of the wired telephone in conjunction with the internet in the late twentieth century are examples of technologies that have become an integral part of the business systems environment.

12.2 Business applications of mobile computing

The primary function, or application, of mobile computing devices and technologies is to support the *mobile workforce*. Many occupations require employees to be mobile, such as sales force teams, architects, real estate agents, and consultants. These mobile workers require access to corporate information resource while they are out of the office. Many mobile workers are permanently in the field, collecting information and data on behalf of their organization, so often use wireless devices to support their job functions. For example, a wireless PDA can be used to access corporate databases on products and prices, and information can be made readily available to customers and clients. Collected data and information can be transmitted back to office databases via a wireless connection. Since the data is input directly to the corporate databases, there is no need to re-input the data when the worker returns to the office. This practice can eliminate data errors and improve data accuracy and user productivity.

The use of e-mail is fundamental to business activity in the twenty-first century. Being able to access e-mail in the field is a considerable business advantage. Many devices are available just to provide access to e-mail servers, so that e-mail can be sent and received remotely from any location and at any time. In addition, general information on the internet, or corporate intranets, can be accessed anywhere and at any time. Location-specific data and information can be accessed about a specific location. The Wireless Application Protocol (WAP) was a global protocol standard for hand-held devices to access online services in the late 1990s. However, WAP has largely been replaced with access to the internet in a style that is similar to PC-based formats. This has opened up the wireless internet to the office systems environment.

The use of mobile computing in the business systems domain is sometimes referred to as *mobile commerce* (m-commerce). It is concerned with the systems use, application and integration of wireless technologies and wireless devices within the business domain. Mobile computing can be defined as the interconnection of portable computing technologies and the wireless telecommunications networking environments necessary to provide 'location-independent connectivity' within the business information systems domain. The use of wireless technologies extends the nature and scope of traditional e-business by providing additional aspects of *mobility* and *portability*. Wireless networks, and the portable mobile technologies that support such network infrastructures, provide flexibility and mobility within the business systems domain.

Location-specific information is data and information based on an awareness of a user's location and point in time. Mobile device users have expectations and requirements that are different to those who are stationary, or back in the office. For example, information can be provided on a geographical location (e.g. a directory of restaurants in a specific location, or requesting the location of the nearest ATM cash machine). Mobile devices can also be used to track a mobile device user and products can be targeted to mobile device users at specific times and for specific locations.

Activity 12.1 Mobile computing environments

Discuss and explain what is meant by the term mobile computing and explain how important mobile computing domains could be to business information systems environments. What are the main business applications of mobile computing and what devices can be used to support mobile computing environments?

12.3 Pervasive computing environments

The term *pervasive computing* is often used interchangeably with the term *ubiquitous computing*. Both indicate that computing power is all around us, freed from the PC desktop, and embedded in static and mobile devices that are in communication with one another via wireless telecommunications (Elliott and Phillips, 2004). In other words, computing technology is available anytime, anywhere and in any device. Embedded devices can range from refrigerators, cookers and motor vehicles to PDAs that detect the presence of networks within their wireless vicinity. These devices can possess embedded microprocessor technology to an extent that we are unaware of the devices interacting with the environment around them. Computing can exist around us without anyone realizing it is there.

What embedded computing devices have in common is the automatic exchange of information via fixed wire and wireless communication channels. Many of these devices are referred to as *information appliances* because they are embedded with the specific aim of supporting a user, or group of users in the work or home environment.

Pervasive computing environments are characterized by client-server networks that utilize microprocessor computing technology and wired and wireless telecommunications. Embedded devices are normally triggered by the relative proximity of another device within their environment. Embedded devices monitor and control the transmission of data and information dependent upon the trigger signal from other mobile devices. Examples include a refrigerator that monitors its product contents and signals when product content levels are falling, or an elevator that can remotely inform a centralized maintenance computer that there is a fault that needs attention or servicing. The three important qualities in pervasive computing environments are:

▶ **Mobility**: moving about easily and in an untethered manner (i.e. unfixed) – computing is everywhere.

▶ **Ubiquity**: existing everywhere, and all around, often at the same time – computing is everywhere.

▶ **Embedded**: subsuming and engendering devices with computerized technology – computing is 'disguised' and subsumed within devices.

According to the National Institute of Standards and Technology (NIST), the three main characteristics of pervasive computing are:

▶ numerous, casually accessible, often invisible computing devices;

▶ frequently mobile or embedded in the systems environment;

▶ connected to an increasingly ubiquitous network infrastructure.

Embedded technology, and in particular, embedded devices are sometimes referred to as *smart devices* because they automatically detect other compatible devices within their wired and wireless environment. In other words these devices are 'smart' and intelligent and able to recognize their location and other networked devices, and maintain relevant data about users. The desirable characteristics of embedded smart devices are that they are:

▶ unobtrusive

▶ constantly connected

▶ intelligent and smart

▶ portable and mobile

▶ constantly available.

Pervasive computing systems development involves building mobile, wireless, networked and unobtrusive information systems environments that support mobile working. For example, many organizations have invested in smart, embedded technologies to create *smart rooms*. These smart rooms are intelligent to an extent that they can monitor and engage with people and devices that are randomly moving about the room. Embedded intelligence is supported by small, powerful devices and sensors, built into the walls, floors and ceilings of a room (or building). Office workers who randomly move about the building are unaware that they are interacting with a computer at all. The devices that engage with these embedded computers are many. They can be portable devices, such as laptops, wireless PDAs and mobile phones. But they can also be wearable devices that could be contained in a person's clothing, in a watch, in shoes, or even in spectacles. These devices can then monitor meetings, by recording and dictating lectures and talks, track individual speakers, and communicate and receive data from various portable and mobile devices belonging to office workers. The portable devices talk to each other over a local area network (LAN) that can support both wired and wireless telecommunications between devices.

Smart rooms in general are referred to as *smart space*. For example, it is possible to have voice recognition software (via an array of microphones) in a conference room or university building, to allow people within a room to dictate lectures and conversations. The embedded devices in the smart space not only record but can also track people within the smart space. People can move around the room without worrying about being near a microphone or a computer.

In office buildings, smart space can be used in various ways to enable workers to move about and still maintain a wireless connection to computer servers, and to engage with computing applications from any location untethered by wires. Wireless mediated environments provide opportunities for increased productivity, better client-server networking relationships, and unbounded computerized connectivity.

Areas where pervasive and embedded technology has taken hold in the twenty-first century information systems environment include:

▶ **smart rooms** (e.g. the smart home and the smart office)

▶ **wearable computing** (e.g. wearable within and without the body)

▶ **automotive telemetry** (e.g. remote systems diagnosis)

▶ **information appliances** (e.g. self-reporting household appliances).

A number of scientists are also looking at ways of embedding computing devices into humans; this is sometimes referred to as *invasive computing*.

Activity 12.2   **Pervasive computing environments**

Discuss and explain what is meant by the term pervasive computing and explain how important pervasive computing domains could be to business information environments. What are the main business applications of pervasive computing? What devices can be used to support pervasive and networked computing environments?

12.4 Computer security

Business organizations spend a large proportion of their ICT budgets on computer security. Customer use of the internet to purchase goods and services is determined by their opinion of the level of security of a website. Computer security must consider:

▶ **Privacy**: ensuring that data and information on people and corporations is secure and safe from illegal access.

▶ **Integrity**: ensuring that the data is accurate and up-to-date and ensuring that data corruption does not occur when data and information is transferred across a network.

▶ **Confidentiality**: ensuring that messages sent across a network are not intercepted and the message gets to the correct person without interference or observation by those who have no rights to see the information; also ensuring that systems do not allow access to data that is held on people.

▶ **Authentication**: ensuring that those that use and access data are who they appear to be on the network; also ensuring that people can be identified accurately so that someone cannot pass themselves off with a false identity.

▶ **Protection**: ensuring that data and information resources cannot be corrupted by computer viruses and other forms of attack from outside the system.

Most systems have barriers to access in the form of passwords and security identification (i.e. IDs). The passwords and IDs are only given out to authorized people. *Hackers* are those people that try to break into systems by attempting to get around password and ID barriers. Hackers try to access information for various reasons. In the business domain a major reason is industrial espionage, where someone tries to obtain the trade secrets of another organization.

Computer networks and computer systems can be attacked in a number of ways. People can try to access data or purchase goods over the internet by pretending to be someone else. They adopt the identity of a real person and use their credit card details, and access codes to buy goods and services illegally. This is often known as 'spoofing'. Other common forms of attack on computer systems are through *viruses* that enter a network and corrupt the data or processing activities of a computer network. A third type of attack is where data and information are intercepted as they pass from node to node on a network. This type of attack is common in wireless networks where the data passes through the air and the signals can be intercepted. For example, mobile cell phone communication can easily be intercepted by receiver dishes that pick up data messages transmitted from one mobile cell phone to another mobile cell phone. It should also be noted that mobile cell phones can be easily tracked: this is sometimes known as 'sniffing'. It is a particular problem with wireless networks where people can intercept wireless networks and use the facilities on a network, such as corporate intranets.

PAUSE FOR THOUGHT 12.1

Security issues won't slow pervasive computing

Concern over data security in enterprise wireless networks is not the obstacle blocking the adoption of pervasive and mobile computing systems, according to the director of IBM's software group. 'No, the key concern for companies mulling mobile computing investments remains the same: business model, business model, business model,' said Steve Mills, senior vice president and group executive of IBM's software group [in September 2003]. 'At the end of the day, as much fun as wireless devices are, you have to be tuned into the business model,' Mills said during a briefing for reporters about IBM's new wireless middleware upgrades. To that end, technology companies such as IBM and others 'have to think through and figure out how to leverage device capability and apply it in a way that is going to deliver value to those customers,' he said. 'The devices themselves, the companies that manufacture those devices, the kinds of applications and solutions that companies and partners work with, will be the key drivers to really getting the market moving around pervasive computing,' said Mills.

In a bid to put some gas in mobile computing's growth engine, IBM is rolling out new versions of its WebSphere family of middleware in order to help partner software providers and developers create applications that can speak to a variety of operating systems, and switch to different wireless network protocols. Called Extension Services for WebSphere Everyplace, the flagship middleware is designed to ease the porting of applications and services to pervasive devices. In the process, Big Blue [IBM] is also staking a claim to building development tools that provide the widest support for handheld operating systems. That includes WebSphere lines that support Palm, Linux, Symbian and Microsoft's Pocket PC operating systems, which collectively represent about 90 percent of the handheld market. Call it a mobile WebSphere line of software for Java-enabled applications that are less chatty than desktop-based applications – but can convey much the same meaning as bigger programs.

Rather than rewriting applications for mobile devices, or calling for a mini-browser to access data or information, the WebSphere suite provides a services-oriented runtime environment that enables connection independent deployment and lifecycle management of applications and network services, officials said. In short, the environment helps push out portlets to do the job with data that bandwidth-hungry browsers do on a desktop. Mills also stressed that authentication and security issues really aren't deal-stoppers for wireless computing deployments. Essentially, customers are forced to re-examine their current corporate security – how many firewalls they have enabled, or who has access to what – when rolling out mobile computing access.

In addition, IBM said its identity management software, such as Tivoli Access Manager, is already embedded in WebSphere Everyplace. Company officials said the Tivoli system helps customers automate management of security policies, whether employees are wired or wireless and regardless of what type of device they are using to access data behind a corporate firewall. IBM also demonstrated another key component of its WebSphere Everyplace suite: its DB2 Everyplace database product for network-connected devices. Streamlined to provide enterprise-level queries for devices, but at a fraction of the processing bandwidth for industry-standard SQL applications, DB2 Everyplace includes a small-footprint database and the DB2 synchronization server. It too runs on the widest variety of mobile platforms in the industry, including embedded Linux, Microsoft's Pocket PC, QNX Neutrino, IBM said. Independent software vendors that have integrated IBM's WebSphere Device Management software include X Point, a managed recovery software vendor. The company said it is using IBM WebSphere

Device Management software to provide carrier-grade services to wireless service providers. Another independent software vendor (ISV), Bitfone, said it plans to integrate its own identity management offering with IBM's (Tivoli-based) WebSphere Device Management software.

Voice-activated applications were not overlooked in the demonstrations either. IBM said it is Voice XML 2.0-compliant in its WebSphere Voice Server 4.2, WebSphere Voice Application Access 4.2 and WebSphere Voice Response 3.1.5 development environments.

Meanwhile, IBM said its multimode development environment for Pocket PC now allows speech and graphics to be used in the same interaction. The upgrade is an extension of IBM's already announced multimodal browser aimed at the Sharp Zaurus Linux PDA that runs on the Opera browser.

Rod Adkins, general manager of IBM's pervasive computing division, said the latest WebSphere upgrade 'expands what is increasingly becoming a louder industry call-to-arms for the creation of an ecosystem that can allow on-demand access to any content from any device on any network.'

Indeed, he added, a key provision in the WebSphere Everyplace platform is that it can help devices navigate different network protocols they are jumping into in order to access data, such as Wi-Fi-based or GPRS networks.

Source: Erin Joyce, 'Mills: security issues won't slow pervasive computing', © Internetnews.com, 24 September 2003.

Activity 12.3 Computer security

Discuss and explain the five main aspects of computer security. What is meant by a secure computer system? Why do business organizations invest in comuter systems security? Who should be responsible for computer security in a business organization? What measures can be used to support the development of secure networked computer systems?

12.5 Security management

Most systems have software tools and applications, such as *firewalls* and anti-virus software, to combat security breaches. Most systems also have authentication mechanisms to allow, or prevent, access to a computer systems environment. *Authentication* is the process of determining a user's identity. Passwords and IDs are used to enable a user to log-on to a computer system. A large and growing area of authentication is *biometrics*, where iris, eye, retina, face, voice intonation and fingerprints are used to determine the identity of a person for access to a computer system. Compaq has manufactured a hand-held PC that integrates biometric fingerprint identification. In modern systems environments *digital certificates* are used as an electronic signature to enable electronic transactions.

When data needs to be transmitted across a computer network a technique known as *encryption* is used. Encryption is a method of secretly encoding messages so that they appear unreadable to anyone that intercepts the message. The message is encoded before it is transmitted and decoded on arrival at its destination. Encryption is a technique that has been used to 'scramble' messages for many centuries. The Romans used encryption techniques to scramble written commands to their legion commanders. Within encryption environments, the password may only be known by the sender and receiver of a message; this password is held in a secure manner. The password is needed to access (and interpret) the message. In e-business transactions a *Public key infrastructure* (PKI) is used to enable the encryption of information without prior exchange of secret information, such as a password. The PKI enables cryptography and secure transactions to take place.

What is a public key infrastrucure (PKI)?

A form of key encryption using digital certificates from certificate authorities that verify and authenticate each person, or body, involved in an electronic transaction.

Digital signatures, in a similar manner to handwritten signatures, are used to identify a person and authenticate an electronic transaction (within e-business). A digital signature is a cryptographic technique that uses PKI to verify the identity of a sender of a message. The digital signature attaches the identity of the sender signature to a transaction. To possess a digital signature, a user must possess both a *public* key and a *private* key. These are not physical keys, but electronic codes.

The PKI generates a matching pair of encoded and decoded strings of numbers. The encoded data through the public key is generally available to the key user. However, the 'private key', or decoded data key, is only kept by the receiver: the private key is unique to the owner of the digital signature. An electronic transaction can be authorized using the private key (i.e. the unique code). This can then be electronically sent to a retailer (on the internet), who can then verify the signature by the corresponding public key code: the public key verifies the user of the private key. The public and private keys are both encrypted.

Did you know?

One of the most common public key infrastructure (PKI) methods used is called RSA encryption. It was invented in 1977 by Ron Rivest, Adi Shamir, and Leonard Adleman. The name RSA comes from their three initials.

To obtain a digital signature (i.e. a private key code and a public key code) a *digital certificate* is required. The digital certificate contains the details of the user, such as holder's name, serial number, public key and date of signature acquisition and expiry date. Essentially, digital certificates are used in PKIs to send and receive secure (i.e. encrypted) electronic messages or transactions. Digital signatures are a means of overcoming a person's inherent mistrust of electronic transactions, both in the fixed wire and wireless networking domains.

Did you know?

Many countries have created and enacted legislation to support the use of digital signatures. This legislation has attributed to digital signatures the same legal force as handwritten signatures. For example, the Global and National Commerce Act in June 2000 in the USA outlined that digital signatures were as legal as normal pen signatures.

The digital signature effectively verifies that the person undertaking the transaction is the rightful owner of the bank card used to make the transaction. A digital signature can be used to verify that a credit card being used to buy goods over the internet is being used by its rightful owner (Elliott and Phillips, 2004). For example, customer X buys a television over the internet using her credit card, but then denies she bought it. The television may have already been acquired by the online retailer from the manufacturer, so he is not too happy! The online retailer is now stuck with the cost of the television. Customer X claims that she did not use her credit card for the transaction. There is no way to prove that customer X used her credit card or that someone else fraudulently used the card to buy the television online. This may lead to a long legal battle between the television retailer and customer X. However, all this is avoided if the online retailer could have proved that customer X used her credit card normally and legally: a digital signature would have verified the credit card user's identity.

Activity 12.4　Computer security management

What is the difference between security and access? What is being secured in computerized systems environments? What is a digital signature and how is it used in the e-business domain? Discuss and explain the term 'sniffing' in wireless security. What techniques are used in security management and what is a digital certificate? What is encryption and how is it used in computer security?

12.6　Security standards

The world of internet security is full of security standards. These standards attempt to ensure secure transactions via wired and wireless electronic communications channels. Standards are essential for networks and data messages being sent across networks. Security standards dictate the manner in which data messages are secured over electronic computer networks, such as the internet. Previous chapters have mentioned the International Standards Organization (ISO), which is one of the oldest standards organizations in the world, founded in 1946. The ISO is responsible for creating international standards in many areas, including computing and telecommunications standards. The American National Standards Institute (ANSI) is a US government body responsible for approving US standards in computing and telecommunications.

The ISO17799 standard of the International Standards Organization covers security in organizations. (This standard even has a web site at www.iso17799-web.com.) The standard provides a rigorous coverage of a number of areas, such as security management, security policy and access control. Other standards include Pretty Good Privacy (PGP). This is a public domain encryption and security standard that can be used within e-mail clients and servers (e.g. Microsoft Outlook). The Data Encryption Standard (DES) is another security standard that was used by the US military. Although DES is not normally used in commercial computing environments, it is identical to the ANSI standard Data Encryption Algorithm (DEA), defined as standard X3.92–1981.

Within the e-business domain the majority of transaction standards and protocols are aimed at eliminating credit and debit card fraud. One major problem is the use of mirror websites that mimic the websites of legitimate online business organizations. The mirror sites appear to reflect the identity of the real online merchant. People are fooled into providing their credit card details by these sites because they believe that they are dealing with a real, known and legitimate website.

> ### Did you know?
> Secure Electronic Transaction (SET) is a security standard for credit card transactions. It was developed by a consortium of organizations including Visa, MasterCard, American Express, Netscape and Microsoft.

A security system known as *Secure Electronic Transaction* (SET) has been established to deal with this type of credit card misuse and fraud. SET uses digital certificates to provide a means for customers to transmit their credit card details to the credit card issuer without the vendor of an online product seeing the credit card information. The X.509 standard is a predominant standard for digital certificates. One card issuer, the Visa corporation, has also developed a system to combat online fraud, using smart cards. The consumer uses their smart Visa card, with its associated identification PIN (personal identification number), to purchase products online. For example, the user views a web page and then decides to buy goods online. The user inserts the smart Visa card into a smart Visa card reader that is attached to their computer. The user is asked to enter their PIN (or password). The money is then securely transferred from the user's account to the online merchant. The website then indicates that the purchase has been securely completed.

Activity 12.5 Security standards

Outline the main security standards available in the world today. What do security standards achieve in the e-business domain? Discuss how the Secure Electronic Transaction (SET) standard for secure transactions works. What are the benefits of secure transactions on the internet? If you have ever bought anything off the web, discuss the methods and manner in which the transaction was conducted.

12.7 Internet misuse and fraudulent transactions

Successful e-business relies on customers feeling confident about using their credit and debit cards online over the internet, through the web pages of online retailers. Fraudulent transactions occur in a number of ways. The main fraudulent activity occurs through criminals trying to gather the credit card details of customers, so that they may use the customer's credit card details to buy products illegally. Many credit card issuers have software that monitors and tracks the transaction activities of customers to determine their spending habits. The software looks for patterns of user purchasing activity that is irregular and may indicate fraudulent use of the credit card.

However, most security software is aimed at preventing the credit card details from falling into the wrong hands over the web. Fraudulent activity over the internet can take many shapes and forms from e-mail scams, such as e-mails requesting bank number details, to identity theft, where someone or some organization masquerades as someone else, thus fooling people to part with secure information, such as PINs and passwords.

Fraud over the internet is sometime referred to as 'dot-cons'. Internet fraud has included:

▶ **Credit card fraud**: an online internet customer has the details of their credit card numbers and passwords illegally lifted. The credit card details are then used by criminals to buy products illegally over the Web.

▶ **Identity theft**: information on a person, or organization, is stolen and used to set up a mirror identity on the web. People are then fooled into buying non-existent products and services because they believe the website to be genuine

▶ **Investor fraud**: stocks and equity prices are artificially boosted by false company reports and company forecasts. An investor receives an e-mail detailing the imminent success of an equity price (or share price) and people start to buy the company's equity, thus raising the price. Equally, a false report can be hosted on the web to fool investors into either buying equities or selling equities.

▶ **Web auction fraud**: false auction websites are set up. The buyer does not receive the product after the auction and the vendor does not receive their money for selling the product.

In addition to fraudulent internet activities, the internet can also be misused by people claiming scientific achievements or people expounding their political views without due regard to the sensitivities of others using the web.

Activity **12.6** Internet fraud

Outline what is meant by internet fraud. What types of internet fraud exist in the world today? Is internet fraud an international problem? What measures can be put into place in organizations to combat internet fraud? Should companies have policies and standards to combat internet fraud? What legislation exists in your country or state to combat internet crime?

12.8 Biometrics, security and systems access

Biometrics is concerned with the use of automated computerized technology to identify people by their physical attributes (e.g. facial features, eye composition and fingerprints) or characteristics of behaviour. Biometrics is mainly used for security identification and authentication; it is used within the systems security environment to verify, identify and authenticate users. Metrics in computing is concerned with *measurement*. Therefore, biometrics is the process of measuring and analyzing the unique differences in individual humans and then, in the future, identifying the human being from their individualistic features and characteristics. One of the main applications of biometrics in the computing security domain is identifying humans for the purposes of authentication and system access.

The main features and attributes measured in biometrics are:

▶ **Facial features**: using digital imaging of human features to develop a facial image of a human user for the purposes of identification. This technique is mainly used as part of the security camera monitoring activities of malls and casinos. A number of casinos use facial feature recognition technology to create databases of fraudsters.

▶ **Fingerprints**: using fingerprint pattern matching. Fingerprint matching is the most common type of biometric because it is a relatively cost-effective security technique. Area access is the commonest application of the fingerprint biometric.

▶ **Hand measurement**: analyzing and measuring the shape and natural characteristics of a human's hand. The applications of hand geometry recognition include monitoring office staff movement through a building (or a security zone) and attendance monitoring.

▶ **Eye-ball features**:
  – Retina analysis: scanning and analyzing the layer of blood vessels situated at the back of the eye. The pattern, size and distribution of the blood vessels form a unique human identifier.
  – Iris analysis: analyzing features found in the coloured ring of tissue that surrounds the retinal pupil. Iris recognition techniques are less intrusive than retinal biometrics.

▶ **Voice features**:
  – Voice recognition: analyzing the wave modulation (and patterns) of a human voice.
  – Voice authentication: relying on voice-to-print authentication, whereby voice is translated to text. Voice authentication involves use of a microphone and voice translation software.

▶ **Handwriting**: analyzing handwriting and signature features. Signature features include speed, flow and pressure as well as the shape and nature of the final signature. A signature is an accepted and natural form of identification that has been used for thousands of years to identify a person and authenticate legal documents.

All these human features and physical characteristics are used to identify people. Biometric technologies are being embedded into the pervasive mobile computing world as solutions to personal verification. The applications affected include network infrastructure security, human user identification, secure data transactions and law enforcement.

Many business organizations use biometric techniques and technologies to limit or allow access to secure office environments. Within a computerized systems environment, human users can be identified by:

▶ something that is known about the user and is personal to the user (e.g. a password or PIN);

▶ possessing something tangible (e.g. security card, smart card or bank card);

▶ personal human features and characteristics (e.g. unique fingerprints or retina features).

In assessing and selecting a biometric technology a number of factors need to be considered:

▶ The technology must be easy to use and unobtrusive.

▶ The accuracy of the recognition technology must be high.

▶ Employees need to accept the technology. For example, many people are afraid and wary of having to put their face into machinery in order to get identified by retina analysis. (The equipment is similar to that used by optometrists and opticians.)

▶ The stability of technology is important. The technology must be robust and at a level of maturity and standardization that invokes user confidence.

The main applications of security biometrics are to restrict or permit access to rooms and buildings, to control virtual access within computerized systems environments, and to authenticate financial transactions. One of the advantages with biometrics is the reduced need for photograph ID cards that need to be verified by a human security guard. Most biometric technologies permit automated access and control. Biometric devices and technologies are therefore useful in environments that cannot rely on accurate security staff screening vast numbers of people, such as at a sporting event or in a sports stadium. Security biometrics is often used in association with other security technologies, such as smart cards, encryption keys and digital signatures.

Wearable computing

Early developments of *wearable computing* used devices similar to eyeglasses and wristwatches; they contained embedded computing applications, but were portable, mobile and conveniently worn on the body. More sophisticated developments of wearable computing involve implanting miniaturized devices into clothing or implanting computing devices into the human body (e.g. implanting computer devices under the skin, or into the organs of a human).

> **Did you know?**
>
> A Canadian academic named Dr Steve Mann is one of the people credited with establishing and conceptualizing the idea of wearable computing.

Examples of wearable computing for information exchange are eyeglasses with lenses that display personal data and information. This is achieved by the integration of a screen display and camera concealed in eyeglasses. Other forms of wearable computing include wrist PDAs and wristwatch videophones. These devices can store and process security software that will identify the wearer in smart space environments. Smart spaces can then identify users, their actions, and even goals, and facilitate interaction with information resources. Smart spaces can also provide data, information and audit trails of systems user activity and support distributed network environments.

Activity 12.7 Biometric identification

What is the use of biometrics in the systems security domain? What human features are analyzed by biometric systems? What are the advantages and disadvantages of the various biometric techniques and technologies? Why are some biometric techniques thought to be more 'invasive' than other techniques? What are the main applications of biometric technology within the business domain?

12.9 Attacks on computer systems

Computer security is not only directed at preventing misuse or unauthorized access; it is also concerned with preventing systems from being attacked by computer hackers and those that try to destroy systems with destructive program code called viruses. Attacks on a business computer system can cause disruption in its simplest form or total systems failure in more drastic forms. Virus attacks are very common in the twenty-first century. Fortunately, so is the availability of software to prevent virus attacks, such as firewalls and anti-virus software that destroys unwanted code in a computerized environment. Virus attacks are aimed at either destroying a computer system's ability to function, or at destroying the data and information on a system, known as *corruption of data*.

Attacks by viruses occur when destructive software is deliberately communicated to a computer system with the intention of interrupting the functioning of that system. Some viruses not only attack a single system but also collect data on e-mail addresses and then communicate the virus on to other computer systems around the world. This sort of virus is often referred to as a *worm* because it burrows into a system and then replicates itself to cause destruction in computer systems around the world. Sometimes the words virus and worm are classified separately: a virus is a destructive piece of software code that damages the data resources and functionality of a computer, while worm is a piece of software that uses up resources on a computer system, thus filling up memory and processing capacity to an extent where the computer system collapses.

> ### Did you know?
> A Trojan Horse computer virus is code that lives inside other code (and applications) and comes out into a networked system when certain conditions are fulfilled, such as a specific date or operation by a computer user.

Viruses are often placed on a computer system by being attached to e-mail messages. The e-mail is innocently read by the person receiving the message and the virus then releases itself on to the e-mail user's computer. This type of hidden virus attack on a computer system is called a *Trojan Horse*. From the first computer system, it then enters all the other computers networked to the user's computer.

Business organizations spend a great deal of money each financial year ensuring that their systems are secure from attack by hackers and viruses. Many business organizations annually lose money or business because their computer systems have been down for days or hours throughout each year due to virus attacks. The consequences of virus attack are systems that become non-operational for long periods and data corruption.

Viruses come in many types. Examples of viruses include ones that:

▶ arrive embedded in e-mail messages that overwrite data files;

▶ attack a user's websites and web pages;

▶ collect e-mail addresses, then send on the virus automatically to all addresses found on the user's networked computer;

▶ hide in the recycle bins of PCs so that they are not detected by some anti-software virus checkers;

▶ degrade computer systems performance by slowing the system down by over-using processor capacity;

▶ are deliberately targeted as a form of vendetta at certain computer software manufacturers, such as Microsoft;

▶ deliberately attack anti-virus software in order to expose computer systems to mass attack from viruses that are constantly roaming computer networks around the world.

To combat viruses many companies produce guidelines and policies that workers and employees must adhere to in their day-to-day business activities. General guidelines may stipulate that employees should:

▶ not open any e-mail messages where the sender's identity is not known;

▶ not accept e-mail attachments unless they know who sent those attachments;

▶ ensure that anti-virus software is constantly updated (however, most computer systems do this automatically when a user starts up their computer each day);

▶ not bring data files on disks or CD-ROMs from other computer systems and attempt to load the software on to their office computer;

▶ only forward e-mail messages that are from known users identified in the organization.

Many computer systems are set up not only to try to prevent virus attacks but also to deal with what is known as *denial of service* attacks over the internet. In this type of attack a website is hit with multiple requests for web pages, thus over-loading the web server. This is achieved by unscrupulous people placing hidden files on a networked computer, sometimes known as 'destructive cookies'. These files are then activated and automatically request thousands of web pages in an attempt to overload the server. This type of attack happens through LANs or, in particular, the internet. The cookies come down from the internet on to a user's computer, following a session of web browsing, and lie dormant until they are activated by a request. This type of attack relies on certain inherent vulnerabili-ties in the internet domain.

Internet *cookies* are used by many organizations to gather data on customer profiles. Although destructive cookies are dangerous and pernicious, cookies can be useful in the marketing domain of e-business. Normal, and harmless cookies are small programs that are placed on a user's computer and gather data on inter-net activity, such as which web pages a user visits. The user is then targeted with specific information on websites that may be of interest. For example, cookies can be activated by a host computer to collect information on web pages visited and keep a record of the type of information normally searched by the user. Cookies can be located remotely, on a host computer, or placed on a user's client PC or even wireless device.

What is a cookie?

A small program that is placed on a user's computer that gathers data on internet activity, such as which web pages a user visits. Cookies can also be used to store passwords and identification profiles on internet users.

Web browsers read a user's cookie files to determine their information prefer-ences and typical search profile. Many websites use cookies to gather targeted and personalized user information or to record the history of sites visited. Another use of cookies is to store passwords and identification profiles, so that a user who regularly visits a secure site does not have to keep re-entering their password or identification code each time they revisit the site. However, sometimes cookies have been used to profile the software on a user's computer or to read data off memory drives – unnecessary misuses of cookies that some users may feel are an invasion of privacy.

The misuse of the internet is often collectively referred to as *cyber-crime*. This covers crimes related to networked computer systems, the largest being the internet. Most countries have legislation to impose severe penalties on those that perpetrate cyber-crime. Pause for thought 12.2 outlines some real cases of cyber-crime and the penalties that followed conviction for cyber-crime at the start of the twenty-first century.

Activity 12.8   Computer systems attack

Outline the various forms of attack on a computer system from viruses and worms. How do these attacks occur within networked computer environments? What can business organizations do to prevent attacks on their networked computer systems through the distribution of virus-infected e-mail communications? Why do many viruses come on to computer systems from the internet?

Activity 12.9   Cookies and internet user profiling

How do cookies collect data and establish a record of a user's computing activity? Provide two reasons why cookies are used in the internet computing world. What commercial value is gained by understanding the habits and interests of internet users? What is the difference between a normal cookie, used for e-business customer profiling, and a destructive cookie?

PAUSE FOR THOUGHT 12.2

Cyber-crime and its penalties

The jailing for two years of a 22-year old virus writer in January 2003 represented a dramatic new get-tough policy on computer crime.

Simon Valler, a web designer from north Wales, in the United Kingdom, confessed to writing the 'Gokar', 'Admirer' and 'Redesi' mass-mailer viruses. The viruses infected 27,000 PCs in 42 countries – not many when compared to the tens of millions of computers infected by the 'Kournikova' worm in 2001. The author of that virus, Dutch programmer Jan de Wit, was ordered to serve 150 hours community service. And while only one person complained to police about Valler's code, dozens of people claiming losses of thousands of dollars testified for the FBI in the de Wit case. In October, de Wit appealed against his sentence – unsuccessfully – for fear the conviction would damage his career. But, as Valler can now testify, it could have been a lot worse.

Nevertheless, a poll of more than 600 business PC users by Sophos, the UK anti-virus software company, found that 46 per cent felt the punishment was not harsh enough and only 16 per cent felt it was too severe. More than 60 per cent felt a prison term was the most appropriate sentence for anyone who writes and distributes a virus.

Meanwhile, one of the world's most notorious computer criminals, Kevin Mitnick, who served five years in a United States prison for wire fraud, computer fraud and intercepting communications, completed his probation last month [January 2003] – and celebrated by surfing the web for the first time in five years.

Source: 'Businesses have little sympathy for jailed virus writer', *Information Age*, February 2003.

12.10 Cyber-crime legislation

Investigate what legislation exists in your country or state to deal with cyber-crime. What does this legislation address in the computer systems domain? Search the internet for cases and histories of computer systems attacks in recent years. What are business organizations and governments doing to fight crime and misuse of the internet? Provide two examples of cyber-crime, reported in newspapers and magazines, and discuss the nature of these activities and how these cyber-crimes affected internet users.

12.10 Chapter summary

Mobile computing uses mobile computerized devices and wireless networks to send and receive data and information. Mobile wireless computing is an important aspect of computerized systems today. Embedded technology in buildings and devices enables computing 'on the move', while mobile computing enables the mobile workforce in the business information systems environment. Wireless computer networks enable the internet to be accessed from small, hand-held devices anytime, anyplace and anywhere: internet and corporate intranet information is available on the move and from anywhere in the world.

Combining the internet with mobile phones and other wireless devices, such as wireless PDAs, enables e-business to be transformed into m-business. Accessing the internet anywhere, anytime and untethered by fixed-location wired technology (e.g. personal computers and laptops) provides business opportunity in the twenty-first century. For example, organizations are able to provide information, intranet applications and other networked computing services, based on awareness of a user's location. The resources are deployed to enhance the various benefits of mobility. Remote, wireless device users who are on the move have expectations and requirements that are different to those who are stationary.

Two types of mobility service predominate in the wireless mobile information systems domain. First, data and information can be provided on a specific geographical location (e.g. calling up a directory of restaurants in a specific location or requesting the location of bank ATM machines in the local vicinity). Second, a mobile device user can be tracked and located (i.e. via their mobile cell phone signals) to determine their specific geographical location anywhere in the world. Such location technology can be used to support location-based services to employees on the move. These are referred to as *location assets*. Figure 12.1 indicates the types of location assets found by using a wireless PDA, or other wireless device, such as a mobile cell phone, within a wireless business information systems domain.

Pervasive computing is a label used to explain the idea that computing today is available anytime, anywhere, and from any portable mobile device. Pervasive computing is a natural evolution of wired client-server networked computing. One of the benefits of pervasive computing is the fact that it can exist around us

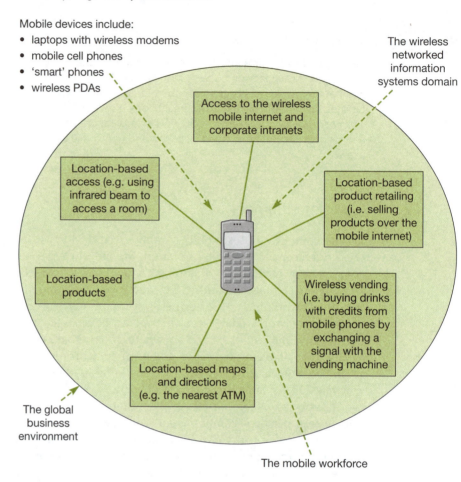

Mobile devices include:
- laptops with wireless modems
- mobile cell phones
- 'smart' phones
- wireless PDAs

The wireless networked information systems domain

Access to the wireless mobile internet and corporate intranets

Location-based access (e.g. using infrared beam to access a room)

Location-based product retailing (i.e. selling products over the mobile internet)

Location-based products

Wireless vending (i.e. buying drinks with credits from mobile phones by exchanging a signal with the vending machine

Location-based maps and directions (e.g. the nearest ATM)

The global business environment

The mobile workforce

Figure 12.1 Wireless mobile information assets

without anyone realizing it is there – it appears to be invisible. The IBM pervasive computing website states that pervasive mobile computing is:

> computing power freed from the desktop – embedded in wireless handheld device automobile telematics systems, home appliances, and commercial tools-of-the-trade. I the enterprise, it extends timely business data to workers in the field ... In our personal lives, it expands our freedom to exchange information anytime, anywhere.

The start of the twenty-first century witnessed a trend in mobile computing that will continue to grow throughout the century. Business information system will become more mobile and so more reliant on wireless information system architectures. Business organizations are developing business information systems environments that accommodate wireless information systems to support an increasingly mobile workforce.

HORT SELF-ASSESSMENT QUESTIONS

12.1   Explain what is meant by *mobile computing* and describe the main characteristics of mobile computing.

12.2   Outline the main business applications of mobile computing and describe the importance of these applications in the wireless business domain.

12.3   Define the term *pervasive computing environments* and describe how such environments provide computing capability and availability 'anytime, anywhere and in any device'.

12.4   Outline the three important qualities in pervasive computing environments and describe how each of these factors is dealt with in the business environment.

12.5   Explain the term *embedded technology* and explain why embedded devices are sometimes referred to as 'smart devices'.

12.6   Outline four areas where pervasive and embedded technology has taken hold in the twenty-first century business information systems domain.

12.7   Outline and describe the five main aspects of computer security and explain how these are dealt with in the business information systems environment.

12.8   Explain what is meant by *authentication* and describe the use of *digital signatures* in computer systems security.

12.9   Explain what is meant by *encryption* and describe the use of *public key infrastructure* (PKI) in the e-business domain.

12.10   Outline the main security standard and protocols used within computerized information systems domains.

12.11   Describe the use of the *Secure Electronic Transaction* (SET) in computer systems security for internet transactions in the e-business domain.

12.12   Explain what is meant by internet misuse and fraudulent internet activity and list two examples of fraud on the internet.

12.13   What is biometrics and how is biometrics used to identify systems users and permit access to computerized systems and locations?

12.14   Outline and describe the main human features and characteristics measured in biometrics and suggest which are the least invasive.

12.15   Outline three ways that computer systems are attacked with viruses and describe two ways that e-mail borne viruses attack a computer system.

EXTENDED STUDENT ACTIVITIES

Group-based activity   Break up into pairs of students and discuss the following:

1 Why is computer systems security so important in the business environment?

2 Why are computer systems apparently so vulnerable to attack from hackers and viruses?

3 What security and controlled access measures are put into a networked computer systems domain?

4 Why do business organizations spend so much money ensuring that their computer systems are secure from attack?

5 What policy guidelines should be adopted by employees using corporate intranets and the internet?

Individual reporting activity   Discuss the use of biometrics in systems access and security. What are the main biometric measures and what are they used for in the business systems domain? How do companies go about securing access to buildings, rooms and other resources? Can smart-room technologies help to monitor and control access to secure areas in a building? Why are biometric technologies referred to as either invasive or non-invasive? How should managers in an organization protect the real (e.g. buildings, equipment and technology) and virtual assets (e.g. data, information and networks) of the 'digital company'?

REFERENCES AND FURTHER STUDY

Books and articles   Amor, D. (2002) *Internet Future Strategies: How Pervasive Computing Will Change the World*, Prentice-Hall, ISBN: 013041803x

Chesbro, M. (2000) *Complete Guide to E-security: Using the Internet and E-mail Without Losing Your Privacy*, Paladin Press, ISBN: 1581601050

Cheswick, W.R. et al. (2003) *Firewalls and Internet Security: Repelling the Wily Hacker*, Addison-Wesley, ISBN: 020163466X

Elliott, G. (2001) 'Defining mobile commerce (M-commerce) within the business information technology domain: a case study approach', proceedings of the 11th BIT Conference, Manchester, UK, October, ISBN: 0905304381

Elliott, G. and Phillips N. (2004) *Mobile Commerce and Wireless Computing Systems*, Addison-Wesley, ISBN: 0201752409

Jones, K. and Johnson, B. (2002) *Anti-hacker Toolkit: Key Security Tools and Configuration Techniques*, Osborne McGraw-Hill, ISBN: 0072222824

Kerry, J. (1998) *The New War: The Web of Crime That Threatens America's Security*, Simon Schuster, ISBN: 0684846144

May, P. (2001) *Mobile Commerce: Opportunities, Applications and Technologies of Wireless Business*, Cambridge University Press, ISBN: 052179756x

McKeown, P. (2003) *Information Technology and the Networked Economy*, Thomson Course Technology, ISBN: 003034851x

Merritt, M. and Pollino, D. (2002) *Wireless Security*, Osborne McGraw-Hill, ISBN: 0072222867

Oppliger, R. (2002) *Internet and Intranet Security*, Artech House, ISBN: 1580531660

Singh, S. (2000) *The Code Book: The Secret History of Codes and Code-breaking*, Fourth Estate, ISBN: 1857028899

Singh, S. (2002) *The Code Book: How to Make It, Break It, Hack It, or Crack It*, Delacorte Press, ISBN: 0385729138

Stoll, C. (2000) *The Cuckoo's Egg: Tracking a Spy Through the Maze of Computer Espionage*, Pocket Books, ISBN: 0743411463

Swaminatha, T. and Elden, C. (2002) *Wireless Security and Privacy: Best Practices and Design Techniques*, Addison-Wesley, ISBN: 0201760347

Wall, D.S. (2001) *Crime and the Internet: Cyber-crimes and Cyber-fears*, Routledge, ISBN: 0415244293

Wayman, J. (ed.) et al. (2002) *Biometric Systems: Technology, Design and Performance Evaluation*, Springer-Verlag, ISBN: 1852335963

Journals

Journal of the International Biometric Society

Journal of Mobile and Ubiquitous Pervasive Computing

Web resources

Pretty Good Privacy (PGP) (global) – promotes the use of Pretty Good Privacy.
www.pgpi.org

Biometric Consortium (USA/global) – a consortium set up to bring biometric technology and users together.
www.biometrics.org

International Standards Organization (global) – telecommunications and network standards.
www.iso.org

IBM pervasive computing website (USA/global) – development in pervasive computing.
www.ibm.com/software/pervasive

Global Mobile Commerce Forum (global) – organization promoting mobile commerce.
www.gmcforum.com

Case study
Information systems analysis, design, implementation and evaluation within the business environment

'The whole is greater than the sum of its parts' (Aristotle, 384–322 BC)

Learning outcomes When you have studied this chapter you will be able to:

▶ work in groups and solve information-systems-related problems within the business environment;

▶ develop a confident knowledge of the scope of networked and integrated ICT environments;

▶ advise on ICT configuration and infrastructure within a business information systems domain;

▶ apply information systems theory and project management ideas within the business environment;

▶ demonstrate an ability to analyze global information systems problems and convey solutions;

▶ link information systems theory to information systems practice in the modern business systems domain.

13.1 Introduction to the case study

The basis of a programme of study in information systems is the ability to integrate a number of discrete business, computing and IT disciplines. This chapter sets out to integrate the various academic disciplines and skills, explored in the previous 12 chapters, into a holistic project. The modern emphasis within business information systems is on end-user information systems development which eliminates the historic need for specific task-related intermediaries such as proprietary programmers and business systems analysts; these two roles are therefore often merged into one role within the modern business systems environment. Careers and job descriptions within the business information systems environment have, through business evolution and technological change, seen an increasing movement away from demarcation in computer-based tasks. Nations require trained and educated ICT specialists who possess a broad vision of how ICT integrates into a business organization, and possess the ability to adapt to dynamic internal and external forces within the business environment.

This case study unit should be used to gain expertise in the analysis, design, implementation and evaluation of information systems and ICT within global business organizations. The case study will develop an understanding of the integration of software applications, information technology, and information systems theory, to form a body of knowledge capable of delivering ICT solutions to general or specific business systems problems. This necessitates not only understanding information systems but also the application of information and communications technology to solve business systems problems. You should see this case study as a systems and ICT project that provides an understanding of the various skills and disciplines studied throughout this book.

13.2 Student remit and requirements

Students using this case study should aim to deepen their understanding of the development and integration of ICT in the following areas:

▶ information systems (IS)

▶ information technology (IT)

▶ networked computing systems environments

▶ information systems development frameworks and methodologies

▶ information systems theory and practice

▶ information and communication technology (ICT) integration and strategy

▶ software and hardware application within fourth generation development environments

▶ project team management and group dynamics

▶ information systems and technology literacy.

The integration of these various disciplines should be focused on achieving a given business goal or set of business objectives.

For the purposes of this case study, students should take on the role of a business information technology specialist or consultant brought into an organization to solve a number of hard and soft business information systems problems as elicited by the case study. This will entail careful reading and absorption of the case study. Students will be required to:

▶ review the position of the company within the business environment;

▶ analyze specific and suggested hard and soft ICT problems;

▶ recommend solutions to achieve company-bound objectives and goals;

▶ use a development methodology to analyze and design appropriate business systems;

▶ use a development framework and tools to implement and evaluate systems;

▶ recommend and integrate software applications and ICT to meet end-user requirements;

▶ present findings as if delivered to the business organization's chief executive officer (CEO).

The evolution of the project should use a systems development methodology as a guiding framework, such as the traditional information systems development life cycle (SDLC), rapid applications development (RAD), dynamic systems development method (DSDM), prototyping or another related methodology. However, you must be careful to justify the use of the methodology chosen in terms of its appropriateness and suitability to the case study scenario.

It is recommended that the case study be undertaken in groups of two, three or four students. Any more than four students would dilute the meaning and purpose of the exercise. However, if the case study is used as an individual activity this is still appropriate, although the final outcome will not be able to address fully issues of group dynamics and group management. If the case study is tackled in groups, then it is strongly recommended that additional skills such as minute taking and apportionment of team member roles and responsibilities be established. The case study could then be used as a vehicle for assessing group dynamics and other softer group-based communication skills. These skills are a valuable asset to any computer-oriented professional working in the business environment where human and technology communication skills are of paramount importance. Pause for thought 13.1 outlines the importance of good communications skills for career progression within the business environment.

The formation of working groups is a common occurrence in the business world. Working groups are formed to achieve a specific or desired outcomes that cannot be achieved by an individual's isolated effort. The successful operation of group dynamics is therefore an essential feature of the ICT domain. Part of the assessment criteria of this case study should have regard to the way a group manages and controls the development of the case study. Groups with a common objective offer an enriched learning experience and, on the basis of the systems theory premise that 'the sum is greater than the parts', group work can enhance the group's overall knowledge and understanding of the subject matter. Therefore, the ability to collaborate to achieve a given objective is an important skill to acquire. In addition to working in groups, the ability to provide technical advice and expertise and to communicate ideas and solutions to an ICT problem are essential qualities in the profile of any business information technology specialist.

The case study project groups can, if desired, make a team presentation in the presence of any other project groups undertaking the same project. It is suggested that the presentations should be of a maximum 15 minutes in length, and groups should be encouraged to use relevant communication and presentation techniques (e.g. slides, hand-outs, OHPs, screen show, graphics etc.). However, the presentations should be delivered as if to the chief executive officer (CEO) of the client firm.

PAUSE FOR THOUGHT 13.1

Are you ready for ICT?

The type of companies offering jobs in ICT now include not only the traditional software and hardware vendors but almost every other type of organization, from advertising to marketing and from tourism to publishing. Although there are plenty of vacancies it seems that not enough people with the right skills are putting themselves forward.

The ICT systems sub-committee of the Association of Graduate Careers Advisory Services, AGCAS, in the UK, looked into the whole area of what employers want and what students expect from ICT jobs. Tom Franks, careers adviser at Birmingham University, says that there is a popular misconception among many undergraduates that an ICT job means having an ICT degree and being tied to the computer screen when, in reality the majority of jobs are 'people-focused' jobs. An international report on *Skills for Graduates in the 21st Century* identified why graduates sometimes do not get the best ICT jobs:

▶ their personal communication skills are weak;
▶ their ability to work in groups is weak;
▶ their ability to write coherent reports under time pressure is weak;
▶ they find complex systems analysis a difficult problem;
▶ they are not good at arranging their time.

This case study will determine whether you can prove that these weaknesses do not affect you!

13.3 The integration of ICT theory and practice

The case study should act as an integrating assignment, incorporating the knowledge acquired over the previous 12 chapters. It contains the following information on Norman Payne Enterprises:

▶ business history
▶ trading interests and market characteristics
▶ information and communication infrastructure
▶ management and systems structure
▶ existing manual and ICT-based information systems
▶ corporate plans and future requirements.

The nature of downsizing and decentralization within the business environment has led to more information-systems-related activities being undertaken through the formulation and management of task-specific project groups. Consequently, the softer skills of project team management, control and coordination are central to the ethos of ICT. The Norman Payne case study attempts to abstract a real-world situation that is characterized by hard and soft information requirements.

The Norman Payne case study aims to develop the capability to identify, analyze and solve a set of business information technology problems that are characteristic of the type facing large and small organizations within the business environment. It is suggested that the project should be developed with reference to the *5-I Model* which emphasizes how most business systems problems require inspirational thought and creative ideas. Business systems problems cannot usually be solved by the application of inflexible or prescriptive solutions. Therefore, the application of ICT principles and disciplines within the business environment requires a significant level of innovation. The strands of the 5-I Model are as follows:

▶ independence (of project management)

▶ identification (of problem areas)

▶ integration (of disciplines, tools and techniques)

▶ implementation (of the project and delivery of outcomes)

▶ inspiration (of thought and attitude to solving an ICT problem).

The case study is intended as a means of integrating various theoretical and practical subjects, and to provide a vehicle for developing skills in business information systems engineering.

13.4 Case study outcomes

The case study aims to provide the knowledge and skills set required for a rounded understanding of the use and application of ICT within the business environment. This will necessitate acting as a conduit between the disciplines of ICT and business, translating the information requirements of the business environment into usable business systems. We understand from a socio-technical perspective that business information systems involve people, organization and technology. Therefore, those engaged in applying business information technology theory and practice must be able to:

▶ work with a variety of information technology and understand the environments and disciplines necessary for the development of integrated business information systems;

▶ communicate effectively and understand the requirements of different business activities and sector-specific procedures and practices;

▶ analyze, design, implement and evaluate ICT-based business information systems within different commercial or organizational constraints;

▶ understand the business environment and the range of disciplines necessary for the development of software-based information systems;

▶ establish information systems within the business environment for strategic, managerial and operational decision making;

▶ manage, control and coordinate ICT-based information systems projects and other related business resources;

▶ recommend, plan and apply appropriate hardware and software applications within a business organization and provide advice on the connectivity and integration of information technology;

▶ perform a knowledgeable liaison role, effectively linking the business domain to the computing and ICT domain within the business environment;

▶ evaluate and determine areas where information systems and information technology might be used to achieve a competitive advantage within the business environment;

▶ establish information requirements for an organization and develop a specification for business information requirements within a business.

13.5 Management and human decision making

The case study illustrates how the fundamental premise of business information systems is that business is a human activity system, which relies on decision making of all forms and at all levels of the organization. Decision-making activity within the business environment is normally supported by information systems. The effectiveness and efficiency of these information systems allow an organization to compete and, in many cases, can often provide a competitive edge within the environment in which business activity and decision making take place.

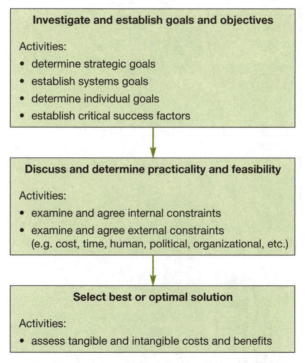

The process of making decisions can be separated into three generic stages. The decision-making philosophy that pervades a business organisation may span the spectrum from autocratic to democratic. Nevertheless, it is essential that the underlying decision-making process concludes with selection of the best, or optimal, solution. It is then important to follow decision making by putting into place within the business environment the control mechanisms to deliver the decision.

Figure 13.1 The process of making decisions

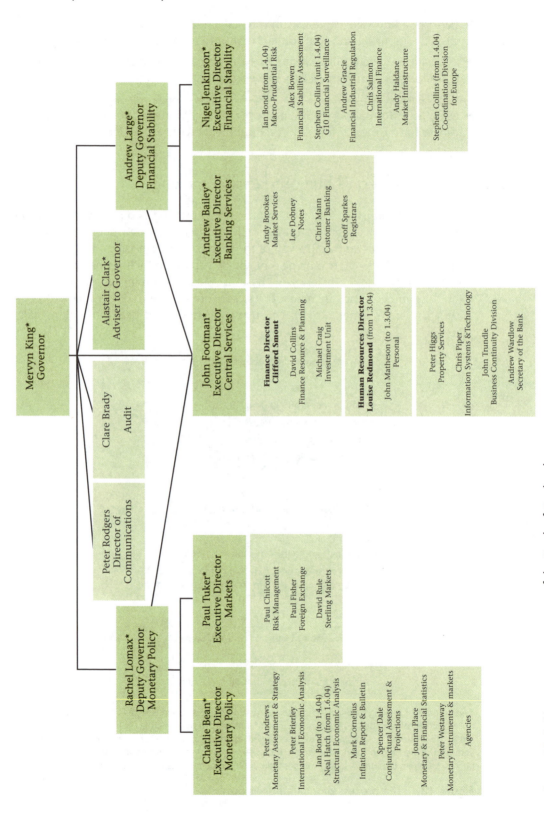

Figure 13.2 Management structure of the Bank of England

*Members of the executive team
Source: ©Bank of England (www.bankofengland.co.uk)

The process of making decisions can be separated into three generic stages. This process is illustrated in Figure 13.1. Earlier chapters have stressed the importance of understanding the nature of decision making within the three generic levels (operational, managerial and strategic) of the organizational hierarchy. The rigidity of an organizational structure will depend upon the culture (or ethos) of the business organization. For example, Figure 13.2 shows the hierarchical management structure that once operated in the Bank of England. The organizational schema shows the lines of authority that existed in the Bank of England. Organizational structures need not be as rigid as that for the Bank of England. Nevertheless, organizational structure often affects the way in which ICT is incorporated into the business environment.

The decision-making philosophy that pervades a business organization can be autocratic or democratic. Nevertheless, it is essential that the decision-making process concludes with the selection of the best solution. It is then important to put into place the *control mechanisms* to deliver the decision. The effective application of management is essential for the control of an organization's three main resources of people, technology and organization. It is the activity of management that is concerned with coordinating and directing the human, technological and financial resources of an organization. Some of the earliest academic work in the area of management science and organizational behaviour was by a French industrialist named Henri Fayol. Fayol's definition of management is still used as the fundamental basis of modern management science and the foundation for many academic courses on management.

Did you know?

Henri Fayol (1841–1925) was one of the founding fathers of management science. Fayol said that 'to manage is to forecast and plan, to organize, to command, to coordinate and to control'.

Henri Fayol described 14 general principles of management that were concerned with management lines of authority and organizational behaviour – these principles are outlined in Figure 13.3. These principles can be utilized and absorbed into all aspects of management and control within the business environment. For instance, the ideas of Fayol form the basis of the planning, decision making and control life cycle studied earlier in this book.

Fayol's principles are a classical approach to management within organizational boundaries. However, not all these principles are recognized as desirable within the context of modern business organizations, particularly the notion of rigid structure for lines of authority and the division of labour. Many organizations operate within flatter (non-hierarchical structures) that devolve much responsibility for decision making to individuals, rather than maintaining a centralized authority. Many of the classical principles also ignore the humanistic aspects of modern ICT within business organizations. Modern approaches to management highlight the human relations aspect of business and recognize the fact that business is a human activity system.

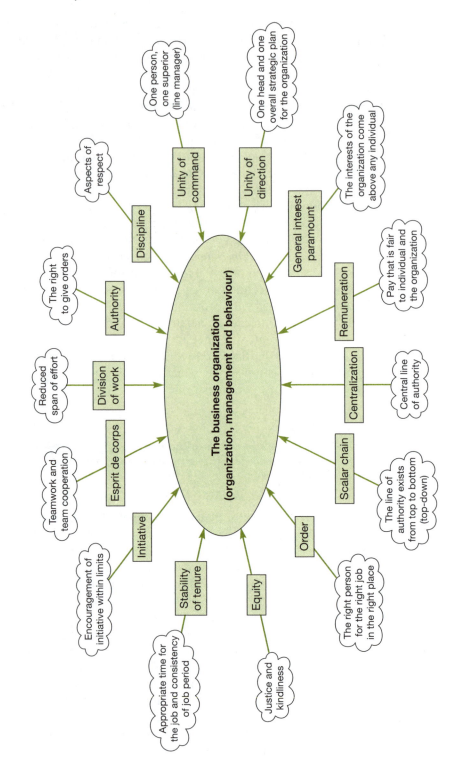

Figure 13.3 Henri Fayol's fourteen principles of management

Source: Fayol, 1949.

CASE STUDY: NORMAN PAYNE ENTERPRISES

Norman Payne Enterprises

100 Enterprise Buildings
Free Trade Road
London

BIT Consultants
Technopark
Farsighted Road
London

5 January

Dear Consultant,

We are inviting your firm of ICT consultants to submit a proposal for the development of the following systems and procedures within our international organization:

1 An ICT-based human resources system.
2 An ICT-based marketing information system.

We would also like you to carry out an investigation and analysis of the following:

1 The cost and benefit of a weekly newsletter.
2 Improved logistical distribution and shipping systems.
3 Improved sales order processing and purchase order processing systems.

Our company has been trading since 1964 and the number of staff employed by our organization has increased from 4 to 15 304, employed in 14 countries. We now feel that our present systems are inadequate to meet the needs of our continually expanding organization.

Your proposal should include detailed system and technical specifications, as well as the associated development and equipment purchase costs. The proposal should also include a review of the organization's business systems to ensure that the business is operating efficiently and effectively.

Your response should reach our offices no later than 1 March. Please do not hesitate to contact me if you require further information.

Yours sincerely,

Norman Payne
President and CEO
Norman Payne Enterprises

Intelligence report – Norman Payne Enterprises

Norman Payne established Norman Payne Enterprises in 1964. In 1996 the company went public and now shares for the company are quoted on the UK Stock Market and the New York exchange. The shares currently trade at $2.00 each. In 1990 Mr Payne was awarded the honour of 'Businessman of the Year' by the Confederation of British and American Industry (CBAI). Norman Payne Enterprises has branch offices in Rome, Paris, New York, Los Angeles and Lagos, Nigeria. A strategic review of operations in 2004 suggested that any future expansion of the business organization would only take place by targeting overseas customers. However, it is the view of Mr Payne that the marketing division of the company has failed to attract overseas customers because of its outdated marketing methods and techniques. Mr Payne believes that the development and integration of an improved, ICT-based marketing information system may address some of these apparent underlying problems.

In a major strategic review of operations, in 2004, the following areas of concern were highlighted:

▶ The marketing division was failing to target a suitable level of customers and to meet its performance standards. However, what these performance standards were is a matter of debate.

▶ The company operates a hierarchical organization structure, with few responsibilities devolved to divisional heads.

The business organization known as Norman Payne Enterprises has two main trading strands that overlap in certain areas:

▶ Buying, selling and fitting of shop fixtures and fittings, including the supply of refurbished business machines and other business organizational equipment.

▶ Auctioning of bankrupt office equipment and fixtures and fittings from premises in Kent, England, and Queens, New York.

Despite the recession, the organization has succeeded in remaining marginally profitable, although profit margins have been squeezed by the high level of costs incurred in the organization's trading operations. The business is computerized in certain areas but not in other areas and there is a concern that the systems that exist are not fully integrated within the business organization. Furthermore, the use and understanding of IT within the business organization is limited. The sales order processing system and purchase order processing systems were updated and computerized in January 1999. The payment of staff salaries has been computerized since 1991.

In August 2000 the organization recruited a marketing consultant from a top advertising firm. The initial improvement in the marketing operations widened the customer base of the organization on a global scale. However, most areas of the organization do not have the benefit of ICT and still rely on old manual systems and procedures. These systems have fuzzy boundaries and staff are often employed in various areas as and when required, with little need for task specialization. In an attempt to keep all his employees informed of the organization's practices, procedures and future direction, Mr Payne believes that the organization should have an employee newsletter of facts and figures. The type of information requirements of the newsletter have yet to be determined. However, Mr Payne has suggested that the newsletter should not be 'chatty', but should be factual and distributed to all employees around the world on a weekly basis (an obvious logistical headache!). The establishment of an organizational newsletter may help to unite the international divisions, and publicize overall business strategy.

In a major review of operations with his executive board, Mr Payne highlighted the following areas of concern within the organization:

▶ the human resources system

▶ telecommunications between international branch offices

▶ the dissemination of information between branch offices across the globe

▶ the distribution of material and goods between branch offices

▶ general integration and linkage of systems within the organization

▶ failure to exploit marketing opportunities and other business advantages.

The function of marketing within Norman Payne Enterprises is concerned with the planning, promotion and sale of products in existing markets, and the development of new products and new markets to serve present and potential customers better. Thus, marketing performs a vital function in the operation of the business organization. Strategic, tactical and operational information systems assist the marketing managers in product planning, pricing decisions, advertising and sales promotion strategies and expenditures, forecasting market potential for new and present products, and determining channels of distribution. Collateral reporting systems support the efforts of marketing managers to control the efficiency and effectiveness of the selling and distribution of products and services.

The human resources system

Norman Payne Enterprises requires an ICT-based human resources system to be developed covering all divisions within the organization on a global scale. The exact content of personnel information will vary from one business division to another, but there a number of items that will always be present (e.g. name, address, telephone number, details of next of kin, unique employee number). Other items are required so that forms required for government departments can be completed (e.g. number of registered disabled employed). Like all organizations, Norman Payne Enterprises is legally bound to keep details of pay, income tax and other information for all staff.

A brief study of Norman Payne Enterprises, in December 2003, found that individuals kept some records of their own for the staff for which they were responsible. These, however, would not be the same as those kept by the personnel department and, in some cases, the personnel department would not keep the same details. For example, the person responsible for booking training courses would keep full details of all courses attended by any member of staff while the personnel staff would only record the dates and titles of the courses. Discrepancies of information flows need to be sorted out quickly to reduce data redundancy in the organization.

PAUSE FOR THOUGHT 13.2

Human resources management

The human resource management function in organizations involves the recruitment, placement, evaluation, compensation, and development of the employees of an organization. Originally, businesses used computer-based information systems to produce paychecks and payroll reports, maintain personnel records, and analyze the use of personnel in business operations. Many business organizations have gone beyond these traditional functions and have developed human resource information systems (HRIS), which also support:

▶ recruitment, selection and hiring
▶ job placement
▶ performance appraisals
▶ employee benefits analysis
▶ training and development
▶ health, safety, and security.

Human resource information systems support the concept of human resource management. This business function emphasizes:

▶ planning, to meet the individual needs of the business;
▶ development of employees to their full potential;
▶ control of all personnel policies and programmes.

The goal of human resource management is the effective and efficient use of the human resources of a company.

The human resource management system within Norman Payne Enterprises has one central office in London with only 35 members of staff located there and all the other staff working in the various other branches and sites around the world. The personnel office currently finds it very difficult to arrange meetings of various groups of staff because the central office does not normally keep information about holidays with the exception of breaks of one or more weeks. As it is not always possible to speak to staff during normal office hours unless they contact the central office during the day, it sometimes takes three or four days before a meeting can be finalized. It has recently become important that the staff at the central office be able to identify qualified (trained) staff as quickly as possible to fill areas with a skills short-fall. It is suggested that the human resources system should be able to provide:

▶ the necessary links with the existing payroll system;
▶ details of training courses attended (and planned) as part of individual staff development programmes.

Certain activities can cause extra strain on the human resources system at particular times of the year. One example of this is salary reviews; since these tend to occur towards the end of March each year, a change could be expected for each employee at about this time. The system should require minimal staff internal re-education or training. Training may have to be outsourced.

PAUSE FOR THOUGHT 13.3

Effective information systems

Some of the major applications of information systems that support human resource management in organizations are:

▶ **Staffing**: recording and tracking human resources through personnel record-keeping, skills inventories, and personnel requirements forecasting.
▶ **Training and development**: planning and monitoring employee recruitment, training, performance appraisals and career development.
▶ **Compensation**: analyzing, planning, and monitoring policies for employee wages, salaries, incentive payments and fringe benefits.
▶ **Governmental reporting**: reporting to government bodies concerning equal opportunity policies and statistics, employee health, workplace accidents and hazards, safety procedures, and so on.

Changes in job assignments and compensation, or hiring and termination, are examples of information that would be used to update the personnel database.

Personnel requirements forecasting is important to ensure that a business organization has an adequate supply of high-quality human resources. Information is required of personnel requirements in each major employment category for various company departments or for new projects and other ventures being planned by management. Team composition must have regard not only to the skills set of each member, but also the personality and softer attributes of each member of the team.

Efficient and effective information systems help managers plan and monitor employee recruitment, training, and development programmes by analyzing the success history of present programmes. They can also be used to address the career development status of each employee to determine whether development methods such as training programmes and periodic performance appraisals should be recommended.

Networking links

It is suggested that with the introduction of a computerized human resources system Norman Payne Enterprises could keep one central personnel record for each member of staff. However, because it is possible to network many terminals to the computer used in the personnel section, other members of staff could also use the information without having to remove it from its central location. It is also suggested that a specialist business IT consultancy firm be employed to advise on the establishment of an effective and efficient human resources system.

The nature of data security and privacy also needs to be addressed. As a large business organization, Norman Payne Enterprises will often have many terminals connected into the system, and staff could be given user numbers and passwords to allow them to use the section(s) of data related to their jobs while, at the same time, they will not be allowed to look at (view) or update data that is not related to their job function. Other functions such as word-processing, e-mail and diary arrangements can easily be linked into this system, as well as the more normal links to other business information systems. This is known as systems integration.

The methods used for such ICT network links will depend largely on the location of the various members of staff, as some firms have all (or most of) their staff located in one office block while other firms have their staff located in many separate offices.

There is a need to investigate the appropriateness of local area networks (LANs) and wide area networks (WANs) within the organizational boundaries of Norman Payne Enterprises. Should the company use internet technology within an intranet environment? Staff are located in many separate sites across the globe and the major advantages of a central integrated system would be that information could be obtained very quickly and collectively.

The newsletter

Mr Payne requires the newsletter to be short and to the point. However, it must contain a balance of hard facts for operational purposes along with personnel news (such as promotions, staff training courses, social events, etc.). The newsletter will be used as a vehicle to communicate facts to the divisions around the world. This will save time and money spent communicating general information on an individual basis. The newsletter should be linked to the organization's human resources system. However, Mr Payne would accept advice on the exact relationship of the newsletter within the organization's integrated information systems as a whole. The hard information requirements of the newsletter include:

▶ delivery dates and times for overseas divisions
▶ work scheduling details
▶ staff scheduling and task changes
▶ reporting structures
▶ information on strategic direction.

Mr Payne suggests that a newsletter with colour graphics would be preferable to a text newsletter, as long as the benefits outweighed the costs. He is also excited about the prospect of possibly putting the newsletter on the web. Many of the competitors of Norman Payne Enterprises already have their own web pages. Could Norman Payne Enterprises transact business over the web?

Improved sales and distribution systems

Currently, Norman Payne Enterprises ships goods to overseas divisions using various sea and air carriers. It has its own cargo plane to ship goods around the world. It also uses a fleet of seven long-distance container trucks.

PAUSE FOR THOUGHT 13.4

Road haulage

Road haulage is the dominant mode of transport used by most business organizations. Such systems consider:

- ▶ vehicle route/load-planning systems
- ▶ fleet management systems
- ▶ tachograph analysis
- ▶ on-board computers
- ▶ fuel management systems
- ▶ on-board communications.

Business organizations are often faced with the problem of optimizing the use of a vehicle fleet to meet a given delivery workload. Determining the optimum route for each vehicle is only a very small part of this problem. It also involves determining which deliveries are allocated to each vehicle. This normally means taking account of the weight and volume of goods for each delivery, as well as its location. Frequently there are also other constraints, such as specific agreed times or 'bookings' for particular deliveries, or early closing days. Finally, not all organizations aim for service levels requiring all available orders to be delivered each day, so that a separate decision has to be made on which orders to include on loads today, and which to defer. Road network databases are now available for most countries in the developed world, and certainly for most countries in Western Europe. Transport operators can pay separately for a license to use most such databases. However, it is far more common for them to buy or rent a route-planning package, including the use of the relevant road network databases.

Norman Payne Enterprises would like to link some of the functions of distribution into its proposed website. For example, the monthly auction catalogue will be placed on the website for customers to browse and view the items to be auctioned. Could the site utilize EFT and EDI technology to conduct business transactions?

Norman Payne Enterprises is also considering automating the sales function, particularly with regard to its team of 50 sales agents within the UK and abroad. In many business organizations the sales force is fitted out with laptop computers, hand-held PCs, or even pen-based tablet computers. This not only increases the personal productivity of sales people, but dramatically speeds up the capture and analysis of sales data from the field to marketing managers at company headquarters. In return, it allows marketing and management to improve the support they provide to their sales people.

Therefore, for Norman Payne Enterprises, salesforce automation may be a way to gain a strategic advantage in sales productivity and marketing responsiveness. For example, sales people could use their desktop PCs to record sales data as they make their calls on customers and prospects during the day. Then each night sales reps in the field could connect their computers by modem and telephone links to the mainframe computer at company headquarters and upload information on sales orders, sales calls, and other sales statistics, as well as send electronic mail messages and other queries. In return, the host computer may download product availability data, information on good sales prospects, e-mail messages, and other sales support information.

Product managers at Norman Payne Enterprises need information to plan and control the performances of specific products, product lines, and brands. Computers could help provide price, revenue, cost, and growth information for existing products and new product development. Information and analysis for pricing decisions is a major function of the sales and marketing system. Information is also needed on the manufacturing and distribution resources required by proposed products. Computer-based models may be used to evaluate the performances of current products and the prospects for success of proposed products.

Marketing managers at Norman Payne Enterprises need information to help them achieve sales objectives at the lowest possible costs for advertising and promotion. Computers could be used for analyzing market research information and promotion models to help:

▶ select media and promotional methods;

▶ allocate financial resources;

▶ control and evaluate the results of various advertising and promotion campaigns.

For example, a marketing analyst may develop an electronic spreadsheet model to analyze the sales response of advertising placed in a variety of media.

PAUSE FOR THOUGHT 13.5

Marketing information systems

The basic functions of sales forecasting can be grouped into the two categories of short-range forecasting and long-range forecasting. Short-range forecasting deals with forecasts of sales for periods up to one year, whereas long-range forecasting is concerned with sales forecasts for a year or more into the future. Managers use market research data, historical sales data, promotion plans, and statistical forecasting models to generate short-range and long-range sales forecasts.

A marketing information system often provides marketing intelligence to help managers make more effective marketing decisions. It also provides marketing managers with information to help them plan and control the market research projects of a business organization. IT often assists the market research activity collect, analyze and maintain an enormous amount of information on a wide variety of market variables that are subject to continual change, including information on customers, prospects, consumers and competitors. Market, economic and demographic trends are also analyzed. Data can be purchased in computer-readable form from external sources, or from gathering data through telemarketing and computer-aided telephone interviewing techniques. Finally, statistical analysis software packages help managers analyze market research data and spot important marketing trends.

Marketing managers use computer-based information systems to develop short-range and long-range plans outlining product sales, profit and growth objectives. They also provide feedback and analysis concerning performance-versus-plan for each area of marketing. The use of variances is an important area of management control. Computer-based marketing models in decision support systems and expert systems are also being used to investigate the effects of alternative marketing plans. In addition, the fast capture of sales and marketing data by salesforce automation systems helps marketing management respond faster to market shifts and sales performance trends and develop more timely marketing strategies.

Current objectives

The following summarizes the goals of six particular information systems found within Norman Payne Enterprises. However, there is concern that the goals and characteristics of these business systems may change if the business organization applies a drastic business process re-engineering (BPR) approach to the holistic integration of business information systems within Norman Payne Enterprises.

▶ **Sales order processing**: an important transaction processing system within Norman Payne Enterprises that captures and processes customer orders and produces invoices for customers. This data is needed for sales analysis and stock control. In many business organizations, it also keeps track of the status of customer orders until goods are delivered. Computer-based electronic data interchange (EDI) of the sales order processing system provides a fast, accurate and efficient method of recording and screening customer orders and sales transactions. EDI is also used to automate the purchase order processing system. Norman Payne Enterprises is trying to establish whether it is possible to merge the two business functions of sales order processing and purchase order processing within one IT-based structure.

▶ **Stock control systems**: process data reflecting changes to items in stock. Once data about customer orders is received from an order processing system, an IT-based stock control system records changes to stock levels and prepares appropriate shipping documents. Then it may notify managers about items that need reordering and provide them with a variety of inventory status reports. Computer-based inventory control systems thus help a business provide a high-quality service to customers while minimizing investment in stock and stock holding costs.

▶ **The accounts receivable process**: part of the financial accounting system which keep records of amounts owed by customers from data generated by customer purchases and payments. The system produces monthly customer statements and credit management reports. ICT-based accounts receivable systems stimulate prompt customer payments by preparing accurate and timely invoices and monthly statements to credit customers. They provide managers with reports to help them control the amount of credit extended and the collection of money owed. This activity helps to maximize profitable credit sales while minimizing losses from bad debts.

▶ **The accounts payable process**: keeps track of data concerning purchases from and payments to suppliers. The system prepares cheques in payment of outstanding invoices and produces cash management reports. ICT-based accounts payable systems help ensure prompt and accurate payment of suppliers to maintain good relationships, ensure a good credit standing, and secure any discounts offered for prompt payment. The system provides tight financial control over all cash disbursements of the business organization. It also provides management with information needed for the analysis of payments, expenses, purchases, employee expense accounts and cash requirements.

▶ **The payroll process**: receives and maintains data from employee time cards and other work records. It produces paychecks and other documents, such as earning statements, payroll reports and labour analysis reports. Other report are also prepared for management and government agencies. ICT-based pay roll systems help businesses make prompt and accurate payments to thei employees, as well as reports to management, employees and governmen agencies concerning earnings, taxes and other deductions. They may also pro vide management with reports analyzing labour costs and productivity.

▶ **The general ledger**: consolidates data received from accounts receivable accounts payable, payroll and other accounting information systems. At the end of each accounting period, it 'closes the books' of a business and produce the general ledger trial balance, the income statement and balance sheet of the firm, and various income and expense reports for management. ICT-based gen eral ledger systems help business organizations accomplish these accounting tasks in an accurate and timely manner. They typically provide better financia controls and management reports and involve fewer personnel and lower cost than manual accounting methods.

In general, business information systems support all areas and hierarchica levels of Norman Payne Enterprises through a variety of ICT-based operational management and strategic information systems.

Written report

It is suggested that your written report should have the following structure (which should only be used as an indicative guide):

1 preamble or abstract
2 project specifications
3 business systems and user requirements
4 problems and conflicts
5 analysis and design
6 implementation and evaluation
7 recommendations and conclusions.

Your report is eagerly anticipated!

EXTENDED STUDENT ACTIVITIES

Return on investment
Stock and equity markets, such as the Dow Jones and the London Stock Market, separate companies into related areas governed by the nature of the business: these are referred to as industry sectors. Examples include technology sector stocks and equities, oil and gas sector stocks and equities and engineering sector stocks and equities. Each sector is expected to provide a return on investment in terms of resources utilized.

Some industry sectors have a higher expected return on resources than other sectors. The resources of an organization are known as its assets. Assets are purchased and managed by a business organization with the intention of producing a profit. The level of profit related to the initial investment in resources can be considered the return on investment for the business organization. The return on investment can be calculated by a ratio of the total value of assets to the profit generated from those assets.

Example
SouthWest Enterprises is a small engineering company located in Nevada, in the USA. The company has five staff and assets that can be separated into buildings, vehicles, plant and machinery, and investment in information systems and information technology. For the previous financial year the business made a profit of $60 000. The investment costs of the business were as follows:

	$
Buildings	40 000
Vehicles	12 000
Plant and machinery	33 000
Information technology	15 000
Employees costs	20 000
Total	*120 000*

In this example the return on investment would be $60 000/$120 000 = 0.5 or 50 per cent. This indicates that 50 per cent of the value of the resources of the business are returned as profit. Therefore, for every $1 spent on resources (assets) there is a return of 50 cents.

Individual reporting activity 1
Discuss how ICT can improve the return on investment within a business organization. Describe the underlying nature of the business base of the top ten performing ICT corporations in your home country. Investigate and discuss the types of products and the types of markets within which these business organizations operate.

Individual reporting activity 2
The profit made by Paisley Corporation is $40 000 for the previous financial year. What is the return on the ICT investment undertaken by the business? The investment costs of the business are:

	$
Buildings	90 000
Vehicles	20 000
Plant and machinery	40 000
Information technology	20 000
Employees costs	30 000
Total	*200 000*

REFERENCES AND FURTHER STUDY

Books Cadle, J. and Yeates, D. (2001) *Project Management for Information Systems*, FT Prentice Hall, ISBN: 0273651455

Fayol, H. (1949) *General and Industrial Management*, trans. by Constance Storrs, Pitman.

Futrell, R.T. et al. (2002) *Quality Software Project Management*, Prentice Hall PTR, ISBN: 0130912972

Henry, J. (2003) *Software Project Management: A Real World Guide to Success*, Addison-Wesley, ISBN: 032122342x

McMahon, P.E. (2001) *Virtual Project Management: Software Solutions for Today and the Future,* CRC Press, ISBN: 1574442988

Whitehead, R. (2001) *Managing a Software Development Team*, Addison-Wesley, ISBN: 0201675269

IT outsourcing study questionnaire

1 COMPANY INFORMATION

Company name _____

Address _____

Tel no: _____ Fax no: _____

Name of participant _____ Position _____ Reporting to: _____

How many people does your company employ?

In total within the UK _____

In IT _____

What is the core business of your company? _____

Are you directly responsible for outsourcing strategy? YES/NO

Are you currently using outsourcing for any IT functions? YES/NO
(IF NO – GO TO QUESTION 11)

2 EQUIPMENT TRANSFERRED

Please identify the equipment type and how currently used:

Please tick the appropriate items

	Mainframes	Servers	Workstations	Other (specify)
Ownership transferred but run on your site				
Ownership transferred but run on your site as a service centre for other customers				
Work transferred to provider's site				
Ownership retained by company				

3 APPLICATIONS

Which applications are involved? (please circle)

Accounting	CAD/CAM	EPOS	Order processing
Production control	Electronic mail	Stock control	Process control

Other (specify) _____

4 SERVICE DESCRIPTION AND QUALITY (please tick as appropriate)

	Service delivered			Service quality			Trends		
	OK	Very poor	Poor	OK	Good	Very good	Improving	Worsening	Static
Processing									
Hardware maintenance									
Software support									
Application development									
Systems conversion									
Network management									
Project management									
Performance review/reporting									

5 THE OUTSOURCING DECISION

Who made the justification for the move to outsourcing?

(please enter as appropriate)

In-house   *Consultants*

Position _____   Company name _____

What were the objectives? (please circle)

Cost reduction   Service improvement   Technical improvement

Space reduction   Control and accountability   Other (specify) _____

Has the implementation met its original objectives? YES/NO

If no, which have not been met? (circle as appropriate)

Cost reduction   Service improvement   Technical improvement

Space reduction   Control and accountability   Other (specify) _____

6 CHOICE OF SUPPLIER

Reasons for choosing current supplier (please circle as appropriate)

Reputation   Recommendation   Technical knowledge

Sales effort   Cost   Other (specify) _____

What selection procedures did you use? (please circle)

Detailed service specification produced   Responses rated by a points system

Evaluation by steering committee   User community involved in decision

What is the length of the current contract? _____

When is the next date for contract review? _____

Do you feel 'locked in' to your current provider? YES/NO

If yes, why? (please circle below)
Technical knowledge Cost of change Termination conditions Other (specify)_____

7 CHANGING SUPPLIERS

Have you changed suppliers since starting outsourcing? YES/NO
(IF NO – GO TO QUESTON 8)

If yes, why did you change? (please circle as appropriate)

Cost saving   Performance dissatisfaction   Technical capability

Specific skills and experience relating to new initiatives

Other (specify) _____

What was the length of the initial contract? _____

Did it run its full term? YES/NO

If no, what was the reason?

_____

Are you using more than one supplier at the same time? YES/NO

If yes, what is the reason? (please circle)

Performance trials   Specific skills in one supplier for a particular service

Dissatisfaction with the existing supplier

Other (specify) _____

Has the initial contract been – (please circle)

Returned to in-house operation   Awarded to the original supplier

8 FUTURE PLANS

What are your future plans for outsourcing? (please circle)

Change supplier   New applications

No change   Additional supplier

What is your timescale for change?

This year   Next year   Later (specify) _____

What do you see happening in the outsourcing budget over the next three years?
(please indicate)

Reduce   Increase   No change _____

9 PERSONNEL ISSUES

How effective would you rate the handling of the employee communication and transfer process? (please indicate)

	Excellent	Good	OK	Poor	Very poor
Initial employer information about intentions					
Communication from the selected supplier before the date of transfer					
Efforts of supplier to deal with the fears and reservations of employees					
Absorption of employees into the supplier's culture and ways of working					
Overall, has the transfer benefitted the employees					
Overall, how successful has the transfer been					

10   SERVICE LEVEL AGREEMENTS

Are service level agreements in operation between your company and the supplier
YES/NO

How are the performance measures structured? (please indicate)

In computing terms, e.g. hours of availability

In terms of the business objectives of the users

Other (please specify) _____

11   FOR THOSE WHO HAVE NOT YET IMPLEMENTED OUTSOURCING

Are you considering using outsourcing? YES/NO
If YES which equipment types will be involved?

Mainframes   Servers   Workstations   Networks

Other (IT) _____   Other (non IT) _____

What type of processing service will you require? (please circle below)

On own site   On supplier's site   With other customers on a customer site

No change

What outsourcing services are you likely to take up? (please circle)

Processing   Hardware maintenance   Software support

Application development   Systems conversion   Network management

Project management

What are the objectives of the change? (please indicate below)

Cost reduction	Service improvement	Technical change
Space reduction	System migration	Accountability

Other (specify) _____

When will this be implemented?

This year / Next year / Other (specify) _____

THANK YOU FOR COMPLETING THIS QUESTIONNAIRE

3G (third generation) An advanced generation of wireless technology that enables data transmission up to 2 Mbps, making possible the integration of voice, data and video over wireless networks.

802. 11 A standard for local area network (LAN) interoperability.

Access To obtain data from the computer. This may be stored inside the CPU or on a remote backing store.

Access time The time interval between the instant at which data is called for from a storage device and the instant delivery begins.

Accounting system An internal (management) and external (financial) transactions system used for collecting, collating, recording and publishing data and information using a monetary base (e.g. £, $, yen).

Ada A programming language developed for the Department of Defense in the USA and designed to be open and portable across all military hardware and software.

Adaptive system A system that senses, monitors and responds to changes in its environment.

Address An identification as represented by a name, label or number, for a location in a storage medium.

ADSL (asynchronous digital subscriber line) Fixed wire modems attached to twisted pair copper wiring that transmit from 1.5 Mbps to 9 Mbps downstream to the subscriber and from 16 Kbps to 800 Kbps upstream.

Algorithm A set of rules that gives a sequence of operations for solving a problem. A set of code to carry out a routine operation or a defined set of rules or processes for solving a problem. An algorithm can be a mathematical procedure as well as a software program.

Alphanumeric Letters of the alphabet A to Z and numbers 0 to 9.

Analysis group A team of people given the task of analyzing a system.

ANSI (American National Standards Institute) A technical standards body in the USA that determines IT and computing standards.

Applet A software application written in Java code to be used and inserted into an HTML program for dynamic content.

Application As in application software package. A program designed to perform a particular task or set of functions (e.g. a database, word-processor, spreadsheet, etc.)

Applications generator A software tool used in high-level development environments to create and generate appropriate applications code from natural language instructions of an end user.

Application service provider (ASP) An organization that provides other organizations with software applications and systems in return for a fee or commercial service agreement.

Arithmetic logic unit (ALU) A component of the CPU that carries out arithmetic and logical operations on data.

Array A linearly ordered set of data items, such as a table of numbers.

Artificial intelligence (AI) A form of computer reasoning that mimics human reasoning and 'intelligence'. AI systems learn from experience.

Artificial intelligence shell Programming environment of an AI system.

ASCII (American Standard Code for Information Interchange) A standard computer code that uses seven-bit digital character code to represent text and numeric characters.

Assembler language A computer program that converts instructions to the computer into machine code.

Asynchronous Not existing or occurring at the same time. A term used often in telecommunications to indicate that data signals are not being transmitted at the same time.

ATM (asynchronous transfer mode) A multimedia high-speed network that allows the transmission of voice, video, pictures, text and graphics data.

ATM (automated teller machine) A machine in the walls of banks that dispenses cash to authorized holders of a cash dispenser card.

Attribute Data concerning an entity. Used in entity relationship context diagrams.

B2B (business-to-business) Represents the electronically mediated business relationship between two commercial organizations.

B2C (business-to-consumer) Represents the electronically mediated business relationship between a business organization and its customers.

Backup file A copy of a file that is used in the event of the original file being corrupted.

Bandwidth The range of frequencies on a particular telecommunications medium. It represents the width of a radio channel measured in hertz that can be modulated to transfer data and information. The range (band) of frequencies that are transmitted on a channel. Frequencies are expressed in hertz (Hz) or millions of hertz (MHz).

Bar code An array of black and white lines used on products and other physical items to be read electronically by OCR scanning technology.

BASIC A high-level programming language. An abbreviation for Beginners All-purpose Symbolic Instruction Code.

Baud The rate data is transferred along a communications line – usually 1 bit per second (bps).

Binary A state of only two possible conditions (e.g. 'yes' or 'no', 'on' or 'off', '1' or '0'). Binary code has a base of 2, using either '1' or '0'.

Binary digit In binary notation either the digits '1' or '0'.

Biometrics The science and technology of measuring human features. Used in network access and security.

Bit Binary digit 0 or 1. The smallest part of a digital data signal, a contraction of **bi**nary dig**it**.

Bit mapping Video graphics technology environment that allows each pixel on a screen to be addressed and organized by a computer.

Bits per second A measure of data transmission rate. For example, a rate of 2 megabits per second would be annotated as 2 Mbps.

Bluetooth™ A standard for wireless networking developed by Ericsson.

Boolean logic A set of logical operators for expressing logical relationships.

Buffer Temporary storage location for data as it is transferred from one device to another.

Bug A mistake or error in a computer program or computer system.

Bus An electrical connection between the components of a computer system along which data is transmitted.

Bus width The number of bits that can be transferred at one time between the CPU and other related peripheral devices.

Business environment (BE) The total of all conditions and aspects of the environment that affect or impact on business activity.

Business functions The generic tasks or activities necessary for an organization to undertake business activity (e.g. sales order processing, purchase order processing or stock controlling).

Business organization The interrelated set of human, technology and systems resources that are managed and coordinated to achieve certain objectives and goals.

Business process re-engineering (BPR) A drastic information systems development approach that looks at the overall goal of an organization and the inherent nature of the processes needed to support that goal.

Byte A set of bits (usually eight) that is used to represent one character.

C++ A common programming language used within the business environment.

Cache High-speed computer memory that temporarily stores data in order to speed data transmission or processing (e.g. of web pages).

CAD (computer-aided design) The use of computer applications to produce technical drawings.

CDMA (code division multiple access) A digital mobile telephony standard used mostly in the USA. A type of cellular digital network where calls are split into packets that are tagged with identifying codes.

CD-ROM (compact disk-read only memory) An optical disk storage technology.

CD-RW A compact disk used for storage where data can be read and written to the disk.

Cellular mobile phone Mobile telephone using radio waves to transmit voice and other data. A wireless telephone device suitable for accessing a cellular network. Normally referred to as a 'mobile phone' in Europe.

CGI (common gateway interface) An approach to linking web pages and server applications.

Character string A sequence of alphanumeric characters joined together.

Chip An integrated circuit that is etched on to a small piece of silicon.

Client-server computing A model of computing that divides the processing tasks to be performed between client and servers on a network. Each machine is given the tasks that it performs the most effectively.

Coaxial cable A telecommunications transmission medium of insulated copper wire.

COBOL An old programming language used mainly in business in the 1980s.

Communications software Software used to communicate data over a telecommunications network.

Compiler A program that converts a high-level language into a low-level language or machine code.

Computer literacy Knowledge and understanding of computing and IT, its role and application.

Configuration The various pieces of hardware and software integrated to complete a computerized system.

Cookie A software application that captures data and information on user activity and websites visited.

CPU (central processing unit) The area or unit of a computer system that includes the main storage and the circuits controlling interpretation and execution of instructions that control other parts of the computer system.

Cursor A blinking square or character that appears on a computer screen to indicate the position of the pointer.

Data The raw facts that can be processed to produce information.

Database A series of files structured and stored for the storage and manipulation of data.

Database management system (DBMS) The software application that acts as an interface between the database and the user. It assists the user in interrogating and manipulating data within a database.

Data capture The technique of collecting data by using various devices and procedures.

Data channel A path along which data can flow electronically.

Data dictionary The part of a DBMS that stores definitions and characteristics of data items.

Data flow The movement of data and information within an information system.

Data flow diagram (DFD) A graphical tool used for documenting the logical design of an information system.

Data redundancy The existence of duplicated data within a database or storage file.

Data retrieval The process of extracting data from a database.

Data security The process and techniques for preventing unauthorized access to computer systems.

Data warehousing A technique of data storage in modern business information environments.

Debug To detect, locate and remove mistakes and errors from a program or computer system.

Decision support system (DSS) A computerized system used to assist human decision making within an organization.

Demodulation The process of converting analog signals to digital signals.

Desk top publishing (DTP) A software application for producing professional-quality reports and documents incorporating text, graphics and pictures for newspapers and magazines.

Digital certificate An electronic file (or document) signed with a digital signature that indicates that a specified public key belongs to a specified person.

Digital signature Uses public key cryptography to produce an electronic signature on data being transmitted over a network. It is used to authenticate the person sending the data.

Directory A list of the names of programs and files stored on a disk area.

Distributed database A database that is used and maintained in more than one location.

Downsizing The miniaturization of hardware technology.

DSL (digital subscriber line) Offers a faster internet connection than a standard dial-up connection.

E-business The conduct of business primarily over the internet.

EDI (electronic data interchange) The automatic electronic transfer of data from one computer system to another computer system.

Edit To modify the form or format of data.

EFT (electronic funds transfer) Communicating and transferring monetary transaction details along telephone wires, satellites and other transmission mediums around the world to transfer money.

EFTPOS (electronic funds transfer at point of sale) The transmission and transfer of money electronically usually at an EFTPOS terminal in a shop (at the point of sale).

E-mail (electronic mail) Process by which text-based messages are sent and received over computer networks.

End user The individual that has responsibility for using information and contributes to the development of the systems to support the processing and delivery of that information.

Entity An object or item on which information is maintained.

Executive information system (EIS) An information system used at the top strategic decision-making level of a business organization.

Expert system (ES) A system that mimics the knowledge, reasoning skills and professional decision making of experts in particular areas (e.g. medicine, geology and financial advice).

Extranet Enabling one organization to use another organization's telecommunications and intranet systems.

FAX (facsimile) A technology that transmits documents containing text and graphics over standard telephone lines.

Feasibility study A formal analysis of whether something is possible and practicable, given the internal and external constraints within an environment.

Feedback The process of obtaining output and then feeding it back into another process or the same process.

Fibre optics A transmission technology medium that uses clear glass fibre to transmit data through the use of pulsing laser beams of light.

Field An area on a record that contains a single string of information.

File A collection of related records treated as a unit.

File server A computer that acts as a repository of data and applications, which allows other computers on a network to share files and applications software.

Firewall Computer programs that secure a networked computer system and prevent attacks on the system by viruses.

Fixed disk A computer storage disk medium that is permanently fixed to a computer system.

Font (or fount) A style and size of typeface character.

FORTRAN A programming language used mainly for mathematical and scientific applications in the 1970s and 1980s (an abbreviation for **For**mula **Tran**saction).

Fourth generation development The tools and techniques used to develop information systems with little or no involvement from technical specialists. Such development environments are more user-friendly and encourage end-user development.

Fourth generation language (4GL) A programming language that uses a high level of natural language rather than mathematical symbolism.

Freedom of information The right of individuals and organizations to have free access to available data and information kept by organizations.

FTP (File Transfer Protocol) A protocol used for downloading data files over a computer network.

Fuzzy logic A concept used in AI and ES to recognize the fact of uncertainty within strategic and managerial decision-making environments.

Gateway A computer system's interface between two computer networks, which may have various access controls. Performs the necessary protocol conversions between networks.

Geographic information systems (GIS) Applications that produce two or three-dimensional maps and graphics, used for modelling.

Gigabyte Computer storage measurement equal to approximately 1,000 million bytes.

Globalization The process of systems and people becoming increasingly more international and integrated.

Global positioning system (GPS) A handheld device that enables the user to locate their exact position on Earth. It uses a series of 24 satellites and is used in personal tracking and navigation.

Graphical user interface (GUI) The computer interface environment of screen icons, cursor and other visual aspects of interaction.

Graphics Diagrams, charts, pictures or graphs produced using a computer system.

Graphics tablet An input device that allows diagrams to be input into a computer.

Groupware Software that assists the activity of project development and team-based activities (e.g. scheduling meetings and sharing ideas).

Hacker A person who tries to break into secure or restricted computer systems.

Hardcopy Printed output from a computer system that can be taken away and studied.

Hard disk The term used to indicate the rigid recording surface used for bulk storage of computer data.

Hardware The physical and electronic components that make up a computerized system.

Heuristic program A computer program that has the facility for self-learning.

Hierarchy The arrangement of individuals in an organization according to rank or authority.

High-level language. A user-friendly programming language that uses natural language (e.g. English, French, Chinese).

Holism The concept of looking at a problem scenario or system in totality rather than focusing on one particular part of the system.

Host computer The main responsible computer on a network.

HTML (HyperText Mark-up Language) A standard web coding language that describes (or 'marks-up') how pages should look when displayed in a web browser.

HTTP (HyperText Transfer Protocol) An internet communications protocol that determines how one computer system communicates with another computer system over the web.

Hypermedia A network of nodes or connections across a set of various data and information.

Icons Symbols and pictures displayed on a screen, often in the form of menu pictures.

Implementation The process of converting a systems solution into a tangible product or outcome.

Index A series of identifiers, each of which characterizes a piece of information.

Indexed file A file that includes an index directory to facilitate random processing.

Index term A word or phrase used to classify a document or item in a database.

Inference engine The rule base of an expert system.

Informatics The study of information and its handling, especially by means of information technology. The term is derived from the French word *'informatique'*.

Information The result of processing data for use and meaningful decision making.

Information and communications technology (ICT) The creation, processing, storage and dissemination of various types of data by means of computerized technology, computer networks and telecommunications technology.

Information retrieval (IR) The process of recovering specific information from stored data (e.g. databases).

Information science The study of all aspects of storage, processing and dissemination of information.

Information system (IS) Interrelated components working together to collect, store, process and disseminate information for decision making.

Information theory The study of the problems and processes of the transmission of information.

Ink-jet printer A printer that works by spraying ink on to the paper to make up the shapes of type characters.

Input Data or information received by a computerized system from outside.

Input device An item of equipment that permits data or instructions to be entered into a computer (e.g. keyboard, scanner or sensor).

Integrated circuit A miniaturization of electronic circuits so that thousands of components are formed on a small chip of silicon.

Integrated software The composition of two or more software applications packages (e.g. spreadsheets, databases and word-processors).

Intelligent agent A program application that performs services or functions on behalf of a user (e.g. intelligent agents for searching information on the World Wide Web).

Internet A network of computer networks spanning the globe.

IR (infrared technology) An invisible band of radiation at the lower end of the electromagnetic spectrum. Infrared transmission requires an unobstructed line of sight between transmitter and receiver. It is used for wireless transmission between computer devices.

IrDA (Infrared Data Association) A standard for infrared communication between devices. It uses a focused ray of light in the infrared frequency spectrum and enables data to be transmitted wirelessly over short distances.

ISDN (integrated services digital network) An international communications standard for sending voice, video, and data over digital telephone lines or normal telephone wires. (ISDN supports data transfer rates of 64 Kbps.)

ISP (internet service provider) An organization that provides internet access.

Iteration To repeat a procedure with data derived from the last run of the procedure (i.e. using feedback) in order to obtain a more accurate value.

Java A dynamic and high-level programming language, developed by Sun Microsystems, that works on any computer. It allows sophisticated client-server applications to be developed for the web and intranets.

JavaBeans A software component model associated with the Java programming language. A JavaBean is an object-based component that can be used repeatedly.

JavaScript A web-based scripting language that enables HTML pages to be created with Java Applets, objects and classes with abridged knowledge of the Java language.

Job A specified group of tasks prescribed as a unit of work for a computer system.

Justify text To adjust the positions of words on a page of text so that the margins are regular. Type can be aligned on the left, or the right, or centred.

Keyboard An input device consisting of standard typewriter keys, numerical keys and often special function keys.

Key field A field within a data record to identify the record.

Kilobyte A measure of microcomputer storage capacity (equal to 1,024 bytes).

Knowledge The set of concepts and cognitive frameworks used by humans to collect, store, process, organize and communicate understanding.

Knowledge-based system (KBS) Part of ES and AI systems technology that comprises the tools, techniques and information sets for use in ES and AI.

Knowledge engineer A specialist in ES engaged to elicit information and expertise from other professionals, which is then used in a knowledge base.

Knowledge management (KM) The coordination and management of human understanding and knowledge within an organization.

LAN (local area network) A term applied to computer networks that operate over a small area, such as one site or building of a business organization. A network of interconnected computers and peripheral devices that are networked within a localized environment (e.g. an office building).

Laser printer A high-quality printer that uses laser beams to form characters on paper.

Linux A version of the Unix operating system, developed by Linus Torvalds in 1991, that is freely available and runs on many hardware platforms.

LISP A programming language used mainly in the field of artificial intelligence in the 1980s.

Load To enter data into storage locations of computer systems.

Logical design A description of the underlying goal of an information system in terms of its purpose and logical information requirements.

LOGO A programming language used in education, particularly for robotics in the 1970s and 1980s.

Loop A loop is used when a process needs to be done more than once (iterations). It takes the last instruction of a process back to the beginning.

Machine code The lowest form of computer programming language, with instructions in binary code, that is used directly by a computer.

Machine cycle The series of operations required to execute a computer instruction.

Macro A set of instructions in a computer language that is equivalent to a specific sequence of computer instructions.

Management information systems (MIS) A system providing information for managers to undertake decision making within a business organization (e.g. used for monitoring and control of an organization).

Megabyte A measure of computer storage equal to approximately 1 million bytes (1,048,576 bytes).

Megahertz A measure of computer clock speed equal to 1 million cycles per second.

Microcomputer A small desktop or portable computer.

Microprocessor A central processing unit (CPU) implemented by means of a single silicon chip.

Microsecond A measure of machine cycle time equal to one millionth of a second.

Microwave A high frequency transmission medium popular with mobile phone technology. It uses electromagnetic waves in a range of 1 to 30 gigahertz.

Middleware Software applications that connect different applications and pass data between applications.

Millisecond One thousandth of a second.

Modem A device that allows electronic information to be transmitted and received through various communication channels.

Modulation The process of converting digital signals into analog.

Mouse An input device that is moved over the table in order to move a cursor on the screen. Icons can be selected by placing the cursor on them and double-clicking a button.

Multimedia The integration of text, graphics, pictures, video, sound and animation into one computer medium.

Multiplexer A technology that allows a single communications channel to transmit from multiple sources simultaneously.

Multitasking The execution of a number of tasks or operations simultaneously.

Nanosecond An order of magnitude of one thousand millionth of a second.

Natural languages Languages that are used by humans (e.g. English, French, Japanese etc.).

Network A set of components within a computerized system, interconnected by telecommunications channels.

Network gateway Link points between different computer networks.

Network topology The configuration of hardware devices within a network (e.g. star, bus, ring topologies).

Neural network A network that emulates the patterns and responses of the human brain.

Object-oriented programming A programming technique that combines data and the specific instructions acting on that data into a defined object.

Object-oriented technology A technology that utilizes the connection of data and information objects.

Online Directly connected to and under the control of a computer network, such as the internet.

Operating system (OS) Software that controls and manages the operation of computer programs on a computer system.

Operational systems Systems found at the lowest functional levels of a business organization, which are used to process routine deterministic data.

Optical character recognition (OCR) A device that reads characters from a page or product (e.g. bar code).

Organizational structure The shape, nature and configuration of information flows and lines of authority within a structured organization.

OS/2 An operating system that allows multitasking, which was usually used with 32 bit microcomputers in the 1990s.

OSI (open systems interconnection) A standard for worldwide communications that defines a framework for implementing protocols in seven layers.

Output The results of data processing activity in a computerized environment.

Outsourcing The use of external computer vendors and sources to develop, maintain or operate a business organization's information systems and information technology.

Parallel processing Processing activity in which more than one instruction is processed at any one time.

Pascal A high-level structured programming language.

Password A word that needs to be typed into a computer system to gain access to data and information.

PDA (personal digital assistant) A small, portable hand-held device that offers functions such as diary, address storage, calendar, office applications, internet access and e-mail. Most PDAs can be synchronized with PCs.

Physical design The physical technology (hardware and software) that manifests itself as a result of the logical design of information systems.

Picosecond A measure of computer machine cycle time equal to one trillionth of a second.

PIN (personal identification number) A secret number used to gain access to cash dispensers known generically as ATMs.

PKI (public key infrastructure) An electronic security architecture that includes digital certificate management applications to create secure networks.

POP (Post Office Protocol) A communications protocol used to retrieve e-mail from a mail server.

Primary key A unique identifying field key of a database record.

Primary storage The part of a CPU that temporarily stores program instructions and related data.

Processing The conversion of raw data into meaningful information.

Program A set of instructions written in a computer language that a computer can recognize and understand.

Programming language A series of statements used for writing computer programs and instructing computer systems.

Project management The art and technique of managing and coordinating information systems projects and teams.

Protocol The set of rules governing telecommunications transmission between two or more computer networks.

Prototyping The building of an experimental model that can be tested and evaluated.

Pseudocode The technique of using natural language statements to describe processing and programming logic.

PSTN (public switched telephone network) A global voice telephony network.

Quality control The monitoring and identification of variances from established standards that affect the manufacturing and production systems of a business organization.

Queue An ordered waiting line of tasks or jobs to be processed through a computer system.

Query language A usually high-level programming language for accessing data in a database.

Qwerty Refers to a keyboard used in the UK and USA, so named because the first row of alphabetic characters is QWERTYUIOP.

RAM (random access memory) Memory where any location can be read from, or written to, in a random access manner. That is, memory where there is no need to go through other records to find the one that is required.

Real time The response of the computer is at the same rate as the data input (e.g. the automatic pilot system in aircraft).

Record A unit of related information, or set of data, forming the basic element of a file

Relational database An organization of data within a database in which a data item in one table can be related to a data item in another table.

Remote access Access gained to a computer system, through data communications from a remote terminal not located at the site of the computer system.

RISC (reduced instruction set computing) Improving microprocessor speed and characteristics by including only the most frequently used instructions on a microchip.

Robotics Physical systems that replicate and replace the manual work undertaken by humans.

ROM (read-only memory) Memory that can be accessed, but not altered.

Routine A sequence of operations for a computer system to perform.

Scanner A data input device that electronically reads text or graphics into a computer system.

Scramble The mixing up of data/information before it is communicated electronically, to avoid the data being interfered with and used.

Scroll The movement of text up and down or across a screen or monitor.

Sector A portion of a magnetic computer disk.

Semiconductor chip A silicon chip containing hundreds of thousands of etched circuits.

Sensors Technology that electronically collects data from the environment to be input into a computer system.

Sequential file A file where records are kept in order or sequence.

SMTP (Simple Mail Transfer Protocol) A protocol for sending and receiving e-mail messages between computer servers.

Socio-technical approach An approach to information systems development that recognizes the impact and involvement of people, organizations and technology.

Software A computer program or suite of programs that are used to direct the operations of a computer.

Sort Arranging data/information into an ordered or structured format, such as in alphabetical or numeric sequence.

Spreadsheet A software package that consists of a grid of cells that can hold alphanumeric data or formulae.

SQL (Structured Query Language) A standardized language for requesting information from a database. (An original version called SEQUEL – Structured English Query Language – was developed by IBM in 1975).

SSL (secure sockets layer) A communications protocol for transmitting private documents over the internet.

Strategic information system (SIS) A system for decision-making at the highest (strategic) level of a business organization, sometimes known as executive information systems.

Supercomputer A very powerful computer that can perform complex and fast computations.

System A method or approach to organization and interaction in the world at large.

TCP/IP (Transmission Control Protocol/Internet Protocol) A set of network transmission protocols that have become a networking standard. Commonly used over the X.25 and Ethernet networks, TCP/IP relates to the third (network) and fourth (transport) layers of the OSI model.

Telecommunications The transmission and reception of data in the form of electronic signals using radio, satellite or transmission lines.

Telecommunications carrier A utility that carries voice and data traffic across communications networks (e.g. AT&T in the USA and Vodafone in Europe and Africa).

Telecommuting The use of information technology to work or operate from home while still being employed and attached to a business organization.

Teleconferencing The use of IT and communications technology to allow individuals to engage in a conference or meeting from remote locations.

Terabyte A unit of measure of approximately 1 trillion bytes.

Terminal A device that is capable of sending and/or receiving data.

Test data Data that is prepared in order to test the functioning of a specified program or computer system.

Topology A description of the shape and nature of a computer network. It shows the logical connection of devices on a network.

Touch screen A sensitive computer screen that allows a user to command the system by touching specific areas of the screen.

Transaction processing system (TPS) Operational systems that process functional transactions at the lowest hierarchical level of a business organization.

Unix An operating system for mainframes and microcomputers that supports multitasking and networking.

Upgrade To improve the specification of a computer system in terms of hardware and software.

Upper case The capital letters of the alphabet (e.g. 'D' instead of 'd').

URL (uniform resource location) Internet address that indicates where a web page is located and identifies the protocol used to locate the web source.

Usability An indication of how easy it is for a user to engage with and use computing technology.

User-friendly A system that users find easy to understand without much formal and lengthy training.

User interface The device or technology that allows a user to interact with a computer-based system.

Value-added network (VAN) A computer network managed by an external organization that charges a fee for usage, thus allowing a business organization access to network technology without outright purchase.

Value chain A series of independent but linked activities that deliver a service or product to a customer (based on Michael Porter's academic work).

VDU (visual display unit) A screen used to display the output from a computer.

Verification To determine whether a data recording operation has been achieved accurately. The computer-based network activity of identifying and authenticating an encrypted communication.

Video conferencing A form of teleconferencing where participants see, as well as hear, other participants at remote locations.

Virtual organization An organization that utilizes computer communications technology to facilitate work and projects among employees and outside agents.

Virus A software program that can destroy or damage a computer system.

Voice mail The digitization of the spoken word, which is then transmitted over a telecommunications network and stored until the receiver is ready to listen to the message in audio format.

VoIP (Voice-over-Internet Protocol) Used for telephone calls over the internet.

W3C (World Wide Web Consortium) An organization that tries to manage and develop standards and practices for the web.

Wafer A thin slice of silicon that forms the basis of a microprocessor.

WAN (wide area network) The wider connection of computers and other peripheral equipment over a set of networks that are not restricted to a local area.

WAP (Wireless Application Protocol) An open wireless standard for mobile internet access. WAP enables mobile cell phone users, and other wireless device users, to access and interact with internet services.

Web An abbreviated version of the World Wide Web.

WiFi (Wireless Fidelity) The WiFi logo is a trademarked logo from the Wireless Ethernet Compatibility Alliance that certifies compliance to Wireless LAN Standard IEEE 802.11b.

Window A sub-domain of a screen. A screen can be split into a number of different areas of variable size known as windows, each area being used for a separate function. These areas are sometimes known as dialogue boxes.

Windows CE A version of the Windows operating system designed for handheld devices. Sometimes known as 'Pocket PC' operating system.

WindowsNT A powerful operating system that supports multitasking and can be used in networked environments. It was popular in the late 1990s and the early twenty-first century.

Wireless network A telecommunications network that uses microwaves rather than fixed wire lines to communicate messages.

WML (Wireless Mark-up Language) An XML language used to specify content and user interface for WAP devices.

Wordprocessor A computer package or application that can store, handle and manipulate written information.

Wordwrap A facility in word-processing applications whereby text can be typed continuously and the processor wraps words on to the next line as the line length is exceeded.

World Wide Web (WWW) Hypertext technology that allows the linking of documents and information sources over the internet.

Worm A computer virus that transfers itself across network connections.

Write To transfer data to a storage device such as the main memory of a computer disk or floppy disk.

WYSIWIG An acronym for 'what you see is what you get', indicating that the text/data seen on the screen will also appear as seen on the printed page (no hidden data/information).

XML (eXtensible Mark-up Language) A mark-up language regulated by WC3 – the World Wide Web Consortium. It can create more advanced links than HTML.

Zero Indicating nothing or nought. Also a state of representation within binary code.

Index